D0850490

PARALLEL COMPUTING
Fundamentals & Applications

Proceedings of the International Conference ParCo99

PARALLEL COMPUTING
Fundamentals & Applications

Delft, The Netherlands   17–20 August 1999

Editors

E. H. D'Hollander
Gent University, Belgium

G. R. Joubert
Technical University of Clausthal, Germany

F. J. Peters
Philips Research, Eindhoven, The Netherlands

H. J. Sips
Delft University of Technology, The Netherlands

Co-Editor

R. Sommerhalder
Delft University of Technology, The Netherlands

ICP   Imperial College Press

Published by

Imperial College Press
57 Shelton Street
Covent Garden
London WC2H 9HE

Distributed by

World Scientific Publishing Co. Pte. Ltd.
P O Box 128, Farrer Road, Singapore 912805
USA office: Suite 1B, 1060 Main Street, River Edge, NJ 07661
UK office: 57 Shelton Street, Covent Garden, London WC2H 9HE

British Library Cataloguing-in-Publication Data
A catalogue record for this book is available from the British Library.

PARALLEL COMPUTING: FUNDAMENTALS AND APPLICATIONS
Proceedings of the International Conference ParCo 99

ISBN   1-86094-235-0

Printed in Singapore by Uto-Print

CONFERENCE COMMITTEE
Gerhard R. Joubert (Germany/Netherlands) (Conference Chair)
Erik H. D'Hollander (Belgium)
Frans J. Peters (Netherlands)
Henk Sips (Netherlands)
Ruud Sommerhalder (Netherlands)

STEERING COMMITTEE
Frans Peters (Netherlands) (Steering Committee Chair)
Bob Hiromoto (USA)
Janusz Kowalik (USA)
Masaaki Shimasaki (Japan)
Dennis Trystram (France)

ORGANISING COMMITTEE
Ruud Sommerhalder (Netherlands) (Organising Committee Chair)
Dick Epema (Netherlands)

FINANCE COMMITTEE
Frans J. Peters (Netherlands) (Finance Chair)

INTERNATIONAL PROGRAM COMMITTEE
Henk Sips (Netherlands) (Program Committee Chair)
Erik H. D'Hollander (Belgium) (Program Committee Vice-Chair)

Adeli, H. (USA)
Arbab, F. (NL)
Arabnia, H. R. (USA)
Bal, H. (NL)
Bjorstad, P. E. (USA)
Bode, A. (D)
Chapman, B. (UK)
Chassin de Kergommeaux, J. (F)
De Bosschere, K. (B)
Deuflhard, P. (D)
Dongarra, J. (USA)
Duff, I.S. (UK)
Ferreira, A. (F)
Fox, G. (USA)
Gemund, A. van (NL)
Gentzsch, W. (D)
Grandinetti, L. (I)

Hempel, R. (D)
Hertzberger, L.O. (NL)
Hiromoto, R. (USA)
Indermark, K. (D)
Li, K. (USA)
Kober, R. (D)
Kroll, N. (D)
Leca, P. (F)
Mellor-Crummey, J. (USA)
Mierendorf, H. (D)
Nagel, W. (D)
Oyanagi, Y. (J)
Paul, W. (D)
Petkov, N. (NL)
Philips, W. (B)
Quinn, M.J.   (USA)
Reuter, A. (D)

Roman, J. (F)
Roose, D. (B)
Schweizerhof, K. (D)
Sloot, P. (NL)
Smith, A. (USA)
Stüben, K. (D)
Sunderam, V.S. (USA)
Tezduyar, T. (USA)
Valero, M. (E)
Van Campenhout, J. (B)
Vorst, H. van der (NL)
Voss, H. (D)
Wesseling, P. (D)
Wittum, G. (D)
Zhang, F. (CDN)
Zhu, C.-Q. (PRC)
Zima, H. (A)

PREFACE

The international conference *ParCo99* was held in August 1999, i.e. during one of the last few months of the century during which the first electronic and parallel computers were developed. The next millennium will see the increased use of parallel computing technologies at all levels of main stream computing. The majority of computer hardware will use these technologies to achieve higher compute speeds, high-speed access to very large distributed databases and greater flexibility through heterogeneous computing. These developments will result in the extended use of all types of parallel computers in virtually all areas of human endeavour. Compute intensive problems in emerging areas such as financial modelling and multimedia systems will, in addition to traditional application areas of parallel computing, such as scientific computing and simulation, stimulate this development. Parallel computing as a field of scientific research and development will change from a niche position concentrating on solving compute intensive scientific and engineering problems to becoming one of the fundamental computing technologies.

The invited and contributed papers gave a retrospective view of what was achieved in the parallel computing field during the past three decades, as well as a prospective view of expected future developments.

From the many papers submitted just more than one third were selected for presentation at the conference. The presented papers were refereed at and after the conference and those finally accepted for publication are included in these proceedings. Abstracts of all papers of which a full version was not accepted or not available in time are also included.

The editors are indebted to the members of the International Programme Committee, the Steering Committee and the Organising Committee for the time they spent in making this conference such a successful event. Special thanks are due to the staff of the Informatics Department of Delft University of Technology for the excellent way in which they organised the event. In this regard, particular mention should be made of the key roles played by Ruud Sommerhalder (Organising Committee Chair), Dick Epema and Toos Brusse in organising this venture. Without their exceptional support, the conference would not have been such a success.

The Editors are especially indebted to Ruud Sommerhalder for agreeing to also act as Co-Editor of the proceedings. Ruud took on this additional task in spite of all the other organisational tasks he executed.

The organisers are grateful to the various organisations, which financially supported the conference.

Erik D'Hollander	Gerhard Joubert	Frans Peters	Henk Sips
Belgium	Germany	Netherlands	Netherlands

January 2000

Contents

Algorithms   233

System Software and Hardware Architecture   409

Industrial Perspective   747

Extended Abstracts 763

Invited Papers

COORDINATION MODELS AND LANGUAGES
FOR PARALLEL PROGRAMMING

PAOLO CIANCARINI

University of Bologna, Italy
E-mail: ciancarini@cs.unibo.it

THILO KIELMANN

Vrije Universiteit, Amsterdam, The Netherlands
E-mail: kielmann@cs.vu.nl

Most conventional approaches to parallel programming are based on some basic kinds of synchronized mechanisms and related models of concurrency control: shared variables, message passing, and remote procedure calls. Whereas these paradigms suffice to program parallel applications, they hardly provide abstractions adequate for programmers or language designers. Hence, parallel programming using these models becomes tedious and error–prone. Another issue is that most modern software engineering methods and techniques exploit component-based software architectures usually designed using some object-oriented approaches, which require specific support for concurrency and/or distribution of software components and architectures. Programming languages based on a formally defined *coordination model* and encompassing a notion of autonomous software components, or *agents*, are emerging as an effective paradigm for designing parallel systems. In this paper we describe the basic ideas behind some research in the field of coordination models and languages for designing and controlling the software architecture of parallel applications.

1 Introduction

For several years programming has been synonymous for sequential programming; the very idea of algorithms was based on the concept of instruction sequences. Non–sequential programming became a research topic when system programmers realized that an operating system could be better designed and built as a collection of independent cooperating processes. This idea gave birth to the concept of concurrent programming languages able to express interactions among independent control threads.

With the introduction of distributed systems, the scope of concurrent settings became broader. The absence of shared memory as well as the presence of significant communication latencies, communication errors, and possible system heterogeneity added a lot of complexity to concurrent programming. Traditional concurrent programming languages are based on three basic kinds of mechanisms and corresponding models of concurrent programming: shared variables, message passing, and remote procedure calls. Whereas these paradigms suffice to program distributed systems, they hardly provide adequate abstractions. Hence, programming using these models becomes tedious and error–prone. These problems as well as the requirements of open systems with dynamically changing configurations make programming models with suitable abstractions inevitable.

Gelernter introduced a fourth basic model called *generative communication*. [1] Concurrent languages based on this concept initiated the research area of *coordination*. Today, the interaction between active entities is typically investigated based on the notion of coordination, and by introducing a variety of non–conventional computing models.

This paper presents a perspective on current research issues in coordination models and languages. It has the following structure: Sect.2 introduces some basic concepts concerning coordination. Sect.3 defines our notions of coordination models and languages. Sect.4 puts in a design perspective coordination and software integration. In Sect.5, we discuss some relevant coordination languages. In Sect.6 we draw our conclusions.

2 What is coordination

Coordination as the key concept for modelling concurrent systems is discussed in a wide range of publications. Due to its fundamentality, this notion has a lot of facets it covers. In the scope of this paper we see coordination from the viewpoint of designers of programming models and languages. The following quotations introduce some important issues within this respect.

Here, coordination is:

- *"the additional information processing performed when multiple, connected actors pursue goals that a single actor pursuing the same goals would not perform."* [2]

- *"the integration and harmonious adjustment of individual work efforts towards the accomplishment of a larger goal."* [3]

- *"the process of building programs by gluing together active pieces."* [4]

As can be seen, coordination is concerned with managing the communication which is necessary due to the distributed nature of a system, with the expression of parallel and distributed algorithms, as well as with all aspects of the composition of concurrent systems. In an effort to give a concise definition, we need to define a number of notions:

Agent Agents are active, self–contained entities performing actions on their own behalf.

Action Actions by agents can be divided into two different classes:

1. *Inter–Agent actions.* These actions perform the communication among different agents. They are the subject of coordination models.

2. *Intra–Agent actions.* These are all actions belonging to a single agent, like e.g. internal computations. In the case of specialized interface agents, intra-agent actions may also comprise communication acts by an agent outside the coordination model, like primitive I/O operations or interactions with users.

Configuration We call a collection (or a system of) interacting agents a configuration. Configurations usually have some structure, that is the *software architecture* of the system of agents.

Coordination Coordination is managing the inter–agent activities of agents collected in a configuration.

3 Coordination models and languages

Coordination of agents can be expressed in terms of coordination models and languages. In the following, we try to clarify these two different notions. For coordination models we prefer the following intuitive definition: *"A coordination model is the glue that binds separate activities into an ensemble."* [4] In other words, a coordination model provides a framework in which the interaction of individual agents can be expressed. This covers the aspects of creation and destruction of agents, communication among agents, spatial distribution of agents, as well as synchronization and distribution of actions over time.

A more constructive approach to describe coordination models is to identify the components out of which they are built:

1. Coordination Entities.
   These are the building blocks which are coordinated. Ideally, these are the active agents.

2. Coordination Media.
   These are the media enabling the communication between the agents. Also, coordination media can serve to aggregate a set of agents to form a configuration.

3. Coordination Laws.
   These laws describe how agents are coordinated making use of the given coordination media.

A coordination model can be embodied in a (software) coordination architecture or in a coordination language. Examples of coordination architectures are the client–server architecture, the software pipeline, or the blackboard: Software components are arranged in some special, well–defined structures that enact specific cooperation protocols. Usually parallel programmers implicitly design a software architecture using low–level communication primitives. Due to this rather intuitive approach to software design, there is the need for high–level coordination languages to simplify the implementation of such systems.

A *coordination language* is "*the linguistic embodiment of a coordination model.*" [4] Thus, a coordination language should orthogonally combine two models: one for coordination (the inter–agent actions) and one for (sequential) computation (the intra–agent actions). The presumably most famous example of a coordination model is the Tuple Space in Linda which encountered several linguistic embodiments like C–Linda or FORTRAN–Linda, both on workstation networks and on massively parallel architectures.

4 Coordination as software integration

Open systems are systems in which new active agents may dynamically join and later leave, i.e. evolving self–organizing systems of interacting intelligent agents. [5,6] More precisely, open systems can be defined as being composed of software components which are *encapsulated* and *reactive*. [7] Components are called encapsulated if they have an interface that hides their implementation from clients; they are called to be reactive if their lifetime is longer than that of the atomic interactions (e.g. messages) which they execute. The fundamental property of open systems is their ability to cope with incremental adaptability, where encapsulation captures spatial incrementality by controlled propagation of local state changes and reactiveness enables temporal evolution by incrementally executing interactions.

A related important notion is the one of *open distributed systems*. It is defined in the ISO reference model of open distributed processing (RM–ODP). [8] In the RM–ODP definition, *distributed systems* have to cope with *remoteness* of components, with *concurrency*, the *lack of a global state*, and *asynchrony* of state changes. In addition, *open distributed systems* are characterized by *heterogeneity* in all parts of the involved systems, *autonomy* of various management or control authorities and organizational entities, *evolution* of the system configuration, and *mobility* of programs and data.

ODP identifies the following properties of systems capable to deal with the above characteristics: *Openness* for new kinds of systems, *integration* of heterogeneous systems, *flexibility* with respect to system evolution, *modularity* of system structure, *federation* for combining separate systems to compound ones, and *trans-*

parency of distribution and heterogeneity.

The requirements of open distributed systems on programming models can be characterized by the notions of heterogeneity in the following senses:

1. Heterogeneity of hardware.

   Open distributed systems may consist of computers of various architectures, from different vendors, with different data representations and capabilities. Furthermore, there may be very different interconnection media and topologies, including dial–up lines, different types of local area networks, and even specific interconnections in tightly coupled systems like parallel computers.

   As a result, coordination models for open distributed systems cannot rely on specific data representations or communication structures.

2. Heterogeneity of software.

   Computers in open distributed systems of course run different operating systems, like MS-DOS, various UNIX-flavours, or some special systems for mainframes, depending on their hardware platform. Also, programming languages in use may vary depending on the purpose of every system in use, ranging from Cobol for business programs, over Fortran in numerical processing to C for text processing or Prolog for knowledge based applications.

   Consequently, coordination models trying to integrate such systems cannot be bound to specific language interfaces or communication protocols.

3. Heterogeneity of configurations over time.

   Besides the different kinds of the involved systems, the most challenging property of open distributed systems is their dynamic nature. Examples are situations in which additional machines will be brought into the system, dial-up lines connect and disconnect, new machines replace older ones, new operating systems or communication protocols have to be integrated etc.

   Thus, agents in an open distributed system must be allowed to appear and disappear completely on their own behalf. This forbids coordination models to rely on specific (central) units or to make use of communication schemes based on static connections or specific identifiers (addresses).

Hence, composition of open distributed systems by modelling the interaction of encapsulated and reactive components, covers concurrency aspects of the more general notion of *software composition* which has recently emerged as an independent research area. [9]

4.1 Open object systems

Encapsulation and reactiveness as central requirements of agents in open systems directly leads to object–based modelling. Objects are by their very nature open interactive systems. They can not (completely) be described algorithmically because they interact while computing. Hence, specification of object–based systems is inherently incomplete and hence reflects openness. [10]

The RM–ODP model which conceptually provides the basis for commercially available systems uses object–based modelling too; also because of the principal object properties of encapsulation and reactiveness. RM–ODP focuses on interaction between objects based on the client/server architecture: "They (objects) embody ideas of services offered by an object to its environments, that is, to other objects." [8] In RM–ODP, coordination between objects takes place via centralized instances, so called *traders*; which are repositories of service type definitions, used to identify offered and requested services.

Presumably the most prominent commercial system for open, object–based systems is the Common Object Request Broker Architecture (CORBA). [11] Its central component, the Object Request Broker (ORB) acts as a trader in the sense of RM–ODP. Like other traders, the ORB provides references to server objects which in case of dynamically changing configurations may quickly turn into void ("dangling") references causing problems in open configurations.

Another well–known commercial system is Microsoft's *Object Linking and Embedding* (OLE). It is a set of so–called *component objects* for advanced document processing. It is based on the Component Object Model (COM), [12] which provides a binary interface standard between possibly heterogeneous application components. Like with CORBA, new interfaces can be introduced at runtime to a simplified form of a trader, called *component object library* (COL).

Today, client/server architectures are seen as the current intermediate step on the way from mainframe–oriented to collaborative (peer–to–peer) computing. [13] Nevertheless, service–oriented communication is an important paradigm for open distributed systems [14] and must hence be captured by coordination models. But because client/server communication is restricted to the exchange of request/reply pairs, other communication forms like e.g. for group communication can not be modelled adequately. Hence, coordination models for open systems need to be more general in their applicability.

Generative communication as initially introduced in [1] is based on an abstractly shared data space, sometimes also called *blackboard*, in which data items can be stored ("generated") and later retrieved. This kind of communication model inherently uncouples communicating agents: a potential reader of some data item does not have to take care about it (e.g. as with rendezvous mechanisms) until it really wants to read it. The reader even does not have to exist at the time of storing. The latter point directly leads to the other major advantage of generative communication: agents are able to communicate although they are anonymous to each other.

This uncoupled and anonymous communication style directly contributes to the design of coordination models for open systems: uncoupled communication enables to cope with dynamically changing configurations in which agents move or temporarily disappear. Anonymous communication allows to communicate with unknown agents. Hence it allows communication with incomplete knowledge about the system configuration which is a crucial demand of open systems. Due to this fact, coordination models based on generative communication are superior to message passing or trader–based schemes because these both rely on knowledge about a receiver's or server's identification.

Based on this observation, the LAURA model [15] has been developed in order to introduce generative communication into the RM–ODP model. In LAURA, agents using and offering services share a so–called *service space*. Here, *offer* and *request* forms are matched by LAURA's service type system which replaces RM–ODP's trading function. This model introduces uncoupled and anonymous communication into RM–ODP, but it does not help to overcome the rather restrictive communication scheme of request/reply pairs. Hence, a general–purpose coordination model for open systems needs further improvements.

4.2   Coordination requirements for open object systems

As we have seen so far, open (distributed) systems impose special requirements over coordination models in order to achieve functionality as well as abstractions suited to cope with very large and complex systems. In the following, we investigate properties necessary to fulfil those requirements.

We have identified the following group of properties being *necessary* for building open distributed systems. Primarily, the requirements of heterogeneity and dynamics are reflected here.

Dynamics It is a central requirement of open distributed systems to allow agents to enter or leave a configuration at any time. Hence, coordination laws must not rely on the existence of specific agents.

Decentralization As a consequence of dynamics, it must be possible in a cordination model to specify an agent's behaviour in a separate program. By definition of open distributed systems, there is no overall compile time. Hence, it must be possible to program new agents during the runtime of an already existing system.

This property not only requires a certain degree of dynamics in the coordination model. Moreover, it forces a particular implementation to be "open–ended" in order to allow new agents to enter a running system.

Generativeness With *generative communication* (meanwhile also known as *uncoupled communication*) as introduced so far, all communication is performed by generating and consuming separate entities, usually contained in a specific computational space. (In the original work, [1] the tuple space of Linda served for this purpose.) The existence of separate communication entities enables the modelling of communication in open distributed systems, because it uncouples communication from the existence of specific agents: Communication may simply be performed by generating a communication entity and putting it into the computational space. This allows agents to enter and leave an open system whenever they want without prohibiting their ability to communicate.

Furthermore, generativeness enables reasoning about the communication of a specific configuration, because it is solely based on the state of the communication entities involved in it.

Interoperability The necessity of coordinating agents which are programmed in different languages and operating on different platforms requires that coordination models, and especially their linguistic embodiments, must not rely on properties of specific programming languages or communication media like data types or their representations.

4.3 Coordination requirements for scalable systems

By identifying the following group we reflect the aspects of open distributed systems concerning scalability to significantly large sizes. Although such systems could be built with coordination models lacking the properties listed below, they are essential in order to build really large but still maintainable systems.

Homogeneity A model suited for coordinating large systems must be as simple as possible. Hence, all agents should be modelled in a uniform way.

Hierarchical Abstraction For the purpose of really large systems, it is vital to divide the overall configuration into smaller subconfigurations. Hence, it must be possible to treat entire configurations like single agents in a more abstract coordination level. This requirement unifies the notions agent and configuration, enabling agents to be composed out of multiple agents. Additionally, this property enables communication based on groups of agents.

Encapsulation In order to maintain a well-defined, consistent state it must be possible for a configuration to be protected from undesired interactions with agents outside.

Separation of Concerns Inter–agent actions have to be cleanly separated from intra–agent actions in order to distinguish between the concerns of coordination on one hand and of computations on the other.

Rigorous Semantics The model should be based on a rigorous formalism in order to allow reasoning about the interactions to be coordinated. Formal semantics should also offer a basis for automatic optimizer tools, which are able to exploit the different features of different hardware available in heterogeneous systems.

5 Sample coordination languages

We will now present some existing coordination languages. Therefore, we identify their coordination entities, media, and laws. We also discuss their suitability for software integration purposes by evaluating them against the requirements identified in the previous section.

5.1 Linda

The Linda coordination model has been introduced to incorporate the idea of generative communication. [1] In Linda, processes (the coordination entities) communicate by writing or reading tuples (in the mathematical sense; consisting of basic data items like numbers and strings) into the so–called "tuple space". The basic communication acts are creating a tuple (by the *out* operation), and reading or removing tuples from it (by the *read* and *in* operations). Synchronization is performed by letting processes wait until a suitable tuple to be read has been inserted into the tuple space. Furthermore, new processes can be invoked by putting active tuples into the tuple space (by the *eval* operation) which are in turn evaluated. Active tuples produce results in form of passive tuples to which they are converted on termination of their computation.

Typically, in the tuple space the main coordination law defines how tuples are selected to be read from the tuple space itslef. The potential reader specifies a template for a tuple he wishes to obtain. The tuple space performs a matching operation in order to find an appropriate tuple. Both tuples and templates may consist of actual fields (values) and formal fields (placeholders for specific data types). A tuple matches a given template if the arities of both correspond and if each actual field matches one of the same type and value or a formal field of the corresponding type.

Although it is not provided by current implementations, the Linda model itself allows dynamic and decentralized concurrent systems. Linda is of course generative and it also enables interoperability on the basis of simple data types being the building blocks for tuples. The separation of concerns between computation and coordination is achieved in an orthogonal way, because the tuple space operations can be added to any given language without interferences with other language properties.

Because Linda fulfils all of these properties, it is a possible model for building open distributed systems. Unfortunately, Linda fails being homogeneous by introducing active and passive tuples, templates, and a tuple space. The original Linda model neither provides hierarchical abstractions nor encapsulation, because there is only one global tuple space. Hence, distributed systems based on Linda are either open or encapsulated, but not both.

For making Linda completely suitable for integrating open distributed systems, we have recently introduced the Objective Linda coordination model. [16] Here, tuples are replaced by encapsulated objects. Object matching is performed based on objects types and interfaces. Objective Linda provides hierarchies of object spaces and a matching-based mechanism for relating object spaces to each other. A formal semantics for Objective Linda as well as its application to component-based parallel programming has been presented recently. [17]

5.2 ActorSpaces

The actor model unifies objects and concurrency. [5] Actors are autonomous and concurrently executing objects which operate asynchronously. Actors may send messages to each other. In response to receiving a message, an actor may take the following types of actions: It may send messages to other actors, it may create new actors, and it may specify its own new behaviour (state) to be used when processing the next incoming message.

In the *ActorSpace* model, [18] coordination entities are the actors, whereas the coordination laws are stated in terms of pattern–directed message passing: The sender of a message directs it to a set of receiving actors by denoting a pattern which has to be matched by the receivers. So, ActorSpaces serve as the coordination media, acting as passive containers for actors, providing a context for matching patterns on actors and their attributes.

ActorSpaces are dynamic, because the creation of new actors and ActorSpaces is allowed in the model. It is also possible to implement decentralization, because actors and ActorSpaces can be realized as self–contained entities. Unfortunately, ActorSpaces are not generative, because communication is based on messages which have no observable state. This leads to semantical problems with messages sent to actors which might not yet exist or may already have left a system, a phenomenon which has also been described elsewhere. [18]

The ActorSpace is quite homogeneous, because there is only one kind of actor, whereas communication is always based on terms of ActorSpaces. It is also possible to overlap or even nest different ActorSpaces which in turn enables the design of large systems using hierarchical abstractions. The latter is strenghtened because ActorSpaces protect the actors they contain because their visibility to the outside is determined by properties of the ActorSpaces. So, it is possible to achieve encapsulation.

The concerns of computation (the intra–agent actions) and coordination (the inter–agent actions) are separated in a very simple manner: Computation is implemented inside the actors themselves while communication is described in terms of ActorSpaces only. Formal semantics for ActorSpaces have already been developed, so reasoning about coordination in ActorSpaces got a rigorous foundation.

5.3 Obliq

Obliq [19] has been introduced as a scripting extension to Modula 3 rather than as a coordination model. Nevertheless, it has some interesting features which contrast the *ActorSpaces* model introduced above.

In Obliq, multiple sites contain objects and threads as their coordination entities. These sites can communicate over a local or even world–wide network. An Obliq site corresponds to an address space, objects contain data in form of their state, and threads perform communication. Threads and objects can move across sites. Sites communicate via globally known name servers which provide locations for given object names.

Every action performed by an Obliq computation (such as method invocation, delegation, object updating or cloning) is performed on a per–object basis. Obliq provides no abstractions for dealing with groups or sets of objects. Hence, threads (special ones acting as so–called "execution engines") can be seen as active agents whereas there is not really a notion of configuration: In Obliq only exist local sites and the whole system of participating sites. As a result, it is impossible to build hierarchical abstractions. Furthermore, it is also difficult to identify coordination media; name servers, sites, object interfaces, and communication channels play this role.

Synchronization can be performed on a per–object basis, too. Operations on objects can be synchronized by monitor–like constructs, namely mutual exclusion and condition variables. Deadlocks caused by recurrent method invocations are avoided using the notion of self–inflicted operations which circumvent the object's mutual-exclusion protection.

Obliq's coordination laws are based on communication channels which are initially set up using the name servers. This allows new agents to enter an active configuration simply by registering them at a name server. This enables decentralized programming. But as a valid channel is needed for communication, it is impossible for a specific agent to leave a configuration at any time he wants to, so dynamics is prohibited. Additionally, communication in Obliq is not generative, because it is based on remote method invocation. As a consequence, there are problems with agents eventually leaving a configuration.

Obliq isn't homogeneous, because the notions of passive objects and active threads are separated, causing the necessity of introducing synchronization constructs in the Obliq language. The encapsulation of objects is performed in two interesting ways. On one hand is Obliq's lexical scope which introduces the necessity of a valid handle in order to access an object. On the other hand, it is possible to implement encapsulation explicitly by so–called "protected objects".

Because Obliq computations are performed by sequences of method calls, both local computations and remote invocations are performed in a unified manner. Unfortunately, this prohibits the separation of concerns between computation and coordination purposes. The lexical scope which is basically used by Obliq computations enables to simply introduce distributed semantics based on the notions of sites, locations, values, and threads. But due to the currently experimental status of Obliq, there already are no formally given semantics, yet.

5.4 Embedding Java in a coordination model

The Java programming language recently attracted manifold interest as a platform for software integration purposes, especially with open distributed (e.g. Web-based) systems. Although Java includes some mechanisms for concurrency control based on monitors and critical regions, it can be combined with a higher level coordination model to support related component techniques. In fact, we have recently introduced a coordination language kernel called Jada, [20] which extends Java with Linda-like coordination primitives.

Jada has been introduced to design object-oriented applications distributed over the WWW, however, especially for applications which need support for rule-based coordination, workflows, and logically distributed transactions, Jada is too simple because it is based on singleton tuple transactions, whereas in several cases programmers need to test, delete, or replace multisets of tuples. Several other projects pursue a similar goal using a similar technology.

Interestingly, the idea of combining Java with Linda-like coordination has been pursued by some important software industries. In fact, both Sun's JavaSpaces [21] and IBM's TSpaces [22] provide mechanisms for distributed persistence and data exchange for code written in Java. Their basic coordination medium consists of flat multiple tuple spaces. In JavaSpaces, a tuple is called an *entry*, defined as typed group of objects. An entry can be written in a JavaSpace, to be later searched or deleted by lookup operations. JavaSpaces support a transaction mechanism to build atomic multiple operations across multiple JavaSpaces. Moreover, active objects can ask a JavaSpace to notify when an entry is written that matches a given template. The actual implementation of JavaSpaces is part of the Jini software architecture. [23] TSpaces exploit a similar coordination model; however such a system has been developed using a relational database management system as support for tuple spaces, so it is clearly more suited for applications where data management is an important issue.

6 Conclusions

Parallel as well as concurrent programming is typically performed using ad-hoc and low-level constructs like message passing, shared variables, or remote procedure calls. Those constructs hardly provide adequate abstractions, making the construction of large parallel software systems tedious and error-prone. The research area of *coordination* studies interaction between active entites or *agents*, aiming at the provision of suitable models for managing the complexity of such systems.

In this paper we identified and discussed the notion of *coordination* itself, as well as of *coordination models* and *languages*. We investigated the role of coordination as a paradigm for software integration in concurrent systems, focusing on open distributed (e.g. Web-based) systems. Here we discussed the importance of objects and of component-based software architectures, and we identified requirements for coordination models suitable for those systems. Finally, we discussed some coordination models and languages and their suitability for open distributed systems.

References

1. D. Gelernter. Generative Communication in Linda. *ACM Transactions on Programming Languages and Systems*, 7(1):80–112, 1985.
2. T. Malone and K. Crowstone. The Interdisciplinary Study of Coordination. *ACM Computing Surveys*, 26(1):87–119, 1994.
3. B. Singh. Interconnected Roles (IR): A Coordinated Model. Technical Report CT–84–92, Microelectronics and Computer Technology Corp., Austin, TX, 1992.
4. N. Carriero and D. Gelernter. Coordination Languages and Their Significance. *Communications of the ACM*, 35(2):97–107, February 1992.
5. Gul Agha. *Actors: A Model of Concurrent Computation in Distributed Systems*. M. I. T. Press, Cambridge, Massachusetts, 1986.
6. Paolo Ciancarini. Coordination Languages for Open System Design. In *Proc. of IEEE Intern. Conference on Computer Languages*, New Orleans, 1990.

7. Peter Wegner. Tradeoffs between Reasoning and Modeling. In Gul Agha, Peter Wegner, and Akinori Yonezawa, editors, *Research Directions in Concurrent Object–Oriented Programming*, pages 22–41. MIT Press, Cambridge, Mass., 1993.

8. ISO/IEC JTC1/SC21/WG7. Basic Reference Model of Open Distributed Processing. International Standard ISO/IEC 10746–1 to 10746–4, ITU–T Recommendation X.901 to X.904, 1995.

9. Oscar Nierstrasz and Dennis Tsichritzis, editors. *Object–Oriented Software Composition*. Prentice Hall, 1995.

10. Peter Wegner. Interactive Foundations of Object–Based Programming. *IEEE Computer*, 28(10), 1995.

11. Object Management Group. The Common Object Request Broker: Architecture and Specification. OMG Document Number 93.12.43, 1993.

12. Microsoft Corporation. The Component Object Model. *Dr. Dobbs Journal*, 12 1994.

13. Ted G. Lewis. Where is Client/Server Software Headed? *IEEE Computer*, 28(4):49–55, 1995.

14. Richard M. Adler. Distributed Coordination Models for Client/Server Computing. *IEEE Computer*, 28(4):14–22, 1995.

15. Robert Tolksdorf. Coordinating Services in Open Distributed Systems with LAURA. In Ciancarini and Hankin [24], pages 386–402. Proc. COORDINATION'96.

16. Thilo Kielmann. Designing a Coordination Model for Open Systems. In Ciancarini and Hankin [24], pages 267 – 284. Proc. COORDINATION'96.

17. Tom Holvoet and Thilo Kielmann. Behaviour Specification of Parallel Active Objects. *Parallel Computing*, 24:1107–1135, 1998.

18. Gul Agha and Christian J. Callsen. ActorSpace: An Open Distributed Programming Paradigm. In *Proc. of the Fourth ACM Symposium on Principles and Practice of Parallel Programming*, pages 23–32, San Diego, Ca., 1993. Published in SIGPLAN Notices, Vol. 28, No. 7, 1993.

19. Luca Cardelli. Obliq: A Language with Distributed Scope. Research Report 122, Digital Equipment Corporation, Systems Research Center, 1994.

20. P. Ciancarini and D. Rossi. Jada: Coordination and Communication for Java agents. In J. Vitek and C. Tschudin, editors, *Mobile Object Systems: Towards the Programmable Internet*, volume 1222 of *Lecture Notes in Computer Science*, pages 213–228. Springer-Verlag, Berlin, 1997.

21. Eric Freeman, Susanne Hupfer, and Ken Arnold. *JavaSpaces, Principles, Patterns, and Practice*. Addison Wesley, 1999.

22. P. Wyckoff, S. McLaughry, T. Lehman, and D. Ford. T spaces. *IBM Systems Journal*, 37(3):454–474, 1998.

23. Ken Arnold, Bryan O'Sullivan, Robert W. Scheifler, Jim Waldo, and Ann Wollrath. *The Jini Specification*. Addison Wesley, 1999.
24. Paolo Ciancarini and Chris Hankin, editors. *Coordination Languages and Models*, number 1061 in Lecture Notes in Computer Science, Cesena, Italy, 1996. Springer. Proc. COORDINATION'96.

EXPLOSIVE ADVANCES IN COMPUTATIONAL CHEMISTRY — APPLICATIONS OF PARALLEL COMPUTING IN BIOMEDICAL AND MATERIAL SCIENCE RESEARCH

LEONID GORB, ILYA YANOV, AND JERZY LESZCZYNSKI

Computational Center for Molecular Structure and Interactions (CCMSI), Department of Chemistry, Jackson State University, Jackson, Mississippi 39217-0510, USA

The efficiency of parallel computations on a CRAY T3E 1200 system with the parallel version of Gaussian 94 has been studied. Several molecular systems (a complex between nitrobenzene and the hydrated surface of clay minerals, a complex of guanosine phosphate with a hydrated magnesium cation, and a fullerene molecule) have been investigated. These species represent the systems of current interest in the fields of environmental, biological, and material science as well as general chemistry and were selected for our benchmark test at the HF and B3LYP levels of theory with the STO-2G, STO-3G, 3-21G*, 4-31G, 6-31G, and 6-31G(d) basis sets. The wallclock time and efficiency of parallelization for links 502 and 703 are tested and discussed.

1 Introduction

While computational chemistry has made spectacular progress in the last couple of decades, the current state of the art nevertheless leaves both room and need for improvement. Many important problems in surface science, pharmacology, and material science require a quantitative description of extended molecular systems. Since experimental information is scarce for many of these chemical systems, a computational approach would be particularly desirable. However, the ultimate breakthrough for computational methods in the study of such systems has been limited by the availability of inexpensive computing power.

That situation is now rapidly changing as the emergence of parallel computing appears to offer a remedy for these concerns. Over the past few years, the evolving computer hardware situation has allowed new areas of chemistry to be explored with computational methods. Many parallel architectures allow for very high nominal performance, measured in GFLOPS, at a very affordable cost. In general, however, the computational methods and algorithms traditionally used do not lend themselves well to efficient implementation on parallel hardware. An extensive development of algorithms and computer codes is therefore mandatory. Indeed, one of the most significant challenges facing contemporary computational quantum chemists involves the restructuring of application software to fully utilize current computer hardware. Considering the wide variety of available computer architectures and the ephemeral nature of the cutting edge technology upon which they are based, this is not a one-time task but rather an ongoing development project.

To take full advantage of a parallel computer, the user needs software coded to run in parallel. This is not a simple task because effective parallel code needs software which can be ported from computers designed for sequential calculations. Nevertheless, due to the tremendous, ongoing efforts of the last 10 years, most well known quantum chemical programs such as GAUSSIAN [1], GAMESS [2], MOPAC [3], HONDO [4], CADPAC [5], and COLUMBUS [6] have been parallelized. Among them the GAUSSIAN series of programs has been established as the most widely used ab initio package [7,8]. This is not only because of the extremely simple internal language which controls the *ab initio* job but also due to the constantly improving performance of this program. This increased performance makes possible the determination of structures, thermochemistry, characterization of IR and UV spectra, and the reaction mechanisms of gas phase, solution, and surface reactions. GAUSSIAN 94 is parallelized using the Linda parallel programming environment [9].

The data reflecting performance of the GAUSSIAN packages on parallel computers are published in several papers [8-10]. Most of them are used as benchmarks for molecules having a basis set consisting of ~300 basis functions. However, calculations with this many basis functions can be performed successfully on a modern machine having a single CPU.

To utilize the power of parallel computing we have chosen tasks which are very difficult to run on a single CPU computer in order to obtain the result within a reasonable amount of time. The systems investigated by our group are chosen because of the significance of their practical applications.

All calculations have been performed at the Army High Performance Computing Research Center [11] using a Cray T3E-1200 LC256-512 system. Each processor element (PE) of this computer uses the DEC Alpha microprocessor running at 600 MHz to give peak performance of over 300 gigaflops. Each PE has 512 megabytes of memory for a total of 131072 megabytes. The memory is logically shared but physically distributed such that any processor can access the memory of any other processor. The processors are connected in 3-D torus by a network capable of a 480 megabytes/second transfer rate in each direction. Among the different numbers of parameters which reflect the efficiency of a programs running in parallel, we have chosen an efficiency (E) which is calculated as follows

$$S = t_1/t_p,$$
$$E = (S/p)*100,$$

where t_p is the time for parallel calculations, and t_1 is the time for the sequential calculations. The Gaussian 94 Revision E2 [1] has been chosen for our testing. It is known that there are two steps which are the most time consuming. These are Link 502 (the closed and open shell SCF solution) and Link 703 (the two-electron integral first and second derivative evaluation). It is also important to note that the time which is needed to complete Link 502 at the Hartree-Fock level is approximately 80% of the CPU time which is typically required to finish one step of the optimization procedure. Because we tested the code which is routinely used by the computational chemists on the Cray T3E computer, the only available way to obtain the time of execution is to measure the total elapsed wallclock time for the entire link. This time includes both parallel and sequential time as well as the I/O and link initiation time. The efficiency of these particular links has been tested below for the calculations of the adsorption complex between nitrobenzene and the hydrated surface of clay minerals, fullerenes, and deoxyguanosine molecules.

We also would like to mention that all results were obtained performing standard calculations on a system running several jobs concurrently. Due to the large number of possible factors affecting time such as operating system, compiler type, speed of disk memory, etc., the readers of this report may not be able to exactly reproduce the indicated times. Finally we would like to mention that nobody from the industry which produced and distributed the software and the hardware has been involved in this investigation.

2 Results

2.1 Adsorption complex between nitrobenzene and hydrated surface of clay minerals.

Pesticides, herbicides, solvents, explosives, dyes, and nitro-aromatic compounds (NAC) are among the 127 "priority pollutants" included in the US EPA priority pollutant list. It has been shown that NACs adsorb strongly and specifically on natural clays [12]. This observation could give a rise to a number of very efficient technologies which are able to expedite the remediation of NAC contaminants. For testing purposes, the cluster having the stoichiometric formula $Si_6Al_6O_{30}H_{18}$ (Figure 1) has been chosen. It consists of pseudohexagonal silica-oxygen and alumino-oxygen rings connected through Si-O-Al bonds in the same way as 1:1 (kaolinite) and 2:1 (montmorillonite) clay minerals. The geometry of the cluster has been fully optimized at the HF/6-31G(d,p) level.

To avoid multiple calculations to locate the most favorable position of the Na^+ cation, we have determined the electrostatic potential in the plane which is parallel to the basal plane and is located 1 Å above the position of the basal oxygen [13]. The Na^+ cation has been placed in the area with the most negative electrostatic potential in the vicinity of atoms O2 and O3 (Figure 1), and the structure was reoptimized. This structure has been used for our testing of efficiency at Hartree-Fock level. It consists of 81 atoms and has the stoichiometric formula $Si_6Al_5MgO_{30}H_{18}(H_2O)_2C_6H_5NO_2$. To complete one SCF step, this system needs 15 SCF iterations. The aim of our testing was to get data regarding the efficiency of Link 502 and Link 703 depending on the number of basis functions and primitive gaussians. The results of our testing are presented in Table 1 (Link 502) and Table 2 (Link 703) and in Figures 2 and 3.

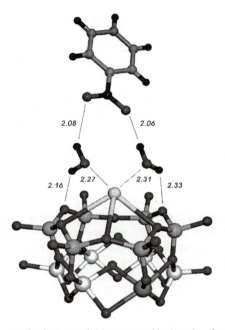

Fig. 1 Adsorption complex between nitrobenzene and hydrated surface of clay mineral:
$Si_6Al_5MgO_{30}H_{18}(H_2O)_2C_6H_5NO_2$ – complex 1.

It is well known that to obtain reliable results for the interaction energy, one should perform the calculations at least at the 6-31G(d) level. As follows from the data collected in Table 1, this level of calculation can be reached only by running the job on 8 and 16 processors of the CRAY T3E computer (the run time at the Computer Center was limited to 8 hours). Considering the total efficiency of the mentioned job, it is assumed that the job utilizes the computer facilities efficiently if the calculated efficiency exceeds 75%. Based on this assumption one may see that efficiency depends dramatically on the number of basis functions used. A job using a relatively small number of functions (basis sets STO-3G and STO-3G*) is running efficiently on not more then 16 processors. The job which is using a relatively large number of basis functions (basis sets 6-31G(d) and 6-31G(d,p)) is efficient up to 32 processors. Neither of the tested basis sets are efficient when a job is running on 64 processors. It should be noted that the parallelization of Link 703 has performed much better that of Link 502 when a job is running on up to 16 processors.

Table 1. The wallclock (Link 502) average time (sec.) per one SCF HF iteration for a clay–nitrobenzene complex.

Basis set	No. of basis functions	No. of primitive gaussians	Number of processors						
			1	2	4	8	16	32	64
STO-3G	349	1047	438	228	120	66	27.6	43.8	24
STO-3G*	414	1112	1050	534	276	174	96	72	42
3-21G*	670	1125	3720[a]	1938	906	504	282	186	142
6-31G	592	1608	3900[b]	-	1008	594	336	192	132
6-31G(d)	916	1932	12900[c]	-	-	1818	990	666	480
6-31G(d,p)	997	2013	15840[d]	-	-	-	1200	720	498

[a]estimated taking into account the 95% efficiency of the job running on 2 nodes
[b]estimated taking into account the 96% efficiency of the job running on 4 nodes
[c]estimated taking into account the 89% efficiency of the job running on 8 nodes
[d]estimated taking into account the 82% efficiency of the job running on 16 nodes

Table 2. The wallclock (Link 703) time (sec.) for two electron integrals, first and second derivatives of a clay–nitrobenzene complex.

Basis set	No. of basis functions	No. of primitive gaussians	Number of processors						
			1	2	4	8	16	32	64
STO-3G	349	1047	3318	1710	840	420	210	180	90
STO-3G*	414	1112	7698	3912	1980	1038	486	492	210
3-21G*	670	1125	18348[a]	-	4704	2352	1206	600	432
6-31G	592	1608	22110[b]	-	5670	2898	1440	810	720
6-31G(d)	916	1932	67200[c]	-	-	-	4392	2298	1518
6-31G(d,p)	997	2013	77280[d]	-	-	-	4986	4338	2958

[a]estimated taking into account the 97% efficiency of the job running on 4 nodes
[b]estimated taking into account the 97% efficiency of the job running on 4 nodes
[c]estimated taking into account the 95% efficiency of the job running on 16 nodes
[d]estimated taking into account the 97% efficiency of the job running on 16 nodes

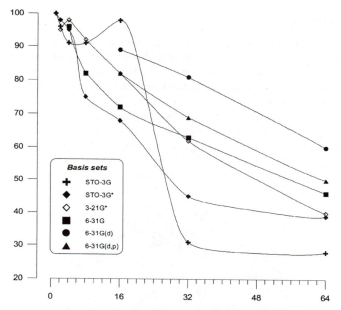

Fig. 2. Efficiency (%) of the computations (Complex 1, Link 502).

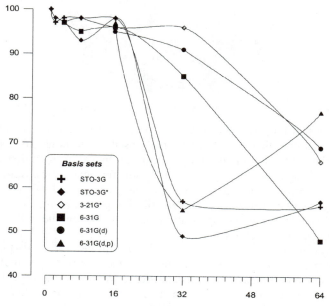

Fig. 3. Efficiency (%) of the computations (Complex 1, Link 703).

2.2   Fullerene (C_{60})

As the amount of memory on the modern parallel computers continues to increase, today it is possible to perform a considerable portion of the calculations entirely in memory. It is well known that this option leads to an increase in the efficiency of the calculations. In this section we present the performance of the Cray T3E system for direct Hartree-Fock SCF calculations (Link 502).

To obtain the actual efficiency of the computations, it is necessary to choose a representative system and the appropriate basis sets and theoretical methods. The geometry of the C_{60} molecule (Fig. 4) was selected as the input data for our benchmark test at the HF and B3LYP levels of theory with the STO-2G, STO-3G, 3-21G*, 4-31G, 6-31G, and 6-31G(d) basis sets.

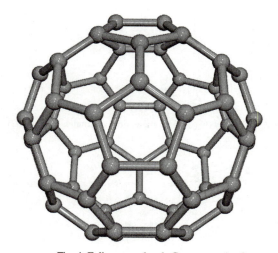

Fig. 4. Fullerene molecule C_{60} — complex 2.

The unusual properties of fullerene molecules and their unique characteristics allow us to assume that they will be widely used in the future for the creation of new materials [14]. Reports on the prospective applications of fullerene structures have been recently published. They include soft ferromagnetics, three-dimensional organic conductors, lubricant materials, etc. Of special significance is the superconductivity discovered in fullerene films doped with alkaline metals [15,16]. It is also of interest in the application of materials on the fullerene basis for nanotechnology and catalysis.

The C_{60} molecule is also interesting for testing because of its high symmetry and uniform structure. In our test along with the regular benchmark data (time, speedup ratio or efficiency of parallelization), we utilize these properties of the fullerene molecule to study the dependencies that are not often discussed in literature.

First of all, the time of the direct (in memory) quantum chemistry computations depends not only on the number of basis functions but also on the number of fitting functions (primitive gaussians) of the system. We address these relationships in this work.

The I_h symmetry of fullerene molecule can be reduced to D_{5D} — one of the highest symmetries allowed in GAUSSIAN94. We compare the efficiency of the parallelization in relation to the symmetry of the system.

The benchmark results for parallel direct HF and B3LYP SCF calculations on the C_{60} molecule are given in Tables 3 and 4 and consequently in Figures 5 and 6. As before, these data are in the tables giving the total run times, and the figures show the percentage efficiency.

Table 3. The wallclock (Link 502) average time for one SCF iteration (sec.). C_{60}, HF level of theory.

Basis set	No. of basis functions	No. of primitive gaussians	Number of processors						
			1	2	4	8	16	32	64
STO-2G	300	600	78	44	26	17	12	9	8
STO-3G	300	900	134	70	39	25	14	10	8
3-21G*	540	900	563	277	156	98	70	48	39
4-31G	540	1200	811	410	225	170	88	78	74
6-31G	540	1320	1091[a]	-	303	219	120	101	52
6-31G(d)	900	1680	5389[b]	-	1497	843	528	378	281

[a]estimated taking into account the 90% efficiency of the job running on 4 nodes
[b]estimated taking into account the 90% efficiency of the job running on 4 nodes

Table 4. The wallclock (Link 502) average time for the one SCF iteration (sec.). C_{60}, B3LYP level of theory.

Basis set	No. of basis functions	No. of primitive gaussians	Number of processors					
			1	2	4	8	16	32
STO-2G	300	600	572	292	147	79	43	26
STO-3G	300	900	754	391	196	105	56	31
3-21G*	540	900	2194	1098	582	317	195	140
4-31G	540	1200	1833[a]	965	504	309	174	108
6-31G	540	1320	2361[b]	-	656	367	185	156
6-31G(d)	900	1680	7441[c]	-	2067	1106	633	392

[a]estimated taking into account the 95% efficiency of the job running on 4 nodes
[b]estimated taking into account the 90% efficiency of the job running on 4 nodes
[c]estimated taking into account the 90% efficiency of the job running on 4 nodes

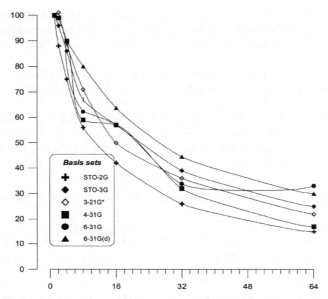

Fig. 5. Efficiency (%) of the computations (Complex 2, Link 502, HF level of theory).

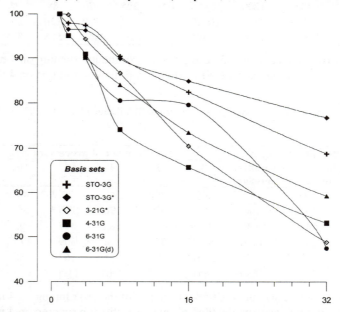

Fig. 6. Efficiency (%) of the computations (Complex 2, Link 502, B3LYP level of theory).

As one can see, an average performance of approximately 75 percent is achieved in jobs running up to the 16 processors. The efficiency of more than 16 processors is less than 30%. It should be noticed that the overall performance and efficiency of the calculations increases with an increase in the size of the problem and the requirements of a more time consuming level of theory (B3LYP).

Fig. 5 shows also the dependence of the efficiency as a function of the number of primitive gaussians in the system with the same number (540) of basis functions.

The time and efficiency of the parallelization in relation to the D_{5D} symmetry of the system are shown in Table 5 and Figure 7. From the data presented here, it is clear that although the use of symmetry considerably reduces the time of the calculations, the efficiency of parallelization is much lower.

Table 5. The wallclock (Link 502) average time for the one SCF iteration (sec.). C_{60}, HF level of theory. D_{5D} symmetry.

Basis set	No. of basis functions	No. of primitive gaussians	Number of processors					
			1	2	4	8	16	32
STO-2G	300	600	16	14	12	12	11	21
STO-3G	300	900	18.	16	13	12	11	15
3-21G*	540	900	89	68	57	52	52	49
6-31G	540	1320	77	59	48	44	44	47
6-31G(d)	900	1680	563	296	233	203	186	188

[a]estimated taking into account the 95% efficiency of the job running on 4 nodes

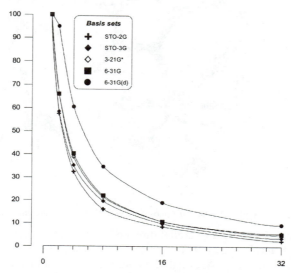

Fig. 7. Efficiency (%) of the computations (Complex 2 with D_{5D}, Link 502, HF level of theory).

2.3   Complex between guanosine phosphate and hydrated magnesium cation

Knowledge of the geometrical structure and electron density distribution in deoxyribonucleotides is of fundamental importance for chemistry and biology. The reason is well justified: the canonical forms of deoxyribonucleotides are the building blocks of DNA and RNA molecules. Being extremely flexible and not inert chemically, deoxyribonucleotides have several potential sites for bonding with different substances such as water and other hydrogen bonding donors and acceptors, metal ions, peptides, etc. It is now well documented that all these properties are tightly connected with the biological functions of DNA [17,18].

For testing purposes, we have chosen guanosine phosphate which has the largest number of atoms between the nucleotides used to construct DNA and RNA molecules. According to the experimental data this system exists as the complex between the nucleotide and magnesium cation coordinated by 5 molecules (Figure 8). It consists of 51 atoms and has the stoichiometric formula $C_{10}O_{12}N_5H_{23}MgP$. The geometry has been optimized at HF/6-31G(d) level.

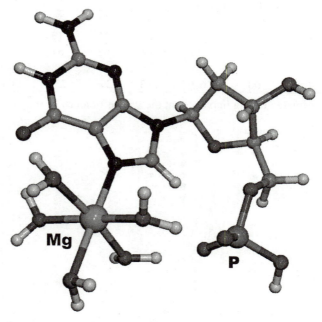

Fig. 8. Complex of guanosine phosphate with $Mg(H_2O)_5^{2+}$— complex 3.

The benchmark results for parallel direct SCF calculations for this complex are given in Table 6 and in Figure 9. The data in the table give the total run times, and the figure shows efficiency. Although the compound system has the lowest number of basis functions among the considered systems, the efficiency of parallel computation has the same tendencies that have been described above for other systems tested at the Hartree–Fock level. From a practical viewpoint the most important is the tendency to increase the efficiency when there is an increase in the number of basis functions. It allows for the assumption that for larger, biologically important species SCF level calculations will be feasible in the near future.

Table 6. The wallclock (Link 502) average time for the one SCF iteration (sec.). Complex between guanosine phosphate and hydrated magnesium cation, HF level of theory.

Basis set	No. of basis functions	No. of primitive gaussians	Number of processors					
			1	2	4	8	16	32
STO-2G	176	352	34	19	10	8	4	3
STO-3G	176	528	69	36	19	10	6	4
3-21G*	327	540	264	135	72	44	26	21
6-31G	315	778	382	197	107	59	37	22
6-31G(d)	489	952	1327	688	363	243	131	72

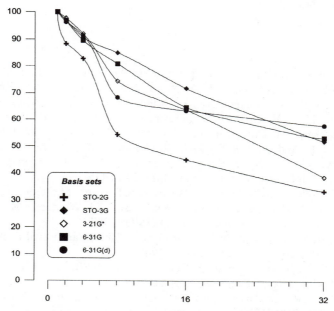

Fig. 9. Efficiency (%) of the computations (Complex 3, Link 502, HF level of theory).

3 Conclusions

The application of commercial parallelized software allows computational chemists to successfully investigate not only simple molecules but to also extend their studies to problems of practical applications. Among the scientific areas which could benefit the most from such studies are material science, molecular biology, and biomedical applications. The available quantum chemical codes are not yet fully parallelized. The progress in this area is expected to be explosive in the years to come.

Acknowledgement

This work was facilitated by the NIH grant No. G12RR13459-21, by the Office of Naval Research Grant No. N00014-98-1-0592 and by the support of the Army High Performance Computing Research Center under the auspices of the Department of the Army, Army Research Laboratory cooperative agreement number DAAH04-95-2-0003/contract number DAAH04-95-C-0008, the content of which does not necessarily reflect the position or policy of the government, and no official endorsement should be inferred.

References

1. Gaussian 94, Revision E.2, M. J. Frisch, G. W. Trucks, H. B. Schlegel, P. M. W. Gill, B. G. Johnson, M. A. Robb, J. R. Cheeseman, T. Keith, G. A. Petersson, J. A. Montgomery, K. Raghavachari, M. A. Al-Laham, V. G. Zakrzewski, J. V. Ortiz, J. B. Foresman, J. Cioslowski, B. B. Stefanov, A. Nanayakkara, M. Challacombe, C. Y. Peng, P. Y. Ayala, W. Chen, M. W. Wong, J. L. Andres, E. S. Replogle, R. Gomperts, R. L. Martin, D. J. Fox, J. S. Binkley, D. J. Defrees, J. Baker, J. P. Stewart, M. Head-Gordon, C. Gonzalez, and J. A. Pople, Gaussian, Inc., Pittsburgh PA, 1995.
2. M.W.Schmidt, K.K.Baldridge, J.A.Boatz, S.T.Elbert, M.S.Gordon, J.J.Jensen, S.Koseki, N.Matsunaga, K.A.Nguyen, S.Su, T.L.Windees, M.Dupois and J.A.Montgomery, J.Comput.Chem., 14 (1993) 1347.
3. J. J. P. Stewart. MOPAC Manual; A General Molecular Orbital Package, Frank J. Seiler Research Labaoratory, Dec. 1988.
4. HONDO. Michel Dupouis, Dept. MLMA/MS078, IBM Corporation, Neighborhood Road, Kingston, New York 12401.
5. CADPAC. Roger Amos, University Chemical Laboratory, Lensfield Road, Cambridge, CB2 1EW, Great Britian
6. H. Lischka, H. Dachsel, R. Shepard, R. J. Harrison. In Parallel Computing in Computational Chemistry. Ed. T. G. Mattson; AC, Washington, DC 1995.

7. W.J. Hehre, L. Radom, P. v. R. Schleyer, J. A. Pople. Ab .initio Molecular Orbital Theory; John Willey & Sons; New York, 1986.
8. Book series "Computational Chemistry: Reviews of Current Trends". Vol. 1-4. Ed. J. Leszczynski. World Scientific. 1997-1999.
9. Scientific Computing Associates Inc. C-Linda User's Guide & Reference Manual; New Haven, CT, 1993.
10. http://www.gaussian.com/wp_linda.htm
11. AHPCRC, http://www.arc.umn.edu/structure
12. S. B. Haderlain, R. P. Schwarzenbach. Environ. Sci Technol. 1996, 30, 612.
13. L. Gorb, J. Gu, D. Leszczynska, J. Leszczynski. (submitted).
14. J. Leszczynski and I. Yanov J. Phys. Chem. A 1999, 103, 396-401.
15. A.F.Hebard, M.J.Rosseinsky, R.C. Haddon. Superconductivity at 18 K in potassium-doped C_{60}. Nature, 1991, 350, 6319, 600.
16. Z. Iqbal, R.H. Baughman, B.L. Ramakrishna. Superconductivity at 45 K in rubidium/thallium codoped fullerene C_{60} and C_{60}/C_{70} mixtures. Science 1991, 254, 5033, 826.
17. W. Saenger. Principles of Nucleic Acid Structure. Springer-Verlag, New-York, Berlin, London, Paris, Tokyo, 1983.
18. Nucleic Acids in Chemistry and Biology. Eds. By G. M. Blackburn and M. J. Gait. Oxford University Press, Oxford, New-York, Tokyo, 1990.

32

THE CHALLENGE OF MASSIVELY PARALLEL COMPUTING

DAVID E. WOMBLE

*Sandia National Laboratories, *Albuquerque, NM, USA, 87185-1110*

Since the mid-1980's, there have been a number of commercially available parallel computers with hundreds or thousands of processors. These machines have provided a new capability to the scientific community, and they been used successfully by scientists and engineers although with varying degrees of success. One of the reasons for the limited success is the difficulty, or perceived difficulty, in developing code for these machines. In this paper we discuss many of the issues and challenges in developing scalable hardware, system software and algorithms for machines comprising hundreds or thousands of processors.

1 Introduction

Massively parallel computing has been around since the mid-1980s and has been used by scientists and engineers with varying degrees of success. Presently, only a few institutions continue to use massively parallel computers. Most institutions are currently investing in machines with smaller numbers of processors or clusters of workstations and are using these machines because of their computing capacity instead of their computing capabilities.

Effective massively parallel computing has the reputation of being difficult to achieve. Whether a specific application or use of these machines is, in fact, difficult will be left up to the reader; however, it is true that there are many issues that must be specifically addressed. It is also true that these issues span the range of hardware, system software, and algorithms, and that many of these issues are beyond most users' control. Nevertheless, users must be familiar with the issues if they are to use these machines effectively [2]. It is the purpose of this paper to discuss the major issues affecting massively parallel computing.

We begin by defining *massively parallel computing*. The working definition for this paper will be the use of a sufficient number of processors that particular attention must be paid to the issues of scalability. Of course, this is application dependent. For example, in some simulations with explicit time steps, 500 processors might not be considered massively parallel. In other applications, such as those that require multidimensional FFTs, 50 proces-

*Sandia is a multiprogram laboratory operated by Sandia Corporation, a Lockheed Martin Company, for the United States Department of Energy under Contract DE-AC04-94AL85000.

sors might be considered massively parallel. In practice, the effects of poor scalability are often seen somewhere between 50 and 100 processors. This is where slow networks, serial bottlenecks and other non-scalable constructs are almost certain to show up.

This definition reduces the challenge of efficient massively parallel computing to one of scalability. In this paper, we will consider three aspects of scalability: algorithms, hardware and system software. Each of these has an impact on overall efficiency of a simulation code as does the interaction between the three. Hardware often gets a lot of attention. Machines with tens of thousands of processors have been built, and these machines are often characterized using things like communication-to-computation ratios and bisection bandwidths.

Scalable algorithms have also been considered at length in the technical literature. Computational scientists work hard to parallelize individual applications codes and pay special attention to computational kernels like the solution of linear systems of equations, FFTs, the solution of tridiagonal systems, and matrix transposition.

The scalability of system software and tools has received somewhat less attention. Even though parallel capabilities have been added to operating systems, they often require $O(p^2)$ time or memory. For example, a system that requires a table entry for each page of memory on each processor requires $O(p^2)$ memory. Also, tools like debuggers designed for thousands of processors are almost non-existent.

In this paper, we will examine each of the three aspects of scalability in more detail. However, in light of the recent industry trend towards the use of commodity components, we first state

Fallacy #1: A massively parallel computer is just a collection of workstations

The fact is that while workstations can be replicated and connected by reasonably fast networks, the issues of scalability discussed throughout this paper must be specifically addressed if the system is to scale to hundreds or thousands of processors. If these issues are not addressed, a cluster of a thousand workstations will be used most effectively by running a thousand small jobs simultaneously. In other words, this cluster provides computing capacity, but it does not provide a new capability to a scientist or engineer.

After the section addressing the scalability of algorithms, hardware and sytem software, we will discuss the Cplant project at Sandia National Laboratories, which is an attempt to develop a scalable cluster of workstations.

2 Algorithms

Before discussing algorithms specifically, we must distinguish between two types of efficiency. The first is the traditional fixed-size parallel efficiency.

$$E_p = \frac{T(n,1)}{pT(n,p)},$$

where n is the problem size and p is the number of processors on which the problem is run. This attempts to measure the effect of the parallelization, including such factors as interprocessor communications.

One of the problems with this measure of performance is that it is not consistent with how parallel machines are used. Scientists and engineers want a new capability, which usually means the ability to solve larger problems faster than would be possible on serial machines. To incorporate the effect of problem size we introduce a second type of efficiency, algorithmic efficiency, which refers to how the computational requirement scales as the number of unknowns increases or as the desired accuracy increases compared to a base problem size n. The algorithmic efficiency can be written as

$$E_a = \frac{mT(n,p)}{T(mn,p)},$$

where m is the scaling factor for the problem size. This is, perhaps, less informative and less formal than traditional algorithm analysis. However, it does have the property that it is similar in style to the traditional parallel efficiency and that it assigns an efficiency of 1 to an algorithm that scales as $O(n)$, which is the goal of many algorithms in modeling and simulation.

Combining these efficiencies, yields

$$E = E_p E_a = \frac{mT(n,1)T(n,p)}{pT(n,p)T(mn,p)},$$

which is the efficiency that scientists would actually see as they scale the problem to match machine capabilities. If $m = p$, that is if the scaling of the number of processors equals the scaling of the problem size, the efficiency becomes

$$E = \frac{T(n,1)}{T(p \times n, p)},$$

which is the traditional definition of scaled efficiency where the problem size is increased in proportion to the number of processors.

An example of an algorithm that achieves good parallel efficiency, but poor algorithmic efficiency, is Jacobi iteration. An example of an algorithm that achieves good algorithmic efficiency, but poor parallel efficiency, is the solution of a tridiagonal linear system. If a choice must be made, an algorithm with good algorithmic efficiency is to be preferred over one with good parallel efficiency in almost all cases. This leads us to state the following.

Fallacy #2: A massively parallel computer can make a bad algorithm good.

In other words, if the algorithm is not the preferred one for a problem of size n on a serial machine, it is not likely to be the preferred one for a problem of the same size on a parallel machine.

We can also divide algorithms into two types. The first type is *solvers.* The term here is used broadly, and includes algorithms that are used both in serial and parallel implementations of codes. The second type is *enabling algorithms.* These algorithms are specific to parallel implementations, and include things like load balancing and algorithms for explicit matrix transposes. In some sense, these algorithms are purely parallel overhead, and the performance of parallel codes requires that special attention be paid to efficient, scalable implementations.

Scalability must receive special consideration when parallelizing either solver or enabling algorithms. There are two very important issues that must be addressed if a code is to be scalable.

1. Load balance. That is, the processors must have the same amount of work

2. Data locality. That is, the data needed by a processor must be in the memory of that processor.

These two issues can be combined into the single issue of data placement, although we prefer to keep them separate.

In the case of load balance, if one processor has more work than others, a serial bottleneck is created. If this extra work does not decrease in proportion to the number of processors (and this is usually the case in real applications where load imbalances are often caused by a serial component of the algorithm orimbalanced communications), scalability is severely limited. Load balancing is often considered when domain decomposition methods are used; however, it seems to receive little attention when master-slave implementations are used, and as a result, many master-slave implementations are not scalable.

The issue of data locality is not unique to parallel machines; it is also essential to good cache performance on serial machines. However, the importance of data locality is magnified on parallel machines because of increased latencies and lower bandwidths between processors (compared to local memory latencies and bandwidths). The goal of the programmer (or compiler) must be to build data structures and distribute data to processors to minimize the time spent in the overhead of interprocessor communication. The desire of programmers to ease the burden of programming parallel machine has made shared memory programming models attractive. But despite the added difficulty of explicit message passing, it has the advantage that it forces the programmer to address the issue of data locality.

Many machines are moving towards a global address space to simplify the task of parallel programming. We would like to point out here that having a global address space, by itself, does not prevent scalability. Rather it is the dependency on compilers and hardware for internode transfers and the illusion that data locality is not important that causes problems. To justify this observation, we can consider memory associated with another node as simply another layer in the memory hierarchy. It is well known that depending on compilers and hardware to restructure a code for cache performance can result in significant performance penalties, even with the relatively small latencies for a cache miss.

3 Hardware

Hardware receives a lot of attention. Indeed, most press releases highlight numbers of processors, theoretical peak speeds, Linpack benchmark results or some other measure of performance that focuses on the hardware capabilities. In view of this, we state

Fallacy #3: Peak FLOPS is a good measure of a machines capabilities,
  and the related

Fallacy #3a: Linpack is a good measure of a machines capabilities.

The truth is that hardware performance is an important ingredient in the high performance equation but is not by itself sufficient. Linpack plays an important role as a widely accepted benchmark and as an acceptance test, but represents accurately the performance of only a few applications.

In any parallel computer, single-processor performance and communication network performance drive overall performance. Single-processor performance, in turn, is limited by processor computing rates and by memory bus bandwidths, where the latter is the limiting factor in most modern processors. To illustrate this, we compare the DEC EV-5 and the DEC EV-6 processors. At a given clock speed, both processors have the same theoretical peak flop (floating point operations) rates. However, based on actual runs of real applications at Sandia National Laboratories, the EV-6 achieves a 2.5 to 3 times performance increase primarily through improvements in the memory bus and the processor integer unit.

The performance of the interprocessor communication network is also important. Unlike computations, interprocessor communication is entirely overhead associated with parallelism. It is generally characterized in terms of latency and bandwidth, where latency is the time required to start a message transfer and bandwidth is the rate at which data can be transferred between processors. Different codes require different capabilities. Codes, like the Linpack benchmark, that are able to collect and send large messages require high bandwidths and are less sensitive to high latencies. However, codes like unstructured finite element-based simulations, tend to send smaller messages and require low latencies.

It is difficult to identify a one-size-fits-all balance between computational speeds and network latencies and bandwidths. However, in the many applications run on massively parallel computers at Sandia National Laboratories, we have found that for the current generation of processors (e.g., DEC EV-5, Intel Pentium II), achievable latencies in the range of ten microseconds and achievable bandwidths of about 300 Mbytes/sec (approximately one byte per second for each achievable floating point operation per second) allow codes to scale to thousands of processors.

In the preceding paragraph, we skirted the issue of network topology by specifying that we use achievable bandwidths during code execution for our comparisons. However, network topology can play a crucial role in bandwidths actually achieved. For example, if a network is organized as a tree, and if the bandwidths near the trunk of the tree are no larger than those near the leaves, a code running on all processors will see significantly lower bandwidths than a code running on just two processors. This is, of course, due to the bottleneck at the trunk of the network tree.

Another important issue is the reliability of the hardware. While this does not affect a machines performance directly, it certainly affects the usability. To illustrate the point, we note that most users find it tolerable that the workstation (or PC) on their desk crashes once a month. But a machine comprising 1,000 of those same workstations would be expected to crash approximately every 45 minutes and a machine comprising 10,000 of those workstations would be expected to crash approximately every 4 minutes. This would make the machine completely unusable. Indeed, some massively parallel computers cannot even load a job in this amount of time.

In this section, we have mentioned several hardware issues affecting scalability of a computer to thousands of processors. In fact, significant progress has been, and continues to be, made by hardware vendors in all of these areas. For exampel, processor performance continues to follow the curve of Moore's law. The greater challenge to vendors of massively parallel computers is system software, which is discussed in the next section.

4 System Software

In this section, we discuss the impact of system software on scalability. We use the term broadly to include, not only the operating system, but also the development environment, e.g., compilers and debuggers. As with algorithms and hardware, there are significant issues that must be addressed in systems scalable to hundreds or thousands of processors.

The operating system has been and continues to be a major limitation in achieving scalablility to thousands of processors. For example, "features" that severely limit scalability include

1. Size of the operating system. Yes, memory is cheap (at present), but enough memory to load an operating system that requires tens of megabytes and that must be replicated thousands of times is still expensive. There are additional reasons to limit the size of the operating system. First, it takes significant time to boot a machine with a heavyweight operating system. Second, increased size usually means increased complexity, which means reduced stability, and it was pointed out in the previous section that the effect of reduced stability is severe in massively parallel computers.

   Increased complexity also means more interactions between the OS and the users code. For example, interrupts can have the same effect as a serial bottleneck in a users code. As an extreme case, suppose a code synchronizes every 100 microseconds, that the code is perfectly balanced, that the OS generates an interrupt randomly but on average once a second, and that the interrupt lasts 10 microseconds. (In fact, Linux on an Alpha generates 1024 interupts per second.) On a two-processor machine, this results in a 0.001% reduction in scaled efficiency, because two out of every 10,000 synchronizations are delayed. (Actually, the reduction in efficiency is slightly less since there is a small chance that the two interrupts occur during the same sychronization interval.) But on a 10,000-processor machine, this results in worst case scaled efficiency of 90% and an expected scaled efficiency of 94%. (The number of syncrhonizations intervals that are not interrupted have a Poisson distribution with mean $10,000/e \approx 3679$.) The fact is that many of the features that drive up the size of the OS are not necessary on the compute nodes of a massively parallel computer.

2. Support for multiple users and time sharing. Time sharing compute nodes

in a massively parallel computer has the same effect (although much more severe) as OS interrupts. To illustrate this, consider a machine with 100 processors that is time shared by two users. Half of the time on each shared processor is allocated to one user who has a code loaded on all 100 processors, and half of the time is allocated to the second user who has a code loaded on 50 processors. If each job requires the same wall-clock time, the total usage of the machine is only 75%. A better way to use the machine is to allocate to users the number of nodes on which their code runs effectively, to guarantee them 100% of the time on those nodes, that is to space share the machine.

3. Support for virtual memory. In principle, virtual memory is a good thing, but only for workstations. The problem is that virtual memory adds a lot of overhead. Even on a workstation, a simulation that uses virtual memory can take many times longer than the same simulation running on a machine with sufficient physical memory. On a parallel computer, the situation is worse. First, swapping often appears as a serial bottleneck, in much the same way as OS interrupts described in item 1, although the effect is much worse. Second, unless there is a disk on each node, there is either network contention or disk contention as processors vie for limited disk resources.

4. Cache coherency across processors and attempts at distributed shared memory. The promise of cache coherency coupled with a global address space and a shared memory paradigm is that the user can worry about the parallelism in the computation without worrying about the parallelism in (location of) the data. The problem is that implementations of cache coherency typically scale as $O(p^2)$ in total memory and work. This may be fine on a very small number of processors but not on thousands of processors. Algorithms that incur $O(p^2)$ overhead are not considered scalable and neither should system software with the same scaling. Another problem with having this capabililty is that users will use it. But as was discussed in the algorithms section, the location of the data and the management of communications is critical in achieving scalable performance. Both of these are left to general purpose system software which is usually much less than optimal.

There are also several problems that persist in system software even though they are known to prevent scalability and have been eliminated in all successful implementations on massively parallel machines. Two examples follow.

1. Linear processor loads. A job is usually started on a massively parallel computer by loading a users code on each processor on which the code is to execute. If this is done in a linear fashion, i.e., one processor at a time, the overhead is $O(p)$. However, since the same code is usually loaded on each processor, a logrithmic load is possible, which has overhead $O(\log(p))$. On a 1000-processor machine, the difference is a factor of 100: a job that should take 30 seconds to load and start would take almost an hour. This is hardly an efficient use of expensive massively parallel computer hardware.

2. Preallocated communication buffers for each processor. There are also some operating system implementations that preallocate a communication buffer corresponding to each processor from which a message is expected during the code execution (at least equal in size to the largest message expected during the execution). The problem is that for codes in which all-to-all communications are expected or possible (or if the OS cannot identify or does not allow the user to specify the communication pattern), $O(p^2)$ memory is required. On a 1000-processor machine, it is possible that hundreds of megabytes of memory must be reserved for communication buffers on each node.

Many of these problems arise from the mistaken view that workstation operating systems that focus on user interactions are also good for massively parallel computing. (We refer to this as a workstation mentality.) One solution is to take advantage of the fact that nodes in massively parallel computers typically serve a particular purpose and to use a partitioned model for the operating system. For example, a workstation operating system can (and should) be used on the service nodes, i.e., nodes on which users log in, compile code, and queue jobs to the compute nodes. A stripped down operating system focusing on a minimal set of services, including efficient interprocessor communications can then be used on compute nodes. A similar philosophy applies to I/O nodes, or other special-purpose nodes.

Parallel development environments and tools also suffer from a workstation mentality, although in a somewhat different fashion. The challenge in this case is to collect, process and present data from many processors in such a way that the user can quickly develop, debug or improve the performance of code for parallel computers. The problem is that most vendors are trying to simply extend current tools without sufficiently addressing the problems of scalability. Some of these challenges are the following.

1. The tools must themselves be efficient, scalable, distributed memory codes.

2. The tools must be able to collect, organize and present much larger datasets to the programmer

3. There is a new set of problems that face programmers and the tools must be able to present data in such a way as to make these problems easy to identify. For example, a debugger must present data such that deadlocks due to message passing problems are obvious. This may not be difficult when programmers are explicitly programming the message passing, but it will become more difficult as compilers attempt to hide more and more of the complexities of distributed memory parallelism from the programmer.

Finally in this section, we mention compilers. Much has been accomplished on compilers that identify parallelism, or otherwise attempt hide or simplify the task of writing parallel code, but they are not able to produce scalable code for massively parallel computers. The problem is that while the parallelism in a simulation may be obvious at the level of the physics or the model (e.g., a domain decomposition approach), it is usually not obvious at the code level. Compilers generally consider fine-grain parallelism at the level of inner loops, whereas the physics-based parallelism is often at the level of the outer loop. As a simple example, a compiler may be able to see that a finite-difference code performs most of its calculations on one-dimensional arrays and partition the work accordingly. But it may miss the fact that the one-dimensional array comes from a three-dimensional problem and that communication may be significantly reduced if a different decomposition is used. Compilers also depend on easily understood, regular data structures to identify parallelism, but data structures are not always regular. For example, finite element simulations usually involve irregular data structures and rely heavily on indirect addressing.

Many of the tools available to programmers are effective for small numbers of processors. This represents one approach: to start with small numbers of processors and attempt to evolve the tools to large numbers of processors as techniques evolve. It is our opinion that the problems of scalability and massive parallelism, both for operating systems and tools, should be addressed up front and specifically. We will then end up with better tools and these tools will port easily to smaller numbers of processors. In other words, just as in the cases of algorithms and hardware, scalability should be addressed first.

5 Cplant

Tightly-integrated, custom designed massively parallel machines have continued to increase in cost until very few institutions or industries are able to afford them or willing to buy them. As a result, the recent trend is to assemble massively parallel machines as much as possible from commodity (workstation and network) components. The trap in this approach is to fall into the workstation mentality, that is that massively parallel computers can be designed and used just like workstations. The result of this thinking is a machine with a large capacity, but one that does not provide a new capability to scientists or engineers. (Of course, to be fair, capacity may be exactly what is needed in many cases.)

Sandia National Laboratories has begun a project to design, build and put into production a scalable machine of commodity components that in fact provides a new capability [1]. The machine is called Cplant. This machine currently consists of over 1,000 DEC EV-5 and EV-6 based workstations with a Myrinet interprocessor network and a version of the Linux operating system on each node. The largest single "piece" of Cplant is currently 604 nodes.

Scalability is being addressed from the start.

1. System designers are working to provide as low latency and as much of the myrinet bandwidth to applications as possible. This has involved developing extensions to Linux focused on message passing. Furthermore, the network has been designed so as not to introduce communication bottlenecks between switches.

2. Designers have addressed the reliability problem both through good hardware design (e.g., proper cooling and power supplies), through strong diagnostics, and by including a diagnostic network that enables management of individual nodes.

3. Designers are building a range of tools, including debuggers and resource management (e.g., queuing) that specifically address the massively parallel computing environment.

4. Designers have used a partitioned approach. Nodes have specific functions (e.g., computation, service, I/O or management), which enables the software on each node to do one thing reliably and well.

The Cplant focus has been on the hardware and system software aspects, and in this they have been successful. Codes that scale well to thousands of processors on machines like Sandia's Teraflops compter currently scale to hundreds of processors on Cplant. It is expected that these codes will scale to thousands of processors with a scheduled doubling of the bandwidth of the communication network and with continued improvements in such areas as operating system design and I/O.

6 Conclusions

The primary conclusion of this paper is that scalability takes extra effort and investment in algorithms, hardware and system software. In the case of algorithms, this responsibilty falls to the user or code developer, although parallel libraries and other common software can greatly reduce the work. The primary issue for the code developer is data placement (data locality and load balance). Also, parallelism is found primarily in the physics of the problem, not in the code, and the most effective code is the product of a developer who understands the problem.

The scalability of hardware and system software is most often the responsibility of the vendor. For hardware, the primary issue is providing communication between processors that matches the computational capabilities of today's processors. For system software, the challenge is to provide a robust operating system with scalable algorithms and without serial bottlenecks that and tools that collect, process and present the large amounts of data generated by massively parallel computers. For both hardware and system software, the issue of reliability must be addressed.

In each of these areas, we have found a "workstation mentality," that is, the desire to ignore the challenge of scalability and to design and use a massively parallel computer in exactly the same fashion as a workstation. This approach almost always leads to failure. Scalability must be designed in from the beginning, and the reward for doing so is a new capability for the scientist and engineer.

Acknowledgement

The author would like to thank the many staff members at Sandia National Laboratories who have contributed their experience to their paper through discussions of scalability. These staff members include Mike Heroux, Bruce Hendrickson, Steve Plimpton, Jim Tomkins, and Rolf Riesen.

References

1. R. Riesen, http://www.cs.sandia.gov/cplant , (1999).
2. D. E. Womble *et al*, Paralel Computing **26**, to appear (2000).

Applications

A COMMUNICATION LIBRARY TO COUPLE SIMULATION CODES ON DISTRIBUTED SYSTEMS FOR MULTI-PHYSICS COMPUTATIONS

R. AHREM, P. POST, K. WOLF

GMD-German National Research Center for Information Technology
Institute for Algorithms and Scientific Computing (SCAI)
Schloss Birlinghoven, D-53754 Sankt Augustin, Germany
E-mail: {regine.ahrem, peter.post, klaus.wolf}@gmd.de

A lot of tools for monodisciplinary simulations are available today. Each environment provides high quality simulation results in a specific physical domain. Now there is also a solution to do multidisciplinary computations. Multidisciplinary simulations are crucially important for realistic predictions in scientific computing and engineering. The code coupling interface COCOLIB opens this field to all parallel simulation tools without the need for significant changes or rewriting of code. This marks a breakthrough for loosely coupled parallel problems with direct industrial impact. The paper presents applications in the field of fluid-structure interaction, that demonstrate the applicability and the advantages of the parallel coupling library for this kind of problems.

1 Introduction

Extremely high demands on designing accurate prototypes in production industry require multidisciplinary simulations. For instance heart valves, airfoils, power plants or torque converters are exposed to powerful loads in their daily use because of the interactions between fluid and structure. Thus the coupled simulation of these problems is highly desirable.

Many complex physical phenomena can be regarded as coupled problems. These are defined as combinations of at least two problems described by systems of partial differential equations. The computation of each single aspect of the problem is usually performed on different, connected domains, in general with different grids. There exist efficient parallelized simulation codes on a high technological standard for monodisciplinary physical problems.

In the framework of multi-physics problems the coupling of separate simulation codes has the potential to solve various such problems. The aim of the COupling COmmunication LIBrary COCOLIB, developed in the European ESPRIT project CISPAR [1], is to enable the simulation of multi-physics problems on distributed systems. This parallel coupling library makes multiphysics computations on the basis of current high standard monodisciplinary simulation codes possible.

2   Concept of COCOLIB

An essential issue in the specification of the MPI-based communication library
COCOLIB [2] was to preserve the independence of the codes as far as possible. The philosophy behind COCOLIB is to elevate MPI to a higher level:
MPI allows communication between single processes, COCOLIB allows data
exchange between two or more parallel codes. The COCOLIB subroutine interface resembles the MPI interface as much as possible. To make COCOLIB
open to new codes no specific programming for particular simulation codes
is done inside COCOLIB. To achieve flexibility with respect to the specific
coupling algorithm used, COCOLIB is algorithm independent as much as possible. Nevertheless to facilitate the coupling of new codes, coupling standards
can be introduced to support specific coupling algorithms.

As there are no assumptions in COCOLIB on the specific codes used, code
specific tasks can be realized separated from the general COCOLIB tasks. The
code specific interface can be implemented as a layer of subroutines on top
of the basic COCOLIB. Due to this flexibility the amount of work required
to couple separately developed codes is minimized. The simulation codes are
linked to COCOLIB and call COCOLIB routines to realize the neccessary
coupling algorithm. The basic component is the exchange of coupling values
arranged on grids within the coupling region carried out transparently through
COCOLIB library calls.

The normal pre- and postprocessors can be used for the individual codes.
Each code simply works with its own local mesh and needs no specific modification for the codes with which it is coupled. The coupling data can be arranged on matching or non-matching, structured or unstructured grids. The
simulation codes must specify their coupling interface to COCOLIB. In the
current implementation the interfaces have to be 2-dimensional surfaces in
3-dimensional space, consisting of triangle or quadrilateral elements. The coordinate systems must be global, to enable COCOLIB to detect the distances
and relations between the specified interfaces. It is allowed that the interfaces
are not identical but distant from each other. The maximal allowed distance
is adjustable by a parameter in the input-file of COCOLIB. In the case of
non-matching grids the data arranged onto the nodes of the source-grid are
interpolated by COCOLIB on the nodes of the target-grid. COCOLIB manages the complex connections between the surface-meshes without the codes
being involved.

Each process of the coupled computation has its own COCOLIB layer.
The information needed to perform communication using the underlying MPI
system is stored in these COCOLIB layers. The code, COCOLIB and MPI
operate in one thread. There is no concurrency between the COCOLIB layer

and the code layer. The COCOLIB layer is only active when the thread of control passes through it. Therefore, when a code is performing computations, the local COCOLIB layer is doing nothing in the background. As a consequence, the codes must explicitly call COCOLIB subroutines to make use of the facilities of COCOLIB.

The communication between the processes of each single code is performed in the coupled computation as before, the MPI calls stay the same. The parallelization technique used for the internal communication of the codes has no influence on the code coupling. COCOLIB does not assume anything about the parallelization strategy of a code. Codes with different parallelization strategies may participate in the same coupled computation. Only a subset of the processes of a code needs to perform COCOLIB communication calls. This is useful for supporting general parallelization strategies like task farming, where some processes perform only low-level tasks and know nothing about the global solution process. MPI has the ability to partition communication space using a communicator concept. This ability allows different parallel codes to participate in the coupled computation without interfering with each other. Furthermore, the communication performed by COCOLIB is completely separated from that of the code it is linked to.

3 Software Realization and Portability

The use of object-oriented technology has led to a very clear and comprehensible internal design. The encapsulation of concepts and methods decouples the development of different parts of COCOLIB and thus facilitates teamwork. Other features like inheritance and polymorphism make it easy to add new functionality and algorithms (e.g. for contact search or interpolation). The code is completely written in C++. The library can be accessed trough C and FORTRAN-77 interfaces. Both interfaces are consistent, i.e. coupled computations where one code is written in C and the other in Fortran, are possible. The FORTRAN-77 interface is based on the C interface and simply forwards its operation to the C interface. The main COCOLIB functionality is in the C++ part, which can theoretically also be accessed directly by C++ programs. However, only the C and FORTRAN-77 interfaces are specified and should be used by a code. The C++, C and FORTRAN-77 interfaces are collectively referred to as the CCL layer. Different UNIX-platforms, various compilers and MPI-versions are supported by COCOLIB. Today COCOLIB is available for SUN Solaris, SGI IRIX, IBM AIX, IBM SP2, CRAY T3E, HP, Windows NT. The developed porting procedures are optimized, so that the expected effort to port COCOLIB onto a new machine – e.g. DEC or a new operating system version on SGI - is less than one week.

COCOLIB has various debug levels and monitor features, which can be switched on or off. Furthermore a dedicated visualization tool called COCO-Vis (cf. [3]) provides full insight into the ongoing coupling process.

The execution of the coupling code begins with a startup-phase. In this phase the COCOLIB input file is read and distributed among all processes. The COCOLIB initialization routine sets the specific environment for each code. The communicators for the code internal communication and the communicators for the communication of the codes between one another are established.

In the coupling definition phase each process of a code announces its interface parts with their nodes and elements of the coupling surface to COCOLIB. Each interface part announcement returns a so-called *interface handle* which must be used in subsequent COCOLIB calls to indicate the involved interface. When each code has specified the grid data of its side of the coupling surface, COCOLIB performs the contact search which is necessary for the interpolation. The basic search method for matching and non-matching grids implemented by COCOLIB consists of four steps:

1. **pre-contact search:** COCOLIB generates pairs of points with elements (non-matching grids) and pairs of points (matching grids) that possibly match.
2. COCOLIB applies a detailed matching criterion to all pairs that were generated in step 1 and selects the best matches.
3. **brute force search:** If desired, COCOLIB performs a brute force linear search for all points that did not occur in step 1 and selects the best matches according to the matching criterion.
4. **reject:** COCOLIB rejects all pairs for which the matching criterion is not fulfilled.

The neighborhood search for non-matching grids is described in the following in a simplified manner. For each node of both grids the element of the opposite grid with the shortest distance to the node has to be computed. First each element of the coupling surface, which is different to a triangle, is split into triangles. For each triangle a bounding box is constructed just large enough to contain all vertices of the element. These bounding boxes are enlarged, so that they are equal in size in all coordinate directions by taking the largest dimension of the bounding box from the previous step. Then the bounding boxes are magnified by multiplying it with an eligible factor with respect to their centers. The algorithm proceeds in computing the average over the sizes of all constructed bounding boxes. Then a regular grid of buckets with the size of this average is superimposed on the volume region. The bounding boxes, which have an overlap with an bucket, are assigned to this bucket.

To detect the element with the shortest distance to a specific point lying in one of these buckets the algorithm has only to consider the triangles of the bounding boxes assigned to this bucket. In the second step COCOLIB computes the minimal distance between the particular point p and all points of each extracted triangle $\triangle ABC$. The rejection criterion for minimal_distance is configurable using the parameters θ_1, θ_2, θ_3, and τ. All points for which $\theta_1 \cdot (|u| + |v| + |w| - 1) + \theta_2 \cdot \frac{d_t^2}{|\triangle ABC|} + \theta_3 \cdot \frac{d_n^2}{|\triangle ABC|} > \tau$ are rejected. In (3), u, v, and w denote the barycentric coordinates of the projection of p' of p onto the plane defined by $\triangle ABC$, $d_n = \|p - p'\|$, and d_t is the distance between p' and the point p'' inside $\triangle ABC$ that has minimal distance to p, see figure 1.

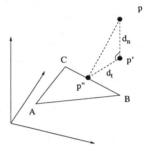

Figure 1. Minimal distance matching and rejection criteria.

The difficulties of the neighborhood search are that coupling interfaces could be distributed over several partitions of several processes and that a distance is allowed between the coupling surfaces of the different codes.

The main computations of the simulation codes are carried out in the coupling phase. In this phase the coupling data are specified to CO-COLIB. COCOLIB sends the data to the receiver code, interpolates the data onto the nodes of the target grid and distributes the interpolated data to the specified arrays. Then the computations of the receiver code, which depend on the coupling data, can start. Communication always occurs pairwise between codes. To indicate the code to send information to or to receive information from, an integer code identifier is used in send and receive calls.

It is difficult to combine all coupling values in COCOLIB communication calls because many different types of coupling values exist for example vectors or scalars which may reside at different locations in the computational grid. Therefore, prior to COCOLIB sends, the coupling values to be exchanged are specified and stored per interface part through interface handles. In the COCOLIB send, COCOLIB will determine which values actually need to be sent to the remote code. Conversely, a COCOLIB receive call receives and stores coupling values per interface parts, which can be retrieved by COCOLIB subroutines. In order to achieve optimal parallel efficiency, the communication between the codes is done as directly as possible, that is, data are exchanged only in the overlap regions.

The interpolation is based on the data of the neighborhood search. A linear and a bilinear interpolation depending on the type of the element are implemented. The user can choose between a conservative and a non conservative interpolation. Furthermore, it is possible to integrate a user-defined interpolation.

In the termination phase the coupled computation is finished and some cleanup is done. After this call it is not allowed to call any COCOLIB function or to start a new initialization.

Due to the flexibility of the coupling library all of the known coupling algorithms of a loose coupling can be executed with COCOLIB. There are several possibilities to determine the next step at which communication will take place. One of these is to use the information specified by the user in the input file. In this case, the user specifies the exact points (e.g. time points for a time integration, iteration numbers for a stationary computation) in the input file. More generally, the user can specify a certain type of coupling algorithm in the COCOLIB input file, and the codes then call COCOLIB subroutines to access this information. It is still unspecified how this is realized. Another alternative is to use a collective operation, which is also offered by COCOLIB. For example, for a transient coupling, each code can specify its next required coupling time to the call of this operation together with a minimum operation.

4 Applications

Different multi-physics problems are computed by COCOLIB. As illustrating examples this paper presents applications in the field of fluid-structure interaction.

Most multidisciplinary simulations in automotive industry are concerned with fluid-structure interactions. The CISPAR project partner Daimler-Chrysler provided two applications: simulation of a wheel spoiler and a torque converter. Both applications were computed with a STAR-CD/PERMAS coupling.

The structure code PERMAS is a general purpose software system to perform complex calculations in engineering using the finite element method. It has been developed by INTES and is available to engineers as an analysis tool worldwide. STAR-CD is a multi-purpose computational fluid dynamics code developed by Computational Dynamics.

In the first example the maximum deformation of a wheel spoiler from a DaimlerChrysler automobile is simulated. The wheel spoiler is attached to the underbody of a car in front of the front wheel. The task of the wheel spoiler is to guide the air which flows under the car around the wheel. This improves drag and lift. If the wheel spoiler is rigid, it would completely fulfill this task, but on the other hand the wheel spoiler has to be soft enough to avoid damage when hitting an obstacle. The simulation is used to find a

compromise between the two conditions for the wheel spoiler. The fluid mesh
for a simplified test case consists of about 278000 elements, the structural mesh
has 120 brick elements. The coupling surface is composed of 120 elements and
168 nodes. The first coupled analysis was performed with the matching version
of COCOLIB on the DaimlerChrysler IBM SP2. After 45 data exchanges
the run was finished. The deformation of the wheel spoiler converged to its
maximum (1.226 mm). The results are shown in Figure 2 and in Figure 3. In

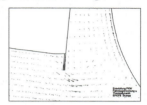

Figure 2. Flow field around the wheel influenced by the wheel spoiler (by courtesy of DaimlerChrysler)

Figure 3. Flow field and displacement of the wheel spoiler (by courtesy of DaimlerChrysler)

a second run the structural mesh is refined to get non-matching grids at the
coupling surface. The modified structural mesh consists of 3240 brick elements
and the coupling surface of 2160 elements and 2318 nodes. The maximum
deformation for this run is 1.256 mm, slightly different to the previous one.
Considering the different stiffnesses of the two structural meshes, the results
of the non-matching and matching run agree with each other.

The second application from DaimlerChrysler is a torque converter. In
this example DaimlerChrysler is interested in the maximum stresses. The
computations should be performed with varying the thickness of the plates
and the type of the material. The aim of the simulation is an improved design
w.r.t. the weight of the torque converter. The fluid mesh for the torque
converter was made to carry out a complete flow analysis of this specific torque
converter and evaluating the performance curve from the flow calculation. One
load case was selected for the coupled analysis (pump speed 2000 rpm, reactor
speed 0 rpm). The fluid mesh was divided into three parts and consists in
total of 239402 elements and 419019 nodes. The structural mesh is build of
9072 brick elements and 12768 nodes. The coupled run was performed with
STAR-CD and PERMAS. (see Fig. 4 and Fig. 5).

The CISPAR project partner Sulzer Innotec provides another application. The design and development of artificial heart valves require a detailed examination of structural mechanics and fluid dynamics. The fluid

3 ELEMENTS TORQUE CONVERTER

COMPUTATIONAL MESH

1 PUMP₂

2 TURBINE₂

3 REACTOR

Figure 4. Structure of a torque converter (by courtesy of DaimlerChrysler)

Figure 5. Computational mesh of the torque converter (by courtesy of DaimlerChrysler)

flow solution and the structural behavior are strongly dependent on each other: The fluid of blood exerts forces on the heart valve, causing the structure to deform. The structural deformation is then fed back into the fluid in terms of a mesh deformation. The coupled simulation provides information about the structural loads, bending of stent cusps, opening and closing of the leaflet and flow conditions during operation. For this simulation the codes STAR-CD and PAM-CRASH were coupled. The solid code PAM-CRASH is a finite element explicit solver developed and validated by the ESI Group and its partners in the transportation industry. The figure 6 shows the pressure of the dynamic heart valve simulation at a specific time point.

5   Conclusions and outlook

The basic software problems for the development of a coupling library are solved in COCOLIB and the practicability for real problems is shown in several industrial applications. Nevertheless, there remains a lot of research to be done in order to achieve more general results in the field of coupled computations. The numerical stability of different coupling algorithms has to be investigated. General rules or algorithms for dedicated application areas are still missing.

Figure 6. Heart valve: pressure distribution during opening phase of valve (by courtesy of Sulzer Innotec)

Furthermore the standard interpolation algorithms implemented today are not sufficient for some problems. Advanced interpolation algorithms must be made available for the users of the communication library. After the implementation of the required interpolation in the coupling library, the new interpolations have to be tested with regard to their exactness, efficiency and necessary numerical stability in the field of the applications. Furthermore, more flexibility and control is necessary for multidisciplinary applications.

Performance w.r.t. the computing time of the coupling library proved to be of minor importance in the CISPAR project: The reason was that because of the loose coupling approach and the fact that the coupling region was only 2-dimensional, the times spent in the individual codes was much larger than the time spent in COCOLIB (about 1%). Nevertheless, for future work performance will play a more important role, especially if volume coupling is included. An important task for this purpose is the integration of more efficient neighborhood search algorithms.

The development of the communication library will be continued in new projects, which will use the library for a wider range of applications. The results and experiences not only by the CISPAR project but also by the GRISSLi project [4] enter the future development of the library. Future development of the coupling library will be done under the trademark MpCCI - Mesh based parallel Code Coupling Interface.

Acknowledgments

The authors gratefully acknowledge the kind cooperation of the following organizations: Computational Dynamics, DaimlerChrysler, ESI, INTES and Sulzer Innotec.

References

1. CISPAR – Open Interface for Coupling of Industrial Simulation Codes on PARallel computers, ESPRIT Project 20161, see also http://www.gmd.de/SCAI/scicomp/cispar/
2. Deliverable 1.1: Specification of the COupling COmmunications LIBrary, ESPRIT Project 20161
3. G.A. Kohring and G. Lonsdale, COCOVIS Design, deliverable 3.5, CISPAR ESPRIT Project 20161
4. Grissli-Abschlussbericht, to be obtained by GMD - Forschungszentrum Informationstechnik GmbH, Institute for Algorithms and Scientific Computing (SCAI), Schloss Birlinghoven, D 53754 St. Augustin, Germany

CELLULAR AUTOMATA MODEL FOR PARALLEL SIMULATION OF CONTAMINATION PROCESSES BY OIL IN POROUS SOILS

M. ANDRETTA, M.A. MAZZANTI, R. SERRA, M. VILLANI

°CRA Montecatini via Menotti, 48 48023 Marina di Ravenna (RA), Italy

S. DI GREGORIO, R. RONGO, W. SPATARO

*Dept. of Mathematics, Univ. of Calabria, 87036 Arcavacata di Rende (CS), Italy

Cellular automata (CA) can be applied for modeling the dynamics of spatially extended physical systems, representing an alternative to the classical PDE approach. Furthermore, CA implementation on large parallel computer is straightforward because of their characteristics of parallelism and acentrism. In this paper, a CA model for simulating the fluid-dynamics of contaminated porous soils is introduced. It is based on an empirical method for modeling complex phenomena from a macroscopic viewpoint; such a choice is motivated by the aim of simulating large scale systems. We report here first significant applications of this model concerning case studies and experiments in pilot plants. The results of the applications and a comparison between case studies and simulations are presented and commented on.

1   Introduction

A main goal in order to face problems concerning polluted soil is the capability of computing the multiphase flows (gas, water, oils) in the soil matrix [2]. Partial Differential Equations (PDE) approach can involve, in many cases, severe computational limits. They occur when, for example, the basic laws of the continuum mechanics cannot be directly applied without adding phenomenological assumptions, or when analytical solutions of the equation system is unknown. In such cases, direct discrete modeling may represent a convenient alternative to the use of continuum models, followed by numerical discretisation. Parallel Computing models [1] sometimes represent such a valid alternative for modeling complex phenomena, whose behaviour can be described in terms of local interactions of their constituent parts (acentrism). Cellular Automata (CA) are a paradigm of the parallel computing; they are based on a regular division of space in cells, each one embedding identical finite automata (fa), whose input is given by the states of the neighbouring cells; fa have an identical transition function, which is simultaneously applied to each cell. At the time t=0, fa are in arbitrary states, representing the initial conditions of the system, and the CA evolves changing the state of all fa simultaneously at discrete times, according to the transition function of the fa.
Cellular automata (CA) can be applied for modeling the dynamics of spatially extended physical systems, and represent an alternative to the classical PDE approach. Applications of CA are very broad; they range from microscopic simulation of physical and biological phenomena to macroscopic simulation of

geological and social processes; furthermore, CA implementation on large parallel computer is straightforward because of their characteristics of parallelism and acentrism [1].

The main features of the method are the following: each characteristic, relevant to the evolution of the system and relative to the space portion corresponding to the cell, is identified as a component of the state (a substate). The values associated to the substates can vary depending on the interactions among substates inside the cell (internal transformation) and local interactions among cells. Local interactions are treated in terms of flows of some quantity (substate) towards the neighbouring cells, in order to achieve equilibrium conditions. In many cases the flows are proportional to the differences of the quantity values between the central cell and each neighbour with lower value. Flows are computed according to an appropriate law, which reduces the differences and fixes a relaxation rate, that depends also on the CA clock and the cell dimension.

In this paper, a macroscopic CA model for simulating the fluid dynamics of contaminated porous soils is introduced. The choice of macroscopic automata is motivated by the aim of simulating large-scale systems. Furthermore, a similar method was applied successfully to the problem of bioremediation of porous soils, contaminated by phenol [5, 6, 7], where the fluid-dynamics was considered in the simplified context of a monophase flow in unsaturated soil [4]. CAMEL, a CA environment for parallel computers was developed, in order to apply this model (and others of similar conception) to real cases [3].

The extension of this model to a more complex phenomenon was not trivial since, if a macroscopic scale of time and space must be considered, interdependent physical variables change their values at very different rates. For example, pressure, which leads the flows in the saturated soil, must be considered to propagate very quickly (and almost instantaneously) in comparison with the remaining physical variables. Then a sequence of CA computation stages with different characteristics must be planned for the transition function of the CA.

The price to pay for this solution is the lack of direct correspondence between the CA step and the physical time, in the sense that an external time must be determined in order to build a link between a period of time and a sequence of steps of the CA. On this basis; first applications of this model have been performed in order to simulate case studies and experiments in pilot plants.

The second section of the paper describes an outline of the CA model; the third section concerns the results of the simulation and case study; at last, conclusions and comments are reported.

2   The Cellular Automata model SOIL

A macroscopic CA was developed; its specification is given by:
SOIL = (R, A, X, Q, σ, γ)

- R = {(x, y, z)| x, y, z ∈ N, $0 \le x \le l_x$, $0 \le y \le l_y$, $0 \le z \le l_z$} is the set of points with integer co-ordinates in the finite region, where the phenomenon evolves. N is the set of natural numbers.

- A ⊂ R, specifies the cells, to which are imposed special conditions, determined by the presence of pumps; the particular transition function γ must be applied to such cells before σ.

- The set X is the geometrical pattern of cells, which influence the cell state change.

X = {(0, 0, 0), (0, 0, 1), (0, 1, 0), (1, 0, 0), (-1, 0, 0), (0, -1, 0), (0, 0, -1)};

- The finite set Q of states of the fa:

$$Q = Q_w \times Q_g \times Q_o \times Q_{pw} \times Q_{po} \times Q_{pg} \times Q_p \times Q_{fw}^6 \times Q_{fg}^6 \times Q_{fo}^6 \times QK_w \times QK_g \times QK_o \times Q_z$$

where are substates:

Q_w, Q_g, Q_o are respectively the water, gas and oil content in the cell.

Q_{pw}, Q_{pg}, Q_{po} are respectively the water, gas and oil pressure inside the cell.

Q_p is the "effective porosity parameter". It depends on physical characteristics of the soil in the cell and individuates the porous volume, which can be filled by water, gas and oil.

Q_{fw}, Q_{fg}, Q_{fo} represent respectively the water, gas and oil flows toward the six neighbourhood directions from the central cell. Note that the inflows Q_{iw}, Q_{ig}, Q_{io} are not explicitly considered, they are obtained trivially by the outflows.

QK_w, QK_g, QK_o are respectively the water, gas and oil efficacious conductivity; their value is depending on the pressure and from the cell contents of the phases.

Q_z is the cell depth from the suface

- $\sigma:Q^7 \to Q$ is the deterministic state transition function for the cells in R; it is specified in terms of internal transformations 'computation of the efficacious conductivity' σ_{T1} and local interactions 'computation of capillary pressure' σ_{I1}, 'computation of the new cell outflows' σ_{I2} and 'computation of the new cell phases content' σ_{I3} :

σ_{T1}: $Q_w \times Q_g \times Q_o \to QK_w \times QK_g \times QK_o$

σ_{I1}: $(QK_w \times QK_g \times QK_o \times Q_{pw} \times Q_{pg} \times Q_{po} \times Q_z)^7 \to (Q_{pw} \times Q_{pg} \times Q_{po})^6$

σ_{I2}: σ_{I1}: $(QK_w \times QK_g \times QK_o \times Q_{pw} \times Q_{pg} \times Q_{po})^7 \to (Q_{fw} \times Q_{fg} \times Q_{fo})^6$

σ_{I3}: $(Q_w \times Q_g \times Q_o) \times (Q_{iw} \times Q_{ig} \times Q_{io})^6 \to Q_w \times Q_g \times Q_o$

- $\gamma:Q_w \times Q_o \times Q_{pr} \times N \to Q_w \times Q_o \times Q_{pr}$ is the additional transition function of cells, to which are imposed forced conditions, determined, e.g., by oil spilling or by the pumps in laboratory experimental devices or in the soil. γ is applied before σ and its effect is depending on the planning of the external interventions for each time interval $s \in N$.

At the CA step 0 the initial configuration is defined, specifying all the starting values of the cell substates. Then a sequence of CA computation stages is applied:

a) the function γ is applied, if there are working pumps,

b) the pressure distribution in the CA is computed in a fixed sequence of steps,
c) the rest of the transition function is applied and the other substates are up-dated.

3   SOIL simulations and case studies.

Many simulations concerning monitored real events and case studies have been performed on the base of the previous model. In the present section we describe a selected simulation from a real case of saturation on data collected from a pilot plant and a selected case study of oil washing [4,5,6].

The following figures (fig. 1.a, fig. 1.b) show, respectively, the cellular automata discretization of the plant and its noteworthy regions (measurement area, injection well, extraction well). The size of the square cells is 21 cm.; the upper layer simulates the atmosphere.

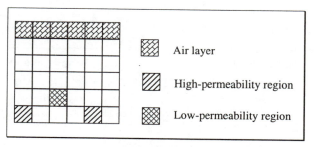

Fig. 1.a Pilot plant permeability profile.

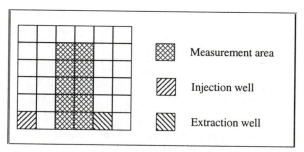

Fig. 1.b Remarkable areas of the pilot plant.

The high-permeability regions represent the gravel which surrounds and protects the openings of the wells. The injection well position includes both the injection well and the filler of the pilot plant base; the extraction well position includes both the extraction well and the outlet of the pilot plant base.

60

The first test is the simulation of the saturation event. The initial humidity of the plant is about 6%, almost uniform in space, and we suppose a pressure of 115000 Pascal (about 1/10 greater than atmospheric pressure) in correspondence to the opening of the filler of the pilot plant base.

In the following figures, we show the flow profile at different steps of the simulation.

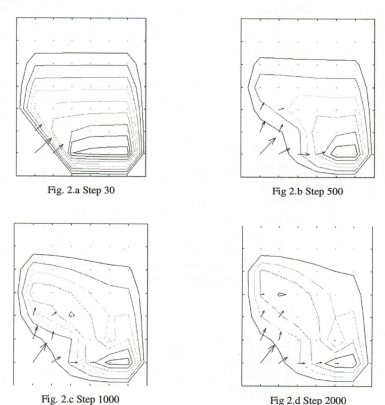

Fig. 2.a Step 30

Fig 2.b Step 500

Fig. 2.c Step 1000

Fig 2.d Step 2000

We can observe the formation of two water flows, which moves around the low permeability region. A quite similar behavior was observed also in the real. In fact, the measurements made during the plant saturation show a slow humidity growth in correspondence to this region, unlike the fast increase found in the high-permeability region (fig.2).

The case study regards of a washing effect in a plant of the same dimensions of the previous one with the soil at the same global permeability and 2 pumps in a symmetric position. Initial conditions are the saturated soil with 0.017 % of soil porosity in oil and water present all over the plant.

The injection well and the extraction well work initially with respectively 200000 Pascal and 0 Pascal pressure values. The injection well injects water, but the extraction well extracts water and oil.

Initially the oil is "repelled" by the injection well in all the directions (fig 3.b) accordingly to the water potential distribution (fig 3.a), and is "adsorbed" in correspondence of the extraction well (right well). So, the maximum oil density will be at the maximum distance of the injection well (oil is repelled) and of the extraction well (oil is absorbed and is not replaced by as much as other oil at the same way of water), with prevailing effect of the extraction well on the injection well. Little by little a corridor is developed between the area to higher oil density to the extraction well determining in the time the partial washing of the plant (fig 3.c, 3.d).

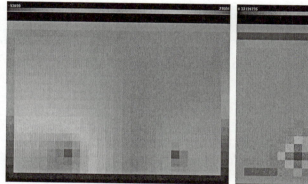

Figure 3.a

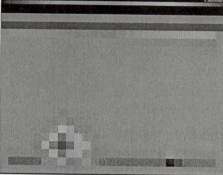

Figure 3.b

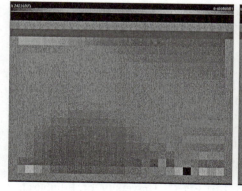

Figure 3.c

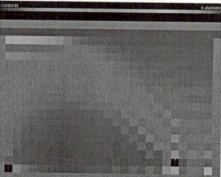

Figure 3.d

4   Conclusions

For the simulations and the case study we used 2D models instead of 3D models, which are too much time and resource demanding, using a single processor architecture, to allow an efficient search of correct parameters and scenarios [3]. However these 2D models, even if running on PC, can reproduce the main trends of the most important physical phenomena and are enough accurate to validate the main features of the theoretical model. For a more deep-in-knowledge study of more complex phenomena applied on large scale fields, the model has been developed using the CAMELot parallel environment [1, 8], which permits a faster and more precise study with respect to a single PC processor architecture. Eventually, the results of a comparison between experimental and simulation are very encouraging.

Acknowledgements

This study has been conducted under the sponsorship of the the UE Esprit project 24907, Colombo.

REFERENCES

1.   S. Di Gregorio, R. Rongo, W. Spataro, G. Spezzano, D. Talia, *A Parallel Cellular Tool for Interactive Modeling and Simulation*, IEEE Computational Science & Engineering, vol. 3, no. 3, Fall 1996, 33-43.

2.   R. Helmig, *Multiphase Flow and Transport Processes in the Subsurface - A Contribution to the Modeling of Hydrosystems* - Springer-Verlag, 1997.

3.   Di Gregorio, R. Rongo, W. Spataro, G. Spezzano, D. Talia, *High performance scientific computing by a parallel cellular environment* , Future Generation Computer Systems n.12, 1997, 357-369

4.   Di Gregorio, R. Rongo, R. Serra, W. Spataro, M. Villani: *Simulation of water flow through a porous soil by a Cellular Automaton model*, ACRI '96, Proceedings of second Conference on Cellular Automata for Research and Industry, Milan, Italy 16-18 October 1996, Springer London, 1997, 79-88

5.   R. Serra, M. Villani, D. Oricchio, S. Di Gregorio, *Recent advances in dynamical models of bioremediation.*, in S. Bandini, R. Serra, F. Suggi Liverani (eds): Proceedings of ACRI'98, London, Springer, 1998, 92-105.

6.   S. Di Gregorio, R. Serra and M. Villani, *Simulation of soil contamination and bioremediation by a Cellular Automaton model* Complex Systems vol. 11 **1**, 1998, 31-54.

7.   *CAMELot Implementation*, Version 1.0. EPCC, University of Edinburgh - COLOMBO Project Deliverable, Report D7.

HIPERPLAST: AN HPCN SIMULATOR FOR REINFORCED THERMOPLASTICS INJECTION PROCESSES

E. ARIAS, V. HERNÁNDEZ, J. E. ROMÁN, A. M. VIDAL

Departamento de Sistemas Informáticos y Computación,
Universidad Politécnica de Valencia,
Camino de Vera, s/n, E-46022 Valencia, Spain.

R. TORRES, I. MONTÓN, F. CHINESTA, A. POITOU, F. MESLIN

Laboratorie de Mecanique et Technologie,
Ecole Normale Superieure de Cachan, France.

Numerical simulation is very important in plastics manufacturing. Plastic injection processes have been simulated for a long time. However, this has not been the case for short fiber reinforced thermoplastics, because the injection of these materials is a much more complex process. This work presents an HPCN-based simulator for this application developed within an 18-month EU-funded project titled *HIPER*PLAST. This simulator comes at a time when cost-effective PC-based parallel systems have become available for SME's.

1   The Industrial Problem

Reinforced plastics have many applications, mainly in situations where there is a restriction regarding the robustness of the piece to some eventual stress. Today we can find these plastics in a great range of industrial products, for example vehicle toys such as cars or bikes. Due to the high stresses supported by these kinds of products it is necessary to make use of some structural pieces made of stainless steel or aluminium. In this way, the toy industry, mainly specialised in plastic forming, strongly depends on the metal industry. The use of assembled metallic pieces poses some industrial problems such as higher production costs and dependence on external suppliers of metallic components. The use of Short Fibre Reinforced Thermoplastics (SFRT) can alleviate these problems, allowing to define the structure as an assembly of metallic tubes and joints made of these plastics. By doing this, the metallic parts are common to several different toy designs. This last issue is important for the toy industry because of the short life cycle of the product.

Design of SFRT pieces implies a trial-and-error prototyping process, in which the operator uses his intuition and expertise to make an initial guess of the appropriate injection parameters (e.g. the shape of the mould or the number and position of the injectors). Once the initial piece has been designed with a CAD tool, the manufacturing of the corresponding mould is ordered.

After that, the prototype can be injected and tested to see if it fulfils the required specifications. From the results of the tests, the initial design must be refined. The process typically takes several iterations until a satisfactory result is achieved. This procedure has many practical drawbacks, because the operator has no means to assess whether his guess is correct until the physical prototype is available. The construction of the prototype is expensive (2000-3000 Euro per mould) and, even worse, it makes the whole design process very lengthy in time (more than fifteen days per mould).

Simulation can help reduce this tedious prototyping procedure by predicting the final fibre orientation in the conformed piece. With the results of the simulation, the user can check the material properties at the critical points and, if necessary, refine the design without needing a prototype. With this new scheme, costs can be considerably reduced since the only required physical prototype corresponds to the last design. More importantly, this new process is much shorter in time, leading to important benefits.

Computer simulators for plastic injection have been available for a long time. However, none of the commercial simulators can cope with reinforced materials. Only a few address this specific problem, but considering only the surface of the mould, without taking into account the flow in its interior. This approach is not sufficient for real applications and a 3D modelling is necessary. Furthermore, these simulations usually take about 30 days to complete since they run on a single processor.

In order for the simulations to be effective for the end user, the response must be relatively fast and the results have to be accurate. Typically, the user requests the simulation of pieces with complicated shapes, which must be treated in a 3D fashion. In addition, the grain of the mesh used in the analysis must be sufficiently fine to reach acceptable accuracy. For these reasons, the algebraic problems which appear, in this case linear systems of equations, are large (more than a million unknowns). In this setting, the use of HPCN techniques is compulsory. A parallel code must be used in order to reduce the response time, or else the simulator is useless. Moreover, the huge memory requirements of the code prevent it from running on a single workstation. Since SME's do not usually have access to supercomputers, the only alternative is to exploit the computing power of a cluster of PC's or workstations.

2 The *HIPER*PLAST Simulator

The injection process can be modelled by the flow equations, which define an anisotropic Stokes problem, coupled with the fibre orientation equation and the volumetric fraction equation. Coupled resolution of the motion and orientation equations are justified, due to the strong influence of fibre orientation on the velocity field. An explicit discontinuous Taylor-Galerkin strategy has been used in order to decouple these equations.

The pressure and velocity fields are denoted by p and $\underline{v}$, respectively. The orientation tensor is $\underline{a}$, whose eigenvalues represent the probability of finding a fibre oriented in the direction of the corresponding eigenvector. The strain rate tensor and the stress rate tensor have been denoted by $\underline{\underline{d}}$ and $\underline{\underline{\sigma}}$. Ω represents the whole domain, i.e. the mould to be filled. It is divided in two parts, domain containing fluid (Ω_f) and domain without fluid (Ω_v). The inflow boundary has been denoted by $\Gamma_{(-)}$.

The following set of partial differential equations describe the behaviour of the suspension [4]:

- Equilibrium equation (neglecting the inertia terms),

$$\text{Div } \underline{\underline{\sigma}} = \underline{0}. \tag{1}$$

- Incompressibility equation for steady regime and incompressible flow,

$$\text{Div } \underline{v} = 0. \tag{2}$$

- Constitutive law for dilute or semi-dilute suspensions in a Newtonian fluid,

$$\underline{\underline{\sigma}} = -p\,\underline{\underline{Id}} + 2\mu\{\underline{\underline{d}} + N_p \text{Tr}(\underline{\underline{a}}\,\underline{\underline{d}})\underline{\underline{a}}\}, \tag{3}$$

where $\underline{\underline{Id}}$ is the identity tensor, μ is the viscosity and N_p is a constant which depends on the shape and concentration of fibers.

- Orientation equation, neglecting Brownian motion and assuming that the particles have a quasi-infinite aspect ratio,

$$\frac{\partial \underline{\underline{a}}}{\partial t} + (\underline{v}\,\text{Grad})\underline{\underline{a}} = \text{Grad } \underline{v}\,\underline{\underline{a}} + \underline{\underline{a}}\,(\text{Grad } \underline{v})^T - 2\text{Tr}(\underline{\underline{a}}\,\underline{\underline{d}})\,\underline{\underline{a}}. \tag{4}$$

Taking into account that $\underline{\underline{a}} = \underline{\underline{a}}^T$ and $\text{Tr}(\underline{\underline{a}}) = 1$, only 5 components of the orientation field need to be computed.

- Equation of evolution of the volumetric fraction,

$$\frac{\partial I}{\partial t} + (\underline{v}\,\text{Grad})\,I = 0, \tag{5}$$

where the fluid fraction I is a scalar field taking the value 1 in Ω_f and 0 in Ω_v. This equation is subject to an initial condition over the inflow boundary: $I(\underline{x}, t) = 1, \forall \underline{x} \in \Gamma_{(-)}, \forall t$.

Until now, numerical simulations of the suspension flows have been carried out by several techniques, but using simplified models or treating particular geometries such as plate moulds [3]. The objective of the *HIPER*PLAST project is the development of a much more general simulator valid for generic 3D moulds. The main algorithm proposed for the simulation is the following:

Given the initial conditions $\underline{v}_0$, I_0, $\underline{\underline{a}}_0$,
While $|\Omega_f| < |\Omega|$ do
1. Update the domain occupied by the fluid, by solving the fluid transport equation (5),

2. Compute the fibre orientation in the updated domain, by solving the fibre orientation equation (4), and

3. Compute the velocity and pressure fields in the new domain with the new orientations, by solving the kinematics equations (1), (2) and (3).

The Finite Element Method (FEM) has been chosen for the solution of this problem, with a non standard interpolation scheme for the velocity components (linear interpolation plus a bubble function with C^0 continuity), a conforming linear approximation for the pressure and a constant approximation for the orientation tensor and the volumetric fraction. To extend the formulation to the whole mould domain, a pseudo-behaviour in the empty domain, defined by $p = 0$ and $v = 0$, is introduced.

The FEM formulation leads to the following element equations,

$$\underline{\underline{K}}^e \begin{bmatrix} \underline{U}^e \\ \underline{P}^e \end{bmatrix} = \begin{bmatrix} \underline{W}_1^e \\ \underline{W}_2^e \end{bmatrix}, \tag{6}$$

where $\underline{P}^e$ is a vector of size 4 and $\underline{U}^e$ has 15 components, 3 of which correspond to the bubble velocities.

The boundary conditions used are Dirichlet-type, in which a particular nodal value of the solution must be enforced. More specifically, the nodal velocities are specified for the nodes corresponding to the injection point, and set to zero in the rest of the border of the mould.

For the discretisation of the transport equations associated with the fibre orientation (4) and evolution of the fluid domain (5), a Lesaint-Raviart scheme (discontinuous Galerkin) is proposed. The behaviour of this method in the simulation of the mould filling process of a Newtonian generalised fluid has been shown in [2]. The explicit time discretisation of the transport equations can be done by using a truncated Taylor series approximation for the unknown quantities, for example with I

$$I(\underline{x}, t + \Delta t) = I(\underline{x}, t) + \frac{\partial I}{\partial t}(\underline{x}, t)\Delta t + \cdots + \frac{1}{n!}\frac{\partial^n I}{\partial t^n}(\underline{x}, t)(\Delta t)^n + \Theta((\Delta t)^{n+1}).$$

3 Solution of Linear Systems of Equations

Figure 1 shows the pattern of the coefficient matrix of the linear system of equations to be solved at each step of the simulation algorithm. It corresponds to a small example case with 2092 elements and 552 nodes.

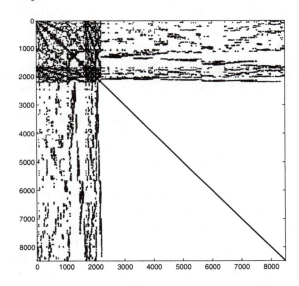

Figure 1. Sparsity pattern of the coefficient matrix.

From the figure, one can easily observe that the degrees of freedom associated with the bubble functions are completely decoupled from the rest of the unknowns. The solution strategy has been strongly biased by this fact.

After applying the boundary conditions, the resulting system of equations can be written in the following form

$$\begin{bmatrix} M & J \\ J^T & D \end{bmatrix} \begin{bmatrix} n \\ b \end{bmatrix} = \begin{bmatrix} w_1 \\ w_2 \end{bmatrix}, \tag{7}$$

where the nodal quantities, velocities v and pressures p, have been grouped in vector n, distinguishing them from the bubble velocities b.

In equation (7), D is a symmetric 3×3 block diagonal matrix, M is a symmetric sparse matrix and J is a rectangular sparse matrix. In order to benefit from the structure of matrix D, a block Gaussian elimination is applied, yielding the following set of equations

$$(M - JD^{-1}J^T)n = w_1 - JD^{-1}w_2 \; , \tag{8}$$

$$J^T n + Db = w_2 \; . \tag{9}$$

Matrix $M - JD^{-1}J^T$ has the same pattern as M and it is also symmetric. In the implementation, this matrix is computed explicitly and the linear system (8) is solved with a preconditioned Conjugate Gradient method.

4 Parallel Approach

Although there are several ways of distributing the different data structures (matrices, vectors, ...) when parallelising solvers for mesh-based problems, domain decomposition (or mesh partitioning) is the preferred strategy because it preserves the locality of the problem, which is of great importance for the efficiency of the implementation. In *HIPER*PLAST, groups of elements are clustered to form aggregations that are mapped to each processor, and inter-processor communications overhead is minimised by appropriate decomposition of the geometric domain. The decomposition process can be idealised as an attempt to form clusters of elements that maximise the ratio of domain volume to surface area of contact between sub-domains. This has been accomplished by a multilevel k-way partitioning algorithm [1].

Scalability of the equation solution task is readily achieved by using parallelisable solvers such as Krylov iteration schemes. The computation of an *inner product* of two vectors can be easily parallelised. Each processor computes the inner product of the corresponding segments of each vector. On distributed memory machines, the local inner products then have to be sent to other processors to be combined for the global inner product.

For *matrix-vector* products, communication is required for components of the vector which are not stored locally. These components correspond to nodes in the inter-processor interfaces. In order to avoid performance degradation, an appropriate ordering of internal, local boundary and external boundary unknowns is necessary. Overlapping between communication and computation has also been implemented.

Preconditioning is the most problematic part of parallelising an iterative method. In a first approach, point Jacobi preconditioning has been used, in which all processors execute their part of the preconditioner solve without further communication.

For the implementation of the prototype in a distributed memory environment, the Message Passing Interface (MPI) has been used. This guarantees the portability of the code to a wide range of platforms, including networks of workstations. In addition, linear algebra kernels such as the BLAS have been used whenever possible. The performance of the prototype has been measured in two different platforms with two test cases, TB2 with a 413392 order coefficient matrix and TB1 with size 955929. Table 1 shows the results in a cluster of 16 PC's (Pentium II 300 MHz with 128 Mb RAM) connected with Fast Ethernet. In this table, speedup and efficiency for p processors are computed relative to $p/2$ processors, since T_1 is not available due to memory requirements. The figures correspond to the first 100 simulation steps.

Table 1. Performance obtained in a cluster of PC's with cases TB2 and TB1.

p	T_p	S_p	$E_p(\%)$	T_p	S_p	$E_p(\%)$
2	15608	-	-	-	-	-
4	7852	1.99	99	23298	-	-
8	4484	1.75	88	13654	1.71	85
16	4750	0.94	47	10750	1.27	64

From the table, one can see that with the medium test case (TB2) there is no point in using 16 processors with respect to 8 processors. This is due to the overhead of communications in this kind of platform, which would likely be reduced in a faster network. In the case of TB1, which is closer in size to a real life case, there is still a speed gain when using 16 processors. Note again that in this case, the minimum number of PC's required to run the simulation is four, meaning that a sequential solution would not have been applicable.

In figure 2, the performance obtained in a SGI Origin 2000 multiprocessor is shown. It can be observed from the picture that efficiency maintains above 70 %. In this figure, speedup and efficiency are computed with respect to execution time in a single processor.

5 Framework

*HIPER*PLAST[a] arises in the Preparatory Support and Transfer (PST) Activities programme[b]. As part of this programme, the European Commission has established a network of 20 centres across Europe to encourage new users to

---

[a] *HIPER*PLAST Project. http://hiperttn.upv.es/hiperplast
[b] HPCN–TTN Network. http://www.hpcn-ttn.org

70

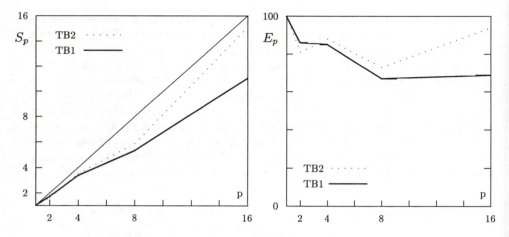

Figure 2. Speedup and efficiency (in %) achieved in an SGI Origin 2000.

adopt HPCN technology. These centres, called Technology Transfer Nodes[c] (TTNs), are coordinating various activities which tackle important industrial applications. There are many TTN-activities (200 activities with some 400 industrial partners altogether), some of them related to the plastic sector. The target of the resulting demonstrators are primarily small and medium sized enterprises (SME's). The focus of all activities is on satisfying business requirements, and also promoting HPCN technology.

References

1. G. Karypis and V. Kumar. Multilevel k-way Partitioning Scheme for Irregular Graphs. *J. Par. and Dist. Comp.*, 48(1):96–129 (1998).
2. E. Pichelin and T. Coupez. Finite Element Solution of the 3D Mould Filling for Viscous Incompressible Fluid. Submitted to *Comp. Meth. in Appl. Mech. and Engin.* (1997).
3. A. Poitou *et al.* Numerical Prediction of Flow Induced Orientation in Anisotropic Suspensions. Application to Injection Molding of Fibers Reinforced Thermoplastics. *J. Mat. Proc. Tech.*, 32:429–438 (1992).
4. A. Poitou and F. Meslin. A Differential Model for Short Fibers Composites. In *12th Annual Meeting of the PPS*, Sorrento (1996).

[c]HIPERCOSME Technology Transfer Node. http://hiperttn.upv.es

PARALLEL NON LINEAR ELECTROMAGNETIC MODELLING WITH FEM

M. AZIZI[1], E.M. DAOUDI[2,*] R. EL HANI[1,†] AND A. LAKHOUAJA[2]

[1] *Ecole Supérieure de Technologie*
B.P. 473, Oujda, Morocco
E-mail: {azizi,elhani}@est.univ-oujda.ac.ma

[2] *Faculté des Sciences, Dépt. de Math. et d'Informatique*
LaRI
Oujda, Morocco
E-mail: {mdaoudi,lakhouaja}@sciences.univ-oujda.ac.ma

In this work, we present a parallel implementation for the electromagnetic modelling of the electrotechnic systems taking into account the saturation effects on a distributed memory architecture composed of p processors. We have used and compared the Newton Raphson and successive approximations methods. The experimental results are obtained on the parallel machine TN310.

1 Introduction

The modelling offers extended possibilities for constructors and operators, it permits design optimization, which leads to high performances. In this context, the numerical computation of spatial and temporal distribution of the magnetic field in the electrotechnic systems, is based on the resolution of the magnetic vector potential equation. The Finite Elements Method (FEM) is one of the more used methods for approximating this type of equation [8]. In order to solve real problems, this method requires a large memory space and a prohibitive computation time. These two constraint can be avoided by parallelizing the problem.

Our aim is to present a parallel implementation of the FEM, taking into account of saturation effects, on a distributed memory architecture composed of p processors. In [1], we have used the successive approximations linearization method, with classical conjugate gradient method (CG). In this work we present the results obtained using the Newton Raphson (NR) and successive approximations (SA) methods with preconditioned modified conjugate gradient (PMCG) based on Chybeshef polynomial.

---

*SUPPORTED BY THE EUROPEAN PROGRAM INCO-DC, "DAPPI" PROJECT
†U.F.R. ELECTRONIQUE ET SYSTEMES

2   Magnetic vector potential formulation

Based on Maxwell's equations [4], we are led to solve a magnetic vector potential
equation [1,3]:

$$curl(\nu curl(\vec{a})) + \sigma\frac{\partial \vec{a}}{\partial t} = -\sigma\overrightarrow{grad}(V)$$

with :
   ν is the magnetic reluctivity $\vec{a}$ is the magnetic vector potential
   V is the electric scalar potential σ is the electric conductivity.
   In the case where the studied system present an invariance character
by translation following one axes (oz for example), the vector $\vec{a}$ becomes
$\vec{a} = a\,\vec{k}$ where $\vec{k}$ is the unitary vector following the oz axes. The problem
to solve by FEM, becomes:

$$-div(\nu\overrightarrow{grad}(a)) + \sigma\frac{\partial a}{\partial t} = J_0$$

on a domain D.
   After spatial discretization by FEM and temporal approximation by the
implicit Euler method, we are led to solve the following matrix equation:

$$(A + \frac{1}{\Delta t}B)P_{t+\Delta t} = \frac{1}{\Delta t}BP_t + F_{t+\Delta t} \tag{1}$$

where A and B are sparse, symmetric and positive definite matrices. P
and F are vectors of size N, with N is the unknown number. P is the unknown
vector of vector potentials a.

3   saturation effects

In the nonlinear material, the magnetic reluctivity ν is a nonlinear function
of magnetic induction. In order to introduce this nonlinearity, the first mag-
netization curve is necessary and generally given by the constructor under
a shape of raising set of magnetic induction and fields. For the numerical
modelling one must dispose of a continuous expression. From the different
methods describing the curve ν, we have retained the Marrocco approach [9].
In this case, A depends on the induction magnetic, therefore on the potential
vector [3]. Hence, it is necessary to use an iterative method. The two main
used methods are SA and NR.

3.1 Successive approximations method

The successive approximations algorithm of resolution of nonlinear systems (1), at every instant $t + \Delta t$, is defined as follow:
1. Computation of $F_{t+\Delta t}$
2. Initialization : $k = 0$ and $P^0_{t+\Delta t} = P_t$.
3. While $err > eps$ (eps is a given precision).
    3.1 Computation of ν.
    3.2 Computation of the matrix A.
    3.3 Computation of $P^{k+1}_{t+\Delta t}$ by CG.
    3.4 Error Approximation.
4. End while.

3.2 Newton Raphson Method

The idea of this method is : if x^k is an approached solution of the equation $g(x) = 0$ then a new approached solution x^{k+1} is given by the relation $g'(x^k)\Delta x^{k+1} = -g(x^k)$ with $\Delta x^{k+1} = x^{k+1} - x^k$.

In our case, we apply Newton Raphson method to equation (1), we obtain:

$$(A^k + N_r^k + \tfrac{1}{\Delta t}B)\Delta P^{k+1}_{t+\Delta t} = -(A^k + \tfrac{1}{\Delta t}B)\Delta P^k_{t+\Delta t} + \tfrac{1}{\Delta t}BP_t + F_{t+\Delta t}$$

Where N_r is a symmetric, positive definite matrix [1].

NR algorithm is the same as SA, with the following modifications:

- at step 3.2, we compute also the matrix N_r.

- at step 3.3, we compute $P^{k+1}_{t+\Delta t}$ using CG, from equation (2).

4 Sequential algorithm

At each step of time we need to compute the vector P using the CG. Note that the matrix B is computed one time while the matrices A and N_r are computed at each iteration of linearization.

Let I_{sa} (resp. I_{nr}) denotes the number of iterations of SA (resp. NR) and I_{cg} the number of iterations of CG.

The execution time of the sequential algorithms, at each step of time, is estimated to:

$$T_{seq}(SA) = (7N + (90N + 28N * I_{cg}) * I_{sa}) * \omega$$
$$T_{seq}(NR) = (21N + (157N + 28N * I_{cg}) * I_{nr}) * \omega$$

where ω is the execution time for one $flop$.

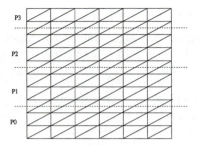

Figure 1. Partitioning domain into strips

5 Parallel implementation

In this section we present a parallel implementation of SA and NR on a parallel distributed machine composed of p processors numbered by $P_i, 0 \leq i \leq p-1$. The communication of m data between two neighbor processors is modelled by $\beta + m\tau$, where β is the start-up time, τ is the time to transmit one data.

5.1 Domain decomposition

The parallelization consists in partitioning the global domain D into p strips each of size N_x by $\frac{N_y}{p}$, where: N_x is the number of nodes in the x axis, N_y is the number of nodes in the y axis [5,6].

At each processor P_i, for $0 \leq i \leq p-1$, we affect one strip as shown in figure 1.

The computation of F and A is highly parallelizable since it does not need any communication between processors. In parallel, each processor computes one part of the matrix A and the vector F. However, the computation of N_r needs communication between neighbor processors. For the computation of the reluctivity ν in each triangle one needs communication between neighbor strips since the calculation of the induction requires the values of the potential vector at each node of the triangle.

5.2 Conjugate gradient method

The conjugate gradient method [2,10] is an iterative method to solve the linear systems equation of type $Ax = b$ where A is a symmetric and positive definite matrix. In the initialization phase, three operation are necessary, two inner products, one matrix-vector product and one vector updates

$(y = y + \alpha x \; , x, y \in I\!\!R^n, \alpha \in I\!\!R)$ and at each step, three major operations: three inner products, one matrix-vector product and three vector updates.

- **Inner product:** The computation of the inner product is done in two steps. Each processor computes its local inner product after that, it exchange the local inner product with the other processors in order to compute the global inner product. Therefore, each inner product implies a synchronization of the processors which is prohibitive in communication cost, especially when the iteration number is great.

- **Matrix-vector product:** Unlike the inner product where global communications are done, the matrix-vector product needs only communication between neighbor processors. For $0 \leq i \leq p - 2$, P_i sends N_x data to P_{i+1} and for $1 \leq i \leq p - 1$, P_i sends N_x data to P_{i-1}.

- **Vector updates:** The vector updates needs only local computation.

In order to decrease the number of synchronizations in each CG iteration, we have used a modified version (MCG) [2] which consists in doing three successive inner products, which implies only one synchronization. In other hand, to improve the convergence of CG, we have used a polynomial preconditioning which consists in solving the system $C(A)Ax = C(A)b$, where $C(A)$ is a matrix polynomial. C is chosen such that $k(C(A)A) << k(A)$, where $k(A)$ is the condition number. $C(A)A$ is constructed by applying scaled and translated Chebyshev polynomials [2]. Since the polynomial preconditioning requires only vector updates and matrix-vector products, the same parallel strategies can be exploited. Note that the number of matrix-vector product increase in each PMCG iteration, however, the number of synchronization decrease.

At each step of time, the computation time is estimated to be:

$$T_{comp} = \frac{T_{seq}}{p}$$

and the communication time is estimated to be:

$$T_{com}(SA) = ((3 + Icg)(\beta + N_x \tau) + \log 2(p)(I_{cg}(\beta + 3\tau) + 2(\beta + 2\tau)))I_{sa}.$$

$$T_{com}(NR) = ((4 + Icg)(\beta + N_x \tau) + \log 2(p)(I_{cg}(\beta + 3\tau) + 2(\beta + 2\tau)))I_{nr}$$

When communication and computation do not overlap, the execution of the algorithm, at each step of time, is $T_{par} = T_{comp} + T_{com}$.

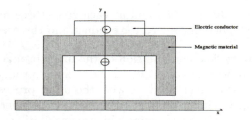

Figure 2. Electromagnetic relay

6 Experimental results

We have implemented this method on the distributed memory architecture T-N310 of Telmat composed of 32 Transputers T9000 under PVM environment with real double precision. Using PVM, the estimated values for communication parameters are $\beta = 0.002s$ and $\tau = 22\mu s$. For computation, $\omega = 0.25\mu s$. This shows that the communication for our system is very expensive. As a test example, we have considered the electomagnetic relay (figure 2) [3], taking into account the saturation effects and assuming that the current in the spool (electrical material) constant. The system is placed in a box of air with Dirichlet conditions. The geometrical structure is symmetric following oy axis, this leads to treat only one half of the domain with Neumann condition on the symmetric axis. Figure 3 shows the equipotential lines obtained for this example.

In [9], it is shown that SA converges only for small values of current density J_0. For $J_0 = 2.0 \ 10^6 A.m^{-2}$ and $N = 975$, SA diverge while NR converge.

In figure 4, we present the execution time obtained for NR using CG and MCG. These results show that MCG is better than CG since the number of synchronization decreases with MCG. In figure 5, we compare the execution times for SA and NR using MCG. The results show that for great values of N, NR is better than SA because NR converges rapidly, even though the computation and communication times, for each step of time, are greater than those for SA. In figure 6, we compare the execution time of SA using MCG and PMCG. The results show that PMCG is better than MCG when the number of processors increases, because with PMCG the computation cost increases but the number of CG iterations decreases.

The figures 7 and 8 show clearly the penalty due to communication which increases with the number of processors and the number of unknown.

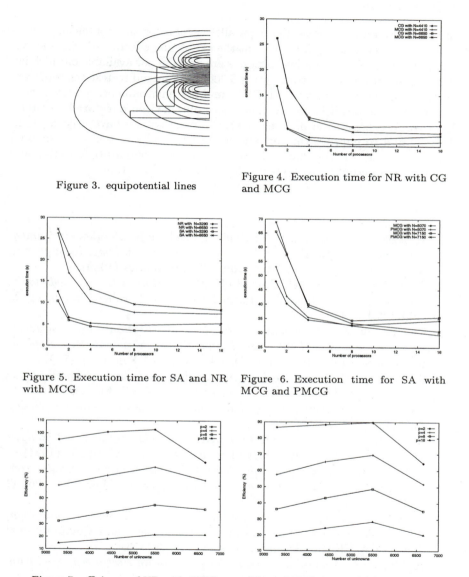

Figure 3. equipotential lines

Figure 4. Execution time for NR with CG and MCG

Figure 5. Execution time for SA and NR with MCG

Figure 6. Execution time for SA with MCG and PMCG

Figure 7. efficiency of NR with MCG

Figure 8. Efficiency of SA with MCG

7 Conclusion

In this work we have presented a parallel version for the nonlinear electromagnetic systems taking into account the saturation effects with SA and NR methods. The effective implementations are done on our available parallel distributed system based on transputers T9000. We intend to test this program on new parallel machines under PVM or MPI environment, we think that the performances will be better than those obtained on our parallel system. In order to decrease the number of synchronization, we have used a modified CG and to improve the convergence of CG we have used a polynomial preconditioning. In other hand, the communication/computation overlapping technics, had permit us to decrease the global execution time.

References

1. M. Azizi, E.M. Daoudi, R. El Hani, A. Lakhouaja, *Parallel electromagnetic modelling for the non linear electrotechnic systems*, to appear in Journal of Computational and Applied Mathematics (1999).
2. A. Baserman, B.Reichel, C.Scheltoff *Preconditioned CG methods for sparse matrices on massively parallel machines*, Parallel Computing 23 (1997) 381-398.
3. F. Boualem, *Contribution à la modélisation des systèmes électrotechniques à l'aide des formulations en potentiels: Application à la machine asynchrone*, PhD Thesis à l'UST de Lille, (1997).
4. R. Dautray, J.L. Lions, *Mathematical analysis and numerical methods for science and technology*, vol.1, Springer-Verlag, New York, 1990.
5. I.T. Foster, *Designing and building parallel programs*, Addison-Wesley Publishing Company (1995).
6. A. Kumar et al *Introduction to parallel computing: design and analysis of algorithms*, The Benjamin/Cummings Publishing Company (1994).
7. F. Hecht, A. Marrocco, *A finite element simulation of an alternator connected to an nonlinear external circuit*, IEEE Trans. Magn. Vol. 26, n2 (1990) 964-967.
8. T. Kawai, *Role of computer simulation in scientific research and engineering development*, Electromagnetic Phenomena and Computational Techniques, Elsevier Science Publishers (1992) 3-18.
9. A. Marrocco, *Analyse numérique des problèmes d'électrotechnique*, Ann. Sc. Math. Quebec, vol.1 (1977) 271-296.
10. Y. Saad, *Iterative methods for sparse linear systems*, PWS Publishing Company, Boston (1996).

HIPERCIR: A SCALABLE PC-BASED PARALLEL SYSTEM FOR MEDICAL IMAGING

I. BLANQUER, V. HERNÁNDEZ, J. RAMÍREZ, A. VIDAL

Departamento de Sistemas Informáticos y Computación, Universidad Politécnica de Valencia,
Camino de Vera s/n, 46022 Valencia, SPAIN.
Phone: 34-963877356, Fax: 34-963877359
e-mail: {iblanque, vhernand, jramirez, avidal}@dsic.upv.es

Clinics have to deal currently with hundreds of 3D images a day. 3D Medical Images contain a huge amount of data, and thus, very expensive and powerful systems are required in order to process them. The present work shows the features of a software integrated parallel computing package developed at the Universidad Politécnica de Valencia, under the European Project HIPERCIR [1.] Project HIPERCIR is aimed at reducing the time and requirements for processing and visualising 3D images with low-cost solutions, such as networks of PCs running standard operating systems (Windows 95/98/NT). HIPERCIR is targeted to Radiology Departments of Hospitals and Radiology System Providers for easing the day-to-day diagnosis. This project is being developed by a consortium formed by medical image processing and parallel computing experts from the Computing Systems Department (DSIC) of the Universidad Politécnica de Valencia (UPV), experts on biomedical software and radiology and tomography clinic experts.

1 The HIPERCIR System

The HIPERCIR integrated parallel package combines a medical image segmentation and reconstruction system. Three-dimensional medical images usually come from Computer Tomography (CT) or Magnetic Resonance (MR). These two systems obtain a set of 2D images that comprise different slices of a patient's body.

Medical image processing typically involves two tasks: segmentation and 3D reconstruction. Medical image segmentation implies to select the regions of interest (ROIs) of the image. Non-interesting tissues are neglected and different organs are showed using different colors. The segmentation of medical image is a very complex task and, unless specific cases, it requires user intervention. 3D reconstruction is the process of projecting the 3D image resulting from the segmentation on a view plane. There are two basic methods for 3D reconstruction, which are surface reconstruction and volume rendering. Surface reconstruction methods obtain a polygon mesh of the surface of the objects in the image and volume-rendering methods directly work with the object data. Surface methods can be sped-up using specialized hardware, whereas volume-rendering methods obtain higher quality and keep the volumetric information of the image.

HIPERCIR implements a parallel segmentation engine and a parallel 3D volume rendering visualization system. The code has been implemented using

Visual C++ and the WMPI message-passing library. The objective of this package is to provide an affordable but high-quality and high-performance tool that can be used for day-to-day work. HIPERCIR provides very realistic views of isolated organs or tissues from any point of view. The platform used for the performance tests shown in this document, consisted on a network of PentiumPro 200Mhz PCs, with 64 MB RAM and running Windows NT, connected by a Fast Ethernet Hub. Results on a network of Bi-processor PentiumII/III PCs are also included.

2   THE PARALLEL SEGMENTATION TOOL

The segmentation is an interactive process and requires very quick interaction with the user. The user generally makes a segmenting operation and can take back the action according to the result. For a realistic interactive use, a parallel version has been developed.

HIPERCIR implements a semi-automatic segmentation system that works on clusters of PCs in parallel. It is a variant of the 3D Region Growing (RG) algorithm, which is suitable for a general-purpose tool. RG algorithms only require enough gray-level differentiation among the frontiers of the different tissues or organs. In this process, the user selects a set of seeds that are expanded attending a criteria of proximity (the nearest 3D neighbors, from 6 to 26) and similarity (gray-level inside an interval centered in the average of the initial set). Figure 1 shows a scheme of the parallelisation approach.

Figure 1: Parallelisation Approach of the Segmentation System.

Different slices are distributed by blocks among the available processors. Segmentation is started by the master processor, which controls the user interaction, but also has the initial set of seeds. The segmentation process is the same as the sequential procedure until it reaches a limit slice. Limit slices are replicated between neighboring processors to avoid communications during the computing of inter-limit slices. The seeds that belong to slices located in other processors are packed in a message that is sent to the neighbor processors. The communication procedure is controlled by the master processor to avoid deadlocks. The seeds are buffered in order to optimize message size. In order to reduce initial idle delays on the processors different from the master one, the z-axis is expanded first. When all processors have finished the region growing process, the resulting information is sent to the master processor, which shows the results to the user. In order to reduce the communication cost, the data is packed using RLE.

The vicinity criteria used are the 3D 6 and 26-neighbors. The homogeneity criterion used is an interval centered on the seeds mean gray-level, with a radius of a constant times the standard deviation plus a tolerance. To improve the segmentation of soft tissues with poor intensity differentiation, a locality criterion has been used. This adaptive criterion modifies the interval radius in order to fill small holes in and to avoid escaping through noisy narrow paths. This criterion has proven to be good for tissues such as brain, metastasis and blood vessels.

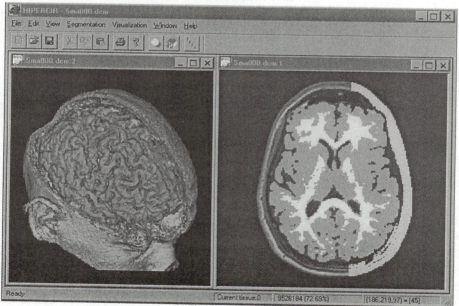

Figure 2 Segmentation of soft tissues and 3D reconstruction using HIPERCIR

Figure 2 shows a 3D image of the white and gray matter of a brain (using yellow and orange colors), as well as part of the skull and the skin (in pink). The realism of the image is very good and has required very low user interaction.

82

In order to analyze the efficiency and quality of the parallel-computing segmentation tool implemented, a test battery was proposed. This test battery comprises real cases from the radiology department of a Spanish Hospital, which have a special medical or computing interest. Table 1 shows a description of the different test cases comprising the size, dimensions and objective.

Case	Size	Size	Description
Liver-1	512x512x32	8Mbytes	A 35 years-old woman with breast cancer. Several small ill-defined metastatic liver lesions were found.
Liver-2	512x512x52	13Mbytes	A 59 years-old woman with breast cancer. Multiple large focal metastatic liver lesions were found.
Chest-1	512x512x31	7.8Mbytes	A 63 years-old woman with gastrointestinal primary adenocarci-noma and abdominal metastatic disease.
Angio-1	512x512x68	17Mbytes	A 75 years-old male with an abdominal pulsatile mass. Infrarenal aneurysm was found.
Angio-2	512x512x68	17Mbytes	A 45 years-old male with lower limb claudication: Popliteal artery entrapment was suspected. No abnormality was found.
Angio-3	512x512x33	8.3Mbytes	A 33 years-old patient with chest pain and an ischemic left lower limb. A toracoabdominal aortic dissection was found.
Brain-1	256x256x200	12Mbytes	MR image of the brain. A patient with no pathology.
Ear-1	512x512x20	5Mbytes	CT image of the ears. Chronic Mastoiditis is found.
Ear-2	512x512x24	6Mbytes	CT image of the ears. A benign osteoma is found.

Table 1: Test battery for the HIPERCIR project

Along with the test-battery a set of experiments were defined. Each one of the experiments produced a different area of different size. All the experiments could be repeated for the comparison of different configurations.

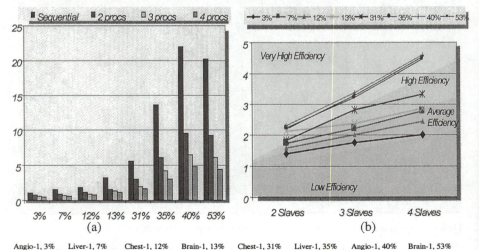

Angio-1, 3%   Liver-1, 7%   Chest-1, 12%   Brain-1, 13%   Chest-1, 31%   Liver-1, 35%   Angio-1, 40%   Brain-1, 53%

Figure 3: Time spent (a) and speed–up (b) for the segmentation of different areas in the test battery.

The results obtained have reached efficiencies close to 100% for costly cases that involve a large area. In this way, HIPERCIR showed in the performance test that it can segment the 50% of a 12 Million voxels image (256x256x200, e.g.) in less than 5 seconds using four PC-based machines.

Super-linear speed-up is achieved for large cases. This phenomenon typically appears with problems that have a high data locality access pattern, as in the case of region growing. The increase of caché memory also affects the performance.

3   THE PARALLEL VISUALISATION TOOL

There are several different approaches for the visualization of images in 3D. In HIPERCIR, a ray-casting volume rendering procedure [3,4] was selected. The reasons for this choice lie on the ability to manage volumetric information and in the high quality of the images obtained. The main drawbacks of ray-casting volume rendering algorithms are the huge demand of computing power and memory requirements. The objective of HIPERCIR is to introduce parallel computing to minimize this constraint. Volume-rendering techniques can be divided on ray-casting and Splatting methods. Ray-casting methods work on the image-space, tracing rays from the image plane towards the object. Splatting techniques work on the volume-space and project the voxels towards the image plane.

The volume-rendering algorithm implemented is ray-casting oriented. It makes use of tri-linear interpolation for obtaining better quality. It takes as input the result of the segmentation tool, and permits to show different segmentation sessions with different colors and opacities or transparencies. Discrete and continuous scaling factors permits to obtain more or less accuracy depending on the purpose of the study. The interface uses parallel-processing real-time low-quality projection for the interactive positioning of the viewpoint. The algorithm makes use of the typical acceleration techniques, such as early ray termination or leaping over empty areas.

The parallel version of the Volume Rendering algorithm has been implemented dividing cyclically the screen area in different blocks of rows to optimize load balancing since medical objects can have very irregular shape. These blocks are equally distributed among the different processors of the system. Communication is only required at two stages: on one hand, at the beginning to exchange the parameters of the operation, and on the other hand, at the end to collect the results of each processor. This results in very short communication overhead, quick performance and good efficiency. The communication is optimized by using a specific cyclic message type. Ray casting is performed using a discrete 3D ray traversal algorithm that takes into account light diffusion.

The system also takes into account if each computer has more than one processor with a finer grain parallelism inside. The data distribution inside each computer is block-row oriented and synchronisation is performed through standard primitives.

84

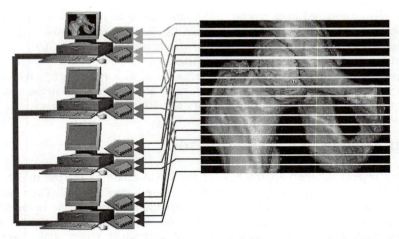

Figure 4: Cyclic block row distribution among computers and block-row intra-computer distribution.

Although medical practitioners usually work with orthogonal projection, perspective projection is also interesting for navigation. Perspective projection can be used for inspecting the inner part of parenchyma areas such as vessels, intestines, trachea, and medullar spine. HIPERCIR combines both projection systems. The cost of perspective is slightly higher since projection direction is not the same for all the pixels in the image, like in the orthogonal projection. In this last case pre-computing of normal intensities and colours in a look-ahead table is performed.

For the validation and testing of the parallel volume-rendering tool, the HIPERCIR test battery was used (table 1). The speed-up obtained is quasi-linear for a moderate number of processors, with a response time of one second for a real large image (256x256x200, 17MBytes). However, although the efficiency decreases when the number of processors increase, the parallel algorithm is scalable and the problem is due to the Hub interconnection system used. If a switch connection system were used, the efficiency would have remain stable.

The following table shows the time consumed by a rotation in the Z-axis for each one of the images of the test battery and different number of processors (from one to five Pentium Pro 200MHz computers) linked with fast-Ethernet.

# Processors	Ear-1	Ear-2	Angio-1	Angio-2	Angio-3	Brain-1
1	0,44	0,38	1,17	2,47	2,69	4,31
2	0,26	0,27	0,61	1,28	1,47	2,22
3	0,20	0,22	0,47	0,92	1,05	1,67
4	0,18	0,20	0,36	0,47	0,88	1,22
5	0,15	0,19	0,33	0,38	0,73	1,00

Table 2 : Time (in sec.) spent in rotating 10° each one of the test battery images

The absolute time spent by HIPERCIR is enough short to reach interactive use. Moreover, time is predicted to continue decreasing for larger number of processors (and large images) and performance would increase with a switched network.

Figure 5 show the speed-up and efficiency obtained. The platform used for the test was a cluster of three bi-Pentium II 400MHz computers, linked with a fast Ethernet hub. Performance shown on figure 5 includes the overhead (redistribution, computation, communication and bitmap reconstruction). Thus, these are the real figures that a user will experiment. The results are much better as in table 2, not only due to the improvement on processor speed, but also on the topology. Inside each computer a fine grain parallelism is performed, whereas a MPI message passing coarser-grain parallelism is implemented among different computers.

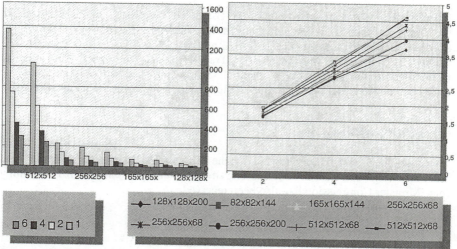

figure 5 : Computing time and Speed-up obtained with the test battery

Scalability is very good, mainly in the larger cases and speed up is very high (around 4.5 in larger cases with 3 bi-processors). Moreover, the absolute value of the time spent is very short. The impact of the collisions in the communication link and the high latency of Ethernet prevent from obtaining higher performance.

4   CONCLUSIONS

The HIPERCIR project has produced a parallel demonstrator that has been designed to promote the use of HPCN by showing the real benefits that could be obtained. HIPERCIR has been focused on improving the knowledge of HPCN in the medical users and technology providers.

The HIPERCIR project has result in an affordable tool that can help the day-to-day work of clinics and Hospitals. The use of parallel computing makes the system very competitive in performance to the current workstation-based systems, which are much more expensive. Clinic experts in Computer Tomography and Magnetic Resonance have tested the usability of the package. The system is scalable and can run efficiently using from one single PC to several, depending on the user demand. There are very few commercial applications that use HPCN for medical imaging, and all of them are based on SMP approaches, which lead to use no more that two or four processors. HIPERCIR demonstrates that it is feasible to introduce low-cost parallel computing to provide high performance with affordable systems.

5   OTHER INITIATIVES IN THE EUROPEAN UNION

HIPERCIR [1,2] is one of the results of the HIPERTTN Project [5] (ESPRIT 24003) in the frame of the METIER (Mechanism for Enabling Technology Transfer in Europe) action, focused on the activities of the HPCN-TTN (High Performance Computing and Networking Technology Transfer Nodes) Network [7]. This network is oriented to the promotion of Parallel Computing in different sectors of the European industry. HIPERCIR is one of the activities aiming at the medical sector [6].

6   ACKNOWLEDGES

This work has been mainly funded by the HIPERCIR Preparatory, Support and Transfer Activity. Additionally, funding from Spanish Science and Technology Inter-Minister Commission has also been received.

7   REFERENCES

1.   HIPERCIR Project. http://hiperttn.upv.es/hipercir
2.   I. Blanquer, V. Hernández, F.J. Ramírez, A. Vidal, et al. HIPERCIR: *Altas Prestaciones y Bajo Coste en la Segmentación y Visualización en 3D de Imágenes*. Proceedings of the Annual Congress of the Spanish Biomedical Society, September 1998, ISBN: 84-7721-664-9.
3.   L. Martí-Bonmatí, I. Blanquer, V. Hernández, F.J. Ramírez, A. Vidal, et al. *The HIPERCIR EU Project: fast MRI processing facilities at low-cost*. MAGMA journal, September 1999, PII: S1325-8661(99)00040-X.
4.   R.A. Drebin, L. Carpenter, P. Hanrahan, *Volume Rendering*, Computer Graphics, Vol. 22,(4) August 1988.
5.   M. Levoy. *Efficient Ray Tracing of Volume Data*, ACM Transactions on Graphics Vol 9. No.3 July 1990.
6.   HIPERTTN Project. http://hiperttn.upv.es
7.   Medical group of the HPCN-TTN. http://www.epcc.ed.ac.uk/ttn-Medical/
8.   HPCN-TTN Network. http://hcpn-ttn.org

BAYESIAN IMAGE RESTORATION: PARALLEL IMPLEMENTATION ON A SGI ORIGIN MULTIPROCESSOR

J. M. CARAZO

BioComputing Unit, Centro Nacional de Biotecnología-CSIC,
Madrid, Spain
E-mail: carazo@cnb.uam.es

R. DOALLO, J. M. EIROA, J. SANJURJO

Departamento de Electrónica e Sistemas, Universidade da Coruña,
A Coruña, Spain.
E-mail: doallo@udc.es, jmeiroa@des.fi.udc.es, josesan@udc.es

Image restoration is an important problem with applications in many fields of science from Medicine to Astronomy. In this work we attempt to improve performance by means of parallel optimization techniques for the restoration process of images affected by zero-mean Gaussian white additive noise by means of a bayesian restoration algorithm. We employ the MAP algorithm, which uses a simulated annealing scheme and a Markov image model. The computational cost of this algorithm justifies the need for its parallelisation on a multiprocessor architecture. A sequential implementation created data dependences, impeding any kind of parallelisation, but it was possible to rewrite the algorithm in such a way that the image was divided into regions that were mapped onto the processors and computed concurrently. The algorithm has proved to be highly scalable.

1 Introduction

Very often in image formation a corrupted image is obtained due to some kind of degradation. This makes the study of methods for recovering the original image, i.e., restoring the image, very interesting. Amongst proposed methods for solving this problem, a statistical approach can be an intuitive one in many cases [1,4].

From the knowledge about the physical principles that govern the image construction process we can build a statistical model in the form of a likelihood function $P(Y|X)$, which estimates the probability of the measure Y given an image X. The statistical approach to the actual image estimation is to find an image that maximizes the likelihood function. However, the problem is often ill-conditioned, i.e., small changes in the measurements can cause relatively important changes in the solution. The normal way of stabilizing this problem is to incorporate *a priori* knowledge in the restoration process. In our case this knowledge can be exploited by formulating a probability function $P(X)$ over all possible image configurations, which defines a prior image model. By using Bayes' theorem, an estimation $\hat{X}$ of the image can be obtained based on the posterior distribution $\frac{P(X)P(Y|X)}{P(Y)}$.

In this work we attempt to improve performance by means of parallel optimisation techniques for the restoration process of an image affected by zero-mean Gaussian white additive noise. A Bayesian restoration algorithm, the MAP (*maximum a posteriori*) algorithm, involving a simulated annealing scheme and based on a definition of a Markov image model [1,2] is used. The computational cost of this algorithm justifies the need to approach their parallelisation on a multiprocessor architecture. In our case, we have used a distributed shared memory system: the SGI Origin system.

This work is the first step in the study of the application of this methodology on electron microscopic images in the setting of our collaboration with the Biocomputing Unit at the Centro National de Biotecnología (CNB, Madrid, Spain).

2 Image model

A Markov image model is associated with a Gibbs distribution [4]:

$$\Pi(X) = \frac{1}{Z}e^{-\beta H(X)} \tag{1}$$

where X is an image, β is a scaling constant, Z is a normalization factor and $H(X)$ is the system energy function or Hamiltonian, by means of which we represent the local properties of our image model. Hamiltonians are defined as a sum of clique potentials:

$$H(X) = -\sum_{C \in \mathcal{C}} V_C(X) \tag{2}$$

where $X = (x_1, \ldots, x_N)$ is an image, C is a clique and $\mathcal{C}$ is the union of all classes of cliques. Potentials $V_C(X)$ represent the energy contribution of every clique, a *clique* being an ordered subset of the pixel set, or equivalently, a subset of the integer set $S = \{1, \ldots, N\}$. In this restoration algorithm we use two clique classes: The first, $C_{2\times 2}$, consists of every index sequence in natural order corresponding with 2×2 contiguous pixel subarrays. The second, $C_{3\times 3}$, consists of every index sequence in natural order corresponding to 3×3 contiguous pixel subarrays. These cliques are shown in figure 1(a).

In our case we define two Hamiltonians (H_1 and H_2) that bring information about homogeneous regions and borders which may surround homogeneous regions [2,3]. The unified model is defined by adding both Hamiltonians,

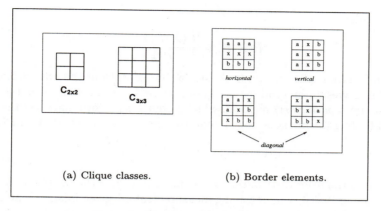

(a) Clique classes. (b) Border elements.

Figure 1. Cliques and border elements.

so it is defined by the following distribution:

$$\Pi(X) = \frac{1}{Z'}e^{-\beta(H_1(X)+H_2(X))} \tag{3}$$

The model properties depend on the magnitudes of the distribution parameters and the clique classes used.

Homogeneous regions are described using $C_{2\times2}$ and $C_{3\times3}$ cliques: the formation of an homogeneous region is favoured when every pixel in the clique have the same gray levels. On the other hand, using $C_{3\times3}$ cliques we can design a Hamiltonian to describe border elements in different orientations. Figure 1(b) shows border elements: the formation of a border is favoured when every pixels labeled by a have the same gray levels, every pixels labeled by b have the same gray levels, too, but different from the one associated with a, and every pixels labeled by x can have one or the other of these two gray levels.

3 Description of the restoration algorithm

In many situations the image formation model is of the form:

$$Y = X_0 + \eta \tag{4}$$

where Y is the observed image, X_0 is the original image and η represents the noise (in our case, zero-mean Gaussian white additive noise). As has previously been mentioned, the posterior distribution of the images, given by

Bayes' rule:

$$P(X|Y) = \frac{P(X)P(Y|X)}{P(Y)} \tag{5}$$

is useful to find different kinds of estimations of X from the observation Y.

The Bayesian method we are going to use for estimating X is the MAP (*maximum a posteriori*) method, which in our case is formulated as the problem of finding the image X that maximizes the posterior distribution $P(X|Y)$:

$$\max {}_X P(X|Y) = \frac{\Pi(X)L(Y|X)}{P(Y)} \tag{6}$$

where Π is the prior distribution of the images X, L is the likelihood function giving the probability of obtaining measurements Y given image X, and $P(Y)$ is the probability of measurements Y (which does not depend on X). For zero-mean Gaussian white additive noise, the likelihood function is given by:

$$L(Y|X) = \prod_{i \in S} \frac{1}{\sqrt{2\pi\sigma^2}} \exp\left(-\frac{(y_i - x_i)^2}{2\sigma^2}\right) \tag{7}$$

where σ is the standard deviation of the noise, $S = \{1, 2, \ldots, N\}$ is the index set of the images $X = (x_1, \ldots, x_N)$ and $Y = (y_1, \ldots, y_N)$. The gray level of a pixel from X and Y is represented by x_i and y_i respectively. The equivalent problem is finding the X that minimizes the following expression:

$$U(X, Y) = -\ln \Pi(X) - \ln L(Y|X) \tag{8}$$

In order to apply this method we use a simulated annealing scheme [2]. The algorithm is shown in figure 2: $X(0)$ is the initial image, $X(k)$ is the image after k iterations, s is an image pixel, $X(k)[s, \alpha]$ is the image $X(k)$ except at pixel s (where which has value α), Λ is the image gray level set, and $\Pi(\cdot)$ is the Gibbs distribution. Temperature T is set based on the expression:

$$T_k = \frac{C}{\log(1 + k)} \tag{9}$$

where k is the number of iterations and C a constant which is set to 4.0 by us [4].

4 Transformation strategy

From an algorithmic point of view, two aspects deserve special mention: the exploration of an image is permitted in any order; and the value of a pixel affects and is affected by the values of the surrounding pixels, depending on the

1. $k = 0$

2. Set a temperature T. T is a parameter that diminishes with each iteration.

3. Choose a pixel s from $X(k)$.

4. Compute the pixel local conditional distribution

$$P_s(\alpha) = \frac{\exp(-U(X(k)[s, \alpha], Y)/T)}{\sum_{\alpha' \in \Lambda} \exp(-U(X(k)[s, \alpha'], Y)/T)}$$

5. Generate a random sample α from the above distribution.

6. $X(k) = X(k)[s, \alpha]$

7. If the whole image has not been swept, go back to step 3. Otherwise, increase k and go back to step 2. The process ends when convergence is reached.

Figure 2. *Simulated annealing* algorithm.

nature of the neighbourhood system that is employed. These considerations are key to improving the computation performance of the implementation. Originally, a sequential exploration order was opted for, which on one hand was simple, but on the other created data dependences between the pixels, which impeded any attempt at parallelisation: the computation of new values for the neighbouring pixels influenced each other mutually and their update could not be realised concurrently. In order to compute various pixels concurrently, it would be necessary that they do not affect each other. To this aim, we resorted to the possibility of exploring the image in any order.

The first step was the transformation of the algorithm in order to break the data dependencies between pixels. This was done by dividing the image into regions, in order that the algorithm could be applied concurrently in independent regions [5]. Two regions are independent if the pixels of one region do not depend on the pixel values in the other region, although they do depend on pixels of other regions that we have called *guard regions*. These regions maintain the separation necessary in order for these to be independent regions and their pixel values are constant throughout the duration of the processing of the independent regions.

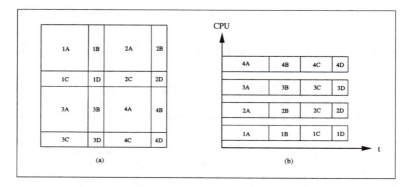

Figure 3. (a) Division in regions of an image on a system with 4 processors. (b) Concurrent processing of the regions.

5 Work distribution

Work distribution is the division of the image in regions which were mapped onto the processors in order to compute them concurrently. Taking advantage of the possibility of the algorithm to explore image pixels in any order, the regions are computed concurrently by steps, computing in each step the regions that are independent among themselves. The procedure for dividing the image and its computation is shown in figure 3.

There exists a natural correspondence between an image and a processor mesh. Every work distribution can be associated with a certain processor mesh. The algorithm for work distribution determines the optimal dimensions of the processor mesh for a given image and then computes the shape of the regions for that mesh.

The central idea is using, in each dimension of the image, a number of processors from the available processors proportional to the size of the image in that dimension (the larger the size of a dimension, the greater the number of processors). Once the mesh has been sized, an area of the image is mapped onto a processor whose position in the mesh corresponds to the positions of the area in the image. This area must in turn be divided in regions to allow parallel processing. Let be (x_0, y_0) coordinates of the top left corner of the subimage, (x_1, y_1) coordinates of the bottom right corner of the subimage, $minX$ minimum size in dimension X, $minY$ minimum size in dimension Y. The subimage is divided into regions according to the scheme in figure 4. We have chosen this division procedure (a main region and several "residual"

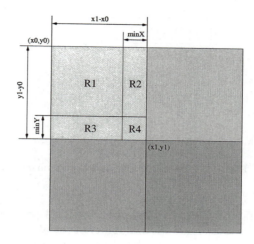

Figure 4. Work distribution.

regions) as it is the most similar to the ideal case, in which there would be just one main region. The procedure for computing image regions concurrently is shown in figure 3: analogous regions are processed simultaneously. This balances the load, i.e., it gives as much work to one processor as to all the other processors.

6 Results

The initial developmental work of the new implementation and the introduction of optimization techniques was carried out on a SGI Origin 200 system (4 processors MIPS R10000 at 180 Mhz). An SGI Origin 2000 system (16 processors MIPS R10000 at 195 Mhz) was used to evaluate performance.

Once the implementation was modified to allow parallel processing, first we considered the effects that scalar optimization techniques could have on it, i.e., performance enhancing techniques for a single processor extensible to multiprocessor environments simply by application to each processor. In this manner we improved performance by 10 % with respect to the original figures (the program executed 10 % faster than the original). Then we used parallel optimization techniques, with which we were able to implement the multiprocessor possibilities that had arisen after the code transformation. Obtained results with 1, 2, 4 and 8 processors are shown in figure 5.

The speedup increases almost linearly with the number of processors, so

94

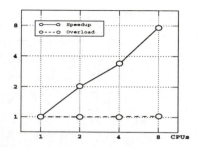

Figure 5. Parallel implementation performance.

the efficiency remains constant. The speedup with 4 processors was 3.5 and with 8 it was 7.74, which shows the scalability of the algorithm. The parallelisation overload is almost inexistent because the start-up for multiprocessing is carried out at the beginning of the program, outside the main loop.

Acknowledgements

The authors wish to thank the University of Málaga (Spain) for providing access to its SGI Origin 2000 system. This work was supported by the Spanish CICYT under the grant TIC96–1125–C03.

References

1. J. Besag. On the Statistical Analysis of Dirty Pictures (with discussion). *Journal of the Royal Statistical Society Series B*, 48(3):259–302, 1986.
2. M. Chan, G. T. Herman, E. Levitan. Bayesian Image Reconstruction Using a High-Order Interacting MRF Model. *Lecture Notes in Computer Science*, ISSN 0302–9743, 974:609–614, 1995.
3. M. Chan, G. T. Herman, E. Levitan. Bayesian Image Reconstruction Using Image-Modeling Gibbs Priors. *International Journal of Imaging Systems and Technology*, 9:85–98, 1998.
4. S. Geman, D. Geman. Stochastic Relaxation, Gibbs Distributions, and the Bayesian restorarion of images. *IEEE transactions on Pattern Analysis and Machine Intelligence*, 6(6):721–741,1984.
5. F. Jeng, J. W. Woods, S. Rastogi. Compound Gauss-Markov Random Fields for Parallel Image Processing. In R. Chellapa and A. Jain, editors, *Markov Random Fields: Theory and Application*, pp. 11–38. Academic Press, San Diego, 1993.
6. R. van der Pas. *SGI porting and optimisation seminar*. Silicon Graphics, Inc., 1998.

A FRAMEWORK FOR PARALLEL MULTITHREADED IMPLEMENTATION OF DOMAIN DECOMPOSITION METHODS

A. S. CHARÃO, I. CHARPENTIER AND B. PLATEAU

Laboratoire de Modélisation et Calcul (LMC-IMAG)
B.P. 53, F-38041 Grenoble Cedex 9, France
E-mail: {charao,charpentier,plateau}@imag.fr

This paper presents a framework that allows easy and efficient exploitation of multithreading techniques in the development of parallel PDE solvers based on domain decomposition methods. Within this framework, users are able to concentrate on actual computations performed by numerical domain decomposition solvers, without having to directly deal with communication and synchronization programming details. The framework relies on object-oriented techniques to provide a modular organization based on a parallel, multithreaded kernel that supports a large variety of domain decomposition methods.

1 Introduction

In the context of solving partial differential equations (PDEs) on parallel computers, increasing interest has been devoted to domain decomposition methods[1,2]. The main idea behind these methods is to split a discrete domain into smaller subdomains that are cheaper in terms of memory and computation requirements. Such methods are well-adapted to parallel computing: subdomain computations can be performed in parallel, although some data must be exchanged to solve boundary value problems along the interfaces between subdomains. Domain decomposition methods are also useful for problems that need special treatment of singularities such as discontinuous media, and for multidisciplinary simulations that couple different mathematical models, each posed on a different domain.

Obtaining good parallel performance when using domain decomposition methods depends on several issues. The main ones are minimization of communication costs and load balancing. These issues can be very difficult to address, specially when we solve problems on irregular domains or when we deal with mesh refinement and adaptive techniques. An interesting way to cope with these issues is multithreading. Threads are useful to mask communication overhead, to ease efficient task scheduling and to overlap load balancing and actual computations when dealing with irregular applications. Multithreading also allows to efficiently exploit symmetric multiprocessor (SMP) architectures that become largely available nowadays. In such platforms, different threads that compose a parallel program can execute simultaneously on different processors. For a thorough discussion on the advantages of using threads for parallel irregular applications see, for example, [3] and [4].

Considering the context described above we have developed AHPIK, a framework which allows for an easy and efficient exploitation of multithreaded programming for the implementation of parallel PDE solvers based on domain decomposition methods. After discussing related research on frameworks for scientific computing, we describe the organization of AHPIK and evaluate its efficiency for a test problem. The final section summarizes our contributions and discusses future work.

2 Related work

The increasing demand for specialized support to parallel scientific computations has motivated the development of a large number of frameworks that encapsulate parallelism, improve portability and simplify programming. Three representative examples of such frameworks are PETSc[5], ScaLAPACK[6] and POOMA[7]. All these tools deal with parallelism and provide common abstractions for solving PDEs. Overture[8], Cogito[9] and KeLP[10] are other interesting similar projects. They treat specialized constructions like structured grids for finite difference parallel PDE computations. When examining current developments in this area, one realizes that an increasing attention has been devoted to the use of object-oriented techniques, since issues like reusability, flexibility and expressiveness of source code become more and more desirable when developing parallel scientific applications.

Even though our work is situated in the same general context as various existing frameworks, there are some important details that distinguish our contribution. While most frameworks focus on scientific computing in general, we restrict our attention to a specific strategy for solving PDEs, i.e., numerical domain decomposition methods. This allows us to invest in optimizations that are not possible in more general-purpose frameworks. In fact, our primary goal is not to offer a complete tool for numerical simulation, but to concentrate on the issues related to efficient parallelization of domain decomposition methods using multithreading techniques. Also, AHPIK currently supports both finite difference or finite element PDE computations over structured and unstructured meshes. As a mid-term goal, we want to cope with load balancing when adaptive refinement techniques are applied to problems involving unstructured meshes. This should confirm the interest of our multithreaded approach.

Most existing frameworks do not integrate multithreading techniques. Some projects, in particular POOMA and Overture, rely on runtime kernels that support threads, but the integration of multithreading into their parallel solving procedures is limited to shared-memory multiprocessors. Using threads for efficient distributed and shared memory parallelism remains an open field of research.

3 The AHPIK framework

The AHPIK framework is composed of C++ classes. These classes provide various abstractions for developing PDE solvers based on domain decomposition methods. Object-oriented programming is employed as a means of providing a highly modular support for parallel solvers, characterized by strong separation between programming interface and parallel, multithreaded implementation. A modular organization also facilitates the integration of existing third-party libraries that provide building blocks for handling linear systems. AHPIK currently uses SparseLib++/MV++ for dealing with sparse matrices and vectors, and IML++ for solving local systems using standard iterative methods. Direct solving capability will be soon available, through integration of the SuperLU package available from the ScaLAPACK framework.

AHPIK classes are organized in three groups: those representing subdomains, those dealing with discrete methods for PDE problems and, those related to domain decomposition solvers for these problems. The classes in the first group provide data structures and functions for dealing with overlapping or non-overlapping, structured or unstructured two-dimensional meshes. In the second group, one finds finite element and finite difference basic procedures that allows assembling a linear equation system corresponding to some PDE problem. Classes belonging to this group contain virtual functions that must be overridden in a derived class to satisfy requirements of each problem to be solved. Even though they are sufficient for implementing simple simulations, these classes do not cover a large set of finite element methods, so AHPIK allows them to be easily replaced by the user.

Most relevant to the AHPIK framework are the classes of the third group, i.e., those offering support to parallel, multithreaded implementation of domain decomposition methods. These classes are distributed in three layers built on top of ATHA-PASCAN[11], a portable communicating threads library which efficiently integrates Posix thread kernels to MPI message passing model on various target architectures. The first layer in our framework corresponds to the AHPIK kernel; such a *generic layer* encapsulates data and control abstractions that can be reused by different domain decomposition solvers. The second layer is the *coordination layer*, where specific communication and synchronization schemes are defined. Finally, the actual computations that have to be performed by domain decomposition solvers are defined by the user in the *domain decomposition layer*. We will now describe each layer in more detail.

3.1 *Generic layer: the* AHPIK *kernel*

The kernel was designed to be as generic as possible, in order to support the implementation of various domain decomposition methods. The key idea is that most domain decomposition methods exhibit similar computation patterns. More specifically, their general behavior can be described as an iterative process composed by two types of interacting tasks: *internal* tasks and *interface* tasks. Internal tasks perform local computations, i.e., computations that require only local data within a subdomain. On the other hand, interface tasks carry out computations over interface variables, and require data from neighboring subdomains. Numerical domain decomposition methods differ in terms of actual operations performed by internal and interface tasks and in the way these tasks communicate and synchronize their execution. They also differ in the amount of overlapping between subdomains: most authors classify domain decomposition methods in *overlapping* or *non-overlapping* methods (see, for example, [1]).

The above task decomposition is well-adapted to multithreading. In the AH-PIK framework, parallel PDE solvers are organized as a set of interacting *internal* and *interface* tasks, each task being performed by a specialized thread. Additional sender/receiver threads are employed to carry out communication of boundary data needed for solving each interface problem. Threads are scheduled based on the availability of the data they depend on. When a subdomain has more than one interface, interface computations can be performed in parallel by different threads as soon as their input data are available.

An important feature of AHPIK is the ability of assigning several subdomains per processor, in the same address space. This technique, known as *clusterization*, is useful for overlapping communication with computation, and allows threads corresponding to subdomains assigned to the same processor to communicate through shared memory. Clusterization is particularly interesting because classic domain decomposition methods are *synchronous*, i.e. they require processors solving neighboring subdomains to synchronize in order to perform interface computations. Without clusterization this means that, face to load imbalances, some processors may be idle waiting for others to finish their local computations. Alternative numerical methods have been proposed to break this strict synchronization (see [12]). These *asynchronous* methods allow to perform interface computations by using the data most recently received from neighboring processors, not necessarily corresponding to the current iteration. AHPIK supports both synchronous and asynchronous methods (see section 3.2).

3.2 Coordination layer

Interaction patterns between internal and interface tasks are defined in this layer. Usually, these patterns depend on the iterative method chosen to solve the interface problem. In practice, one notices that some patterns can be reused to implement different methods.

The implementation of synchronous or asynchronous methods differ in terms of interaction patterns. In synchronous methods, interface threads wait for neighboring subdomains to send interface data corresponding to the current iteration. They may block if their neighbors have not yet finished local computations. On the other hand, asynchronous methods allow to perform interface computations with the data most recently received, so interface threads never block.

Another issue concerning the coordination layer is convergence control of the domain decomposition methods. Distributed convergence control is usually required when solving interface problems by conjugate gradient methods. For other methods, centralized convergence control may be more adequate. Both schemes are supported in AHPIK. In a centralized scheme, an additional thread is created in one of the processors, and the global convergence control follows a master-slave model. A distributed scheme, on the other hand, relies on collective communication to allow global error computation.

AHPIK encapsulates interaction patterns in base classes containing virtual functions that have to be overridden in derived classes. Several interaction patterns are currently available. To implement a new solver, the user chooses one of these predefined patterns or, eventually, writes a new one.

3.3 Domain decomposition layer

After choosing an interaction pattern, writing a new domain decomposition solver involves the definition of a derived class from the base interaction pattern class. Figure 1 shows an example using the base class `GenericSyncDDSolver`, which encapsulates a generic synchronous scheme. This class has been used to implement both a *Schur complement* and an *additive Schwarz* domain decomposition method. The derived class must override some virtual functions declared in the base class. These functions essentially manipulate the linear equation system associated to each subdomain. The base solver class drives the construction of this linear system, using information from both subdomain representation class and discrete PDE specification class. Following this general framework, one can easily develop parallel multithreaded domain decomposition applications without having to directly deal with communication and synchronization programming details.

4 Experimental results

The AHPIK framework has been used to develop parallel, domain decomposition solvers for some test problems. In this paper, we consider the numerical solution of a convection-diffusion problem over a 257×257 finite element grid. We chose a Schur complement method to solve the interface problem, and a bi-conjugate gradi-

```
#include <Ahpik.h>
#include <SyncDDSolver.h>

class NewSolver : public GenericSyncDDSolver
{
    public:
        // Specifies local computations over a subdomain.
        void InternalComputation();

        // Specifies interface computations over variables associated
        // to interface k. Vector v represents data received from
        // neighboring subdomain.
        void InterfaceComputation(int k, const Vector& v);

        // Specifies data that must be sent to neighboring
        // subdomain associated to interface k.
        void LocalContribution(int k, Vector& v);
};
```

Figure 1. Declaration of a derived class from `GenericSyncDDSolver`.

ent method preconditioned with incomplete LU-factorization for the local problems.

Our goal in this experimental study is to analyze the behavior of AHPIK for different mesh decompositions and different mapping schemes. We consider decompositions of the original domain in 2, 4, 8 and 16 non-overlapping subdomains of equal size. Table 1 shows speedup of the parallel domain decomposition solver for a number of processors ranging from 2 to 16. To compute speedup, we made a sequential implementation of the same domain decomposition solver, and measured the CPU consumption for each decomposition. We chose the fastest sequential execution (i.e., with 16 subdomains) as a reference.

Table 1. Speedup of the test solver for different mesh decompositions and different mapping schemes.

Number of subdomains	Number of processors			
	2	4	8	16
2	0.81	-	-	-
4	1.22	1.83	-	-
8	1.78	2.77	3.99	-
16	1.86	3.57	6.07	8.01

When interpreting table 1, one must take into account that using a bi-conjugate gradient method for local problems gives rise to load imbalances, since the number of iterations to achieve convergence may vary from one subdomain to another, even though all subdomains have equal size. Also, the domain decomposition solver has a highly synchronous behavior. These two factors together explain the low speedup when assigning only one subdomain per processor. As we increase the number of subdomains per processor, speedup approaches the optimal. These results show that the overhead of using a multithreaded, generic domain decomposition framework is kept at a low level.

5 Concluding remarks

We have presented an object-oriented framework which exploits intensive multi-threading techniques for the implementation of parallel applications based on domain decomposition methods. The general abstractions provided by the framework are suitable for both overlapping and non-overlapping, synchronous and asynchronous methods. The use of multiple threads leads to programs that are flexible in terms of data exchange and efficient to overlap communication with computations. Concerning parallel performance, promising speedup results have been obtained when solving our test problems on an IBM SP. We plan to implement more realistic applications as soon as we finish integration of adaptive techniques into AHPIK. Mesh refinement procedures are already available, but some work must still be done to link computation and adaptation phases together in a parallel solver. Our experiences in the context of adaptive PDE computations will lead to the inclusion of dynamic load balancing strategies into AHPIK.

Acknowledgments

This research work is part of APACHE and IDOPT projects sponsored by CNRS, INPG, INRIA and UJF. The first author holds a grant from CAPES/COFECUB.

References

1. B. Smith, P. Bjørstad, and W. Gropp. *Domain Decomposition: Parallel Multi-level Methods for Elliptic Partial Differential Equations*. Cambridge University Press, 1996.
2. C. Farhat and F.-X. Roux. Implicit parallel processing in structural mechanics. *Computational Mechanics Advances*, 2:1–124, 1994.

3. N. Chrisochoides. Multithreaded model for dynamic load balancing parallel adaptive PDE computations. *Applied Numerical Mathematics Journal*, 6:1–17, 1996.

4. P.-E. Bernard and D. Trystram. Report on a Parallel Molecular Dynamics Implementation. In E. H. D'Hollander, G. R. Joubert, F. J. Peters, and U. Trottenberg, editors, *Advances in Paralle Computing*, volume 12, pages 217–220. North Holland, 1998.

5. S. Balay, W. Gropp L. C. McInnes, and B. Smith. Efficient management of parallelism in object-oriented numerical software libraries. In E. Arge, A. M. Bruaset, and H. P. Langtangen, editors, *Modern Software Tools in Scientific Computing*. Birkhauser Press, 1997.

6. L. S. Blackford, J. Choi, A. Cleary, E. D'Azevedo, J. Demmel, I. Dhillon, J. Dongarra, S. Hammarling, G. Henry, A. Petitet, K. Stanley, D. Walker, and R. C. Whaley. *ScaLAPACK Users' Guide*. Society for Industrial and Applied Mathematics, Philadelphia, PA, 1997.

7. J. V. W. Reynders et al. POOMA: A framework for scientific simulations of paralllel architectures. In *Parallel Programming using C++*, Cambridge, MA, 1996. MIT Press.

8. D. L. Brown, W. D. Henshaw, and D. J. Quinlan. Overture: An object-oriented framework for solving partial differential equations. *Lecture Notes in Computer Science*, 1343:177–187, 1997.

9. M. Thun, E. Mossberg, P. Olsson, J. Rantakokko, K. Ahlander, and K. Otto. Object-oriented construction of parallel pde solvers. In E. Arge, A. M. Bruaset, and H. P. Langtangen, editors, *Modern Software Tools in Scientific Computing*. Birkhauser Press, 1997.

10. S. J. Fink, S. B. Baden, and S. R. Kohn. Efficient run-time support for irregular block-structured applications. *Journal of Parallel and Distributed Computing*, 50(1):61–82, 1998.

11. J. Briat, I. Ginzburg, M. Pasin, and B. Plateau. Athapascan runtime: Efficiency for irregular problems. In *Proceedings of the Europar'97 Conference*, pages 590–599, Passau, Germany, Aug 1997. Springer Verlag.

12. L. Giraud and P. Spiteri. Implementation of parallel solutions for nonlinear boundary value problems. In D. J. Evans, G. R. Joubert, and H. Leddel, editors, *Advances in Parallel Computing*, volume 4, pages 203–212. North Holland, 1992.

PERFORMANCE EVALUATION OF A FD-TD PARALLEL CODE FOR MICROWAVE OVENS DESIGN

GIOVANNI ERBACCI, GIANNI DE FABRITIIS·✦
CINECA, Interuniversity Computing Centre
Via Magnanelli 6/3, 40033 Casalecchio di Reno, Bologna, Italy

GAETANO BELLANCA♥, PAOLO BASSI
Dipartimento di Elettronica Informatica e Sistemistica (D.E.I.S.)
University of Bologna, Viale Risorgimento 2, 40136 Bologna, Italy

RUGGERO ROCCARI
De' Longhi Italia, Treviso, Italy

A parallel Finite Difference-Time Domain (FD-TD) electromagnetic simulator for the design of domestic microwave ovens has been implemented to run both on a CRAY-T3E massively parallel computer and a PC cluster. In this paper, the main features of the code are described and the adopted parallelisation scheme is briefly illustrated. Then, the performances of the simulator are tested on a real case. The high efficiency obtained on the PC cluster clearly demonstrates the possibility to "bring" HPCN at low cost directly into the R&D department of industrial end-users, leaving the use of massively parallel systems available at big computer centres only for the simulation of huge dimension problems corresponding to special cases which require very fine mesh.

1   Introduction

The standard sequence of a microwave oven design begins with the definition of the cavity dimensions. Then, a prototype is built and a series of heating tests need to be performed, in order to assess the output power and the field uniformity with a number of defined loads as, for example, frozen minced meat, sponge cakes and batters representing ready chilled food. Every modification to the structure of the oven means rework of the prototype and complete re-testing. Obviously this cut-and-try procedure is very tedious and can last up to one year. Considering that a complete design also requires to define other aspects as compliance to the safety standards, compliance to the electromagnetic compatibility (EMC) regulations and the development of the oven controls, it is evident that for an oven with electronic controls the time-to-market can easily reach two years. This is no longer acceptable nowadays, as time to market of new products should be reduced as much as possible.

The use of computer simulation techniques, allowing to investigate the behaviour of the oven before the realisation of any prototype, is therefore a

---

✦ Present address: Centre for Computational Science, QMW College, University of London, Mile End road, London E1 4NS, UK.
♥ Present address: Dept. of Engineering - University of Ferrara, Via Saragat 1, I 44100, Ferrara, Italy, Tel. +39-0532-293838, Fax +39-0532-768602, e-mail: gbellanca@ing.unife.it

fundamental tool for the design of these devices. The first problem to be tackled is the determination of the electromagnetic (e.m.) field distribution into the cavity, as the heating generation inside the food depends on the local distribution of the microwaves. The approach must be compulsorily numerical, because of the complicated nature of both the equations and the geometry of the structure representing the oven and the food. For this purpose different techniques, such as the Finite Difference in the Time Domain (FD-TD) or the Finite Element Method (FEM), can be used [1]-[2]. Unfortunately the long computer time needed to run the simulations limited, up to now, the effective application of these methods by the manufacturers of microwave power devices. This is particularly true when complicated shapes of the cavity are present or high dielectric constant loads are considered into the oven. In fact, in these two situations very fine grids should be used, in order to obtain accurate results, thus increasing the dimension of the mathematical problem and making each simulation very time consuming. This drawback is very important in practice, as the best possible configuration of the oven can be identified only after several computation runs.

To overcome this problem, the HPCN approach offers a convenient solution [3]. By this technique, distributing the complexity of the computation among different processor elements (PEs), a reduction of the total simulation time (proportional to the increase in the number of the dedicated PEs) can be expected. Therefore, HPCN seems the only way to tackle the problem of modelling large applicators without introducing simplifying assumptions, which reduce the accuracy of the obtained results [4]. In the past, the exploitation of its advantages required both a dedicated hardware, with very fast processors connected by a high-speed/fast-switched network, and a careful rewriting of the code, to obtain the expected increase in the computational speed. Nowadays, the continuous growth in the performance of the processors installed in standard personal computers (PC) and the higher data flow-rate offered by the connecting networks allow the implementation of effective parallel systems in form of a "computer cluster" (i.e. Personal Computers or Workstations connected in a high-speed network). Moreover, this powerful hardware is also supported by efficient compilers, mathematical libraries and other tools useful for the final optimisation of the code. Therefore, it can be envisaged that HPCN will spread out of highly specialised computer centres to industrial Research and Development facilities.

In this paper, after a short description of the FD-TD technique, which is really effective to solve the e.m. problem on a parallel system, the fundamental aspects of the parallel implementation of the code using the standard *Message Passing Interface* (MPI) paradigm are illustrated. Then, the performances obtained running the code on two platforms, a CRAY-T3E 1200e massively parallel computer and a PC cluster, are reported in detail and analysed considering different dimensions of the computational domain. Results confirm that medium dimension problems can be efficiently solved implementing a PC cluster directly in the R&D of an industrial end-user whereas, as can be expected, the simulation on massively parallel computers is still the best way to cope with huge dimension cases.

2   The FD-TD method

The electromagnetic field inside a metallic microwave cavity representing the oven has been described by the Time Domain Maxwell's curl Equations. Differential operators have been written in difference form following the Yee's scheme [5]. The resulting equations for all the 6 field components (electric **E** and magnetic **H** ones) have the same form and differ only from the values of the multiplication coefficients, which are evaluated according to the dielectric properties of materials in each cell of the computational domain. As an example, the equation of the E_x field component can be written as:

$$
\begin{aligned}
E_x^{n+1}(i,j,k) = {} & C_1(i,j,k)E_x^n(i,j,k) + \\
& C_2(i,j,k)\left[H_z^{n+\frac{1}{2}}\left(i+\tfrac{1}{2},j+\tfrac{1}{2},k\right) - H_z^{n+\frac{1}{2}}\left(i+\tfrac{1}{2},j-\tfrac{1}{2},k\right)\right] + \\
& C_3(i,j,k)\left[H_y^{n+\frac{1}{2}}\left(i+\tfrac{1}{2},j,k+\tfrac{1}{2}\right) - H_y^{n+\frac{1}{2}}\left(i+\tfrac{1}{2},j,k-\tfrac{1}{2}\right)\right]
\end{aligned}
\tag{1}
$$

where n is the iteration time step, (i, j, k) represents the generic node of the discrete computational domain and the coefficients C_1, C_2 and C_3 are functions of both the local values of the dielectric properties and the spatial step increments along y and z.

This six triple vector loop, which performs the temporal update of all the electromagnetic field components in every point of the mesh representing the structure to be investigated, is the core of the solving algorithm. These equations are well suited to be solved on a parallel computer because of their simple and explicit nature. In fact, as it is easy to observe, the three electric field components do not depend from each other, but are only functions of the previous value of themselves in the same cell and of the magnetic field components in the surrounding cells. A similar result holds also for the three magnetic field equations. Therefore, all the unknowns are evaluated using known variables, thus making the computations very fast as no matrix inversion is needed.

Inter-processor communication is required to solve the field equations on the boundaries between sub-domains belonging to different PEs. This communication activity is not required when the simulator runs on only one PE and represents extra time due to the execution on a parallel system. As it will be shown in the following, the final performance of the code strongly depends on this task; therefore, its careful optimisation is fundamental.

The field evaluation on the outer grid boundaries of the overall computational domain requires the implementation of suitable *Absorbing Boundary Conditions* (ABC) [6]. Moreover, to ensure the stability of the algorithm, the time step must be chosen accordingly to the Courant criterion [7] which forces a relationship between the smallest increment used for the lattice describing the geometry to be simulated and the speed of the computed temporal evolution; the finest the mesh, the smallest the time step. Therefore, to reach a final defined time instant, the field equations must be solved for an increased number of intervals, thus producing longer runs.

3   The parallel implementation

The original FD-TD code has been parallelized splitting the field update tasks among all PEs using a spatial decomposition scheme. The *MPI message passing paradigm* has been chosen as a programming model, allowing a general portability of the simulator on different parallel architectures and the direct comparison of the performances obtained. In order to realise an efficient parallelization of the code, it is important to evenly share the work among all the PEs. In fact, the computation time required to complete the global task (the parallel simulation), strongly depends on the time required by the slowest unit to complete its local work. Moreover, as the synchronisation among all the PEs is fundamental for the correct execution of the code, a slight load imbalance could produce an undesired idle time when the fastest (or less loaded) PE is waiting for the other processors to complete their operations. As anticipated, to obtain a good performance, it is also mandatory to keep the communication limited. This activity becomes necessary when the e.m. fields on the shared surface boundaries among the domain of each PE must be computed. In fact, due to the nature of the algorithm, this evaluation needs data exchange with remote PEs. The structure of the parallel code is shown in the following scheme:

> *Initialization*
> *Loop {*
>> *Update E fields*
>> *Barrier*
>> *Exchange E fields*
>> *Update E boundary conditions*
>> ***Barrier***
>> *Exchange E boundary conditions*
>> *Update H fields*
>> ***Barrier***
>> *Exchange H fields*
>> *Update H boundary conditions*
>> ***Barrier***
>> *Exchange H boundary conditions*
> *}*
> *Collect and print results*

The first part of the FD-TD simulator consists of the initialisation procedures. The overall computation domain, loaded to the solver by a structured-binary file, is decomposed depending on the number of the PEs required by the user. This operation is performed only by the "*master processor*" of the parallel system, and accomplished trying to have the same number of cells on each PE in order to guarantee the optimum load balance in both computing and communication. Other serial and parallel tasks, related to the array allocation and the variable initialisation, are executed once the data structure has been assigned to each PE. The efficiency of this section is important but not fundamental for the overall performance of the code, as it is executed only once at the beginning of the simulation. The computation of the e.m. field starts after this module and is the truly parallel section. Its main tasks are the evaluation of fields inside each sub-domain and on the outer boundaries, the excitation of the same fields and data exchange among different processors. These procedures are executed from the first time step until the end of the simulation for both the three **H** and the three **E** field components and represent the core of the FD-TD simulator.

During the simulation, all the field components needed to perform the computation on the boundaries must be communicated correctly. This is obtained creating a map of the computational domain at the beginning of each simulation and using properly some ghost cells defined around the "true" domain of each PE. The communication takes place only among the PEs who have faces of their local computation domain in common. The PEs which have plane faces on the outer boundaries, corresponding to the border of the overall computational domain adopt an *ABC* formulation to evaluate the e.m. field on these planes which needs only the local values of **E**. As communication is not required, outer boundaries are computed while other PEs are involved in these tasks, thus optimising the use of the resources.

Field extraction for data analysis is performed when required by the user. Being a serial task executed during the computation procedure, it must be optimised as much as possible. The best results are achieved writing structured binary files.

4 Results

The electromagnetic field distribution inside a microwave oven cavity loaded with frozen minced meat has been calculated first on the CINECA's CRAY-T3E 1200e, (600MHz) massively parallel computer using a pitch of 5mm to describe the geometry of the computational domain. This choice produced a $58 \times 72 \times 84$ lattice (350784 cells). The simulation must run for about 6000 time steps to compute the e.m. field pattern need to evaluate the uniformity of the heat generation inside the considered load.

The improvements due to the increase in the number of the used PEs have been quantified by means of the Speed-Up parameter, obtained as the ratio between the simulation times required to run the program on one PE and on N PEs. Results are reported in Fig. 1, where the contribution to the overall Speed-Up of each portion of the code is highlighted. For the field calculation alone, which is the core of the FD-TD algorithm, the resulting increase in speed with the number of the used PEs follows an almost linear law, showing both a good implementation of the code and the high efficiency of the solving equations on a parallel computer. Unfortunately, as pointed out before, the Speed-Up can not be exactly proportional to the number of computation units, because of the presence of serial tasks and communication activity. The serial tasks, mainly connected to data file reading/writing and domain decomposition procedures needed for the parallel execution of the code, don't affect significantly the performance of the simulator being the time required for the execution of these operations a small percentage (always less than 15%) of the total computation time. On the contrary, a very important role is played by the communication. In fact, as illustrated in Fig. 2, the plot of the total Speed-Up shows the same trend of the ones corresponding to the Speed-Up of the field computation procedures evaluated considering also the time required for data exchange on the boundaries of each computation domain. The communication activity is therefore responsible of the increased deterioration of the expected improvement. The extent of the saturation depends, in turn, on the overall dimensions of the problem (i.e. the number of cells used to describe the model).

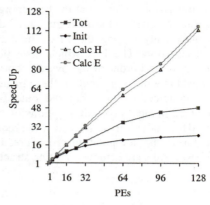

Figure 1 Speed-Up on the CRAY-T3E for a computation domain of 58×72×84 cells. Tot is the overall Speed-Up; Calc E and Calc H the field computation procedures (without communication) and Init the initialisation tasks. The total elapsed time for the simulation is reduced from 2900 seconds on one PE to 420 seconds for 8 PEs, where the efficiency begins to degrade.

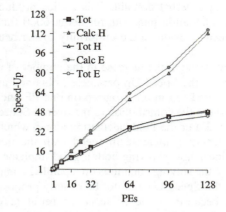

Figure 2 Comparisons among the Speed-Up of the field computation procedures excluding (**Calc E** and **Calc H**) and considering (**Tot E** and **Tot H**) the communication time on the CRAY-T3E. The overall Speed-Up (**Tot**) is strongly influenced by the communication activity.

For small computational domains like a 58×72×84 one, the high speed of the CRAY-T3E processors can not be completely exploited but, simulating the same structure using smaller cells, in order to achieve a better precision, the increased weight of the calculations respect to the communication yields a better performance of the parallel system. This is shown in Fig. 3a by the plots labelled as BD (Big Domain $\approx 1.2 \cdot 10^6$ cells obtained using a 80×116×139 lattice) compared to those labelled SD (Small Domain $\approx 350 \cdot 10^3$ cells). As a consequence, when solving a problem with a mesh adequate to guarantee a given precision, it is possible to obtain a parameter indicating the number of processors for the maximum efficiency.

Fig. 3b reports the plots of the efficiency η, as a function of the number of processors. This parameter has been evaluated as the ratio between the simulation time required by the code on one PE and the time on N PEs times N. For the small domain, a relative maximum equal to 0.86 is obtained with both 4 PEs or 8 PEs whereas, for the bigger domain, the maximum is 0.89 with 8 PEs.

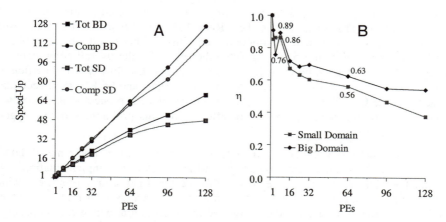

Figure 3 Speed-Up (**A**) and Efficiency (**B**) on the CRAY-T3E 1200e as a function of the number of PEs for a small (SD $\approx 350 \cdot 10^3$ cells) and a big (BD $\approx 1.2 \cdot 10^6$ cells) computation domain.

The circumstance that, for the design of a typical microwave oven, the efficiency peak is reached with a small number of PEs suggests as convenient the implementation of a parallel computing system with a reduced number of PCs, to be used directly on a R&D department of an industry. A "non homogeneous" cluster (i.e. realised using processors with different clock frequencies) has then been implemented connecting 4 Pentium II by a 100 Mbit/s link equipped with the Linux Operating System. Table 1 reports the comparison between the simulation time on the CRAY-T3E and a PC cluster for the previously described small computational domain. As this machine is not natively parallel, but implemented with "discrete components" designed to work independently, it can not guarantee the same performances of the massively parallel system mentioned before (in particular for huge dimension problems because of the slower interconnection network).

Table 1 Comparisons among the computation time for the simulation of a microwave oven (about $6 \cdot 10^3$ time steps) on a CRAY-T3E 1200e and on a PC cluster (SD $\approx 350 \cdot 10^3$ cells). The third column shows the time required to compute the e.m. field, the fourth one the time spent for the communication activities. The last two columns illustrate the total CPU time for the simulation.

PE	Clock (MHz)	Calc (s)	Comm (s)	Tot PC (s)	Tot Cray (s)
1	233	5550	0	5723	2900
1	350	3896	0	4002	2900
1	400	3496	0	3595	2900
2	350-350	1929	430	2427	1700
3	233-350-350	1350	770	2182	1300
4	233-350-350-400	964	393	1404	840

Nevertheless, the PC system shows a good Speed-Up: about 2.85 referred to the PC with a frequency clock of 350 MHz, which can be considered as the one with the average speed. The Speed-Up on the CRAY-T3E was 3.6 with 4 PEs and results only 1.67 times faster than the implemented cluster. This result can be explained with the particular nature of the FD-TD scheme, where the overall computation of the EM field is plagued by many accesses in memory that slow down the efficiency of the Alpha processor (only 8 KByte of primary cache and 96 KByte of secondary cache) of the CRAY. On the contrary, the slower Intel PII processor, equipped with 512 KByte of secondary cache is not affected by this problem, showing a good overall performance.

If compared to a remote massively parallel computer, the "home-made" HPCN system provides important advantages which make its implementation very attractive. The first one is the availability at the final user's premises, which eliminates queues and relevant waiting time for the access to a remote computer centre. Another advantage is the set-up and reconfiguration, which can be managed easily via software. Moreover, one must also consider the low cost of the overall system, due to the fact that all the hardware components for both the computers and related link devices (network cards, network switches, etc.) are cheap and ready available on the market. On the other hand, massively parallel computers are still advantageous when dealing with huge dimension problems. In this case, both the availability of a higher number of processor units and of a very efficient communication network can reduce the computation time to the low limits required for an industrial application of this technique. To show this, the last simulated microwave cavity has been described using a 2.5mm mesh, producing a lattice of about $2.8 \cdot 10^6$ cells ($116 \times 144 \times 168$). In this case, the 4 PC cluster requires 2.75 hours to simulate the oven, whereas the CRAY can solve the problem in 1.6 hours using 4 PEs. This time is reduced to about 4.5 minutes using 128 processors to run the simulation. Results are reported on Table 2.

Table 2 *Computation times as a function of the used PE on the PC cluster (BD $\approx 1.2 \cdot 10^6$ cells). The third column shows the time required to compute the e.m. field, the fourth one the time spent for the communication. whereas the last column illustrate the total CPU time for the simulation*

PE	Clock (Mhz)	Calc (s)	Comm (s)	Tot PC (s)
1	350	30000	0	31000
2	350-350	15000	2800	19000
4	233-350-350-400	7500	2020	9900

5 Conclusions

A parallel Finite Difference-Time Domain (FD-TD) electromagnetic simulator for the design of domestic microwave ovens has been implemented to run both on a CRAY-T3E massively parallel computer and a PC cluster using the MPI *Message Passing* paradigm. The obtained results show the good performance of the code on both the architectures and the very interesting efficiency obtained on the PC cluster clearly demonstrates the possibility to "bring" HPCN at low cost directly into the R&D department of industrial end-users, leaving the use of massively parallel systems available at big computer centres only for the simulation of huge dimension problems corresponding to special cases which require very fine mesh like, for example, the simulation of big microwave power applicators used in industry.

Acknowledgements

This work was supported by the "POPCORN" ESPRIT Project n° EP 27213.

References

1. M. Sundberg, P.O Risman., P.S Kildal., T. Ohlsson, *Analysis and Design of Industrial Microwave Ovens Using the Finite Difference Time Domain Method*, J. M.wave Power and E.M. Energy, **31**, 3, (1996), 142-157.
2. D. Dibben, A.C. Metaxas, *Finite Element Analysis of Multimode Applicators using Edge Elements*, J. M.wave Power and E.M. Energy, **29**, 4, (1994), 242-51.
3. C.H. Cap, V. Strumpen, *Efficient Parallel Computing in Distributed workstation environments*, Parallel Computing, **19**, (1993), 1221-1234.
4. G. Bellanca, S. Botti, P. Bassi, G. Falciasecca, *Sensitivity of FD-TD simulations to small mesh modifications in microwave ovens design*, Proc. 6th Int. Conf. on M.wave and High Frequency Heating, Fermo (I), Sept. 1997, 60-63.
5. K.S. Yee, *Numerical Solution of initial boundary value problems involving Maxwell's equations in isotropic media*, IEEE Trans. A.P., **14**, 5, (1966), 302-7.
6. Z. Bi, K. Wu, J. Litva, *A Dispersive Absorbing Boundary Condition for Microstrip Component Analysis using the FD-TD Method*, IEEE Trans. Mic. Theory Tech., **40**, 4, (1992), 774-77.
7. J.C. Strikwerda, *Finite Difference Schemes and partial Differential Equations*, Wadsworth & Brooks/Cole Adv. Books & Software, Pacific Grove, Cal, 1989.

MPEG 1 AND MPEG 2 COMPRESSION BASED ON A WORKSTATION CLUSTER

MASSIMO FERRERO, LORENZO CAVASSA

CSP – Centre of Excellence for Research, Development and Experimentation of Advanced Computer Science and Telematics Technologies

Corso Unione Sovietica, 216 – IT-10134 – Torino, ITALY

M.Ferrero@CSP.it - L.Cavassa@CSP.it

Compressing video sequences into MPEG format requires a significant amount of computation power. This is the reason why the encoding of MPEG sequences is performed by a specialized hardware equipment.

In order to satisfy personal needs, a software encoder permits the management of more parameters. This is why a software encoder is more flexible than a hardware solution.

A sequential encoder was parallelized on a workstation cluster using MPI standard library. We have also performed some encoding of significant test sequences in order to get specific data about the improvement in encoding speed.

In this paper, we will introduce the MPEG standard to put in evidence the algorithms that need a significant amount of computation power. We will also describe some algorithms that we have implemented to improve the speed of sequential encoder. Finally, we will describe the implementation of a parallel MPEG encoder on a workstation cluster.

In addition, there will be the introduction of the cluster hardware, based on a classical Beowulf-like COTS architecture and on a Flextel fast proprietary architecture.

Our software choices will be examined in terms of OpenSource operating system and libraries, in order to run the MPEG encoder as fast as possible and in a reliable way.

1 MPEG Standard

The television standard defines the number of pictures per second (25 for system PAL) and the number of lines per picture (625 for system PAL). However, a part of video information is used. Picture synchronization reduces visualized lines (576 for system PAL).

The directive CCIR 601 establishes a sampling frequency of 13.5 MHz for each line that corresponds to a resolution of 720 pixel per line. The resolution for each RGB component is 8 bit.

Each color is coded in a space YUV, where Y corresponds to the luminance (black and white signal) and U,V are the two components of chrominance.

The luminance component is sampled at a frequency of 13.5 MHz. A halved frequency (6.75 MHz) is usually used for the chrominance components.

For system PAL the bit rate needed is:

Luminance Y	$\rightarrow$	720x576x25x8 = 82944000 bps
Chrominance U	$\rightarrow$	360x576x25x8 = 41472000 bps
Chrominance V	$\rightarrow$	360x576x25x8 = 41472000 bps

The total bit rate, obtained by summing each bit rate, is 166 Mbps. This is the bit rate used for video information. It's the same used in video broadcasting and DVD applications.

74.6 Gbyte (more or less) are needed for an hour of video sequence. Using MPEG-2 compression it is possible to reduce this amount of data to about 3 Gbyte.

1.1 MPEG-1 and MPEG-2

Over the last 10 years the Moving Picture Expert Group (MPEG) has proposed two compression algorithms: MPEG-1 and MPEG-2. MPEG-2 is an extension of MPEG-1. However for video compression in video broadcasting, HDTV and DVD applications. It's not an enhanced version of MPEG-1

Below 3.5 Mbps $\Rightarrow$ MPEG-1 (Source Input Format resolution - 352x256 pixel)
Above 5.5 Mbps $\Rightarrow$ MPEG-2 (CCIR-601 resolution - 720x576 pixel)

The standard doesn't define how the encoder must be implemented. It only defines the syntax of the stream in order to permit the decoding by all standard decoders.

A video sequence is coded using 3 types of picture: Intra picture, Predicted picture and Bi-directional picture.

The Intra picture is used to reduce the frequency redundancy. It is coded using only information present in the picture itself and provides moderate compression.

Predicted and Bi-directional pictures are used to reduce spatial redundancy. The Predicted picture is coded using the nearest previous Intra or Predicted picture. The Bi-directional coding is performed using both a previous and a future picture reference.

1.2 Intra Picture

The Intra picture encoding is most similar to JPEG encoding. The image is divided into 8x8 blocks of pixel. Then a Discrete Cosine Transform is performed on each block to obtain coefficients in the frequency domain. These coefficients are then quantized by a special low-pass matrix. The result is a matrix that has a lot of zero coefficients especially at high frequencies (on the right bottom of the matrix). The algorithm sorts the coefficients in order to have the low frequency before the high frequency coefficients. This is performed by a zig-zag scanning.

Then a run-length encoding is performed to get a couple of values that indicate the amplitude of the coefficient and the number of zeros before this coefficient.

The last step consists of Huffman encoding (entropy encoding).

1.3 Motion Compensation

Motion compensation is used in Predicted and Bi-directional picture to eliminate temporal redundancy. Motion compensation improves compression by about a factor of three to Intra picture coding. The algorithms that perform Motion Compensation work at the macroblock(16x16 pixel block) level.

The compressed file contains the information about the spatial vector between the reference macroblock and the macroblock being coded (motion vector). It also contains the differences between the reference macroblock and the macroblock being coded (error terms).

When a macroblock in a Predicted picture cannot be represented efficiently by motion compensation, it is coded in the same way as a macroblock in an Intra picture.

The difference between Bi-directional and Predicted picture is that a macroblock in a Predicted picture uses the previous reference only, while a macroblock in a Bi-directional picture is coded using any combination of a previous and future reference picture.

Each macroblock is then coded as an Intra block using the Discrete Cosine Transform, the quantization and the Run-length encoding.

In order to find the best reference macroblock, The encoder performs a search over an area around the macroblock being coded. This is the algorithm that needs a lot of computational power.

2   Cluster Architecture

During the development of the software encoder, we started to design and implement the cluster architecture needed by the project.

Because our organisation is involved in the development and the promotion of the OpenSource and Freeware philosophy in Italy, we selected two low-cost hardware solutions that guarantee us the capability to run OpenSource and Freeware software: a COTS (Component Off The Shelf) Beowulf-like cluster and a Flextel 1200 multi-gigabit bus proprietary architecture.

We are going to integrate the two architectures in the same cluster to speed-up the encoding process.

We began the implementation around the COTS cluster, delaying the implementation on the Flextel platform after the working on TCP/IP stack and device-drivers fine-tuning.

The COTS cluster solution offers us an extended selection of hardware components, the choice over a huge software base with a general good quality, the capability to run well known operating systems and good implementations of the MPI library.

2.1   Cluster Hardware

Figure 3. shows the topology of the cluster. At the moment we run a cluster with 4 nodes each one built around a Pentium-II CPU, a 33 MHz PCI Bus, 128MB Ram, an Adaptec 2940 SCSI-II PCI controller, one IBM DDRS-34560W 4.4 GB disk and a Digital 21140 based Fast Ethernet card.

One node, the master node, mount an additional SCSI-II disk, a Fujitsu MAA3182SP model with a capacity of 17.4GB and one other Fast Ethernet controller that links the cluster to the CSP laboratory network.

We selected that solution because we need to load the uncompressed stream only one time for each elaboration on the 17.4GB disk of the master node and this can be done via the master node himself, leaving free the switch from the load of this network activity.

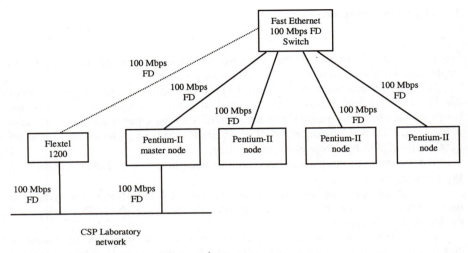

Figure 3. Cluster topology

2.2 Cluster Software

In order to maintain a future compatibility with the configuration and the software that can be run on the Flextel 1200 machine, we chose to install a standard Linux distribution, the RedHat 5.0, and the 2.0.35 release of the Linux kernel.

Needing MPI libraries to run the encoder on cluster nodes, we chose to compile and install the freeware MPI implementation of the Argonne National Laboratory & Mississippi State University named MPICH.

We run the Network File System (NFSv3) protocol over UDP to move a significant amount of uncompressed and compressed data between the master node and the others computing nodes.

The Linux NFS is known to be a good implementation so, after little performance tests, we have checked 8192 bytes are the best compromise in the size of NFS read and write block.

With these values, we achieve a read and write throughput of about 80 Mbps.

Uncompressed images and the resulting MPEG stream are hosted only on the 17.4GB disk on the master node. From the CSP network, using a simple FTP client, we can upload and download data on or from the cluster via the master node.

3   The Parallel encoder

The Discrete Cosine Transform and the search algorithm need a lot of computational power. This is the reason why the commercial encoders were implemented at hardware level. However a software encoder is more flexible than a hardware solution.

The optimised sequential encoder has been parallelized on a workstation cluster. Each worker encodes a Group of picture and sends the result to MPEG WRITER module that makes the final MPEG stream and stores it.

More workers can run on each workstation in order to minimise the idle time of the CPU. A JOB EMITTER sends information about what sequence of picture each worker must encode and synchronises them.

The communication between JOB EMITTER, MPEG WRITER and the Workers is performed by MPI Standard library. Each worker reads the uncompressed picture from a network disk using a Network File System protocol. We have not used MPI to send uncompressed images because NFS is more efficient in terms of speed.

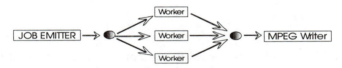

Figure 4. Encoder model

We have also decided to put the uncompressed images on a master disk and not on local disk. The uncompressed images on the local disk of each workstation is not a good solution for future industrial design review.

Each worker encodes a number of GOP, fixed by a parameter, to permit to the control bit rate algorithm to work well. This is why we have decided to encode, on each worker, a number of picture that is a multiple of a GOP.

4   Simulation

We have performed some simulations to obtain specific data about the performance of the sequential and the parallelized encoder. We have used a sequence in SIF format (352x240 pixel with a resolution of 24 bit for each pixel) and CCIR-601 (720x576 pixel with a resolution of 24 bit for each pixel).

We have used 4 workstations connected together by a 100 Mbps Fast Ethernet Switch.

4.1   Sequential encoder

We have used a sequential encoder on a workstation of the cluster to perform the encoding. We have not performed the encoding using the parallelized encoder with only 1 worker in order to obtain information about the speed of the encoder without the effect of the structure described before: JOB-EMITTER – Worker – MPEG-WRITER.

	Length	Elaboration time	Real time coefficient
Seq. SIF	32 Sec	198 Sec	6.18
Seq. CCIR-601	180 Sec	10083 Sec	56.01

We can notice that we need 6.18 times the time of a sequence in SIF format and 56.01 times in CCIR-601 format. Those values are unacceptable for industrial application. Here is the reason to implement the encoder by means of an hardware equipment.

4.2   Parallel Encoder

As we said before, the time needed to perform an encoding by a MPEG software encoder is unacceptable for industrial application. So the only way to perform a faster encoding would be a hardware implementation. However, there is another way: perform the encoding using more than one workstation. We have encoded the same sequence using a cluster of 4 workstations.

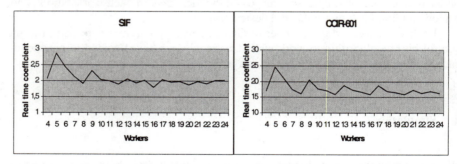

Figure 5. Real Time Coefficient

We can notice that there is a minimum of real time coefficient when we use 16 workers. The irregularity of the result depends on the environment variability due to hardware interrupts, hard disk speed, collisions on the interconnection network.

However, the results are very comfortable. We can hope that with a higher performance network like ATM network or, better, Gigabit Ethernet, and a greater number of workstation, we can obtain a near real time encoding for the CCIR-601 sequence at low cost.

In the near future we are going to use MMX library to improve the speed of the Discrete Cosine Transform algorithm. In this way, we hope to obtain real time encoding for SIF format and reduce by a factor of 2 the encoding time for CCIR-601 format.

References

1. Mitchell J. L., Pennebaker B. W., Fogg E. C., LeGall J. D., *MPEG video compression Standard* (Chapman and Hall – New York, 1997)
2. *Information technology – Generic coding of moving picture and associated audio: Video* (ISO/IEC 13818-2, 1996)
3. Moore J., Lee W., Dawson S., Smith B., *Optimal Parallel MPEG encoding* (Department of Computer Science 4130 Upson Hall, Cornell University, Ithaca, NY 14853-750, USA)
4. Shen K., Rowe A. L., Delp J. E., *A parallel implementation of an MPEG-1 Encoder: Faster than real time* (Computer Vision and Image Processing Laboratory – School of Electrical Engineering, Purdue University, West Lafayette, Indiana and Computer Science Division – Department of Electrical Engineering and Computer Science, University of California, Berkeley, California)
5. Tiwari P., Viscito E., *A parallel MPEG-2 Video encoder with look ahead rate control* (IBM Corporation, Thomas J. Watson Research Center, P.O. Box 218, Yorktown Heights, NY 10598, USA)
6. *MPI: A Message Interface Standard* (Message Passing Interface Forum, June 12, 1995)
7. *MPI-2: Extensions to the Message Interface Standard* (Message Passing Interface Forum, July 18, 1997)
8. *MPICH - A Portable Implementation of MPI* (Argonne National Laboratory and Mississippi State University, http://www-unix.mcs.anl.gov/mpi/mpich)
9. http://www.Flextel.it
10. http://www.Beowulf.org

Acknowledgements

Special thanks to David Quaglia and Domenico Ventura for the support during the design and implementation of the encoder.

PARALLEL IMPLEMENTATION OF A 3D BJT DEVICE SIMULATOR

ANTONIO J. GARCIA–LOUREIRO AND TOMAS F. PENA

Departamento de Electrónica e Computación, Univ. de Santiago de Compostela, Campus Sur, 15706 Santiago de Compostela, Spain
E–mail: antonio,tomas@dec.usc.es

JUAN M. LOPEZ–GONZALEZ AND LLUIS PRAT

Departament d'Enginyeria Electrónica, Univ. Politécnica de Catalunya Campus Nord, c/Jordi Girona,1–3, 08034 Barcelona, Spain
E–mail: jmlopezg@eel.upc.es

This work presents a 3D parallel bipolar junction transistors (BJT) device simulator. This simulator was implemented using the MPI library on distributed memory multicomputers. We have studied a GaAs BJT using the Fujitsu AP3000 multicomputer. We have used domain decomposition methods to solve the linear systems. Performance obtained with this simulator has been measured and several electrical results are showed.

1 Introduction

The development of semiconductor device simulators is currently an important research area.[1] The first programs enabled one–dimensional simulations to be carried out. Nevertheless, with the reduction of the physical dimensions of the devices to be simulated, the need for carrying out 3D simulations in order to be able to study the diverse factors that affect the devices in a more precise manner has become evident.[2] The main problem here is that the development of 3D simulators requires the use of computers with high memory requirements and calculation speed, due to the high number of nodes being worked with. This is due to the fact that calculation time increases exponentially with the number of nodes, and obviously, this number is very high in the case of 3D simulation.

In the next section we introduce the physical model of the semiconductor devices. Section 3 presents the mathematical model, where we describe the simulator and the domain decomposition methods. Then, in section 4, some numerical results for a GaAs BJT are showed. In the final section the main conclusions of this work are presented.

2 Physical Model

The object of the 3D simulation is to relate electrical characteristics of the device with its physical and geometrical parameters.[3,4] The basic equations to be solved are Poisson and electron and hole continuity equations, in a stationary state:

$$div(\varepsilon\nabla\psi) = q(p - n + N_D^+ - N_A^-) \tag{1}$$

$$div(J_n) = qR \tag{2}$$

$$div(J_p) = -qR \tag{3}$$

where ψ is the electrostatic potential, q is the electronic charge, ε is the dielectric constant of the material, n and p are the electron and hole densities, N_D^+ and N_A^+ are the doping effective concentration, and J_n and J_p are the electron and hole current densities, respectively. The term R represents the volume recombination term, taking into account Schokley–Read–Hall, Auger and band–to–band recombination mechanisms.[5]

The expression for the electron and hole concentrations are:

$$n = n_{\text{ien}} \exp\left(\frac{q\psi - q\phi_n}{kT}\right) \tag{4}$$

$$p = n_{\text{iep}} \exp\left(\frac{q\phi_p - q\psi}{kT}\right) \tag{5}$$

where n_{ien} and n_{iep} are parameters that are affected by material characteristics and device bias, and ϕ_n and ϕ_p are the quasi–Fermi potentials of electrons and holes.

3 Mathematical Model

We have applied the finite elements method[6,7] in order to discretise the Poisson, hole and electron continuity equations by using tetrahedral elements. Initially a pre–processing is carried out, which consists of meshing the structure of the semiconductor in the Figure 1 into tetrahedrons. This meshing has been carried out using the QMG program.[8] The result is an unstructured mesh in which we place more nodes in the areas of union between different areas of the transistor. More nodes are situated in these areas, because it is here where the gradients of the unknown quantities are greatest. Using the METIS program,[9] we have divided the domain into sub–domains, in such a manner that we have a sub–domain for each processor. We subsequently use this program in order to achieve an improved ordering of the nodes of each sub–domain.

122

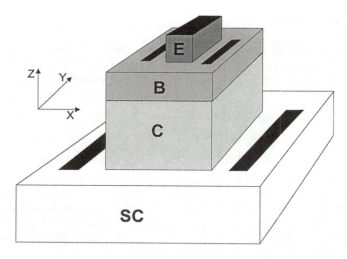

Figure 1. Structure of the BJT.

We then went on to decouple the Poisson, hole and electron continuity equations, and, after linearising them using Newton method, for each sub–domain, the part corresponding to the associated linear system is constructed in parallel. Each one of these systems is solved using domain decomposition methods.[10] These methods involve a collection of techniques which revolve around the divide and conquer principle. They combine ideas from partial differential equations, linear algebra, mathematical analysis and graph theory techniques.

If we consider the problem of solving a linear system on a domain Ω partitioned in p subdomains Ω_i, then a domain decomposition or substructuring method attempt to solve the problem on the entire domain from the solution on each subdomain Ω_i.[11] This means that Ω_i's are such that

$$\Omega = \bigcup_{i=1}^{p} \Omega_i \tag{6}$$

There are several domain decomposition techniques, and we have studied them using the library of parallel iterative solvers PSPARSLIB.[12] The best result was obtained with the Additive Schwarz decomposition technique.

This procedure is similar to a block–Jacobi iteration and consists of updating all the new components from the same residual. The basic additive Schwarz iteration would therefore be as follows:

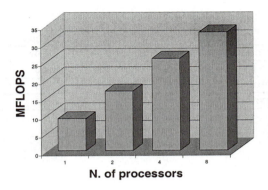

Figure 2. Parallel Performance.

1.- Obtain $y_{i,ext}$
2.- Compute local residual $r_i = (b - Ax)_i$
3.- Solve $A_i\delta_i = r_i$
4.- Update solution $x_i = x_i + \delta_i$

To solve the linear system $A_i\delta_i = r_i$ a standard ILUT preconditioner combined with GMRES for the solver associated with the blocks is used.[10] In the ILUT preconditioners, a fill–in parameter is used to control the zero entries which become nonzeros during the factorization process. A factor which can affect convergence is the tolerance used for the inner solver. As accuracy increases the number of outer steps may decrease. However, since the cost of each inner solver increases, this often offsets any gains made from the reduction in the number of outer steps to achieve convergence. It is interesting to observe that the required communication, as well as the overall structure of the routine, is identical with that of matrix–vector products.

4   Some Numerical Results

The simulator was developed for distributed–memory multicomputers, using the MIMD strategy (*Multiple Instruction–Multiple Data*) under the SPMD paradigm (*Simple Program–Multiple Data*). Our program has been parallelized, and tested on a Fujitsu AP3000 multicomputer using the MPI communications library.[13]

We have measured the performance obtained with this simulator on various transistors with different meshes. In Figure 2 values of MFLOPS are

Table 1. Doping profile of GaAs BJT.

	$N_{eff}(\text{cm}^{-3})$	Δ X(μm)	Δ Y(μm)	Δ Z(μm)
Emitter(n)	$5.0\ 10^{17}$	0.5	1.0	0.3
Base (p)	$1.0\ 10^{18}$	1.5	3.0	0.12
Collector (n)	$5.0\ 10^{16}$	1.5	3.0	0.5
Subcollector (n)	$2.0\ 10^{18}$	3.0	6.0	0.3

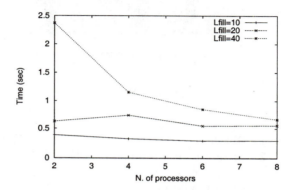

Figure 3. Influence of fill–in parameter (dim. Krylov=15).

shown for a GaAs BJT transistor (such as the one in Figure 1) with the electrical parameters shown of the table 1. As can be seen, the program is highly scalable. This result is the consequence of the high degree of parallelism that is afforded by domain decomposition methods. It should also be noted that the use of parallel libraries, such as PSPARSLIB, has enabled us to easily analyse the different alternatives for solving and to select the methods that are best suited to each situation.

Figure 3 shows the performance results using the Additive Schwarz preconditioner for different values of the fill–in parameter, and in Figure 4 the influence of the size of Krylov subspace for the resolution of only a linear system associated to the Poisson equation is shown. For this preconditioner, using low levels of fill–in and a small size of Krylov subspace leads to lower execution time.

With respect to the electrical results, in Figure 5 we show the values of the potential in equilibrium in the plane $y = 0$. Semilogarithmic graphics for the values of the concentration of holes and of electrons are shown in 6 and 7,

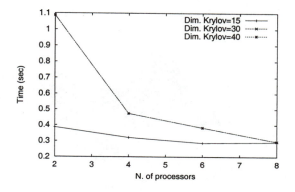

Figure 4. Influence of size of Kirlov subspace (fill–in=10).

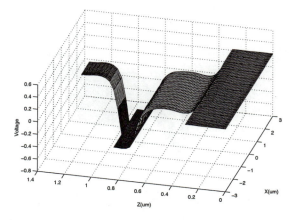

Figure 5. Voltage in equilibrium.

respectively, using $V_C = 0.1, V_B = 0.1$ and $V_E = 0.0$. We have also included into the simulator the capability for calculating low signal parameters, such as g_m, C_T, f_t, etc., as well as the current density in different contacts.

5 Conclusions

In this work we have presented a 3D BJT device parallel simulator, which has been used to study a GaAs device on the Fujitsu AP3000 multicomputer.

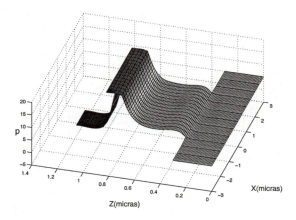

Figure 6. Concentration of holes.

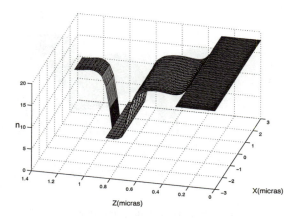

Figure 7. Concentration of electrons.

It is necessary to use multicomputers owing to the fact that calculation time increases exponentially with the number of nodes, and obviously, this number is very high in the case of 3D simulation.

We have applied domain decomposition methods to solve the Poisson and electron and hole continuity equations. We have applied the finite element method (FEM) in order to discretise these equations by using tetrahedral mesh. We have studied the influence of fill–in level and size of Krylov subspace in the performance of the solvers.

We have shown several electrical results and some measures of the parallel performance. We have obtained a highly scalable simulator. It is the consequence of the high degree of parallelism that is afforded by domain decomposition methods.

References

1. Kevin M. Kramer and W. N. G. Hitchon, *Semiconductor Devices: A Simulation Approach*, Prentice Hall, (1997).
2. Hiang-Cheong Chan and Tsay-Jiu Shieh, A three-dimensional semiconductor device simulator for GaAs/AlGaAs heterojunction bipolar transistor analysis, *IEEE Trans. on Electron Devices*, 38(11):2427–2432, (1991).
3. P. A. Markowich, *The Stationary Semiconductor Device Equations*, Springer–Verlag, (1986).
4. S. Selberherr, *Analysis and Simulation of Semiconductor Devices*, Springer, (1984).
5. C. M. Wolfe, N. Holonyak, and G. E. Stillman, *Physical Properties of Semiconductors*, chapter 8, Ed. Prentice Hall, (1989).
6. T. F. Pena, J. D. Bruguera, and E. L. Zapata, Finite element resolution of the 3D stationary semiconductor device equations on multiprocessors, *J. Integrated Computer-Aided Engineering*, 4(1):66–77, (1997).
7. J. Tinsley and Graham F. Carey, *Finite Elements*, Prentice–Hall, (1983).
8. Stephen A. Vavasis, *QMG 1.1 Reference Manual*, Computer Science Department, Cornell University, (1996).
9. George Karypis and Vipin Kumar, *METIS: A software package for partitioning unstructured graphs, partitioning meshes, and computing fill–reducing orderings of sparse matrices*, Univ. of Minnesota, (1997).
10. Y. Saad, *Iterative Methods for Sparse Linear Systems*, PWS Publishing Co., (1996).
11. Barry Smith, Petter Bjorstad, and William Gropp, *Domain Decomposition*, Cambridge University Press, (1996).
12. Y. Saad, Gen-Ching Lo, and Sergey Kuznetsov, PSPARLIB users manual: A portable library of parallel sparse iterative solvers, Technical report, Univ. of Minnesota, Dept. of Computer Science, (1997).
13. University of Tennessee, *MPI: A Message-Passing Interface Standard*, (1995).

IMPLEMENTATION AND PERFORMANCE EVALUATION FOR A COMPUTATION-INTENSIVE CLIMATE SIMULATION APPLICATION

HAO WANG [1,2,3], G.M. PRABHU [2], E.S. TAKLE [3] AND R. TODI [2]

[1] *IBM, Rochester, MN 55901, USA;* [2] *Department of Computer Science,*
[3] *Department of Geo.& Atmospheric Sciences, Iowa State University, Ames, IA50011, USA;*
E-mail: haowang@us.ibm.com prabhu@cs.iastate.edu

In this paper, we design, implement, and compare several parallel version codes of our shelterbelt turbulent flow model system which involves extremely strong non-linear processes, solid-air interactions, flow-pressure linkages, and turbulent feedback mechanisms. We evaluate the performance of each implementation and show that the parallel code's performance depends on its design and coding strategies. The performance gains of the domain decomposition parallel version of our model system are quite satisfactory. For functional decomposition, we even obtained parallel performance loss. We analyze the speedup and its change with domain size and number of processors. There is tradeoff between reduced computation load and increased communication load, and the relative weight, which is related to domain size, number of processors, and problem specific features, determines the speed ratio and load balance ratio.

1 Introduction

Fast computers have stimulated the rapid growth of a new way of doing science. The two broad classical branches of theoretical science and experimental science have been joined by computational science. Computational scientists simulate on supercomputers phenomena too complex to be reliably predicted by theory and too dangerous or expensive to be reproduced in the laboratory. With the rapid development of microcomputers and fast networking with high-speed switches, parallel processing on distributed networks of workstations has emerged as a cost-effective method of high-performance computing – cluster computing.

Previous work on parallelizing old climate models under USDOE "grand challenges" project was focused mainly on relatively simple linear shallow water model with very low spatial resolution. In the past several years, we were developing non-linear shelterbelt turbulent flow model with strong flow-pressure and solid-air interactions. This new model is very computation-intensive. In this paper, we describe our work to seek the better prallellelization of this non-linear, strong flow-pressure and very-high-resolution model system. This problem can be widely used in real applications.

2 The Shelterbelt Turbulent Flow Model

This model system was developed to solve the real-world complex turbulence and flows around vegetation and climate problems. The real earth's surface is not an ideal homogeneous flat surface as required by classical atmospheric boundary-layer theory. Ideal flows and turbulence are themselves complex, but this complexity is significantly increased for boundary-layer flows and turbulence around vegetation. We derived a general set of equations for a porous medium and developed a model system. Limited by the length of this paper, we could not describe it in details. Please refer our previous journal papers [4-10] for the model's physics and mathematics.

3 Problem Analyses and Sequential Computation Timing

In order to understand the roles of various processes in this application and the corresponding computational requirements, we analyze the sequential code before we parallelize it.

3.1 The solver and Computation Time

Most people who work on parallel computing focus on the solver. Recently, there are a few publications that describe parallel algorithms of linear algebra (tridiagonal system). We also began with parallelizing this solver in our model system in the last year. However, no significant speedup was achieved by parallelizing this solver, no matter what kind of parallel algorithms were used. Therefore, it is necessary for us to find out why.

We also know that the solver function is called most frequently. The solver is called 636 times more than other functions! Therefore, we also thought that most frequently called function also would be most important. But, that is not true, especially for a complicated nonlinear system with feedback and interactions. Usually the solver only accounts for 1-5% length of the system code, and the linear equation solver is very fast.

3.2 Non-linear Processes and Theoretical Analyses

The interactions and feedback between different variables complicate the computation and theoretical analyses. For large spatial scales, the simple and linearized shallow-water equation is used to analyze the theoretical performance of parallel computing. That is feasible because there exist few and weak feedback and interactions for large spatial scale. As dx (spatial resolution) is large, both u du/dx (nonlinear advection) and dp/dx (pressure driving force) are small. When dx is small, the nonlinear term and driving force term become extremely large. Moreover, what we want to study and reproduce (simulate) are interaction mechanisms and processes. Therefore, if we simplify the equations by linearizing them, we cannot get the mechanisms and nonlinear processes from our simulations.

We try to analyze our nonlinear feedback model system. We list the main functional parts: (1) parameters inputs, (2) grid generator, (3) initialization, (4) compute TKE, (5) compute dynamic pressure perturbation, (6) compute U, (7) compute V, (8) compute W, and (9) the solver. Please keep in mind that we cannot isolate each part and ignore feedback and interactions between different parts. Assume the domain size is n x n, we estimate computation of each part as (1) parameters input $O(1)$ – constant time; (2) grid generator $O(n)$; (3) initialization $O(n^2)$; (4) compute TKE $O(n^2)$; (5) compute dynamic pressure perturbation $O(n^2)*M$ -- consider feedback and interactions between wind and pressure, this term may cause $O(n^3)$, where M depends on domain size and magnitude of physical forcing; (6) compute U $O(n^2)$; (7) compute V $O(n^2)$; (8) compute W $O(n^2)$; and (9) the solver $O(n)$. Therefore, the total sequential computation time is $O(Mn^2)$ $+O(n^2)$ $+O(n)=O(Mn^2)+O(n^2)$, where M is not a small number, it depends on physical conditions.

3.3 Computation of Dynamic Pressure Perturbation

From above estimates, we see that the dynamic pressure perturbation module is very time-consuming and it depends on the magnitude of physical forcing. We calculated the various magnitudes of physical forcing (shelterbelts). For a porous shelterbelt, the computation time of dynamic pressure perturbation accounts for 66% total computation time; however, for a dense shelterbelt, the computation time of dynamic pressure perturbation accounts for as high as 91.4% total computation time (Tables omitted). For medium-dense shelterbelt, the computation time of dynamic pressure perturbation accounts for 88.5%. The denser the shelterbelt, the stronger interactions between flow and pressure. Pressure gradient force drives the flow, and the change in flow also modifies the pressure. So, when wind (U, V, or/and W) changes, we need compute the divergence or convergence; the divergence or convergence causes the changes of pressure; after computing new pressure perturbation, we also need adjust wind according to current pressure field.

4   Functional Decomposition Parallel Programming (FDPP)

4.1 Functional Decomposition

Functional parallelism computations are based on different operations and functions. Separate tasks or functions must be executed at the same time on different processors for achieving higher speed. Before decomposing the functional modules, we must understand the relationships and data dependency between different functions.

As we discussed in the above section, we mainly have 9 different functional modules. The functions outside the time-step iteration loop are not worth parallelizing because they execute only once for the whole run. Also these functions must process the large amount of data. If we parallelize them, they will have heavy communication overhead because all data needed are sent to all processors in the group. We let the root processor handle all these functions and transit between time steps, while other six functions take 6 different machines. These functions take inputs from the previous time-step values, and run independently within the same time step. They are synchronized at the end of completion of each time step so that for every time step, different functions use the same previous time-step values as inputs. At the end of completion of the function for each time step, the processor will broadcast the updated values to all other processors so that other processors can use the newest values computed by other processors.

In our original sequential code, we used just-computed values for the same time step but the computation was done before another variable's prediction began. By using newest available values of variable, we can improve the performance. When we rewrote the sequential code into functional parallel code, we did not use currently available new values of the same time step for minimizing the computation overhead.

4.2 Speedup, Communication Overhead, and Analyses

As shown in Figure 1, the communication overhead took most of CPU time. For 6 of 7 nodes, the communication overhead took more than 97% of CPU time. It is difficult to see any details from Figure 1 since the communication overhead bars cover most of them. In summary, serial execution time =23137.430, parallel execution time =29696.437. Therefore, speedup = 23137.430/29696.437 = 0.779, which is less than 1. That means that the parallel code took more time than the serial one. What cause such inefficiency?

The major portion of the computation time is consumed by calculating dynamic pressure perturbation. Computing dynamic pressure perturbation consumed 17424.77 seconds for the functional decomposition parallel code and 20468.309 seconds for the serial code, thus gaining 14.9% speedup in terms of computation of dynamic pressure perturbation. However, node 5 which computed dynamic pressure perturbation needs extra 11922.345 seconds to broadcast and receive the whole updated new time-step values to/from all other processors which also compute other functions independently. Because u, v, and w affect TKE and p, p drives u, v, and w, and TKE also affect u, v, and w; there exist very complicated interactions and feedback. Computing any of these variables needs the information of other variables. Therefore, there are $O(n^2)$ message passing.

132

Moreover, the program should be synchronized at the completion of each function to the same starting point so that all functions can get the same time-step values as new initial values. The computation of pressure is time-consuming, so other processors just sit there to wait for the completion of the pressure computation. The average load balance ratio is only 51%. The parallel time is determined by the maximum time of the most time-consuming function computing plus communication overhead.

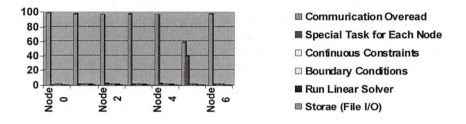

Figure 1. Graphical display of timing for functional decomposition parallelism

5 Domain Decomposition Parallel Programming (DDPP)

One of the most critical design decisions in any parallel program is how to partition your problem. A poor or rigid partitioning choice might result in disastrous parallel performance. As we saw from the last section, functional decomposition not only is not flexible (dependent on how many main function components; we had 7 main functions for shelterbelt turbulent flow problem), but also causes very poor performance (parallel processing with 7 processors needs longer time than serial processing with only one processor). A flexible partitioning choice, designed to optimize real world problems will result in much better parallel performance.

5.1 Domain Decomposition and Efficiency

Domain decomposition refers to spatially partitioning the computational domain. The effectiveness of spatial decomposition methods can be explained in terms of volume and surface area. When we consider partitioning a numerical grid problem spatially, the volume enclosed by a particular partition will correspond roughly to the number of cells. And the surface area of the section will correspond roughly to the communications needed for that partition to communicate with its neighbors. The domain is vertically sliced in our application (Figure omitted). Let us assume the domain size is n x n. We sliced it into m small regions, each region has size n/m x n (we can divide it into different size regions; but for convenience of analysis, we assume the regions have the same size). Then we distribute each region to a processor, so the computation load is reduced and performance is enhanced; however, this region needs to exchange information with its neighbors, and communication load increases, with additional message complexity of $O(2n)$ (please note that the functional decomposition brings additional messages of $O(n^2)$). Therefore, there are tradeoffs also for domain decomposition, and the final performance depends on the relative effects of both factors.

We run our domain decomposition MPI parallel version shelterbelt turbulent flow model with different processors and different sizes. The parallel performance gains are significant for all runs. Because the timing data are huge, we summarize the key performance here. We also evaluate the correctness and errors of multiple processing. As shown in Table 1, the differences of computed results by using different number of processors are very small.

Table 1. Comparisons of Computed Mean Kinetic Energy (MKE)

#PROCESSORS	1	2	4	8
MKE	16.3762	16.3739	16.3735	16.3731
#PROCESSORS	16	32	64	
MKE	16.2728	16.3729	16.3726	

5.2 Speedup Ratio and Its Changes with Domain Size and Number of Processors

Figure 2 shows the changes of speedup ratio with number of processors and domain size. The curve with squares is for the domain size of (128+2) x (64+2), and the curve with solid circles is for the domain size of (256+2)x(128+2). We also plot the ideal 1 to 1 line. As shown from the Figure, speedup increases with increasing number of processors. For small number of processors, the curves are close to the ideal line; but, with the increasing number of processors, the curves depart from the ideal line, and the performance gains slow down, especially for small domain size. This is the result of tradeoffs between reduced computation load and increased communication load after the domain is decomposed. When the number of processors is small or the domain is large, the reduced computation dominates. When the number of processors is large, each processor processes only a few grids, the performance gains are limited, but the increased communications dominate.

134

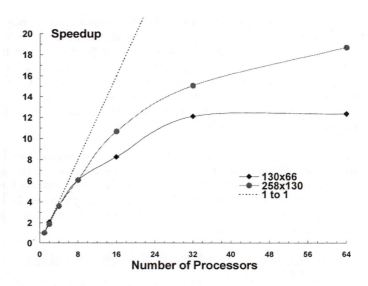

Figure 2. Speedup and its changes with domain size and number of processors

5.3 Load Balance and Analyses

Table 2 lists the changes of load balance with the number of processors. We can see that the load balance ratio improves a little bit with large number of processors.

Table 2 Load balance ratio for domain size of (256+2)*(128+2)

Processors	2	4	8	16	32	64
Load Balance	0.89	0.90	0.89	0.91	0.93	0.91

6 Summary and Conclusions

We designed, implemented, and compared several parallel version codes of our shelterbelt turbulent flow model system which involves extremely strong non-linear processes, solid-air interactions, flow-pressure linkages, and turbulent feedback mechanisms. There is a need for running this code in parallel because this code is very time-consuming and because we can use it to research many cutting-edge scientific problems. This paper described the implementation and performance evaluation on a cluster of workstations. The code used MPI for message passing and three design approaches were implemented: most-frequently-used module, functional decomposition, and spatial decomposition. The spatial decomposition was found to give the best performance for our application.

7   Acknowledgements

This research was supported by the US Department of Agriculture Grant 96351083892, the US Department of Energy NIGEC Grant DE-FC 0390ER61010, and the NRI Competitive Grant 93-37101-8954. The final work was done on the ALICE network of workstations in the Scalable Computing Laboratory. The ALICE computer facility was maintained by the USDOE Ames Laboratory.

References

1. Baker, L. and B.J. Smith, *Parallel Programming*. (McGraw-Hill, New York, NY, 1996), Pp.381.
2. Gropp, W.,   E. Lusk, and A. Skjellum, *Using MPI: Portable Parallel Programming with the Message-Passing Interface* (The MIT Press, Cambridge, MA,1994), Pp1-169.
3. Pritchard, D. and J. Reeve (Eds.), *Euro-Par'98 Parallel Processing.*   Lecture Notes in Computer Science, No.**1470** (1998), 1-1152.
4. Wang, H. and E.S. Takle, Boundary-layer flow and turbulence near porous obstacles: I. Derivation of a general equation set for a porous medium. *Boundary-Layer Meteorology*, **74**(1995), 73-88.
5. Wang, H. and E.S. Takle, A numerical simulation of boundary-layer flows near shelterbelts. *Boundary-Layer Meteorology*, **75**(1995), 141-173.
6. Wang, H. and E.S. Takle, On three-dimensionality of shelterbelt structure and its influences on shelter effects. *Boundary-Layer Meteorology*, **79**(1996), 83-105.
7. Wang, H. and E.S. Takle, On shelter efficiency of shelterbelts in oblique wind. *Agric. Forest Meteorology,* **81**(1996), 95-117.
8. Wang, H. and E.S. Takle, Numerical simulations of shelterbelt effects on wind direction. *Journal of Applied Meteorology*, **34**(1996), 2206-2219.
9. Wang, H. and E.S. Takle, Momentum budget and shelter mechanism of boundary-layer flow near a shelterbelt. *Boundary-Layer Meteorology*, **82**(1997), 417-435.
10. Wang, H. and E.S. Takle, Model-simulated influences of shelterbelt shape on wind-sheltering efficiency. *Journal of Applied Meteorology*, **36**(1997), 695-704.

MODELLING HEAD BIOMECHANICS
ON PARALLEL PLATFORMS

ULRICH HARTMANN

NEC Europe Ltd. C&C Research Laboratories
Rathausallee 10, D-53757 Sankt Augustin, Germany
E-mail:hartmann@ccrl-nece.technopark.gmd.de

In this paper a new FEM-based approach to model the mechanical response of the head is presented. To overcome restrictions of previous approaches our head model is based on individual datasets of the head obtained from magnetic resonance imaging (MRI). The use of parallel computers allows to carry out biomechanical simulations based on FE meshes with a spatial resolution about five times higher than that of previous models. A totally automatic procedure to generate FE meshes of the head starting from MR datasets is used. Models for individual clinical cases can be set up within minutes. Here, we focus on the performance of several parallel platforms for our demanding FE simulations.

1 Introduction

In recent years the finite element method (FEM) has gained growing interest in the medical field. Because of its versatility and flexibility the finite element method is currently becoming a powerful tool in the neurosciences.

About twenty-five years ago FEM was first utilised to study the biomechanics of the head. A detailed review of the progress made ever since is given in[1]. Most head models have been designed to find mechanisms describing brain injury after impact as occuring in accidents. The other models deal with investigating the consequences of structural alterations within the head (e.g. tumor growth). Though these head models have proven their general applicability to the field of head biomechanics they are still far from being a tool for the neurologist in clinical practice. This situation is mainly explained by the following shortcomings of existing models:

1. Most models are based on a crude representation of brain anatomy. Many head models are two-dimensional and of poor spatial resolution. Their geometry is based on images which are taken either from anatomical textbooks or adapted from medical image data.

2. Current models are not flexible. Finite element meshes of the head are often generated by hand and designed to reproduce the average geometry of the human head. Thus, they do not allow neurological pathologies or deviations from the average head geometry to be taken into account.

3. The material models reflecting the biomechanical behaviour of head tissue under load are very simple because of the lack of accurately measured parameters.

Only two mechanical head models have been presented to the high performance computing (HPC) community: Subramaniam and coworkers[2] have created a model dedicated to the phenomenon of hydrocephalus. An obstruction of an aqueductal site within the brain leads to a water accumulation and likewise to an increased hydrostatic pressure. Though their simulations are carried out on a supercomputer the underlying two-dimensional FE mesh comprises only several hundreds of finite elements. Nevertheless the authors ensure that their concept leads to physically reasonable results.

The Wayne State University (WSU) head model can considered to be the most detailed concerning brain anatomy. The three-dimensional (3D) WSU model[3]. has been created to establish a relationship between mechanical stress caused by impact and neurological deficit. Recently, it has been further developed in collaboration with PAM System International (PSI)[4]. The WSU model consists of 22000 mesh nodes and the slightly more complicated PSI model comprises 26000 nodal points. Though the spatial resolution seems relatively high, the WSU/PSI model still suffers from a rather poor FE representation of the complex-shaped anatomical structures. In particular the ventricles, large cavities within the brain (see Figure 2), are barely recognisable. Another drawback of the WSU model can be seen in the costly mesh generation process. The geometry of the mesh is defined once only to represent an average human head. This geometry is then used for all impact simulations.

In this paper, we present a new FEM-based approach to model the mechanical response of the head. To overcome the abovementioned restrictions this head model is based on individual datasets of the head obtained from magnetic resonance imaging (MRI). The use of parallel computers allows us to carry out biomechanical simulations based on FE meshes with a spatial resolution about five times higher than that of previous models. These meshes guarantee (i) a precise FE representation of neuroanatomical structures (see Figure 2) and (ii) a high numerical accuracy of the results. In contrast to previous models a totally automatic procedure to generate FE meshes of the head is used. Models for individual clinical cases can be created within minutes. In the future this technique will also allow the incorporation of additional knowledge about the brain's mechanical behaviour delivered by more sophisticated imaging techniques (see Chapter 5).

2 Neuroanatomical Basics and Imaging Aspects

From a macroscopic viewpoint the brain that occupies the top half of the skull consists of two materials, grey and white matter (see Figure 1). The brain is embedded in a cushion of cerebrospinal fluid (CSF). The complex shaped inner cavities of the brain (see Figure 2) -the ventricles- are filled with CSF which leads to a mechanical behaviour different from that of the brain (see Chapter 4). For a better understanding of the remainder of this article some

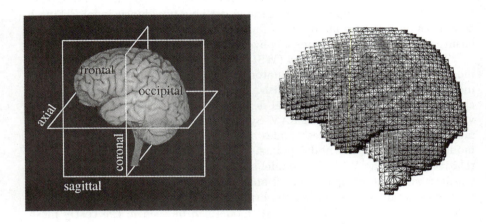

Figure 1. *On the left: Illustration of some basic medical terms used throughout the text. On the right: Depiction of a FE representation of the brain obtained with the modelling approach to be explained in the next chapter.*

medical terms are clarified in Figure 1. There are three easy ways to cut a 3D brain dataset by a plane. According to the orientation of the cutting plane a slice through the dataset is called coronal, sagittal or axial. The area around the upper back of the brain is the occipital region and the opposite area is called the frontal region.

Modern imaging techniques such as magnetic resonance imaging (MRI) generate high resolution datasets of the human head and its internal structures. Current MR scanners reach a spatial accuracy of about 1 mm. A typical dataset consists of 256^3 three-dimensional (3D) cubical image elements (voxels).

Figure 2. *A finite element mesh of the ventricles generated with the methods described in Chapter 3.*

3 Solution Methods and Material Modelling

Body deformation evoked by a time-dependant force $\mathbf{F}(t)$ is modelled by the following system of differential equations

$$\mathbf{M\ddot{U}}(t) + \mathbf{D\dot{U}}(t) + \mathbf{KU}(t) = \mathbf{F}(t). \tag{1}$$

$\mathbf{U}$ denotes the nodal displacement vector and its time derivatives are symbolized by dots. The global matrices $\mathbf{M}$, $\mathbf{D}$ and $\mathbf{K}$ reflect the mass, the damping and the stiffness of the elastic system. 3D MRI raw datasets (see Figure 3,

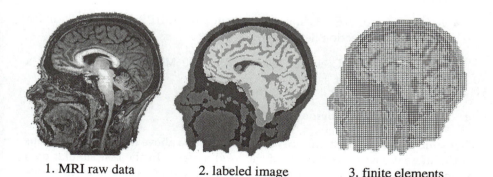

1. MRI raw data   2. labeled image   3. finite elements

Figure 3. *From MRI data to finite elements: By the means of image processing we obtain a segmented image which serves as input for our mesh generator. The images show sagittal slices through the 3D datasets.*

left image) of the brain provide a precise geometric description of the head and its structures. Starting from an MRI dataset head meshes with cubes and tetrahedra as finite elements (see Figure 3, right image) are generated[5]. As an intermediate stage a labeled dataset is created in which all voxels belonging to the same neuroanatomical structure share a common grey value (see Figure 3, middle image) thus defining materials in the dataset.

In the linear elastic case the material behaviour of human tissue is modelled by three parameters only; Young's modulus, Poisson's ratio and density. The majority of existing head models makes use of this approach. Some authors implemented a vicoelastic tissue model. However, in a comparative study[6] Kuijpers et al. observed no significant difference between the simulations results obtained with a viscoelastic material model and those generated with a linear elastic model.

After the head meshes have been partitioned with a geometric algorithm, the system matrices are set up in parallel and the arising equation system (1) is then solved with Newmark's implicit integration scheme (time step = 0.05 ms). In principle, an explicit method is indicated for this kind of simulation, but as this project is striving to provide a compact toolbox applicable also to low velocity processes in the head (e. g. tumor growth), an implicit solver system[7] has been chosen capable of covering all user requirements. The FE code has been installed on three different parallel platforms:

- A 128 processor NEC Cenju-3 supercomputer (MIPS R4400 in a multi stage interconnection network)

- A 64 processor NEC Cenju-4 supercomputer (MIPS R10000 in a multi stage interconnection network)

- A 32 processor PC cluster (PentiumPro 200 MHz interconnected by a high speed myrinet switch).

4 Application/Performance-Analysis

Dynamic impact simulations are carried out on the above described platforms with different spatial resolutions of the head meshes. In the test simulation a time-dependant force is applied to the forehead and the subsequent intracranial pressure distribution is computed. Theoretically one expects increased pressure in the frontal brain region and decreased pressure in the occipital brain area. Figure 4 shows that the model fulfills the theoretical expectation. The ventricles are subjected to a complicated pattern of high and low stress during the pressure wave propagation because their mechanical properties are different from those of brain matter (see Chapter 2). Figure 5 depicts the relative timings for an impact simulation based on a mesh comprising 200000 unknowns. Expectedly, the Cenju-4 is a factor of three to four faster than the other machines. One of the interesting results of the analysis is that the PC cluster can compete with the Cenju-3 system. On the average the Cenju-3 system is only 30% faster than the cluster. This result shows that PC clusters are becoming a serious challenge for medium scale parallel systems.

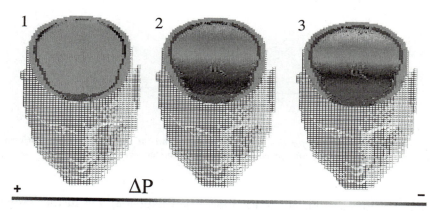

Figure 4. *Coup-contrecoup phenomenon: Stress distribution in the brain caused by a time-dependent force applied in the frontal region. An axial slice through the 3D pressure data is mapped on the FE mesh of head.*

No. of processors	24	32	48	64
Time in [s]	47.4	35.9	24.4	19.0
relative speed-up	1.00	1.32	1.94	2.50

Table 1. *Absolute timings and speed-up for one Newmark iteration on the Cenju-4.*

The timings given in Table 1 make clear that Newmark's scheme is efficiently parallelisable and that it yields computation times of less than half a minute for one time step (i.e. Newmark iteration) if an equation system of more than 400000 unknowns is solved on 64 processors of the Cenju-4. The total computation time for this dynamic analysis with 50 time steps (see snapshots of the FE analysis in Figure 4) takes 20 minutes. Though this value is far away from real-time it is nevertheless an astonishing value for such a large

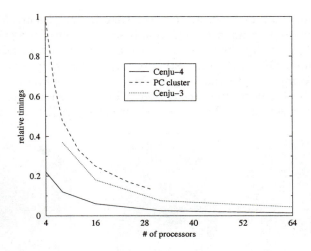

Figure 5. *Relative timings for one Newmark iteration on the different parallel platforms. The computation time for four processors of the PC cluster was set to one.*

problem. Optimisation of the FE tools (see Chapter 5) will further reduce this computation time.

5 Discussion and Outlook

This study is part of a research programme aiming at a comprehensive FE head model applicable to a wide range of medical problems stemming from such fields as traumatology and neurosurgery. In its current state the model allows to correctly reproduce clinical findings. By designing our model as a supercomputer application, a high spatial resolution and a short solution time have been achieved. The possibility to generate highly resolved models of individuals is a key feature for an extensive validation study planned together with forensic physicians and partners from the automobile industry. An extension of the modelling environment into another direction will be the possibility to predict structural changes in the head caused by space-consuming processes and to pre-operatively plan neurosurgeries. As mentioned above the achievement of these ambitious goals is currently hindered by the lack of precisely measured material parameters. It is obvious that the demand for techniques yielding individually measured material properties is very strong in the modelling community. Very recently, a new imaging method called elastography has been developed[8]. This combination of ultrasound and MRI yields an individual image dataset encoding the elastic properties of the tissue types under examination. If this novel technique is applied to the head the resulting image dataset can be directly incorporated into our meshing process. As the elastography datasets will have a high spatial resolution the use of parallel computing technology becomes indispensable to carry out simulations on such high resolution meshes. Having achieved this decisive step, the modelling toolbox has to be further developed by adding more elaborate finite element features. Finally, the clinical user will have a powerful tool at hand that supports him in everyday clinical life.

References

1. Sauren, A.A.H.J. and Claessens, M.H.A. (1993) Finite Element Modeling of Head Impact: The Second Decade. *Proceedings of the International IRCOBI Conference on the Biomechanics of Impact*, 241-254.
2. Subramaniam, R.P., Neff, S.R., and Rahulkumar, P. (1995) A numerical study of the biomechanics of structural neurologic diseases. *High Performance Computing-Grand Challenges in the Computer Simulation Society in Computer Simulations, San Diego* 552-560
3. Zhou, C., Khalil, T.B and King, A.I. (1995) A New Model Comparing Impact Responses of the Homogenous and Inhomogenous Human Brain. *Proceedings of the 39th Stapp Car Crash Conference*, (available via <http://www.sae.org>), 121-138.
4. Haug, E., Beaugonin, M. and Tramecon, A. (1998) Current Status of Articulated and Deformable Human Models for Impact and Occupant Safety Simulation at ESI Group, *PAM'98 User's Conference*
5. Hartmann, U. and Kruggel, F. (1998) A Fast Algorithm for Generating Large Tetrahedral 3D Finite Element Meshes from Magnetic Resonance Tomograms. *Proceedings of the IEEE Workshop on Biomedical Image Analysis* ISBN 0-8186-8460-7, 184-192
6. Kuijpers, A.H.W.M., Claessens, M.H.A. and Sauren, A.A.H.J. (1995) The Influence of Different Boundary Conditions on the Response of the Head to Impact: A Two-dimensional Finite Element Study. *Journal of Neurotrauma*, **12**, 715-724.
7. Hutchinson, S.A., Prevost, L.V., Shadid, J.N. and Tuminaro, R.S. (1998) Aztec User's Guide Version 2.0β, SAND95-1559
8. Chenevert, T.L., Skovoroda, A.R., Donnell, M.O., Emelianov, S.Y. (1998) Elasticity Reconsstructive Imaging via Stimulated Echo MRI. *Magnetic Resonance in Medicine*, in print

HIPERWATER: A HIGH PERFORMANCE COMPUTING DEMONSTRATOR FOR WATER NETWORK ANALYSIS

V. HERNÁNDEZ, A. M. VIDAL, F. ALVARRUIZ, J. M. ALONSO, D. GUERRERO, P. A. RUIZ

Department of Information Systems and Computing, Universidad Politécnica de Valencia, Camino de Vera s/n, Valencia 46022. Spain.
e-mail: vhernand@dsic.upv.es

This paper presents the development of a demonstrator (HIPERWATER) based on High Performance Computing for simulation and optimisation of water networks. EPANET package has been the starting point for the demonstrator. The paper discusses the approach used in the application of parallel computing to the hydraulic and water quality simulations, and to a method for leakage reduction.

1 Introduction

Last two decades have seen an important progress in the modelling of water supply systems. Extended period dynamic models, which take into account the evolution of hydraulic and water quality variables, are currently of wide use. Geographical Information Systems allow to produce more complete network models, although their analysis is significantly more complex. On the other hand, optimisation problems require the solution of multiple simulation problems, and they are therefore complex and computationally-intensive. A consequence of that is the need of more powerful computing resources, and hence the interest in the use of parallel computing.

In this context, the HIPERWATER project (ESPRIT project 24003, http://hiperttn.upv.es/hiperwater/) (Hernández et al. 1999a; 1999b) has been carried out aiming at two main objectives: firstly, to introduce High Performance Computing in the simulation and analysis of water networks; secondly, to introduce leakage modelling and develop a parallel optimisation module to reduce leakage by controlling network pressures.

The starting point for the development of the demonstrator has been the package EPANET. EPANET (Rossman 1993a) is one of the most extended water network simulation packages in the world, due both to the good performance of its calculation module, and to the fact that it is freely available.

HIPERWATER tackles three different types of problems making use of HPCN solutions: firstly, the solution of the hydraulic problem by means of the Gradient Method (Todini and Pilati 1987); secondly, the Discrete Volume Element Method, in the context of the water quality problem (Rossman et al 1993b); and thirdly, the use of Sequential Quadratic Programming algorithms (Lawrence et al 1997) in the context of water network optimisation.

The first two problems are the subject of sections 2, 3 and 4, while the problem of leakage minimisation is presented in section 5. Finally, section 6 is devoted to results and section 7 to conclusions.

2 Hydraulic Simulation

Given a pipe network defined by its topology, pipe characteristics and system constraints, the problem consists in determining all the flowrates Q in the pipes, as well as all the unknown heads H at the nodes, on the assumption of steady state conditions.

The equations that model water networks (and piping networks in general) are non-linear and therefore require an iterative solution, i.e. the problem is reconducted to the solution of a sequence of systems of linear equations. One of the most effective methods to perform this reconduction is the *Gradient Method*, proposed by Todini (Todini 1979; Todini and Pilati 1987). This method requires in each iteration the solution of a linear system $Ax = b$, where A is a sparse, symmetric positive definite matrix.

The major concern in the implementation of a parallel algorithm for hydraulic simulation has been the parallelisation of the solution of those linear systems. This is done by means of a Cholesky multifrontal method consisting of 4 different stages: ordering, symbolic factorisation, Cholesky numerical factorisation and triangular systems solution.

During the ordering phase, a permutation matrix P is computed so that the matrix PAP^T incurs a minimal fill-in, and its factorisation presents a high degree of cuncurrency. This is done by means of the *Multilevel Nested Dissection* (MND) algorithm (Bui and Jones 1993; Heath et al. 1991).

During the symbolic factorisation phase the non-zero structure of the triangular Cholesky factor L is determined. The role of the symbolic factorisation phase is to increase the performance of the numerical factorisation phase. The necessary operations to compute the values in L that satisfy $P AP^T = LL^T$, are performed during the phase of numerical factorisation (Liu 1992). Finally the solution to $Ax = b$ is computed by solving two triangular systems, $Ly = b'$ followed by $L^Tx' = y$, where $b' = Pb$ and $x' = Px$. The final solution is $x = P^Tx'$.

The first two phases depend only on the non-zero pattern of the matrix A, which in the case of hydraulic simulation is the same for all the linear systems. Thus, these two phases need to be done only once, as an initialisation process prior to the simulation.

3 Water Quality Simulation

Water quality simulation can be used to obtain information about different parameters, such as substance concentrations, water age analysis, or percentage of flow from a determined source. There are various methods that can be used for water quality simulation. In particular, EPANET uses the *Discrete Volume Element Method* (DVEM) (Rossman et al. 1993b).

The DVEM method proceeds by first dividing the pipes of the network into segments, and then simulating the propagation of mass through the segments in a series of time steps, each consisting of four phases, as shown in Figure 1:

- *Reaction*. If the substance is reactive, its reaction is measured in this step.
- *Transport into the nodes*. Water is transported from the last segment of each pipe to its connecting node.
- *Transport along the pipes*.
- *Transport out of the nodes*. Mass is moved out of each node into the first segment of the pipes.

Since the different DVEM steps have to be performed sequentially, the parallel approach must be based on the parallelisation of each DVEM step. The basic idea is to divide the water network in several parts, one for each processor in our system. This initial network partitioning plays an important role to minimise communications and balance the computational load. Two are the desired objectives to be accomplished by the partitioning algorithm: a similar number of elements (nodes) should be assigned to each processor, and the number of pipes with nodes belonging to different processors should be minimum.

Graph partitioning algorithms can be used for that purpose. In particular, the graph partitioning algorithm used is known as *Multilevel Recursive Bisection* (Bui and Jones 1993; Hendrickson and Leland 1993). Briefly, the algorithm involves gradual coarsening of a graph to a few hundred vertices, then partitioning this smaller graph, and finally, projecting the partitions back to the original graph by gradually refining them.

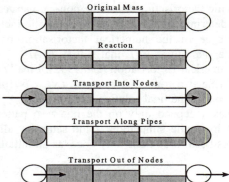

Figure 1. Phases of a DVEM step for a network pipe and its two end nodes. Shadowed areas represent the substance considered in the water quality simulation.

Once the partition of the network has been established, simulation can begin. Each processor performs in parallel the DVEM steps, taking into account that communications take place in each DVEM step, for those pipes with nodes belonging to different processors.

4 Overlapping Hydraulic and Water Quality Simulations

This section presents a parallel approach complementary to that presented in the previous two sections. The idea is to overlap hydraulic and water quality simulations, so that both take place simultaneously.

Hydraulic and water quality simulations are performed separately in EPANET, i.e. hydraulic simulation is first completely carried out and its results written to a file. Then quality simulation is performed, reading the hydraulic results from that file.

An alternative approach is to overlap both simulations. In this case, we have one or several processors in charge of the hydraulic simulation and another group of processors in charge of the quality simulation. As soon as the first group completes the simulation of a hydraulic step, the results are sent to the other group, which carries out the quality simulation. If the system is adequately balanced, which can be done by choosing the number of processors for the hydraulic and quality simulations, an effect of overlap takes place, as shown in figure 1.

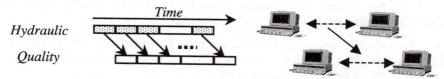

Figure 2. Overlapped hydraulic and water quality simulations in HIPERWATER.

5 Leakage Minimisation

Different experiences have shown that leakage is very sensitive to network pressures. The problem of leakage minimisation consists in using Pressure Reducing Valves (PRVs) so as to keep network pressures (and consequently leakage) as low as possible, while at the same time satisfying minimum service pressures at particular (or all) nodes.

Taking into account that hydraulic simulation consists of a series steady-state simulations at different instants, leakage must be minimised at each of those instants. The problem of leakage minimisation at each time instant is formulated directly as the following non-linear constrained minimisation problem (for another formulation of the leakage minimisation problem, see (Germanopulos 1995)).

$$min \ f(x) = \sum_{j=1}^{NH} q_j(x)$$

subject to: $p_j(x) \geq Pmin_j, \qquad j \in I_c$

where:

> x: PRV settings, a column vector of NV elements,
> NV: Number of PRV valves that we can act on,
> NH: Number of nodes in the network,
> $q_j(x)$: leakage flow at node j, expressed as a function of the PRV settings,
> $p_j(x)$: pressure at node j,
> $Pmin_j$: Minimum pressure imposed on node j,
> I_c: subset of nodes where a minimum pressure is imposed.

An alternative, more standard way to express pressure constraints is:

$$g_j(x) = Pmin_j - p_j(x) \leq 0, \qquad j \in I_c,$$

where constraint functions $g_j(x)$ are introduced.

The optimisation problem stated is solved by means of the *Sequential Quadratic Programming Method* (SQP). We make use of the general-purpose implementation of the method in CFSQP (Lawrence et al. 1997). The SQP method is based on finding a step away from the current point by minimising a quadratic model of the problem. The elements that we have to provide for application of the SQP method are:

- The objective function $f(x)$ and the constraint functions $g_j(x)$. The evaluation of this function requires the solution of the steady-state hydraulic analysis problem (in the presence of leakage).
- Gradients of the previous functions with respect to the decision variables x: $\nabla f(x)$ and $\nabla g_j(x)$. These gradients are calculated by finite differences, although a deeper analysis could lead in the future to an analytical formulation of them.

In order to make a parallel implementation of this optimization process, we could think of applying parallelism to the part of hydraulic analysis, using the scheme outlined in section 2.

However, an alternative approach is to take advantage of the time step sub-problems being independent of each other, thus assigning each of them (or a group of them) to a different processor. This has been the option chosen, leading to a simple yet efficient coarse-grain parallel implementation.

The problem is very suitable to be handled by a master-slave paradigm. The master is a process whose only task is to distribute the time intervals among the different slave processes. The latter are continuously waiting for an optimisation problem, in order to process it and return the results to the master.

6 Results

Results shown in this section have been obtained on a cluster of Pentium-Pro PCs linked with a Fast-Ethernet network. Operating system is Windows, and MPI (Message Passing Interface) communication library is used. Each PC has 64 Mb RAM and runs at 200 MHz.

Three water networks (referred to as Test 1, 2 and 3) have been used for evaluating the performance of the parallel algorithms for hydraulic and water quality simulations. On the other hand, tests 4, 5 and 6, correspond to water supply networks used for the algorithms of leakage minimisation. The main features of the networks are given in table 1.

Table 1. Water networks used for performance evaluation

	# Pipes	# Nodes	# PRVs
Test 1	4,901	2,501	-
Test 2	19,801	10,001	-
Test 3	34,516	32,404	-
Test 4	1,345	1,241	3
Test 5	805	770	3
Test 6	126	66	2

Figure 3 shows the time spent on the simulation (both hydraulic and water quality simulations) by the HIPERWATER demonstrator, and also the time spent by EPANET. The demonstrator (with overlapping of hydraulic and water quality simulations) is run on 2, 3 and 4 processors (HW-2p, HW-3p and HW-4p respectively). It is easily appreciated that the computing time is notably reduced by the use of High Performance Computing in the HIPERWATER demonstrator.

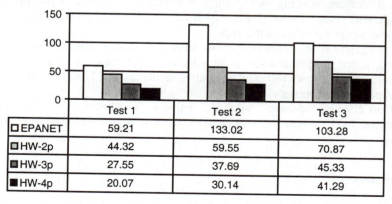

	Test 1	Test 2	Test 3
□ EPANET	59.21	133.02	103.28
□ HW-2p	44.32	59.55	70.87
■ HW-3p	27.55	37.69	45.33
■ HW-4p	20.07	30.14	41.29

Figure 3. Simulation time (in seconds) of the HIPERWATER demonstrator, compared with EPANET.

Figure 4 shows the computing time spent on the leakage minimisation process for the networks, considering from 1 to 5 processors. It can be observed the

150

important reduction in execution time achieved by means of High Performance Computing technology.

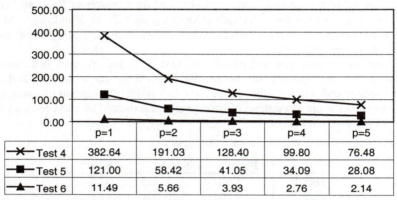

	p=1	p=2	p=3	p=4	p=5
✕ Test 4	382.64	191.03	128.40	99.80	76.48
■ Test 5	121.00	58.42	41.05	34.09	28.08
▲ Test 6	11.49	5.66	3.93	2.76	2.14

Figure 4. Computing time (in seconds) for leakage minimisation process as a function of the number of processors used.

7   Conclusions

This paper shows the application of HPC techniques in water network analysis processes. Both hydraulic and water quality simulations are approached from the point of view of parallel computing, and results obtained show the interest in the application of parallel computing in processes of simulation of water networks.

On the other hand, a parallel method is presented for the determination of optimal pressure reducing valve settings minimising leakage. This process requires considerable computational power, which can be provided by means of the parallel implementation described in this paper.

Geographical Information Systems allow to produce more complete network models, although their analysis is significantly more complex. A consequence of that is the need of more powerful computing resources, and hence the interest in the use of parallel computing.

Cost-effective parallel systems, namely a cluster of Pentium PCs interconnected by a Fast-Ethernet network, have been used for obtaining the results shown.

References

BUI, T., and JONES, C. (1993). "A Heuristic for Reducing Fill in Sparse Matrix Factorisation", *6th SIAM Conf. Parallel Processing for Scientific Computing*, 711-718.

GERMANOPOULOS, G. (1995) "Valve Control Regulation for Reducing Leakage". *Improving Efficiency and Reliability in Water Distribution Systems*, 212-240.

HEATH, M. T., NG, E. G.-Y., and PEYTON, B. W. (1991). "Parallel Algorithms for Sparse Linear Systems", *SIAM Review*, 33: 420-460.

HENDRICKSON B., and LELAND R. (1993). "A Multilevel Algorithm for Partitioning Graphs". *Technical Report SAND93-1301*, Sandia National Laboratories.

HERNÁNDEZ, V., VIDAL, A.M., ALVARRUIZ, F., ALONSO, J. M., GUERRERO, D., RUIZ, P. A., MARTÍNEZ, F., VERCHER, J., and ULANICKI, B. (1999a). "Parallel Computing in Water Network Analysis and Optimization Processes". 26th *Ann. Water Resources Planning and Management Conf.*, ASCE, Arizona.

HERNÁNDEZ, V., MARTÍNEZ, F., VIDAL, A.M., ALONSO, J.M., ALVARRUIZ, F., GUERRERO, D., RUIZ, P.A., VERCHER, J. (1999b). "HIPERWATER: A High Performance Computing EPANET-Based Demonstrator for Water Network Simulation and Leakage Minimisation", International Conference on Computing and Control for the Water Industry (CCWI'99), Exeter, UK.

LAWRENCE, C. T., ZHOU, J. L., and TITS, A. L. (1997). "User's Guide for CFSQP Version 2.5: A C Code for Solving (Large Scale) Constrained Nonlinear (Minimax) Optimization Problems, Generating Iterates Satisfying All Inequality Constraints", *Technical Report TR-94-16r1*, Institute for Systems Research, University of Maryland.

LIU, J. W. H. (1992). "The Multifrontal Method for Sparse Matrix Solution: Theory and Practice", *SIAM Review*, vol. 34, no.1.

ROSSMAN, L. A. (1993a). *EPANET User's Manual*, US Environmental Protection Agency.

ROSSMAN, L. A., BOULOS, P. F., and ALTMAN, T. (1993b). "Discrete Volume-Element Method for Network Water-Quality Models", *J. of Water Resources Planning and Management*, ASCE, 119(5), 505-517.

TODINI, E. (1979). "Un Metodo del Gradiente per la Verifica delle Reti Idrauliche", *Bolletino degli Ingegneri della Toscana*, No. 11, 11-14.

TODINI, E., and PILATI, S. (1987). "A Gradient Method for the Solution of Looped Pipe Networks", *Proc. Int. Conf. Computer Applications for Water Supply Distribution*, Leicester Polytechnic, UK.

Acknowledgments

The authors wish to acknowledge the financial support provided by the ESPRIT programme of the European Commission, and also by research staff training grants from the Spanish government and the autonomous government of the Comunidad Valenciana, in Spain. We must also acknowledge André L. Tits for providing access to the CFSQP package.

PARALLEL GROUND WATER FLOW MODELLING

L. HLUCHÝ, V. D. TRAN, L. HALADA, G. T. NGUYEN

Institute of Informatics, Slovak Academy of Sciences
Dúbravská cesta 9, 842 37 Bratislava, Slovakia
E-mail: upsyhluc@savba.sk

In this paper we present the HPCN ground water flow modelling. It requires the solution of a partial differential equation representing a 3-D diffusion process. Its numerical solution by a finite difference method leads to a very large sparse, well-structured system of linear algebraic equations. Two parallel methods: the parallel Strongly Implicit Procedure and the preconditioned Conjugate Gradient are analyzed. We also present our experiments in a cluster of Pentium workstations, which compare the methods from the viewpoint of speedup and computation time.

1 Introduction

Planning and management of ground water resources, environmental protection of ground water recharge including pollution control and measures, require a tool for predicting the response of the aquifer system and processes in the aquifer system to the planned activities.

The tool for achieving such comprehensive goals is the model, which can represent the real nature processes by a system of partial differential equations. However, the real natural aquifer system and the water quality processes in this system are very complicated. The best suited modelling tools are the numerical methods where differential equations are replaced by a set of algebraic equations of the state variables at the discretization points in space and time. Thus, the problem is that the number of the algebraic equations to be solved simultaneously is very large and to reach the required accuracy of decision, rather large computations are required.

Solving diffusion and convection differential equations, which describe the fluid flow, is one of the most widely studied problems in scientific computations. With the arrival of parallel computers, this became possible for large 3D tasks as well. The effort to find stable and efficient parallel algorithms and/or program codes for various types of parallel computers became of primary interest for various research groups.

There are several numerical methods allowing to solve these equations. One is the finite difference method, which proved to be suitable for numerous 2D and 3D applications. Application of this technique results in solving a large system of linear equations $Ax=b$, approximately of the order 10^5-10^6, where the system matrix is sparse, symmetric and quasi-bounded. This is very time consuming so that parallel methods are of great importance. For the solution of such systems, the mostly used methods are relaxation methods, Alternating Direction Implicit (ADI) and Strongly Implicit Procedure (SIP) method. During the last decade, preconditioning techniques have become attractive because parallelizing the sparse matrix-vector product is much easier than the sparse triangular solver. Therefore a comparison of the above mentioned techniques, especially SIP [1], [2] and preconditioned Conjugate Gradient (CG) is very interesting.

The paper is organized as follows: in section 2 the theoretical background if the ground water model is given. In section 3 the parallel version of SIP is proposed. The CG method is described in section 4 and the experimental results are shown in section 5.

2   The mathematical model and its discretization

The fluid flow model can be described by the partial differential equation:

$$\frac{\partial}{\partial x}\left(K_x \frac{\partial H}{\partial x}\right) + \frac{\partial}{\partial y}\left(K_y \frac{\partial H}{\partial y}\right) + \frac{\partial}{\partial z}\left(K_z \frac{\partial H}{\partial z}\right) = S\frac{\partial H}{\partial t} + f(x,y,z,t) \tag{1}$$

where K_x, K_y, K_z are the hydraulic conductivity coefficients in the direction of corresponding coordinate axes, $H=H(x,y,z,t)$ is the piezometric level to be found, $f(x,y,z,t)$ is the function characterizing water infiltration and specific yield in a given point, and $S=S(x,y,z,t)$ is the coefficient with variable piezometric level H of elastic storage. The boundary conditions of Equation (1) are given by the initial values of the function $H(x,y,z,t)$ at time t_o in any point of the area considered. The coefficients K_x, K_y, K_z and S are determined by the constant geological properties of the aquifer at any point, and by the piezometric level H.

Numerical solution of this equation will be based on the finite difference method using space and time discretization. For the considered area of Equation (1), a grid containing N_x, N_y, N_z nodes in the direction of coordinate axes x, y, z, respectively, will be created. The corresponding difference equations resulting from (1) will be applied to every node of the grid and we shall have a system of $N_x.N_y.N_z$ linear equations in the following form:

$$A_{i,j,k}H_{i,j,k-1} + B_{i,j,k}H_{i-1,j,k} + C_{i,j,k}H_{i,j-1,k} + D_{i,j,k}H_{i,j,k} +$$
$$E_{i,j,k}H_{i,j+1,k} + F_{i,j,k}H_{i+1,j,k} + G_{i,j,k}H_{i,j,k+1} = Q_{i,j,k} \tag{2}$$

where $1\leq i\leq N_x$, $1\leq j\leq N_y$, $1\leq k\leq N_z$. In the equations of this system, the coefficients $A_{i,j,k}$, $B_{i,j,k}$, $C_{i,j,k}$, $D_{i,j,k}$, $E_{i,j,k}$, $F_{i,j,k}$, $G_{i,j,k}$ with the unknowns, and the known values of $Q_{i,j,k}$, are related to time moment t, and the values of H are calculated for the following moment $t+\Delta t$ (for simplicity, subscripts will be omitted in the sequel).

The equations in system (2) can be interpreted on the basis of water balance in blocks into which the investigated real space area can be divided. Note that, because the form of physical environment space blocks need not be rectangular but may be quasi-rectangular, the investigated area may always be interpreted as ideal parallelepipeds composed of identical cubes. Each of these boxes (grid nodes), determined by integer coordinates i, j, k corresponding to coordinate axes x, y, z, has the parameters $A_{i,j,k}$ $B_{i,j,k}$ $C_{i,j,k}$ $E_{i,j,k}$ $F_{i,j,k}$ $G_{i,j,k}$ which characterize water diffusion through all cube walls in time from t to $t+\Delta t$, and by the parameter $H_{i,j,k}$ representing its piezometric level in time $t+\Delta t$. Although the parameters $A_{i,j,k}$ $B_{i,j,k}$ $C_{i,j,k}$ $E_{i,j,k}$ $F_{i,j,k}$ $G_{i,j,k}$ depend upon the value of piezometric level H (in time t), their change in a time interval is slow enough and thus it can be considered that they do not change in every such interval. In finite difference equations system, the parameters $D_{i,j,k}$ and $Q_{i,j,k}$ are used as well. The first one determines summary diffusion from a block plus block storage change for the moment $t + \Delta t$, and the second one characterizes the sum of block storage in time t and the infiltration value. In matrix form, this equation system is represented by

$$MH = Q \tag{3}$$

where M is symmetric 7-diagonal matrix, as results from the interpretation of the coefficients $A_{i,j,k}$ $B_{i,j,k}$ $C_{i,j,k}$ $D_{i,j,k}$ $E_{i,j,k}$ $F_{i,j,k}$ $G_{i,j,k}$ and Equation (2).

3 The Parallel Strongly Implicit Procedure (SIP) algorithm

After analyzing several algorithms for solving sparse system of linear equations, we have chosen Strongly Implicit Procedure (SIP) algorithm for solving Equation (3). SIP is especially designed for full exploitation of the regularity (nonzero elements are only on 7 diagonals) of the sparse matrix M for efficient solution. The main idea of this method is in performing fast low-cost approximate LU decomposition of matrix M into two 4-diagonal triangular matrices (lower matrix L, and upper matrix U) in linear time:

$$LU \approx M \tag{4a}$$
$$\text{or} \qquad LU = M + N \tag{4b}$$

where N is "close" to zero matrix. By substitution $M = LU - N$ from Equation (4b) to Equation (3), we have:

$$(LU)H = Q + NH \tag{5}$$

Equation (5) will be solved by iteration:

$$(LU)H^i = Q + NH^{i-1} \tag{6}$$
$$\text{or} \qquad (LU)(H^i - H^{i-1}) = Q - MH^{i-1} \tag{7}$$

Letting $X^i = H^i - H^{i-1}$ and $R^{i-1} = Q - MH^{i-1}$, Equation (7) can be solved in two steps:

$$LY^i = R^{i-1} \tag{7a}$$
$$\text{and} \qquad UX^i = Y^i \tag{7b}$$

Because L and U are sparse 4-diagonal triangular matrices, Equations (7a) and (7b) can be solved in linear time. The iteration process (7a) and (7b) will be repeated, until the X^i vector is close enough to zero vector.

In summary, SIP consists of two parts: the approximate LU decomposition (4a) and the iteration process, which involves solving two sparse triangular matrices (7a) and (7b). It is well known that the SIP method convergence rate increases when, instead of one LU decomposition, two different ones are used, where the second LU decomposition differs from the first one by inverted re-numbering order of index values in one of the i,j,k directions.

In order to parallelize SIP, the data dependency of each step of SIP has been investigated in detail. Each step of SIP has the form of 3-dimensional nested loop. In LU decomposition (4a) and solving $LY^i = R^{i-1}$ (7a) the computation has the following form:

```
for i = 1 to Nx
    for j = 1 to Ny
        for k = 1 to Nz
            Zi,j,k = f(Zi-1,j,k, Zi,j-1,k, Zi,j,k-1);
```
where Z is a set of variables.

In solving $UX^i = Y^i$ (7b) the computation has the opposite direction:

```
for i = Nx to 1
    for j = Ny to 1
        for k = Nz to 1
            Zi,j,k = f(Zi+1,j,k, Zi,j+1,k, Zi,j,k+1);
```

In both cases, the loops have the Uniform Recurrence Equation (URE) form with dependence vectors $d_1=(1,0,0)$, $d_2=(0,1,0)$, $d_3=(0,0,1)$. Different techniques for parallelizing URE are proposed in [10], [11], [12]. In [3], Megson and Chen have analyzed existing methods and proposed a systematic way to parallelize and distribute URE on parallel environment. The simulation space is divided in the direction of x axis. Each processor computes nodes of the grid in a row, sends the value of the last node to the next processor and continues on the next row. The computation behaves as pipeline. We can also create pipeline in direction y or z. If e is the computation time of a node, and c is the communication delay, the speed-up of a p-processor system is:

$$sp = \frac{T_1}{T_p} = \frac{N_x N_y N_z e}{\dfrac{N_x}{p} N_y N_z e + (p-1)(c + \dfrac{N_x}{p} e)} \tag{8}$$

where start-up overhead $st=(p-1)(c+N_x e/p)$ is the time, when the last processor starts. Equation (8) can be transformed to the form:

$$sp = \frac{p}{1 + \dfrac{st}{N_x N_y N_z e}} \tag{9}$$

From (9) we can see that the algorithm can reach near optimal speed-up, given that the scale of the simulation space is large enough.

If the network bandwidth is small, the system does not have enough time to transfer messages after computing each row. In this case, we have to increase the granularity of computation by grouping nodes - N_{grain}. Processors compute N_{grain} rows and send all N_{grain} values in one package. By this way, the communication overhead can be reduced. However, increasing N_{grain} also increases the start-up overhead and decreases the speed-up. The optimal N_{grain} depends on the scale of the simulation space, the speed of processors, the type and the bandwidth of interconnection network.

4 The Preconditioned Conjugate Gradient algorithm

In our paper, we used the modified CG method with diagonal scaling preconditioner, which is simple but very effective. The modified CG algorithm can be described in the following form [13]:

```
1.  Init: H⁰, R⁰ = Q - MH⁰, T⁰ = R⁰
2.  i = 0,1, ...
3.            Yⁱ = MTⁱ
4.            δⁱ = (Rⁱ)ᵀ Rⁱ
5.            αᵢ = δᵢ/((Tⁱ)ᵀ Yⁱ)
6.            βᵢ = αᵢ(Yⁱ)ᵀ Yⁱ/((Tⁱ) Yⁱ) - 1
7.  Hⁱ⁺¹ = Hⁱ + αⁱTⁱ
8.            Rⁱ⁺¹ = Rⁱ - αⁱYⁱ
9.            Tⁱ⁺¹ = Rⁱ⁺¹ + βⁱTⁱ
10. until convergence
```

CG contains only matrix and vector operations, which have natural parallelism. Let us show more details of the communication among processors at each iteration. The data distribution is similar to SIP. The operation in line 3 can be written in the form:

$$Y^{(i)}_{i,j,k} = A_{i,j,k}\, T^{(i)}_{i,j,k-1} + B_{i,j,k}\, T^{(i)}_{i-1,j,k} + C_{i,j,k}\, T^{(i)}_{i,j-1,k} + D_{i,j,k}\, T^{(i)}_{i,j,k}$$
$$+ E_{i,j,k}\, T^{(i)}_{i,j+1,k} + F_{i,j,k}\, T^{(i)}_{i+1,j,k} + G_{i,j,k}\, T^{(i)}_{i,j,k+1} \quad (10)$$

where, A, B, C, D, E, F, G are diagonals of M in Equation (2). If i, j, k are the indices of a node on the right border of the iteration space of a processor, the value of $T^{(i)}_{i+1,j,k}$ has to be sent form the next processor in order to compute $Y^{(i)}_{i,j,k}$. So CG needs to exchange the values of T in the borders at each iteration, but it can be overlapped with computation (the inside nodes can be computed during the communication). The operations in line 3, 4, 5 require to compute the vector products $(R^i)^T\, R^i$, $(D^i)^T\, Y^i$, $(Y^i)^T\, Y^i$. If R_j is the part of vector R on processor j, the vector product $R^T\, R$ can be written in the form:

$$R^T\, R = R^T_1\, R_1 + R^T_2\, R_2 + \ldots + R^T_p\, R_p \quad (11)$$

It means that all partial products have to be sent to a "master" processor, which calculates their sum and sends it back. When the number of processors is large, the "master" processor may be the bottleneck of CG because it has to receive a large amount of packages. The problem can be solved using multilevel tree architecture, a processor collects the partial products of a group, calculates the sum and then sends it to "master".

If the interconnection network allows processors to communicate with each other independently, the speed-up of CG is given as follows:

$$sp = \frac{T_1}{T_p} = \frac{N_x N_y N_z e}{\dfrac{N_x N_y N_z}{p} e + c} \qquad (12)$$

where e is the computation time of each node at each iteration and c is the communication delay. For mesh architecture, the communication delay in (12) is $c.p^{1/2}$ instead of c, where p is the number of processors.

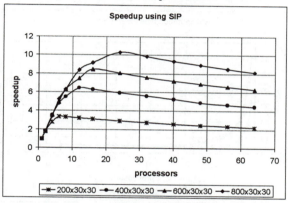

Fig. 1. The dependency of the speed-up of SIP on the number of processors

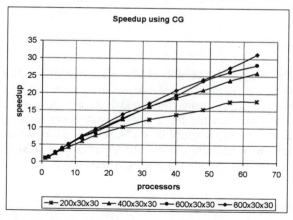

Fig. 2. The dependency of the speed-up of CG on the number of processors

158

5   Experimental results

Experiments have been done on the cluster of Pentium workstations. The speedup of SIP strongly depends on the size of the simulation space and on the number of processors. It increases with the number of processors to a given threshold, then decreases (Fig. 1). The speedup of CG is nearly linear with the number of processors (Fig. 2). However, the computation time of CG on a single processor is 2-2.5 times larger than the computation time of SIP, so despite the good speedup, CG is slower than SIP in smaller systems (Fig. 3).

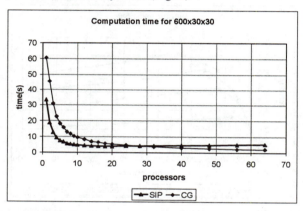

Fig. 3. Computation time of SIP and CG

6   Conclusion

We have presented the parallel version of SIP and preconditioned CG methods and demonstrated them on numerical solution of the partial differential equation (diffusion type) of the ground water flow model. As our experiments have shown, the SIP method is more suitable for a system with lower number of processors whereas CG can achieve better speed-up on large systems. Concretely, we use the cluster of 16 Pentium workstations with SIP algorithm for modelling the ground water flow in the river-basin of the Danube in Slovakia.

Acknowledgements

We thank the Slovak Scientific Grant Agency which supported our work within Research Project No.2/4102/99.

References

1. J. A. Alden, R. G. Compton, R. A. W. Dryfe, "Modelling electrode transients: the strongly implicit procedure", Journal of Applied Electrochemistry, Vol. 26, 1996, pp. 865–872.
2. H. I. Stone, "Iterative solution of implicit approximations of multidimensional partial differential equations", SIAM J. Numer. Anal., Vol. 5., No. 3, September 1968, pp. 530–558.
3. G. M. Megson, X. Chen, Automatic parallelization for a class of regular computations. World Scientific, 1997.
4. L. Hluchý, A. Godlevsky, L. Halada, M. Dobrucký, V. D. Tran, "Ground Water Flow Modeling in Distributed Environment", Proc. of DAPSYS'98, Workshop on Distributed and Parallel Systems, Budapest, 1998, pp. 155–161.
5. L. Hluchý, A. Godlevsky, L. Halada, M. Dobrucký, "Ground water flow modeling on PC cluster", ASIS 98 - Advanced Simulation of Systems, XXth International Workshop, Krnov, 1998, pp.15–20.
6. N. I. M. Gould, J. A. Scott, "Sparse approximate-inverse preconditioners using norm-minimization techniques", SIAM J. Sci. Comput., Vol. 19, No. 3, May 1998 pp. 605–627.
7. M. Benzi, M. Tuma, "A sparse approximate inverse preconditioner for nonsymetric linear systems", SIAM J. Sci. Comput., Vol. 19, No. 3, May 1998, pp. 968–994.
8. E. Chow, Y. Saad, "Approximate inverse preconditioner via sparse-sparse iterations", SIAM J. Sci. Comput., Vol. 19, No. 3, May 1998, pp. 995–1023.
9. P. Tsompanopoulou, E. Vavalis, "ADI method cubic spline collocation discretizations of elliptic PDEs", SIAM J. Sci. Comput., Vol. 19, No. 2, March 1998, pp. 341–363.
10. M. Rim, R. Jain, "Valid Transformation: A New Class of Loop Transformations for High-Level Synthesis and Pipelined Scheduling Applications", IEEE Trans. on Parallel and Distributed Systems, Vol. 7, No. 4, April 1996, pp. 399–410.
11. A. Agarwal, D. A. Kranz, V. Natarajan, "Automatic Partitioning of Parallel Loops and Data Arrays for Distributed Shared-Memory Multiprocessors", IEEE Trans. on Parallel and Distributed Systems, Vol. 6, No. 9, September 1995, pp. 943–962.
12. A. Darte, Y. Robert, "Constructive Methods for Scheduling Uniform Loop Nets", IEEE Trans. on Parallel and Distributed Systems, Vol. 5, No. 8, August 1994, pp. 814–822.
13. A. Basemann, B. Reichel, C. Schelthoff, "Preconditioned CG methods for sparse matrices on massively parallel machines", Parallel Computing, vol. 23, 1997, pp. 381-398.

PARALLEL COMPUTATIONAL MAGNETO-FLUID DYNAMICS

R. KEPPENS

FOM-Institute Rijnhuizen, P.O. Box 1207, 3430 BE Nieuwegein, The Netherlands,
E-mail: keppens@rijnh.nl

G. TÓTH

Department of Atomic Physics, Eötvös University, Pázmány Péter sétány 1, 1117
Budapest, Hungary, E-mail: gtoth@hermes.elte.hu

J.P. GOEDBLOED

FOM-Institute Rijnhuizen, E-mail: goedbloed@rijnh.nl

In a Priority Program on Massively Parallel Computing, eight Dutch research groups (http://www.phys.uu.nl/~mpr/) cooperate since 1995 to develop new algorithms and software to simulate the non-linear dynamics of thermonuclear, geophysical, and astrophysical plasmas. As one result of this collaboration, the general-purpose **Versatile Advection Code** (http://www.phys.uu.nl/~toth/) has demonstrated excellent scaling properties across a variety of shared and distributed memory architectures. VAC uses various shock capturing numerical methods with explicit, semi-implicit, or fully implicit time stepping on 1, 2, or 3 dimensional finite volume grids. Portability to different hardware platforms is achieved by preprocessors that can translate the code from Fortran 90 both forwards to High Performance Fortran and backwards to Fortran 77. With this code, we simulate complicated magnetized plasma phenomena where simultaneous large-scale and small-scale structures evolve on different timescales. We investigate fundamental hydromagnetic instabilities in multi-dimensional, fully non-linear regimes, as well as astrophysically oriented applications. An overview of recently investigated phenomena includes: the role of the magnetic field in Rayleigh-Taylor and Kelvin-Helmholtz instabilities, stellar wind models and solar coronal mass ejections, and accretion flows onto compact objects (black holes).

1 Introduction

The cluster project on Parallel Computational Magneto-Fluid Dynamics of the Dutch Science Organization (NWO) has developed and applied powerful numerical tools to CPU-intensive research applications. The eight groups involved are collaboratively progressing in nonlinear magnetohydrodynamical (MHD) simulations of astrophysical, thermonuclear and geophysical interest, in tailoring parallel eigenvalue solvers to MHD spectroscopy, and in implementing sophisticated parallel ocean circulation codes. A series of annual reports document our achievements[a]. The coding efforts of the past three years resulted in various optimized, scalable codes. Both the data parallel and the message passing paradigms have led to successful implementations on various vector and parallel platforms.

A particular highlight in this collaboration is the continued development of the Versatile Advection Code (VAC [13,16]) to simulate nonlinear fluid or plasma dynamics. The code is versatile with respect to (1) applications (shallow water, Euler, Navier-Stokes, or magnetohydrodynamic equations), (2) geometry (1D, 1.5D, 2D, 2.5D or 3D), (3) computer platforms (PC, workstation, vector to distributed memory platform [17]), (4) high resolution spatial [14] and (5) temporal discretizations [18,8]. This state-of-the-art software package has grown out of intense collaboration between researchers from the astrophysics and thermonuclear physics groups with specialists in numerical analysis and computer science. A wide variety of applications has been or can be addressed, thanks to VAC's versatility for choosing a problem-specific optimal solution strategy. The philosophy behind VAC is using a single software with options and switches for various problems, rather than developing a different method or version for each problem separately. The advantage of such a general approach is a reduction of overall time for software development, easier maintenance, compatibility of different parts, automatic extension of new features to all existing applications. The price of the general approach is some added complexity in the source code.

2 Numerical and parallel aspects

VAC aims to *solve a set of conservation laws with source terms.* Implemented are: the simple transport equation for test purposes, the Euler equations of compressible hydrodynamics with adiabatic or full energy equation, and the resistive MHD equations with isothermal or full energy equation. Source terms for external gravity, heat conduction, and viscosity can be included as library subroutines, e.g. the Euler equations with the viscosity source terms are the compressible Navier-Stokes equations. Other source terms can be defined in user written subroutines.

All equation-modules are written in the original *Loop Annotation Syntax* (LASY [15]). The LASY notation essentially generalizes the Fortran 90 array syntax with patterns that are expanded according to dimensionality. This source code is then translated to Fortran 90 by a Perl preprocessor for a D-dimensional simulation of the selected physics problem. As a result, the

---

[a]Rijnhuizen Report 98-234, MPP-CMFD team, eds. R. Keppens and J.P. Goedbloed, 1998, available at http://www.phys.uu.nl/~mpr/mpr98.ps.gz.

number of spatial dimensions $1 \leq D \leq 3$ and the number of components $D \leq C \leq 3$ for the vector variables (e.g. the momentum and the magnetic field) may have 6 different combinations. The equations can be solved on a 1, 2 or 3D structured grid with *conservative finite volume discretization*. Structured grids include Cartesian, polar and spherical grids as trivial examples, but they can be used in more complicated geometries as well. In 1D and 2D both slab and cylindrical symmetry may be assumed for the ignored dimension(s). Boundary conditions are implemented by two layers of *ghost cells* around the mesh. For each boundary and each variable the type of the boundary can be defined as periodic, symmetric, antisymmetric, open, fixed, etc. Time dependent or more complicated boundary conditions can be realized via user defined subroutines.

Several algorithms are available for solving the differential equations: The Flux Corrected Transport scheme (FCT [2]), two Total Variation Diminishing schemes with a Roe-type Riemann solver (TVD [3] and TVD-MUSCL [21]), and a Lax-Friedrichs type TVD scheme (TVDLF [22,14]) with no Riemann solver. The TVD schemes maintain monotone profiles by appropriately limiting the slopes of the variables. Since they make use of an approximate Riemann solver, they resolve discontinuities without spurious oscillations, but the Riemann solver is specific to the equation module. The TVD Lax-Friedrichs scheme has proven to be more robust, but slightly more diffusive. All these schemes are *second order in space and are able to simulate shocks and other discontinuities* as well as smooth flows. Multidimensional equations are solved either by Strang-type dimensional splitting [12], or by adding the fluxes from all directions simultaneously. Source terms may be included in a time split fashion or added together with fluxes.

When the MHD equations are solved, the solenoidal condition on the magnetic field can be enforced in several ways. We only mention the possibility of using a projection scheme [1] which requires the solution of a Poisson equation. The Poisson equation is solved by the Conjugate Gradient (CG) and the stabilized Bi-Conjugate Gradient (BiCGSTAB [20]) methods, both implemented in LASY syntax. Fully implicit and semi-implicit time integration schemes [8,18] are also available, both for time accurate and steady state problems. The Jacobian matrix is then evaluated numerically. The resulting linear system is solved by a block tridiagonal solver in 1D, while in multidimensional simulations, preconditioned [19] iterative schemes are used.

We compared the performance of the code [17] on different computer platforms, including work stations and vector and parallel supercomputers. We make use of High Performance Fortran (HPF) to run on distributed memory architectures. Therefore, the Perl script `f90tohpf` inserts HPF distribution directives into the translated LASY source code for all arrays defined over the computational grid. This automatic insertion allows one to experiment with different distributions, like (BLOCK,BLOCK) or (*,BLOCK) for a 2D problem. The optimal distribution for the particular problem and computer platform is then easily determined from scaling experiments and then used for production simulations. We reported scaling for HPF execution on a Cray T3D, Cray T3E and IBM SP platforms. Timing results for the latter two platforms for a specific 3D MHD problem are given below, alongside the vector Cray C90 performance.

3 Research Achievements with VAC

VAC has been applied to investigate non-linear plasma dynamics, like Rayleigh-Taylor [9] and Kelvin-Helmholtz instabilities [5,4], stellar winds [6] and accretion disks [11], and solar physics applications like prominences and waves in coronal loops. The number of applications is still increasing. Here, we briefly discuss some of these recent results.

- *Rayleigh-Taylor instability.* We simulated the development of the Rayleigh-Taylor instability [9], causing a heavy compressible gas to mix into a lighter one underneath, in an external gravitational field. We compared the development of this instability in two and three spatial dimensions, without and with magnetic fields. Adding an initial horizontal magnetic field, the mixing process is slowed down and may suppress the development of secondary Kelvin-Helmholtz instabilities in shear flow regions entirely.

- *Kelvin-Helmholtz instability.* We performed a numerical study of this instability occuring at the interface of a shear flow configuration in compressible magnetohydrodynamics. The calculations cover 2D [5] and 3D [4] configurations. The 2D results considered an initial magnetic field aligned with the shear flow, and analyzed the differences between cases where the field is unidirectional everywhere and where the field changes sign at the interface. In the latter case, the initial current sheet gets amplified by the vortex flow and can become unstable to tearing instabilities forming magnetic islands. Thereby, the evolution of such a current-vortex sheet eventually transits to magnetically modified turbulence (Fig. 1). The 3D simulations considered shear flow in a cylindrical jet configuration, embedded in a uniform magnetic field. The growth of linear perturbations at specified poloidal and axial mode numbers demonstrated intricate non-linear coupling effects. We identified the physical mechanims leading to induced secondary Kelvin-Helmholtz instabilities at higher mode numbers (Fig. 2). The initially weak magnetic field becomes locally dominant in the non-linear dynamics before and during saturation.

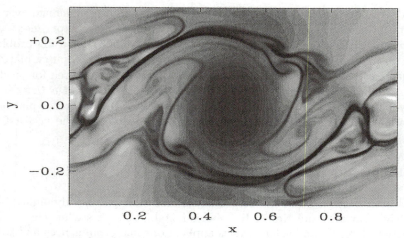

Figure 1. This figure displays the density structure in a two-dimensional current-vortex sheet evolution when it transits to magnetically modified turbulence. This occurs when a Kelvin-Helmholtz unstable shear flow triggers small-scale reconnection events.

In Table 1, we list execution times per time step for this 3D MHD problem (8 unknowns per grid point) on several platforms. The resolution was held fixed at $50 \times 100 \times 100$ (alltogether 4 million unknowns), which is still a modest resolution. The code requires roughly 400 MB memory on the Cray C90, where we reach 388.4 Mflops on a single CPU which is 40 % of the theoretical peak performance. When we exploit autotasking on the shared

Table 1. Timings on various platforms and number of PEs, in seconds per time step for the Kelvin-Helmholtz 3D ($50 \times 100 \times 100$) MHD simulation. Speedup factors are given between brackets and the percentage of time spent on the Poisson solver is indicated.

Platform	1PE	2PE	4PE	8PE	16PE
Cray C90	8.40	4.32 [×1.9]	2.27 [×3.7]	–	–
	19.5%	19.4%	19.4%	–	–
Cray T3E	–	–	–	24.3	12.9 [×1.9]
	–	–	–	16.4%	16.6%
IBM SP	–	–	14.3	7.7 [×1.8]	4.2 [×3.4]
	–	–	15.2%	15.6%	16.6%

Figure 2. The three-dimensional density structure for a magnetized, jet-like shear flow. Kelvin-Helmholtz instabilities disrupt the originally circular jet cross-section, and cause localized density depletions (dark) and enhancements (bright). At the time shown, non-linear magnetic effects play a dominant role, with the strongest fields coinciding with low density regions.

memory C90 (using `f90 -O scalar3,vector3,task3,inline3`), we reach an efficiency (Speedup/Number of PEs) of 97 % on 2 CPUs and 91 % on 4 CPUs. For the distributed memory platforms IBM SP and Cray T3E, we find similarly good speedup (see Table 1). For these HPF runs, the distribution was set to (`*,BLOCK,BLOCK`). On both platforms, the Portland Group `pghpf` 2.4-4 compiler was used with optimization level `-O3`. The $\nabla \cdot \mathbf{B} = 0$ condition was enforced through a projection scheme using 20 iterations of the Conjugate Gradient method to solve the Poisson equation. The table lists the percentage of time spent on the Poisson problem as well: it clearly scales both in shared and distributed memory execution.

• *Stellar wind and accretion flow.* We simulated stellar winds [6] and accretion flows [11]. Current modeling efforts include both steady-state and time-dependent transonic outflows from magnetized, rotating stars [7]. For steady-state models, we efficiently exploit implicit time stepping. Specifically, Fig. 3 presents an axisymmetric, stationary solar wind solution that takes into account both the solar rotation and the presence of an equatorial dead zone.

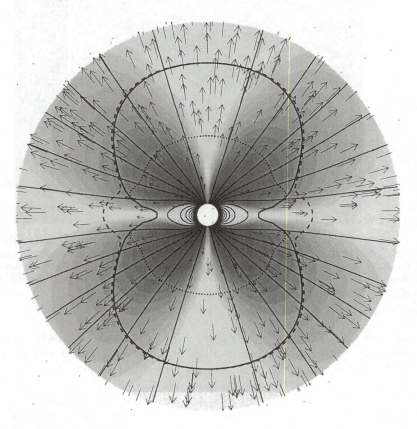

Figure 3. An example of a stellar wind calculated with the Versatile Advection Code. Solid lines indicate the coronal magnetic field structure, with both open and closed field line regions. Thermally driven plasma escapes freely (vectors) along the open field lines, thereby continuously accelerating from subslow to superfast speeds. The three MHD transonic critical curves are indicated (hourglass curves). The grey-scale gives the absolute value of the toroidal magnetic field, built up by the stellar rotation.

4 Conclusions

We have tackled various hydrodynamic and magnetohydrodynamic physics issues where powerful numerical tools are a necessity. The examples presented here, all calculated with the Versatile Advection Code, show how we succesfully modeled axisymmetric solar and stellar winds, exploiting implicit time stepping strategies, or how we use parallel computing to investigate the non-linear evolution of Kelvin-Helmholtz instabilities in 3D MHD. We are extending our stellar wind simulations to fully 3D, time-dependent phenomena, along the lines of recent work by Linker et al [10], and we can now study Kelvin-Helmholtz behaviour in driven plasma loops. Large-scale computing for plasma physics and astrophysics research promises to yield enormous assets in the coming millenium.

Acknowledgments. VAC is developed in the project on *Parallel Computational Magneto-Fluid Dynamics* funded by NWO. Computer time is sponsored by NCF. GT is supported by OTKA D 25519 and a Bolyai Fellowship.

References

1. J. U. Brackbill and D. C. Barnes, *J. Comput. Phys.* **35**, 426 (1980).
2. J. P. Boris and D. L. Book, *J. Comput. Phys.* **11**, 38 (1973).
3. A. Harten, *J. Comput. Phys.* **49**, 357 (1983).
4. R. Keppens and G. Tóth, *Phys. of Plasmas* **6**, 1461 (1999).
5. R. Keppens et al , *J. Plasma Phys.* **61**, 1 (1999).
6. R. Keppens and J. P. Goedbloed, *Astron. Astrophys.* **343**, 251 (1999).
7. R. Keppens and J. P. Goedbloed, *Astrophys. J.* **530**, February 20 (2000).
8. R. Keppens et al , *Int. J. for Numer. Meth. in Fluids* **30**, 335 (1999).
9. R. Keppens and G. Tóth, *Lect. Notes in Comp. Sci.* **1573**, 680 (1999).
10. J.A. Linker et al , *J. Geophys. Res.* **104**, 9809 (1999).
11. D. Molteni et al , *Astrophys. J.* **516**, 411 (1999).
12. G. Strang, *SIAM J. Numer. Anal.* **5**, 506 (1968).
13. G. Tóth, *Astrophys. Lett. & Comm.* **34**, 245 (1996).
14. G. Tóth and D. Odstrčil, *J. Comput. Phys.* **128**, 82 (1996).
15. G. Tóth, *J. Comput. Phys.* **138**, 981 (1997).
16. G. Tóth, *Lect. Notes in Comp. Sci.* **1225**, 253 (1997).
17. G. Tóth and R. Keppens, *Lect. Notes in Comp. Sci.* **1401**, 368 (1998).
18. G. Tóth et al , *Astron. Astrophys.* **332**, 1159 (1998).
19. A. van der Ploeg et al , *Lect. Notes in Comp. Sci.* **1225**, 421 (1997).
20. H. A. van der Vorst, *SIAM J. Sci. Statist. Comput.* **13**, 631 (1992).
21. B. van Leer, *J. Comput. Phys.* **32**, 101 (1979).
22. H. C. Yee, *NASA TM-101088*, (1989).

PARALLEL PROCESSING OF NATURAL LANGUAGE PARSERS

M. P. VAN LOHUIZEN

Parallel and Distributed Systems Group – ITS – Delft University of Technology
E-mail: mpvl@acm.org

In this paper we describe an implementation of a parallel parser for natural language. We first indicate why these applications are typically hard to parallelize. We then present a work stealing approach for symmetric shared-memory multiprocessors that minimizes overhead by dynamically controlling the granularity of work distribution. In addition, we will explain how we deal with concurrent access of the centralized chart.

1 Introduction

The increasing demand for accuracy and robustness for today's natural language processing brings on an increasing demand for computing power. Almost all of today's NLP systems use unification-based parsers. A unification-based parser is basically a context-free parser augmented with unification (cf. Prolog), which can be seen as an extra constraint on the context-free backbone. Such parsers are mostly used for syntactical analysis, but can also be used for, e.g., semantical analysis. Unification-based parsers are often also the most computationally expensive component. In order to let NLP systems be responsive, NLP systems are often limited to what extent they cover a certain domain of discourse. Therefore, speeding up parsers cannot only allow for faster response times, but also allow for a better linguistic accuracy and robustness. In this paper we will present a technique for parallelizing unification-based parsers.

Typically, processing unifications accounts for the bulk of the processing time. One could therefore attempt to parallelize this operation. Even though unification is known to be hard to parallelize (it is not in Nick's Class),[1,2] some researchers have taken this approach.[3,4] A disadvantage of this approach, however, is that the context-free part remains sequential. In addition, the fine-grained parallelism potentially yields a lot of overhead.

For several of the reasons mentioned above, most research has focussed on exploiting parallelism at the context-free level by distributing the individual unification operations evenly amongst the processors. Most of the attempts, however, were not very successful, sometimes even obtaining a slowdown for a two-processor setup.[5,6,7] Some of our experiments[8] indicate that many of the failed attempts can be attributed to the nature of the parallelism inherent in unification-based parsers. In this paper, we will present some of these experimental results. In addition, we will present a work stealing approach that minimizes overhead to a maximum by incorporating a mechanism to dynamically adapt the granularity of distribution.

2 Related Work

Parallel parsing for NLP in specific has been researched extensively. For example, Tomita[9] presented a parallel LR parser, and Thompson[5] presented some implementations of parallel chart parsers. Nijholt[10] gives a more theoretical overview of parallel chart parsers. There has also been research focusing on the parallelization of alternatives for conventional parsing.[11,12] Adriaens and Hahn[13] give an extensive survey of parallelism in NLP.

Nevertheless, the presented solutions usually either did not yield acceptable speedup or were very specific to one application. Recently, however, several NLP systems have been parallelized successfully. Pontelli et al.[14] show how two existing NLP applications were successfully parallelized using the parallel Prolog environment ACE. Even though a great deal of NLP applications are written in Prolog, the ones that are not cannot benefit from this approach. Our approach can bring a solution to this category of systems. We even suspect that our parallelization technique can be used to parallelize tabular Prologs (like XSB and Dialog).

Manousopoulou et al.[15] discuss a parallel parser generator based on the EuPAGE system. This system builds on top of Orchid and PVM, using a distributed shared-memory model. Besides being very specific to parsing, this solution exploits coarse-grained parallelism which proved to be unusable for the Delta system (the subject of our research). Many other natural language parsers will not be able to benefit from this approach either.[6] Our approach provides a solution in case fine-grained parallelism is required.

On the scheduling side, our approach shows close resemblance to the Cilk-5 system.[16] It implements work stealing using similar techniques and also minimizes overhead according to principle of moving as much of the overhead as possible from the workers to the thieves. An important difference, though, is that our scheduler was designed with tabulation algorithms in mind (cf. memoization and dynamic programming). This means it had to be optimized for frequent locking by all threads of central repository of intermediate results. In addition, our approach allows to steal categories of tasks depending on the need for more fine-grained distribution.

3 Analysis of Parallelism

One of the most popular techniques to parse natural language is *chart parsing*. It is often preferred over extended LR techniques, because it provides a more natural approach to deal with the tremendous amount of ambiguities inherent in natural language grammars. The chart in chart parsing refers to a global table in which all intermediate parsing results (called *items*) are stored. The chart is often accompanied with an agenda, which records all items that still need processing. In this case, the

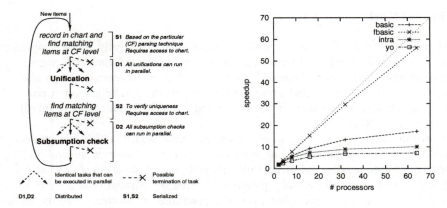

Figure 1. Left: A typical cycle in the parsing process. It shows where the possibilities for parallelism lie. Figure 2. Right: Maximum attainable speedups for several distribution schemes. Both basic and fbasic use the agenda as a work queue, implementing dynamic load-balancing. basic, however, implements a less fine-grained distribution by grouping certain unification operations, unconditionally. basic is probably the most used distribution technique. Both yo and intra implement a static load-balancing technique. Obviously, only fbasic yields a scalable solution. See Van Lohuizen[8] for more details.

parsing process may proceed as follows. First an item is fetched from the agenda. For each matching item in the chart (based on the CF rules), a unification operation is performed. If it succeeds, the chart is used to verify the uniqueness of the item. Finally, if the item had not been derived before, it is added to the chart and recorded on the agenda to repeat the cycle. As can be seen, chart parsing is similar in concept to techniques like memoization and dynamic programming. An outline of one complete parsing cycle is sketched in figure 1.

There are several problems that make chart parsers particularly hard to parallelize: contention, highly stochastic task graphs, and a lack of locality. The contention problem directly follows from the need to record all intermediate results in a centralized chart. It is required that the operation of adding an item to the chart and finding all its matches at the CF level be an atomic operation, mainly to prevent doing double work. Although intelligent indexing can reduce the cost of this operation considerably, it can still be large enough to cause significant holdup.

The highly stochastic task graphs characteristic for unification-based parsing also form a problem. Both the number of tasks being spawned by each task and the execution times of the different tasks can vary widely. The first variation is caused by the great variation in the number of items that can match an item that is being added to the chart (from none to many thousands). The second variation is caused by the great variation in the execution time of unifications. (It is possible that some operations execute in the order of several percent of the total parsing time, whereas many others terminate after a single comparison.[6]) The latter variation poses the biggest problem by far, moreover because predicting the execution times of tasks takes about as much time as actually executing the tasks (both run $O(n)$).

We have performed a thorough analysis of task graphs derived from our natural language parser, Delta.[8] Delta uses a double dotted chart parser and an average sized wide-coverage grammar for the Dutch language, comprising 120 morphological rules, 360 syntactical rules, and about 3600 dictionary entries. The task graphs were used to simulate a variety of distribution techniques. The simulations produced a scheduling of the tasks amongst the processors, using best case scenarios. This allowed us to investigate the maximum attainable speedup for the respective distribution technique. If even the best case scenarios did not yield a well-balanced scheduling, we would know that it would be impossible to attain acceptable speedup. As we expected, most distribution techniques were not suitable. Some of the results are illustrated in figure 1. The results showed that only a centralized, dynamic load-balancing scheme—allowing each unification operation to be scheduled independently—yields a scalable distribution technique.

4 Implementation

In this section, we will describe the implementation of our parallel parser, which is aimed at circumventing the problems described in the previous section. First we will give a description of the overall architecture. After that we will describe the most important details.

Considering the frequent access to the shared chart, and given the need for dynamic load-balancing, we have chosen to base the design on a shared memory model. In addition, we have chosen a work stealing approach, rather than spawning a new thread for each task: From Graham[17] we know that if we create a new thread for each task, it will be possible to achieve at least half the optimal speedup. However, as we just mentioned, the only way to achieve acceptable speedup is to distribute each individual unification. For typical NLP systems, this can amount to hundreds of thousands of threads per sentence. We would really like to avoid the overhead that is incurred by this. Therefore, each processor is assigned a single thread.

At the parsing level each thread corresponds to a worker, which functions much like a sequential parser. Each worker holds enough context to complete an entire parsing cycle (see figure 2). Although the chart is shared amongst the workers, each worker maintains its own agenda. Only a small amount of initial work (one task for each word) is stored in a centralized agenda. A single worker processes all work associated with a word, during which it puts newly derived work on its agenda. So far, apart from synchronizing through the chart, each worker operates independently.

Obviously, since a sentence typically consists of only a dozen of words, some threads are bound to be out of work at an early stage. At this point, threads may start stealing work from other threads. The philosophy behind the design of the work stealing scheme was to incur as little overhead as possible in the case threads are not stealing, and to make sure that thieves return to normal operation as soon as possible.

In order to achieve the latter, we implemented the following stealing scheme. We know that stealing of work should be able to take place at the granularity of unification and subsumption operations. However, for large grammars typically 80% of the unification operations fail,[4] meaning no new work will be derived. A stolen subsumption will only yield new work when it is the last completed. Typically, the chances of a steal resulting in new work decreases as work is stolen further down the parsing cycle. In order to circumvent this problem, we allow stealing at multiple points. Each thread maintains a *stealing stack* with multiple entry points that indicate what work can be stolen. Typically, a thief will steal work from the lowest valid entry point on the stack, representing the tasks most likely to result in new work.

The entry points are filled as follows. The parser's code contains several for loops that can be performed in parallel. Before entering a loop, the parser puts a *signature* at the appropriate level of the stack to indicate how work can be stolen. On completion of the loop, the signature is removed. A worker's agenda is permanently marked for stealing at the lowest entry point.

When a thief steals work from a victim, it copies all necessary data from the victim to proceed independently. The benefit of this approach is that no context need to be saved at the worker side. Copying typically gets more expensive at a further stage in the parsing cycle (although it does not involve copying large structures), whereas fetching from the agenda incurs no extra overhead. The stealing stack also functions to let thieves perform the cheapest stealing operations possible.

Synchronization between worker and thief has been optimized to move as much of the overhead as possible to the thief by using a Dijkstra like mutual exclusion protocol.[18,16] The protocol is illustrated in figure 3. As long as no stealing is taking place, workers will not have to resort to an expensive lock. In addition, a worker will only need to lock if a thief is stealing at the same or higher stealing level (as defined by the stack). This prevents, for example, a thief from holding up a worker that is quickly iterating over small subsumption tasks while the thief is fetching work from the victim's agenda. The protocol is provided by the scheduler by means of macros.

Until now we have discussed how we deal with highly stochastic task graphs. We will now discuss our approach to the before mentioned problem of contention for access to the chart. The solution is quite straightforward. Instead of locking the chart unconditionally, the worker uses a trylock. If it succeeds it will proceed as usual. If it fails, it will simply record the associated work in a serializer queue, and defer its processing to the worker currently holding the lock. This is much like synchronizing

Worker/Victim	Thief

```
before loop:                        steal work:
1   stack[L].sig = someSig;         12  Determine victim
                                     13  victim.lock;
each iteration                       14  victim->L = S;
2   isBusy=YES;                      15  while (!victim->isBusy) {}
3   if (L >= A)                      16  Iterate using victim->stack[L].sig;
4       isBusy=NO;                   17  victim->L = 0;
5       self.lock;                   18  victim.unlock;
6       Iterate
7       self.unlock;                 perform obtained work:
8   else                             19  self.invoke;
9       Iterate
10      isBusy=NO;
```

Figure 3. Simplified pseudocode of Victim/Thief protocol. A and S represents the current granularity level of the worker and victim, respectively. L represents the smallest level of granularity at which threads are currently stealing from the victim. stack[L].sig indicates whether there is work and how it can be stolen from the victim at the respective level. Line 3 enables a worker to only lock when a thief is stealing from the same or higher entry point on the stack. In the current implementation, a busy loop is used as part of the mechanism that ensures a thief will always steal at the coarsest level of granularity. Note that *Iterate* means obtaining a new task, not executing it. Obviously, executing a task is done outside the critical region. For this reason, variables used for iterating may not be used inside the body of the loop. In this case, a copy must be maintained. Apart from this fact, only lines 1, 2, 3, and 10 and a memory fence between line 2 and 3 contribute to a worker's overhead.

by sending messages. After the work has been queued, the worker can continue by fetching new work from its agenda.

Crucial to a good functioning of the scheduler is an efficient work queue for both the agenda and serializing. The scheduler provides a generic FIFO queue which allows thread-safe, independent operation of reader and writer without locking. It is implemented by a cyclic buffer, which may grow dynamically. Only when the buffer is enlarged, readers and writers need to be briefly synchronized with a lock.

5 Performance

Both the parser's and scheduler's implementation are in a preliminary stage of development. There are several points of interest in this initial phase. Firstly, we investigated the overhead in the one processor case. To measure this, we compared the execution time T_S of the sequential parser with the execution time of a one-processor parallel version T_1, the major difference between the two versions being the mutual exclusion protocol surrounding each iteration (up to the subsumption level). The result was $T_1/T_S = 1.03$, which is completely acceptable.

Secondly, we investigated whether there was enough parallelism to allow speedup. This depends for a great deal on the grammar and the length and type of sentence. We were able to obtain speedups of 1.7 to 1.8 for an average sized sentence on a two processor 266 MHz Pentium-II.[a] Running multiple threads on a single processor yielded scalable behavior for more than 2 threads. Considering the early stage of development, however, it is difficult to give accurate performance results.

On the other hand, these results were obtained while there is still a lot of room for improvement. Firstly, there are still a lot of platform specific optimizations to be done. Also, the parser does not yet allow distributing at the finest level of granularity (the measurements for T_1/T_S, however, did include the mutex protocol in the iteration). Considering that there are many more optimizations left to do we are optimistic that an even better speedup can be obtained.

6   Conclusions and Future Research

The first performance results are encouraging. In addition, we will investigate the following possible improvements. Currently, the scheduler ensures a thief will always steal at the coarsest level of granularity provided by *any* worker. This is basically accomplished by cycling past all threads for one level, before entering the next. It might be much more efficient to just ensure a thief will steal from a worker's lowest entry point, disregarding whether other workers have lower entries.

The serializer is also still far from optimized. Apart from optimizing the interface to the work queues we also need to find a good balance between efficiency and processing work as soon as possible. Finally, we want to generalize the scheduler so that it allows for different agenda's per worker.

On the parsing side we can remark the following. The most complex issue of parallelizing a chart parser is to make sure that no work is done twice. Once a clear parallelization scheme was set, it proved to be fairly straightforward to parallelize the parser, given the functionality provided by the scheduling package. The changes entailed maintaining copies of some iteration variables, queueing work at some continuation and serialization points, among other things. Another requirement was that the unification algorithm be non-destructive (thread-safe). Such algorithms are known however.

The resulting parallel parser will be used for further research on parallel parsing such as the ability to efficiently parse a variety of sentences, behavior for different grammars, and computationally expensive extensions to natural language parsers.

---

[a] Unfortunately, we did not have a machine with more processors at our disposal at the time of measuring.

References

1. Cynthia Dwork, Paris Kanellakis, and John Mitchell. On the sequential nature of unification. *Journal of Logic Programming*, 1(1):35–50, 1984.
2. Hiroto Yasuura. On parallel computational complexity of unification. In *Proc. of the Int. Conf. on Fifth Generation Computer Systems*, pp. 235–243, Amsterdam, 1984.
3. T. Fujioka, H. Tomabechi, O. Furuse, and H. Iida. Parallelization technique for quasi-destructive graph unification algorithm. In *Information Processing Society of Japan SIG Notes 90-NL-80*, 1990.
4. H. Tomabechi. Quasi-destructive graph unifications. In *Proc. of the 29th Annual Meeting of the ACL*, Berkeley, CA, 1991.
5. Henry S. Thompson. Parallel parsers for context-free grammars–two actual implementations compared. In Adriaens and Hahn [13].
6. Günther Görz, Marcus Kesseler, Jörg Spilker, and Hans Weber. Research on architectures for integrated speech/language systems in Verbmobil. In *The 16th International Conf. on Computational Linguistics*, volume 1, pp. 484–489, Copenhagen, DK, 1996.
7. J.P.M. de Vreught. A practical comparison between parallel tabular recognizers. In *Proc. of the 6th Twente Workshop on Language Technology (TWLT6)*, pp. 63–70, 1993.
8. Marcel P. van Lohuizen. Simulating communication of parallel unification-based parsers. Parallel and Distributed Systems Reports Series PDS-1998-008, Delft University of Technology, 1998.
9. M. Tomita. *Efficient parsing for natural language*. Kluwer Academic Publishers, Boston, MA, 1985.
10. A. Nijholt. Overview of parallel parsing strategies. In M. Tomita, editor. *Current Issues in Parsing Technology*. Kluwer Academic Publishers, Norwell, MA, 1991.
11. Hiroaki Kitano. *Speech-To-Speech Translation: A Massively Parallel Memory-Based Approach*. Natural Language Processing and Machine Translation. Kluwer Academic Publishers, Dordrecht, The Netherlands, 1994.
12. Peter Neuhaus and Udo Hahn. Restricted parallelism in object-oriented lexical parsing. In *Proc. of the 16th Int. Conf. on Computational Linguistics*, Copenhagen, DK, 1996.
13. Geert Adriaens and Udo Hahn, editors. *Parallel Natural Language Processing*. Ablex Publishing Corporation, Norwood, New Jersey, 1994.
14. E. Pontelli, G. Gupta, J. Wiebe, and D. Farwell. Natural language multiprocessing: A case study. In *Proc. of the 15th Nat. Conf. on Artifical Intelligence*, 1998.
15. A.G. Manousopoulou, G. Manis, P. Tsanakas, and G. Papakonstantinou. Automatic generation of portable parallel natural language parsers. In *Proc. of the 9th Conf. on Tools with Artificial Intelligence (ICTAI '97)*, pp. 174–177. 1997.
16. Matteo Frigo, Charles E. Leiserson, and Keigh H. Randall. The implementation of the Cilk-5 multithreaded language. *ACM SIGPLAN Notices*, 33(5):212–223, May 1998.
17. R.L. Graham. Bounds on multiprocessing timing anomalies. *SIAM J. Appl. Math.*, 17(2):416–429, 1969.
18. E. W. Dijkstra. Solution of a problem in concurrent programming control. *Communications of the ACM*, 8(9):569, September 1965.

THREE-DIMENSIONAL DIRECT NUMERICAL SIMULATION OF FLOW PROBLEMS WITH ELECTROMAGNETIC CONTROL ON PARALLEL SYSTEMS

O. POSDZIECH AND R. GRUNDMANN

Institute for Aerospace Engineering, Dresden University of Technology,
D-01062 Dresden, Germany
E-mail: {posdzie|grundman}@tfd.mw.tu-dresden.de

S. SEIDL AND W.E. NAGEL

Center for High-Performance Computing, Dresden University of Technology,
D-01062 Dresden, Germany
E-mail: {seidl|nagel}@zhr.tu-dresden.de

Direct Numerical Simulation is used to study the impact of electromagnetic forces on flows with low electrical conductivity. The numerical solution of the governing equations requires a maximum on computational power. Parallel systems with a large number of processing elements are predestined to realize extensive parameter studies in a justifiable time. As this application consumes a significant part of the high performance computing capacity at Dresden University of Technology, it is obvious to analyze the parallel performance to reveal possible improvements in terms of MFLOPS and scalability. We present the parallelization of a spectral element code for an efficient solving of the 3D Navier-Stokes equations by means of the message passing system MPI. Based on VAMPIR, we have analyzed computation/communication patterns, performance and scalability behavior. Finally, the paper describes the analysis process and the applied optimization techniques.

1 Introduction

Computational Fluid Dynamics takes up an increasing share in the ubiquitous problem of flowing materials. The numerical solution of the governing equations requires a maximum on computational power and memory capacity. One branch of CFD deals with the Direct Numerical Simulation of flows, where all physically relevant scales have to be resolved. Large vector computers or massively parallel systems are used to perform this task. During the last decade, DNS has become an important tool in the field of flow control. Active or passive methods to reduce the drag or increase the heat transfer are of enormous technological importance. External flows of electrically conducting fluids can be controlled by means of electromagnetic forces. Even if the conductivity is very modest, crossed electric and magnetic fields generate a Lorentz force (Fig. 1) that alters the flow structure near the surface.

The proposal of using electrodes and magnets to prevent boundary layer

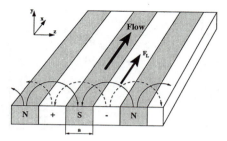

Figure 1. Generation of Lorentz force F_L by means of crossed electric and magnetic fields

growth in saltwater was made by Gailitis and Lielausis[1]. Tsinober[2] showed the postponement of flow separation on a circular cylinder. Several research groups have investigated experimentally or numerically electromagnetic flow control mainly on the turbulent boundary layer. They used either alternating pairs of electrodes and magnets to induce a streamwise Lorentz force (Henoch and Stace[3]), or a chessboardlike arrangement to induce a wall-normal force (O'Sullivan and Biringen[4]). It is well-known that the flow separation on bluff bodies can be postponed by means of suction or blowing, and that this mechanism leads to a considerably decrease of drag. Here, electromagnetic forces are used in order to prevent or delay separation. This has been studied on a circular cylinder within the regime of wake transition to turbulence.

After the description of the application of the spectral element method to flow control on a circular cylinder, the discretization method and the parallelization scheme are presented. The performance of the code has been analyzed by means of the tool VAMPIR (Nagel et al.[5]), where parallel performance and communication patterns are part of the findings. It will be shown that besides of the coarse-grain parallelization, a fine-grain part at critical sections of the code can improve the overall scalability. This is accomplished by a proper choice of parallel matrix operations, where the overall increase on communications is balanced by the faster algorithm.

2 Control of Flow Separation on a Circular Cylinder

The flow around infinitely long circular cylinders has, in spite of the simple geometry, a variety of flow phenomena in a small scope of Reynolds numbers (relation between inertial and viscous flow forces). Patterns like flow separation, the Kármán vortex street, or the transition to three-dimensionality and turbulence in the wake contribute mainly to the drag. By means of alternating

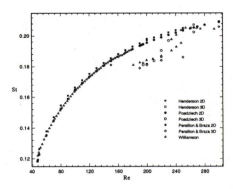

Figure 2. Strouhal number in dependence on Reynolds number

pairs of electrodes and magnets, wrapped around the cylinder surface, a tangentially induced Lorentz force is able to change this patterns and control the drag. The spectral element code *PRISM3D* was used for the DNS. The mesh consists of 186 spectral elements, and a polynomial order of 10 has been used. In order to minimize blocking effects, the outer boundaries have been located $70\,D$ from the cylinder (diameter D). Boundary conditions along the outer edges of the computational domain are uniform flow ($u = 1, v = 0$) across the inflow, top and bottom boundaries, and outflow ($(\mathbf{n} \cdot \nabla)\mathbf{u} = 0$) downstream. The pressure is set to zero at the outflow boundary, otherwise a high-order pressure condition of Neumann-type is used. The fluid velocity satisfies the no-slip condition at the cylinder surface. 3D calculations have been performed with 32 physical planes (16 Fourier modes) in the spanwise direction, where a FFT could be used due to periodicity. Runs were performed on a SGI Origin2000 and a CRAY T3E. The use of fine grids and a large number of spanwise planes is needed to correspond with the experiments. Besides, the code has to be executed for about 20,000 time steps to obtain sufficiently averaged flow statistics.

In order to validate the code, 2D and 3D calculations of the cylinder flow at Reynolds numbers from 47 to 280 have been carried out and compared to different numerical and experimental works (Henderson[6,7], Persillon and Braza[8], and Williamson[9]). The Strouhal number St, a nondimensional frequency of vortices in the unsteady wake, is used to compare the results. It can be seen in Fig. 2 that the 2D results corresponds accurately to the measurements, whereas 3D data show a bigger scatter. Curves for the drag coefficient show a similar trend compared to Fig. 2. We were mostly inter-

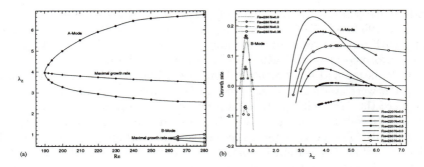

Figure 3. Spanwise wavelength of 3D instability in dependence on (a) Reynolds number and (b) interaction parameter

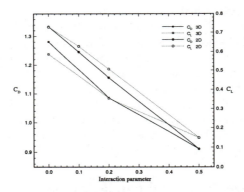

Figure 4. Comparison of drag and lift versus interaction parameter for 2D and 3D flow control at $Re = 220$

ested in the regime of 3D wake transition ($190 \leq Re \leq 300$), characterized by mode A and B instabilities (see Williamson[10]), under the effect of a Lorentz force. First, critical spanwise wavelengths λ_Z, where 3D perturbations are amplified, have to be determined. The stability analysis has been carried out on Navier-Stokes equations with only two Fourier modes in the spanwise direction. A small perturbation was introduced, and the temporal growth rate μ ($\mu < 0$ stable, $\mu > 0$ unstable) was determined. Lines of neutral stability and maximal growth rates in dependence on Reynolds number are shown in Fig. 3 (a). The mode A wavelength is approximately four times larger than that of mode B. At $Re > 260$, both mechanisms exist in parallel, but mode B determines the dynamics of the wake. Critical Reynolds numbers $Re_{C_A} \approx 190.2$, $\lambda_{Z_A} \approx 3.966\,D$, $Re_{C_B} \approx 261.1$, $\lambda_{Z_B} \approx 0.825\,D$ agree excellently with results presented in Barkley and Henderson[11]. Full 3D DNS have been performed at wavelengths with maximal growth rates.

Calculation and fundamental effects of the Lorentz force in terms of drag reduction were studied in Posdziech and Grundmann[12]. From numerical solutions of the Maxwell equations, a force profile $F_L(y) = J_0 \cdot B_0 \cdot e^{-\frac{\pi}{a}y}$ was obtained (y wall-normal coordinate, J_0 current density, B_0 magnetic induction at the wall). The Lorentz force accelerates near-wall fluid and stabilizes the velocity profile. Separation is postponed and the total drag decreases. The strength of electromagnetic forces is characterized by the interaction parameter $N = J_0\,B_0\,D\,\rho^{-1}\,U_\infty^{-2}$. The effect of the Lorentz force on the spanwise unstable wavelength was studied. It can be seen from Fig. 3 (b) that in case of mode A, the growth rate is lowered with increasing N, but the unstable regime broadens. At both Reynolds numbers (220, 280), the 3D flow returns to a 2D pattern, if the force is strong enough. The mode B instability shows a slightly different behavior. If the Lorentz force is weak ($N = 0.2$), the growth rate increases compared to the case without force ($N = 0.0$). This behavior has not been expected. It will need further investigations to explain the phenomena. Again, the maximal growth rate at each interaction parameter has been used to run full 3D DNS at $Re = 220$. In Fig. 4, 2D and 3D drag and lift coefficients are shown versus N. Both values decrease due to the applied electromagnetic force. The decrease in the 3D case is larger compared to the 2D calculations: $\Delta C_D = 15.2\%$ versus 13.4% and $\Delta C_L = 39.6\%$ versus 30.5%.

3 Computational Issues and Parallelization

The analyzed code solves 3D time-dependent incompressible Navier-Stokes equations on the basis of a parallel spectral element-Fourier discretization. The spectral element method combines the generality of finite element methods in handling of complex geometries with the fast convergence and high accuracy of global spectral models. The governing equations are momentum and continuity equations

$$\frac{\partial \mathbf{u}}{\partial t} + (\mathbf{u} \cdot \nabla)\mathbf{u} = -\frac{1}{\rho}\nabla p + \nu\nabla^2\mathbf{u} + \frac{1}{\rho}(\mathbf{J} \times \mathbf{B})\,, \quad \nabla \cdot \mathbf{u} = 0 \tag{1}$$

where $\mathbf{u}$ is the flow velocity, p the pressure, ν the kinematic viscosity, ρ the density, and $\frac{1}{\rho}(\mathbf{J} \times \mathbf{B})$ the Lorentz force per unit volume. It can be calculated decoupled from the Navier-Stokes equations and was added to the nonlinear term. A splitting scheme and a high-order time stepping method are used.

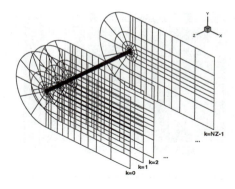

Figure 5. Parallel two-dimensional X-Y-planes in physical space

Further details of the code can be found in Henderson and Karniadakis[13].

The 3D velocity field is represented by Fourier interpolation through a set of evenly spaced planes in the spanwise (periodic) direction of the computational domain (see Fig. 5). The velocity field is determined in physical space by M planes, and in Fourier space by M+1 complex Fourier coefficients. Due to symmetries, the Fourier transform has the same number M of degrees of freedom as the physical space, so the same storage is required for both. The semi-discrete equations of the splitting scheme are transformed in Fourier space. Only the nonlinear interactions are computed in physical space and transformed back to Fourier space to finish a time step. The computation of each mode m can be done independently once the nonlinear terms have been calculated. The obvious parallelization is to compute mode m on processor m, so that the 3D computation becomes a set of M 2D problems computed in parallel. The identical meshes on each processor promise load balancing and good scalability. To form the nonlinear terms in physical space, we need to compute the Fourier transform of an array distributed across the processors. For each point, independent FFT's are performed in parallel, and after calculation of the nonlinear terms the field values are restored to its original frequency decomposition. This operation requires global communications that are performed by means of the message passing interface MPI.

Surprisingly, an appropriate VAMPIR testcase output, Fig. 6, reveals that the initial implementation is not load balanced although there is no theoretical necessity for that at first glance. The performance of the parallel code was determined on a CRAY T3E with up to 32 processing elements and different

182

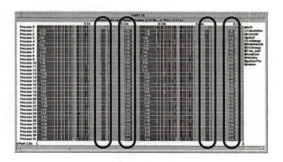

Figure 6. Two time steps of DNS code *PRISM3D* (initial implementation)

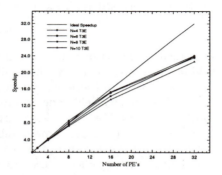

Figure 7. Speedup measured on a CRAY T3E for different problem sizes N (initial implementation)

problem sizes (increasing polynomial order N) as shown in Fig. 7. The runs with a coarse grid showed a good scalability up to 16 processors, but became poorer on larger numbers of PE's. A modest speedup was analyzed even on a small number of processors (4, 8) on finer grids. Deeper insight in the visualizations showed a nonsufficient balancing between processor 0 that solves the $0th$ Fourier mode and the other processors working on higher modes. Since mode 0 corresponds to the physical space, it contains the boundary conditions, where matrix operations are required. On the higher modes, only the interior is solved in Fourier space, and the processors finish its tasks considerably faster. After this solver routines, all PE's have to communicate in order to calculate the nonlinear term, so a Barrier arises. Ways to increase the parallelization in that part of the code are searched. The coarse-grain

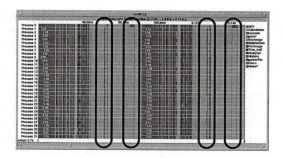

Figure 8. Two time steps of DNS code *PRISM3D* (load balanced implementation)

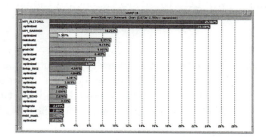

Figure 9. Comparison of the two versions of DNS code *PRISM3D*

parallel approach with weakly coupled x-y-planes has to be supplemented by a fine-grain part. But it should be kept in mind that the necessary rise on communication between the processors does not decrease the overall performance.

VAMPIR output Fig. 8 shows two time steps of *PRISM3D* after reaching full load balance. The critical section of the code *Solve_Boundary*, only entered by Fourier mode 0, solves a system of linear equations $\mathbf{A} \cdot \mathbf{x} = \mathbf{b}$. The original solver version has been replaced by a parallelized one. Now, the matrix is to be partitioned in blocks and mapped onto a two-dimensional grid of processors. Fortunately, the new matrix solver, with 32 processors, has the same speed as the old one, although it is massively communicating. Fig. 9 demonstrates that the application does not spend any longer a lot of time waiting on a Barrier. In order to obtain maximum speed, the code firmly uses LAPACK[14] and BLAS. Furthermore, the new version of the matrix solver uses ScaLAPACK (Scalable LAPACK) and PBLAS (Parallel BLAS) with BLACS (Basic Linear Algebra

184

Communication Subprograms) under cover. Therefore, as a result, a 32 CPU *PRISM3D* runs with 53 MFLOPS sustained on each processor of a T3E-900.

4 Conclusions

The effect of Lorentz force on the flow around circular cylinders in the wake transition regime was studied by means of DNS. It could be shown that lift and drag forces are reduced due to the control of flow separation. The DNS of turbulent wakes on bluff bodies and turbulent channel flows requires the usage of a large number of processors $(64, 128, \ldots)$. Therefore, the improved solver which avoids the scalability problem of its predecessor is a basic requirement. Additionally, gained by dexterous usage of well optimized packages, the high per-node performance will help to tackle turbulent problems in the future.

Acknowledgments

We thank G.E. Karniadakis (Brown University) for the donation of the spectral element code. The support of Deutsche Forschungsgemeinschaft (DFG INK 18 B1-1 TP A2) is gratefully acknowledged, and we thank F. Hoßfeld from Research Center Jülich for providing access to the CRAY T3E-900.

References

1. A. Gailitis and O. Lielausis, *Appl. Magnetohydrodyn., Reports Phys. Inst. Riga* **12**, 143 (1961).
2. A. Tsinober, in *Viscous drag reduction in boundary layers*, eds. D.M. Bushnell, J.N. Hefner (AIAA 1989).
3. C. Henoch and J. Stace, *Phys. Fluids* **7**(6), 1371 (1995).
4. P.L. O'Sullivan and S. Biringen, *Phys. Fluids* **10**(5), 1169 (1998).
5. W.E. Nagel *et al*, *Supercomputer 63* **12**(1), 69 (1996).
6. R.D. Henderson, *Phys. Fluids* **7**(9), 2102 (1995).
7. R.D. Henderson, *J. Fluid Mech.* **352**, 65 (1997).
8. A. Persillon, M. Braza, *J. Fluid Mech.* **365**, 23 (1998).
9. C.H.K. Williamson, *J. Fluid Mech.* **206**, 579 (1989).
10. C.H.K. Williamson, *J. Fluid Mech.* **328**, 345 (1996).
11. D. Barkley and R.D. Henderson, *J. Fluid Mech.* **322**, 215 (1996).
12. O. Posdziech and R. Grundmann, *Europ. J. Mech. B/Fluids*, submitted.
13. R.D. Henderson and G.E. Karniadakis, *J. Comp. Phys.* **122**, 191 (1995).
14. http://www.netlib.org.

USING PVM ON COMPUTER NETWORK TO PERFORM FAST PRE-PROCESSING OF LARGE MEDICAL DATA SET

V. POSITANO, M.F. SANTARELLI AND A. BENASSI

C.N.R. Institute of Clinical Physiology, Via Savi, 8 - 56126 Pisa Italy
positano@ifc.pi.cnr.it

L. LANDINI

Department of Information Engineering: EIT, University of Pisa,
Via Diotisalvi, 2 - 56126 Pisa, Italy

In the present paper a parallel algorithm for medical image processing has been proposed, which allows anisotropic diffusion filtering of large data set. Anisotropic filtering is a fundamental task in the pre-processing of medical images, in order to solve the problem of gray scale inhomogeneities that reduces the accuracy of the segmentation algorithms applied to images. The anisotropic filtering algorithm was implemented on a heterogeneous computer network using PVM libraries, in order to exploit the computational resources typically available in a hospital. To test the developed system in actual medical environment, dynamic sequences of 3D data volume, derived from Magnetic Resonance cardiac images, have been processed.

1 Introduction

Today available medical imaging systems collect a massive amount of data in short time and require fast computers for both image reconstruction and analysis [1, 2]. Due to the large amount of data provided by acquisition devices, the traditional way to perform data analysis (i.e. sequential examinations of images and mental three-dimensional reconstruction) becomes ineffective. On the other hand, automated segmentation and quantitative analysis of medical images is still an open challenge.

One of the most important drawbacks in image segmentation is the presence of gray scale inhomogeneities, which affect the measured gray level values so that pixels representing a specified tissue class have different gray level in different regions of image.

In particular, in Magnetic Resonance Imaging (MRI), radio frequency wave attenuation by tissue, inhomogeneities in the main magnetic field, magnetic susceptibility of tissue and many other effects increase the gray scale variance of the tissue classes that reduce the accuracy of the segmentation algorithms applied to MRI.

A powerful algorithm to reduce the gray scale inhomogeneities, based on a nonlinear anisotropic diffusion filter, was proposed by Perona and Malik [3]. This filter was used by several researchers to enhance MRI before segmentation operation [4, 5, 6]. This filter can also be used to enlarge the coherence of a medical image data set in order to increase the performance of volume rendering algorithms based on run-length encoding approach [7].

Unfortunately, anisotropic diffusion filtering is a very time consuming task, especially for analysis of large amount of medical volumetric data. For example, a 64-steps filtering operation on a dynamic sequence of 24 128x128x14-voxel images requires about 26 minutes of total computation time using a SGI O2 with an R10000 CPU at 200 MHz.

In order to exploit the resources available in a typical medical structure, we have implemented the anisotropic diffusion filtering of a dynamic sequence of medical image data on a heterogeneous computer network. The PVM [8, 9] freely available libraries allows to implement such application both reducing financial effort and using all available Operative Systems along the network.

2 Algorithm Description

Perona and Malik [2] formulate the anisotropic diffusion filter as diffusion process that encourages intra-region smoothing while inhibiting inter-region smoothing:

$$\frac{\partial}{\partial t} I(\bar{x}, t) = \nabla \bullet \left(c(\bar{x}, t) \nabla I(\bar{x}, t) \right).$$

$I(\bar{x}, t)$ is the image, $\bar{x}$ refers to the image axes and t refers to the iteration step. $c(\bar{x}, t)$ is called the *diffusion function* and is a monotonically decreasing function of the image gradient magnitude. The edges in the image are smoothed or enhanced based on the diffusion function value. In our algorithm implementation, we use the following diffusion function:

$$c(\bar{x}, t) = e^{-\frac{|\nabla I(\bar{x}, t)|^2}{2K^2}}$$

K is referred as the diffusion constant and the filter behavior depends on K. Fig. 1.a shows the monotonical decrease of the diffusion coefficient c($\bar{x}$,t) with increasing gradient (dot curve). The parameter K is the diffusion constant and it is chosen in order to preserve edge strength at object boundary and to reduce the noise contribute. In order to exploit the relation between the K parameter and the discontinuity value ∇I, it is preferable to discuss the flow function $\phi(\nabla I)$ defined as the product $c \bullet \nabla I$ (fig. 1.a – continue curve). The flow strength is dependent on the relationship between K and ∇I. The maximum flow is produced at image location with $\nabla I = K$. When ∇I is below K, the flow function reduces to zero because in almost homogeneous regions the flow is minimal. For ∇I larger than K the flow function again decreases to zero, halting diffusion at locations of high gradients. Therefore, a proper choice of the diffusion function not only preserves, but also enhances object edges usually situated at high gradient values. Obviously, it requires setting the K parameter correctly. The figure 1.b shows the effect of anisotropic filter on a noised blurred edge. It is clear that the anisotropic filter not only reduces the noise but also enhances the edge slope.

The application discrete diffusion process to bidimensional images consists of updating each pixel in the image by a quantity equal to the contributed flow of its four nearest neighbors. The process will be repeated until the desired result is reached.

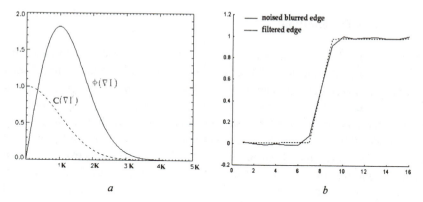

Figure 1: a) anisotropic diffusion (C(∇I)) and flow functions($\phi(\nabla I)$) and b) effect of anisotropic filter on blurred edge.

The figure 2 shows the effect of the anisotropic filter on the edge definition in a MR image of the hearth left ventricle. The fig 2.a shows the edge map extracted from the original image, the fig 2.b shows the edge map extracted from the image filtered by means of anisotropic diffusion. The anisotropic filter reduces the noise contribute and also enhances object edges.

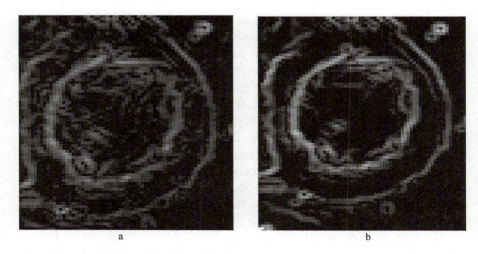

a   b

Figure 2: effect of anisotropic filter on edge definition

3   Parallel Implementation

A typical set of 3D medical image data consists of a series of parallel slices, covering the zone of interest. A 3D set can be acquired several times, to follow the evolution of physiological phenomena, as cardiac cycle. So that, a dynamic 3D data set can include hundreds of images. Each one of these images can be filtered independently, so that the parallel implementation can be based on a master process that distributes the images on the slave processes. We named in the following this approach as SMSA (Standard Master-Slave Algorithm). When a slave process ends its task, the master provides a new image to the slave process. If the number of processed images is high with respect to the number of slave processes, this approach is able to obtain a good load balancing.

For small data sets, the algorithm performances will be reduced due the starting and ending phases. In the starting phase the master process have to load the data on all slave processes and this phase requires a sort of startup time; a tree-structured communication was used in order to reduce the loss of performance. About ending phase, it should be stressed that, using an heterogeneous network of computers, the performance of each machine can vary in a wide range of values in dependence by the peak performance of the machine and the use of the same machine by other users. Because the master process has to wait for the end of all slave processes, the presence of a slow process can delay the termination of the whole application. The same problems can reduce the application scalability increasing the number of processes using larger networks. To solve this problem, the filtering operation applied on each image can be split into several steps. In fact, anisotropic filtering is an additive process, so that a process consisting of a number N of iterations can be split in K processes each with N/K iterations. We named in the following this approach as MMSA (Modified Master-Slave Algorithm). This approach reduces the performance loss due to starting and ending phases but requires an additional data exchange. The figure 3 shows the utilization diagram extracted from XPVM interface for a data set of 128x128x14-voxel images using both approaches; it is clear from the figure that the loss of performances in the starting and ending phase of the algorithm can be reduced using the MMSA.

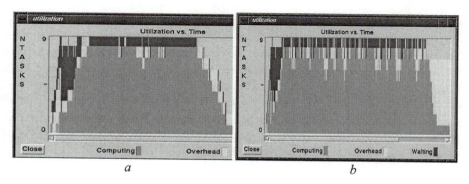

Figure 3: Normalized utilization vs. time diagram: standard master-slave algorithm (a) and modified master-slave algorithm (b).

The application has been tested on a local network composed of several machines based on Unix and WinNT Operative Systems by means of PVM libraries. In particular, an SGI O2 workstation has been used to run the graphical user interface, the master process and one slave process. The other slave processes run on a double PPRO machine with Linux OS, on a Pentium 75 based machine whit Linux OS, on a SPARC 20 workstation and on two Pentium2-based machines with WinNT OS. The LAN is a standard Ethernet at 10 Mbit/sec. The table 1 shows the CPU95 benchmarks relevant to the previous described machines provided by the Standard Performance Evaluation Corporation (SPEC).

190

Table 1. SPEC benchmarks for the machines used in the network.

Processor type	# processors	CINT 95	CFP 95
SPARC 20	1	4.02	4.71
R10000	1	10.1	8.77
Intel PPRO 200	4	8.08	6.34
Intel Pentium 75	1	2.39	2.06
Average	7	5.82	4.94

The application was also tested using MPICH [10] implementation of MPI libraries on a smallest network including only the UNIX-based machines.

4   Results and Conclusions

To test the application performance we used cardiac MR studies, each one consisting of 14 slices of 128x128 pixels covering the heart. The size of one MR study is about 0.5 Mbytes. Each slice was acquired a number of times (from 1 to 24) during the cardiac cycle. Figure 4.a shows the processing time for different data sizes, corresponding to a different number of MR studies. The test was performed on the sequential algorithm running on SGI machine, the SMSA and the MSMA versions of the parallel implementation of the algorithm.

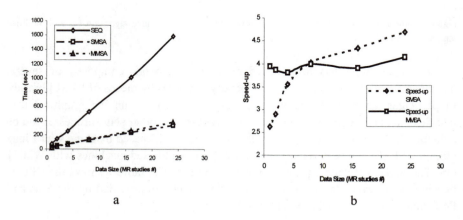

a   b

Figure 4.a: Time vs. Data Size; Figure 4.b: Speed-up vs. Data Size

Figure 4.b shows the Speed Up related to figure 4.a; from the table 1 we expect a speed-up value from 4 to 5, using the SPEC benchmarks as index for the performance of each machine in the network. The results seem to confirm this statement. The fig 4.b also shows that the MMSA ensures an acceptable speed-up value for every data size; on the other hand, the SMSA provides a better speed-up value for large data size but becomes inefficient for small data size.

Table 2 shows the processing time for different data size, obtained by processing a different number of MR studies, for the SMSA and the MMSA versions of the algorithm implemented with PVM and MPICH libraries. This test was performed on a smallest network including only UNIX-based machines (i.e. 5 processors).

Table 2: time performance of PVM and MPICH implementation

# MR studies	SMSA			MMSA		
	PVM	MPI	Diff. (%)	PVM	MPI	Diff. (%)
1	30.74	30.24	- 1.6	30.88	32.32	+ 4.66
4	106	105	- 0.94	110	117	+ 6.36
8	209	211	+ 0.95	212	228	+ 7.54
16	419	438	+ 4.53	431	460	+ 6.72
24	619	630	+ 1.77	628	682	+ 8.59

For the SMSA algorithm version, only negligible differences were found. For the MMSA version, the MPICH version seems to be a bit slower respect to the PVM version. However, the difference of performance between the two versions is always less than 10%.

In conclusion, the reduction of the processing time in the anisotropic filtering of large data set of medical images, achieved by using parallel computing, greatly increases the application effectiveness in medical image processing. The use of the message-passing programming technique, based on PVM libraries, seems to achieve good algorithm efficiency.

In addiction, the use of existing heterogeneous LAN to increase the algorithm performance allows to spread the use of parallel computing technique on the medical community using the resources available in a typical medical environment.

References

1. Santarelli M.F., Positano V. and Landini L., *IEEE Transactions on Information Technology in Biomedicine*, Vol. 1, n 3, Sep 1997, 171-178

2. Stacy M., Hanson D., Camp J. and Robb R. A., *Parallel Computing* 24 (1998) 1287-1321.
3. Perona, P and Malik, J., *IEEE Trans. On Pattern Analysis and Machine Intelligence*, 12(7): July 1990, 629-639.
4. Geric G., Kubler O., Kinikis R. and Jolesz F. A., *IEEE Transaction on Medical Imaging*, 11(2), June 1992, 221-232.
5. Alvarez L., Lions PL. and Morel J.M., *SIAM J. Number. Anal.*, 29(3), 1992, 845-866.
6. Atkins M.S. and Mackiewich B., *IEEE Transactions on Medical Imaging*, 17(1), Feb. 1998, 98-107,.
7. Santarelli M.F., Positano V., Landini L. and Benassi A., *Computers in Cardiology, IEEE Comp. Soc. Press, Los Alamitos*, 1997; 323-6
8. Sunderam V. S., *Concurrency: Practice and Experience*, 2, 4, December 1990, 315--339.
9. Beguelin A., Dongarra J., Geist A. and Manchek B. and Sunderam V., *International Journal for Supercomputer Applications,* Vol. 9, No. 2, summer 1995.
10. Gropp W., Lusk E., Doss N. and Skjellum A., *Parallel Computing*, vol. 22, n.6, Sept 1996, 789--828.

FINE GRAIN PARALLELIZATION OF MULTIBODY SYSTEM EQUATIONS OF MOTION

T. POSTIAU, P. FISETTE[1], J.-D. LEGAT

Université catholique de Louvain
CEREM: Centre for Research in Mechatronics
Departments of mechanical and electrical engineering
B-1348 Louvain-la-Neuve
e.mail: tpostiau@prm.ucl.ac.be

This paper deals with the efficien&t modeling and computation of articulated mechanical systems ("multibody systems"). The symbolic approach is used to generate kinematical or dynamic equations in a recursive formulation - Newton-Euler for instance - ready for any numerical process. The symbolic process deals with equations in scalar form rather than in a classical matrix/vector formulation. The fine grain parallelisation of the recursive set of operations is analyzed and the development of a vector architecture is investigated in order to be able to generate a dedicated HDL file ready for silicon compilation. A multi-FPGA board [6] will be used as prototyping system for an implementation of this architecture.

Introduction

The generation of the kinematical and dynamic equations of multibody systems is a quite tedious task because of both the size and the complexity of the mathematical models corresponding to real physical applications: robots, vehicles, mechanisms, machine tools or even human body. This is why a large variety of "multibody" programs have been developed all over the world [1], whose recent developments aim at improving their universality and computer efficiency. The latter feature is fundamental for two different classes of applications: the numerical analysis of multibody systems and the real time control of mechanical devices. Indeed, in the first case, the trend is presently to enlarge the capabilities of multibody simulations by incorporating them into an optimization process: the latter being highly time consuming, it requires, to be effective, a very fast computation of the multibody equations. In case of real time control, the need of compact mathematical models (mainly the dynamics) is more than obvious and the performances of modern DSP or FPGA devices strongly motivate the developments of formalisms and algorithmic techniques, parallelization for instance, able to speed up the computation of dynamic models.

---

[1] Chercheur qualifié FNRS

1   Symbolic generation

Among the possible options to generate the equations of motion, the symbolic approach, which appeared in the eighties, is a powerful tool to drastically simplify the equations and, secondarily, to give them a high legibility in their final form. In this context, the ROBOTRAN program (see [1]) has been developed in our laboratory. It is a stand-alone C program entirely dedicated to the study of multibody systems.

Starting from the *symbolic* description of the mechanical system (topology, articulations, geometrical and dynamic parameters of bodies, ...), the equations of motion are generated symbolically by ROBOTRAN in scalar form, in readiness for any numerical process. The program has been already used abundantly for many applications and is internationally recognized in the field of multibody dynamics [2].

Coming back to the model performances, a simulation using our symbolically generated equations of motion runs about 10 times faster than if it was computed with a pure numerical program. This is the consequence of the symbolic "tricks" endowing ROBOTRAN to remove all the superfluous sub-expressions or equations from the final symbolic form. Among the ROBOTRAN capabilities, let us mention :

- elimination of 0 - addition/multiplication and 1 – multiplication,
- location and processing of identical expressions (simple or complex),
- recursive simplification of complex trigonometric expressions,
- location and elimination of superfluous equations in a recursive computation.

All these simplification procedures are performed via pointer manipulations strongly controlled to minimize the memory requirements : this allows to deal with very large models (up to 100 d.o.f.^{2}), contrary to commercial symbolic packages.

Let us considers the computation of the inverse dynamics of a general 6 d.o.f. robot manipulator like the PUMA 560, generated using the "Newton/Euler recursive algorithm" [3]. It requires approximately 1200 arithmetical operations in matrix form, such as used by classical numerical programs. By using the ROBOTRAN symbolic generator, this reduces to 337 operations, i.e. less than 30 percent !

2   Fine grain parallelization

The "recursive" nature of the equations generated by ROBOTRAN is such that each equation of the type < auxiliary variable = symbolic expression > depends on some of the previous equations (auxiliary variables), but not necessarily on the last ones in the sequence (see [4]): this will initiate the proposed symbolic vectorization process. Contrary to the approach proposed in the literature (see [5] for instance) where matrix/vector parallelization is achieved, we consider in the present study a fully "exploded" recursive set of equations, generated symbolically in scalar form, which

---

^{2} degree of freedom

consist of a set of binary operations like: $Var_k = Var_i \blacklozenge Var_j$ where $\blacklozenge$ denotes 'mult', 'add' or 'sub' and possibly 'div' for direct dynamic models.

This requires the introduction of some new auxiliary variables and sometimes other simplifications. For instance, the original ROBOTRAN symbolic equation

```
Fs22 = m(2)*(ALPHA22-OMp12*L(3,2));
```

becomes once exploded :

```
Fs22dd = OMp12*L(3,2);
Fs22d  = ALPHA22-Fs22dd;
Fs22   = m(2)*Fs22d;
```

Once this process is achieved, the exploded equations still form a recursive scheme, a longer one, in which it is obvious that the serial dependency is preserved. One notes, by inspecting the interdependency of the resulting exploded equations (337 for our 6 d.o.f. robot), that they can be scheduled in a vectorized scheme to reach a minimal number of steps (47 for the robot), being in fact the "depth" of the binary tree representation of the whole set of equations or the length of the critical path of the data dependency graph. Let us emphasize that, this scheduling process is automatically performed by ROBOTRAN whatever the complexity of the application (from a double pendulum to a 80 d.o.f. vehicle model).

In the context of parallel processing, one must always have in mind the final hardware/software implementation envisaged for a given algorithm. In the present case, the goal being to download the vectorized equations in a FPGA-based reconfigurable system, the number of vector steps is not the only criterion to be satisfied. Indeed, since arithmetical operations such as a multiplication are quite consuming for such a chip (in terms of gates of a FPGA), the number of arithmetical units required simultaneously *must be minimized* as much as possible. Fortunately, we have some freedom at our disposal to handle how the vectorization process is performed, while still ensuing the minimum number of vector steps.

Indeed, to compress the serial scheme, an "as soon as possible" (asap) principle could be used [4], by evaluating a given equation as soon as all the elements of its right-hand-side are known. Intuitively, each equation is "pushed" towards the data.

In such an asap vector scheme, the first vector step consists of all the equations involving the original data (i.e. the geometrical, inertial and dynamic parameters and the joint coordinates, sine and cosine). The second step consists of all the equations depending on those from the first step, and so on. Each equation is then assigned an asap number corresponding to the soonest vector step at which it can be scheduled.

By considering the opposite, an "as late as possible" (alap) principle, each serial equation could be "pushed" towards the results to end up with another vector scheme, also with the minimal number of steps. No equation will be computed sooner than necessary. In that alap vector scheme, the last vector step consists of the equations providing the final results. All the equations needed by those from the last step are then scheduled on the last but one step, and so on. Each equation receives an alap number corresponding to the latest vector step at which it can be scheduled.

Experiments showed that these two extreme ordering processes induce a vector scheme which is ill-balanced in terms of arithmetical units. In other words, there is a very high disparity of the vector scheme width. For instance, in case of the robot, an "asap" re-ordering induces a vector scheme (47 steps) containing a step of width 23. Actually, the number of required units is given by the sum of the maximum number of occurrence for each operator 'mult', 'add' or 'sub' and for each step of the vector scheme. In this case, 28 arithmetical units are required simultaneously: 5 'add', 3 'sub' and 20 'mult'. To avoid this problem, we take advantage of the freedom we have to find an optimal ordering (in terms of arithmetical unit minimization) of the equations, between the asap and alap extreme solutions.

The problem is to find a method allowing us to schedule the equations with respect to their interdependency and providing us with a "minimal width" and a "minimal length" vector scheme. We first tried to do this by using a method based on the mobility being the difference between the alap and asap indices of the equations. The ones with the lowest mobility are scheduled first. This method provides us with a vector scheme of the required (minimal) length and gives us the amount of arithmetical units needed for its computation. Unfortunately, this quite simple method does not result in the best possible scheme. So, we presently have chosen a more flexible, but iterative, way of doing this by using a 'list scheduling' algorithm. This method needs the list of operations to be sorted by increasing value of alap number, then by asap number in case of the same value of the alap number. Then, according to a given number of available arithmetical units, the list scheduling algorithm provides us with a vector scheme whose length depends on the given units number. So, given a initial number of arithmetical units, coming from an estimator or from the previously described scheduling method, one can iterate on the number of needed 'mult', 'add' or 'sub' units by decreasing their number while the length of the resulting vector scheme remains equal to the known minimal number of steps.

This method ends up with very interesting results. For robot dynamics, for instance, the 47 vector steps, once optimally re-ordered, only require 11 simultaneous arithmetical units : 3 'add', 2 'sub' and 6 'mult'. Furthermore, experiments show that with very large multibody models[3] (~100 d.o.f.) which require approximately 15000 scalar symbolic operations, the final vector scheme contains 740 steps and requires *only* 25 arithmetical units ('add', 'sub' and 'mult'). This is a very encouraging result since, of course, the larger the models, the longer the required computation of the original serial scheme and the higher the need of CPU performances (e.g. for optimization or simulator applications).

To briefly illustrate the method, let us take, as 'academic' example, a planar double pendulum for which the inverse dynamics is computed symbolically by ROBOTRAN.

Figure 1 presents, in Matlab® syntax, the symbolic serial recursive scheme (from which superfluous equations have already been removed by ROBOTRAN). The exploded equations are then generated and alap/asap sorted. Let us emphasize that this process intrinsically preserves the serial dependency of the exploded equations.

---

[3] ex. : full railway vehicle, system with flexible elements, …

```
%
%                 ROBOTRAN 6.0 : double_pendulum
%
function [Qq] = dyninvner(q,qp,qpp,D,L,m,I,g)
%
S1 = sin(q(1)); C1 = cos(q(1)); S2 = sin(q(2)); C2 = cos(q(2));
%
BS91 = -qp(1)*qp(1);
ALPHA21 = g(3)*S1;
ALPHA31 = g(3)*C1;
OM12 = qp(1)+qp(2);
OMp12 = qpp(1)+qpp(2);
ALPHA22 = C2*(ALPHA21-qpp(1)*D(3,2))+S2*(ALPHA31+BS91*D(3,2));
BS92 = -OM12*OM12;
ALPHA32 = C2*(ALPHA31+BS91*D(3,2))-S2*(ALPHA21-qpp(1)*D(3,2));
Fs22 = m(2)*(ALPHA22-OMp12*L(3,2));
Fs21 = m(1)*(ALPHA21-qpp(1)*L(3,1));
Fs32 = m(2)*(ALPHA32+BS92*L(3,2));
Cq12 = -Fs22*L(3,2)+I(1,2)*OMp12;
Cq11 = Cq12+qpp(1)*I(1,1)-Fs21*L(3,1)-D(3,2)*(Fs22*C2-Fs32*S2);
%
Qq(2) = Cq12;
Qq(1) = Cq11;
%
```

Figure 1 : inverse dynamics of a double pendulum ; 13 serial equations

```
%
%                 ROBOTRAN 6.0 : double_pendulum
%
function [Qq] = dyninvner(q,qp,qpp,D,L,m,I,g)
%
S1 = sin(q(1)); C1 = cos(q(1)); S2 = sin(q(2)); C2 = cos(q(2));
%
z1(1:5)=[qp(1)*qp(1), g(3)*S1, g(3)*C1, qpp(1)*D(3,2), qp(1)+qp(2)];
z2(1:6)=[z1(1)*D(3,2), z1(5)*z1(5), qpp(1)*L(3,1), qpp(1)*I(1,1),
         qpp(1)+qpp(2), z1(2)-z1(4)];
z3(1:5)=[C2*z2(6), z2(5)*L(3,2), S2*z2(6), z2(2)*L(3,2),z1(3)-z2(1)];
z4(1:4)=[S2*z3(5), C2*z3(5), I(1,2)*z2(5), z1(2)-z2(3)];
z5(1:3)=[m(1)*z4(4), z3(1)+z4(1), z4(2)-z3(3)];
z6(1:2)=[z5(1)*L(3,1), z5(2)-z3(2)];
z7(1:2)=[m(2)*z6(2), z5(3)-z3(4)];
z8(1:3)=[m(2)*z7(2), z7(1)*L(3,2), z7(1)*C2];
z9(1:2)=[z8(1)*S2, z4(3)-z8(2)];
z10(1:2)=[z9(2)+z2(4), z8(3)-z9(1)];
z11(1:2)=[D(3,2)*z10(2), z10(1)-z6(1)];
z12(1:1)=[z11(2)-z11(1)];
%
Qq(2) = z9(2);
Qq(1) = z12(1);
%
```

Figure 2 : inverse dynamics of a double pendulum ; 12 vector equations

Finally, they are vectorized to end up with the final "well-balanced" vector scheme shown in figure 2. One can see that starting from the original serial equations containing 37 arithmetical operations, the process has re-ordered them in 12 vector steps which require at most (step number 2) 1 'add', 1 'sub' and 4 'mult' simultaneous arithmetical units[4]. The smaller the model, the lower the benefits but this is of course the correct trend since only large models (see above) are of practical interest. Moreover, it could seem that the scheme is not so "well-balanced" since a lot of steps do not contain so many operations. This will be discussed later and is, in this particular case, due to the small size of the system with regard to its number of d.o.f. The double pendulum is only shown here to illustrate the proposed vectorization process.

3   Optimization

The resulting vector scheme can still be optimized. Indeed, we can improve the resulting scheme by considering an arithmetical unit able to compute both additions and subtractions. So the 'add' and 'sub' operations can be handled as 'add/sub' operations and no longer as two different ones: this introduces more flexibility in the scheduling. The minimal time vector scheme of our 6 d.o.f. robot arm becomes now 6 'mult' units and 4 'add/sub' units rather than 3 'add' and 2 'sub', for the same number of 47 execution steps. One can notice that we need one 'add' or 'sub' less than before. Sometimes, this new flexibility induces a reduction of the number of required 'mult' units too. In the sequel, we will consider that the 'add' and 'sub' operations can thus be performed by the same arithmetical units.

On the other hand, up to now, we have only focused on minimal time vector scheme. One could accept to "relax" the (implicit) constraint on the minimum number of vectorized steps, in so far as this could allow us to reduce the number of required units.

Reducing the number of available arithmetical units, our 'list scheduling' method will of course produce a 'longer than minimal' vector scheme. But now, how to choose how many units to use and how much more steps will be necessary to compute the new vector scheme ? Here, one needs to run the scheduler a few times with different number of units to know how the vector scheme will be with regard to its length and width. We have grouped in table 1 and 2 a few scheduling results of the inverse dynamics of our 6 d.o.f. robot and of the double pendulum respectively.

The first two columns of those tables contain the number of arithmetical units. The third column contains the number of steps needed to compute the vector scheme with the given number of arithmetical units.

---

[4] One notes that 'mult' is the most required operator in multibody dynamics, and also the most "consuming" one.

The 'speed ratio' column contains the ratio of the minimal number of steps of the system, by the number of steps resulting from the scheduling mentioned in the third column. This ratio of course is equal to 1 when the number of steps is minimal and it decreases when there are less arithmetical units at ones disposal.

The last column 'use ratio' is the ratio of the total number of operations to perform for the computation of the model, by the maximum number of operations which could be done i.e. the product of the number of steps by the number of arithmetical units.

For instance, in case of the 6 d.o.f. robot, if you plan to use 4 'mult' and 3 'add/sub', the scheduler produces a scheme with 54 steps, so 378 operations could theoretically be processed, while the corresponding inverse dynamics computation only requires 337, thus the 'use ratio' is 337 / 378 = 0,89.

One can notice that the reduction of the available arithmetical units, while resulting in a slight increase of the number of computation steps, brings a noticeable improvement of the use ratio of the scheme: from 65..70% to almost 90% for the 6 d.o.f. robot inverse dynamics.

Of course if one reduce too much the number of arithmetical units, the length of the vector scheme will increase considerably and the use ratio will be worse. There is thus an optimum in term of use ratio. A good tradeoff has to be found with respect to the needs, keeping in mind that using a lot of units leads to a shorter vector scheme but implies more logic cells use for the implementation and obviously a more complex circuit.

#mult	#add/sub	# steps	speed ratio	use ratio
6	4	47	1	0.72
5	4	48	0.98	0.78
5	3	50	0.94	0.84
4	4	52	0.9	0.81
4	3	54	0.87	0.89
3	3	68	0.69	0.82
3	2	72	0.65	0.93
1	1	199	0.24	0.84

Table 1 : 6 d.o.f. robot inverse dynamics vectorization

#'mult'	#'add/sub'	# steps	speed ratio	use ratio
3	2	12	1	0.62
3	1	15	0.8	0.62
2	2	14	0.86	0.66
2	1	15	0.8	0.82
1	1	24	0.5	0.77

Table 2 : double pendulum inverse dynamics vectorization

4   Prospects

The present symbolic vectorization task, performed through symbolic data dependency analysis, represents a fundamental part of the proposed research, and is at the root of future developments, which will focus on the chip implementation. We are now working on the design of the parallel architecture on which the vector scheme will be mapped. ROBOTRAN capabilities has been increased to automatically generate an hardware description file of the architecture for any multibody system. The compilation of these text description file with a tool like MAX+PLUS$^{©}$ II from Altera$^{©}$, allows us to refine our architecture design. Preliminary compilation results show that it should almost be possible to fit in a device like an Altera$^{©}$ FLEX 10K100 FPGA, a vector processor with seven 24 bits floating point units, able to compute our 6 d.o.f. robot inverse dynamics in 54 steps (see table 1).

In terms of mechanical modeling, the results obtained here are momentarily restricted to open structures but the generalization to closed systems with kinematical loops between bodies, whose models involve both symbolic and numerical computations, will be envisaged in a close future, using the same philosophy as that pursued in the present work.

References

1. *"Multibody Systems Handbook"*, Schiehlen, W., ed.Berlin : Springer-Verlag, 1989
2. *"Multibody Computer Codes in Vehicle System Dynamics"*, Kortüm, W.; Sharp, R.S., Supplement to Vehicle System Dynamics, vol. 22, Swets and Zeitlinger, Amsterdam, 1993
3. *"Symbolic Generation of Large Multibody System Dynamic Equations using a New Semi-Explicit Newton/Euler Recursive Scheme"*, Fisette, P., Samin J.C., Archive of Applied Mechanics, vol. 66 (1996), pp 187-199
4. *"Contribution to Parallel and Vector Computation in Multibody Dynamics"*, Fisette, P., Péterkenne, J.M., Parallel Computing, vol. 24 (1998), pp 717-728
5. *"Parallel computation of Manipulator Dynamics"*, A. Fijany, A. K. Bejczy, Journal of Robotic System, vol. 8/5 (1991), pp 599-635
6. *"A 400Kgates 8 Mbytes SRAM multi-FPGA PCI System"*, David, J.P., Legat, J.D., int. Workshop on Logic and Architecture Synthesis, Grenoble, dec. 1997, pp 133-117

Acknowledgments

This work has been supported by the Belgian Program on Interuniversity Attraction Poles initiated by the Belgian State – Prime Minister's office – Science Policy Programme (IUAP – 24). The scientific responsibility is assumed by its authors.

VEHICLE ROUTING WITH TIME WINDOWS AND STOCHASTIC DEMAND

MATTHEW PROTONOTARIOS, IOANNIS VYRIDIS,
CHRISTOS NIKOLAIDIS AND THEODORA VARVARIGOU
National Technical University of Athens
Department of Electrical and Computer Engineering
Division of Computer Science
GR-157 73 ATHENS
GREECE

This paper deals with a real-life vehicle routing problem concerning the distribution of products to customers with stochastic demands. The objective is to minimize distribution costs while maximizing customer satisfaction and respecting certain constraints, like vehicle capacity, time windows for customer service, driver working hours per day, predetermined or non-compatible pairings amongst customers and vehicles and others. A significant feature of the problem is the fact that the demand of each customer is stochastic. A model describing all these requirements has been developed as well as a heuristic genetic algorithm to solve the problem. High Performance Computing has been used to allow the pursuit for a near-optimal solution in a sensible amount of time, as the parallelization counterbalances the increased size and complexity of the problem. The system solves complex logistics planning problems, optimizing for a non-homogenous fleet of trucks and multiple products. The nature of the operations involved in our genetic algorithm in combination with the use of dynamic population permits the asynchronous processing of individuals by sending newborn individuals to a pool from where they can be distributed over several processors for evaluation and then return to the population. Additionally a heuristic mechanism was engineered in order to preserve the generation of individuals that satisfy as many constraints as possible.

1 Introduction

This work has been developed in the framework of the ESPRIT project "DYNALOG" which stands for DYNAmic LOGistics. The DYNALOG project develops a dynamic, integrated system to meet the current needs in the field of logistics. As transportation costs represent a large percentage of the total costs in a company, managers require the amount of time to make routing decisions to be as short as possible, to give them superior reactivity and cost-effectiveness compared with their competitors. The use of HPCN enables the use of advanced software systems to fulfil these requirements within the minimum amount of time.

The end-users in the project are MEVGAL (Greece) and FIEGE (Germany), which have complementary problems that reflect the diversity of needs across Europe. MEVGAL produces and delivers ultra-fresh dairy products while demand is not always known at departure time. FIEGE offer large volume logistic services throughout Europe and they are of the largest logistics companies in Europe. In their case the demand is known just a few hours before route scheduling. Here the stochastic router will be used for strategic purposes.

The Vehicle Routing Problem with Time Windows (VRPTW), besides retail distribution as in our case, applies in a variety of situations like mail delivery, newspapers delivery, waste collection and consequently has taken up the time of many researchers. However, there is still a lot of space for further research due to the high complexity of the problem, which allows only search for better and computationally faster approximations of the optimal solution. It is worth mentioning that even finding a feasible solution for a given number of vehicles is NP-hard (see Savelsberg[2]). The use of Genetic Algorithm techniques to encounter the problem seems to be a very promising. Thangiah [4] has followed this approach with GIDEON to face VRPTW with deterministic customer demands. We follow a similar rationale, taking further into account that demand is stochastic.

2   Problem description

A dairy company is engaging a non-homogenous fleet of trucks (some owned by the company and some are franchised trucks) in order to distribute a variety of dairy products to a large number of customers situated in a dense geographic region. The trucks, initially located at a given depot(s), have to serve (some of) the customers within specified periods of time. Each customer's demand is stochastic, respecting historical data and current trend as well as external factors that influence the demand. The target is to create a number of baseline routes on a weekly basis for the vehicles, within a user-defined period that respect certain additional constraints like driver working hours per day, franchised drivers' revenue, predetermined or non-compatible pairings amongst customers and vehicles. Hence, our objective is to consider all expected fluctuations in demand across the predefined period, while keeping customer satisfaction high and distribution costs to a minimum.

3   The model

Here, we present a mathematical formulation of the problem on which our approach was based. This model is an initial simplified mathematical description of the problem. However it might prove useful for a better understanding of the problem and of the difficulties that would arise if analytical methods were to be used.
We use the following notation:

- Customers: $1, 2, \ldots, n$ (usually denoted by i, j)
- Vehicles: $h_1, h_2, \ldots, h_m$
- Week-days (Mon, Tues, ...) will be used and denoted in indices by l.

- Time: t , we assume that time takes discrete values within a specified time period

- Volume capacity of vehicle $h_k : V_k$

- Expected product volume by customer j on week-day l (probabilistic): $\tilde{v}_{jl}$

- and associated cost per unit of volume: c_{jl}

- It is $v_{jl} = \begin{cases} v_{jl1} & with & p_{jl1} \\ \vdots & \vdots & \vdots \\ v_{jlN} & with & p_{jlN} \end{cases}$

- That is, $p_{jlr} \equiv P(v_{jl} = v_{jlr})$

- Time window of customer j : $W_j = [e_j, l_j]$

- Penalty when customer j with time window $W_j = [e_j, l_j]$ is served at time

$$t : p(t, W_j) = \begin{cases} 0, & t \in W_j \\ \lambda_j \left| t - \dfrac{e_j + l_j}{2} \right| & t \notin W_j \end{cases}, \text{ where penalty weight } \lambda_j \text{ is}$$

defined by the user and depends on customer j , (when the time window for a customer should not be violated, it is $\lambda_j = \infty$).

- Maximum working time for vehicle/driver h_k: K_k (this could be the same for all vehicles, i.e. $K_k = K$, $\forall k$)

- Time distance between customers i and j when the departure occurs at time $t : d_{ijt}$ (see next paragraph)

- Time spent on serving customer j on day l: T_{jl}

Decision variables:

- $x_{ijk}^t = 1$, if vehicle k goes from customer i to customer j and departs at time t , $= 0$ otherwise and

- y_{jlk} = product volume loaded on vehicle h_k for customer j on week-day l.

The objective function

The objective function to be minimised incorporates the following terms alongside weight factors that show the contribution of each term o the general distribution cost. The user will be given the limited freedom to modify the weight factors according to their policy.

- Total time spent travelling time: $\sum\limits_{i,j,k,t} x_{ijk}^t d_{ijt}$

- Cost for returned products for vehicle h_k: $\sum\limits_{j} [y_{jlk} - \tilde{v}_{jl}]^+ c_{jl}$

- Cost for unsatisfied demand for vehicle h_k: $\sum\limits_{j} [\tilde{v}_{jl} - y_{jlk}]^+ c_{jl}$

- Now, let us expand the stochastic variables. Set

$$y_{jlk} - v_{jlr} = Y_{jklr}^+ - Y_{jklr}^-$$ where Y_{jklr}^+, Y_{jklr}^- are nonnegative variables.

The two costs above become

$$\sum\limits_{k,j,r,l} Y_{jklr}^+ c_{jl} p_{jlr} \quad \text{and} \quad \sum\limits_{k,j,r,l} Y_{jklr}^- c_{jl} p_{jlr} \qquad \text{respectively.}$$

<u>Constrains</u>

- From each customer i departs at most one vehicle just once:

$$\sum\limits_{t}\sum\limits_{k}\sum\limits_{j} x_{ijk}^t \leq 1, \ \forall i$$

- There exists a vehicle going to customer j at time t if and only if there exists a vehicle leaving customer j at time $t + T_j$

$$\sum\limits_{i} x_{ijk}^t = \sum\limits_{l} x_{jlk}^{t+T_j}, \ \forall j,k,t$$

- Vehicle h_k must visit customer i : $\sum\limits_{j}\sum\limits_{t} x_{ijk}^t = 1$,

- Vehicle h_k should not visit customer i : $\sum\limits_{j}\sum\limits_{t} x_{ijk}^t = 0$,

- Customers j and l should be in the same route:

$$\sum\limits_{i}\sum\limits_{t} x_{ijk}^t = \sum\limits_{i}\sum\limits_{t} x_{ilk}^t, \ \forall k$$

- Customers j and l should be in different routes:

If $\sum\limits_{i}\sum\limits_{t} x_{ijk}^t = 1$, then $\sum\limits_{i}\sum\limits_{t} x_{ilk}^t = 0$ (and vice-versa)

- $y_{jlk} - Y_{jklr}^+ + Y_{jklr}^- = v_{jlr}$, $\forall j,l,k$

- if $v_{jl} = 0$ then $y_{jlk} = 0$, $Y_{jklr}^+ = 0$, $Y_{jklr}^- = 0$:

$$y_{jlk} \le v_{jl}A \quad , \; Y_{jklr}^+ \le v_{jl}A \quad , \; Y_{jklr}^- \le v_{jl}A$$

- $x_{ijk}^t \in \{0,1\}$, $\forall i,j,k,t$ and $y_{ilk}, Y_{jklr}^+, Y_{jklr}^- \in R$

4   The use of a Heuristic Genetic Algorithm Model

In contrast to classical search, with GAs the possibilities are not explored in an exhaustive way in some order, but a current set of candidate solutions is improved by stochastically selecting one or more parents and using them to generate one or more children by applying a genetic operator. The advantage of a GA is that of genetic diversity: each step in the search process considers a set of candidates, instead of a single one, selected on the basis of their quality, for the creation of new candidates. Hence, a GA explores and exploits the relationship between the inner structure and the quality of candidate solutions automatically. The so-called *building block hypothesis* states: a GA detects simple patterns within candidates, the building blocks, that contribute to the quality, and composes candidate solutions consisting of high quality building blocks.

Traditional GAs are primarily applicable for problems where there is no interaction (epistasis) between the variables of a candidate solution. However, as it is also obvious from the mathematical model presented earlier, this is not the case with DYNALOG, which can be characterised as a Constraint Optimisation Problem (COP). Hence, it is inevitable that classical GAs must be modified to be able to cope with a COP. The essential modification is that of the representation of the individuals (single solutions – chromosomes) and the child generation mechanisms, the genetic operators. Our approach is to replace classical representations and genetic operators with representations and mechanisms that take (some of) the constraints into account. In defining such mechanisms we adopt heuristics aiming at the best of two worlds, creating a heuristic GA that will execute a directed search while being able to discover candidates outside the scope of search heuristics, due to the occasional random steps.

Particular attention is paid on dealing with constraints. We relax the constraints that cannot be embedded into the operators, penalise them and finally include them into the objective function. In this case an infeasible solution becomes a feasible one but it gets penalised in the objective so that it becomes a "bad" solution. Next we describe our method of solving the particular VRPTW problem in question.

4.1   Representation

An order-based representation is used in a form of a 3-D matrix. The third dimension is used only for supplementary information relevant to time bookkeeping that was calculated during initialization. Each sub-chromosome, represented by a row of the matrix, is a permutation of a subset of customers, e.g. $\{1,\ldots,K\}$, assigned to a specific truck. The maximum number of customers a truck can visit is set and the maximum number of trucks is the maximum that appears in the initial population.

4.2   Selection

A practical solution to the problem should involve trucks visiting nearby customers in one neighborhood and gradually proceeding into other neighborhoods, rather than jumping from one area to another just for one or two customers. Taking into account the above additional constraint, that would be difficult to quantify otherwise, a heuristic sampling algorithm was employed, based on local tournament selection. In tournament selection, n individuals are chosen at random from a subset of the population, the fittest being selected for reproduction (we will refer to this individual as "female"). But instead of repeating the same process for the other parent, n individuals are chosen at random from the population and then each one is assigned a probability to be chosen for reproduction that is proportional to its "compatibility" to the female. We will refer to this individual as "male" (the two terms being interchangeable).

The evaluation of the mating "compatibility" is performed by choosing one time window at random (upper, lower bound) for each sub-chromosome of each candidate father. Then each string of adjacent genes that is located between the two time splices is tested on how well it fits into the equivalent "female" sub-chromosome, taking into account the time distances from the genes of the "female" sub-chromosome that are located adjacent to the edges of the time window. The "male" with the best overall performance gets a higher probability of being selected.

The main idea is to speed up convergence (combined with replacement) trying to improve fairly fit individuals while allowing the selection of weaker individuals for breeding. Since the above algorithm involves local sampling it does not need to be carried centrally but it is suitable for parallel processing so that each processor can carry out selection independently and proceed with crossing.

4.3   Crossing & Mutation

Since the initial constrained optimisation problem is represented as a GA-suited counterpart, the original set of constraints is divided into a subset of indirect and one of direct constraints. The first group is incorporated into the objective function of the GA-suited counterpart as a soft constraint. Infeasible solutions to the original problem are feasible in the GA-suited counterpart but severely penalised in the objective function. In such a case it is expected that new generations will include a large number of weaker individuals that represent unfeasible solutions. A heuristic mechanism would be preferable in order to preserve the generation of individuals that satisfy an as many direct constraints as possible.

The mechanism incorporates the following characteristics:

- If a truck has a compulsory assignment to a customer that is represented by a specific value of a gene, this value must never appear in a different row than the one that represents the route of this truck.
- If it is compulsory that a truck must not be assigned to a customer that is represented by a specific value of a gene, this value must never appear in the row represents the route of this truck.
- The upper time bound of customers should not be violated, including the bound of the legal total working time of each truck.
- If a truck must visit at least m customers, there should not exist any sub-chromosomes in the resultant child chromosome with less than m genes.
- Any attempt to mix gene values between the equivalent sub-chromosomes of the parents should not result in duplicate or absent gene values to appear in the resultant child chromosomes.

Therefore, a mechanism was engineered, based on the Linear Order Crossover and a heuristic best-fit insertion mutation in order for all initial chromosomes to represent feasible solutions and for the rest of the above-defined requirements to be met.

4.4 Replacement

With weak parent replacement, a weaker parent is replaced by a stronger child or vice versa. This keeps improving the overall fitness of the population taking into account that weaker individuals have fair chances in being selected for breeding and subsequently be replaced. Additionally it does not require to be carried centrally (e.g. scan of static ordered population in order to locate the weaker individual) but it is suitable for parallel processing as it favours dynamic populations.

4.5 Population characteristics

A dynamic population is used. A large population was required in order to avoid the loss of genetic diversity. On the other hand, the initialisation was very expensive (a heuristic was used repetitively that first generates baseline routes using random walk on edge maps of a selected subset of customer nodes and then employs a cheapest insertion heuristic to add the rest of the customer nodes to the existing routes; constraints should be met in all cases). Using a dynamic population solved partially this problem since a smaller population was initially created and then the genetic algorithm took over, initially without replacement. Finally, using a dynamic population permitted the asynchronous processing of individuals by sending newborn individuals to a pool, from where they can be distributed over several processors for evaluation and then return to the population.

5   Conclusion

In this paper we have presented a model for solving a real-life vehicle routing problem which meets the requirements of a dairy company. However, the same model applies to many other situations where similar needs and restrictions occur. The latter include: limited vehicle capacity, time windows of serving customers, restricted duration of each route, combination of customers in the same or in different routes, allocation of customers to specific vehicles/drivers, exclusion of customers from specific vehicles/drivers. A significant feature of the problem is the fact that the demand of each customer is not known in advance. It may vary according to expected factors (e.g. seasonality) and unexpected ones (e.g. strikes) and so it is given probabilistically. The possible fluctuations in the demand should be taken into account as they affect the return cost for the remaining products as well as the satisfaction of the customers, and subsequently, in connection with the capacity constraint for the vehicles, they may dramatically influence the scheduling of the routes. In the last section, a strategy that uses genetic algorithms is presented. As the problem depends on a great deal of factors and has quite a few constraints, the size and the complexity of the problem are quite large. The method proposed implies the segmentation of the problem in smaller parts. Distinct, almost independent procedures are required for each part so that parallelization can play a key-role in our approach. Problems of this size and this form constitute an ideal area for the exploitation of capabilities provided by HPCN techniques.

REFERENCES

1. Michalewicz, Zbigniew, Genetic Algorithms + Data Structures = Evolution Programs (3rd edition) Springer-Verlag, 1996
2. Savelsbergh M.W.P., Local Search for Routing Problems with Time Windows. Annals of Operations Research 4, 285-305, 1985.
3. Solomon, Marius M., Algorithms for the Vehicle Routing and Scheduling Problems with Time Window Constraints. Operations Research 35 (2), 254-265, 1987.
4. Thangiah, Sam R., Vehicle Routing with Time Windows using Genetic Algorithms, submitted to the book on "Applications Handbook of Genetic Algorithms: New Frontiers".
5. Thangiah, Sam R. – Osman, Ibrahim H. – Vinayagamoorthy, Rajini – Sun, Tong, Algorithms for the Vehicle Routing Problems with Time Deadlines. American Journal of Mathematical and Management Sciences, 13 (3&4), 323-355.

PARALLEL CLOUD MODELING

ROBERT REILEIN* AND GUDULA RÜNGER

Institut für Informatik, Universität Leipzig, Germany
E-mail: {reilein,ruenger}@informatik.uni-leipzig.de

Atmosphere simulation programs are composed of several submodels, each of which is based on a separate physical model. In this paper we describe parallel implementations of one of those submodels: cloud modeling. We study procedural and data dependencies and investigate different parallelization schemes on clusters of workstations and symmetric multiprocessors (SMPs), respectively.

1 Introduction

Atmosphere or water simulations are time consuming applications which can benefit from parallel computing. There already exists a large variety of sequential and parallel programs in this area, running on a wide range of parallel platforms including workstation clusters and parallel supercomputers, see e.g. [1,2,3]. Still, there is need for a more efficient exploitation of parallel machines as more advanced models will be used to get more realistic simulations of the problem. A careful analysis of the application problem and the parallel programming model of the target machine has to be performed. For distributed memory machines, reducing load imbalances and communication overhead are the main goals.

In this paper, we consider the modeling of cloud behavior which is an important subproblem of most atmosphere simulation programs [4]. Cloud modeling describes the creation, development and breakup of clouds and is commonly used for weather prediction, climate research and environmental pollution studies. The parallel programming model of existing parallel programs is the message-passing paradigm or data parallelism.

We concentrate on the parallelization of cloud modeling with an emphasis on exploiting the algorithmic structure for task or data parallel implementations. The underlying sequential version is the cloud module of the non-hydrostatic mesoscale model GESIMA [5]. The goal is not only to get a very efficient parallel version of the module but also to investigate the characteristics that lead to good parallelization strategies which can be used for further more elaborate cloud models, e.g. spectral models. The spectral modeling is based on cloud modeling, but will contain a larger number of different cloud particles leading to an increase of computation time. Possible generalizations

---

*SUPPORTED BY DFG

of the parallel implementation for spectral cloud models are described in [6]. Our investigations include tests for different parallelization strategies using both the message-passing and the thread programming paradigm. The target machines are clusters of workstations and symmetric multiprocessors (SMPs).

The rest of the paper is organized as follows: Section 2 summarizes the cloud model and the sequential simulation program. Section 3 describes the parallelization strategies and Section 4 presents runtime results on a SUN workstation cluster, a SUN E6000 system and a HP X-Class.

2 Cloud modeling

Meteorological and atmospheric behavior is modeled by a system of partial differential equations derived from conservation laws for mass, heat, motion, water and gases or aerosols. The simulation programs are based on a discretization of the underlying physical space resulting in a three-dimensional grid or graph structure on which approximations of the continuous equations are computed. Dynamical processes are approximated by discretizing the time-dependent partial differential equations on the three-dimensional grid. Physical processes such as radiation and influences of the surface are modeled on smaller scale. When considering mesoscale models the physical processes are included in a parameterized way. Due to the complexity of meteorological simulations each phenomenon is considered in isolation and is realized in a separate submodule. Meteorological and atmospheric simulation programs consist of several submodules simulating subproblems of the atmospheric behavior which interact according to the functionality of the entire model. Those submodules include the simulation of air pressure, temperature, wind, influences of the surface and cloud modeling.

The cloud model contains processes related to the movement of cloud particles and to the cloud micro physics describing the interaction between particles. The number and types of particles simulated in a model depend on the underlying micro physics model. We consider the cloud simulation of the atmospheric simulation program GESIMA (GEesthachter SImulationsModell der Atmosphäre). GESIMA is a non-hydrostatic mesoscale model to simulate atmospheric phenomenons in the scale from a few hundred up to ten thousand meters. To simulate this scale area, so-called anelastic Boussinesq equations for the conservation of mass, impulse and energy are used [5] considering the air as incompressible. The cloud model in GESIMA was introduced to simulate the circulation in an land-sea environment. Currently, there are several versions of the cloud model for GESIMA simulating the cloud physics in different ways. We have chosen the model described in [7].

2.1 Implementation of the cloud model

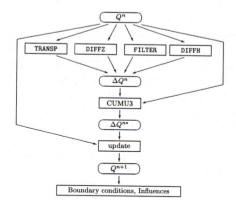

This figures illustrates the control flow of the main submodules and the data flow of the arrays describing and updating the hydrometeors. Q^n denotes an array for one hydrometeor at simulation time step n, ΔQ denotes a temporary array with changes to a hydrometeor array and Q^{n+1} denotes the updated hydrometeor array at simulation time step $n+1$.

Figure 1. Flow graph of the cloud driving module CLOUDP in GESIMA.

The cloud model in GESIMA is implemented as a separate submodule which may be called in each time step of the simulation if the modeling of clouds is required. The input data needed from other parts of the simulation include the pressure, the temperature, and the velocity of the wind. The result of the cloud module are changes to atmospheric data caused by the cloud process. Those atmospheric data are the centered vertical velocity, the potential temperature or input data to the radiation simulation. Internally, the cloud module simulates the creation, development and movement as well as the dispersion of clouds.

The simulation of clouds does not consider clouds as a homogeneous material or object but simulates the behavior of clouds in terms of cloud particles which are cloud water, cloud ice, rain, graupel or snow. The basic data structure of the entire GESIMA simulation model is a three-dimensional staggered grid resulting in a decomposition of the physical space into three-dimensional cells. For each cell all variables including cloud and precipitation particles are defined. We consider a model with 5 particle types which are cloud water, cloud ice, rain, snow, and graupel. Each type is described in two ways which are the mass relation to the air in a cell and the number of particles in the cell. In addition, the aerosol concentration (i.e. the concentration of air particles not containing water) is given in terms of the number of those particles per cell. For all of those 11 particle descriptions, called hydrometeors, an additional temporary array is needed.

The simulation of clouds is subdivided into several submodules each of which is devoted to a different phenomenon. The transport of particles caused by atmospheric fluxes is splitted into the advection realized in submodule TRANSP and the turbulent fluxes in horizontal and vertical direction realized in the submodules DIFFZ and DIFFH, respectively. The movement caused by gravity and the creation and transition of precipitation and cloud particles is done in the micro physics module CUMU3. The subroutine FILTER smoothes the grid values. In each time step the transport subroutines have to be performed for every type of the particles. The micro physics is called only once for each time step after the dynamics has been computed and treats all particle types together. In addition, there are other smaller subroutines to calculate the influence of the cloud particles on the temperature, pressure and vertical velocity. The dependence structure of the cloud submodules in the cloud driving module CLOUDP is illustrated in Figure 1.

3 Parallelization strategies

3.1 Data parallel implementation

Our first implementation is a standard realization of the cloud model with static load balancing in the message-passing paradigm. The distribution of work is based on a partitioning of the three-dimensional grid and the corresponding owner-computes rule. For the grid partitioning horizontal cuts were chosen as data dependencies are stronger in the vertical direction, especially in the micro physics module. The granularity of vertical columns seems to be appropriate for the chosen target machine. The program code was rewritten to support the grid partitioning in terms of columns. The implementation has the following characteristics:

- We provide a subroutine for converting grid data from a standard x-oriented storage scheme into a z-oriented storage scheme, see Figure 2. The program is left unchanged with the exception of access functions to the grid. The advantage is the possibility of static and dynamic irregular grid partitionings.

- At the border of the subgrid of one processor, data in form of columns have to be exchanged. A subroutine selects the boundary data from the z-oriented storage scheme of the subgrid and an encapsulated border exchange performs the non-blocking communication.

- Local arrays of pointers of the size of the horizontal grid describe the irregular data distribution. Local columns are described by non-zero entries which give the position in the z-oriented storage scheme.

- As the new storage scheme destroys the cache-optimized behavior, we have exchanged the order of loops such that the z-loop is the inner loop.

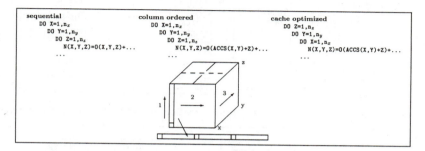

Figure 2. Conversion of the storage-scheme and exchange of the loop order.

From the application programmers point of view it is not visible which set of columns is assigned to a processor. Because of this modular style of programming, it is possible to change the sequential GESIMA code and to combine it with the message-passing program for the cloud module. The message-passing implementation is illustrated in Figure 3.

3.2 Task parallel implementation

The task parallel implementation uses tasks which are created according to the cloud particle types, i.e. for each of the particle arrays Q there is one task which computes the dynamic subroutines, see Figure 4. Each of those tasks is completely independent from the other tasks. In the MPI realization, the appropriate data are send to the corresponding tasks. As the micro physics needs all particle data the corresponding module is executed sequentially. In the POSIX threads implementation the call to the cloud driving module in GESIMA is replaced by a thread creation program in C which creates threads and encapsulates the corresponding data. The underlying functions are the original Fortran routines of the cloud modules which only have to be recompiled for multithreaded programming.

The scalability of the task parallel version is eleven according to the number of particle fields. When using less than eleven processors an automatic load balancing is given by the system thread scheduler. The parallel implementation can potentially handle an arbitrary number of particle types, so that more elaborate modules be supported.

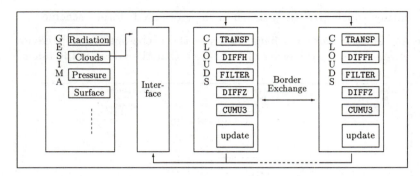

Figure 3. A C-interface organizes the thread creation according to the particles types.

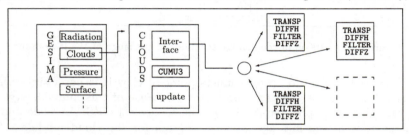

Figure 4. The GESIMA main program sends data to the data parallel cloud module.

4 Experiments

For our runtime experiments we use a geographical area of the Oderhaff, Germany, with size $160km \times 120km$. The initial parameters and data for the mesoscale model are measurements from the 25th July 1997 taken by the weather station at Greifswald, Germany. The special weather situation describes a hot summer day with convective clouds and local precipitation. The nonhydrostatic mesoscale model GESIMA simulates the amount of precipitation on every horizontal grid cell.

The message-passing program was tested on a SUN workstation cluster up to eight workstations. We achieve good performance results using four workstations and medium on eight, see Figure 5. Using message-passing on an SMP machine like HP X-Class Server with eight processors the results are very good, even including superlinear speedups due to cache effects, see Figure 6. The SMP implementation is developed on a SUN E6000 with 16 processors achieving medium performance results, see Figure 6. On this machine, the thread implementation reaches similar speedups as the MPI implementation.

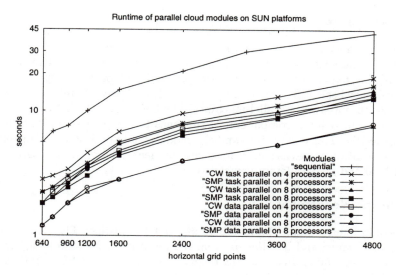

Figure 5. Runtime values for the data and task parallel implementation using MPI on a SUN E6000 (SMP) with 250MHz UltraSPARC-II processors and a SUN workstation cluster (CW) with 300MHz UltraSPARC-IIi processors.

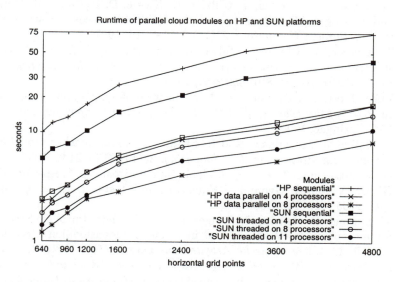

Figure 6. Runtime values for the task parallel implementation with POSIX threads on a SUN E6000 with 250MHz UltraSPARC-II processors and for the data parallel implementation using MPI on a HP X-Class server with 180 MHz HP 8000 processors.

5 Conclusion

We have realized several task and data parallel versions of cloud modeling showing good speedup values on small numbers of processors. The contribution of this paper is not only to show that efficient parallel implementation for grid-based scientific applications is possible on lowly parallel platforms (in contrast to massively parallel machines) like SMPs and workstation clusters, but also to provide a comparison of runtimes for different parallel programming models. This comparison and the modular way of designing our parallel implementation serves as a basis for a development of more sophisticated cloud models aimed at parallel implementations.

6 Acknowledgement

We would like to thank the members of our DFG project TE 51/11-1, especially M. Simmel and N. Mölders from the Institut für Meteorologie, Leipzig, and the Max-Planck-Institut MIS Leipzig for access to the SUN E6000.

References

[1] M. Ashworth, F. Fölkel, V. Gülzow, K. Kleese, D. P. Eppel, H. Kapitza, and S. Unger. Parallelization of the GESIMA mesoscale atmospheric model. *Parallel Computing*, 23(14):2201–2214, 1997.

[2] T. Kindler, K. Schwan, D. Silva, M. Trauner, and F. Alyea. A parallel spectral model for atmospheric transport processes. *Concurrency: Practice and Experience*, 8(9):639–666, 1996.

[3] Luka Onesti and Tor Sørevik. Parallelization of a local area ocean model. In *Proc. of the 1996 Applied Parallel Computing Conference*, pages 543–554. Springer, 1996.

[4] C. Baillie, J. Michalakes, and R. Skålin. Regional weather modeling on parallel computers. *Parallel Computing*, 23(14):2135–2142, 1997.

[5] H. Kapitza and D. P. Eppel. The Non-Hydrostatic Mesoscale Model GESIMA. Part I: Dynamical Equations and Tests. *Beitr. Phys. Atmosph.*, 2(65):129–146, 1992.

[6] M. Simmel, R. Reilein, G. Rünger, and G. Tetzlaff. Parallele Strategien für ein spektrales Wolkenmodul in einem 3-dimensionalen Mesoskalenmodell. In *Meteorologische Arbeiten aus Leipzig (IV)*, 12:217-224, 1999.

[7] R. Devantier. *Wolkenbildungsprozesse über der südwestlichen Ostsee — Anwendung eines neuen Wolkenschemas in einem mesoskaligen Modell.* PhD thesis, Institut für Meteorologie, Universität Leipzig, 1995.

HYBRID SCHEDULING FOR REALISTIC IMAGE SYNTHESIS

ERIK REINHARD

ALAN CHALMERS

Dept. of Computer Science, University of Bristol, Bristol, UK.

E-mail reinhard\alan@cs.bris.ac.uk

FREDERIK W. JANSEN

Fac. of Information Technology and Systems, Delft University of Technology, Delft,

The Netherlands. E-mail: F.W.Jansen@twi.tudelft.nl

Rendering a single high quality image may take several hours, or even days. The complexity of both the model and the lighting simulation may require excessive computer resources. In order to reduce the total rendering time and to accommodate large and complex models that exceed the size of a single processor system, a parallel renderer may provide a viable alternative to sequential computing.

In this paper, a data-parallel strategy is applied to allow large models to be distributed over the processors' memories. The resulting uneven workload is then balanced by scheduling demand driven tasks on the same set of processors. Whether tasks are scheduled demand driven or data parallel, is dependent on the amount of data coherence in the task. Implications of this hybrid algorithm with respect to performance, caching and memory usage are investigated.

1 Introduction

Ray tracing[1] simulates the behaviour of light by shooting rays from the eye point into the scene. Pixels are coloured according to the object that was hit. Shading and shadowing is computed recursively by shooting rays from the intersection point of the ray and the object towards the light sources and into reflected and refracted directions. Some ray tracers extend this "ray tree" by also sampling the indirectly reflected diffuse light by shooting a large number of rays from the intersection point into random directions (ambient sampling)[2].

Lighting simulations are expensive algorithms, whose irregular data access patterns complicate parallel distributed memory solutions, especially on distributed memory computers. In this paper, data access patterns are analysed for a hybrid scheduling solution and its memory usage is evaluated.

Previous parallel ray tracing approaches tend to fall into one of two classes: data parallel and demand driven scheduling. Demand driven[3], usually equivalent to image space partitioning, subdivides the screen into a number of regions. Whenever a processor finishes a task, it requests a new one from the master until the image is complete. Data accesses to most of the scene geometry require scene replication for this method to be most effective. Caching could be used to some extent to salvage performance loss due to excessive data communication (see also section 2).

Data parallel approaches[4] partition object space by distributing the geometry over the processors. Ray tasks are then migrated to the processors that hold the relevant data. A single ray may therefore pass through multiple processors before an intersection is found. At the cost of efficiency, this method allows very large scenes to be rendered.

Hybrid scheduling techniques may overcome the disadvantages of both these methods. One such scheme separates the work into ray traversal and intersection tasks[5]. The former would require only a limited amount of data in the form of the spatial subdivision structure, while for the latter the full object geometry would be required. The ray intersection tasks are scheduled data parallel and provide a basic but uneven load, while the ray traversal tasks are scheduled demand-driven to compensate for this load imbalance. However, ray traversal typically takes less than 10% of the total computation time, and is therefore not computationally intensive enough to effectively balance the load.

Alternatively, coherence could be used to subdivide tasks into data parallel and demand driven components[6]. Coherent ray bundles, which require a relatively small data set while being sufficiently expensive, are for example good candidates for demand driven scheduling, while the remainder of the tasks is handled in a data parallel fashion. Both primary and shadow rays can be grouped into coherent bundles.

This paper first shows the behaviour of object accesses during ray tracing and explains why neither demand driven nor data parallel solutions are likely to be efficient when the scene geometry is distributed. Then our parallel algorithm is briefly described in section 3. Memory and cache management is discussed in section 4, followed by experiments and conclusions.

2 Scene analysis

Assuming that no super-sampling is performed to reduce aliasing artifacts, the computations associated with different pixels are independent. Demand driven algorithms exploit this independence by farming out different parts of the image to different processors. However, sampling an entire ray tree for a single pixel may involve a potentially large and unpredictable subset of the scene geometry. Demand driven algorithms therefore give best performance when the scene data is replicated with each processor. In the case that the processors' local memories are too small, the scene will have to be distributed. In order to reduce the number of data fetches, object caches are normally employed. These caches work under the assumption that object accesses are coherent.

On the other hand, data parallel algorithms distribute the scene over the processors' memories and ray tasks are migrated to the processors that store the relevant data. These algorithms assume that an object distribution can be found which equalises the workload associated with each processor. Unfortunately, predicting object distributions which equalise both workload and memory consumption for each processor, is a non-trivial problem which is as yet unsolved.

The validity of these assumptions can be assessed by collecting statistics during sequential rendering. Counting the number of intersection tests performed for each object provides insight in the distribution of work over the scene. For these tests, the Radiance package[2] was modified. The test scenes are depicted in figure 1.

Figure 1. Left to right: studio model (5311 objects), conference room (3951 objects), colour cube and transparent colour cube (11026 objects each).

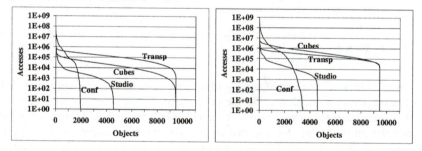

Figure 2. Object accesses sorted by frequency without (left) and with (right) diffuse inter-reflection. Note the logarithmic scale on the vertical axis.

As Radiance has the capability to sample diffuse inter-reflection, its effect on the distribution of work over the scene is measured as well. Results for the four test scenes are depicted in figure 2. In all cases, besides increasing the workload by an order of magnitude, the number of object accesses and the spread over time is larger when diffuse inter-reflection is sampled, thus showing less data locality and thereby reducing cache efficiencies.

For all scenes a small subset of the objects is intersected three orders of magnitude more often than the majority of the objects. This peak is good for demand driven algorithms, provided these objects are cached by all processors. However, the remainder of the objects is still intersected quite often, and hence cache efficiencies can still be low. For data parallel processing, the peak to the left of the figures normally causes severe load imbalances, but a large majority of the objects are accessed more or less evenly. This peak is mainly caused by the light sources, which attract a large portion of the workload, but unfortunately other objects cause load imbalances too.

The temporal access pattern is assessed by looking at the median objects. For the colour cube model, the data accesses per second for one of its objects near the median is given in figure 3. These graphs show that sampling diffuse inter-reflection destroys temporal coherence. But even without ambient sampling, the data accesses for this object are spread out over a considerable amount of time. For other scenes temporal coherence can be better without diffuse inter-reflection, but when ambient sampling is performed, temporal coherence is always lost, irrespective of which scene is rendered.

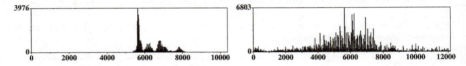

Figure 3. Temporal behaviour for a typical object of the colour cube without (top) and with (bottom) diffuse inter-reflection.

In all, a lack of data locality exists which prevents the design of efficient caches in demand driven algorithms. On the other hand, the peak of object accesses for some objects leads to poor efficiency in data parallel approaches. Hence, we propose to split the problem into demand driven and data parallel components (section 3). Caching will be used to serve objects for the demand driven part (sections 4 and 5).

3 Hybrid scheduling

We propose to implement ray tracing in parallel by using a hybrid scheduling algorithm, consisting of a demand driven and a data parallel part. Each processor handles both types of tasks, but gives data parallel tasks a higher priority, thus achieving automatic load balancing.

Bundles of primary rays and shadow rays are executed as demand driven tasks, while specular reflection and refraction, as well as any diffuse inter-reflection is executed data parallel. The majority of ray tasks is therefore computed in demand driven mode, ensuring load balancing capability until the end of the computation. This was not yet achieved in previous research presented in[6].

The demand driven tasks in this system require objects to be fetched, and a caching mechanism is implemented to reduce overall communication requirements. Because the most unpredictable rays are now executed as data parallel tasks, cache consistency is expected to be better than in pure demand driven approaches. Its details and behaviour are explained in the following two sections, while a more general overview can be found in[7].

4 Memory management

In our hybrid algorithm we would like to be able to fetch data for certain demand driven tasks and have the data parallel component benefit from these fetches without any additional overhead. For this reason, the cache is incorporated into the main spatial subdivision structure, which is based upon an octree (figure 4). All the non-empty leaf nodes in the octree point to an index in a hash table, the hash function being the sum of the objects contained within the leaf node. The hash table contains a set of pointers to objects. Hence, leaf nodes containing the same objects, will address the same index in the hash table. In order to determine which processor stores the data in this object set, a flag field is added to each of these sets, which stores the processor number, as well as a flag indicating whether this object set is cached or not. A non-resident voxel can therefore be requested from the processor which is indicated by this flag field. Currently, the octree and the object sets are replicated with each processor. The objects themselves are distributed.

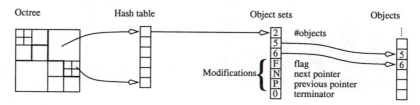

Figure 4. Radiance's data structure, including modifications required for parallel rendering.

During ray traversal, for each new voxel traversed, the flag field is checked to determine whether the data for this voxel is available or not. If not, the ray task is migrated to the processor indicated by the flag field. Otherwise, the objects are intersected with the ray.

When memory is full, some of the object data is freed. To this extent, the cached voxels all link to each other using a doubly linked list, for which the next and previous fields are used (figure 4). When a voxel is traversed, the object set is unlinked

222

from this list and re-inserted at the front. Clearing voxels proceeds from the end of the list, effectively implementing a Least Recently Used (LRU) scheme.

5 Experiments

During the course of the computation, two different types of data need to be stored: objects that can be removed at any time to create more storage space, and data that can not be freed. The resident set belongs to the latter category, as well as storage of intermediary results (intersection points that await results from other processors before shading can be performed) and input buffers. As the size of the object cache is changed, variations in performance and memory consumption can be expected. The smaller the cache, the more data fetches are required, resulting in longer idle time and reduced efficiency. At the same time, intermediary results may need to be stored longer, and therefore memory consumption may be negatively affected. If a processor becomes a bottleneck, then the number of tasks being queued for that processor may become rather large as well.

In order to test this, the studio model (figure 1) was rendered on a Parsytec PowerXplorer. This machine consists of 32 PowerPC 604 nodes running at 133 MHz with 96 MB of memory per node, connected by a 27 MB/s network.

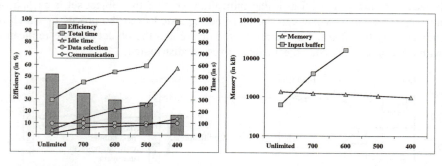

Figure 5. Efficiency and timing (and its components) for the studio model on 8 processors (left) and the associated maximum memory consumption (right).

Linear speed-ups with an efficiency of around 50-60% are obtained when the object cache is large enough to hold whatever data is required by each processor. In that case the algorithm is scalable at least up until 32 nodes. The efficiency is not higher because overhead is incurred for selecting the relevant data for each of the demand driven tasks. However, this overhead is scene and parameter dependent and therefore affects efficiency, but not scalability.

When the cache size is artificially limited to a fixed size, efficiency, scalability and memory consumption does change. Figure 5 (left) shows the efficiency for the studio model on 8 processors with an object cache size that ranges from unlimited to 400 kB along the horizontal axis. The same graph also shows the total rendering time as well as idle time, data selection time and time spent in communication routines. By reducing the object cache size, the loss of efficiency is almost entirely due to an increase in idle time, which is mainly the result of one processor being overloaded. A load balancing bottleneck arises because the smaller the object cache, the less the capability of the demand driven component to balance the workload. Hence, the importance of the demand driven component varies according to the size of its object cache, which makes that this hybrid scheduling algorithm sits in-between pure demand driven and pure data parallel approaches.

When the size of the object cache is reduced to under 400 kB for the studio model, the rendering time increases disproportionately. It appears that this is the point when the most important objects of the studio model, as discussed in section 2, cease to fit in the object caches.

The total memory consumption (figure 5 right), which includes both the object cache and storage of intermediary results, but excludes PVM's input buffers, shows that generally the memory overhead is acceptable and reduces when the object cache is made smaller. This pattern is well-behaved and according to expectation, although with smaller cache sizes, intermediary results may be in memory longer before shading occurs. Unfortunately, for smaller cache sizes, the data parallel component becomes more important (as argued above), and the resulting processing bottleneck is accompanied by a large input buffer of tasks awaiting execution (also depicted in figure 5 right[a]). This is a problem which could be solved by carefully monitoring the amount of work in the system at any one time. By reducing the total amount of work, the processing bottleneck at one processor is not resolved, but the input buffer should be shorter.

As it generally is cheaper for an overloaded processor to serve data to another processor than to execute ray tasks, another possible solution would be to allow data to be fetched more than once for those tasks that required data that was once cached but already replaced by new data. Currently, this memory problem is the most important remaining issue that prevents this algorithm to render very large scenes.

6 Conclusions

In this paper, we have analysed the spatial and temporal behaviour of ray tracing and it is shown that the ray tracing algorithm shows a low degree of data locality, in

---

[a]Measuring the size of a PVM input buffer is inefficient and affects the performance of the algorithm. For this reason, these measurements were carried out separately on a cluster of 8 SGI O2's.

particular when diffuse inter-reflection is sampled. This complicates parallel implementations, assuming the memory associated with each processor is not sufficient to replicate the scene data. Most current parallel implementations are not suitable for efficiently rendering large scenes. When memory permits, our hybrid scheduling algorithm resembles an efficient demand driven approach, but when larger scenes need to be rendered, the algorithm's performance progressively deteriorates towards a data parallel solution. It is therefore more capable of exploiting the available memory than pure data parallel implementations, while also being more efficient than demand driven approaches for those cases where the scene data can not be completely replicated. A gradual trade-off between memory use and performance is therefore possible, thus optimising efficiency when large scenes are to be rendered. However, before this can be achieved within our implementation, we have to implement a mechanism to control the work-flow in order to avoid flooding any input buffers.

Acknowledgements

This work was sponsored by the European Commission under TMR grant number ERBFMBICT960655 and by the Stichting Nationale Computerfaciliteiten (National Computing Facilities) for the use of supercomputer facilities, with financial support from the Nederlandse Organisatie voor Wetenschappelijk Onderzoek (Netherlands Organisation for Scientific Research).

References

1. T Whitted. An improved illumination model for shaded display. *Communications of the ACM*, 23(6):343–349, June 1980.
2. Greg Ward Larson and Rob A Shakespeare. *Rendering with Radiance*. Morgan Kaufmann Publishers, 1998.
3. S A Green and D J Paddon. Exploiting coherence for multiprocessor ray tracing. *IEEE Computer Graphics and Applications*, 9(6):12–26, November 1989.
4. Mark A. Z. Dippé and John Swensen. An adaptive subdivision algorithm and parallel architecture for realistic image synthesis. ed. Hank Christiansen, *Computer Graphics (SIGGRAPH '84 Proceedings)*, pages 149–158, July 1984.
5. I D Scherson and C Caspary. Multiprocessing for ray tracing: A hierarchical self-balancing approach. *The Visual Computer*, 4(4):188–196, 1988.
6. Erik Reinhard and Frederik W Jansen. Rendering large scenes using parallel ray tracing. *Parallel Computing*, 23(7):873–886, July 1997.
7. Erik Reinhard, Alan Chalmers, and Frederik W Jansen. Hybrid scheduling for parallel rendering using coherent ray tasks. In *Proceedings Parallel Visualization and Graphics Symposium*, 1999.

A PARALLEL ARCHITECTURE FOR INTERACTIVE FEM COMPUTATIONS IN A SURGERY SIMULATOR

A. RHOMBERG, C. BRECHBÜHLER, G. SZÉKELY, AND G. TRÖSTER

Department of Electrical Engineering
Swiss Federal Institute of Technology (ETH)
CH-8092 Zürich, Switzerland

For a laparoscopic surgery simulator, large deformations of soft tissue are computed in real time using the explicit Finite Element Method (FEM). Stability issues impose $100\,\mu s$ time steps. The required performance of several GFLOPS can only be achieved with a parallel computer. This paper describes tools and methods for partitioning and scheduling as well as the design of parallel hardware and algorithms. Emphasis is put on a communication concept that provides the necessary low latency and high bandwidth.

1 Introduction

In comparison to open surgery, endoscopic operations, also termed "keyhole surgery", can greatly reduce the tissue damage necessary to reach the operation site and shorten the recovery time for the patient. The price for this improvement is paid by the surgeon, whose task is more difficult due to the loss of direct access to the operation site, monocular view, loss of tactile feedback, and the need for indirect movements. A significant amount of training is required to develop a reasonable dexterity in working under these conditions. In today's training there is a big step from manipulating matches and rubber foam in a box to the participation as an assistant in an actual surgery. Our group is developing a simulator based on virtual reality technology[3] to bridge this gap. We want to achieve more realistic elastic organ behavior than earlier systems[4].

Like a surgeon, the user of the simulator holds in his hands the back ends of an optic device and an instrument, both entering through holes in the phantom belly wall. In real surgery, the optic device consists of a light source and a miniature camera. The instrument may be a blunt probe, an electric coagulator, a tongue, or scissors. The handles of both devices on the simulator are the same as in the operation room. Inside the phantom, the current position and orientation of the devices are encoded and sent both to the mechanics and graphics engines. The mechanics engine determines any contacts between the instrument and inner organs and computes the resulting deformations of the organs and the according reaction forces. It sends the latter back to the instrument device for force feedback. The graphics engine receives the new shape of the deformed organs and renders them with high realism, as seen from the current point of the camera. The resulting inside view of the abdomen appears on a monitor in front of the surgeon, just like in an actual surgery[5].

2 System Overview

The simulator is modularly built of five components, which are implemented as separate programs. The central controller starts up both devices, instrument and optics, and the engines for the mechanics computation and graphics. Physically based mechanical behaviour is achieved by explicit FEM simulation[6]. Stability dictates that the time step be smaller than the time a sound wave takes to traverse the smallest element. In our application the time step is $100\,\mu s$, and computations must be completed in this interval for interactive speed. This can only be achieved with parallel computation for any reasonable number of elements[7]. Consequently the mechanics engine runs on a network of parallel processors[2].

The hardware to run the whole surgical simulator consists of two parallel computers. One is a Silicon Graphics Onyx-2 8 processor SMP machine that is used for rendering photorealistic graphics and for the top level co-ordination of different software parts. About 4 processors along with dedicated render pipes are needed for the graphics alone. The second parallel computer is a Beowulf-type cluster that is needed for the power consuming real time Finite Element calculations. This machine consists of 64 workstations connected over an Ethernet switch for normal cluster operation and a Myrinet network for high bandwidth/low latency communication[8,1].

3 Parallel Computer Topology

The 3D structure of the FE model suggests distributing computation to a 3D lattice of processor elements, each connected to its direct neighbours (over local channels) as well as to a global bus. The problem is divided into clusters

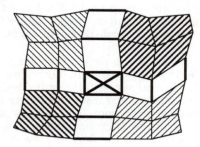

Figure 1. Distribution of FE on processors with communication lines

of elements, which are distributed among the processors. As most of the data is exchanged between processors with elements that share nodes, the local channels can handle most of the data transfer

Some data is also exchanged between arbitrary processors, requiring a global method of communication. The whole structure is mapped on a packet switched network with Myrinet cards.

We shall call the three local communication directions west↔east (or x), north↔south (or y), and above↔below (or z). These directions only refer to the organisation of processors and not to any spatial direction.

When we use a grid of $n_x \times n_y \times n_z$ processors, a processor is identified by its co-ordinates i_x, i_y, and i_z, where $0 \leq i_x < n_x$, $0 \leq i_y < n_y$, and $0 \leq i_z < n_z$. A processor can have up to six local communication channels, but processors on the border of the grid lack some neighbours.

4 Partitioning and Scheduling

We distribute the elements of the FE model to the processors in the grid, assuming this mapping from elements to processors as given. Each processor is assigned a number of elements, the internal reaction forces of which is has to compute, as exemplified in Fig. 2. One node is usually shared by several

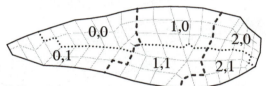

Figure 2. Distributing elements to processors. The large numbers are the processor coordinates i_x, i_y. Between elements, x borders are dashed, y borders are dotted.

elements. All elements incident in a node exert a force on that node; the resulting force accelerates this lumped mass. When the contributing elements reside on different processors, all those processors update their copy of the node and need the resulting force to update its position. This force is accumulated in the course of the communication between the processors involved, using local communication where possible.

To minimise the effects of communication latency, we schedule concurrent computation and data transfer between elements. Computation happens element-wise and is divided into four batches. Elements with any node on the x border make the first batch (Fig. 3(a)). The x communication phase follows, sending border nodes in x direction. While this data transfer is in progress, remaining elements with nodes on a y border are computed: this is the second batch (Fig. 3(b)). The partial forces now received from x direction add to the own forces of each processor. The y communication phase follows similarly, concurrent with the third batch, and then z communication and the fourth, "inner" batch. At the end of the time step, all instances of a node have accumulated the total force from all elements acting on that node (Fig. 4). The presented parallelization / splitting scheme does not change the result.

Given a distribution of finite elements to processors, we have the tools to automatically schedule what computations will be carried out in what batch on each processor, and which nodes to send in what particular order in the

228

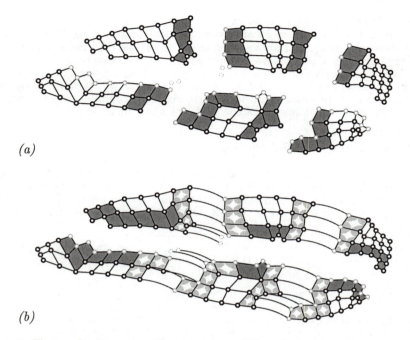

(a)

(b)

Figure 3. Phases of a time step. The elements on different processors are moved apart. Inertial and gravitational forces act initially on thickly lined nodes. Initial forces of the gray copies of nodes are zero.
(a): Batch 0 computes ("recovers") reaction forces for elements on the x border (dark shade means ongoing computation).
(b): Some forces of computed elements on their nodes are now known, indicated by a light shade in the respective corners. Now the processors exchange results from batch 0 on x border nodes; arcs show communication. Concurrently, batch 1 computes elements on the y border. In the next step, the "inner" elements are recovered while forces are communicated in y direction

three communication phases. A given mapping of elements to processors allows force accumulation through *local* channels if and only if for all nodes, the co-ordinates of the involved processors differ at most by one in any communication direction. Otherwise, the forces of the offending nodes must be accumulated using the global bus.

Any node may need communication in x, y, and/or z direction; this means its forces will be transferred up to three times. This node is then on a x, y, and/or z border. The border nodes imply the classification of the elements into four batches: An element having any node on an x border belongs to the "x" batch. An element having a node on a y border (but none on an x border) belongs to the "y" batch. Similarly the remaining elements belong to

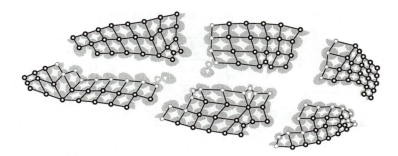

Figure 4. After the last batch of elements is computed and all incoming forces have been added, all nodes have the correct resulting force.

the "z" batch if they have any node on a z border, otherwise to the "inner" batch.

A working prototype demonstrates the validity of the parallelisation strategy and tools. It implements processing elements as separate Unix processes communicating over MPI or sockets, while the construction of the parallel hardware is in progress. The program also runs on the first implementation of the parallel computer, two alphas connected over a Myrinet and controlled via Internet by an SGI machine.

5 Communication

The main concerns for communication are low latency of messages and low overhead in the processors. Sufficient bandwidth is needed to guarantee that the network doesn't saturate. A major concern is minimal work for the processors, as several small messages have to be transferred during a $100\,\mu s$ time step. To optimise the communication the properties of the problem and the network are exploited. The network has a very low error rate and high reliability and it preserves the order of the communication. The problem has repetitive and symmetric data transfer that can be predicted at the time the model is distributed to the processors.

5.1 Sending and Receiving

Direct Channels To send data on a direct channel, a CPU stores the information directly in the memory of the Myrinet card. As the program can do this right after the results are computed, the stores are from cache or even from register. This method thus uses less time and introduces less latency than setting up a DMA. Additionally, there is no sharing of the DMA between outgoing and incoming messages. Once all the data of packet is queued up, the communication function tells the Myrinet processor to send it off. This first sends out the route and the header with the length of the packet and then sets up the DMA that puts the data out the door. In the receiving

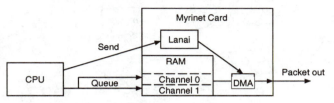

Figure 5. Outgoing data

Myrinet card, a DMA to receive packet is always set up. Once the packet is completely in local memory, the Lanai analyses its header and sets up a host DMA to forward it to the correct location in the host's main memory. The main program waits for the data by polling a memory location until the correct number has arrived.

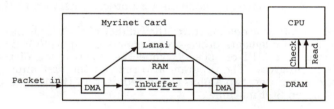

Figure 6. Incoming data

Global Communication The sending of global data is essentially the same. First, the sender initialises a packet with the target address and length. After queuing up the data, the CPU tells the Myrinet processor to send the data to a certain processor. The receiving Myrinet card analyses the packet and determines the correct buffer space to store the data by adding the received address to the base address of the buffer for global data. All Data transfers are executed by a user space program, which runs without system calls and therefore needs no expensive context switches.

5.2 Communication Protocols

We use two different communication protocols, one for data exchange between neighbours and the other between arbitrary processors. On the direct channels, the processors send data in a fixed order. The receiving processor identifies the data by the order in which it reads it, so no additional administrative information has to be transmitted. The receiving Myrinet card needs information about the length of the packet, so this is stored right after the header. The protocol for global communication needs something for identification, as global data can arrive in any order at a particular processor. This additional data is an offset within the receiving buffer, where this message is to be stored. Both protocols have an additional data word, which makes

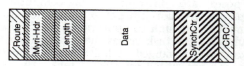

Figure 7. Direct Channel Protocol

up the protocol for the processor. The communication part of the program attaches to each packet a running number (SynchCtr) which the receiver then waits for to determine that the correct packet has arrived.

Figure 8. Global Bus Protocol

5.3 Co-ordination/Synchronisation

Different types of co-ordination are necessary: The correct data has to be used in every time step, and we have to make sure that no data is overwritten before it's used. Further, every processor has a fixed amount of memory that the Myrinet card DMA can access. This memory has to be managed, as up to six neighbouring processors write on the local channels and any other processor could want to write on the global bus into this buffer.

Different CPUs have to stay synchronous. The application calls for a barrier synchronisation at the beginning of each time step, but this is very slow. As data is always written to the same memory location, we have to make sure that the receiving processor has already processed a piece of information before we overwrite it with the next one. To allow for a loose and less expensive synchronisation, we can use one important property of our problem: Communications are always symmetrical. For every packet sent, there is one received. When we receive data from another processor, we know that it has processed the information from the preceding time step, so we can overwrite that buffer. By using two alternating receive buffers for every channel and the symmetrical property of the communication, we are sure to have adequately synchronised processes without additional overhead.

The memory for inbound global data is simply managed by assigning a part of it to every remote processor. As communication is highly predictable, there is not much need for flexibility.

6 Conclusions

To realistically simulate the mechanical behaviour of human organs during virtual surgery, a physically based calculation is needed. The preferable explicit

232

Finite Element Method poses hard constraints on the computer on which it runs. The main problems are the short time step needed for stability, close interaction between elements, and high computational needs that require a parallel computer. Parallelising the task leaves the programmer with lots of short messages that have to be exchanged within a single time step. Traditional parallel computers are not suited for such a task. By exploring the special properties of our problem concerning parallelisation, communication, and synchronisation, we are able to fit this problem on standard workstations with a fast interconnect. We use communication and synchronisation that need virtually no processor involvement and constrain each data transfer to a small part of the network, thus getting a scalable parallel computer optimally suited for the task.

References

1. H. Vonder Mühll. *Concept and Implementation of a Scalable Architecture for Data-Parallel Computing*. Diss. (phd thesis) eth nr. 11787, ETH Zürich, Konstanz, 1996.
2. A. Gunzinger, U. Müller, W. Scott, B. Bäumle, P. Kohler, H. Vonder Mühll, F. Müller-Plathe, W.F. van Gunsteren, and W. Guggenbühl. Achieving supercomputer performance with a DSP array processor. In *Supercomputing '92*, pages 543–550, Minneapolis, 1992. IEEE/ACM, IEEE Computer Society Press.
3. M. Sagar, D. Bullivant, G. Mallinson, and P. Hunter. A Virtual Environment and Model of the Eye for Surgical Simulation. In *Computer Graphics Proceedings*, Annual Conference Series, pages 205–212, 1994.
4. U. Kühnapfel et al. Endosurgery with KISMET. In *Virtual Reality World*, pages 165–171, 1995.
5. Gábor Székely, Christian Brechbühler, Roland Hutter, Alex Rhomberg, Nicholas Ironmonger, and Peter Schmid. Modelling of soft tissue deformation for laparoscopic surgery simulation. In William M. Wells et al., editors, *First International Conference on Medical Image Computing and Computer-Assisted Intervention MICCAI'98*, number 1496 in Lecture Notes in Computer Science, pages 550–561. Springer Verlag, 1998.
6. Klaus-Jürgen Bathe. *Finite element procedures*. Prentice Hall, Englewood Cliffs, New Jersey, 1996. Rev. ed. of *Finite element procedures in engineering analysis*, 1982.
7. V.E. Taylor. *Application-Specific Architectures for Large Finite-Element Applications*. PhD thesis, Dept. El. Eng. and Comp. Sci., Univ. ov California, Berkeley, California, 1991.
8. Alex Rhomberg, Rolf Enzler, Markus Thaler, and Gerhard Tröster. Design of a fem computation engine for real-time laparoscopic surgery simulation. In *Proceedings of the First Merged International Parallel Processing Symposium and Symposium on Parallel and Distributed Processing*, pages 711–715. IEEE Comput. Soc, Los Alamitos, CA, USA, 1998.

Algorithms

HIPERBUILD: AN EFFICIENT PARALLEL SOFTWARE FOR 3D STRUCTURAL ANALYSIS OF BUILDINGS

JOSÉ M. ALONSO, VICENTE HERNÁNDEZ AND ANTONIO M. VIDAL

Universidad Politécnica de Valencia, Departamento de Sistemas Informáticos y Computación, Camino de Vera s/n, 46022 Valencia, SPAIN
E-mail: {jmalonso,vhernand,avidal}@dsic.upv.es

Nowadays, the need of efficient software able to analyse and design 3D structures of large buildings in a very reduced time is clearly required by architects and civil engineers. Moreover, an understanding and real-time 3D visualisation is also demanded. However, computational power and memory requirements to fulfil these goals can become enormous. This paper enables this possibility by means of *HIPER*BUILD, an approach based on parallel computing. The system has been designed to work efficiently, even by using cost-effective PC-based platforms.

1   Introduction

Structural analysis of buildings is the process to determine the response of a structure to specified external loads or actions. This response is usually measured by establishing the forces and displacements at any point of each structural member.

This structural analysis plays a central role during the preliminary design stage of a building, when several alternatives have to be considered (see Figure 1). Each design involves a thorough consideration of the loads and actions that the structure will have to support, including the conditions that will occur during the construction phase. For each design, a structural analysis is necessary, determining the forces and deformations throughout the structure. Frequently, these preliminary designs are based on simplified models to minimize the time and effort invested in this phase.

Before proceeding to the next phase, a selection among the alternatives is necessary. However, all the alternatives are rejected in some cases, and a return to the design stage must be carried out. The structural analysis that is now required for this final design stage must be carried out with great accuracy. All the simplifications of the preliminary design stage have to be eliminated. This requirement of accuracy is due to a need of structural safety. Simplified models such as 2D, can constitute a satisfactory approach when used on simple structures. Nevertheless, they have been found inadequate when applied to complex structures, where more accurate 3D models are needed. It is obvious that unless the mathematical model is sufficiently realistic the results will be of questionable value.

Whereas 2D models involve $3N$ degrees of freedom (number of nodal displacements to be found during the analysis), 3D models deal with $6N$ degrees, where N is the number of nodes considered in the structure. Taking into account that the 3D analysis of a building structure implies the sum of all the flat subsystems

236

involved, the complexity of the problem to be solved increases substantially. As an example, complex buildings or buildings designed with two way floors or continuous slabs can reach up to 15,000 or 20,000 nodes. As six degrees of freedom have to be considered, linear systems of about 100,000 equations must be solved.

The requirement of speed in the structural analysis is imposed by the need of having comprehensive information of the structure in the preliminary design cycle, when several alternatives are analyzed. Moreover, the most appropriate design is then selected for detailed study in the final design phase. Thus, a large number of different structural configurations have to be analyzed quickly to achieve the most efficient solution (the cheapest and safest one). A trial-error process is developed by the structural engineer, where different proportions are given to the members of the building, the whole structure is analyzed and the results are interpreted.

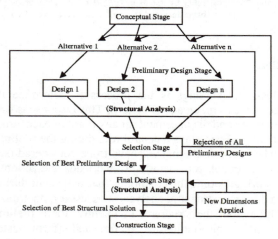

Figure 1: Flow diagram describing engineering design process.

Therefore, it is clear that the structural analysis is one of the most time-consuming phases in the design cycle of a building. Obviously, the demanded speed to efficiently manage large systems requires the application of advanced techniques, such as parallel computing, able to reduce the time spent on this analysis.

2 *HIPER*BUILD Demonstrator

*HIPER*BUILD is a parallel prototype that combines a very powerful and efficient 3D static structural analysis tool with a graphic tool able to manage both the data input (pre-processing) and the post-processing of realistic images in real-time [8,9]. The parallel platform required can be a cluster of Fast-Ethernet linked PCs, running under an easily available operating system such as LINUX or WINDOWS NT. MPI library has been used to perform the communications among the processors that collaborate in different phases of the analysis. Besides, the application is portable and can be run on a wide range of more powerful supercomputers or workstations.

2.1 The Method of Analysis

The matrix methods [1] represent the most powerful design tool in structural engineering and they are very suitable to be implemented on parallel computers. These methods are based on the concept of replacing the actual continuous structure by a mathematical model made up from structural elements of finite size having known elastic and inertial properties that can be expressed in matrix form. The matrices representing these properties are considered as building blocks, which, when fitted together according to a set of rules derived from the theory of elasticity, provide the static and dynamic properties of the actual structural system. Such finite-sized particles have a specified shape, and are referred to as *the structural elements*, and they are specified somewhat arbitrarily by the analyst in the process of defining the mathematical model of the continuous structure. The properties of each element are calculated, using the theory of continuous elastic media, whereas the analysis of the entire structure is accomplished for the assembly of the individual structural elements. When the size of the elements is decreased, the deformational behavior of the mathematical model converges to that of the continuous structure. One of these matrix methods of analysis, called *the stiffness method*, has been parallelised in *HIPER*BUILD. This method employs the stiffness properties of the structural elements to form a set of simultaneous equations that represents the relationship between nodal forces acting on the structure and displacements. The unknown joint movements are computed by solving the equilibrium equations at the joints. At each joint, the loading conditions are specified by six force components, and the response is described by six displacement components. The method is based on the following distinct phases:

2.2 Generation of Stiffness and Force Matrices

First of all, the stiffness matrix of the whole structure $K_E \in \Re^{6N \times 6N}$, which models the building, is derived from assembling the individual member stiffness matrices of all the structural elements, where N represents the total number of joints or nodes (points where two or more structural elements are joined). On the other hand, the force matrix $Q_G \in \Re^{6N \times M}$ is composed of all the different applied forces (dead loads, live loads, wind, snow, rain, soil, and so on), where M is the total number of loads.

Both matrices are generated in parallel in the following way: firstly, the processor P_0, which is in charge of reading from disk the geometry of the building or which had initially stored this information in memory, broadcasts it to the rest of processors $P_1, ..., P_{p-1}$, where p is the total number of processors. Then, the N joints of the structure are divided into p groups of N/p contiguous elements. Each such group composed of the nodes with indices $(N/p)i, (N/p)i+1, ..., (N/p)(i+1)-1$ is assigned to each processor P_i that will be responsible for assembling its local part of the matrices K_E and Q_G in parallel by generating the rows with indices *(6N/p)i, ..., (6N/p)(i+1)-1*. No communications are required in this phase of the structural analysis, and as a result, the global stiffness and force matrices have been partitioned among the processors following a rowwise block-striped distribution. This data-mapping scheme has been chosen taking into account the initial distribution of data needed by the next step of the structural analysis.

2.3 Joint Movement Calculation

In response to the forces that act on it, a structure undergoes deformations. At the joints of the structure, these deformations are manifested by a set of displacements. In the case of 3D structures, there are six independent displacement components for each joint, one translational component along each of the three co-ordinate axes, and a rotational component about each axis. The relationship between the external forces Q_G and displacements q_G is given by:

$$Q_G = K_E.q_G \qquad (1)$$

Thus, a linear system must be solved to calculate the joint movements. It must be pointed out that this step represents the most time-consuming part in the whole structural analysis. A very good precision is also desirable to be obtained. Since the coefficient matrix K_E is sparse, symmetric and positive definite, a parallel approach of the Cholesky factorization has been applied. This direct method comprises the following four steps: *ordering, symbolic factorization, numerical factorization* and *solution of triangular systems*. Owing to the high degree of sparsity in the stiffness matrix of the structure, K_E, efficient data storage formats have been used, substantially reducing the memory requirements. Although an iterative method could have been selected, a direct method has been preferred because of its robustness. Since structural matrices are usually very ill-conditioned, the use of an iterative method would imply to compute a good preconditioner. The effort involved in it may outweigh the cost of direct factorisation and the parallel performance of computing this preconditioner in parallel, e.g. in the case of incomplete LU or Cholesky factorisation preconditioners, is not good in distributed memory computers at the moment.

During the ordering phase, a permutation matrix P is chosen in order to reduce the fill-in during the numerical factorization phase of the new coefficient matrix PK_EP^T. On sequential computers, the primary goal of reordering the matrix is simply to reduce the number of operations and the space required for the numerical factorization. The number of operations required is usually related to the number of non-zero elements in the Cholesky factor. Serial algorithms in nature such as *Multiple Minimum Degree* or *Cuthill-McKee* produce very good orderings. However, on a parallel platform, a fill reducing ordering, besides minimizing the number of flops must also determine an ordering appropriate for efficiently performing the factorization in parallel, with a good load balance. In our case, a parallel version of *Multilevel Nested Dissection* algorithm, based on the *Multilevel Graph Bisection* partitioning algorithm has been applied [2,3]. The *supernodal elimination tree* [4] is also generated by this ordering phase.

During the symbolic factorization step, the non-zero structure of the triangular Cholesky factor L is computed ($PK_EP^T = LL^T$). In the parallel algorithm applied, the supernodal elimination tree is distributed among the processors using the *subtree-to-subcube* mapping and the columns of K_E of each supernode are distributed using a *bitmask based block-cyclic strategy*. The structure of L is computed in a bottom-up fashion, where the non-zero structure of the leaf nodes is firstly computed and sent upwards in the elimination tree to the processors that store the next level supernode. These processors compute the non-zero structure of their supernode and join it with the structure received from their children nodes.

The values of the non-zero elements in L that satisfy $PK_EP^T = LL^T$ are computed in the numerical factorization stage. A parallel version of the *multifrontal algorithm* has been applied [5,6,7]. Broadly speaking, there are two levels of parallelism in this numerical phase. Firstly, the processing of the frontal/update matrices associated with two nonoverlapping subtrees can be treated as completely independent tasks. Secondly, since the amount of computation involved in the assembly and partial elimination of a frontal matrix can be quite substantial, a further subdivision of the task into smaller subtasks must be considered. In this way, the supernodal elimination tree is distributed among the processors following the same subtree-to-subcube strategy mentioned in the symbolic factorisation phase, and the frontal matrix of each supernode is assigned to them using the same bitmask based block-cyclic strategy. With this distribution, the extend-add operations of the algorithm are computed in parallel and each processor exchanges approximately half of its data with its partner from the other subcube. The parallel factor operation at each supernode is based on the dense column Cholesky factorisation.

Finally, two triangular systems $Ly = Q_G'$ and $L^Tq_G' = y$ must be solved by using a forward elimination and backward substitution respectively, where $Q_G' = PQ_G$ and $q_G' = Pq_G$. At last, the joint displacements q_G are achieved by using $q_G = P^Tq_G'$. The parallel version of the algorithm is again governed by the supernodal elimination tree and it uses the same subtree-to-subcube mapping and the same two-dimensional distribution of the matrix L as mentioned in both factorizations. Whereas for the forward elimination the computation proceeds in a bottom-up fashion, the parallel backward substitution proceeds from the top supernode of the tree down to the leaf.

2.4 Member End Action Calculation

Once the movements in all the nodes of the building are known and the part calculated by each processor has been sent to the rest of processors, the member end actions of all the structural elements (Eq. 2) (forces generated within the structure in response to the applied loads) and the support reactions (Eq. 3) (forces at points attached to the rigid foundation to equilibrate the effects of the applied loads) are also calculated in parallel.

The members of the structure have been previously divided into p groups composed of (B/p) consecutive elements, where B is the total number of structural elements in the whole structure. Each processor P_i is assigned one such group, with the members whose indices are $(B/p)i$, $(B/p)i+1$, ..., $(B/p)(i+1)-1$ and calculates, without communications, the member end actions and the support reactions for all the different load hypotheses applied to the structure [1]. End actions (axial, shearing, torsion and bending moments) Q_i and Q_j for a member b connecting the nodes i and j verify the equation:

$$
\begin{pmatrix} \{Q_i\}_b \\ \{Q_j\}_b \end{pmatrix}_L = \begin{pmatrix} \{Q_i^e\}_b \\ \{Q_j^e\}_b \end{pmatrix}_L + \begin{bmatrix} [K_{ii}][R^T][K_{ij}][R^T] \\ [K_{ji}][R^T][K_{jj}][R^T] \end{bmatrix} \cdot \begin{pmatrix} \{q_i\}_b \\ \{q_j\}_b \end{pmatrix}_G
$$

(2)

where Q_i^e and Q_j^e stand for the member b end equivalent loads in local axes. K_{ii}, K_{ij}, K_{ji} and K_{jj} are the compound elementary matrices of the member b stiffness matrix K in local axes, R the rotation matrix and q_i, q_j are the global movements in the nodes i and j, previously worked out. As seen, 12 internal forces are computed for each member, 6 corresponding to its initial node i and 6 corresponding to its final node j. Support reactions Q_i for a node i are simply the internal forces of this node in global axes, as indicated by the Eq. 3:

$$
\{Q_i\}_G = [R]\{Q_i\}_L
$$

(3)

2.5 Deformations at any Point of the Structure

Finally, the deformations at the predefined division points of the members, are evaluated in parallel to check that they do not exceed the design limitations. Deflections are caused in members by various types of forces such as axial, shear and bending moments. However, owing to deflections caused by shear and axial forces are usually small, just deflections caused by bending moments are evaluated.

From the studies of strength of materials it may be recalled that the differential equation of an elastic curve is that of the Eq. 4, where $M(x)$ is the bending moment in the point x of a member, $y(x)$ is the function of deflection in the member and E and I represent respectively its modulus of elasticity and the moment of inertia.

$$
\frac{\partial^2 y(x)}{\partial x^2} = \frac{M(x)}{EI(x)}
$$

(4)

The deflections can be obtained by successively integrating twice the $M(x)/EI(x)$ function, but to avoid this integration, the finite difference method has been used. As a result, two tridiagonal systems of linear equations must be solved for each member, one of them performing the deformations in the XY plane and the other one in the XZ plane. The parallelism that takes place is straightforward. Taking into account the previous distribution of the structural elements among the processors, each one is in charge of calculating the deformations at all the predefined division points of the assigned group of members.

3   Experimental Results

Three large buildings have been chosen to compare the performance of the new parallel demonstrator with respect to a well-known 3D serial package. In this serial package, Cholesky decomposition is applied to solve the linear system, previously reordered by using *Minimum Degree* or *Cuthill-McKee* algorithms. Features of these buildings are shown in Table 1.

Table 1. Features of the buildings to be analysed.

	Nodes	Members	Degrees of Freedom	Forces Applied
Building No. 1	5308	8827	31848	3
Building No. 2	10007	17724	60042	1
Building No. 3	9619	17525	57714	7

Table 2 shows the whole analysis times (in seconds) for these buildings. The platform utilized has been a 12-processor Power Challenge Silicon Graphics (SGI), where each processor is a 200 MHz R10000. Time taken by the 3D serial package and *HIPER*BUILD by using 2 and 4 of these processors are compared in the table. *HIPER*BUILD has also been run on a PC-based platform composed of 2 PENTIUM-II biprocessor systems, interconnected with a Fast-Ethernet local network and under LINUX operating system. Each PC has 256 Mb RAM memory and runs at 400 MHz. Analysis time for the 3D serial package is also given on this platform.

Table 2. Execution time needed to analyse the structures.

	Building No. 1	Building No. 2	Building No. 3
3D Package (SGI 1 p.)	451.20	368.20	1093.16
*HIPER*BUILD (SGI 2 p.)	7.77	13.54	29.15
*HIPER*BUILD (SGI 4 p.)	5.02	8.94	12.96
3D Package (PC 1 p.)	455.81	574.23	1560.56
*HIPER*BUILD (PC 2 p.)	7.85	15.65	37.83
*HIPER*BUILD (PC 4 p.)	6.32	10.84	26.79

Finally, the speed-up between the computing time needed by the 3D serial package with respect to the time taken by *HIPER*BUILD is presented in Table 3. When a PC-based platform is employed, *HIPER*BUILD is able to analyse the structure between 36 and 72 times faster than the 3D serial package.

Table 3. Speed-up between the 3D package and *HIPER*BUILD.

	Speed-up	Building No. 1	Building No. 2	Building No. 3
SGI	2 Processors	58.07	27.19	37.50
	4 Processors	89.88	41.18	84.35
PC	2 Processors	58.06	36.69	41.25
	4 Processors	72.12	52.97	58.25

4   Conclusions

In this paper, the heart of *HIPER*BUILD, a parallel software for calculating 3D building structures has been presented. Thanks to the parallel computing and the numerical methods applied, *HIPER*BUILD has demonstrated to be a tool able to reduce substantially the time spent on the structural analysis and improve the accuracy of the solution. These advantages together with the reduction in the memory requirements imply the possibility of studying any kind of structure in a very short time, without the need of using 2D simplified models. As a consequence, a very fast, realistic and accurate analysis of large buildings is now enabled, even using cost-effective PC-based platforms. SMEs in construction can now easily improve their productivity, profits and volume of business.

References

1. Livesley R. K., Matrix Methods of Structural Analysis (Pregamon, 1962).
2. Bui T. and Jones C., A Heuristic for Reducing Fill in Sparse Matrix Factorization, *6th SIAM Conf. Par. Proc. for Scient. Comp.* (1993) pp. 711-718.
3. George A., An Automatic Nested Dissection Algorithm for Irregular Finite Element Problems, *SIAM J. Numer. Anal.* **15** (1978) pp. 1053-1069.
4. Liu J. W. H., The Role of Elimination Trees in Sparse Factorization, *SIAM J. Matrix Anal. Appl.* **11** (1990) pp. 134-172.
5. Heath M. T., Ng E. and Peyton B., W., Parallel Algorithms for Sparse Linear Systems, *SIAM Review* **33** (1991) pp. 420-460.
6. Liu J. W. H., The Multifrontal Method for Sparse Matrix Solution: Theory and Practice, *SIAM Review* **34** (1992) pp. 82-109.
7. Duff I., Gould N., Lescreiner M and Reid J. L., The Multifrontal Method in a Parallel Environment, *Ad. in Num. Comp.*, (Oxford Univ. Press, Oxford, 1990).
8. Alonso J. M., Hernandez V., Vidal A. M., High Performance Computing in the Building Construction Sector, *CIB W78, The life-cycle of Construction IT Innovations* (Stockholm, 1998) pp. 45-54.
9. Alonso J. M., Hernandez V., Vidal A. M. and Abdilla E., Parallel Computing and 3D Structural Analysis of Buildings, *MICAD'99* (Hermes Science Publications, Paris, 1999) pp. 247-254.

PARALLELIZATION OF THE
UMBRELLA MONTE CARLO ALGORITHM

G. ARNOLD[A], TH. LIPPERT[A], TH. MOSCHNY[B] AND K. SCHILLING[A,B]

[a] *Department of Physics, University of Wuppertal, D-42097 Wuppertal, Germany*
[b] *John von Neumann-Institut für Computing, c/o Research Center Jülich, D-52425*
Jülich and DESY, Hamburg, Germany

We present a novel general method to parallelize umbrella and multicanonical Monte Carlo algorithms which are extensively used in statistical physics and lattice field theory. We demonstrate that substantial progress can be achieved in the study of the phase structure of 4-dimensional compact QED by a joint use of the Hybrid Monte Carlo algorithm and multicanonical simulation techniques, through an efficient parallel implementation. Our approach leads to a general parallelization scheme for the efficient stochastic sampling of systems where (a part of) the Hamiltonian involves the total action or energy in each update step.

1 Introduction

It is embarrassing that lattice simulations of compact QED still have not succeeded to clarify the order of the phase transition near $\beta = 1$, the existence of which was established in the classical paper of Guth [1]. This is mainly due to the failure of standard updating algorithms, like metropolis or heatbath to move the system at sufficient rate between the observed metastable states near its phase transition. Due to supercritical slowing down (SCSD) the tunneling rates decrease exponentially in L^3 and exclude the use of lattices large enough to make contact with the thermodynamic limit by finite size scaling techniques (FSS) [2].

A clarification of the order of the phase transition on the Wilson line requires the design of more powerful updating algorithms. A promising method is based on simulated tempering [3], enlarging the Lagrangian by a monopole term whose coupling is treated as an additional dynamical variable. Multiscale update schemes in principle can alleviate critical slowing down (CSD) which is associated with the increase of the correlation length ξ (as measured in a non-mixed phase) near the critical coupling, β_c [4]. However, SCSD cannot be overcome by such type of scale-adapted methods.

Torrie and Valleau [5,6] used arbitrary "non-physical" sampling distributions in their method, termed "umbrella sampling", to improve the efficiency of stochastic sampling for situations when dynamically nearly disconnected parts of phase space occur by biassing the system to frequent the dynamically depleted, connecting regions of configuration space. Berg and Neuhaus [7,8] applied the idea of "umbrella sampling" under the name "multi-canonical algorithm" (MUCA) to the simulation of a variety of systems exhibiting first-order phase transitions. In this procedure, the biassing weight of a configuration with action S is dynamically adjusted such as to achieve a near-constant overall frequency distribution over a wide range of S within a *single* simulation.

Obviously, MUCA in principle offers a powerful handle to deal with SCSD. It remains then a practical question whether one can indeed proceed to large lattices by boosting tunneling rates. This leads us to the key point of this paper: it is a severe shortcoming of the multi-canonical algorithm that its implementation is seemingly restricted to sequential computers, as it requires knowledge of the *global* action, even during local updating. We will show that HMC is from the very outset able to implement MUCA in a parallel manner.

2   Multicanonical Hybrid Monte Carlo

The hybrid Monte Carlo (HMC) algorithm [9,10,11] produces a global trial configuration by carrying out a molecular dynamics evolution of the field configuration very close to the surface of constant action. Subsequently, a Monte Carlo decision is imposed which is based on the global action difference ΔS, being small enough to be frequently accepted. Within HMC, all degrees-of-freedom can be changed simultaneously and hence in parallel. This then provides the straightforward path to implement MUCA as part of HMC on parallel machines: one just uses the values of the global action, as provided by HMC, to compute the bias weight for the MUCA algorithm.

2.1   Multicanonical Algorithm

"Canonical" Monte Carlo generates a sample of field configurations,$\{\phi\}$ according to the Boltzmann weight $P_{\text{can}}(\phi) \sim e^{-\beta S(\phi)}$. The canonical action density which in general exhibits a double peak structure at a first-order phase transition, can be rewritten as

$$N_{\text{can}}(S, \beta) = \rho(S) \, e^{-\beta S}, \tag{1}$$

with the spectral density $\rho(S)$ being independent of the inverse temperature β. The multicanonical approach aims at generating a flat action density

$$N_{\text{MUCA}}(S, \beta_c) = \text{const.}, \text{ for } S_{\text{max1}} \le S \le S_{\text{max2}}, \tag{2}$$

in a range of S that covers the double peaks located at S_{max1} and S_{max2}. Therefore one modifies the sampling weights introducing a multicanonical potential $V_{\text{MUCA}}(S)$,

$$P_{\text{MUCA}}(S) \sim e^{-\beta_c S - V_{\text{MUCA}}(S)}, \tag{3}$$

$$V_{\mathrm{MUCA}}(S) = \begin{cases} \log N_{\mathrm{can}}(S_{\mathrm{max1}}, \beta_c) & S < S_{\mathrm{max1}} \\ \log N_{\mathrm{can}}(S, \beta_c) & S_{\mathrm{max1}} \le S \le S_{\mathrm{max2}} \\ \log N_{\mathrm{can}}(S_{\mathrm{max2}}, \beta_c) & S > S_{\mathrm{max2}} \end{cases}$$

which is constant outside the relevant action range. Since $V_{\mathrm{MUCA}}(S)$ is unknown at the begin of the simulation, it is instrumental for MUCA to bootstrap from good guesstimates. We shall do so by starting from an observed histogram of the canonical action density, $\hat{N}_{\mathrm{can}}(S, \hat{\beta}_c)$, see eq. (1), at the supposed location of the phase transition, $\hat{\beta}_c$. From the action density, we compute $\hat{V}_{\mathrm{MUCA}}(S)$. The sampling then proceeds with the full MUCA weight,

$$\hat{P}_{\mathrm{MUCA}}(S) \sim e^{-\hat{\beta}_c S - \hat{V}_{\mathrm{MUCA}}(S)}$$

$$\sim e^{-\left(\hat{\beta}_c + \hat{\beta}(S)\right) S - \hat{\alpha}(S)}. \tag{4}$$

In order to compute expectation values of observables, one has to reweight the resulting action density to reconstitute the proper canonical density $P_{\mathrm{can}}(S, \hat{\beta}_c) \sim \hat{P}_{\mathrm{MUCA}}(S) \, e^{\hat{V}_{\mathrm{MUCA}}(S)}$. The computation of the multicanonical weights requires the knowledge of the global and not just the local change in action for each single update step. As a consequence, MUCA is not parallelizable for local update algorithms. For remedy, we propose to utilize the HMC updating procedure.

2.2 Hybrid Monte Carlo

The HMC consists of two parts: the hybrid molecular dynamics algorithm (HMD) evolves the degrees of freedom by means of molecular dynamics (MD) which is followed by a global Metropolis decision to render the algorithm exact.

In addition to the gauge fields $\phi_\mu(x)$ one introduces a set of statistically independent canonical momenta $\pi_\mu(x)$, chosen at random according to a Gaussian distribution $\exp(-\frac{\pi^2}{2})$. The action $S[\phi]$ is extended to a guidance Hamiltonian

$$\mathcal{H}[\phi, \pi] = \frac{1}{2} \sum_{\mu, x} \pi_\mu^2(x) + \beta S[\phi]. \tag{5}$$

Starting with a configuration (ϕ, π) at MD time $t = 0$, the system moves through phase space according to the equations of motion

$$\dot{\phi}_\mu = \frac{\partial \mathcal{H}}{\partial \pi_\mu} = \pi_\mu,$$

$$\dot{\pi}_\mu = -\frac{\partial \mathcal{H}}{\partial \phi_\mu} = -\frac{\partial}{\partial \phi_\mu}[\beta S], \tag{6}$$

leading to a proposal configuration (ϕ', π') at time $t = \tau$. Finally this proposal is accepted in a global Metropolis step with probability

$$P_{acc} = \min\left(1, e^{-\Delta\mathcal{H}}\right), \quad \text{with } \Delta\mathcal{H} = \mathcal{H}[\phi', \pi'] - \mathcal{H}[\phi, \pi]. \tag{7}$$

The equations of motion are integrated numerically with finite step size Δt along the trajectory from $t = 0$ up to $t = N_{\text{md}}$. Using the leap-frog scheme as symplectic integrator the discretized version of eq. (6) reads:

$$\phi^{n+1} = \phi^n + \Delta t \cdot \pi^n - \frac{\Delta t^2}{2} \frac{\partial}{\partial \phi}\left(\beta S[\phi^n]\right)$$

$$\pi^{n+1} = \pi^n - \frac{\Delta t}{2} \frac{\partial}{\partial \phi}\left(\beta S[\phi^n]\right) - \frac{\Delta t}{2} \frac{\partial}{\partial \phi}\left(\beta S[\phi^{n+1}]\right). \tag{8}$$

Here we have presented the scheme with both the momenta and the gauge fields defined at full time steps[a], $t = n\Delta t$.

To ensure that the Markov chain of gauge field configurations reaches a *unique* fixed point distribution $\exp(-S[\phi])$ one must require the updating procedure to fulfil *detailed balance*, which is guaranteed by the iterative map of eq. (8) $f : (\phi, \pi) \to (\phi', \pi')$ being

- time reversible: $f(\phi', -\pi') = (\phi, -\pi)$

- and measure preserving: $[d\phi'][d\pi'] = [d\phi][d\pi]$.

Note that the guidance Hamiltonian, eq. (5), defining the MD may differ from the acceptance Hamiltonian in eq. (7), which produces the equilibrium distribution proper. In the following, we shall exploit this freedom to develop two variant mergers of MUCA and HMC.

2.3 Merging MUCA and HMC for Compact QED (MHMC)

We consider a multicanonical HMC for pure 4-dimensional $U(1)$ gauge theory with standard Wilson action defined as

$$S[\phi] = \sum_{x, \nu > \mu} \left[1 - \cos\left(\theta_{\mu\nu}(x)\right)\right], \tag{9}$$

where

$$\theta_{\mu\nu}(x) = \phi_\mu(x) + \phi_\nu(x + \hat{\mu}) - \phi_\mu(x + \hat{\nu}) - \phi_\nu(x)$$

is the sum of link angles that contribute to one of six plaquettes interacting with the link angle $\phi_\mu(x)$.

---

[a] Note that the actual implementation computes the momenta at half time steps initialized and finished by a half-step in π [9]. Each integration step approximates the correct $\mathcal{H}$ with an error of $O(\Delta t^3)$.

Eq. 4 suggests to consider an effective action $\hat{S}$ including the "multicanonical potential" V_{MUCA}

$$\hat{S} = \hat{\beta}_c S + \hat{V}_{\text{MUCA}}(S, \hat{\beta}_c) = (\hat{\beta}_c + \hat{\beta}(S))S + \hat{\alpha}(S). \quad (10)$$

There are two natural options to proceed from here:

MHMC1 performs molecular dynamics using the canonical guidance Hamiltonian

$$\mathcal{H}_{md} = \frac{1}{2} \sum \pi^2 + \hat{\beta}_c S,$$

with standard action S. The resulting gluonic force is given by

$$\dot{\pi}_\mu(x) = \hat{\beta}_c \sum_{\nu \neq \mu} \left[\sin\theta_{\mu\nu}(x - \hat{\nu}) - \sin\theta_{\mu\nu}(x) \right]. \quad (11)$$

MHMC2 makes use of the multicanonical potential as a driving term within the Hamiltonian,

$$\mathcal{H}_{md} = \frac{1}{2} \sum \pi^2 + \hat{S},$$

inducing an additional drift term

$$\dot{\pi}_\mu(x) = \left(\hat{\beta}_c + \hat{\beta}(S) \right) \sum_{\nu \neq \mu} \left[\sin\theta_{\mu\nu}(x - \hat{\nu}) - \sin\theta_{\mu\nu}(x) \right] \quad (12)$$

For both options, the Hamiltonian governing the accept/reject decision, eq. (7), reads equally:

$$\mathcal{H}_{\text{acc}} = \frac{1}{2} \sum \pi^2 + \hat{S}. \quad (13)$$

The latter method is governed by the dynamics underlying the very two peak structure: V_{MUCA} is repelling the system out of the hot (cold) phase towards the cold (hot) phase, thus increasing its mobility and enhancing flip-flop activity.

We comment that the implementation of MHMC2 requires the computation of the global action (to adjust the correct multicanonical weight, eq. (4)) at each integration step along the trajectory of molecular dynamics to guarantee reversibility. In the polygon approximation, this amounts to a determination of the coupling $\hat{\beta}(S)$ at each time step in MD. Note that $\hat{\alpha}$ does not influence MD but enters into the global Metropolis decision, eq. (7). MHMC1 is much simpler, running at *fixed* trial coupling $\hat{\beta}_c$ and avoiding the effort of computing $N_{\text{md}} - 2$ global sums while travelling along the trajectories. It turned out that of both versions, MHMC2 performs better than MHMC1, when autocorrelation and difference in computational effort are taken into account. Thus, we continue our analysis by investigation of MHMC2.

3 Results

In order to quantify the efficiency of the MHMC, we introduce the *average flip time* τ_{flip} defined as the inverse number of the sum of flips between the two phases multiplied by the total number of trajectories. For reference, we additionally measured τ_{flip} from the Metropolis algorithm with reflection steps (MRS) which is considered as a very effective local update algorithm for U(1)[12].

L	β	$\tau_{\text{flip}}^{\text{MRS}}$	$\tau_{\text{flip}}^{\text{MHMC}}$
6	1.001600	508(12)	650(20)
8	1.007370	1023(60)	1173(50)
10	1.009300	2474(117)	2006(84)
12	1.010143	5470(770)	3260(440)
14	1.010668	16400(3300)	5090(630)
16	1.010753	44800(9700)	6350(860)

Table 1. τ_{flip} for MRS and MHMC measured at the simulated β's.

With the results for τ_{flip} on lattices up to 16^4 we are in the position to estimate the scaling behaviour of MHMC in comparison to standard MRS updates. Fig. 1 shows τ_{flip} both for MHMC and MRS as a function of the lattice size L at their respective β-values, as listed in Tab. 1. According to the expected exponential behaviour of $\tau_{\text{flip}}^{\text{MRS}}$ which, in the asymptotic regime $L \to \infty$, should be given by $\tau_{\text{SCSD}} \sim \exp\left(2\sigma L^3\right)$, we perform a χ^2-fit with the ansatz:

$$\tau_{\text{flip}}^{\text{MRS}} = a \, L^b \, e^{cL^3}. \tag{14}$$

which yields $\chi^2_{\text{per d.o.f.}} = 0.897$. As a result, we find a clear exponential SCSD behaviour for the MRS algorihm. On the other hand, for the tunneling times of the MHMC, we expect a monomial dependence in L:

$$\tau_{\text{flip}}^{\text{MHMC}} = p \, L^q \tag{15}$$

The power law ansatz is well confirmed by the fit quality with $\chi^2_{\text{per d.o.f.}} = 0.795$. We also took the pessimistic ansatz and tried to detect a potentially exponential increase of $\tau_{\text{flip}}^{\text{MHMC}}$. The exponential fit gives $\chi^2_{\text{per d.o.f.}} = 0.975$.

In order to compare the efficiency we have to take into account the computational effort. The complexity of the local Metropolis is given by $t_{\text{MRS}} \sim V$ whereas the optimized leapfrog scheme in MHMC scales as $t_{\text{MHMC}} \sim V^{5/4}$ [13].

We extrapolate the sustained CPU time in Tflop-hours required to generate one flip.

As can be seen in Fig. 2, the exponential contribution remains suppressed in the extrapolation. A potentially dominating exponential behaviour for MHMC can only be detected in future MHMC simulations on larger lattices.

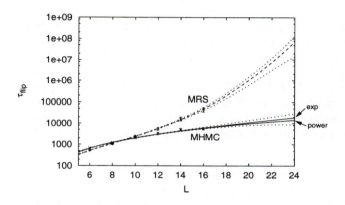

Figure 1. Tunneling times for MRS (exponential fit) and MHMC (lower convex curve is power law, upper convex curve is exponential fit). The errors of the two exponential fits are depicted as dotted lines. The error of the power law fit, eq. (15), is not visible on this scale.

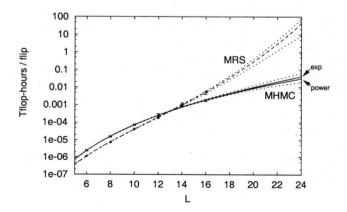

Figure 2. Sustained CPU time in Tflop-hours to generate one flip.

4 Summary and Outlook

We proposed to make use of the multicanonical (MUCA) algorithm within the hybrid Monte Carlo (HMC) updating scheme in order to boost the tunneling rates. Since both algorithms are inherently of global nature, their combination allows the parallelization of MUCA which could not be achieved otherwise.

We have demonstrated that the fully parallel MHMC algorithm is a very effective tool which is able to overcome SCSD as present in the pronounced metastabilities of 4-dimensional $U(1)$ gauge theory. On a 24^4 lattice we predict a gain factor of about 1000 for MHMC over standard local algorithms as the metropolis algorithm with additional reflection. So far, we have encouraging experiences on the 18^4 lattice well confirming the extrapolation results. The investigations presented form part of an ongoing study that aims at a conclusive FSS analysis of compact QED on the Wilson line [14].

References

1. A. H. Guth: Phys. Rev. **D21** (1980) 2291.
2. M. E. Fisher and M. N. Barber: Phys. Rev. Lett. **28** (1971) 1516.
3. E. Marinari and G. Parisi: Europhys. Lett. 19 (1992) 451.
4. S. L. Adler, G. Bhanot, Th. Lippert, K. Schilling, and P. Ueberholz: Nucl. Phys. **B368** (1992) 745.
5. G. M. Torrie and J. P. Valleau: J. Comp. Phys. **23** (1977) 187.
6. J. P. Valleau: J. Comp. Phys. **91** (1996) 193.
7. B. A. Berg and T. Neuhaus: Phys. Lett. **267B** (1991) 249.
8. B. A. Berg: Proceedings of the International Conference on Multiscale Phenomena and Their Simulations (Bielefeld, October 1996), edited by F. Karsch, B. Monien and H. Satz (World Scientific, 1997).
9. S. Duane et al.: Phys. Lett. **195B** (1987) 216.
10. S. A. Gottlieb, W. Liu, D. Toussaint, R. L. Renken, and R. L. Sugar: Phys. Rev. **D35** (1987) 2531.
11. Th. Lippert in: H. Meyer-Ortmanns and A. Klümper (edts.): Proceedings of *Workshop of the Graduiertenkolleg at the university of Wuppertal on 'Field Theoretical Tools for Polymer and Particle Physics'* (Springer, Berlin, 1998), p. 122.
12. B. Bunk: proposal for U(1) update, unpublished, private communication.
13. G. Arnold, Th. Lippert and K. Schilling: Phys. Rev. **D59** (1999)
14. G. Arnold, Th. Lippert, Th. Neuhaus and K. Schilling: to appear.

A TWO-DIMENSIONAL PARALLEL QUADTREE FINITE ELEMENT MESH GENERATOR

A.J. BARRAGÁN*, J.S. REEVE

Department of Electronics and Computer Science, Southampton University, Southampton, SO17 1BJ, Hants, UK

Corresponding author, email: ajbg96r@ecs.soton.ac.uk

In this work we implement a parallel finite element mesh generator for two-dimensional regions, based on recursive spatial division techniques. The main formulation is based on spatial recursive decomposition techniques (RSD) combined with the MPI library. A data structure has been developed aimed at the reduction of inter-processor communication. Results are presented for generation of meshes with a varying number of processors. The extension to the work to 3D regions is also considered.

1   INTRODUCTION

Finite element mesh generation has come a long way since its beginnings, having evolved from being manual procedures for feeding data to finite element programs, to becoming integral part of the solution process. Nowadays, mesh generation is also linked to sophisticated methods for representing complex three-dimensional geometries in an attempt to wholly automate the design-analysis process. Recently, the availability of high performance computing (HPC) has opened the door to the use of more refined meshes. This may allow for more accurate geometric representations in some cases, and more precise iterative methods in others. HPC has become more available for two main reasons: On one side, the increasing ratio performance/cost in hardware, and in the other, the increased availability of programming tools such as the Message Passing Interface Library (MPI), that have lightened the task of writing parallel programs for different computing environments.

2   RELATED WORK

Saxena and Perucchio [4] give definitions of algorithmic parallelism in automatic meshing. They argue that the properties of recursive spatial decomposition (RSD) can be exploited to design a meshing algorithm capable of operating in parallel processing environments. They present a definition of a meshing operator for parallel processing and also algorithms for various stages of the automatic meshing.

Lohner, Canberros, and Merriam [3] developed a system for parallel unstructured grid generation based on the background mesh concept, using a relatively coarse starting mesh whose elements are distributed to the processors for further meshing. Likewise, Hodgson and Jimack [9] use also the same approach in which elements of the background mesh are assigned to each processor to be meshed individually. Load balancing is accomplished by estimating the number of vertices that will be generated within each background element, and splitting the mesh accordingly.

deCougny et al [5] give some details of a parallel mesh generator based on the RSD approach in a MIMD environment. The approach used for load balancing is a bisection-based algorithm that splits portions of the data according to geometric co-ordinates. The main data structures are the mesh and the tree, which must be built initially in a single processor to be distributed afterwards over all the processors.

Spatial subdivision techniques (see [1,2] and references therein) require its own approach to parallelism, as in Simone et al [10,11]. They discuss on tools and techniques for handling octree-based mesh generation in a distributed computing environment. Issues addressed are load balancing procedures based on the partitioning of the data and the migration of the octants from highly loaded to lightly loaded processors.

Vidwans and co-workers [7] develop an algorithm for load balancing three-dimensional unstructured meshes in adaptive processes for fluid dynamics. Their approach employs migration of cells from heavily loaded processors to less loaded neighbouring processors. Later, Globisch [8] presents a program for the parallel generation of tetrahedral meshes in bodies with symmetry of revolution. The strategy is based on the initial decomposition of the region into simply connected sub-domains and then scattering them among the processors.

3   DESCRIPTION OF THE TECHNIQUE

The use of recursive spatial division for finite element mesh generation has been pioneered by Yerry and Shephard [1]. To generate a mesh with this technique, first a quadtree/octree representation is obtained of the region of interest. As a result of this step, the shape of the region is approximated by a set of regions of varying size, stored in a tree-like structure. The shape of these regions is square, in 2D problems, and cubic, in 3D. This has given place to the terms "modified quadtree/octree". In what follows, they will be termed "nodes", to use the tree nomenclature. Nodes that have been divided are termed "branch" and those not divided "leaf" ones. (See fig. 1 for a two-dimensional example)

As the tree is created, the subdivision is applied only to the nodes that intersect the boundary of the region (ON nodes). Unless otherwise specified, the inside nodes are not subdivided to the same level, resulting in adjacent nodes of different size. As a consequence, a given node may have one or more of its corners lying along the sides/faces of an adjacent one. From a finite element point of view, the location of a neighbour's corner along the side of a node must meet some limitations, so a maximum difference of level equal to unity is usually enforced. As a consequence, location of intermediate nodes will be at the middle of a side/face, which is allowed.

The following step is to transform the tree structure into a finite element mesh in such a way to make the ON nodes conform to the boundaries. To achieve this, they have to be modified to make them "fit" to the boundaries of the region. Figure 1 shows both a two-dimensional region and its quadtree subdivision.

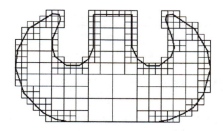

Figure 1. a region and its quadtree representation

4   IMPLEMENTATION.

The parallelisation strategy chosen in this work is based in the master-worker paradigm, which in turn is based in a Single-Program, Multiple-Data (SPMD) model of computation, using the MPI library [6]. In this type of computing environment, interprocessor communication can be very expensive, and as a consequence, a desirable feature of the software to be developed is that such communications are reduced as much as possible.

The main feature of the parallelisation based on the master-worker model of programming is its impact on the design of the program. Initially, the program has been based on recursive data structures based on dynamic memory allocation and being pointer-based, require absolute memory addresses, which are local by nature and lose meaning when sent out of the machine. After an investigation into the nature and the types of data that can be handled by the MPI standard, it was concluded that an adequate message passing could be achieved using static data structures.

This led to the definition of the main data structures for the parallel program which are based in the quadrant as the fundamental type, but now, the tree is stored in an array of structures (quadrants). The role of the master processor is to create the initial array, and then to split it into sub-arrays, which are sent to the worker processors. Thereafter, every processor works on a local queue where the more computationally intensive operations are carried out.

254

A key issue in the mesh generation process is the identification of those steps in which is required to locate the quadrants adjacent to a given one, because it is very likely that at least some of them may have been allocated to another processor, and consequently, some amount of inter-processor communications will become unavoidable. This situation has been addressed in the present work by sorting of the queue created in the first stages (Figure 2), combined with a splitting of the array (Figure 3) according to discrete ranges of the values of the x coordinate.

Figure 2 Sorting of the data structure according to ascending values of x-coordinates (increasing from left to right)

This may create a slight imbalance in the number of quadrants allocated to each processor, but on the other hand, it does produce an organisation of the data that reduces the amount of interprocessor communications.

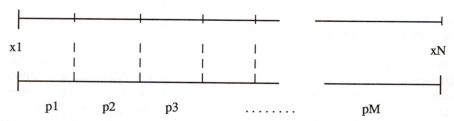

Figure 3. Allocation of the data structure to processors p1 to pM

As a consequence, each processor receives a sorted sub-queue in which only those quadrants "close" to the ends will be likely to have adjacent quadrants in another processor's local queue, but by virtue of the sorted nature of the local queues, it will only be in those processors containing the immediately adjacent queues (Fig 4).

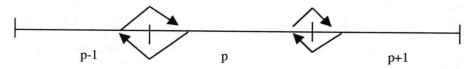

Figure 4. Exchange of information between a processor "p" and its adjacent processors "p-1" and "p+1". The arrows show the flow of information.

As a consequence of all this, a topology is induced among the processors, according to which each processor will only require communications with its two adjacent neighbouring processors (Fig 4).

5   RESULTS AND DISCUSSION

Several environments were used in the development of the software: In the first stages a SPARC machine with simulated distributed memory and where up to eight processors can be simulated was used. Another machine used as a following step was an Meiko CS2, which is also limited to a maximum of eight processors, and finally, the definitive runs were made on an IBM SP2. This machine consists of 23 nodes, having each one a single 66MHz RS6000 processor.

To assess the performance of the program, test runs were made on three different geometries, with a varying number of boundary points ranging from 12 to 237 and, as it can be seen, their complexity varies accordingly (See figs. 5a-5c). Sample meshes for each region are shown in Figure 7.1 to 7.3.

For all the examples the program was timed to obtain the speed-up as a function of the number of processors, and so a number of runs were done for each example with a number of processors ranging from 7 to 20, and the results are shown in figure 6, where each curve corresponds to each one of the example regions.

From the curves shown, it can be seen a marked decrease in time as the number of processors grows, as it was expected. Also is important to note that the shape of the curves is roughly the same, although example 3 displays a steeper decrease in required time in the range of processors from seven to around 12. This could make worthwhile to try this region of low number of processors with bigger meshes. Another feature worth of mention is the flattening of the curves as the number of the processors grows to the maximum.

6   FURTHER WORK

The results obtained are considered to be encouraging to extend the scope of the present work consists of the in order to generate three-dimensional meshes. One of the advantages of the tree-based data structures is that the concepts employed in the generation of two-dimensional meshes can be directly applied to three-dimensional ones. However, special care must be given to some critical issues that arise when handling 3D models, basically due to the inherently superior complexity that such models convey

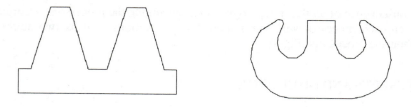

Figure 5.a. Example 1   Figure 5-b. Example 2

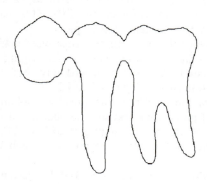

Figure 5-c. Example 3

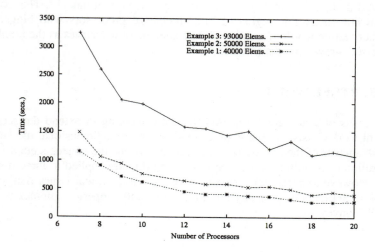

Figure 6. Runtime vs no. of processors

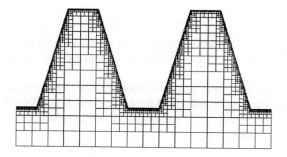

Figure 7.1. Mesh for example 1

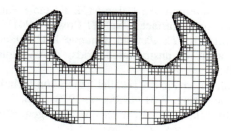

Figure 7.2. Mesh for example 2

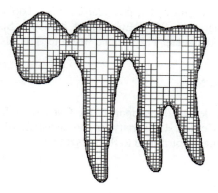

Figure 7.3. Mesh for example 3

REFERENCES

1. Yerry, M.A.; Shephard, M.S.: Automatic mesh generation for three-dimensional solids. Computers & Structures Vol 20 No. 1-3 (1985) pp 31-39.
2. Shephard, M.S.; Georges, M.K.; Automatic three-dimensional mesh generation by the finite octree technique. IJNME Vol 32 (1991) pp 704-749.
3. Lohner, R.; Camberros, J.; Merriam, M.: Parallel unstructured grid generation. CMAME, V95 (1992) pp 343-357.
4. Saxena, M.; Perucchio, R.: Parallel FEM algorithms based on recursive spatial decomposition-I. Automatic mesh generation. Computers & Structures, Vol. 45, No. 5/6 (1992), pp 817-831.
5. de Cougny, H.L.; Shephard, M.S.; Ozturan, C.: Parallel three-dimensional mesh generation. Computing Systems in Engineering, Vol 5, No. 4-6 (1994), pp 311-323.
6. Grop, W.; Lusk, E.; Skjellum, A.: Using MPI: Portable Parallel programming with the Message Passing Interface. The MIT Press (1994).
7. Vidwans, A.; Kallinderis, Y.: Parallel dynamic load-balancing algorithm for three-dimensional adaptive unstructured grids. AIAA Journal, V. 32 No 3 (1994), pp 497-505.
8. Globisch, G.: On an automatically parallel generation technique for tetrahedral meshes. Parallel Computing, V 21 (1995), pp 1979-1995.
9. Hodgson, D.C.; Jimack, P.K.: Efficient parallel generation of partitioned, unstructured meshes. AES Vol. 27 (1996) pp 59-70.
10. Simone, M.L.; Loy, R. M.; Shephard, M.S.; Flaherty, J.E.: A Distributed Octree and its application to Parallel Mesh Generation. SCOREC Report #23-1996, Scientific Computation Research Center, Rensselaer Polythecnic Institute, Troy, NY, USA.
11. Simone, M.L.; de Cougny, H.; Shephard, M.S.: Tools and Techniques for parallel Grid Generation. SCOREC Report #5-1996, Scientific Computation Research Center, Rensselaer Polythecnic Institute, Troy, NY, USA.

ACKNOWLEDGEMENTS

The first author acknowledges the support of the Consejo de Desarrollo Cientifico y Humanistico of the Central University of Venezuela, whose support for the realization of his PhD has contributed to the present paper.

DYNAMIC MULTI-PARTITIONING FOR PARALLEL FINITE ELEMENT APPLICATIONS

A. BASERMANN, J. FINGBERG AND G. LONSDALE

C&C Res. Lab., NEC Europe Ltd., Rathausallee 10, 53757 St. Augustin, Germany

B. MAERTEN

K. U. Leuven, Dept. Comp. Science, Celestijmemlaan 200A, B-3001 Heverlee-Leuven, Belgium

C. WALSHAW

U. Greenwich, Centre for Num. Modelling and Proc. Analysis, Wellington St., Woolwich, London SE18 6PF, UK

1 Introduction

The DRAMA project [1] has been initiated to support the take-up of large scale parallel simulation in industry by dealing with the main problem which restricts the use of message passing simulation codes — the inability to perform dynamic load balancing. The central product of the project is a library comprising a variety of tools for dynamic repartitioning of unstructured Finite Element (FE) applications. The starting point for the DRAMA library is a discretisation mesh distribution into sub-domains that results in imbalanced costs of the application code. The core library functions then perform a parallel computation of a mesh re-allocation that will re-balance the costs based on the DRAMA cost model. We discuss the basic features of this cost model which allows a general approach to load identification, modelling and imbalance minimisation. First results are presented which show the necessity for multi-phase/multi-constraint partitioning components.

2 DRAMA Cost Model

The DRAMA cost model [7] explicitly considers calculation costs w_i per sub-domain i and communication costs $c_{i,j}$ between sub-domains i and j of the parallel application code. For the load-balancing re-partitioning algorithms, it results in an objective cost function F. The model provides a measure of the quality of the current distribution and is used for the prediction of the effect on the computation of moving some parts of the mesh to other sub-domains.

The essential feature is that the cost model is mesh-based, so that it is able to take account of the various workload contributions and communication dependencies that can occur in finite element applications. Being mesh-based, the DRAMA cost model includes both per element and per node computational costs and element-element, node-node, and element-node data dependencies for communication. The DRAMA mesh consists of nodal coordinates and of a list of nodes per element which is a native data structure (element connectivity) in most finite element applications.

In addition to data dependencies between neighbouring elements and nodes in the mesh, dependencies between arbitrary parts of the mesh can occur. For the PAM-CRASH code,[4] such data dependencies originate within the contact-impact algorithms when the penetration of mesh segments by non-connected nodes is detected and corrected. The DRAMA cost model allows the construction of *virtual elements* [2,7] which represent the occurring costs of such dependencies (see also 4). A virtual element is included in the DRAMA mesh in the same way as a real element: as an additional connectivity list of its constituent nodes.

Types u identify calculation cost parameters per element or per node that refer to different kinds of elements, different material properties, or generally different algorithmic parts of the application code requiring different kinds of operations. Communication cost parameters per element-element, node-node, and element-node connection depend on the amount of data that potentially have to be transferred for a link between two objects of type u_1 and u_2.

Different algorithmic parts in parallel application codes that are separated by explicit synchronisation points are defined as *phases* within the DRAMA cost model. DRAMA evaluates the costs per phase *iphase*. The PAM-CRASH code, e.g., can be considered to consist of essentially two sections; stress-strain computations including time integration (FE phase) and contact treatment (contact phase) with a global synchronisation in between and also at the end of each computing cycle.

Cost parameter determination requires application code instrumentation. Numbers of operations per element/node of type u, $nop_i(u)$, can be specified by counting operations **or** by time measurements. The sum over all phases of total calculation times per phase and counting total numbers of computational operations allow the determination of calculation speeds s_i^{calc}. For communication, the number of bytes $noc(u_1, u_2)$ that have potentially to be transferred for a link between two objects of type u_1 and u_2 and communication speeds $s_{i,j}^{comm}$ have to be specified (latency is not considered). $s_{i,j}^{comm}$ essentially depends on the specific communication protocol. A suited communication model considering the message length has to be chosen. Moreover, a correspondence between types and phases must be given.

With these parameters, the DRAMA cost model has the following form.

$$F = \sum_{iphase} \max_i F_i^{iphase} \quad , \quad F_i^{iphase} = w_i^{iphase} + \sum_j c_{i,j}^{iphase}$$

$$w_i^{iphase} = \sum_u N_i(u) \frac{nop_i(u)}{s_i^{calc}} \quad , \quad c_{i,j}^{iphase} = \sum_{u_1 u_2} N_{i,j}(u_1, u_2) \frac{noc(u_1, u_2)}{s_{i,j}^{comm}}$$

$N_i(u)$ is the number of elements/nodes of type u and $nop_i(u)/s_i^{calc}$ is the computational cost of an object of this type. Since only the ratio is relevant both $nop_i(u)$ and s_i^{calc} may be specified as relative values if this makes instrumentation easier. $N_{i,j}(u_1, u_2)$ is the number of elements/nodes in a sub-domain boundary region, and $noc(u_1, u_2)/s_{i,j}^{comm}$ is the potential communication cost for a link between two objects of type u_1 and u_2.

3 DRAMA Library Interface

The interface between the application code and the library is designed around the DRAMA cost model and the instrumentation of the application code to specify current and future computational and communication costs.[2] Thus the application code has to provide DRAMA, per sub-domain, with the current mesh description, i.e., the element-node connectivity including the type information. The elements can be either real or virtual elements. The nodal coordinates are given in addition.

Moreover, the application code places the calculation and communication cost parameters per type at DRAMA's disposal as well as the correspondence between types and phases.

DRAMA returns the new partition in terms of a new numbering of local elements and nodes together with the relationships between old and new numbering systems and the coordinates of the new set of nodes local to a process. The relationships between old and new numbering systems support the application code in building send and receive lists.

4 Dynamic Load Balancing with DRAMA

The goal of any load balancing method is to improve the performance of applications which have computational requirements that vary with time. The DRAMA library is targeted primarily at mesh-based codes with one or more phases. It offers a multiplicity of algorithms allowing the different needs of a wide range of applications (Finite Element, Finite Volume, adaptive mesh refinement, contact detection) to be covered. The DRAMA library contains

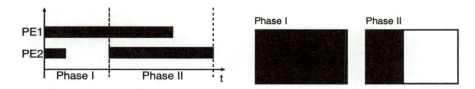

Figure 1. Left: Load imbalance in two phases separated by two sychronisation points. Right: Operations in two phases on different parts of the same mesh.

geometric (RCB), topological (graph) and local improvement (direct mesh migration) methods.[3] It enables the use of leading graph partitioning algorithms through internal interfaces to ParMetis and PJostle.[5,8]

Over using the graph partitioners directly, DRAMA has the following advantages.

1. DRAMA's interface is mesh-based. Since an element-node connectivity list is an essential component of mesh-based application codes DRAMA can be easily integrated. Mesh to abstract graph conversion is performed within DRAMA.

2. Beside graph partitioners, DRAMA offers local improvement (migration) and geometric methods. Thus DRAMA is more general.

3. DRAMA supports cost capturing and cost monitoring.

4. DRAMA supports the application code in building new mailing lists after the re-partitioning.

5. DRAMA allows different element/node type managment.

Thus, DRAMA provides pre-defined solutions for most mesh-based codes.

Many applications consist of several phases separated by explicit or implicit global synchronisation points. This is a challenging problem that requires each phase to be balanced independently. Figure 1 (left) illustrates the situation for two processors and two phases. Both phases show distinct load imbalance. If both phases depend on each other as for the stress-strain and contact phase in PAM-CRASH — the computations refer to the same mesh in both phases — balancing the aggregate costs of both phases is of no use, both phases have to be balanced separately. There are two approaches to this problem, one is to work with a separate division of objects for each phase, the other is to balance each phase on a common partition. The first strategy is advantageous if all computational sections (phases) of the code work on the entire model. It requires fast communication between the different decompositions in each computing cycle. If the code works on different parts of the model (mesh) in different phases it can be favourable to maintain a single mesh decomposition and save communication time. The latter situation is displayed in Figure 1 (right). The first phase refers to the whole mesh, the second only to the left part of the mesh. For a frontal car crash simulation against a rigid wall with PAM-CRASH, stress-strain is computed for the whole mesh whereas contact detection and correction is mainly performed in the front part of the car model.

Here we follow the single mesh decomposition strategy because it is much easier to implement in existing applications. We show first results for the FE phase and contact phase of PAM-CRASH exploiting the new multiphase/multi-constraint options of Jostle and Metis.[6]

The graph-partitioning is built upon a combined graph of elements and nodes [3] because a part of the computation is node-based and a part element-based. The basic objects during contact detection are pairs of nodes and segments of a surface, the segment being defined by four nodes. These objects are passed to the DRAMA library as virtual five-node elements in the DRAMA mesh format.[2]

5 Evaluation of different partitioning techniques

To demonstrate the viability of the DRAMA approach we show first results obtained with multi-constraint (mc) Metis and multi-phase Jostle (MJostle) for a box-beam model with PAM-CRASH. We start from an initial partition with 44% imbalance ($\lambda = 1.44$). The reason for this imbalance are contact calculations in the lowest domain. The cost weights for contact calculations are artificially increased for this small test case to illustrate the effect of multi-partitioning. For the industrial models AUDI and BMW below, realistic weights are applied. After 10,000 simulation cycles, we compute a repartitioning with single-phase/uni-constraint ParMetis static (stat) as well as PJostle diffusion and compare the resulting distribution with the multiphase/multi-constraint approaches.

The load imbalance factors are defined as

$$\lambda^1 = \frac{\max_{i=0..p-1}(\,w_i^1\,)}{\overline{w_i^1}} \quad \text{(FE)}\,, \quad \lambda^2 = \frac{\max_{i=0..p-1}(\,w_i^2\,)}{\overline{w_i^2}} \quad \text{(contact)}\,,$$

Table 1. Distribution of shell elements and contact pairs (CPs) per sub-domain for different partitioning methods together with the load imbalance factors for the box-beam model.

PE	initial		ParMetis stat		PJostle diff		Metis mc		MJostle	
	shell	CPs	shell	CPs	shell	CPs	shell	CPs	shell	CPs
0	512	118	415	61	330	91	512	30	515	30
1	512	0	599	0	516	27	512	30	515	29
2	512	0	445	57	601	0	512	28	507	30
3	512	0	589	0	601	0	512	30	511	29
$\lambda_{1,2}$	1.00	4.00	1.17	2.07	1.17	3.09	1.00	1.02	1.01	1.02
λ_{tot}^1	1.442		1.026		1.004		1.002		1.007	
λ_{tot}^2	1.442		1.302		1.455		1.002		1.007	

$$\lambda_{tot}^1 = \frac{\max_{i=0..p-1}(\sum_j^{nphases} w_i^j)}{\overline{\sum_j^{nphases} w_i^j}} \quad , \quad \lambda_{tot}^2 = \frac{\sum_j^{nphases} \max_{i=0..p-1} (w_i^j)}{\overline{\sum_j^{nphases} w_i^j}} \quad .$$

$\overline{x_i}$ denotes the mean value of all x_i, $i = 0..p-1$. λ_{tot}^1 neglects synchronisation points, whereas λ_{tot}^2, the real load imbalance, considers them.

From Table 1 we see that only multi-partitioning methods can improve the performance of the application; they are the only schemes giving a total imbalance λ_{tot}^2 close to one. Of course, the other schemes minimised the aggregate cost-function as can be seen from the values of λ_{tot}^1 but neglecting the two synchronisation points only results in an increased idle time.

To evaluate the performance of different partitoning methods for more realistic cases we compare results obtained with test meshes of an AUDI and a BMW car model which originate from PAM-CRASH simulations of a frontal impact with a rigid wall. The mesh data are stored after 10,000 cycles from a total of around 80,000 cycles. The two models consist of 4-node shell and 2-node beam elements. The initial total load imbalance of the AUDI model is 12.1%, the initial total load imbalance of the BMW model is 3.1%. For the graph representation of the mesh we use a combined graph [3] consisting of elements and nodes where the connections are only between elements and nodes. We consider the methods listed in Table 2.[5,6,8]

Method 6 is a single phase partitioner and is added for comparison reasons, all other methods are multi-phase/multi-constraint algorithms. Methods 1 and 2 are sequential multi-partitioners, all other methods are parallel. MOC_PARMETIS_SR is a re-partitioner that should minimise load-imbalance and the difference between the current and the new partition. The latter was not investigated here but will be checked in detail in future tests. Tables 3 and 4 show minimum, maximum, and mean total computational weights per

Table 2. Re-partitioning methods.

method	partitioner
1	METIS_mCPartGraphkway, sequential
2	MJostle, sequential
3	MOC_PARMETIS_Partkway
4	MOC_PARMETIS_SR
5	MJostle, parallel
6	PARMETIS_RepartGDiffusion, single phase

phase of 16 sub-domains for the AUDI and the BMW model with all partitioning methods considered. *FE* and *CO* are the costs for the stress-strain phase and the contact phase. Cut edges as well as load imbalance factors per phase and total load imbalance factors are given in addition.

The results in Tables 3 and 4 demonstrate that all multi-partitioning methods are able to achieve nearly perfect load balance. The multi-partitioners reach a load imbalance of around 1% and less for both models whereas the single phase partitioner ends up with a load imbalance of about 15% for the AUDI and of about 9% for the BMW.

6 Conclusions

As demonstrated by tests with meshes from a real industrial simulation code, all multi-partitioning methods achieve nearly perfect load balance whereas single phase partitioners fail to improve the initial imbalance. The new mesh distribution balances both computational phases simultaneously with small remaining imbalance.

Acknowledgements

First, the authors would like to thank all our colleagues from the DRAMA project. Particular thanks go to ESI for providing access to the PAM-CRASH code. The support of the European Commission through ESPRIT IV (Long Term Research) Programme is gratefully acknowledged.

References

1. The DRAMA Consortium, Project Homepage:
   http://www.cs.kuleuven.ac.be/cwis/research/natw/DRAMA.html

Table 3. Total computational weight per phase, cut edges, and imbalance, AUDI.

meth.	FE [min max]	CO [min max]	edge cut	imbalance [FE CO] tot.
1	[10428 10437]	[126 134]	2193	[1.000 1.011] 1.001
2	[9354 10536]	[132 134]	3116	[1.001 1.011] 1.010
3	[10095 10548]	[128 136]	2308	[1.011 1.026] 1.011
4	[10158 10632]	[126 136]	2682	[1.019 1.026] 1.019
5	[10380 10518]	[130 136]	2641	[1.008 1.026] 1.008
6	[9075 11070]	[0 1128]	4154	[1.061 8.513] 1.155
	mean: 10432.1	mean: 132.5		

Table 4. Total computational weight per phase, cut edges, and imbalance, BMW.

meth.	FE [min max]	CO [min max]	edge cut	imbalance [FE CO] tot.
1	[19647 19653]	[232 246]	4018	[1.000 1.006] 1.000
2	[17238 19992]	[238 246]	8472	[1.017 1.006] 1.017
3	[19281 19857]	[220 248]	4096	[1.010 1.014] 1.011
4	[19245 19848]	[234 250]	4017	[1.010 1.022] 1.010
5	[19422 19953]	[238 252]	5029	[1.015 1.030] 1.016
6	[18525 20706]	[0 982]	6863	[1.054 4.014] 1.090
	mean: 19650	mean: 244.6		

2. The DRAMA Consortium, *Updated Library Interface Definition*, DRAMA Project Deliverable D1.2b,[1], 1999.

3. The DRAMA Consortium, *Report on Re-Partitioning Algorithms and the DRAMA Library*, DRAMA Project Deliverable D1.3a,[1], 1998.

4. J. Clinckemaillie, B. Elsner, G. Lonsdale, S. Meliciani, S. Vlachoutsis, F. de Bruyne and M. Holzner, *Performance issues of the parallel PAM-CRASG code*, Int. J. Supercomputer Applications and High Performance Computing, **11 (1)**, page 3-11, 1997.

5. G. Karypis and V. Kumar, *ParMetis: Parallel graph partitioning and sparse matrix ordering library*, University of Minneapolis, tech. rep. #97-060.

6. G. Karypis and V. Kumar, *Multilevel Algorithms for Multi-Constraint Graph Partitioning*, University of Minneapolis, tech. rep. #98-019.

7. B. Maerten, D. Roose, A. Basermann, J. Fingberg, and G. Lonsdale, *DRAMA: A library for parallel dynamic load balancing of finite element applications*, Proceedings of the *Ninth SIAM Conference on Parallel Processing for Scientific Computing*, SIAM, Philadelphia, CD-ROM, 1999.

8. C. Walshaw, M. Cross, and M. Everett, *Parallel Dynamic Graph Partitioning for Adaptive Unstructured Meshes*, J. Par. Dist. Comput., Vol. 47, No. 2, pp. 102-108, 1997.

FACTORIZED APPROXIMATE INVERSE PRECONDITIONING OF A PARALLEL SPARSE EIGENSOLVER

LUCA BERGAMASCHI, GIORGIO PINI

Dipartimento di Metodi e Modelli Matematici per le Scienze Applicate, Università di Padova, Via Belzoni, 7, 35131 Padova PD, Italy
E-mail: berga, pini@dmsa.unipd.it

FLAVIO SARTORETTO

Dipartimento di Informatica, Università di Venezia, Via Torino 155, 30172 Mestre VE, Italy
E-mail: sartoret@dsi.unive.it

In this paper we analyze the parallel efficiency of the *approximate inverse pre-conditioners* AINV and FSAI as DACG preconditioners for the solution of Finite Element and Finite Difference eigenproblems. DACG is an optimization method which sequentially computes the smallest eigenpairs of a symmetric, positive definite, generalized eigenproblem, by CG minimizations of the Rayleigh quotient over subspaces of decreasing size. Numerical tests on a Cray T3E Supercomputer were performed, showing the high degree of parallelism attainable by our code. We found that AINV and FSAI are both effective preconditioners for our parallel DACG algorithm.

1 Introduction.

An important task in many scientific applications is the computation of a small number of the leftmost eigenpairs (the smallest eigenvalues and corresponding eigenvectors) of the problem $Ax = \lambda Bx$, where A and B are large, sparse, symmetric positive definite matrices.

In this paper we analyze the performance of two preconditioning techniques when applied to an optimization method, called DACG (Deflation-Accelerated Conjugate Gradient) [1]. DACG sequentially computes a number of eigenpairs by CG minimizations of the Rayleigh quotient over subspaces of decreasing size. When effectively preconditioned, we found [2] that the efficiency of DACG well compares with that of established packages, like ARPACK. We exploit two preconditioners, FSAI [3] and AINV [4], falling into the class of *approximate inverse preconditioners*. Let A be a symmetric positive definite (SPD) matrix. AINV, which was developed in [4] for linear systems, relies upon the following ideas. One can evaluate A^{-1} by a biconjugation process applied to an arbitrary set of linearly independent vectors. A convenient choice is the canonical basis $(e_1, \ldots e_N)$. This process produces a unit upper triangular matrix $\tilde{Z}$, and a diagonal matrix D such that $A^{-1} = \tilde{Z}D^{-1}\tilde{Z}^T$. Actually, even with sparse A, the factor $\tilde{Z}$ is usually dense. The AINV preconditioner is based on the idea of building a sparse approximation to $\tilde{Z}$ by reducing the amount of fill-in occurring in the computation. This is obtained by annihilating all the elements whose absolute value is smaller than a drop tolerance ε. If the process is completed successfully, which is guaranteed for example when A is an H-matrix [4], a unit upper triangular matrix $\bar{Z}$ and a diagonal matrix with positive diagonal entries $\bar{D}$, are obtained. Thus, a sparse approximate inverse of A, $M = \bar{Z}\bar{D}^{-1}\bar{Z}^T = ZZ^T$ is produced, being $Z = \bar{Z}\bar{D}^{-1/2}$.

The FSAI preconditioner [3] consists of computing a lower triangular matrix $\hat{G}_L$ by solving the matrix equation $(\hat{G}_L A)_{ij} = \delta_{ij}$, $(i,j) \in S_L$, S_L being a prescribed lower triangular sparsity pattern, including the main diagonal. We set $S_L = \{(i,j) : A_{ij} \neq 0, i \geq j\}$, i.e. the same pattern as A. The final approximate inverse $M = G_L^T G_L$ comes from the preconditioning factor G_L, which is obtained by setting $G_L = D\hat{G}_L$, where the diagonal matrix D is computed in order to have $(G_L A G_L^T)_{ii} = 1$.

A parallel implementation of the DACG algorithm has been performed via a data-parallel approach, allowing preconditioning by any given approximate inverse. Ad-hoc data-distribution techniques allow for reducing the amount of communication among the processors, which could spoil the parallel performance of the ensuing code. An efficient routine for performing matrix-vector products was designed and implemented. We have exploited the parallel AINV-DACG and FSAI-DACG algorithms in the solution of Finite Element (FE) and Finite Difference (FD) eigenproblems, both in two and three dimensions. Numerical tests on a Cray T3E Supercomputer show the high degree of parallelism attainable by our code, and its good scalability level.

2 Parallel DACG algorithm.

The s leftmost eigenpairs, (λ_j, u_j), $j = 1, \ldots, s$, of the generalized eigenvalue problem $Ax = \lambda Bx$, are computed by the following Conjugate Gradient procedure. Let $U_j = \{u_1, \ldots, u_{j-1}\}$, $j > 1$, $U_1 = \emptyset$.

DO $j := 1, s$

1. Start with an initial vector x_0 such that $U_j^T Bx_0 = 0$, set $k = 0$, $\beta_0 = 0$. Set tolerances $\varepsilon_1, \varepsilon_2$.
2. Compute $x_0' := Ax_0$, $x_0'' := Bx_0$, $q_0 \equiv q(x_0) := x_0^T x_0' / x_0^T x_0''$.
3. REPEAT

   (a) $g_k \equiv \nabla q(x_k) := (2/x_k^T x_k'')[x_k' - q_k x_k'']$.

(b) $g'_k := Mg_k,$ $\qquad$ M SPD preconditioner.

(c) IF $k > 0$ THEN $\beta_k := g_k^T(g'_k - g'_{k-1})/g_{k-1}^T g'_{k-1}.$

(d) $\tilde{p}_k := g'_k + \beta_k p_{k-1}.$ $\qquad$ $p_k := \tilde{p}_k - \sum_{i=1}^{j-1} (v_i^T \tilde{p}_k) u_i.$

(e) $p'_k := Ap_k,$ $\qquad$ $p''_k := Bp_k.$ $\qquad$ $\alpha_k := \arg\min_t\{q(x_k + tp_k)\}.$

(f) $x_{k+1} := x_k + \alpha_k p_k,$ $\qquad$ $x'_{k+1} := x'_k + \alpha_k p'_k,$ $\qquad$ $x''_{k+1} := x''_k + \alpha_k p''_k.$

(g) $q_{k+1} \equiv q(x_{k+1}) := x_{k+1}^T x'_{k+1}/x_{k+1}^T x''_{k+1},$ $\qquad$ $k := k + 1.$

UNTIL $\qquad$ $|q_k - q_{k-1}|/q_k < \epsilon_1$ $\qquad$ or $\qquad$ $\|x'_k - q_k x''_k\|_2/\|x'_k\|_2 < \epsilon_2.$

4. $\lambda_j := q_k,$ $\qquad$ $u_j := x_k/\sqrt{x_k^T x''_k},$ $\qquad$ $v_j := Bu_j.$

END DO

One can see that each new eigenpair, (λ_j, u_j), $j > 1$, is computed by minimizing the Rayleigh Quotient over the subspace B-orthogonal to $u_1, \ldots, u_{j-1}$.

The algorithm can be decomposed into a number of scalar products, daxpy-like linear combinations of vectors, $\alpha v + \beta w$, and matrix–vector multiplications. We focussed on parallelizing these tasks, assuming that the code is to be run on a machine with p identical, *powerful* processors, our model machine being a Cray T3E Supercomputer.

Scalar products, $v \cdot w$, are distributed among the p processors by a uniform block mapping. The results are combined via a global reduce operation. For any vector combination $z = \alpha v + \beta w$, each processor j computes only a sub-block consisting of $[N/p]$ elements.

Each $N \times N$ matrix is uniformly row-partitioned among the p processors.

The implementation of each matrix-vector product Cv, where C is either A, B, Z, or Z^T, is tailored for application to sparse matrices, by minimizing data communication between processors [5]. Let $C = (c_{ij})$, $h = [N/p]$. Define the sets $R_j = \{h(j-1)+1, \ldots, hj\}$, for each $j = 1, \ldots, p-1$, together with $R_p = \{h(p-1)+1, \ldots, N\}$. R_i encompasses the indices of rows belonging to processor i. Let $P^i = \{c_{rj} \neq 0, \ r \in R_i\}$ be the set including the nonzero elements stored into processor i. Define $P_1^i = \{c_{rj} \in P^i, j \notin R_i\}$. Let $F_k^i = \{j : c_{rj} \in P_1^i, j \in R_k\}$; $G_k^i = \{j : c_{rj} \in P_1^k, j \in R_i\}$. Recall that processor i has in its local memory the components $v^{(j)}$, $j \in R_i$. One can see that to complete a matrix-vector product Cv, the elements $v^{(j)}$, $j \in F_k^i$ must be received from processor k. At the same time the elements $v^{(j)}$, $j \in G_k^i$ must be sent to processor k. Our matrix-vector routine exchanges precisely these elements and no more, thus providing a large saving in the communication time.

3 Numerical tests.

We now report the numerical results obtained applying the DACG procedure to a number of FE and FD problems. The procedure was carefully implemented in Fortran 77, using MPI for executing the parallel tasks. The computations were performed on the Cray T3E 1200 machine at CINECA Computing Center, located in Bologna, Italy.

#	problem	N	N_{nz}
1	2d – FE	10,593	72,737
2	2d – MFE	28,600	142,204
3	3d – FE	42,189	602,085
4	3d – FD	64,000	438,400
5	3d – FD	216,000	1,490,400
6	3d – FE	268,515	3,926,823

Table 1. *Main characteristics of the sample problems. N = matrix size, N_{nz} = nonzero elements in matrix A; FE = Finite Elements, FD = Finite Differences, MFE = Mixed Finite Elements.*

The machine is a *stand alone* system made by a set of DEC-Alpha 21164 processors, performing at a peak rate of 1200 Mflop/s, which are interconnected by a 3D toroidal network having a 480 MByte/s payload bandwidth along each of 6 torus directions. In the present configuration there are 256 processing elements, half of them have a 256-MByte RAM, the others a 128-MByte RAM.

Table 1 lists the main features of the selected test problems, which arise from the discretization of parabolic and elliptic equations in two and three space dimensions. They are representative of a larger set of tests that we performed.

Table 2 shows the number of non-zero elements in each preconditioning factor, together with the number of iterations performed to compute the smallest $s = 10$ eigenpairs. In all but one problem we set $\epsilon_1 = 10^{-8}$, $\epsilon_2 = 10^{-3}$. When $N = 268,515$, to get an accuracy which is comparable to the other cases, we set $\epsilon_1 = 10^{-15}$, leaving $\epsilon_2 = 10^{-3}$. T(M) is the CPU time (in the sequel, all CPU times are measured in seconds) spent to compute the preconditioning factors. IC(0) is the standard incomplete Cholesky preconditioning factor, with the same sparsity pattern as A. The FSAI factor has the same pattern, too, but needs more iterations than IC(0) to converge. With respect to IC(0), a larger number of non-zero elements in AINV is needed to achieve convergence in quite the same number of iterations. On the other hand, IC(0) is not suitable to parallel computations, so it was run only on a single processor. Jacobi preconditioning needs a larger number of iterations to achieve convergence. Incidentally, note that running the un-preconditioned DACG is not worth, requiring much more iterations than with Jacobi. As an example, when N=268,515, the un-preconditioned DACG does not attain convergence

#		IC(0)	Jacobi	FSAI	AINV(ε)		
					$\varepsilon = 0.1$	$\varepsilon = 0.05$	$\varepsilon = 0.025$
1	$N_{nz}^{(M)}$	41,665	10,593	41,665	34,468	97,051	219,818
	iter.	1,285	3,411-3,533	1,676	2,234	1,407	1,019
	T(M)	0.01	-	0.08	0.16	0.20	0.37
2	$N_{nz}^{(M)}$	85,402	28,600	85,402	201,765	464,705	790,632
	iter.	1,978	7,621	4,056	2,276	1,614	1,381
	T(M)	0.02	-	0.18	0.31	0.54	0.90
3	$N_{nz}^{(M)}$	322,137	42,189	322,137	141,956	341,523	601,360
	iter.	913	2,981	1,414	1,527	1,024	824
	T(M)	0.11	-	0.81	0.53	0.69	1.08
4	$N_{nz}^{(M)}$	251,200	64,000	251,200	251,200	251,200	798,640
	iter.	751	2,005-2,164	1,116-1,271	1,145	1,145	945
	T(M)	0.07	-	0.51	0.65	0.65	1.61
5	$N_{nz}^{(M)}$	853,200	216,000	853,200	853,200	853,200	2,732,760
	iter.	1,133	3,002-3,526	1,681-1,925	1,672	1,672	1,308-1,321
	T(M)	0.26	-	1.74	1.94	1.94	5.89
6	$N_{nz}^{(M)}$	2,097,669	268,515	2,097,669	985,304	1,626,471	4,421,002
	iter.	1,605	8,325-8,330	4,431-4,435	3,649	3,493	2,229
	T(M)	4.88	-	5.07	3.34	4.55	13.42

Table 2. *Number of nonzero entries, $N_{nz}^{(M)}$, in the preconditioning factors. The number of iterations (iter.) needed to achieve convergence when computing $s = 10$ leftmost eigenpairs of the sample problems is also shown. When the number of iterations changes with the number of processors, the minimum and maximum values are reported. T(M) gives the CPU seconds spent to compute each preconditioner.*

to the smallest eigenpair within 2000 iterations. In some cases the number of iterations changes with the number of running processors. AINV is more robust than Jacobi and FSAI, since the change in the number of iterations occurs only in one case ($N = 216,000$, $\varepsilon = 0.025$), and the variations with Jacobi and FSAI are much larger.

Concerning the efficiency of our matrix-vector routine, Table 3 reports the average number of elements sent (received) by one processor to perform the products Av and ZZ^Tv, when $N = 28,600$. The amount of data exchanged by each processor, for performing one matrix-vector product, is far smaller than $[N/p]$ values sent to (received from) each other processor, which applies to the unoptimized approach. Using our approach, when the pattern of the matrix is not much dispersed away from the diagonal, each processor sends/receives data to/from a small number of processors. Table 4 reports the CPU time, T_p, spent for computing $s = 10$ eigenpairs, on p processors, together with the speedups, $S_p = T_1/T_p$. The time for performing data input

p	# data					
	Av		$ZZ^T v, \varepsilon = 0.1$		$ZZ^T v, \varepsilon = 0.025$	
	opt.	unopt.	opt.	unopt.	opt.	unopt.
2	179	14,300	240	28,600	910	28,600
4	269	21,450	359	42,900	1,355	42,900
8	314	25,025	418	50,050	1,579	50,050
16	336	26,812	448	53,624	1,691	53,624
32	348	27,706	463	55,412	1,718	55,412

Table 3. *Average number of floating point values (#data) sent (received) by a single processor, in a p-processor run, when performing the products Av and $ZZ^T v$. "opt." stands for our optimized matrix-vector routine, compared with the unoptimized (unopt.) product. Z is the AINV factor for $\varepsilon = 0.1$, $\varepsilon = 0.025$. (Problem 2, $N = 28,600$).*

is not included, nor is the time for computing the preconditioners. When $N = 268,515$ the one-processor run with AINV(0.025) was not performed, due to storage limitations. The corresponding speedups cannot be computed. Due to its slower convergence, Jacobi-DACG usually requires larger CPU times than AINV-DACG and FSAI-DACG in multiprocessor runs, despite its good parallel performance. This result shows that AINV and FSAI are effective preconditioners for our DACG algorithm.

Comparing Table 2 with Table 4, one can see that the time spent for evaluating the AINV and FSAI preconditioners is a small fraction of the overall CPU time, thus on this ground neither FSAI can be preferred to AINV, nor the cost of their computation makes Jacobi preconditioning far superior.

Inspecting Table 4, one can see that good speedups are obtained for the larger problems, scoring up to $S_{32}=24.48$ for FSAI-DACG, when $N=268,515$, which can be considered very satisfactory. The speedup values increase with N, showing that our approach for parallelization is well suited to large problems. When $N = 216,000$, and $N = 268,515$, in some cases $S_2 > 2$ was experimented, due to a smaller number of iterations performed when $p = 2$. AINV and FSAI produce similar speedups, sometimes being better the former ones, sometimes the latter ones. Good speedups are scored exploiting Jacobi, which confirms its good parallel performance. To compare AINV efficiency with FSAI, we observe that the ε value allowing the smallest AINV-DACG CPU time is problem, and p, dependent. However, inspecting Table 4, we see that a convenient choice is $\varepsilon = 0.05$. For this setting, when $p = 1$ AINV-DACG runs faster than FSAI-DACG. On the other hand, when $p=32$, due to

#	precond.	T_1	T_2	T_4	T_8	T_{16}	T_{32}	S_2	S_4	S_8	S_{16}	S_{32}
1	Jacobi	75.64	39.18	23.14	14.28	10.83	10.42	1.93	3.26	5.29	6.98	7.25
	AINV(0.1)	45.96	25.74	14.98	9.44	7.06	6.20	1.79	3.07	4.87	6.51	7.41
	AINV(0.05)	35.18	19.14	11.20	7.36	6.10	4.50	1.84	3.14	4.78	5.77	7.82
	AINV(0.025)	36.64	18.84	10.49	6.41	5.00	4.45	1.94	3.49	5.72	7.33	8.23
	FSAI	35.01	19.52	11.18	7.00	5.13	3.88	1.79	3.13	5.00	6.82	9.02
2	Jacobi	264.66	138.31	78.58	45.90	28.83	21.49	1.91	3.36	5.76	9.18	12.31
	AINV(0.1)	122.74	66.55	36.98	21.52	13.56	10.64	1.84	3.32	5.70	9.05	11.54
	AINV(0.05)	126.42	64.48	34.96	20.55	13.16	10.31	1.96	3.62	6.15	9.61	12.26
	AINV(0.025)	147.89	76.93	40.81	22.88	14.09	10.21	1.92	3.62	6.46	10.50	14.48
	FSAI	177.29	92.39	52.41	31.32	20.06	15.37	1.92	3.38	5.66	8.84	11.53
3	Jacobi	209.77	109.21	61.16	34.90	21.17	14.30	1.92	3.42	6.01	9.90	14.66
	AINV(0.1)	129.73	67.94	37.59	21.89	13.97	10.27	1.91	3.45	5.93	9.29	12.63
	AINV(0.05)	106.23	55.99	29.55	17.64	10.53	8.50	1.90	3.59	6.02	10.09	12.50
	AINV(0.025)	99.31	52.68	29.09	16.69	10.73	7.98	1.89	3.41	5.95	9.26	12.44
	FSAI	141.45	74.25	40.94	23.35	14.48	10.71	1.91	3.46	6.06	9.77	13.21
4	Jacobi	191.52	95.93	48.71	27.84	16.91	11.01	1.99	3.93	6.87	11.32	17.39
	AINV(0.1),AINV(0.05)	133.58	69.09	38.03	21.54	13.31	9.28	1.93	3.51	6.20	10.04	14.39
	AINV(0.025)	154.86	80.52	43.74	24.32	14.92	11.25	1.92	3.54	6.37	10.38	13.77
	FSAI	135.35	69.84	36.65	23.43	13.37	8.41	1.94	3.69	5.78	10.12	16.09
5	Jacobi	992.44	452.15	272.93	138.96	80.79	49.24	2.19	3.63	7.14	12.28	20.15
	AINV(0.1),AINV(0.05)	644.71	339.43	176.38	95.24	53.45	31.49	1.90	3.66	6.77	12.06	20.47
	AINV(0.025)	750.03	372.77	201.75	103.69	55.59	34.54	2.01	3.72	7.23	13.57	21.71
	FSAI	654.73	384.80	179.52	91.46	54.55	31.12	1.70	3.65	7.16	12.00	21.04
6	Jacobi	3,678.90	1,896.71	961.27	503.28	269.41	155.99	1.94	3.83	7.31	13.66	23.58
	AINV(0.1)	2,276.42	1,196.96	627.63	349.51	202.20	132.97	1.90	3.63	6.51	11.26	17.12
	AINV(0.05)	2,567.57	1,311.78	689.65	398.58	235.32	158.12	1.96	3.72	6.44	10.91	16.24
	AINV(0.025)	*	1,146.68	624.08	364.06	263.13	180.56	*	*	*	*	*
	FSAI	2,994.49	1,453.11	798.01	388.93	210.49	122.33	2.06	3.75	7.70	14.23	24.48

Table 4. CPU time, T_p, spent for computing $s = 10$ eigenpairs on p processors. The corresponding speedups, S_p, are also reported. When $N = 64,000$, $N = 216,000$, the AINV(0.1) and AINV(0.05) factors are equal. An asterisk means that the value could not be computed, due to storage limitations.

slightly better parallel performance, FSAI-DACG may run faster than AINV-DACG ($N \geq 64,000$). When $p \leq 16$, AINV-DACG and FSAI-DACG running times are smaller than Jacobi-DACG. However, with $p=32$ processors, the three preconditioners require comparable CPU times, in the larger problems. Summarizing, AINV and FSAI can be considered equally effective preconditioners for our DACG algorithm. They are more suitable for moderately parallel computations, while for massive parallel ones, also the easier and less memory requiring Jacobi preconditioner can be competitive. Note that when a large (say $s > 40$) number of eigenpairs is sought, the cost of each DACG iteration relies essentially on the orthogonalization process, rather than on the preconditioner. The CPU time is driven by the number of performed iterations, thus Jacobi preconditioning, which requires far more iterations than the other techniques, can be far more CPU demanding.

Acknowledgments.

This work has been supported in part by the Italian MURST Project "Analisi Numerica: Metodi e Software Matematico", and CNR contract 98. 01022. CT01. Free accounting units on the T3E Supercomputer were given by CINECA.

References

1. G. Gambolati, F. Sartoretto, and P. Florian. *Comp. Methods App. Mech. Eng.* **94**, 13 (1992).
2. L. Bergamaschi, G. Pini, and F. Sartoretto. Technical Report 78, Dipartimento di Metodi e Modelli Matematici per le Scienze Applicate, Università di Padova, (May 1999).
3. L. Yu. Kolotilina and A. Yu. Yeremin. *SIAM J. Matrix Anal.* **14**, 45 (1993).
4. M. Benzi, C. D. Meyer, and M. Tůma. *SIAM J. Sci. Comput.* **17**, 1135 (1996).
5. L. Bergamaschi and M. Putti. In *Proceedings of the Ninth SIAM Conference on Parallel Processing for Scientific Computing*, (March, 1999). (CD–ROM).

A PARALLEL FINITE ELEMENT SURFACE FITTING ALGORITHM FOR DATA MINING

PETER CHRISTEN

Institut für Informatik, Universität Basel, 4056 Basel, Switzerland,
E-mail: christen@ifi.unibas.ch

IRFAN ALTAS

School of Information Studies, Charles Sturt University, Wagga Wagga,
NSW 2678, Australia, E-mail: ialtas@csu.edu.au

MARKUS HEGLAND AND STEPHEN ROBERTS

Computer Science Laboratory, RSISE, Australian National University,
Canberra, ACT 0200, Australia, E-mail: Markus.Hegland@anu.edu.au

KEVIN BURRAGE AND ROGER SIDJE

Department of Mathematics, University of Queensland, St. Lucia,
QLD 4072, Australia, E-mail: kb@maths.uq.edu.au

A major task in data mining is to develop automatic techniques to process and to detect patterns in very large data sets. Multivariate regression techniques form the core of many data mining applications. A common assumption is that the multivariate data is well approximated by an additive model involving only first and second order interaction terms. In this case high-dimensional nonparametric regression is reduced to the determination of a coupled set of first and second order interaction terms, that is the determination of a coupled set of curves and surfaces. *Thin plate splines* provide a very good method to determine an approximating surface. Obtaining standard thin plate splines requires the solution of a dense linear system of equations of order n, where n is the number of observations. For data mining applications the number of observations is often in the millions, so standard thin plate splines may not be practical. We have developed a finite element approximation of a spline that can handle data sizes with millions of records. The resolution of the finite element method can independently be chosen from the number of observations. The observation data can be read from a secondary storage once, and does not need to be stored in memory. In this paper, we discuss the parallel implementation of this method in an MPI environment.

1 Introduction

In the last decade, there has been an explosive growth in the amount of data being collected. The computerisation of business transactions and use of bar codes in commercial outlets have provided businesses with enormous amounts of data. Revealing patterns and relationships in a data set can improve the goals, missions and objectives of many organisations. For example, sales records can reveal highly profitable retail sales patterns. As such it is important to develop automatic techniques to process and to detect patterns in very large data sets[1]. This process is known as *Data Mining*.

Data mining techniques are used to spot trends in data that may not be easily detectable by traditional database query tools that rely on simple queries to produce results. Data mining tools reveal hidden relationships and patterns as well as uncover correlations that are not detected by simple queries[2]. A typical data mining application is the analysis of insurance data where there may be more than several hundred thousand policies with tens of variables each. Insurance companies analyze such data sets to understand claim behaviour. Some insurants lodge more claims than others do. What are the typical characteristics of insurants who lodge many claims[1]? Would it be possible to predict whether a particular insurant will lodge a claim and accordingly offer an appropriate insurance premium? A major task in data mining is to find out answers to these types of questions.

An important technique applied in data mining is multivariate regression which is used to determine functional relationships in high dimensional data sets. A major difficulty which one faces when applying nonparametric methods is that the complexity grows exponentially with the dimension of the data set. This has been called *curse of dimensionality*. Additive and interaction splines can be used to overcome this curse[3]. In the case where interaction terms in the splines are limited to order two interactions, the model consists of a sum of functions of one or two variables and the fitting problem thus is reduced to fitting a sum of functions of two variables. One could call this problem surface fitting of a set of coupled surfaces.

We have developed a generic surface fitting algorithm that can handle data sizes with millions of records. The algorithm combines the favourable properties of finite element surface fitting with the ones of thin plate splines. The surface fitting technique that is called the *thin plate spline finite element method* (TPSFEM) is presented in Section 2. We discuss the numerical solution of the linear equations arising from the TPSFEM technique in Section 3. In order to interactively analyze large data sets, a considerable amount of computational power is needed in most cases. High-performance parallel and distributed computing are crucial for ensuring system scalability and interactivity as data sets grow considerably in size and complexity. The parallel implementation of the algorithm is presented in Section 4 whereas first test results are given in Section 5. Conclusions and future work are discussed in Section 6.

2 Surface Fitting Algorithm

Surface fitting and smoothing splines techniques are widely used to fit data. We have developed a surface fitting algorithm, TPSFEM, that can be used for various applications such as data mining and digital elevation models. For example, it can be used to model interaction terms in very large data sets for data mining. The TPSFEM algorithm can handle data sizes with millions of records. It can be viewed as a discrete thin plate spline. The following is a brief summary of the derivation of the method. However, the interested reader can refer to[4,5] for details.

The standard thin plate spline is the function f_α that minimises the functional

$$M_\alpha(f) = \frac{1}{n} \sum_{i=1}^{n} (f(\mathbf{x}^{(i)}) - y_i)^2 + \alpha \int_\Omega \left(\frac{\partial^2 f(\mathbf{x})}{\partial^2 x_1} \right)^2 + 2 \left(\frac{\partial^2 f(\mathbf{x})}{\partial x_1 \partial x_2} \right)^2 + \left(\frac{\partial^2 f(\mathbf{x})}{\partial^2 x_2} \right)^2 d\mathbf{x} \quad (1)$$

where the predictor and response variables of observations are respectively given by $\mathbf{x}^{(i)} \in \mathbb{R}^2$, and $y^{(i)} \in \mathbb{R}$ for $i = 1, ..., n$. An appropriate value for the smoothing parameter α can be determined by generalised cross validation.

The smoothing problem will be solved with finite elements. In order to reduce the complexity of the problem we suggest that very simple elements are used, namely, tensor products of piecewise linear functions. For these functions, however, the required second derivatives do not exist. Thus one has to use a non-conforming finite element principle and a new functional is introduced which only consists of second derivatives.

Consider $\mathbf{u} = (u_1, u_2)$, which will represent the gradient of f. The function f can essentially be recovered from $\mathbf{u}$ as follows.

Let H^1 denote the usual Sobolev space and $u_0 \in H^1(\Omega)$, such that

$$(\nabla u_0, \nabla v) = (\mathbf{u}, \nabla v), \text{ for all } v \in H^1(\Omega) \quad (2)$$

and

$$\int_\Omega u_0 \, d\mathbf{x} = 0. \quad (3)$$

Let the function values of u_0 at the observations points be denoted by

$$P u_0 = [u_0(\mathbf{x}^{(1)}) \cdots u_0(\mathbf{x}^{(n)})]^T. \quad (4)$$

Furthermore let

$$X = \begin{bmatrix} 1 & \cdots & 1 \\ \mathbf{x}^{(1)} & \cdots & \mathbf{x}^{(n)} \end{bmatrix}^T \in \mathbb{R}^{n,3} \quad \text{and} \quad \mathbf{y} = [y^{(1)}, \dots, y^{(n)}]^T. \quad (5)$$

We now consider the minimiser of the functional

$$J_\alpha(u_0, u_1, u_2, \mathbf{c}) = \frac{1}{n}(P u_0 + X\mathbf{c} - \mathbf{y})^T(P u_0 + X\mathbf{c} - \mathbf{y}) + \alpha(|u_1|_1^2 + |u_2|_1^2) \quad (6)$$

where the minimum is taken over all functions $u_0, u_1, u_2 \in H^1(\Omega)$ with zero mean and constants $\mathbf{c} = [c_0 \; c_1 \; c_2]^T \in \mathbb{R}^3$ subject to the constraints (2) and (3). The functional has exactly one minimum if the observation points $\mathbf{x}^{(i)}$ are not collinear. The function defined by $f(\mathbf{x}) = u_0(\mathbf{x}) + c_0 + c_1 x_1 + c_2 x_2$ provides a smoother which has essentially the same smoothing properties as the original thin plate smoothing spline. Note that the smoother has been defined in terms of $\mathbf{u}$. Formal proofs of these results can be found in[6].

After some manipulations and discretization[5] one gets the equivalent linear system of equations of (6):

$$
\begin{bmatrix}
\alpha A & 0 & 0 & 0 & -B_1^T \\
0 & \alpha A & 0 & 0 & -B_2^T \\
0 & 0 & M & F & A \\
0 & 0 & F^T & E & 0 \\
-B_1 & -B_2 & A & 0 & 0
\end{bmatrix}
\begin{bmatrix}
\mathbf{u}_1^h \\
\mathbf{u}_2^h \\
\mathbf{u}_0^h \\
\mathbf{c} \\
\mathbf{w}^h
\end{bmatrix}
=
\begin{bmatrix}
0 \\
0 \\
n^{-1}N^T \mathbf{y} \\
n^{-1}X^T \mathbf{y} \\
0
\end{bmatrix}
\tag{7}
$$

where $\mathbf{w}^h$ is the Lagrange multiplier vector associated with the discretization of the constraints (2) and (3). $\mathbf{u}_i^h$ are the discrete approximations to u_i, $i = 0, 1, 2$. The index h denotes the discretization level and will be omitted in the subsequent discussions.

3 Solution of Linear Systems

The size of the linear system (7) is independent of the number of observations, n. The observation data are visited only once during the assembly of the matrices M, E and F and the vectors $N\mathbf{y}$ and $X\mathbf{y}$ in (7). Thus, the time complexity is $O(n)$ to form (7). If the number of nodes in the finite element discretization is m, then the size of (7) is $4m + 3$ which is independent of n. All sub-systems in (7) have the dimension m, except the fourth one that has dimension 3. Thus, the total amount of the work required for the surface fitting algorithm is $O(n)$ to form (7), plus the work required to solve it.

It can be seen that the system matrix (7) is symmetric indefinite and sparse. One of the efficient techniques to solve such systems is the Uzawa algorithm[7,8]. We have applied a modified version of the Uzawa algorithm to (7). If several adjacent elements do not contain any observation points, the matrix M in (7) becomes singular, hence, the Uzawa algorithm becomes inapplicable. In order to avoid this problem we make a block row interchange of the third and fifth block row of the system (7). Then, the variant of the Uzawa algorithm used here has the form of a block Gauss-Seidel iteration and can be written as

$$
\begin{bmatrix} \alpha A & 0 & 0 & 0 & 0 \\ 0 & \alpha A & 0 & 0 & 0 \\ -B_1 & -B_2 & A & 0 & 0 \\ 0 & 0 & F^T & E & 0 \\ 0 & 0 & M & F & A \end{bmatrix} \begin{bmatrix} \mathbf{u}_1^{k+1} \\ \mathbf{u}_2^{k+1} \\ \mathbf{u}_0^{k+1} \\ \mathbf{c}^{k+1} \\ \mathbf{w}^{k+1} \end{bmatrix} = \begin{bmatrix} B_1^T \\ B_2^B \\ 0 \\ 0 \\ 0 \end{bmatrix} \mathbf{w}^k + \begin{bmatrix} 0 \\ 0 \\ 0 \\ n^{-1} X^T \mathbf{y} \\ n^{-1} N^T \mathbf{y} \end{bmatrix} \tag{8}
$$

This system requires the solution of four equations with matrix A for each iteration step. The convergence behaviour and some variations of this approach are discussed in[5]. In the next section, we will discuss the parallel implementation of this approach.

4 Implementation and Parallelization

The original implementation of the TPSFEM algorithm has been done in Matlab[4,5]. For increased performance and parallelization, C and MPI[9] were chosen for a second implementation. The main purpose of this implementation is to analyze parallelization aspects of the TPSFEM algorithm.

Several matrices are needed within this algorithm. Matrices M and A consist of nine diagonals with non-zero elements. They are symmetric, so only the upper part (five diagonals) have to be stored. B_1 and B_2 also have nine diagonals with non-zero elements, but as these matrices are non-symmetric all nine diagonals need to be stored. The chosen data structure for all matrices consists of a two-dimensional array of m rows and 5 or 9 columns, respectively. Each of the columns contains one of the diagonals with non-zero elements. With this packed data structure, a good data locality and thus good cache utilization can be achieved. Finally, the matrix F is of dimension $m \times 3$ and matrix E is a small 3×3 matrix. The dot product and vector addition (DAXPY) implementations use loop unrolling for better RISC pipeline usage.

As the data sets can be quite large, file reading and assembly of the matrices M, F and E as well as the vectors $N\mathbf{y}$ and $X\mathbf{y}$ are time consuming steps. Fortunately, this assembly process can be parallelized easily. First, the data file is split equally into P smaller files by a cyclic distribution. Then, these files can independently be processed by the P processors, which each assembles local matrices and vectors.

After the assembly, these local matrices and vectors have to be collected and summed to get the final matrices M, F, E and vectors $N\mathbf{y}$ and $X\mathbf{y}$. The amount of data to be communicated depends on the dimension of the matrices m, but not on the number of observations. If the amount of communicated data is small compared to the number of observations to process from file, an almost ideal speedup can be achieved for the assembly process. The assembly of the matrices A, B_1 and B_2 only depends on the matrix dimension m and takes much less time than the assembly of M and E.

The resulting linear system (8) to be solved contains five sub-systems, four having a dimension of m and one having dimension 3. As can be seen from (8), the first and second sub-systems can be solved in parallel, and only the resulting vectors have to be communicated.

The parallel implementation applies a functional parallelism in the following way:

- The assembly of matrices M, F, E and vectors $N\mathbf{y}$ and $X\mathbf{y}$ is done by all P processors, where each of them reads one locally stored data file with n/P observations. After the assembly, the local matrices and vectors are collected and summed on the host processor P_0 (with a simple call to MPI_Reduce). Two messages are communicated, one containing M ($5m$ floating point values), the other one containing F, E, $N\mathbf{y}$ and $X\mathbf{y}$ (containing $4m + 12$ floating point values).

- The matrices A, B_1 and B_2 are assembled on both processors P_0 and P_1.

- The iterative solving with the Uzawa's algorithm is only started on P_0 and P_1. After the initialization, processor P_0 starts solving the first sub-system in (8). Processor P_1 solves the second sub-system in (8) and sends the resulting vector $\mathbf{u}_2$ to processor P_0, which then can solve the third and fifth sub-systems. The fourth sub-system has dimension 3 and, thus, its solution cost is negligible. After the convergence check, processor P_0 sends the vector $\mathbf{w}$ to P_1 which then starts the next solving of the second sub-system.

Applying Amdahl's law, the solver part of the algorithm can achieve at most a speedup of about 1.333 if the communication of vectors is neglected and all four large sub-systems need the same time to be solved.

5 Tests Results from Parallel Implementation

The TPSFEM algorithm has already been applied to fit surfaces to large data sets from insurance, flow field, digital elevation and magnetic field areas. In this section, although we demonstrate the efficiency of the parallel implementation of the TPSFEM algorithm by using two large digital elevation data sets, the algorithm can equally be applicable as a nonparametric regression technique used in data mining. Elevation data is an important data component required to transform a Geographical Information System (GIS) from a

2-dimensional map storage system to a 3-dimensional information system[10]. Hence, an efficient surface fitting algorithm such as TPSFEM is an important tool for GIS applications. The involvement of end-users in this area is usually interactive. Therefore, they can benefit significantly from a fast surface fitting algorithm.

Two digital elevation data sets are obtained by digitizing the map of the Murrumbidgee region in Australia. The first and second data sets have $n = 547453$ and $n = 1887250$ observation points, respectively. The test platform is a 10 Sun Sparc-5 workstation cluster networked with a 10 Mbit/s twisted pair Ethernet. We did the test runs for $m = 2601$, 10201, and 63001. The following table shows timings in milliseconds for the assembly stage of the first data set. All timings presented here are average of ten test runs on an otherwise idle platform.

m	Serial Assembly	Parallel Assembly on 10 Processors		
		Computation	Communication	Total
2601	87159	8781	1258	10039
10201	86809	8770	5162	13932
63001	87250	8935	29827	38762

In the second table we present timings for the second data set with $m = 2601$. The serial assembly and solution steps took $285780 \ ms$ and $40893 \ ms$, respectively. The parallel solution step with two processors is $32384 \ ms$. As is explained in the previous section, the parallel solution stage employs only two processors.

Number of Processors	Parallel Assembly		
	Computation	Communication	Total
3	97231	1123	98354
7	41653	1524	43177
10	28187	1800	30987

Finally, in the third table we introduce timings for the second data set with $m = 10201$. The serial assembly and solution steps took $284939 \ ms$ and $624287 \ ms$, respectively. The parallel solution step with two processors is $548180 \ ms$.

Number of Processors	Parallel Assembly		
	Computation	Communication	Total
3	98143	1762	99905
7	41856	4382	46238
10	29374	5769	35143

6   Conclusions

In this work, we concentrated on a parallel version of the TPSFEM algorithm. The TPSFEM method can handle very large data sets to fit smooth surfaces.

There are two main parts of the algorithm that consume most processing time: Forming matrices M, F, E and vectors $N\mathbf{y}$ and $X\mathbf{y}$ in the system (7) and solving the system (8). We demonstrated that an almost ideal speedup can be achieved in the assembly of matrices for very large data sets. Unfortunately, the solver part of this parallel implementation is not scalable contrast to the assembly part. Our future research therefore will concentrate on how to achieve scalability by using distributed algorithms to solve the linear systems. On the other hand, as we deal with sparse matrices, parallel solver routines generally do not scale well. In order to solve the system (7) we are developing a generalized cross validation technique. The work is under progress and will be reported elsewhere.

References

1. Data Mining: An Introduction, Data Distilleries, DD19961, 1996
2. A.A. Freitas and S.H. Lavington, Mining Very Large Databases with Parallel Processing, Kluwer Academic Publishers, 1998.
3. T.J. Hastie and R.J. Tibshirani, Generalized Additive Models, Monographs Chapman and Hall, 1990.
4. M. Hegland, S. Roberts and I. Altas, Finite Element Thin Plate Splines for Data Mining Applications, in Mathematical Methods for Curves and Surfaces II, M. Daehlen, T. Lyche and L.L. Schumaker, Eds., pp. 245-253, Vanderbilt University Press, 1998
5. M. Hegland, S. Roberts and I. Altas, Finite Element Thin Plate Splines for Surface Fitting, in Computational Techniques and Applications: CTAC97, B.J. Noye, M.D. Teubner and A.W. Gill, Eds., pp. 289-296, World Scientific, 1997
6. S. Roberts, M. Hegland and I. Altas, H^1 Finite Element Thin Plate Splines, in preparation, 1999.
7. M. Fortin and R. Glowinski, Augmented Lagrangian Methods: Applications to the Numerical Solution of Boundary-Value Problems, North-Holland, 1983.
8. H.C. Elman and H.G. Golub, Inexact and Preconditioned Uzawa Algorithms for Saddle Point Problems, SIAM J. Numer. Anal., **31**, 1994, pp. 1645-1661.
9. W. Gropp, E. Lusk and A. Skjellum, Using MPI – Portable Parallel Programming with the Message-Passing Interface, The MIT Press, Cambridge, Massachusetts, 1994.
10. L. Lang, GIS Goes 3D, Computer Graphics World, March 1989, pp. 38-46.

External Selective Orthogonalization for the Lanczos Algorithm in Distributed Memory Environments **

A. Cooper, M. Szularz, J. Weston

School of Information & Software Engineering, University of Ulster, Coleraine, BT52 1SA, Northern Ireland

November 4, 1999

Abstract. The k-step explicit restart Lanczos algorithm, LExpRes, for the computation of a few of the extreme eigenpairs of large, usually sparse, symmetric matrices, computes one eigenpair at a time using a deflation technique in which each Lanczos vector generated is orthogonalized against all previously converged eigenvectors. The computation of the inner products associated with this external orthogonalization often creates a bottleneck in parallel distributed memory environments. In this paper methods are proposed which significantly reduce this computational overhead in LExpRes, thereby effectively improving its efficiency. The performances of the implementations of these methods in a massively parallel, distributed memory, MIMD environment (Cray-T3D) are assessed and critically compared with that of the original algorithm.

1 Introduction

The Lanczos algorithm is one of the principal methods for the computation of a few of the extreme eigenvalues and their corresponding eigenvectors of large, usually sparse, real symmetric matrices. Given a symmetric matrix $A \in \Re^{n \times n}$, the standard Lanczos method generates a sequence of tridiagonal matrices $T_j \in \Re^{j \times j}$ and Lanczos vectors $q_j \in \Re^n$ with the properties that $T_{j-1} \in \Re^{j-1 \times j-1}$ is a principal submatrix of $T_j = Q_j^T A Q_j$ where $Q_j = [q_1, \ldots, q_j]$ is orthonormal and that for $j \ll n$, the extreme eigenvalues of A are well approximated by the corresponding eigenvalues of the Lanczos matrices T_j [2].

However, one of the main drawbacks of the Lanczos method is that when the classical three-term recurrence is used in a machine environment orthogonality

---

** This work was carried out using the facilities of the University of Edinburgh Parallel Computing Centre

of the Lanczos vectors is lost. Consequently, spurious eigenvalues are generated and the process fails to terminate. A number of approaches have been suggested for overcoming this problem, one of which adopts a full orthogonalization scheme in which each newly generated Lanczos vector is orthogonalized against all of its predecessors [5]. This, however, is computationally expensive since it is not known in advance how many steps are required before an accurate solution is computed. In an attempt to further reduce this overhead researchers have also developed a number of Implicit and Explicit restart strategies which restart the process at certain points using better approximations to the required eigenvectors [6, 7, 8, 9, 10].

LExpRes is a k-step explicit restart variant of the Lanczos algorithm which incorporates full orthogonalization of the Lanczos vectors [9]. Further, in order to prevent the recomputation of eigenvalues that have already been computed, each newly computed Lanczos vector is also orthogonalized against all previously converged eigenvectors, a process known as full external orthogonalization. The computational effort and communication overhead associated with this process increases as the number of eigenvalues requested and processors used increases, often creating a bottleneck in parallel distributed memory environments. In this paper an alternative *selective* external orthogonalization scheme is proposed which significantly reduces this overhead and which enables two new variants of LExpRes to be constructed, each of which may be efficiently implemented in a distributed memory MIMD environment. A detailed description of the scheme is given in §3. In §2, a brief description of the LExpRes algorithm is presented and in the remaining sections implementation, numerical experiments, results, and conclusions are discussed.

2 Lanczos with Explicit Restart, LExpRes

In the explicit restart method, LExpRes, the p largest eigenvalues of A, together with their corresponding eigenvectors, are computed one at a time in descending order of magnitude. A brief description of LExpRes, in which a restart of the Lanczos process occurs after the computation of each eigenpair, is given below. Suppose that approximated eigenpairs $(\lambda_1, x_1), \ldots, (\lambda_i, x_i)$ are given for $i < p$. Let $\mathcal{X}_i = \text{span}\{x_1, \ldots, x_i\}$ and let its orthogonal component in $\Re^n$ be $\mathcal{X}_i^\perp$. The Lanczos algorithm will converge to the eigenvalues, $\lambda_{i+1}, \lambda_{i+2}, \ldots$, of A in the invariant subspace $\mathcal{X}_i^\perp$, if the Lanczos vectors $q_1, q_2, \ldots$ are constrained to stay in the subspace $\mathcal{X}_i^\perp$. This may be accomplished by projecting newly generated Lanczos vector, q_j, into the subspace $\hat{\mathcal{X}}_i^\perp \neq 0$: a process which may be achieved by orthogonalizing each q_j against the previously computed $x_1, \ldots, x_i$. Let Lanczos_for_one_eig($A, q_1, tol, \hat{\mathcal{X}}_i$) be a function which computes only the largest eigenvalue in the subspace $\mathcal{X}_i^\perp$, viz λ_{i+1}, using the approach described above. Then LExpRes may be described as in Figure 1.

The user supplied tolerance (normally set to some multiplicity of ϵ, the relative

function $[(\lambda_1, x_1), \ldots, (\lambda_p, x_p)] = \text{LExpRes}(A, p, tol)$

$\hat{\mathcal{X}}_0 = 0$

for $i = 1 : p$

    select q_1

    $(\lambda_i, x_i) \leftarrow \text{Lanczos\_for\_one\_eig}(A, q_1, tol, \hat{\mathcal{X}}_{i-1})$

    $\hat{\mathcal{X}}_i \leftarrow [\hat{\mathcal{X}}_{i-1}, x_i]$

end_for

Figure 1: LExpRes

machine accuracy) is denoted by *tol* and the accuracy of the approximations to the required eigenpair in Lanczos_for_one_eig( ) may be made on the basis of the usual error bounds $\parallel Ay - \theta y \parallel_2$ where θ and y are the appropiate Ritz value and Ritz vector, respectively.

LExpRes may be enhanced by incorporating a further restart strategy into Lanczos_for_one_eig( ). Since this function computes *only* the largest eigenvalue within a given subspace using the Lanczos process it may be restarted after k steps using the Ritz vector associated with the appropiate approximation to the required eigenvalue. k is independent of p and may be chosen to be arbitrarily small. However, for the purposes of this paper k is always chosen so that this enhancement strategy is not invoked.

3 Orthogonalization

Algorithms 1 and 2 are variants of LExpRes which incorporate similar schemes to that of Grimes *et al* [3] for reducing external orthogonalization. The differences occur in the function Lanczos_for_one_eig( ). In Algorithm 1 (Algorithm 2) this function is modified so that external orthogonalization does not take place until the level (approximate level) of orthogonality between the required Ritz vector and the previously computed eigenvectors exceeds $\sqrt{\epsilon}$. Further, immediately the appropiate condition is satisfied, the Lanczos process is restarted using the most recently computed required Ritz vector, y, as the start vector. Thereafter, Lanczos_for_one_eig( ) behaves as in the original algorithm. The justification for the new algorithms is outlined below.

Assume that $X = [x_1, \ldots, x_m]$ is the set of all previously computed eigenvectors and that no external orthogonalization has taken place up to the jth step in Lanczos_for_one_eig( ) in the $(m + 1)$th iteration of LExpRes. Let the level of orthogonality be determined by $z = X^T y = (\omega_1, \ldots, \omega_m)$. The question now arises: if the Lanczos process is restarted with the approximation to the eigenvalue being computing assumed to be $\alpha_1 = q_1^T A q_1$ as usual, what is the impact of ω_i on the difference $|\alpha_1 - \theta_1|$ if no external orthgonalization is performed? Since each starting vector is orthogonalized against $[x_1, \ldots, x_m]$ it follows that

$$q_1 = \frac{(I - XX^T)y}{\|(I - XX^T)y\|_2} = \frac{1}{\sqrt{1 - z^T z}}(I - XX^T)y$$

Hence,
$$\alpha_1 = \frac{1}{\sqrt{1 - z^T z}} y^T (I - XX^T)^T A (I - XX^T)y$$
$$= \frac{1}{\sqrt{1 - z^T z}}(\theta_1 - 2y^T AXz + z^T \Lambda_m z)$$

where $\Lambda_m = diag(\lambda_1, \ldots, \lambda_m)$.
Since $AX = X\Lambda_m + R$, where $R = [r_1, \ldots, r_m]$, the m residuals corresponding to the m eigenvectors, it follows that

$$\alpha_1 = \frac{1}{\sqrt{1 - zz^T}}(\theta_1 - z^T \Lambda_m z - 2y^T Rz)$$

If $\max_i |\omega_i| \le \sqrt{\epsilon}$, then with relatively small m,

$$\frac{1}{\sqrt{1 - zz^T}} \simeq \frac{1}{\sqrt{1 - m\epsilon}} = 1$$

Thus
$$|\alpha_1 - \theta_1| = |z^T \Lambda_m z + 2y^T Rz|$$
Assuming that the i-th eigenpair has been computed with accuracy $\|r_i\|_2 = \|Ax_i - \lambda_i x_i\|_2 = |\lambda_i| \epsilon\psi_i$, where $\psi^* \ge 0$ is a small constant corresponding to the 'worst' eigenvector, and that tolerance has been set to $|\lambda_i| \epsilon$, it follows that

$$
\begin{aligned}
|\alpha_1 - \theta_1| &\le \|z\|_2^2 \|\Lambda_m\|_2 + 2\|y\|_2 \|R\|_2 \|z\|_2 \\
&\le m|\lambda_1| \max_i |\omega_i|^2 + 2\sqrt{m} \max_i |\omega_i| \max_j \|r_j\| \\
&\le m|\lambda_1| \max_i |\omega_i|^2 + 2\sqrt{m} \max_i |\omega_i| |\lambda_1| \epsilon\psi^*
\end{aligned}
$$

Thus, since $\max_i |\omega_i| \le \sqrt{\epsilon}$

$$
\begin{aligned}
|\alpha_1 - \theta_1| &\le m|\lambda_1| \epsilon + 2\sqrt{m}\sqrt{\epsilon} |\lambda_1| \epsilon\psi^* \\
&\le m|\lambda_1| \epsilon\left(1 + \frac{\sqrt{m}}{m}\sqrt{\epsilon}\psi^*\right)
\end{aligned}
$$

Hence, since $1 + \frac{\sqrt{m}}{m}\sqrt{\epsilon}\psi^* \approx 1$, $|\alpha_1 - \theta_1|$ is within round-off error with respect to λ_1 if m is reasonably small. This result shows that the level of orthogonality, ω_i, may be estimated by taking the 'single guilty' vector (the one with the highest ψ) into account and that external orthogonalization is completely unnecessary unless ω_i exceeds $\sqrt{\epsilon}$. The result is also very pessimistic since it assumes that ψ^* corresponds to λ_1. In reality the largest eigenvalue will be computed with the highest accuracy. Thus, the subscript i will now be dropped.

Consider now the computation of ω. Since $y = Q_j s$, where s is the eigenvector of the projected A associated with θ, ω may be defined as

$$\omega = \mid x^T y \mid = \mid y^T x \mid = \mid s^T Q_j^T x \mid = \mid s^T v \mid$$

where $v = Q_j^T x = [q_1^T x, q_2^T x, \ldots, q_j^T x] = [\rho_1, \rho_2, \ldots, \rho_j]$. Thus, it is not necessary to explicitly compute the Ritz vector in each step. Further, the explicit computation of v may be easily avoided by using the Lanczos recurrence

$$\beta_j q_{j+1} = A q_j - \alpha_j q_j - \beta_{j-1} q_{j-1} \tag{1}$$

in the computation of v. Clearly

$$
\begin{aligned}
\rho_{j+1} &= x^T q_{j+1} = \frac{1}{\beta_j}(x^T A q_j - \alpha_j x^T q_j - \beta_{j-1} x^T q_{j-1}) \\
&= \frac{1}{\beta_j}(q_j^T r + (\lambda - \alpha_j)\rho_j - \beta_{j-1}\rho_{j-1})
\end{aligned}
\tag{2}
$$

Since equation (2) shows that the loss of orthogonality is propogated in exactly the same manner for all eigenvectors it is sufficient to monitor w for the least exact eigenvector only. In Algorithm 1, henceforth referred to as LExpExt, the term $q_j^T r$ in (2) is computed explicitly. This corresponds in exact arithmetic to the exact level of orthogonality between the Ritz vector and the Lanczos vectors. If $q_j^T r$ is estimated using norms the computation of one inner product can be avoided in each step. Algorithm 2, henceforth referred to as LExpEst, adopts this approach. In both algorithms ρ_0 is initialised to zero.

4 Implementation

The algorithms were implemented on the CRAY-T3D using FORTRAN 77 and make extensive use of the LAPACK, BLAS, and MPI libraries. The classical Gram-Schmidt method with iterative refinement is used to perform all orthogonalization since this method guarantees orthogonalization to working precision and has been shown by Hoffman [4] to be numerically stable. All vectors of length n are distributed across the processors while computations involving the T matrices are inexpensive and are performed locally on each processor.

5 Numerical Experiments

The performance of LExpExt and LExpEst have been compared with that of LExpRes using four sparse symmetric matrices selected from the Harwell Boeing collection [1]. A selection of results for p ranging from 1 to 64, are presented in Tables 1 - 4. (Recall from §2 that the algorithms compute the p largest eigenvalues of A). The headers in Tables 1 and 2 give the size of the matrix and

	PLAT1919			BCSSTRUC16		
	$n = 1919$ ($nz = 32399$)			$n = 4884$ ($nz = 290378$)		
	$\lambda_1 = 2.9216371$			$\lambda_1 = 4.943166 \times 10^9$		
	$\lambda_{64} = 1.3470323$			$\lambda_{64} = 2.2621854 \times 10^9$		
p	LExpRes	LExpExt	LExpEst	LExpRes	LExpExt	LExpEst
1	0	0	0	0	0	0
2	81	20	17	103	92	87
4	732	607	602	740	648	652
8	3806	3301	3434	3794	3220	3408
16	18594	16693	17266	20180	17602	18490
32	87492	79841	82956	108346	97996	101794
64	415879	395735	400408	552332	501694	514528

Table 1: Number of inner products required for external orthogonalization for matrices PLAT1919 and BCSSTRIC16 from the PLATZ and BCSSTRUC2 collections, respectively, using 32 processors

the number of nonzero elements stored, denoted by nz. k has been chosen to be 300, thereby ensuring that the enhanced restart strategy referred to in §2 was never invoked. The requested tolerance has been set to the relative machine accuracy which, for the Cray, is 1.110E-16. In all cases, the value of q_1 has been chosen to be $\frac{1}{\sqrt{n}} \times [1, 1, \ldots, 1]$.

6 Conclusion

The results of the numerical experiments show that, in general, the new algorithms require fewer inner products for external orthogonalization than the original. In particular, LExpExt proved to be superior in this respect whenever the number of eigenvalues requested exceeded 4. However, the percentage reduction in the number of inner products required by both new algorithms proved to be greatest when the number of eigenvalues requested was small. In the majority of cases the new algorithms were more efficient than the original. It was also observed that, in general, there existed very little difference in the number of Lanczos steps performed in corresponding iterations of the new algorithms before external orthogonalization was required. This demonstrates that the level of orthogonality, ω, is well estimated in LExpEst.

References

[1] Duff, I.S., Grimes, R.G., and Lewis, J.G., User's Guide for the

	NOS3			NOS6		
	$n = 960 \ (nz = 15844)$			$n = 675 \ (nz = 3255)$		
	$\lambda_1 = 6.89904 \times 10^2$			$\lambda_1 = 7.6506 \times 10^6$		
	$\lambda_{64} = 4.8160914 \times 10^2$			$\lambda_{64} = 3.5729837 \times 10^6$		
p	LExpRes	LExpExt	LExpEst	LExpRes	LExpExt	LExpEst
1	0	0	0	0	0	0
2	219	269	199	146	179	143
4	1366	889	1232	864	837	846
8	6392	5005	5842	4198	3439	4124
16	27540	23541	25306	17986	15511	17694
32	115246	101131	106820	76440	67959	75028
64	475938	429999	446650	320022	295947	313964

Table 2: Number of inner products required for external orthogonalization for matrices NOS3 and NOS6 from the LANPRO collection using 32 processors

	PLAT1919			BCSSTRUC16		
p	LExpRes	LExpExt	LExpEst	LExpRes	LExpExt	LExpEst
1	4.248	4.294	4.232	2.578	2.56	2.568
2	5.782	6.646	6.738	5.638	5.336	5.117
4	13.633	15.681	13.462	15.043	13.324	13.075
8	33.58	32.586	31.19	38.007	31.04	32.649
16	94.44	85.067	86.147	116.82	94.801	101.819
32	269.962	240.907	250.942	411.983	344.807	371.621
64	851.96	799.53	808.425	1385.737	1224.704	1311.342

Table 3: Time (in seconds) for matrices PLAT1919 and BCSSTRIC16 using 32 processors

	NOS3			NOS6		
p	LExpRes	LExpExt	LExpEst	LExpRes	LExpExt	LExpEst
1	11.618	11.332	11.496	4.513	4.468	4.506
2	22.927	44.354	20.928	9.256	16.814	9.000
4	48.614	66.288	41.995	18.611	32.202	17.862
8	100.441	108.697	86.235	40.537	50.088	38.882
16	213.347	201.01	182.554	88.301	91.184	84.972
32	473.665	416.867	409.374	208.775	197.058	200.725
64	1120.374	989.409	996.641	545.508	514.115	528.204

Table 4: Time (in seconds) for matrices NOS3 and NOS6 using 32 processors

Harwell-Boeing Sparse Matrix Collection (release I), available online ftp orion.cerfacs.fr, (1992).

[2] Golub, G, and Van Loan C.F., Matrix Computations, John Hopkins University Press, London, (1989).

[3] Grimes, R.F., Lewis, J.G., and Simon, H.D., (1994), 'A Shifted Block Lanczos Algorithm for Solving Sparse Symmetric Generalized Eigenproblems', SIAM J. Matrix Anal. Appl., 15,1, 228-272.

[4] Hoffman, W., (1989), 'Iterative Algorithms for Gram-Schmidt Orthogonalization', Computing, 41, 335-348.

[5] Paige, C.C., (1970), 'Practical use of the Symmetric Lanczos Process with Reorthogonalization Method', BIT 10, 183-195.

[6] Saad, Y., (1984), 'Chebyshev Acceleration Techniques for Solving Nonsymmetric Eigenvalue Problems', Math. Comp., 42, 568-588.

[7] Saad, Y., (1992), 'Numerical Methods for Large Eigenvalue Problems', Halsted Press-John Wiley & Sons Inc., New York.

[8] Sorensen, D.C., (1992), 'Implicit Application of Polynomial Filters in a k-step Arnoldi Method', SIAM J. Matrix Anal. Appl., 13. 357-385.

[9] Szularz, M., Weston, J., Clint, M., (1999), 'Explicitly Restarted Lanczos Algorithms in an MPP Environment', Parallel Computing, Vol 25, 613-631.

[10] Szularz, M., Weston, J., Clint, M.(1999), 'Restarting Techniques for the Lanczos Algorithm and their Implementation in Parallel Computing Environments: Architectural Influences', Parallel Algorithms and Applications, Vol 14 (1), 57-77.

IMPLEMENTATION OF PARALLEL ONE-SIDED BLOCK JACOBI METHODS FOR THE SYMMETRIC EIGENVALUE PROBLEM

JAVIER CUENCA

Departamento de Ingeniería y Tecnología de Computadores
Universidad de Murcia. 30071 Murcia. Spain.
javiercm@ditec.um.es

DOMINGO GIMÉNEZ

Departamento de Informática, Lenguajes y Sistemas Informáticos
Universidad de Murcia. 30071 Murcia. Spain.
domingo@dif.um.es

In this work we study the implementation of two one-sided block Jacobi algorithms for the Symmetric Eigenvalues Problem. We prove experimentally that the one-sided algorithms are better suited to parallel computers, obtaining a bigger reduction of the execution time than the reduction obtained by the two-sided algorithms.

1 Introduction

The Symmetric Eigenvalue Problem (SEP) can be solved in at least three different ways [10]: 1) methods working by reduction of matrices into certain condensed form, like the QR-algorithm, 2) Jacobi-like methods, and 3) spectral division methods. Jacobi method is the oldest but the interest in Jacobi's approach is renewed due to its inherent parallelism and good stability [3]. Traditional implementations of dense linear algebra algorithms encounter a bottleneck in modern architectures due to limited bandwidth between the CPU and main memory. Using algorithms by blocks, matrix-matrix operations can be arranged so that more computation is performed between memory accesses. As a result, these operations can take advantage of hierarchical memories. A suite of such matrix-matrix operations are part of the basic linear algebra subprograms (BLAS) [4]. An algorithm coded in terms of calls to BLAS becomes a portable high performance implementation. The use of blocks also allows us to design parallel algorithms with low communication necessities.

In this work we study the implementation of two one-sided block Jacobi algorithms for the Symmetric Eigenvalues Problem. These algorithms were designed using as a basic the one-sided Jacobi algorithms proposed in [2] and the two-sided block Jacobi algorithm proposed in [7]. We prove experimentally that the one-sided algorithms are better suited to parallel computers, obtaining a bigger reduction of the execution time than the reduction obtained by the two-sided algorithms. This reduction of the execution time is obtained because in one-sided Jacobi algorithms there is less communication among the processors than in two-sided algorithms and also because in one-sided algorithms the data are always accessed in the same order they were stored. In contrast to other block methods [1], these algorithms work with several sizes of blocks independently of the size of the matrix and the number of processors used.

In Section 2, the two-sided Jacobi method, a blocks version and a parallel algorithm are described. In Sections 3 and 4 the same with the first and the second version of one-sided Jacobi algorithm is made, respectively. Finally, in Section 5 a theoretical comparison of the three methods is made and the experimental results obtained in different multiprocessors systems are shown.

2 A two-sided block Jacobi algorithm

A Jacobi method works with two matrices: matrix A and matrix V where the rotations are accumulated. Matrix V is initially the identity matrix. This method constructes a matrix sequence $\{A_l\}$ by means of $A_{l+1} = Q_l A_l Q_l^t$ $l = 1, 2, \ldots$, where $A_1 = A$ and Q_l is a plane-rotation that anhilates a nondiagonal element of matrix A_l.

In a block version, both matrices A and V are divided into columns and rows of square blocks of size $s \times s$, and these blocks are grouped to obtain bigger blocks of size $2s \times 2s$. Each Q_l represents a set of rotations that nullify elements in a block of A_l. In each block the algorithm works by making a sweep over the elements in the block. The subdiagonal elements belonging to diagonal blocks will not be zeroed. To correct it, blocks corresponding to the first Jacobi set are considered to be of size $2s \times 2s$, adding to each block the two adjacent diagonal blocks and the symmetrical block.

The work over each block can be performed using level-1 BLAS. The corresponding rotations are accumulated to form a matrix Q of size $2s \times 2s$. Finally, the corresponding columns and rows of blocks of size $2s \times 2s$ of matrix A and the rows of blocks of matrix V are updated using Q. These matrix-matrix multiplications can be performed using level-3 BLAS. After completing a set of block rotations, a swap of column and row blocks is performed, according to the order we are using. The odd-even order has been used because it simplifies a block based implementation of the sequential algorithm, and allows parallelization. The data movement can be included in the updating of the matrices if it is done on the rotation matrix before updating them. This data movement brings the next blocks of size $s \times s$ to be zeroed to the subdiagonal, and the process continues similarly to operations performed in the first step.

However, in this case the elements to be nullified are in square blocks of size $s \times s$ inside diagonal blocks of size $2s \times 2s$. This data movement will imply data transferences in the parallel version of the algorithm.

The cost per sweep of this block algorithm when computing eigenvalues and eigenvectors is:

$$8k_3 n^3 + (12k_1 - 16k_3)\, n^2 s + 8k_3 n s^2 \quad flops, \tag{1}$$

where k_1 and k_3 represent the cost of an arithmetic operation performed using BLAS 1 and BLAS 3, respectively.

2.1 A parallel algorithm

Parallel versions could be developed for a square mesh or a triangular mesh [6], but, in order to compare the algorithm with the block one-sided algorithms that we have developed, an implementation for a ring topology will be analised. A ring of processors is the more logic topology for one-sided Jacobi algorithms, although more scalable implementations can be dessigned for a mesh[9].

Considering $q = \frac{n}{2sk}$, and a ring with $p = \frac{q}{2}$ processors: $P_0, P_1, ..., P_{p-1}$, a balanced algorithm can be obtained assigning to each processor P_i, with $0 \le i < p$, the rows i and $q - 1 - i$ of matrices A and V. So, each processor P_i contains blocks A_{ij} and $A_{q-1-i,j}$, with $0 \le j \le i$, and V_{ij} and $V_{q-1-i,j}$, with $0 \le j \le q$.

The arithmetic cost per sweep when computing eigenvalues and eigenvectors is:

$$8k_3 \frac{n^3}{p} + (12k_1 - 8k_3)\,\frac{n^2 s}{p} + 12k_1 \frac{n s^2}{p} \quad flops, \tag{2}$$

and the cost per sweep of the communications is:

$$(p+3)\frac{n}{s}\beta + \left(10n^2 + 4ns - \frac{n^2}{p}\right)\tau, \tag{3}$$

where β and τ represent the start-up and the word-sending time, respectively.

3 A one-sided block Jacobi algorithm. First version

The first one-sided algorithm we analyse works on matrices $B_0 = A$ and $W_0 = I$, obtaining $B_{r+1} = Q_r B_r$ and $W_{r+1} = Q_r W_r$, with Q_r the rotation matrix nullifying a nondiagonal element of matrix $A_r = B_r W_r^t = Q_{r-1} Q_{r-2}....Q_0 B_0 W_0^t Q_0^t....Q_{r-1}^t$.

To nullify a_{ij} it is necessary to compute a_{ii}, a_{jj} and a_{ij}, because the algorithm works on matrices B_r and W_r, and not on matrix A_r. These elements are obtained with three dot products. After that, rows i and j of B_r and W_r are updated. If the diagonal elements are stored in an auxiliary vector, it is not necessary to compute a_{ii} and a_{jj} each time, and the cost per sweep is:

$$7n^3 - \frac{15}{2}n^2 + \frac{n}{2} \quad flops. \tag{4}$$

A one-sided block algorithm is obtained by combining the previous ideas with the ideas of the two-sided block algorithm [5]. The matrices A and W, of size $n \times n$, are divided in blocks of size $s \times n$, and the blocks of $A = BW$ are treated using the odd-even ordering. Initially the $\frac{n}{2s}$ blocks corresponding to the first Jacobi set are treated, making a two-sided sweep on blocks of size $2s \times 2s$ of matrix A, and accumulating the rotations. These operations are done using BLAS 1. After that, matrices A and W are updated multiplying the rotation matrices, of size $2s \times 2s$, by the corresponding blocks of B and W, of size $2s \times n$, using BLAS 3. After completing a set of block rotations, a movement of rows is done like in the two-sided algorithm. In successive steps it is necessary to compute A_{ii}, A_{jj} and A_{ij}, because the work is not done directly with matrix A, using them a block of size $2s \times 2s$ is formed and the process continues as above. If the diagonal blocks are stored it is not necessary to compute A_{ii} and A_{jj}, and then the cost per sweep is:

$$9k_3 n^3 + (12k_1 - 9k_3)\, n^2 s \quad flops. \tag{5}$$

3.1 A parallel algorithm

A parallel version of this algorithm in a ring of p processors consists of assigning to each processor k consecutive blocks of size $2s \times n$, with $n = 2skp$, of matrices B and W.

The arithmetic cost per sweep is:

$$9k_3 \frac{n^3}{p} + 12k_1 \frac{n^2 s}{p} + 12k_1 \frac{ns^2}{p} \quad flops. \tag{6}$$

In this method it is not necessary to broadcast the rotation matrices because each processor updates the rows of blocks it contains. The only communications are those between steps to group data according to the next Jacobi set. In odd steps blocks of size $s \times n$ of B, and W, and a diagonal block of size $s \times s$ of matrix D are sent from P_i to P_{i-1}, with $1 \leq i < p$ and in even steps the same communications are done from P_i to P_{i+1}, with $0 \leq i < (p-1)$. Therefore, the cost of communications per sweep is:

$$3\frac{n}{s}\beta + \left(4n^2 + 2ns\right)\tau, \tag{7}$$

4 A one-sided block Jacobi algorithm. Second version

The second one-sided Jacobi algorithm proposed in [2] has the advantage of a lower cost, but also has the disadvantage of a worse precision [11]. This algorithm works by diagonalizing matrix $B = A^2$ without constructing B. Rotations nullifying elements b_{ij} of B are applied to A. If iniatilly $A_1 = A$ and $B_1 = A_1 A_1^t$, we will have $A_{r+1} = Q_r A_r$, where Q_r is a plane-rotation that anhilates a nondiagonal element of matrix B_r, so A must be updated only by one side. Because $B_r = A_r A_r^t$, it is necessary to perform dot products to obtain b_{ij}, b_{ii} and b_{jj}, which are needed to obtain the next Jacobi rotation.

To design an algorithm by blocks the matrix A is divided into consecutive blocks of size $s \times n$. Before each subsweep on a block, B_{ii}, B_{jj} and B_{ij}, are computed (or only B_{ij} if the diagonal blocks are stored). The reduction is terminated when no rotation is applied in a sweep, in this moment all pairs of rows of A are mutually orthogonal, i.e., A is of the form DW with D a diagonal matrix and W a matrix whose rows are the eigenvectors of A, and the eigenvalues of A are obtained as the square roots of the norms of these rows. So, this method has worse precision due to we do not calculate directly the eigenvalues of A.

The cost per sweep is:

$$5k_3 n^3 + (12k_1 - 5k_3)\, n^2 s \quad flops. \tag{8}$$

Even if the diagonal blocks are stored, in the first step all the blocks must be computed with an additional cost of order $n^2 s$, because the algorithm works with A and not with B.

4.1 A parallel algorithm

A parallel version of this algorithm in a ring of p processors consists of assigning to each processor k consecutive blocks of size $2s \times n$, with $n = 2skp$, of matrix A.

The arithmetic cost per sweep is:

$$5k_3\frac{n^3}{p} + 12k_1\frac{n^2 s}{p} + 12k_1\frac{ns^2}{p} \quad flops. \tag{9}$$

The only communications are those between steps to group data according to the next Jacobi set. In odd steps $s(n + s)$ elements are sent from P_i to

P_{i-1}, with $1 \leq i < p$, and in even steps the same quantity is sent from P_i to P_{i+1}, with $0 \leq i < (p-1)$. Therefore, the cost of communications per sweep is:

$$2\frac{n}{s}\beta + \left(2n^2 + 2ns\right)\tau. \qquad (10)$$

5 Comparison and Experimental Results

The first version of the one-sided algorithm has higher arithmetic cost than the two-sided method, but the level-3 BLAS operations in the two-sided algorithm are made along rows and columns; however, in the one-sided algorithm these operations are made only along rows, therefore are less costly. The second one-sided algorithm has the lowest cost, but, as we have previously mentioned, also has worse precision.

Communications are less costly in the one-sided algorithms because it is not necessary to broadcast the rotation matrices. Also in the communications the second one-sided algorithm is better than the first one-sided algorithm because it works with one matrix and only half of the data must be transferred.

Consistently, we can predict that when the number of processors increase or/and when the values of the communication constants τ and β are high the execution time of the first one-sided algorithm will be less than that of the two-sided algorithm.

The algorithms have been compared in different parallel systems using MPI[8] and matrices generated randomly with values between -10 and 10. The parallel systems we have used are:

1.- PenFEt : 6 PC Pentiums 200Mhz connected by a Fast Ethernet 100 Mbps.

2.- SunEt : 5 workstations Sun Ultra1 143Mhz connected by a Ethernet 10Mbps.

3.- SP2Sw : a multiprocessor IBM-SP2 with 32 thin160 640Mflops/s connected by a switch network 120 MB/s.

In table 1 we can see the good efficiency obtained when we parallelize one-sided Jacobi methods, because the cost of the communications does not increase so much as in the two-sided one.

In table 2 we can see the second one-sided algorithm is faster than the two others. The first one-sided algorithms is better than the two-sided algorithm mainly in systems where the communications are more costly (SunEt), this difference decreases in systems where the cost of the communications is less in relation to the arithmetic cost (SP2Sw).

In table 3 we can see the time execution of the one-sided algorithms

Table 1. Execution time, in seconds, per sweep and efficiency of different parallel block Jacobi algorithms in PenFEt.

$Proces.$	1	1	1	2	2	2	4	4	4
$size/alg$	$t-s$	$o-s,1$	$o-s,2$	$t-s$	$o-s,1$	$o-s,2$	$t-s$	$o-s,1$	$o-s,2$
$Execution time$									
256	7.72	10.12	5.94	4.46	4.86	2.43	2.81	2.74	1.52
384	25.82	36.83	19.27	16.41	18.73	7.55	12.40	11.77	4.18
640	120.82	171.80	92.95	82.31	88.72	44.45	55.52	51.42	27.54
$Efficiency$									
256	1.0	1.0	1.0	0.9	1.0	1.2	0.7	0.9	1.0
384	1.0	1.0	1.0	0.8	1.0	1.3	0.5	0.8	1.2
640	1.0	1.0	1.0	0.7	1.0	1.0	0.5	0.8	0.8

Table 2. Execution time, in seconds, per sweep of different parallel block Jacobi algorithms in SunEt and in SP2Sw.

$Processors$	2	2	2	4	4	4
$size/alg$	$t-s$	$o-s,1$	$o-s,2$	$t-s$	$o-s,1$	$o-s,2$
$SunEt$						
256	3.40	2.68	1.30	4.21	3.50	1.75
512	31.89	18.36	7.01	32.53	15.78	7.77
1024	211.83	89.00	66.14	165.62	91.60	56.14
$SP2Sw$						
256	0.60	0.59	0.33	0.50	0.35	0.18
512	4.26	4.05	2.26	3.05	2.43	1.39
768	12.85	13.46	7.47	8.29	7.44	4.29

increases more slowly than the time execution of the two-sided one when the size of the problem is increased proportionally.

Acknowledgments

Partially supported by Comisión Interministerial de Ciencia y Tecnología, project TIC96-1062-C03-02.

The IBM-SP2 at the CESCA (Centre de Supercomputació de Catalunya) was used to carry out some of the experiments.

Table 3. Comparison of times per sweep of different parallel block Jacobi algorithms with a scaled problem: $n = 64p$.

Processors	2	3	4	5	6	8	10	12	14
PenFEt									
two − sided	0.63	1.45	2.81	4.59	6.97				
*one − sided, version*1	0.64	1.49	2.75	3.92	5.80				
*one − sided, version*2	0.36	0.93	1.52	1.20	1.79				
SunEt									
two − sided	0.67	1.72	4.21	12.86					
*one − sided, version*1	0.48	1.27	3.50	6.86					
*one − sided, version*2	0.21	0.65	1.75	3.66					
SP2Sw									
two − sided	0.12	0.20	0.39	0.24	1.03	4.35	12.70	11.04	27.38
*one − sided, version*1	0.08	0.16	0.35	0.12	0.48	1.81	3.69	5.55	7.13
*one − sided, version*2	0.05	0.10	0.18	0.30	0.22	0.94	1.74	2.60	4.82

References

1. P. Arbenz and M. Oettli. *Block Implementations of the Symmetric QR and Jacobi Algorithms*. Technical Report 178. Institute for Scientific Computing, ETH Zürich, 1992.
2. B. A. Chartres. *Adaptation of the Jacobi Method for a Computer with Magnetic-tape Backing Store*. The Computer Journal, 5:51-60, 1963.
3. J. Demmel and K. Veselić. *Jacobi's method is more accurate than QR*. SIAM J. Matrix Anal. Appl., 13, 1204-1245 (1992).
4. J. J. Dongarra, J. Du Croz, S. Hammarling and I. Duff. *A set of level 3 basic linear algebra subprograms*. ACM Trans. Math. Softw., 16, (1), 1-17 (1990).
5. D. Giménez, J. Cuenca, R. M. Ralha and A. J. Viamonte. *One Sided Block Jacobi Methods for the Symmetric Eigenvalue Problem*. Proceedings of the 3rd International Meeting on Vector and Parallel Processing. 1998, Porto (Portugal). 687-692.
6. D. Giménez, V. Hernández and A.M. Vidal. *A Unified Approach to Parallel Block-Jacobi Methods for the Symmetric Eigenvalue Problem*. Proceedings of the 3rd International
   Meeting on Vector and Parallel Processing. 1998, Porto (Portugal). 139-151.
7. D. Giménez, V. Hernández, R. Van de Geijn and A. M. Vidal. *A block Jacobi method on a mesh of processors*. Concurrency: Practice and Experience, 9(5):391-411. 1997.
8. *MPI2: a message-passing interface standard*. The International Journal of High Performance Computing Applications, volume 12, number 1/2, 1998. Sage Science Press
9. D. Royo, M. Valero and A. González *A Jacobi-bases Algorithm for Computing Symmetric Eigenvalues and Eigenvectors in a Two-dimensional Mesh*. Proceedings of the Euromicro Workshop on Parallel and Distributed Processing 1998. Madrid. 463-469
10. Xiaobai Sun. *Parallel Algorithms for Dense Eigenvalue Problems*. High Performance Computing and Gigabit Local Area Networks. Essen, Germany. 1996. 202-212.
11. A. J. Viamonte. *Metodos de Jacobi para o Calculo de Valores e Vectores proprios de Matrizes Simetricas*. Tesis de Mestrado. Universidade do Minho. 1996.

COMMUNICATION OVERHEAD FOR PARALLEL SPARSE CHOLESKY FACTORIZATION ON A RECONFIGURABLE NETWORK*

EL MOSTAFA DAOUDI[1], PIERRE MANNEBACK[2], MOSTAPHA ZBAKH[1]

[1] *Université Mohammed Ier,Faculté des Sciences*
Laboratoire de Recherche en Informatique
60 000 Oujda, Morocco
E-mail:{mdaoudi, zbakh} @sciences.univ-oujda.ac.ma
[2] *Faculté Polytechnique de Mons*
Service d'Informatique
7000 Mons, Belgium
E-mail:Pierre.Manneback@fpms.ac.be

We present an efficient multi-phase parallel algorithm for Cholesky factorization of sparse matrices arising from PDE discretization by finite differences on $3D$ regular grids. The classical nested dissection ordering is used to number the grids. The target architecture is a $d - reconfigurable$ network of p processors, where d is the number of bidirectional links per processor. The algorithm is composed of $log\ p$ phases, each phase being computed on a $d-ary$ tree topology following three steps: gathering of the required columns by the root processor, data distribution to the nodes and computation. Overlapping between communication and computation is exploited to reduce the total execution cost. The processor allocation strategy is the subtree to subcube mapping. The communication overhead of the algorithm is shown to be of order $O(N^{\frac{4}{3}} log\ p)$, where N is the matrix's size. This overhead is of lower order than the algorithm proposed by Gupta and al. in 1997 which was of $O(N^{\frac{4}{3}} \sqrt{p})$.

Keywords sparse Cholesky factorization, elimination tree, d-reconfigurable networks, nested dissection ordering, d-ary tree topology.

1 Introduction

Many sparse linear systems $Ax = b$ arising in applications have a symmetric positive definite (SPD) coefficient matrix A. Such systems are usually solved using the Cholesky factorization, which consists of four consecutive phases : ordering, symbolic factorization, numerical factorization and resolution of triangular systems [6]. The ordering phase computes a permutation

---

*THIS WORK IS SUPPORTED BY THE KEEP-IN-TOUCH PROJECT 972644 "DEVELOPMENT OF PARALLEL ALGORITHMS FOR IRREGULAR PROBLEMS" (DAPPI), INCO-DC PROGRAM, DG III, COMMISSION OF THE EUROPEAN COMMUNITIES, NOV.1, 1998-OCT. 31, 2001

matrix P so that the matrix PAP^t has a low fill-in; the symbolic factorization phase determines the non-zero structure of the Cholesky factor L such that $PAP^t = LL^t$; the numerical factorization computes L and, finally, the triangular systems $Ly = Pb$ and $L^t z = y$ are solved, where $x = P^t z$.

Recently, an efficient parallel package, PSPASES (Parallel SPArse Symetric dirEct Solver) has been designed for this problem [3]. This package uses a multilevel nested dissection ordering [5] and a multifrontal numerical factorization [8]. A parallel runtime analysis has been developed for some specific problems referred as 2D and 3D constant node-degree graphs. These problems arise from PDE discretization by finite differences or finite elements on regular grids $N^{\frac{1}{2}} \times N^{\frac{1}{2}}$ (2D) or $N^{\frac{1}{3}} \times N^{\frac{1}{3}} \times N^{\frac{1}{3}}$ (3D). The authors of [3,8] obtained a total communication overhead in the numerical phase respectively of $O(N\sqrt{p})$ for 2D and $O(N^{\frac{4}{3}}\sqrt{p})$ for 3D problems, where p is the number of processors.

In [1], a reconfigurable parallel algorithm for sparse Cholesky factorization has been proposed, that provides a lower communication overhead of $O(N \log p)$ of 2D problems.

In this work, our aim is to adapt and extend this algorithm to 3D problems. We obtain a communication overhead of $O(N^{\frac{1}{3}} \log p)$ using a $d - reconfigurable$ network of p processors, where d is the number of bidirectional links per processor. In section 3, we present this algorithm. Section 4 is devoted to the evaluation of the communication overhead and the scalability analysis. Finally, some conclusions are drawn in section 5.

2 Left-looking sparse Cholesky factorization

We focus here on the numerical factorization phase. We consider that we have to compute a lower triangular sparse matrix L such that $LL^t = A'$, where A' is an already reordered sparse SPD matrix of size N.

We use the left-looking variant of the Cholesky algorithm (jki-factorization)[6]. In order to describe this algorithm let $struct(L_{j*})$ (resp. $struct(L_{*j})$) denote the set of column (resp. row) subscripts of nonzeros in row j (resp. column j) of L. These sets are computed during the symbolic factorization phase. Let $Tcol(j)$ be the task that computes the j-th column of L. It is composed of two sub tasks: $Cmod(j, k)$, which updates column j by column k, and $Cdiv(j)$, which divides column j by $\sqrt{l_{jj}}$.

The sparse column-oriented Cholesky $jki - factorization$ can be described as follows [6]:

for $j := 1$ to N do
{
    $for\ k\ \in\ struct(L_{j*})\ do\ Cmod(j,k);$ $\left.\vphantom{\begin{array}{c}a\\b\end{array}}\right\}$ $Tcol(j)$
    $Cdiv(j);$
}
Where:
    $Cmod(j,k)$

        for $i \in struct(L_{*k}) \cup \{j\}$ do $l_{ij} := l_{ij} - l_{ik} * l_{jk};$
    $Cdiv(j)$

        $ljj := \sqrt{l_{jj}};$
        for $i \in struct(L_{*j})$ do $l_{ij} := l_{ij}/l_{jj};$

3 Parallel left-looking Cholesky algorithm for 3D constant node-degree graphs

In order to present our parallel algorithm, we recall first some notions which we will have to use, namely, elimination tree, nested dissection ordering and subtree to subcube mapping.

3.1 Elimination tree

Elimination trees have been introduced by Liu [9]. They provide a useful information concerning the factorization process. An elimination tree corresponding to the structure of the Cholesky factor L is a tree with N vertices labelled from 1 to N such that the parent of vertex j is the row subscript of the first off-diagonal nonzero in column j. If there are no off-diagonal nonzeros in column j, then vertex j is a root node.

3.2 Nested dissection ordering for 3D problems

We use the nested dissection ordering [5] to number the nodes of the 3D grids because it has a capacity to produce well balanced large trees of small depth, implying more concurrency and small execution time. Given a 3D regular grid of size $N^{\frac{1}{3}} \times N^{\frac{1}{3}} \times N^{\frac{1}{3}}$, the nested dissection ordering consists to divide the initial grid, called the level 0 grid, into eight subgrids (the level 1 subgrids) each of size $\frac{N^{\frac{1}{3}}}{2} \times \frac{N^{\frac{1}{3}}}{2} \times \frac{N^{\frac{1}{3}}}{2}$ by three orthogonal plans, called separator of level 0, each one of size $O(N^{\frac{1}{3}} \times N^{\frac{1}{3}})$. The 2D nested dissection can be used to number the nodes for each plan of the separators. The nodes of the

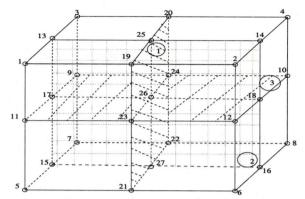

Fig.1 : nested dissection ordering for $3 \times 3 \times 3$ grid

subgrids are numbered first and then the nodes of the separator. This process can be recursively applied to the eight subgrids, leading finally to a complete ordering, as depicted in Figure 1. The level s of a separator is defined as the level in this recursive process. The elimination tree (Figure 2) generated by this ordering [9] is characterized by the following features :

- Each separator of level s contains $O(\frac{N^{\frac{1}{3}}}{2^s} * \frac{N^{\frac{1}{3}}}{2^s})$ nodes and it has eight children which are the separators of level $s + 1$;

- Each separator of level s is composed of three levels of supernodes, where a supernode is a group of consecutive nodes having one child. Each supernode of level l is composed of $O(\frac{1}{2^l} * \frac{N^{\frac{1}{3}}}{2^s} * \frac{N^{\frac{1}{3}}}{2^s})$ nodes;

- At level s, the size of a subgrid is $O(\frac{N^{\frac{1}{3}}}{2^s} \times \frac{N^{\frac{1}{3}}}{2^s} \times \frac{N^{\frac{1}{3}}}{2^s})$.

3.3 Subtree to subcube mapping strategy

In order to reduce the communication cost, we use the mapping scheme called subtree to subcube mapping [4,7]. This scheme is based on the structure of the elimination tree. Although a binary tree is ideal for this method, any tree associated with a nested dissection ordering can be used. Similarly, the method assumes that the number of processors p is a power of two. Starting with the root of the tree, the method assigns the nodes in the initial supernode to all processors. Since the elimination tree is produced by a nested dissection ordering, the initial supernode has two children supernodes. These are in turn

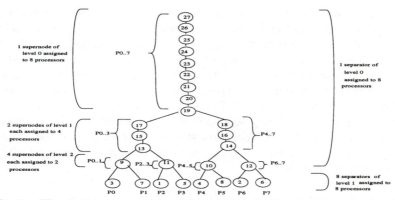

Fig.2 : Elimination tree associated with the grid in the figure 1 and the allocation strategy using 8 processors

split into two and so on, until the bottom of the tree. The method uses this feature in its mapping. It divides the processors into two equal groups and assigns each of the supernodes to each group. The method recursively goes on until only one processor remains in each of the p groups. It then assigns the portion of the tree below each group to that processor (Figure 2).

Each separator level s, $0 \leq s < \log_8 p$, is made of 8^s separators. The allocation strategy consists to assign the nodes of each separator of level s to a set of $\frac{p}{8^s}$ processors. Each separator is composed of three supernodal levels (Figure 2). Each supernodal level l, $0 \leq l \leq 2$, is composed of 2^l supernodes. Therefore, each supernode of level l is assigned to a set of $\frac{p}{2^l 8^s}$ processors organized in the form of a $d - ary$ tree topology (Figure 3).

3.4   Parallel algorithm

A supernode of level l associated with a level s separator is initially assigned to the root processor of a $d-ary$ topology and will be processed on all processors. The root processor acts as a controller for all the nodes of the supernodes in order to compute the tasks $Tcol(j)$ (j in the supernode) according to the following tasks (Figure 3):

- **task 1:** the root processor receives columns k which are necessary to compute $Tcol(j)$, for all j belonging to the supernode.

- **task 2:** the different columns j are partitioned and distributed on all processors assigned to the supernode.

- **task 3:** in order to compute $Tcol(j)$, the root processor sends simultaneously to its children columns k, exploiting pipelining. Then, each one of its children compute $Cmod(j, k)$ on its local subblocks of columns j and simultaneously, sends column k to its children. It is clear that during the computing phase of $Cmod(j, k)$, the root processor can send an other column, overlapping therefore communication and computation [2]. For each column j, when all $Cmod(j, k)$ operations are performed, each processor in the $d - ary$ topology will accomplish $Cdiv(j)$ on its local subblock. A reduction operation started in order to put the column j in the pipe. This latter operation must be done simultaneously with the pipeline of the column k.

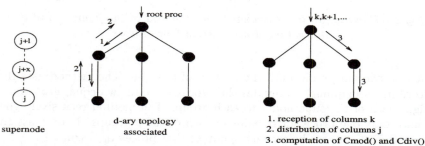

Figure 3: Illustration of tasks 1, 2 and 3 for a supernode on a $d - ary$ tree

The algorithm requires $3\log_8 p$ ($= \log p$) phases. Each phase is composed of the three elementary tasks(1,2,3).

4   Communication overhead and scalability

In this section, we derive expressions for the communication overhead of the algorithm, obtained using three lemmas, the first and the latter taken respectively from [1] and [4], the second one being a generalization of the 2D case described in [4].

4.1   Preliminaries

Lemma 1 [4]: The number of nonzeros from columns associated with the $i \times i \times i$ subgrid that are required by nodes on the subgrid boundary (for column modifications) is bounded by $O(i^4)$.

Lemma 2 (generalization of the 2D case): The number of nonzeros associated with the first level of separator on a $i \times i \times i$ subgrid is bounded

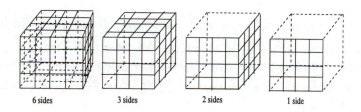

| 6 sides | 3 sides | 2 sides | 1 side |

Figure 4: Scheme illustrating the recurrence on f

by $O(i^4)$.

Proof: Consider an $i \times i \times i$ subgrid bounded by six sides. Let $f(i, 6)$ be the number of nonzeros from this subgrid that are required by the nodes on the six sides. Similarly, we define the quantities $f(i, 3), f(i, 2)$ and $f(i, 1)$, to be the number when the subgrid is bounded by three, two and one sides respectively (Figure 4). Let x be the number of nonzeros to find.

The recurrence relations on f can then be formulated as follows (Figure 4):
$f(i, 6) = x + 8f(\frac{i}{2}, 3)$; $f(i, 3) = x + f(\frac{i}{2}, 3) + 3f(\frac{i}{2}, 2) + 3f(\frac{i}{2}, 1)$
$f(i, 2) = x + 2f(\frac{i}{2}, 2) + 4f(\frac{i}{2}, 1)$; $f(i, 1) = x + 4f(\frac{i}{2}, 1)$
We can deduce that: $f(i, 6) = -7x + 8f(i, 3) - 12f(i, 2) + 12f(i, 1)$
hence : $x = \frac{1}{7}\{8f(i, 3) - 12f(i, 2) + 12f(i, 1) - f(i, 6)\}$
The result follows since $f(i, 3), f(i, 2), f(i, 1) < f(i, 6)$ and $f(i, 6)$ is a $O(i^4)$(lemma 1).

Lemma 3: [1]If a reduction operation has to merge a message of size m distributed among q processors, the communication overhead of this procedure on a $d - ary$ tree is bounded by $O(m \log_d q)$.

4.2 Communication overhead

Consider a separator of level s assigned to a set of $\frac{P}{8^s}$ processors.
This separator is composed of three supernodal levels (Figure 2). Each supernode of level l is assigned to a $d - ary$ tree of $\frac{P}{2^l 8^s}$ processors. Consider a supernode of level l, we have :
Communication overhead associated with task 1: According to lemma 1, at most $O((\frac{N^{\frac{1}{3}}}{2^s})^4)$ nonzeros are required for the root processor, and according to lemma 3 this operation requires, on a $d - ary$ tree topology, a communication overhead of $O(\frac{N^{\frac{4}{3}}}{2^{4s}} \log_d \frac{P}{2^l 8^s})$. Since there are three supernodal levels,

the overhead corresponds to the level s separator will be $\sum_{l=0}^{2} O(\frac{N^{\frac{4}{3}}}{2^{4s}} \log_d \frac{p}{2^{l}8^{s}})$ which is of order $O(\frac{3N^{\frac{4}{3}} \log_d(\frac{p}{8^{s}})}{2^{4s}})$, which is of order $O(N^{\frac{4}{3}} \log p)$.

Recall that this operation is applied $\log_8 p$ times ($\log_8 p$ separator levels), we get a communication overhead of $\sum_{s=0}^{\log_8 p - 1} O(\frac{3N^{\frac{4}{3}} \log_d(\frac{p}{8^{s}})}{2^{4s}})$, which is of order $O(N^{\frac{4}{3}} \log p)$.

Communication overhead associated with task 2: Following the lemma 2, there are at most $O((\frac{N^{\frac{1}{3}}}{2^{s}})^4)$ nonzeros that must be sent to $\frac{p}{2^{l}8^{s}}$ processors by the root processor. This requires, on a $d - ary$ tree, a total communication overhead of:

$$\sum_{s=0}^{\log_8 p - 1} \sum_{l=0}^{2} \left(\frac{p}{2^{l}8^{s}} * \frac{\overbrace{O(\frac{N^{\frac{4}{3}}}{2^{4s}})}^{\text{average size of a subblock}}}{\frac{p}{2^{l}8^{s}}} \right) \log_d \frac{p}{2^{l}8^{s}} \text{ which is of}$$

order $O(N^{\frac{4}{3}} \log p)$.

Communication overhead associated with task 3: Finally at most $O(\frac{N^{\frac{4}{3}}}{2^{4s}}) + O(\frac{N^{\frac{4}{3}}}{2^{4s}}) = O(\frac{N^{\frac{4}{3}}}{2^{4s}})$ elements are pipelined to $\frac{p}{2^{l}8^{s}}$ processors of a $d - ary$ tree. This leads to a total communication overhead of $O(N^{\frac{4}{3}} \log p)$. The total communication overhead of this algorithm, which is the sum of the three previously computed times, is of order $O(N^{\frac{4}{3}} \log p)$. This improves the results obtained by Kumar and al. [8] which was of order $O(N^{\frac{4}{3}} \sqrt{p})$.

4.3   Scalability analysis

Following notations given by [8], let $W(N)$ be the sequential execution time of the algorithm and $T_p(N, p)$ be the parallel execution time with p processors. We define the overhead function by $T_0(N, p) = pT_p(N, p) - W(N)$, and the efficiency by $E = \frac{W(N)}{W(N) + T_0(N,p)} = \frac{1}{1 + \frac{T_0(N,p)}{W(N)}}$. Then, in order to have a constant efficiency, it is necessary that $W(N) = \gamma T_0(N, p)$ (1) where γ is a constant. The sequential execution time to factorize a $N \times N$ matrix arising from a three dimensional grid of finite differences elements ordered by a nested dissection ordering is of $O(N^2)$[8]. Equation (1) leads to :

$$N^2 \propto N^{\frac{4}{3}} \log p$$
$$\Rightarrow N^{\frac{2}{3}} \propto \log p$$
$$\Rightarrow N^2 = W(N) \propto (\log p)^3$$

i.e the size of the problem must be increased as $(\log p)^3$ to maintain a constant efficiency. Therefore, the isoefficiency of this algorithm is better than that obtained by Kumar, Gupta and Karypis which is of order $O(p^{1.5})$[8].

5 Conclusion

We have presented an efficient multiphase parallel algorithm. This algorithm is dedicated for the $d - reconfigurable$ machines and factorizes an $N \times N$ sparse matrix associated with an $N^{\frac{1}{3}} \times N^{\frac{1}{3}} \times N^{\frac{1}{3}}$ regular finite difference grid ordered by a nested dissection method with a communication overhead of $O(N^{\frac{4}{3}} \log p)$. The implementation of this algorithm is currently in progress under PVM environment. We intend to compare it with the PSPASES solver. We are also investigating a block variant of this algorithm.

References

1. A. Benaini, D. Laiymani, G. R. Perrin, "A Reconfigurable Parallel Algorithm for sparse Cholesky Factorization", In Ferreira and J.Rolim editors, Parallel Algorithms for Irregularly Structured Problems, LNCS980,261-274, Springer, 1995
2. F. Desprez, "Procédures de base dans le Calcul Scientifique sur Machines Parallèles à mémoire Distribuée", PhD thesis, Institut National Polytechnique de Grenoble 1994
3. M. Joshi, G. Karypis, V. Kumar, A. Gupta, F. Gustavson George, " PSPASES: An Efficient and Scalable Parallel Sparse Direct Solver ", In Proc. Int. Workshop on Frontiers of Parallel Numerical Computation and Application, Frontiers'99, Annapolis, Maryland, February 1999
4. A.George, J.W.H.Liu, E. Ng, "Communication results for parallel sparse Cholesky factorization on a hypercube", Par. Comput. 3, 327-342, 1989
5. A. George, "An automatic nested dissection algorithm for irregular finite element problems",Siam J. Number. Anal., 15(1978), pp. 1053-1069
6. A. George,M. T. Heath, J. Liu, E. NG, "Sparse Cholesky factorization on a local-memory multiprocessor", SIAM J.Sci. Stat. Comp. Vol.9, 327-340, 1988
7. G. A. Geist, E. Ng, "Task scheduling for parallel sparse cholesky factorization", Int.J. of Parallel Programming, 18 : 291-341, 1989
8. A. Gupta, G. Karypis, V. Kumar, "Highly scalable parallel algorithm for sparse matrix factorization", IEEE Transactions on Parallel and Distributed Systems, Vol.8, 502-520, May 1997
9. J. W. Liu, "The role of elimination trees in sparse factorization", SIAM J.Matrix Anal, Appl, 11, 134-172, 1990

TOWARDS A FAST PARALLEL SPARSE MATRIX-VECTOR MULTIPLICATION

ROMAN GEUS AND STEFAN RÖLLIN

INSTITUTE OF SCIENTIFIC COMPUTING, ETH ZÜRICH

The sparse matrix-vector product is an important computational kernel that runs ineffectively on many computers with super-scalar RISC processors. In this paper we analyse the performance of the sparse matrix-vector product with symmetric matrices originating from the FEM and describe techniques that lead to a fast implementation. It is shown how these optimisations can be incorporated into an efficient parallel implementation using message-passing.

1 Performance analysis of the sparse matrix-vector product

In this paper we focus on large symmetric sparse matrices stored in SSK format[a] [1], that do not fit into the memory cache. However our ideas can be applied to general sparse matrices stored in other formats.

Algorithm 1 shows a matrix-vector multiplication code $y := Ax$ for a matrix stored in SSK format. The accesses to the matrix data structure are in a stride-1 loop, the access pattern on x and y is irregular and depends on the sparsity structure of A.

Algorithm 1

```
for (i = 0; i < n; i ++) {        /* loop over rows of lower triangle*/
  xi = x[i];                      /* load x[i] */
  s = 0.0;
  k2 = ia[i+1];
  for (k = ia[i]; k < k2; k ++){  /* loop over nonzero elems of row i*/
    j = ja[k];                    /* load column index j */
    v = va[k];                    /* load matrix element A[i,j] */
    s = s + v*x[j];               /* s = s + A[i,j] * x[j] */
    y[j] = y[j] + v*xi;           /* y[j] = y[j] + A[j,i] * x[i] */
  }
  y[i] = da[i]*xi + s;            /* y[i] = A[i,i] * x[i] + s */
}
```

To compute an upper bound for the performance of the sparse matrix-vector product for a given architecture, profound knowledge of the design of the processor and the memory subsystem is required. Our approach is more portable and gives comparable results. We compute the ratio η of the number of floating point operations to the number of bytes of memory traffic. For the best case scenario where x and y are read only once from memory and then kept in-cache we get $\eta \approx 0.31$ flops/byte for our test matrices (see section 2)[b]. If we multiply η by the memory bandwidth of

---

[a] For matrices in symmetric sparse skyline (SSK) format the strictly lower triangular is stored in the widely used CSR (compressed sparse row) format[1] (arrays ia, ja, va). The diagonal is stored separately in array da.

[b] For this approximation we assume a very large write-back cache and double precision arithmetic.

System	Processor	Measured Bandwidth Mbytes/s	Max. MFlops	Measured MFlops
Sun Enterprise 3500	336MHz Ultra SPARC	248.71	76.52	28.59
DEC Workstation	500MHz Alpha 21164	245.74	75.61	42.66
HP Exemplar X-Class	180MHz PA-8000	558.14	171.74	48.22
IBM SP2	160MHz POWER2 SC	1165.05	358.49	56.33
Intel Paragon	50MHz i860 XP	N/A	N/A	N/A

Table 1. **Machines used for numerical experiments, their measured memory bandwidth, the predicted maximal performance and the measured performance of Alg. 1.** *Because the Intel Paragon at ETH Zürich suddenly died during the time we conducted our experiments, we don't have all results available for that machine. The numbers in the last column are measured using the matrix cav2 (see Tab. 2).*

the system we get an upper bound of the performance of the sparse matrix-vector product. We determine the memory bandwidth by benchmarking a highly optimised computational kernel tuned for the given hardware[c]. This gives more realistic results than using the peak memory bandwidth reported by the vendor.

From Tab. 1 one can observe that the measured performance is far below the optimal performance. The compiler is unable to generate efficient code, mainly because of data dependencies and irregular loops. Additional cache misses generated by accesses on x and y further degrade performance. On the other hand the upper bound computed for the IBM SP2 is unrealistic because its memory cache is too small (128 KBytes) to keep the vectors x and y in-cache.

2 Design of a fast sparse matrix vector product for one processor

We applied three techniques to improve the implementation of Alg. 1.

1. By use of *software pipelining* (reorganising the code in such a way that the processor pipelines are better filled) we are able to load data into registers earlier (data prefetching) and reduce data-dependencies in the innermost loop iteration. This increases the instruction level parallelism.

   These optimisations cannot be performed by compilers in a satisfactory way. Often compilers do not have the information necessary to move up load instruction safely. Due to the lack of type information, compilers have to generate code conservatively. Also, the compiler technology simply is not yet advanced enough to perform more sophisticated optimisations. E.g., revisiting Alg. 1, a compiler would never load the column index j a loop iteration in advance. Such optimisations have to be carried out "by hand". Current compilers are able to generate efficient code only for simple loops.

2. We reduce the number of memory accesses by *register blocking*, i.e. splitting the matrix A into a sum of matrices, consisting of small dense blocks of a fixed size [2]. When multiplying with a matrix consisting of small dense blocks the

---

[c]We used the vendor supplied BLAS routine daxpy.

Name	*cav1*	*cav2*
Size of matrix	17215	54295
# nonzeros	929159	3172021
Storage	4.41 MBytes	18.46 MBytes
Properties	symmetric	symmetric

Table 2. **Matrices used in numerical experiments.** *Both matrices originate from a FEM code that solves Maxwell's Equations in 3D* [5].

code has to load fewer indices j because only one is needed per block. When multiplying with a dense block, elements of x and y can be loaded once and reused several times.

In our approach we store at least two matrices: one contains the small dense blocks of equal size and the other contains the remaining non-zero elements. In [3] another approach is presented: the authors store the *whole* matrix in small dense blocks, at the expense of having to store some zero entries explicitly.

To store the matrix of small dense blocks we use the same data structure as for the original matrix (SSK format), with the exception that we store a whole block for each coordinate pair (i, j) instead of just one value. We build this data structure using a linear-time greedy algorithm that scans the matrix row by row.

3. We use Cuthill-McKee *reordering* [4] on the matrix to reduce its bandwidth. This can reduce cache misses that accesses to x and y generate [2] and more importantly also lowers the number of messages to be sent in the parallel implementation (see section 3).

For the numerical experiments we use matrices listed in Tab. 2. The experiments are carried out on five different machines as listed in Tab. 1. First we benchmark the three optimisations separately (Figs. 1-3), then we measure the best performance by applying all optimisations at once (Fig. 4). For all experiments we compile the codes with all optimisations flags turned on.

Fig. 1 shows the performance of software-pipelined code in comparison with the original code from Alg. 1. The benefit is substantial on all platforms. The improvement ranges from 27% on the DEC Alpha Workstation to 110% on the IBM SP2 (for matrix *cav2*).

Fig. 2 shows the impact of the block size on the performance of the register-blocked code. For the matrix *cav2* the maximal improvement is 48% on the IBM SP2. On the other platforms the improvement is not remarkable, it lies between 10% and 23%. As can be seen by the lighter colored bars in Fig. 2 the performance of the code would even be higher for matrices consisting solely of small dense blocks. Fig. 3 shows the performance of the unoptimised code when multiplying matrices with different orderings. Compared with the original ordering the performance cannot be increased substantially with Cuthill-McKee-type reorderings. The experiments with random ordering indicate that the performance depends heavily on the matrix ordering. In cases, where the original ordering is not so well suited for matrix-vector multiplication as in our case, the improvement of Cuthill-McKee-type

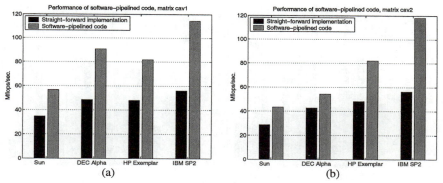

Figure 1. **Performance of the software-pipelined code and the straight-forward code (a) for matrix** *cav1* **and (b) for matrix** *cav2*. *These experiments are carried out on a single processor.*

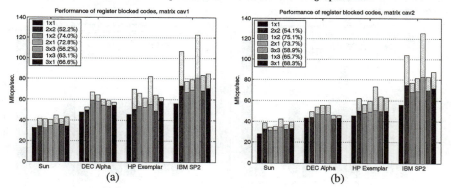

Figure 2. **Performance of the codes that use register blocking.** *Fig. (a) shows the results for matrix* cav1, *Fig. (b) shows the results for matrix* cav2. *The bars in light color (top) represent the performance of the code portion that multiplies the blocked part of the matrix. The darker colored bars (bottom) show the overall performance of the code, including the blocked portion and the unblocked portion. The number in brackets is the percentage of non-zero elements that are stored in dense blocks of the given size. These experiments are carried out on a single processor.*

reorderings is more substantial [2].

For each platform we choose the fastest code that takes all discussed optimisations into account and compare it with the corresponding unoptimized version. The results are shown in Fig. 4. On the SP2 we achieve an overall improvement of 151%, on the HP Exemplar, DEC Alpha Workstation and Sun Enterprise Server we get a performance increase of 80%, 43% and 73%.

3 Parallelisation using message-passing

For the parallel implementation we distribute the lower triangular part of the matrix A by block-rows (see Fig. 5). To balance the load we assign the same number of

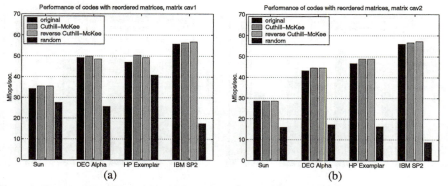

Figure 3. **Performance of the codes when working on matrices with different orderings.** *Fig. (a) shows the results for matrix* cav1*, Fig. (b) shows the results for matrix* cav2*. These experiments are carried out on a single processor.*

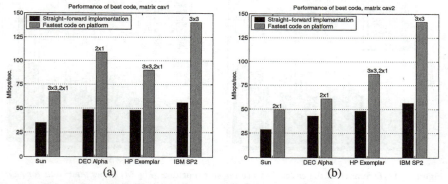

Figure 4. **Performance of the best code and the unoptimised code.** *Fig. (a) shows the results for matrix* cav1*, Fig. (b) shows the results for matrix* cav2*. For each architecture we use the code that performs best and compare it against the unoptimised code. The labels on top of the bars show the block size that yields the best performance for register blocking.*

nonzeros to each processor. The distribution of the vectors x and y corresponds to the distribution of the matrix rows.

During a preprocessing step each processor identifies the vector elements to receive from and send to other processors. For the actual parallel matrix-vector code we implemented three slightly different routines:

1. Without latency-hiding: Exchange parts of x-vector, then multiply with local part of matrix, then exchange parts of y-vector and form resulting vector.

2. With latency hiding: Exchange parts of x-vector and at the same time multiply with local block-column in the upper triangle. Send the y-vector to the other processors. Upon arrival of the remote parts of the x-vector the local block-row in the lower triangle can be multiplied. Upon arrival of the y-vectors form

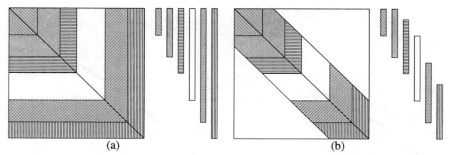

Figure 5. **Data distribution for parallel implementation.** *The figure shows how the matrix is distributed across the processors for* (a) *a non-banded and* (b) *a banded matrix. Because the matrix is symmetric, only its lower triangle is stored. The vectors depicted on the right show which parts of the x-vector must be known to each processor for the multiplication of the local part. This also corresponds to the parts of the y-vector that have to be sent to other processors.*

resulting vector.

3. With latency hiding: Exchange parts of x-vector and at the same time multiply with local diagonal block of the matrix [6]. Upon arrival of the remote parts of the x-vector, multiply with the remaining local part of the matrix, then exchange parts of y-vector and form resulting vector.

Routine 1 is a reasonable choice for machines that do not support latency-hiding. Routine 2 has the disadvantage that it does not exploit the symmetry of the matrix well, since the matrix has to be read from memory twice. Routine 3 has the disadvantage that the diagonal block of the matrix has to be stored separately to make the implementation efficient.

The parallel algorithm benefits from the matrix reordering done for the optimisation of the serial code. As can be seen from Fig. 5 the number of messages is reduced.

We carried out the parallel experiments on three platforms: the Intel Paragon, the HP Exemplar X-Class and the IBM SP2. The software-pipelining optimisation described in section 2 was incorporated into the parallel version. Although it would be entirely possible to implement register blocking also for the parallel version, we did not do that, mainly because of the limited time available.

Fig. 6 shows the measured speedups for the Intel Paragon. For this experiment the matrices are reordered using the Cuthill-McKee algorithm. The code scales well, especially for the matrix *cav2*. Fig. 7 shows the measured speedups for the HP Exemplar X-Class. For the smaller matrix *cav1* we get super-linear speedup due to cache-effects. Fig. 8 shows the measured speedups for the IBM SP2. The code does not scale as well as on the Intel Paragon, because the SP2 has much faster processors and the slower interconnection network. When the matrices are left in their original ordering the performance is unacceptably low, because of the increased number of

314

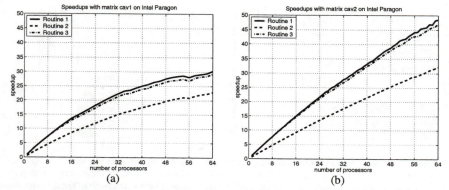

Figure 6. **Speedups of the parallel matrix-vector multiplication code on the Intel Paragon.** *The matrices* (a) cav1 *and* (b) cav2 *are reordered using the Cuthill-McKee algorithm.*

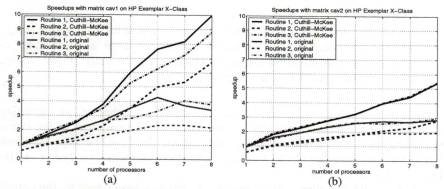

Figure 7. **Speedups of the parallel matrix-vector multiplication code on the HP Exemplar X-Class** *Speedups are reported for matrices* (a) cav1 *and* (b) cav2 *using their original ordering and Cuthill-McKee ordering.*

messages (see Figs. 7 and 8). In the worst case every processor has to communicate with all other processors (see Fig. 5).

4 Conclusions

We computed an upper bound for the performance of the sparse matrix-vector product and showed that straight-forward implementations perform poorly. The three techniques we presented in this paper improved the performance by up to 151%. Our message-passing implementation also benefits from these optimisations and scales reasonably. We think that future work should go into automatic generation of sparse matrix-vector multiplication codes which are optimised to a given matrix and a given target architecture. This approach has been successfully applied to other applications, such as the FFT [7] and the dense BLAS [8].

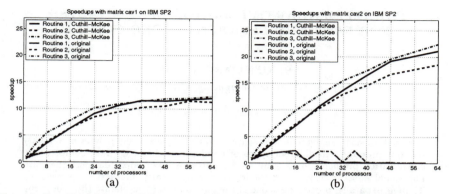

Figure 8. **Speedups of the parallel matrix-vector multiplication code on the IBM SP2.** *Speedups are reported for matrices* (a) cav1 *and* (b) cav2 *using their original ordering and Cuthill-McKee ordering.*

5 Acknowledgments

We would like to thank Peter Arbenz for improvements and corrections of a draft of this paper. We would also like to thank Rolf Strebel for explanatory discussions on the subject of software pipelining.

References

1. Y. Saad. SPARSKIT: A basic tool kit for sparse matrix computations. Technical Report 90-20, Research Institute for Advanced Computer Science, NASA Ames Research Center, Moffet Field, CA, 1990.

2. S. Toledo. Improving memory-system performance of sparse-matrix vector multiplication. In *Proceedings of the Eighth SIAM Conference on Parallel Processing for Scientific Computing*. SIAM, 1997.

3. E. Im and K. Yelick. Optimizing sparse matrix-vector multiplication on SMPs. In *Ninth SIAM Conference on Parallel Processing for Scientific Computing*. SIAM, March 1999.

4. A. George and J. W. Liu. *Computer Solution of Large Sparse Positive Definite Systems*. Prentice-Hall, Englewood Cliffs, NJ, 1981.

5. P. Arbenz and R. Geus. A comparison of solvers for large eigenvalue problems occuring in the design of resonant cavities. *Numerical Linear Algebra with Applications*, 6:1–13, 1999.

6. Y. Saad and A. Malevsky. P-SPARSLIB: A portable library of distributed memory sparse iterative solvers. Technical Report UMSI 95-180, MSI, 1995.

7. M. Frigo and S. Johnson. FFTW: An adaptive software architecture for the FFT. In *ICASSP*, page 1381, 1998.

8. R. Whaley and J. Dongarra. Automatically Tuned Linear Algebra Software (ATLAS). In *SC '98 Proceedings*, 1998.

PARALLEL ADAPTIVE 3-D WAVELET ANALYSIS FOR FAST AND EFFICIENT VIDEO CODING

R. KUTIL*AND A. UHL

RIST++ & Dept. of Scientific Computing, University of Salzburg, Austria

E-mail: {rkutil,uhl}@cosy.sbg.ac.at

Adapted wavelet analysis in the sense of wavelet packet algorithms is a highly relevant procedure in different types of applications, like e.g. data compression, classification problems, data analysis etc. Given a 3-D (video) data set the computational demand is too high for interactive or "nearly-interactive" processing. Therefore, parallel processing is one of the possibilities to accelerate the processing speed. In the 3-D case special attention has to be paid towards handling of the large amount of data. We investigate different data decomposition approaches, border handling techniques and programming paradigms. The memory consuming decomposition into a given arbitrary basis after adaptive basis choice is resolved by a localized decomposition strategy.

1   Introduction

Wavelet packets[1] represent a generalization of the method of multiresolution decomposition and comprise the entire family of subband coded (tree) decompositions. Whereas in the wavelet case the decomposition is applied recursively to the coarse scale approximations (leading to the well known (pyramidal) wavelet decomposition tree), in the wavelet packet decomposition the recursive procedure is applied to all the coarse scale approximations and detail signals, which leads to a complete wavelet packet tree (i.e. binary tree and quadtree in the 1D and 2D case, respectively) and more flexibility in frequency resolution.

Whereas a significant amount of work has been already done concerning parallel algorithms for the fast wavelet transform, only few papers have been devoted to parallel wavelet packet decomposition and its specific features and demands (e.g. approaches for performing the best basis algorithm and the irregular decomposition into such a basis on parallel MIMD architectures[2,3,4,5], application of parallel wavelet packet decomposition in numerics[6]).

Most video compression algorithms rely on 2-D based schemes employing motion compensation techniques. On the other hand, rate-distortion efficient 3-D algorithms exist which are able to capture temporal redundancies in a

---

*PARTIALLY SUPPORTED BY THE AUSTRIAN SCIENCE FUND FWF, PROJECT NO. P11045-ÖMA.

more natural way (e.g. 3-D wavelet/subband coding and hybrid 3-D fractal/subband coding).

Recently, wavelet packet based compression methods[7,8] have been developed which outperform the most advanced wavelet coders (e.g. SPIHT[9]) significantly for textured images in terms of rate-distortion performance. A similar development in the area of video compression may be observed for 3-D subband[10] or 3-D wavelet packet[11] video coding. Therefore, wavelet packet decomposition currently attracts much attention and a thorough examination of parallelization possibilities for the 3-D case is desirable.

2   Sequential Algorithm

In the 3-D case the decomposition of a subband produces eight new subbands by convolving the data with a low pass and a high pass QMF filter along each of the three dimensions. In pyramidal wavelet transforms only one subband (the coarse scale approximation) is decomposed further, whereas in complete wavelet packet decompositions each subband is decomposed, leading to a so called full decomposition tree which produces 8^n subbands at a decomposition depth of n.

As we want to use the transformed data for compression purposes, we have to estimate, how suitable it is for this purpose, by evaluating an information cost function. An example is the entropy $H(X) = -\sum_j p_j \log p_j$ where $p_j = \frac{|x_j|^2}{||X||^2}$ and $X = (x_0, x_1, x_2, \dots)$ are the coefficients in the subband. An additive analogue is $\lambda(X) = -\sum_j |x_j|^2 \log |x_j|^2$ by the use of which $\sum_i \lambda(X_i)$ can be compared to $\lambda(X)$ if X is decomposed into $X_1 \dots X_8$.

To determine the best basis one has to perform a complete decomposition and to compute for each subband on each depth its *best information cost* by comparing its *information cost* with the sum of its subbands *best information costs*. After that the subbands, that minimize the *overall information cost*, have to be selected by either accessing subband data kept in memory (high memory requirements) or performing a second decomposition run according to the best basis tree. We present a strategy how to avoid the second run by backing up and restoring subbands and by walking through the decomposition tree in depth first order. Pseudo Code 1 implements this strategy as a recursive procedure.

```
SequDecompose (Subband S) return InformationCost :=
    C = InformationCost (S)
    -- end of recursion
    if DecompositionLevel (S) = MaxLevel then return C
    Backup S
    Filter S to get Subbands S[1] .. S[8]
    -- decompose the subbands recursively
    D = 0
    for i = 1 .. 8
        D = D + SequDecompose (S[i])
    -- decide whether the best basis tree branches
    if   C < D
    then Restore S; return C
    else return D
```

Pseudo code 1: Sequential Algorithm

3 Parallel Algorithm

3.1 Message Passing

The main idea is to split the data into several parts along one or more axes and to distribute them among the PE. But at a certain depth subbands get too small to be processed efficiently in parallel. This stage is of course dependent on the number of processor elements (PE) employed and is denoted "redistribution level"[4,5]. At this stage data has to be redistributed so that entire subbands are located on single PE which enables to perform the remaining computations without any additional computations. Therefore the concept of the sequential algorithm cannot be completely adapted to the parallel algorithm.

We choose a mixed approach: Below the redistribution level data is completely decomposed to that level and recomposed if it is necessary to satisfy the best basis (which can be interpreted as partial reverse second run). Redistributed subbands are decomposed using the sequential algorithm from the previous section. Figure 1 shows a simplified (binary instead of octtree) example distribution scheme for three PE. Pseudo code 2 shows, how this can be implemented.

The memory requirement of this algorithm for a node PE is therefore $(\frac{t}{\#PE} + (2^r - 1)(f - 2))xy$ floating point numbers for the first phase (t, x and y are the video data sizes along the corresponding axes, f is the filter length and r is the redistribution level) plus $txy8^{-r}(1 + b)$ for the second phase (where b

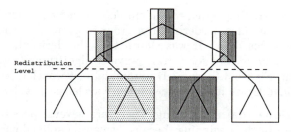

Figure 1. Example data/work distribution at several stages in the decomposition tree (simplified) – different colors symbolize different PE

```
-- Phase 1: split decomposition
for t = 1 .. NumberOfNodes
    Send Part of data to Node t
for l = 1 .. RedistributionLevel
    for all subbands S at level l
        Exchange border data
        Filter S into 8 new subbands
-- Phase 2: subband based decomposition
Redistribute subbands to responsible node
for all subbands S at RedistributionLevel
    SequDecompose (S)
-- Phase 3: partial reverse second run
Determine part of best basis tree below RedistributionLevel
Recompose subbands below RedistributionLevel if necessary
```

Pseudo code 2: Parallel Algorithm

stands for the memory needed to backup the subbands before decomposition) which should be rather small for $r > 1$. In our case $b = 1 + \frac{1}{8} + \frac{1}{8^2} + \ldots \approx \frac{8}{7}$. If we performed a second run, backing up the subbands would not be necessary, therefore $b = 0$. The conventional algorithm (storing all subbands) would imply $b = d - r$, where d is the maximum decomposition depth.

Boundary problem A classical problem in parallel wavelet and wavelet packet algorithms is the question of how to handle the exchange of the necessary border data. In the literature two approaches[12,13] for the boundary problems have been discussed and compared. During the *data swapping* method each PE calculates only its own data and exchanges these results with the appropriate neighbour PE in order to get the necessary border data for the next decomposition level. Employing *redundant data calculation* each PE computes also necessary redundant border data in order to avoid additional communication to obtain this data. It was shown that the decision, which method to apply, is very important for certain wavelet algorithms (e.g. the á trous algorithm[14] and Figure 3 (a) for 3-D pyramidal fast wavelet decomposition). Therefore we investigate its influence on the wavelet packet decomposition.

Multidimensional data splitting There are several possibilities to distribute the data in the beginning, because it can be split along several axes. It can be shown, that by splitting the data not only in time domain but also in spatial domain it is possible to reduce the amount of border data that has to be exchanged, but it increases the communication complexity.

3.2 Data Parallel Approach

Data parallel programming on a shared memory architecture is easily achieved by transforming a sequential algorithm into a parallel one by simply identifying areas which are suitable to be run in parallel i.e. in which no data dependencies exist and different iterations access different data.

Here we choose parallelization of a decomposition step along the time axis of the video data. Because one has to take care, that parallel regions are not too short with regard to execution time, we have to change this strategy at a certain decomposition depth. This leads to a simulation of the message passing algorithm (data redistribution).

4 Experimental Results

We conduct experiments on an SGI POWERChallenge GR (at RIST++, Salzburg Univ.) with 20 MIPS R10000 processors. The size of the video data is 128×128 pixels in the spatial domain, combined to a 3-D data block consisting of 512 frames. QMF filters with 8 coefficients are used. The PVM version employed is a special shared memory variant for SGI systems.

Figure 2 (a) shows clearly, that a too low redistribution level limits the subbands that are redistributed, leaving some PE without work (load balancing problem). A too high redistribution level increases the communication complexity of the redistribution. This shows, that redistribution based on subbands is necessary.

Comparing this Figure with Figure 2 (b) one can see, that although execution time is about 25% shorter if best basis computations are omitted, the speedup behaviour is the same. The reason is, that the computational demand for each subband is increased in the same way over all decomposition levels

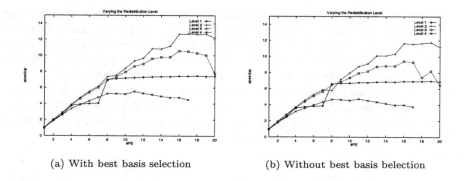

(a) With best basis selection (b) Without best basis belection

Figure 2. Effect of subband based redistribution

and the only additional communications are the exchange of subband statistics and subtree information, which is negligible compared to the exchange of subband data itself.

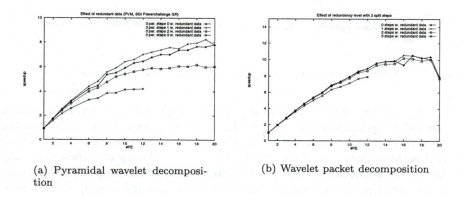

(a) Pyramidal wavelet decomposition (b) Wavelet packet decomposition

Figure 3. Effect of different data decomposition techniques

Figure 3 shows, that whereas for pyramidal wavelet decomposition (a) the choice of the border handling strategy does affect the performance, it turns out to be of almost no relevance for wavelet packet decomposition (b). ("n steps with redundant data" means, that the first n steps of the decomposition do not have to exchange border data.) The reason is that in the pyramidal case the entire processing time is in contrast to the wavelet packet case dominated by the first decomposition level (where the choice of border handling strategy is crucial). The computations above the redistribution level are not affected by any border problem at all which explains the different behaviour.

For the same reason multidimensional data splitting shows little influence on the speedup, as can be seen in Figure 4 (b). (The notation "p:q:r" means, that the video data is split p times in time domain and q and r times along the two spatial axes. PE is the number of processor elements.)

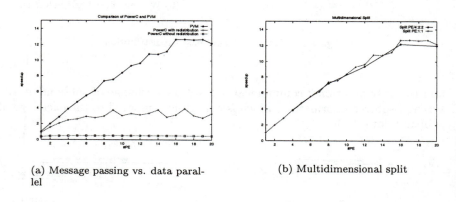

(a) Message passing vs. data parallel

(b) Multidimensional split

Figure 4. Message passing vs. data parallel and multidimensional split

Finally we compare the message passing approach with a version of data parallel programming (see Figure 4). A straightforward approach (denoted "PowerC without redistribution" in the plot) does not even show any speedup across the entire range of processors. Only by simulating the message passing approach (which is very expensive in terms of implementation effort) we reach some speedup but still significantly below the message passing implementation.

5 Conclusion

The experiments show, that in contrast to the pyramidal wavelet transform the border data problem can be neglected. A subband based redistribution is necessary to gain reasonable speedups. The data parallel approach is not able to compete against the message passing paradigm. A localized decomposition strategy can avoid the need for a second run and load balancing problems.

References

1. M.V. Wickerhauser. *Adapted wavelet analysis from theory to software.* A.K. Peters, Wellesley, Mass., 1994.
2. E. Goirand, M.V. Wickerhauser, and M. Farge. A parallel two-dimensional wavelet packet transform and some applications in computing and compression analysis. In R. Motard and B. Joseph, editors, *Applications of Wavelet Transforms in Chemical Engineering*, pages 275–319. Kluwer Academic Publishers Group, 1995.
3. A. Uhl. Adapted wavelet analysis an moderate parallel distributed memory MIMD architectures. In A. Ferreira and J. Rolim, editors, *Parallel Algorithms for Irregular Structured Problems*, volume 980 of *Lecture Notes in Computer Science*, pages 275–284. Springer, 1995.
4. A. Uhl. Wavelet packet best basis selection on moderate parallel MIMD architectures. *Parallel Computing*, 22(1):149–158, 1996.
5. M. Feil and A. Uhl. Algorithms and programming paradigms for 2-D wavelet packet decomposition on multicomputers and multiprocessors. In P. Zinterhof, M. Vajtersic, and A. Uhl, editors, *Parallel Computation. Proceedings of ACPC'99*, volume 1557 of *Lecture Notes on Computer Science*, pages 367–376. Springer-Verlag, 1999.
6. L. Bacchelli Montefusco. Parallel numerical algorithms with orthonormal wavelet packet bases. In C.K. Chui, L. Montefusco, and L. Puccio, editors, *Wavelets: Theory, Algorithms and Applications*, pages 459–494. Academic Press, San Diego, 1994.
7. Z. Xiong, K. Ramchandran, and M.T. Orchard. Wavelet packet image coding using space-frequency quantization. *IEEE Transactions on Image Processing*, 7(6):892–898, June 1998.
8. F.G. Meyer, A.Z. Averbuch, J.O. Strömberg, and R.R. Coifman. Fast wavelet packet image compression. In *Proceedings of the Data Compression Conference DCC'98*, page 563. IEEE Press, March 1998.
9. A. Said and W.A. Pearlman. A new, fast, and efficient image codec based on set partitioning in hierarchical trees. *IEEE Transactions on Circuits and Systems for Video Technology*, 6(3):243–249, 1996.
10. R.L. Lagendijk, F. Bosveld, and J. Biemond. Subband video coding. In A.N. Akansu and M.J.T. Smith, editors, *Subband and Wavelet Transforms*, pages 251–286. Kluwer Academic Publishers Group, 1996.
11. W.L. Hsu and H. Derin. Video compression using adaptive wavelet packets and DPCM. In H.H. Li, S. Sun, and H. Derin, editors, *Video Data Compression for Multimedia Computing*, pages 55–94. Kluwer Academic Publishers Group, 1997.
12. M-L. Woo. Parallel discrete wavelet transform on the Paragon MIMD machine. In R.S. Schreiber et al., editor, *Proceedings of the seventh SIAM conference on parallel processing for scientific computing*, pages 3–8, 1995.
13. S. Sullivan. Vector and parallel implementations of the wavelet transform. Technical report, Center for Supercomputing Research and Development, University of Illinois, Urbana, 1991.
14. M. Feil and A. Uhl. Real-time image analysis using wavelets: the "à trous" algorithm on MIMD architectures. In D. Sinha, editor, *Real-Time Imaging IV*, volume 3645 of *SPIE Proceedings*, pages 56–65, 1999.

UG - A PARALLEL SOFTWARE TOOL FOR UNSTRUCTURED ADAPTIVE MULTIGRIDS

S. LANG

IWR, University of Heidelberg, Germany
`Stefan.Lang@iwr.uni-heidelberg.de`

High level parallel applications based on the message passing paradigm are difficult to design and implement, especially when solution adaptive techniques are used and threedimensional problems on complex geometries are faced. Many of these difficulties are addressed inside the *UG* platform, e.g. dynamic load migration and load balancing, parallel grid adaption, basic grid management, and parallel IO.

Main idea during the design process of *UG* a multigrid code for the computation of partial differential equations, was to find proper abstractions for each of the different functionality parts of a parallel, adaptive and unstructured software system. This assures a maximal degree of code reuse.

In a parallel context grid adaption involves the need to rebalance the computational load. This stage involves both determining a new load balancing and dynamically redistributing the objects of the grid parts. A key feature of *UG* is the capability to dynamically migrate grid objects between the processors during run time. This difficult task is supported by *DDD* (dynamic distributed data), a new parallel programming model. Parallel adaptive calculations of complex real-world problems, two-phase flow and densiy driven-flow in porous media, are presented.

1 Introduction

Whilst in the field of sequential unstructured grids various related code developments take place, e.g. [2,6], parallel developments of unstructured, adaptive multigrid codes, especially for nonlinear 3D problems, are rare.

In this paper some mayor parts of *UG* will be presented. *UG* is a powerful, quite flexible environment for solving PDEs on unstructured multigrids using massively parallel computing resources. Main idea during the design process of *UG* was to find proper abstractions for each of the different functionality parts of a parallel, adaptive and unstructured code. This assures a maximal degree of code reuse and therefore the treatment of various partial differential equations without superfluous coding is possible.

Mayor (sub)systems of parallel *UG* applications, in this paper two-phase and density driven flow, are shown in figure 1, the complete design is given in [3]. These consist of a *problem dependent* part, which realizes a more or less complex numerics and can be subdivided into the application (App) itself with boundary conditions, domain description and proper initialization, discretization of the problem (Problem Class) and adequate linear/nonlinear

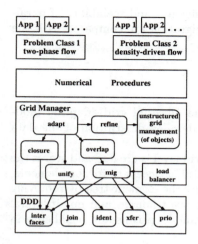

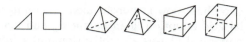

Figure 2. Element types supported by grid manager.

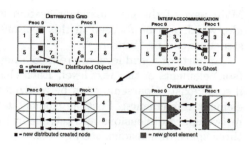

Figure 1. System and subsystem design of parallel *UG* applications.

Figure 3. The different phases of the grid adaption process.

solvers for the equation/discretization, composed with tools from Numerical Procedures. On the other hand a problem *independent part* is needed, which does all the grid and geometry related stuff needed, including

- parallel grid adaption subsystem (adapt, closure, unify, refine, overlap),

- unstructured grid manager for manipulation of the local grid objects,

- load balancer, which determines the redistribution of the grid,

- load migration part (mig), which handles load transfers of grid objects,

- the new parallel programming model *DDD* (dynamic distributed data) on which most of the parallel parts of the code are based.

The structure of an adaptive computations for linear and/or nonlinear problems is characterized by iteratively calculating the solution and adapting the computational grid according to the needs of the solution phenomena.

The remainder of the paper is organized in the following way. The next section explains the process of grid adaption, then an overview of the realized load balancing and load migration concepts is given. In the following section the parallel programming model *DDD* is described. Finally we show parallel adaptive calculations of complex real-world problems, density-driven flow and two-phase flow in porous media. Timings, efficiency and scalability of parallel grid adaption, load balancing and load migration are compared with the numerical phases, discretization and solution.

2 Grid Adaption

Main part of the grid manager system is the powerful grid adaption module, which will be focused in this section. A detailed description of the data structure can be found in [3].

If parts of a grid level are refined a new grid level is created and stores the (son) elements of the next level. Each element has access to its son elements, if some exist. Coarsening can be realized using the element tree by removing element refinements. Possible element types are triangles and quadrilateral in two space dimensions and tetrahedra, pyramids, prisms and hexahedra in three space dimensions, see figure 2.

Grid adaption allows refinement and/or coarsening of grids consisting of mixed elements, ensuring a conforming grid closure, therefore the resulting multigrid is always kept consistent. The algorithmic approach of adapting a complete multigrid is v-cyclic: One sweep is done starting at the finest and ending at the coarsest level to determine a conforming closure, then a sweep follows in the opposite direction to modify (refine/coarsen) the grid levels, doing unification and recreating the element overlap.

In our implementation the calculation of the closure shows local behaviour, since no iterative process is needed to compute the grid closure. Thus it is well suited for parallelisation. The phases of distributed adaption of one grid level are shown in figure 3, the left upper situation shows the starting configuration with two elements, which are marked for refinement:

- closure: calculation of the grid closure, only neighbors of elements marked for refinement are involved, here interface communications are invoked,

- refine: local refinement (and coarsening) of the elements according to marks from the estimator and the closure phase,

- unify: unification of the local objects to form distributed objects with unique global ids and proper interfaces for them. In this phase join and ident modules of *DDD* are used.

- overlap: last phase is the transfer of the new overlap. Thus the adapted grid fulfills the data partitioning model with overlapping.

3   Load Balancing and Load Migration

In a parallel context grid adaption involves the need to rebalance the computational load. This stage involves both determining a new load balancing and dynamically redistributing the objects of the grid parts.

UG provides access to several simple load balancing scheme like a minial move load balancer and recursive coordinate bisection (rcb). Since several load balancing tools are already freely available, we use *Chaco* [7] for load balancing with more sophisticated schemes.

Since *Chaco* is not parallelized, the computation of a new load balancing is done by a central scheme on a designated processor. Note that this is *not* a sequential bottleneck, see figure 5. Load balancing during runtime starts with a clustering step. Hereby several elements are stored in one cluster traversing the element tree. These clusters are then collected at a designated processor, which invokes one of *Chaco*'s partitioneers. The assignment information of the clusters is then spread out to all processors, to set the new destination processor on the elements.

A key feature of *UG* is the capability to dynamically migrate grid objects between the processors during run time. Thus the computation need not be interrupted, but continues after load transfer with a balanced work load on each processor. This difficult task is supported by *DDD* (dynamic distributed data), a new parallel programming model. The migration process has various stages: packing the data objects into buffers, sending and receiving the message buffers and unpacking the data structure.

The coupling between the application, in this context *UG*, and *DDD* is managed by handler functions. These handlers are dependent on the application and are called by *DDD* in the packing and unpacking phases, each to reach a certain level of consistency on the migrated data structure. Calling of handlers depends on the object's state and its priority situation on the receiving processor, since different work has to be done when the object is locally new, ugraded or rejected.

4   The Programming Model DDD

An abstract programming model supporting high-level operations on the distributed grid data has been designed and integrated into the *UG* library. From the architecture's viewpoint this *Dynamic Distributed Data (DDD)* model [5] is implemented as a *UG* subsystem; a standalone version is nevertheless available in order to allow parallelization of other applications as well.

- interfaces: Supports communication operations on existing static data topologies. Interfaces are subsets of distributed objects at inter-processor boundaries and can be used in a transparent manner after their initial definition. They are kept consistent despite all dynamic data changes.

- xfer: Provides procedures for creating object copies on remote processors or deleting local object copies. This enables dynamic changes of the data topology at runtime. The most important task is the transparent transfer of DDD objects across local memory boundaries without troublesome address space conversions. This component allows implementation of dynamic load balancing techniques with arbitrary grid overlap.

- ident: Creation of distributed objects via identification of local objects. This is possible during the complete program run making dynamic grid changes possible (e. g. for adaptive grid refinement).

- join: An extension of the identification functionality. Join allows new objects to join into already existing distributed objects.

- prio: Changing the priority of distributed objects in a consistent way is needed during transfer and coarsening, this is done here very efficiently.

By using DDD the parallel grid manager is the same as the sequential one, both in terms of its usage interface and its program code. The former is advantageous for a clear algorithmic and hierarchical abstraction, the latter is necessary with respect to ongoing code development and maintenance. Apart from the grid manager subsystem, noticeable code adaptions have been necessary only for the numerics subsystem.

5   Two-phase Flow in Porous Media

The flow of two immiscible fluids in a porous medium is described by two coupled non-linear time-dependent partial differential equations [1]. A problem class has been developed that solves the two-phase flow equations in a fully implicit/fully-coupled manner using either phase pressure-saturation or a global pressure-saturation formulation [4]. In the simulations below, a multigrid method with truncated restriction, point-block ILU smoother [11] and a V-cycle has been used.

Figure 4 shows pictures from a *UG* computation in the area of immiscible displacement. Immiscible displacements are characterized by viscosity and density differences between the fluids and surface tension forces involved [8], the fluid interface tends to be instable and under specific conditions immiscible fingering will develop from small perturbations at the interface.

procs	$T_{num}(32)$	$T_{adapt}(32)$	T_{num}	T_{adapt}	job time	rel. perf.
32	379.4	106.1	10015	2349	12364	$\doteq$ 100%
64	191.8	65.0	5119	1492	6611	93.5%
128	102.3	57.8	2734	1225	3959	78.1%

Table 1. Two phase flow: computations on fixed sized problem

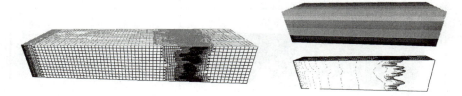

Figure 4. Adaptively refined multigrid with hexa/tetrahedra and pyramids; 16×16 stripped load balancing in flow direction; Vertical cutted domain with isolines of concentration.

The difficulty of simulating such phenomena is a matter of computing power, since the describing equations have to be discretized on a very fine scale to wipe out numerical diffusion leading especially in 3 dimensions to very large equation systems. Moreover since the equations are instationary, many time steps have to be calculated to get immiscible fingering visible.

The problem computed here is a quadratic channel with inflow and outflow boundary conditions, where the wetting phase, water, displaces the nonwetting phase, oil. The combination of several UG inherent features are used to calculate this application: multigrid, adaptivity, parallelism and mixed element types. 209 grid adaptions have been done during the computation of 203 time steps on about 1 million unknowns per timestep. The calculation was performed on 256 T3E processors and needed 12 hours of computing time.

Table 1 shows calculations on a fixed-sized problem, similar to the one described above, with 411068 unknowns in timestep 32. Time for discretization/solution and grid adaption are given for this timestep and accumulated up it. The relative job performance is calculated towards 32 processors. Computations and development were done on Cray T3E-900/1200 at HLRS/Stuttgart and HLRZ/Jülich.

6 Density–driven Flow in Porous Media

Density–driven flow problems can be described by two nonlinear, coupled, time–dependent differential equations, a continuity equation for the fluid and

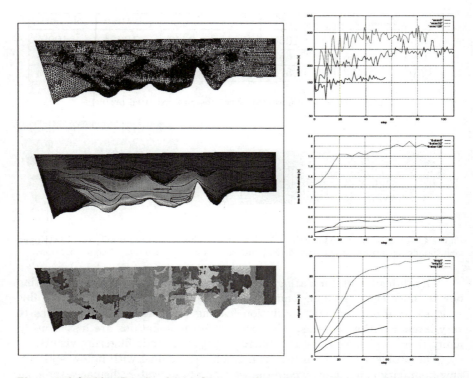

Figure 5. left side: Density–driven flow around a saltdome. From top to bottom: the adaptive multigrid, salt mass fraction ($t = 10a$) and its distribution on 32 processors. right side: Execution times of different phases in comparion: time for discretization and solution, time for load balancing, time for load migration. Timing in seconds.

a continuity equation for the solute transport. The fluid continuity equation is written in terms of pressure, assuming that Darcy's law is valid. Both equations are discretized on vertex-centered finite volumes using different constructions for the control volumes. The transient equations are solved with a fully implicit time-stepping scheme with time step control. The nonlinear equations are solved in a fully coupled mode using an approximative Newton multigrid method where the linearized system is solved with a linear multigrid method. Discretization, estimator and (non)linear solver are described in [9,10].

Figure 5 shows the flow around a saltdome residing on the bottom boundary of the domain. The top picture illustrates the adaptive multigrid, middle picture shows the salt distribution at time $t = 10a$, also the 49 subdomains

processors	minlevel	maxlevel	elements (last step)
8	2	4	82,000
32	3	6	339,000
128	4	7	1,300,000

Table 2. Density–driven flow around a saltdome: configuration of scaled computations.

of the geological layering are visualized, the bottom picture shows the grid distribution on 32 processors. Grid adaption is done between grid level 3 and 6. For performance reasons, the coarse grid with 2932 elements is not agglomerated on one processor, but remains distributed and a parallel amg method is used to avoid slow down in the solution phase due to the coarse grid load.

The time measurements in figure 5, right side, give performance results of a scaled computation, the left sided pictures show the situation after 100 timesteps. The number of elements is scaled with the number of processors see table 6. Each measurement shows the time in seconds needed for discretization and solution, load balancing and load migration in each step drawn over the step count. After an initial adaption process, the times reach quite constant values for each phase/processor configuration. The efficiency of the discretization and solution phase is about 50% comparing 8 to 128 processors. The slowdown is caused both by the degradation of the convergence rate in the solver, since with increasing element and processor count the problem becomes harder and more decoupled, and the degradation of the parallelization itself, longer interfaces and more neighborships lead to more communication over complexer topologies. Times of the loadbalancing step are subcritical (below 1% of the numerical phase), the increase of time in the 128 processor case is a result of the central load balancing scheme. Load migration scales from 8 to 128 processor with an efficiency of about 30%. Times are not constant, but increase slightly because this phase involves a sorting process over increasing interface lengths.

7 Conclusion

Solving partial differential equations of real world problems in an efficient way requires the combination of several techniques developed in the last decades: fast solvers, grid adaption, complicated geometries and parallelism.

The implementation of all these up-to-date techniques for the numerical solution of partial differential equations in a single parallel code is a major software engineering problem. Over years we developed programming abstractions that allow to solve complex two- and three-dimensional problems in an efficient way both in terms of development time and computer run-time.

This paper describes the parallel aspects of such a code and introduces concepts and abstractions for the mayor algorithmic parts grid adaption and load migration, which arise beside the numerical code parts in solution adaptive computations. As a fundamental tool for parallelization, the innovative programming model *DDD* is introduced, which can be used in a quite general manner for codes using irregular graph data structures.

UG is one of the first codes which addresses the development challenge of a parallel, adaptive and unstructured design by introducing clear and reuseable abstractions and concepts. In the near future the development of the parallel framework will be finished after a final efficiency tuning phase and further stability testing and the production phase of the code will start, still allowing to introduce new problem classes on top of it.

References

1. K. Aziz and A. Settari. *Petroleum Reservoir Simulation*. Elsevier, 1979.
2. R. Bank. *PLTMG Users Guide Version 7.0*, SIAM, 1994.
3. P. Bastian, K. Birken, K. Johannsen, S. Lang, N. Neuss, H. Rentz-Reichert, and C. Wieners. UG – a flexible software toolbox for solving partial differential equations. *Computation and Visualization in Science*, (1), 1997.
4. P. Bastian, R. Helmig. *Efficient Fully-Coupled Solution Techniques for Two-Phase Flow in Porous Media*. Advances in Water Resources Research, 1997.
5. K. Birken. Ein Modell zur effizienten Parallelisierung von Algorithmen auf komplexen, dynamischen Datenstrukturen. PhD, Universität Stuttgart, 1998.
6. P. Deuflhard, P. Leinen, and H. Yserentant. *Concepts of an adaptive hierarchical finite element code*, IMPACT of Comp. in Science and Eng., 1 (1989).
7. B. Hendrickson and R. Leland. *The chaco user's guide version 1.0*, Tech. Rep. SAND93-2339, Sandia National Laboratory, October 1993.
8. B. H. Kueper, E. O. Frind. *An Overview of Immiscible Fingering in Porous Media*, J. of Contaminant Hydrology, 2, 1988, 95-110, Amsterdam.
9. K. Johannsen. *Robuste Mehrgitterverfahren für die Konvektions-Diffusions Gleichung mit wirbelbehafteter Konvektion*, PhD, Universität Heidelberg, 1999.
10. P. Knabner, P. Frolkovic, Ch. Tapp, K. Thiele. *Adaptive Finite Volume Discretization of Density Driven Flows in Porous Media*, Preprint No. 220, IAM, Universität Nürnberg, 1997.
11. G. Wittum. *On the robustness of ilu smoothing*, SIAM J. Sci. Statist. Comput., 10, 1989, pp. 543–563.
12. *UG* homepage. *http://cox.iwr.uni-heidelberg.de/~ug*
13. *DDD* homepage. *http://cox.iwr.uni-heidelberg.de/~ddd*

A FRAMEWORK FOR ANALYZING AND DESIGNING PARALLEL ALGORITHMS FOR TRIDIAGONAL SYSTEMS

H.X.LIN

Faculty of Information Technology and Systems
TU Delft, P.O. Box 356, 2600 AJ, Delft, The Netherlands,
email: h.x.lin@its.tudelft.nl

A framework based on graph theoretic notations is described for the design and analysis of a wide range of parallel tridiagonal matrix algorithms. It comprises three basic types of graph transformation operations: partition, selection, elimination and update. We use the framework to present a unified description of many known parallel algorithms for the solution of tridiagonal systems.

1 Introduction

The solution of tridiagonal systems forms an important part in many numerical simulation problems. In the past three decades a large number (over 200, see e.g. online bibliography [4]) of research papers on this topic has appeared in literature. Among the most known parallel algorithms are: the cyclic reduction [1], the recursive doubling [7], the block partitioned elimination [9,2], and the twisted factorization algorithms [8]. These and other algorithms are designed in an ingenious way and by different researchers in parallel computing through the years. The different approaches are often presented in a different way like partition of rows or columns of the matrix, index permutation and elimination tree. In this paper we present a framework based on graph transformation which allows us to describe many of these algorithms in an unified way.

2 Gaussian elimination and graphs

An adjacency or elimination graph associated with A is an undirected graph with the set of edges defined as $E = \{(i,j) \mid a(i,j) \neq 0 \text{ or } a(i,j) \neq 0\}$. Note that we use the term *edge* and *arc* for *undirected* respectively *directed* connections between two nodes. Parter [5] has studied the relationship between fill-ins[a] in the matrix and the addition of new edges in the associated elimination graph. A very important fact is that two non-adjacent nodes in an elimination graph can be eliminated independently. Peters [6] has studied

---

[a]A fill-in is a coefficient which is zero in the original A, but become nonzero during the elimination/factorization.

the parallel pivoting algorithms for sparse symmetric matrices. Lin [3] studied the use of quotient elimination graphs for parallel factorization of block structured sparse matrices obtained from domain decomposition of finite element meshes. These aforementioned researches deal with sparse symmetric matrices and undirected graphs.

The undirected graph has been successfully used for minimizing fill-ins and parallel factorization of sparse symmetric matrices. However, it cannot describe many operations in a parallel matrix algorithm. For instance the recursive doubling algorithm [7] and the partition method [9] cannot be described in terms of eliminating each column or row exactly once during the elimination process. Some rows are modified several times and the final form is here not an upper triangular matrix. Therefore, we use directed graph in our framework. We consider the parallelism in eliminating an arc (j, i) associated with $a(j, i)$ using $a(i, i)$ instead of eliminating an entire column i. Note that we don't assume $i > j$ or $j > i$ here, i.e., we don't assume any pre-determined elimination ordering. Throughout the paper, we ignore numerical cancellations when considering fill-ins and fill-arcs during an elimination process.

Given an $n \times n$ matrix A, a corresponding directed graph $G(V, E)$ is defined as a graph with the set of nodes $V = \{1, 2, ..., n\}$ and the set of arcs $E = \{(i, j) \mid a(i, j) \neq 0, i \in V \wedge j \in V\}$. Arc (i, j) is said to have a *begin node i* and *end* (or *terminal*) *node j*. (i, j) is an *outgoing arc* from i, and an *incoming arc* to j. The set of predecessors and successors of i node i are denoted by $PRED(i)$ and $SUCC(i)$. Note that if $a(i, i) \neq 0$ then there is a self-loop on node i. We assume that the matrices are diagonally dominant, such that we always have $a(i, i) \neq 0$ throughout the elimination or factorization process. Therefore, the self-loops always exist on all nodes and we will not draw them explicitly in the illustrations and figures.

Theorem 1 Consider the elimination of arc (j, i) using node i, arc (j, k) exists if and only if (j, k) or (i, k) exists before the elimination.

Proof Elimination of arc (j, i) corresponds to using row i to eliminate element $a(j, i)$ in the matrix. This means adding $-\frac{a(j,i)}{a(i,i)} \cdot (row\ i)$ to $(row\ j)$, which yields $a^{new}(j, k) = a(j, k) - \frac{a(j,i)}{a(i,i)} \cdot a(i, k)$. Because $\frac{a(j,i)}{a(i,i)} \neq 0$, so $a^{new}(j, k) \neq 0$ if and only if $a(j, k) \neq 0$ or $a(j, k) \neq 0$.

The corresponding numerical operations on the matrix can be defined on this graphical representation. We denote the coefficient $a(i, j)$ as the weight of arc (i, j), an non-exist arc is equivalent to having zero weight. The elimination of arc (j, i) corresponds to the following operations in the graph: 1) for each $k \in SUCC(i)$: $a(j, k) = a(j, k) - a(j, i) * a(i, k)/a(i, i)$. 2) remove arc (j, i).

Algorithm 1
  Initialize $G(V, E)$; $k = 1$;
  WHILE $E \neq$ DO
    SELECT all possible arcs $S(k)$ for parallel elimination (Lemma 1.1);
    ELIMINATE $S(k)$ from E;
    UPDATE E according to Lemma 1.2;
    $k = k + 1$;
  END

Figure 1. A greedy algorithm for parallel elimination.

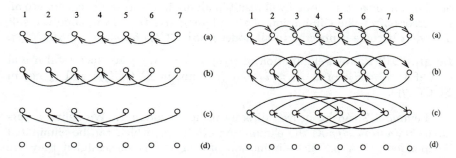

Figure 2. (Left) Application of Algorithm 1 to a bi-diagonal system leads to the recursive doubling scheme. (Right) Application of Algorithm 1 to a tridiagonal system.

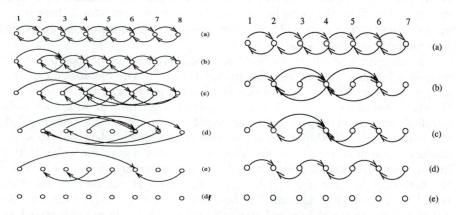

Figure 3. (Left) A parallel elimination scheme free of update conflict. (Right) Illustration of the cyclic reduction algorithm. (b)-(c): reduction phase; (d)-(e): back-substitution phase.

Since we are only interested in the parallelism and the structure of the parallel operations in this paper, we will omit the discussion on the numerical operation of the coefficients. We omit the weight of the arcs except that we define an arc (i, j) only exists when $a(i, j)$ is logically non-zero.

Lemma 1.1 A fill-arc (j, k) occurs when eliminating arc (j, i) if and only if there is a path from j to k through i, and (j, k) does not exist before the elimination of (j, i).

Lemma 1.1 follows straightforward from Theorem 1. Thus the elimination of all incoming arcs to node i will result in all predecessors of i connected to all successors of i. The elimination of all outgoing arcs (i, j) from node i, result in node i become connected to all nodes in $SUCC(j)$ for each $j \in SUCC(i)$.

Lemma 1.2 Parallel elimination of (i_1, j_1) and (i_2, j_2) are successful if and only if 1. $i_1 \neq i_2$; or 2. $i_1 = i_2$ and j_1 is not in $SUCC(j_2)$ and j_2 not in $SUCC(j_1)$.

Lemma 1.2 can be proved directly using Theorem 1. We define a *parallel elimination step* as the elimination of all arcs which can be eliminated independently. A parallel elimination of two arcs is successful if they are both eliminated after the parallel elimination step. This is of course not always possible because the elimination of arc (i_2, j_2) may cause the return of (i_1, j_1), and vice versa. Lemma 1.2 tells us that parallel eliminations of two arcs initiating from the same begin node can only be successful if there is no arc between the terminal nodes of these two arcs. This conclusion can easily be extended to a set of arcs.

An algorithm which determines the parallel elimination of arcs in G until all nodes become isolated is given in Algorithm 1. The elimination of the arcs in each set $S(k)$ comprises one elimination step. The key issue is the Selection operation. Algorithm 1 is a greedy algorithm in which at each parallel elimination step as many as possible arcs are selected for parallel elimination. Fig. 2L shows the application of the greedy algorithm to a bidiagonal system of equations resulting in a parallel algorithm which is the known recursive doubling algorithm [7] for first order linear recurrence. At the first step, all arcs $(i + 1, i)$ for $i = 1, 2, ..., (n - 1)$ can be eliminated in parallel. According to Lemma 1.1 the elimination of $(i + 1, i)$ causes a fill-arc $(i + 1, i - 1)$. In the second step, all arcs $(i + 1, i - 1)$ are eliminated in parallel and resulting in fill-arcs $(i + 1, i - 3)$, etc. In general, at step k, all arcs $(i + 1, i - 2^k + 1)$ are eliminated in parallel and fill-arcs $(i + 1, i - 2^{k+1} + 1)$ are added. This is exactly what the recursive doubling algorithm does for a bidiagonal system.

Fig. 2R shows the results of applying the algorithm to an example. It can be observed that the number of parallel elimination steps achieved with the greedy algorithm is smaller than the cyclic reduction algorithm. However, in some of the steps the elimination of several arcs initiating from the same node causes update conflict. A parallel update conflict occurs when the same coefficient is modified/updated more than once in a parallel elimination step.

Theorem 2 The elimination of arcs (i_1, j_1) and (i_2, j_2) are free of update conflict if 1. $i_1 \neq i_2$; or 2. if (i_1, i_2) and $SUCC(j_1) \cap SUCC(j_2) = \emptyset$.

If we require in each parallel elimination step the elimination of arcs is free of update conflict, we can add the above update conflict test in the selection operation of Algorithm 1. Applied to the example in Fig. 2R, the result of parallel eliminations free of update conflict is shown in Fig. 3L. The number of elimination steps is now increased to 5 in Fig. 3L compared to 3 in Fig. 2R. However, there are update conflict in the first two steps in Fig. 2R which implies a larger parallel execution time in these two steps.

The tests of parallel elimination (Lemma 1.2) and the test of update conflict (Theorem 2) can be simplified by allowing each node being an initiating node at most once in a single parallel elimination step. Furthermore, additional conditions in selecting arcs for parallel elimination is sometimes preferred. Such additional conditions can be limiting the number of fill-arcs, or requiring the number of fill-arcs must be smaller than the number of arcs being eliminated in each step (i.e., to ensure the finiteness of the elimination process), or imposing more regularity and control on the parallelism. In fact many of the known parallel algorithms in literature corresponds to applying a certain heuristics or imposing some structure in the elimination process. The general algorithm can be described as consisting of three basic type of operations: 1. partition; 2. selection; and 3. elimination and update.

3 Application to parallel tridiagonal algorithms

3.1 The cyclic reduction algorithm

The cyclic reduction algorithm consists of two phases: (I) the reduction phase, during which selective elimination of variables is done; and (II) the back-substitution phase, during which the values of the eliminated x_i's are recovered. Denote the dimension of the matrix $n = 2^k - 1$.

(I) The reduction phase: in the first step all the odd-indexed variables $x_1, x_3, x_5, ..., x_{2^k-1}$ are eliminated, resulting in $2^{k-1} - 1$ equations. In the second step, variables with indices that are odd multiples of 2, i.e.,

$x_2, x_4, x_6, ..., x_{2(2^k-1)}$, are eliminated, resulting in $2^{k-2} - 1$ equations. At the mth step, all the variables with indices that are odd multiples of 2^{m-1}, are eliminated, resulting in $2^{(k-m)} - 1$ equations. Thus, at the $(k-1)^{th}$ step, $x_{2^{k-2}}$ and $x_{3 \times 2^{k-2}}$ are eliminated, leaving only one equation in the unknown $x_{2^{k-1}}$.

(II) The back-substitution phase: In this phase values of x_i are computed by back-substitution.

Let $h = 2^{m-1}$ and define,

$$a_{i,i-1}^{(m)} = -a_{i-h,i-h-1}^{(m-1)} \cdot a_{i,i-1}^{(m-1)} / a_{i-h,i-h}^{(m-1)} \tag{1}$$

$$a_{i,i}^{(m)} = a_{i,i}^{(m-1)} - a_{i-h,i-h+1}^{(m-1)} \frac{a_{i,i-1}^{(m-1)}}{a_{i-h,i-h}^{(m-1)}} - a_{i+h,i+h-1}^{(m-1)} \frac{a_{i,i+1}^{(m-1)}}{a_{i+h,i+h}^{(m-1)}} \tag{2}$$

$$a_{i,i+1}^{(m)} = -a_{i+h,i+h+1}^{(m-1)} \cdot a_{i,i+1}^{(m-1)} / a_{i+h,i+h}^{(m-1)} \tag{3}$$

$$b_i^{(m)} = b_i^{(m-1)} - b_{i-h}^{(m-1)} \cdot a_{i,i-1}^{(m-1)} / a_{i-h,i-h}^{(m-1)} - b_{i+h}^{(m-1)} \cdot a_{i,i+1}^{(m-1)} / a_{i+h,i+h}^{(m-1)} \tag{4}$$

Then the cyclic reduction algorithm can be described in Fig. 4. The loop FOR $i \in$ *Index_set* DO PARALLEL means that the statements in the loop can be executed in parallel for all i in the *Index_set* simultaneously.

FOR $m = 1$ TO $k - 1$ DO /* reduction phase */
    FOR $i \in \{2^m, 2 \cdot 2^m, ..., 2^k - 2^m\}$ DO PARALLEL
       evaluate equations (1-4)
    END
END
FOR $m = k - 1$ TO 1 DO /* back substitution phase */
    $h = 2^{m-1}$
    FOR $i \in \{h, 3 \cdot h, 5 \cdot h, ..., 2^k - h\}$ DO PARALLEL
       compute $x_i = \frac{b_i^{m-1} - a_{i,i-1}^{m-1} \cdot x_{i-h} - a_{i,i+1}^{m-1} \cdot x_{i+h}}{a_{i,i}^{m-1}}$
    END
END

Figure 4. Description of the cyclic reduction algorithm.

Using the framework, we can now generate the cyclic reduction algorithm as shown in Fig. 5. The parallel elimination proceeds by starting with the elimination of all arcs initiated from even numbered nodes in the first step, followed by repeatedly eliminates the set of arcs initiated at even numbered nodes with a distance of 2^{k-1} to the end node at step k Fig. 3R illustrates

FOR $m = 1$ TO $log(n) - 1$ DO /* reduction phase */
   $h = 2^{m-1}$
   SELECT $S(m) = \{(2ih, 2ih - h), (2ih, 2ih + h)|i = 1, ..., (n/h - 1)\}$
   for parallel elimination;
   ELIMINATE the arcs in $S(m)$ from the graph;
   UPDATE: add fill-arcs $\{(2ih, 2ih - 2h), (2ih, 2ih + 2h)|$
                    $i = 1, ..., (n/h - 1)\}$;
END
FOR $m = log(n) - 1$ TO 1 DO /* back substitution phase */
   $h = 2^{m-1}$;
   SELECT $S(m + log(n) - 1) = \{((2i - 1)h, (2i - 1) - h),$
                        $((2i - 1)h, (2i - 1) + h)|i = 1, ..., (n/h - 1)\}$;
   ELIMINATE arcs in $S(m + log(n) - 1)$ from the graph;
   UPDATE: there are no fill-arcs;
END

Figure 5. The cyclic reduction algorithm in terms of the framework.

the different elimination steps in the reduction- and back substitution phase of the reduction algorithm.

3.2   The cyclic elimination algorithm

Fig. 6 shows a description of the cyclic elimination algorithm (here $n = 2^k$). This algorithm can be directly generated by the greedy algorithm (Fig. 1). The graphical illustration of the cyclic elimination algorithm is shown in Fig. 2. The cyclic elimination algorithm reduces the tridiagonal system to a diagonal system in $log(n)$ elimination steps each consisting of 6 floating-point execution (assume that eq's.(5), (6), (7) and (8) are executed in parallel). So the parallel time complexity of the cyclic elimination is $6log(n) + 1$ (the last division by the diagonal takes 1 time unit). The time complexity is smaller than the cyclic reduction algorithm which has a time complexity of $11log(n) - 11$. The price to be paid is the additional fill-arcs and thus a larger total amount of floating point operations (when counted sequentially).

3.3   The block partition algorithms

The partition algorithm [9] starts by dividing the matrix into p groups each of $k = n/p$ consecutive rows which corresponds to first partitioning the initial graph into p subgraphs (Fig. 7a). Then each subgraph is eliminated by a sequential Gaussian elimination scheme, except that now fill-arcs occur due to the boundary between the subgraphs. The graph transformation according

FOR $m = 1$ TO k DO
  FOR $i \in \{1, 2, 3, ..., n\}$ DO PARALLEL
    evaluate equations (1-4)
  END
  FOR $i \in \{1, 2, 3, ..., n\}$ DO PARALLEL
    compute $x_i = \frac{f_i^k}{a_{i,i}^k}$
  END

Figure 6. The cyclic elimination algorithm.

to the partition algorithm is illustrated in Fig. 7. In the partition algorithm at step d the arc $d1$ is eliminated before $d2$, and at step e the arc $e1$ is eliminated before $e2$. These two sequential steps result in a time complexity of $O(c_1 \cdot log(n) + c_2 \cdot p)$. Using Lemma 1.2 we can easily see that the arcs $d1$, $d2$, $e1$ and $e2$ can be eliminated in parallel. With such modifications in the partition algorithm the time complexity can be reduced to $O(c_1 \cdot log(n) + c_2 \cdot log(p))$.

The cyclic reduction and cyclic elimination algorithms are based on the principle of Gaussian elimination, whereas the recursive doubling [7] is based on the principle of first factorize the matrix A into a lower triangular matrix and an upper triangular matrix (i.e., LU-factorization). The computation of the factors are equivalent to solving a pair of linear recurrence equations [7], and the computation of these linear recurrence can be performed in the same way as for the bidiagonal system discussed in the previous section (Fig. 2L). The twisted factorization corresponds to the eliminations of the outgoing arcs from node 1 to node $n/2$, and incoming arcs from node n to node $n/2$.

4 Concluding remarks

We have presented a graph theoretic framework which unifies many parallel algorithms for tridiagonal systems. The results regarding the property of parallel elimination of multiple arcs and the test on the update conflict enable us now to design different variants of parallel algorithms. An important application of the framework is that it provides us a simple mechanism to optimize and modify the known parallel algorithms. This makes not only the task of manually designing a parallel algorithm simpler, but it also provides us a means to automatically generate and optimize parallel algorithms for tridiagonal systems. The next step in our research will deal with the use of the framework for the compiler to automatically generate parallelism in a sequentially implemented program. Furthermore, the framework can be readily

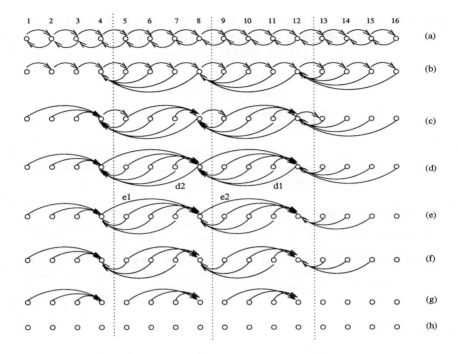

Figure 7. Graph transformations corresponding to the partition algorithm. ($p = 4$)

extended to the banded matrices and general sparse matrices.

References

1. R.W. Hockney, *Journal of ACM*, 1965, pp. 95-113.
2. S.L. Johnsson, *SIAM J. Sci. Stat. Comput.*, 8 (3), 1987, pp. 354-392.
3. H.X. Lin, *Ph.D. thesis*, Delft University of Technology, 1993.
4. A Bibliography on Parallel Solution of Tri-diagonal Systems of Equations. http://ta.twi.tudelft.nl/PA/lin/tri_sol.html
5. S. Parter, *SIAM Review* 3, 1961, pp. 119-130.
6. F.J. Peters. *Parallel Computing*, Vol. 1, 1984, pp. 99-110.
7. H.S. Stone, *Journal of ACM* 20(1), 1973.
8. H.A. van der Vorst. *Parallel Computing*, Vol. 5, 1987, pp. 45-54.
9. H.H. Wang, *ACM TOMS* 7(2), 1981, pp. 1670-183.

LEFT-LOOKING STRATEGY FOR THE SPARSE MODIFIED CHOLESKY FACTORIZATION ON NUMA MULTIPROCESSORS

MARÍA J. MARTÍN

Dept. Electrónica y Sistemas, Univ. A Coruña, SPAIN
E-mail: mariam@udc.es

INMACULADA PARDINES AND FRANCISCO F. RIVERA

Dept. Electrónica y Computación, Univ. Santiago de Compostela, SPAIN
E-mail: {inma,fran}@dec.usc.es

In this work the left-looking algorithm for the Cholesky factorization is adapted to the modified Cholesky factorization on NUMA systems. The proposed algorithm is intended to reduce idle times and to increase data locality which are the main factors that limit the performance. Our proposal is based on an efficient use of a distributed task queue whose implementation is based on the elimination tree of the matrix. A variant form of this method allowing task preemption techniques is also evaluated. Results on the SGI O2000 are presented.

1 Introduction

In this paper we propose an efficient implementation of the modified Cholesky factorization [5] using a left-looking orientation on a NUMA system. Recently great efforts have been made to find efficient implementations of sparse codes on distributed memory systems, examples being the SCALAPACK [1] and PSPASES [6] libraries, among others. On the other hand, there exist very few parallelization proposals on NUMA shared memory systems. An example is the SPLASH2 [10] library, which includes a parallel code for the standard Cholesky factorization based on a blocked right-looking algorithm. The main problem with the right-looking implementation on a NUMA system is the high number of conflicts in the access to memory generated [9]. We propose to lighten this problem by using the left-looking orientation of the algorithm.

This paper is organized as follows. Sec. 2 presents the modified Cholesky factorization. In Sec. 3 the strategies found in the bibliography to carry out the left-looking orientation of the standard Cholesky factorization on a shared memory system are revised. In Sec. 4 the main characteristics of our parallel proposal are described. In Sec. 5 the experimental results that are obtained on the NUMA system SGI O2000 are shown. We end with some conclusions derived from this work.

2   The Modified Cholesky Factorization

The modified Cholesky factorization (MCF) of a symmetric matrix $A \in \mathbf{R}^{n \times n}$ that is not necessarily positive definite is a Cholesky factorization of $A' = A + E$, where E is a non-negative diagonal matrix such that A' is positive definite. Modified Cholesky factorization is widely used in non-linear optimization by quasi-Newtonian method [5].

Due to its similarity to the standard algorithm, the techniques of parallelization used for the Cholesky factorization can be adapted to the MCF. Two approaches can be distinguished depending on the access and updating order of the matrices: the right-looking and the left-looking algorithms.

3   Left-looking algorithm

A parallel version of the left-looking Cholesky factorization on a shared memory system can be found in [3]. In this version a linked list is used to store the columns that are ready to modify other columns [4].

In parallel implementations, a task queue that specifies a task ordering is normally used. When a processor becomes free, it immediately seeks another task from the queue. In general, a factor that highly influences the execution time is this task ordering. Obtaining the optimal scheduling of the tasks is a NP-complete problem. There are, however, several heuristic algorithms to approach this problem, one of them is the critical path scheduling. An application of this method to the standard Cholesky factorization is studied in [7]. We used this method to build a former parallel version of the left-looking algorithm. From now on, we will refer to this algorithm as LCP (**L**eft-looking algorithm using the **C**ritical **P**ath method) and it will be used for comparisons.

4   Our parallel proposal for the left-looking algorithm

Two essential factors limit the program performance of the LCP algorithm: The idle times and the data locality. We propose the following strategies to minimize the influence of these factors:

1. The use of a set of n queues instead of the linked list, one queue for each column.

2. A variant form of this method allowing task preemption techniques to minimize idle times.

3. A new scheduling strategy based on the elimination tree of the matrix [8] with the aim of increasing data locality.

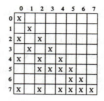

Figure 1. Example matrix: pattern of the L factor

4.1 Using n task queues

The linked list is not appropriate for parallel processing since it does not pick up well all the possible independences and therefore it limits the amount of parallel work. Let us consider, for example, the matrix given in Fig. 1. Let us suppose that column zero of this matrix has been processed. This column modifies columns 2, 4 and 7 and this modifications could be carried out in parallel. However, due to the way in which the linked list is built, there is no evidence that column 0 is ready to modify column 4 until it has modified column 2. Equally, column 0 is not available to modify column 7 until columns 2 and 4 have been modified.

To avoid this, and increase the parallelism, the linked list is replaced by a set of queues. Specifically, for each column a queue of available columns is considered. In these queues the columns that are ready to modify the target column are stored. Thereby, in the example matrix, once column 0 is processed it is introduced in queues 2, 4 and 7. When columns 2, 4 or 7 are accessed to be processed, their respective queues are consulted in order to identify the columns that are ready to modify them. Column 7 will be able to be modified by 0 at the same time as columns 4 and 2. From now on, we will call this algorithm LNQ (**L**eft-looking algorithm using **N Q**ueues).

4.2 Task preemption strategy

In order to minimize idle times we propose that each processor considers more than one column for processing. Let us suppose that at any time each processor has assigned r different columns, $j_1, j_2, ...j_r$. If there are not available columns to modify j_1, then it processes j_2 until there are no columns available for modifying it, then it processes j_3 and so on until j_r; then it returns to j_1 in a round robin fashion. Thus, the possibilities that the processor is stopped decrease. But in contrast, the implementation of this scheme adds complexity to the algorithm which produces overhead. From now on, this proposal is refered to as *LNQr* (**L**eft-looking algorithm using **N** **Q**ueues and assigning **r** tasks to each processor).

4.3 Increasing data locality

At this point, n task queues will be accessed and modified by all the processors. This causes a high data movement and coherence operations. A way to minimize this overhead is to make, as far as possible, the same processor modifies those queues. This is equivalent to assigning to each processor those columns which belong to the same subtree in the elimination tree [8]. The prioritized list of tasks is built considering this strategy.

Initially a leaf node is assigned to each processor. The idea is to select those nodes that are as far from each other as possible. We introduce a distance function between pairs of nodes and we use the Prim's method to select P nodes that have the greatest distance among them, P being the number of processors. The process begins with the deepest node in the tree. We assign each one of these nodes to each processor as initial node. Then, each processor creates its own prioritized list of columns starting with the initial node and going up through the tree. The prioritized lists will be local lists. Each processor will have all the columns of the matrix ordered in a different way inside their own list. Each processor will access to its own list, but global labels indicating what columns have already been processed are needed. Those labels are protected with LOCKs.

The distance function must represent a measure of the potential parallelism between two nodes. For this, the number of levels between nodes and the height of the first common predecessor should be taken into account. Let i and j be two nodes with their first common predecessor k. We define the distance between them as the contribution of three terms:

$$d_{ij} = d_{ji} = \alpha \cdot min\{P_{ik}, P_{jk}\} + \beta \cdot (P_{ik} + P_{jk}) + \gamma \cdot L_k \qquad (1)$$

Where P_{ik} is the number of levels between nodes i and k. L_k is the height of node k, that is to say, the number of levels from the deepest node to node k. Therefore the first term of equation 1 reflects the work in parallel that can be carried out when processing the nodes i and j. This is what will have the greatest influence on the parallel program. The second term takes into account the number of levels existing between both nodes. The greater this number, the greater the parallel work will be and the conflict between them will be lesser. The third term reflects the height of the first common ancestor. The greater it is, the less nodes it will have to update and so the conflict will be lesser. α, β and γ are parameters which emphasize the relative influence of the three factors. We suggest: $\alpha = n$, $\beta = 1$ and $\gamma = 1$.

5 Results

We have implemented the codes on the SGI 02000 using *parmacs*. To avoid false sharing, a macro has been included which allows the allocation of globally shared memory and the alignment of shared information with the secondary cache lines. The main source of conflicts comes from the array of values of the matrices and the array that contains the number of modifications in each column (*nmod*). Both arrays are frequently accessed and modified by different processors causing many cases of false sharing. To minimize this effect the values of the matrix are stored in a two-dimensional array in such a way that each column is mapped at the beginning of a cache line. The objective is to decrease, wherever possible, false sharing, at the cost of a light increment in the memory used due to the alignment. With regards to the *nmod* array, when column j is modified, the counter $nmod(j)$ is also updated. It is therefore advantageous to store $nmod(j)$ just next to the values in column j.

A set of symmetric matrices from the Harwell-Boeing library [2] was selected to analyze the behavior of the codes. The minimum degree algorithm was previously applied in order to reduce the fill. Table 1 shows the characteristics of the matrices, where n_z is the number of nonzero entries.

Table 1. Characteristics of the benchmark matrices

MATRIX	n	n_z in A	n_z in L
BCSSTK14	1806	36630	116071
BCSSTK15	3948	60882	707887
BCSSTK18	11948	80519	668217
BCSSTK23	3134	24156	450953
BCSSTK24	3562	81736	291151
BCSSTK30	28924	1036208	4677146
LSHP3466	3466	13681	93713

Table 2 shows the execution times (in ms) obtained for the LCP algorithm. Note that there is a point in which the execution times increase with the number of processors mainly due to the two factors pointed out in Sec. 4.

Table 3 shows the execution times for the LNQ algorithm. Note that the times for the sequential program increase due to the overhead associated with the management of the n queues. However, the scalability is much better due to the decrease in idle times.

Tables 4 and 5 show the execution times obtained for the $LNQ2$ and $LNQ3$ codes respectively. The decrease in the execution times is more appre-

Table 2. Execution times for the LCP algorithm

MATRIX	P=1	P=2	P=4	P=8
BCSSTK14	360	450	700	1100
BCSSTK15	5900	4400	5500	9200
BCSSTK18	4300	3300	4100	7000
BCSSTK23	3800	2900	3600	6200
BCSSTK24	1200	1100	1700	3000
BCSSTK30	42800	28600	30000	51400
LSHP3466	210	290	460	700

Table 3. Execution times for the LNQ algorithm

MATRIX	P=1	P=2	P=4	P=8
BCSSTK14	370	280	280	350
BCSSTK15	6100	3600	2700	2600
BCSSTK18	4400	2700	2300	2400
BCSSTK23	3900	2400	2000	1900
BCSSTK24	1200	800	850	1100
BCSSTK30	44300	25300	17100	16400
LSHP3466	210	180	210	300

ciable as the number of processors increase, since in this case the idle times are more critical. The best behavior is obtained using $r = 2$. For $r = 3$ the potential parallelism decreases.

Table 4. Execution times for the LNQ2 algorithm

MATRIX	P=1	P=2	P=4	P=8
BCSSTK14	350	270	230	230
BCSSTK15	6000	3700	2400	1900
BCSSTK18	4300	2700	1900	1600
BCSSTK23	3800	2300	1500	1200
BCSSTK24	1100	830	630	630
BCSSTK30	43200	26100	16900	13500
LSHP3466	200	180	180	220

Fig. 2 shows the idle times for the *LCP*, *LNQ* and *LNQ*2 codes using 4 processors and the matrices BCSSTK15 and BCSSTK30. Note that the idle times for the LNQ2 algorithm and 4 processors decrease 80% for the matrix BCSSTK15 and 70% for the BCSSTK30 in relation to the *LCP*. Similar results can be obtained for other matrices. This behavior is translated into a drastic decrease in the execution times as shown in Table 4.

Table 6 shows the execution times for the program using the new schedul-

Table 5. Execution times for the LNQ3 algorithm

MATRIX	P=1	P=2	P=4	P=8
BCSSTK14	340	270	230	260
BCSSTK15	6000	3600	2400	1900
BCSSTK18	4300	2700	2000	1600
BCSSTK23	3800	2300	1700	1300
BCSSTK24	1100	890	760	630
BCSSTK30	43300	28400	18400	13900
LSHP3466	200	210	210	250

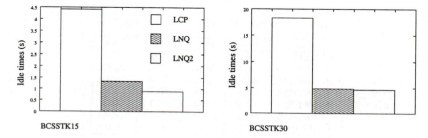

Figure 2. Idle times for the LCP, LNQ and LNQ2 codes and 4 processors

ing algorithm (LNS). Our proposal increases the locality and thus the efficiency of the parallel code. The improvement is more appreciable as the number of processors increases.

Table 6. Execution times for the LNS code

MATRIX	P=1	P=2	P=4	P=8
BCSSTK14	340	290	190	190
BCSSTK15	5900	3500	2100	1400
BCSSTK18	4200	2500	1600	1300
BCSSTK23	3800	2500	1600	1000
BCSSTK24	1100	810	560	430
BCSSTK30	42300	26400	15500	9900
LSHP3466	210	160	130	130

6   Conclusions

In this work we have presented an efficient parallel implementation of the left-looking algorithm for the modified Cholesky factorization on NUMA systems.

The main characteristics of our proposal are the minimization of the idle times and the increase of the data locality achieved through the use of a new scheduling algorithm based on the Prim's method and taking the elimination tree of the matrix into account.

The strategies here described can be generalized to other irregular problems such as factorizations or the solvers of triangular systems. In general they are applicable to all those sparse codes whose dependencies can be represented by a tree.

References

1. J. Choi, J. Demmel, I. Dhillon, J. Dongarra, S. Ostrouchov, A. Petitet, K. Stanley, D. Walker and R. C. Whaley, *ScaLAPACK, a portable linear algebra library for distributed memory computers-design issues and performance*, Computer Physics Communications, 97(1-2), 1996, pp.1-15.
2. I.S.Duff, R.G.Grimes, and J.G.Lewis, *User's guide for the harwell-boeing sparse matrix collection*, Technical Report TR-PA-92-96, CERFACS, 1992.
3. A. George, M. Heath, J. Liu, E. Ng, *Solution of sparse positive definite systems on a shared memory multiprocessor*, Int. J. Parallel Programming, 15, 1986, pp.309-325.
4. A. George and J. Liu, *Computer Solution of Large Sparse positive Definite Systems*, Prentice-Hall Inc., Englewood Cliffs, New Jersey, 1981.
5. P.E. Gill, W. Murray and M.H. Wright, *Practical optimization*, Academic Press, London, 1981.
6. A. Gupta, F. Gustavson, M. Joshi, G. Karypis and V. Kumar, *Design and Implementation of a Scalable Parallel Direct Solver for Sparse Symmetric Positive Definite Systems: Preliminary Results*, In Proc. 8th SIAM Conference on Parallel Processing for Scientific Computing, 1997.
7. Joseph W.H. Liu, *Computational models and task scheduling for parallel sparse Cholesky factorization*, Parallel Computing, 3, 1986, pp.327-342.
8. J.W.H. Liu, *The role of elimination trees in sparse factorization*, SIAM J. on Matrix Anal. Appl., 11, 1990, pp.134-172.
9. M. J. Martín, I. Pardines and F.F. Rivera, *Scheduling for Algorithms Based on Elimination Trees on NUMA Systems*, Lecture Notes in Computer Science, 1685, 1999, pp.1068-1072.
10. S. C. Woo, M. Ohara, E. Torrie, J. P. Singh and A. Gupta, *The SPLASH-2 Programs: Characterization and Methodological Considerations*, In Proc. of the 22nd Annual Int. Symposium on Computer Architecture, pp.24-37, 1995.

A PARALLEL TRIANGLE OPERATOR FOR NOISE REMOVAL IN TRUE COLOUR IMAGES

ODEJ KAO

Department of Computer Science, Technical University of Clausthal
38678 Clausthal-Zellerfeld, Germany

In this paper a new parallel method for impulse noise cleaning in true colour images is discussed. The introduced triangle operator is a non linear smoothing filter. The components of the RGB vector are transformed into two-dimensional co-ordinates and connected giving a triangle. The triangle attributes reproduce the correlation of the colour channels and can be used for colour matching. The absolute differences between the triangles are added to give a sum describing the similarity of the represented colours. This process is repeated for each pair of points in the local neighbourhood. The colour of the noisy pixel is replaced by the colour of the point with the smallest difference to the other colours in the neighbourhood. A disadvantage of the triangle method is its high computational complexity. Therefore a parallel algorithm was developed in order to make the triangle operator available for image and video processing. The parallel algorithm is based on separation of the image into sections and distribution of the data blocks over a number of processing elements. Performance measurements in a PVM environment result in a reasonable speedup factor.

1 Introduction

Impulse noise is a special type of noise which can have many different origins. Thus, in the case of satellite or TV images it can be caused through atmospheric disturbances. In other applications it can be caused by strong electromagnetic fields, transmission errors, etc. Impulse noise is characterised by short, abrupt alterations of the colour values in the image. The concerned points are changed through overlay of a coincidence value such that they differ significantly from their local neighbourhood and disturb the natural colour run. Thereby the subsequent image processing, analysis and evaluation can be affected, regardless whether these actions are done by a human viewer or as part of an automated process.

Early work on noise removal was based on low pass filtering in the frequency domain. A low pass filter separates and removes the high frequencies from the image. A problem is that besides the impulse noise also other picture elements with high frequencies, which represent finer details and edges, are filtered out resulting in a blurred image. Another standard method for impulse noise removal is the median filter. The filter consists of a *nxn* sliding window, usually 3x3, encompassing an odd number of pixels. The pixels in the window are sorted and the center pixel is replaced by the median of the sorted sequence. The median filter is easy to implement and preserves the edges. On the other hand it is compute intensive and particular small image details can be lost [1]. In addition to these operators there exist many other filters for noise removal in halftone images [2,3].

For noise removal in colour images only few operators are available [4]. Some of the reasons for this are the mathematical complexity of methods for direct application to colour images and the required high compute performance.

2 Methods for noise removal in colour images

A colour image is usually represented in the RGB colour space, because most of the computer input and output devices use this colour system. An important disadvantage of the RGB colour system is that adequate means for measuring colour similarity is not available. In case of halftone images two grey levels can be classified as similar, if the difference between their identifiers is not too big, for example grey levels 100 and 110.

There are three common approaches for noise removal in colour images:
1. Separate noise cleaning of each RGB colour component with one of the existing halftone methods
2. Transformation in other more suitable colour systems like HSI and
3. Vector median operator.

The first approach is known as pseudo colour image processing. A RGB image is separated into three halftone images and each image is smoothed with a halftone noise cleaning method such as the median filter. The results are then combined to give a smoothed RGB image. This approach is easy to implement, because the existing and tested halftone methods can be used. A disadvantage is the loss of the correlation between the colour channels resulting in colour shifts, that is a substitution of a noisy pixel colour through a new false colour, which does not fit into the local neighbourhood.

Other colour systems like HSI offer an advantage that a major portion of the colour information is represented by only one component. This component is smoothed, combined with the other two components and finally converted to a RGB image. Colour shifts are, however also possible in this case. A further disadvantage is the compute intensive transformation between the colour systems and the possible occurrence of singularity points.

A further method is the vector median filter, which is an extension of the median filter for halftone images. Let c_i denote a RGB colour vector in a local 3x3 neighbourhood, with $c_i = (r_i, g_i.b_i)$, i=1,..,9, and c_5 the center pixel in the sliding window. The median filter is calculated as:

$$c_5 = \min_{j=1,..,9} \left\{ \sum_i |c_i - c_j| \right\} \tag{1}$$

For each RGB vector the distances to all other vectors in the neighbourhood are computed and added together. The vector with the smallest sum is the vector median. The colour of the noisy point is then replaced by the colour of the vector median. An important disadvantage of the vector median filter is the non unequivocal distance calculation. Furthermore there exist colours in the RGB colour system, which are separated by a small distance, but are completely different.

3   The Triangle Operator

The triangle operator is a novel non linear smoothing filter. It is based on an improved method for colour matching, and restores noisy true colour images without loss of quality due to colour shifts. The dependencies between the three colour channels are considered in the calculation of the replacement colour. All operations are performed on the original RGB vectors. The creation of colours, which do not occur in the local neighbourhood of the pixel being processing, can be avoided by copying the original—if not noisy—colour values into the result image.

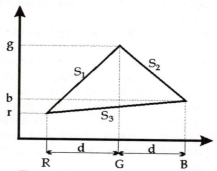

Figure 1: Construction of a colour triangle

The basic idea is simple: a special co-ordinate system with only three positions on the x-axis is constructed with the first position for the red, the second for the green and the third for the blue component (*see Figure 1*). The number of positions on the y-axis is the same as the amount of intensity levels per channel available, usually 256. The components of the RGB vector are transformed into two-dimensional co-ordinates, where d is the distance between the positions on the x-axis:

$$
\begin{aligned}
r_i &\rightarrow (0, r_i) \\
g_i &\rightarrow (d, g_i) \\
b_i &\rightarrow (2d, b_i)
\end{aligned}
\tag{2}
$$

The optimal choice of the distance d between the positions must guarantee a regular colour distribution over the range of available slopes. The application of basic trigonometry gives as result that the distance d is approximately 2028. Each pair of points defines a line, and each vector results in a triangle, which represents the colour. For a given image point $p_1 = (r_1, g_1, b_1)$ following lines are calculated:

$$S_1 : y = \frac{g_1 - r_1}{d}(x) + r_1$$

$$S_2 : y = \frac{b_1 - g_1}{d}(x - d) + g_1 \tag{3}$$

$$S_3 : y = \frac{b_1 - r_1}{2d}(x) + r_1$$

The representation of the colour vector is univocal along the x-axis due to the constant distance. All lines must begin in one of the three fulcrums so a parallel movement in horizontal direction is not possible. Each triangle is characterised by attributes such as area, slopes, side lengths and position. These attributes reproduce the correlation of the colour channels and can be used for colour matching. Colour matching is achieved by use of template matching methods, which are standard methods in digital image processing. They are often used for finding particular objects in images. The triangle matching is much simpler, because the triangles are computer generated without noise, shifts, rotation, etc.

The goal of triangle matching is to find the overlay degree *(Figure 2)*. If the overlay degree is small, the colour does not fit in the neighbourhood, otherwise the overlay degree is large and similar colours are represented.

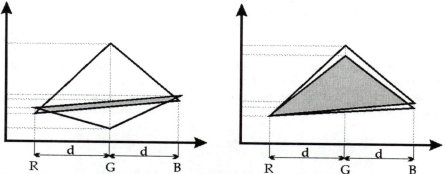

Figure 2: Small overlay degree by non similar colours (left), big overlay degree by similar colours (right)

The first step in the application of the triangle matching method is the calculation of the triangle surface. This can be done with methods from computer graphics, for example the scan line method [5], which is usually used for the filling of graphic primitives. The result for a given pixel p is an array A_p with the following properties: an array element is set with a constant value w, if the point is in the triangle and zero otherwise.

$$A_p(k,l) = \begin{cases} w & \text{if } (k,l) \text{ is inside the representing triangle} \\ 0 & \text{otherwise} \end{cases} \tag{4}$$

354

The constant value w can be specified by the user. In the current implementation a value of $w=10$ was found to give good results. At the end of this phase each triangle is represented by such an array. Afterwards the matching of the representing triangles for the pixels p_i and p_j follows, which is achieved by subtracting the values of the arrays. If the analysed point is part of both triangles the result is zero:

$$u(i, j) = \sum_{k=1}^{|G|} \sum_{l=1}^{|G|} \left| A_{p_i}(k,l) - A_{p_j}(k,l) \right| \tag{5}$$

Instead of the absolute difference other metrics e.g. Euclidean distance can be used. All absolute values of the difference are added to give a sum describing the similarity of the triangles. This process is repeated for each pair of points in the local neighbourhood:

$$U(i) = \sum_{j=1}^{n^2} u(i, j), \qquad i = 1,...,n^2 \tag{6}$$

The colour of the noisy pixel is replaced by the colour of the point with the smallest difference to the other colours in the neighbourhood. This point can be found easily, because it results in the smallest sum:

$$p_{replace} = p_i \quad \text{with} \quad U(i) = \min\left\{ U(j) \mid j = 1,...,n^2 \right\} \tag{7}$$

Figure 3 shows an example for the noise removal in true colour images with the triangle method. The correlation of the image channels are incorporated in the calculation and the method can be easily extended to four and more dimensions. These are, for example, needed for the processing of multispectral images.

Figure 3: Example for noise cleaning with the triangle operator: a) noisy image; b) restored image

4 Complexity and Parallelisation of the Triangle Operator

A disadvantage of the triangle method is its high computational complexity. The calculations involved in the application of the triangle operator can be estimated as follows: Consider a single frame of a PAL video clip consisting of 728 x 576 = 419328 pixels. The number of complex operations executed is:

1. For each pixel three lines must be calculated $\Rightarrow$ 419328 x 3 = 1,2 M lines.
2. The surface of each triangle must be computed $\Rightarrow$ 0,4 M applications for example of the scan line method are needed.
3. The local neighbourhood of a pixel must be examined: 36 matching operations for each pixel and 419328x36 = 15 M matching operations for a whole frame.

The sum of the non elementary operations for only one frame is approximately 16,6 million. A video clip runs at 25 frames per second, thus 16,6x25 = 415 million non elementary operations are needed to remove impulse noise from a one second video clip. Thus noise cleaning in real time with this method is not possible with presently available processors. Therefore fast methods must be examined in order to make the triangle operator suitable for image and video processing.

4.1 Parallel algorithm for the triangle operator

In the case of distributed memory systems, for example PVM running on a network of workstations, the application of the triangle operator can be parallelised through data partitioning. This means that the image is subdivided into sections or image blocks which are then processed in parallel by slave processes. A master process determines the amount and the size of the image blocks. The size of the individual image blocks can be adapted to the performance capabilities of the various processing elements. Thus the available computing resources can be used more efficiently. Each slave process applies the triangle operator to its particular image section(s). The smoothed image parts are sent back to the master process, which collects and combines all segments into the result image.

This approach of data distribution is commonly used in parallel image processing, because it needs no significant modification of the operator structure. A problem is the processing of the section borders in the case of local operators. On each image or image section border a part of the filter window is undefined with the result that the last $(n-1)/2$ pixels cannot be processed. This leads to noisy lines or disturbing strips in the colour run of the smoothed image. A simple solution to this problem can be achieved by periodic extension of the image or image section such that a sufficiently wide neighbourhood of each image section is available.

4.2 Speedup Measurements in a PVM Environment

The performance increase and the time savings achieved with the parallel triangle algorithm were measured in a PVM environment. The run times of the parallel algorithm are compared with those achieved with the conventional triangle operator. The network used consists of five workstations (3xDEC Alpha 21064 processors 433/433/500 MHz and 2xDEC Alpha 21264 processors 500 MHz) with a 10 Mbit Ethernet connection. The smoothing operations are performed on standard test images (256x256, see Figure 3a) and 1000x1000) with a 3x3 filter window. For the measurements configurations with 2, 3, 4 and 5 processing elements were used. The number of available processors corresponds to the number of the distributed image sections. Table 1 shows the measurement results on a single workstation (1-3) and in the PVM environment (4-9). The displayed times are mean values of ten passes:

Table 1: Average run times on a single workstation (1-3) and in the PVM environment (4-9)

Nr.	Configuration	Run Times (256x256)	Run Times (1000x1000)
1	21164 / 433 MHz	7,862 s	241,437 s
2	21164 / 500 MHz	6,406 s	210,626 s
3	21264 / 500 MHz	4,321 s	132,937 s
4	2 x 21164	4,059 s	103,422 s
5	2 x 21264	2,495 s	62,829 s
6	2 x 21164 + 1 x 21264	2,731 s	46,372 s
7	1 x 21164 + 2 x 21264	2,708 s	45,461 s
8	2 x 21164 + 2 x 21264	2,264 s	62,846 s
9	3 x 21164 + 2 x 21264	2,051 s	52,539 s

A graphic representation of the run time measurements is shown in figure 4. The performance diagram corresponds to the expectations: a parallelisation with two PE's leads to approximately 50% faster run times. If four PE's are used another 50% (75% of the single PE time) can be saved. If a larger number of PE's is integrated in the PVM environment the management effort and the influence of the less powerful PE's grow resulting in a slow down in the improvement rate. Thus, no essential performance increase, especially in the 1000x1000 case, with more PE's and similar image size can be assumed.

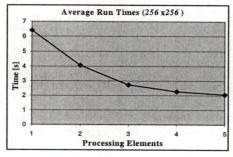 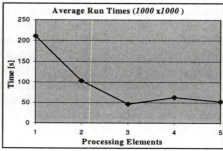

Figure 4: Average run times for the smoothing of the 256x256 (left) and the 1000x1000 (right) image

Table 2 shows the speedup and the efficiency of the parallel algorithm. In the first column the configuration (column Nr. in Table 1) is described. An analysis of the measurement results for the 256x256 image shows the best speedup factor ($\approx 3,1$) is achieved with five PE's, followed by $\approx 2,8$ and $\approx 2,6$ in the case of four and two PE's. The last result is coupled with the best efficiency value of approximately 1,58. In the case of the 1000x1000 image much better speedup ($\approx 4,6$ with 3 PE's) and efficiency ($\approx 1{,}68$ with 2 PE's) values can be reached. On the other hand large run times differences between the single PE's in the PVM can be observed which are mainly depending on the current workload of the workstations. These results are not so reliable as the results achieved with the smaller image.

Table 2: Average speedup and efficiency values of the parallel algorithm

Nr.	164/500/256x256 Speedup (Efficiency)		264/500/256x256 Speedup (Efficiency)		164/500/1000x1000 Speedup (Efficiency)		264/500/1000x1000 Speedup (Efficiency)	
4	1,578	(0,789)	1,064	(0,532)	2,037	(1,018)	1,285	(0,643)
5	2,567	(1,283)	1,731	(0,865)	3,352	(1,676)	2,115	(1,058)
6	2,345	(0,781)	1,582	(0,527)	4,542	(1,514)	2,866	(0,956)
7	2,365	(0,788)	1,596	(0,531)	4,633	(1,544)	2,924	(0,975)
8	2,828	(0,707)	1,908	(0,470)	3,351	(0,838)	2,115	(0,529)
9	3,123	(0,624)	2,106	(0,421)	4,009	(0,802)	2,530	(0,506)

5   Conclusions

In this paper a new method for noise removal in true colour images is proposed. It can be applied directly to the original RGB data and smoothes the image without colour shifts. The components of the RGB vector are transformed into two-dimensional co-ordinates and connected giving a triangle which represents the colour. The colour of a noisy pixel is replaced by the colour of the point with the smallest difference to the other colours in the neighbourhood. A disadvantage of the triangle method is its high computational complexity. Therefore a parallel algorithm was developed. It is based on data distribution over a number of processing elements. Performance measurements in a PVM environment result in a reasonable speedup factor. Future work includes the development of more powerful strategy for the definition and distribution of the image sections. Furthermore other methods for the computation of the overlay degree of the triangles as well as the advantages offered by shared memory systems must be examined.

References

1. O. Kao, New Impulse Noise Cleaning Methods for Monochrome and Colour Images. Dissertation, Papierflieger-Verlag, Clausthal-Zellerfeld, 1997
2. W. K. Pratt, Digital Image Processing, John Wiley & Sons, 1991
3. M. Gabbouj, E. Coyle, N.C. Gallagher Jr., Overview of median and stack filtering, Circuit System Signal Processing, 11(1):7-45,1992
4. J. Zheng, K. P. Valavanis, J. M. Gauch, Noise removal from colour images, Journal of Intelligent and Robotic Systems, 7(3):257-285, 1993
5. J.D. Foley, Computer Graphics: Principles and Practice, Addison-Wesley, Reading, 1990

A NEW SCALABLE ARRAY PROCESSOR FOR TWO-DIMENSIONAL DISCRETE FOURIER TRANSFORM

SHIETUNG PENG, STANISLAV SEDUKHIN, AND HIROSHI NAGATA

Department of Computer Software
The University of Aizu
Aizu-Wakamatsu, Fukushima, 965-8580 Japan
Email:{peng,sedukhin}@u-aizu.ac.jp

In this paper the design of systolic array processors for computing 2-dimensional Discrete Fourier Transform (2-D DFT) is considered. We present a new computational scheme for designing systolic array processors using a systematic approach. The systematic approach guarantees to find optimal systolic array processor(s) from a large solution space in terms of the number of processing elements and I/O channels, the processing time, topology, pipeline period, etc. The optimal systolic array processor obtained in this paper is fully scalable, therefore, suitable for VLSI implementation and highly-parallel computing.

Keywords: Array processors, discrete Fourier transform, systolic algorithm, scalability, VLSI architectures

1 Introduction

In this paper, we consider the problem of computing 2-dimensional Discrete Fourier Transform (2-D DFT). The 2-D DFT is of practical use in many important areas including signal/image processing, speech processing, spectrum analysis, tomography, computer modeling, computer graphics, and computer vision. It is a powerful tool for analyzing and understanding multidimensional signals in the frequency space. Real-time applications require very fast computation of the 2-D DFT. Therefore, it is desirable to design scalable, high-performance array processor(s) for computing the 2-D DFT. There were many systolic array processors for computing the 2-D DFT proposed in the literature [1,2,4,6,8,10,11]. Some array processors are based on FFT (Fast Fourier Transform) algorithm for which long connections are needed for data communication/distribution using the interconnection networks such as shuffle-exchange, butterfly, etc. It was practically shown that for advanced GaAs technology, the direct DFT algorithm is more attractive than the FFT [3]. Furthermore, the array processors based on the FFT are difficult to scale. Systolic arrays for computing the 2-D DFT were proposed in [1,8].

We present an I/O efficient, fully scalable systolic array processor for computing the 2-D DFT. The scalability is one of the most important criteria for highly-parallel computing. A systematic approach based on linear transformations of data dependency graphs (DDGs) of the computational schemes [9] is used to design optimal systolic array processors. Therefore, the time-space optimality of the array processors in the systolization step can be verified.

The rest of this paper is organized as follows. Section 2 gives a new computational scheme for computing 2D-DFT. Section 3 shows an optimal systolic array processor based on the new scheme and a systematic approach. In Section 4, we conclude this paper by discussing the scalability of the proposed systolic array processor.

2   A New Computational Scheme for the 2-D DFT

The $n_1 \times n_2$-point 2-D DFT is given by

$$y_{i_1 i_2} = \sum_{k_2=0}^{n_2-1} \sum_{k_1=0}^{n_1-1} x_{k_1 k_2} \omega_{n_1}^{k_1 i_1} \omega_{n_2}^{k_2 i_2}, \tag{1}$$

where $\omega_{n_i} = e^{2\pi j/n_i}$, $i = 1, 2$, $j = \sqrt{-1}$, $0 \le i_1 \le n_1 - 1$, $0 \le i_2 \le n_2 - 1$.

The design of systolic array processors always starts from the DDG of the given computational scheme. For mapping from DDGs to systolic arrays, there are many research works [5,7,9]. One approach is to map directly the DDGs onto systolic arrays [7,9]. Another approach is to map a DDG to an SFG (Signal Flow Graph), and then apply a systolization procedure to convert an SFG to a systolic design [5]. For systolic array design using the first approach, the schedule vector $\vec{\lambda}$ must satisfy the conditions: $\vec{\lambda}^T \vec{e} > 0$ and $\vec{\lambda}^T \vec{\eta} > 0$, where $\vec{\eta}$ is the designated projection vector and $\vec{e}$ is any dependence vector in the DDG. In this paper, we adopt the first approach. A software package for generating automatically all permissible systolic linear schedules for certain numerical algorithms using the first approach has been developed [9].

Consider first the 1-D DFT, $y_i = \sum_{k=0}^{n-1} x_k \omega_n^{ik}$. The idea of our scheme is to compute the item $x_k \omega_n^{ik}$, $0 \le i \le n - 1$, through pipeline: starting with x_k and then multiplied by ω_n^k, once a time, at each location of the pipeline. The recursive formula of the scheme for 1-D DFT is as follows:

$$x_k^{(0)} = x_k \text{ and } x_k^{(i)} = x_k^{(i-1)} \omega_n^k, \quad 1 \le i, \le n - 1, \ 1 \le k \le n - 1;$$
$$y_i^{(-1)} = 0, \ y_i^{(k)} = y_i^{(k-1)} + x_k^{(i)}, \text{ and } y_i = y_i^{(n-1)}, \quad 0 \le i, k \le n - 1.$$

To compute the 2-D DFT, the required items $\omega_{n_1}^{k_1 i_1}$ and $\omega_{n_2}^{i_2 k_2}$ for each node in the DDG will be generated properly through pipelining and updating steps as in the 1-D case. We first perform an index transformation on Equation (1) to reduce the 4D index space (i_1, i_2, k_1, k_2) into a 3D index space (j_1, j_2, j_3). The index transformation is as follows: $j_1 = i_1$, $j_2 = k_2$, and $j_3 = k_1$ or $i_2 + n_1$, where $0 \leq j_3 \leq n_1 + n_2 - 1$. The Eq. (1) can then be rewritten as Eq. (2) and Eq. (3) below

$$z_{j_1 j_2} = \sum_{j_3=0}^{n_1-1} x_{j_3 j_2} \omega_{n_1}^{j_3 j_1}, \quad 0 \leq j_3 \leq n_1 - 1, \tag{2}$$

$$y_{j_1 j_3} = \sum_{j_2=0}^{n_2-1} z_{j_1 j_2} \omega_{n_1}^{j_2(j_3-n_1)}, \quad n_1 \leq j_3 \leq n_1 + n_2 - 1. \tag{3}$$

Next, we use the indexed (local) variables x, s, z and z, t, y for Eq. (2) and Eq. (3), respectively, to specify the scheme formally as follows. Notice that s and t are constant variables which are used to update variables x and z.

- **Input**
$x(0, j_2, j_3) = x_{j_3 j_2}$, $s(-1, j_2, j_3) = \omega_{n_1}^{j_3}$,
$0 \leq j_3 \leq n_1 - 1$, $0 \leq j_2 \leq n_2 - 1$;
$z(j_1, j_2, -1) = 0$, $0 \leq j_1 \leq n_1 - 1$, $0 \leq j_2 \leq n_2 - 1$;
$y(j_1, -1, j_3) = 0$, $t(j_1, -1, j_3) = \omega_{n_2}^{j_3}$;
$0 \leq j_1 \leq n_1 - 1$, $n_1 \leq j_3 \leq n_1 + n_2 - 1$;

- **Computation**
for $j_1 = 0$ **to** $n_1 - 1$ **do**
  for $j_2 = 0$ **to** $n_2 - 1$ **do**
    for $j_3 = 0$ **to** $n_1 - 1$ **do**

$$z(j_1, j_2, j_3) = z(j_1, j_2, j_3 - 1) + x(j_1 - 1, j_2, j_3);$$
$$x(j_1, j_2, j_3) = x(j_1 - 1, j_2, j_3) \times s(j_1 - 1, j_2, j_3);$$
$$s(j_1, j_2, j_3) = s(j_1 - 1, j_2, j_3); \tag{4}$$

  for $j_1 = 0$ **to** $n_1 - 1$ **do**
    for $j_2 = 0$ **to** $n_2 - 1$ **do**
      for $j_3 = n_1$ **to** $n_1 + n_2 - 1$ **do**

$$y(j_1, j_2, j_3) = y(j_1, j_2 - 1, j_3) + z(j_1, j_2, j_3 - 1);$$
$$z(j_1, j_2, j_3) = z(j_1, j_2 - 1, j_3) \times t(j_1, j_2 - 1, j_3);$$
$$t(j_1, j_2, j_3) = t(j_1, j_2 - 1, j_3); \tag{5}$$

- **Output**
$y_{j_1 j_3} = y(j_1, n_2 - 1, j_3)$, $0 \leq j_1 \leq n_1 - 1$, $n_1 \leq j_3 \leq n_1 + n_2 - 1$.

The DDG of this computational scheme can then be presented in the 3-D index space as shown in Figure 1. Figure 1-(a) shows the topology of the

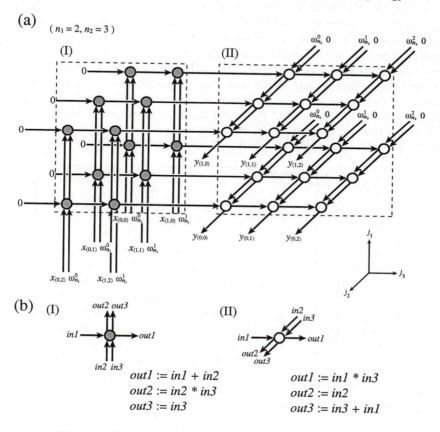

Figure 1. The DDG of the new scheme for computing 2-D DFT

DDG, and Figure 1-(b) shows the computations associated with each node of the DDG. In both Figures 1-(a) and 1-(b), part (I) corresponds to the computations in Eq. (4), and part (II) to the computations in Eq. (5).

3   An Optimal Array Processor for the 2D-DFT

The mapping of the DDG into the 2-D space along all permissible projection directions defines the set of 2-D array processors, which differ in the number of processing elements (PEs) and I/O channels, the time of processing, topology, pipeline period, array size, etc. The allocation function $\mathbf{place}(p) : \mathbf{Z}^3 \rightarrow \mathbf{Z}^2$ is defined in the following linear form $\mathbf{place}(p) = \Lambda_\eta \cdot p$, where Λ_η is a (2×3) matrix of linear transformation corresponding to a *projection direction* $\eta \in \mathbf{kernel}(\Lambda_\eta)$ and which has $\mathbf{rank}(\Lambda_\eta) = 2$, and p is a node in the 3-D index space. The allocation functions must guarantee that a PE executes at most one computation at any given time step. This requires the condition $\lambda \cdot \eta \neq 0$ to be held. For the 3-D DDG there are 17 possible projection directions. However, only 13 of them are permissible according to the condition $\lambda \cdot \eta \neq 0$. Table 1 show the numbers of PEs, and the *data pipelining period* $\alpha = |\lambda \cdot \eta|$ (the time interval separating the neighboring items of input or output data) in the projected mesh for each space allocation schedule.

Direction η	Period α	Number of PEs
$(0,0,1)$	1	$n_1 n_2$
$(0,1,0)$	1	$(n_1 + n_2)n_1$
$(1,0,0)$	1	$(n_1 + n_2)n_2$
$(0,1,1)$	2	$(n_1 + 2n_2 - 1)n_1$
$(1,0,1)$	2	$(2n_1 + n_2 - 1)n_2$
$(1,1,0)$	2	$(n_1 + n_2 - 1)(n_1 + n_2)$
$(1,1,1)$	3	$n_1^2 + n_2^2 + 3n_1 n_2 - 2n_1 - 2n_2 + 1$
$(-1,-1,1)$	1	$n_1^2 + n_2^2 + 3n_1 n_2 - 2n_1 - 2n_2 + 1$
$(1,-1,1)$	1	$n_1^2 + n_2^2 + 3n_1 n_2 - 2n_1 - 2n_2 + 1$
$(-1,1,1)$	1	$n_1^2 + n_2^2 + 3n_1 n_2 - 2n_1 - 2n_2 + 1$
$(-1,1,2)$	2	$n_1^2 + 2n_2^2 + 8n_1 n_2 - 5n_1 - 6n_2 + 4$
$(1,1,2)$	4	$n_1^2 + 2n_2^2 + 8n_1 n_2 - 5n_1 - 6n_2 + 4$
$(1,-1,2)$	2	$n_1^2 + 2n_2^2 + 8n_1 n_2 - 5n_1 - 6n_2 + 4$

Table 1. Projects characteristics

From Table 1, it is clear that the systolic array obtained along the projection direction $\eta = (0,0,1)^T$, i.e. along j_3 axis, is optimal in terms of number of PEs $N = n_1 n_2$, the total computing time $T(n_1, n_2) = 2(n_1 + n_2) - 3$, and data pipelining period $\alpha = 1$. We show this optimal systolic array processor in Figure 2. Figure 2-(a) shows the 2-D array processor and the input arrangement for the case $n_1 = 2$ and $n_2 = 3$. The total computing time $T(2,3) = 2 \times (2 + 3) - 3 = 7$ which equals to the longest path in the DDG. Figures 2-(b) and 2-(c) show the computations in each PE of the array processor which correspond to the computations in Eq. (4) and Eq. (5), respectively. These two modes of computations are activated by the availability of inputs:

the first by the vertical inputs and the second by the horizontal inputs. The details for the implementation of the PE structure are omitted because of page limit.

(a)

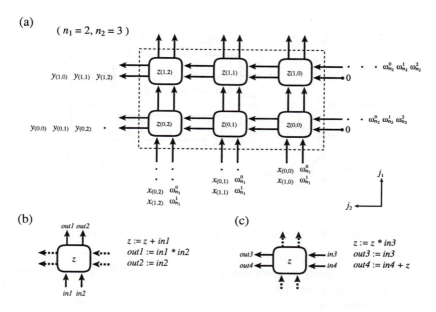

Figure 2. The optimal array processor for computing 2D-DFT

4   Scalability of The Optimal Systolic Array

Most recently, with changing computing environment and emerging of new highly-parallel computer systems, the concept of *scalability* has been reemphasized. The scalability is important for both traditional special-purpose computer systems and the new highly-parallel computer systems since they use commodity components, and therefore, easily scale up (to accommodate ever-increasing performance) or scale down (to reduce cost). The proposed systolic array processor for 2D-DFT can also be implemented in these highly-parallel computer systems in which a set of simple processors are connected through a mesh-like network. Therefore, the proposed systolic array has some advantage over other designs that cannot be scaled.

In Figure 2-(a), we provide n_2 copies of vector $v_1 = (\omega_{n_1}^0, \omega_{n_1}^1, \ldots, \omega_{n_1}^{n_1-1})$

364

and n_1 copies of vector $v_2 = (\omega_{n_2}^0, \omega_{n_2}^1, \ldots, \omega_{n_2}^{n_2-1})$ as inputs to the array processor. Another implementation is to use only two vectors v_1 and v_2 as inputs, and then provide shift registers to feed the inputs in a pipelined fashion as shown in Figure 3.

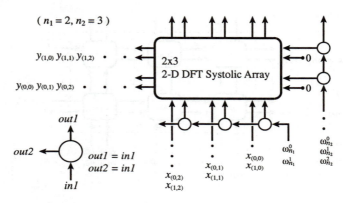

Figure 3. The optimal array processor with shift registers

Finally, in Figure 4, we show that four identical systolic arrays in Figure 3 can be used to compute the 2-D DFT with $n_1 = 4$ and $n_2 = 6$. The shift registers are used only for the bottom and the right most array processors.

References

1. Aravena, J.L., "Triple Matrix Product architecture for Fast Signal Processing", *IEEE Trans. Circuits Syst.* 35(1), pp. 119–122, 1988.
2. Choi, J., and Boriakoff, "A new Linear Systolic Array for FFT computation", *IEEE Trans. Circuits Syst.* 39(4), pp. 236–239, 1992.
3. Gimarc, C., Milutinovic, V., Ersoy, O., "Time Complexity Modeling and Comparison of Parallel Architectures for Fourier Transform Oriented Algorithms", *Proc. Hawaii Int'l Conf. System Sciences, HICSS-22*, Kailua-Kona, Hawaii, pp. 160-170, 1989.
4. Gertner, I., and Shamash, M., "VLSI Architectures for Multidimensional Fourier Transform Processing", *IEEE Trans. on Computers*, Vol. C-36, No. 11, pp. 1265–1274, 1987.
5. Kung, S.Y., *VLSI Array Processors*, Prentice Hall, 1988.
6. Marwood W., Clarke A.P. "Matrix product machine and the Fourier transform", *IEE Proc.*, Vol.137, Pt.G, No.4, August 1990, pp.295–301.
7. Moldovan, D.I., *Parallel Processing: From Applications to Systems*, Morgan

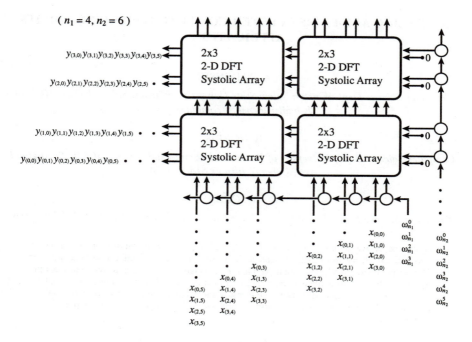

Figure 4. The scalability of the optimal array processor

Kaufmann Publishers, 1993.

8. Peng, S., Sedukhin, I., and Sedukhin, S., "Design of Array Processors for 2-D Discrete Fourier Transform", *IEICE Trans. on Information and Systems*, Vol. E80-D, No. 4, pp. 455–465, 1997.

9. Sedukhin, S.G., and Sedukhin, I.S., "Systematic Approach and Software Tool for Systolic Design", *Lecture Notes in Computer Science*, 854, pp. 172–183, 1994.

10. Thompson C.D. "Fourier transform in VLSI", *IEEE Trans. Comput.*, Vol.C-32, No.11, 1983, pp.1047–1057.

11. Zhang, C. and Yun, D., "Multi-dimensional Systolic Networks For Discrete Fourier Transform", *Proc. Int'l. Conf. on Parallel Processing*, pp. 215–222, 1984.

A GENERIC ALL-PAIRS CLUSTER-COMPUTING PIPELINE AND ITS APPLICATIONS

A. RADENSKI

Computer Science Dept. Winston-Salem State University, Winston-Salem, NC 27110, USA
E-mail:radenski@computer.org

B. NORRIS

Computer Science Dept., University of Illinois at Urbana-Champaign, 1304 W. Springfield Ave., Urbana, Illinois 61801, USA

W. CHEN

Computer Science Dept. Winston-Salem State University, Winston-Salem, NC 27110, USA

In this paper we propose a generic pipeline for *all-pairs computations* on a cluster of workstations. We use this generic pipeline to derive specific cluster algorithms for three different all-pairs problems: n-body simulation, bubble sort, and Gaussian elimination. We implement the generic pipeline and its derivatives on a cluster of Intel Pentium II workstations using C and the PVM cluster computing environment. We measure and evaluate the performance of the derived algorithms. The n-body and bubble sort algorithms achieve super-linear speedup for large problems.

1   Introduction

An *all-pairs computation* performs the same *operation* on every possible set of two elements chosen from a system of n elements [7, 4]. The operation changes a pair of elements independently of the remaining elements and is called for this reason *interaction* between the two elements. Examples of all-pairs computations include n-body simulation [4, 3], bubble sort [2], Gaussian elimination [1], and Householder reduction   [4]. An all-pair sequential computation over a large number of elements may become prohibitively complex. Interactions between pairs of elements happen in the order specified by a precedence graph [4]; fortunately, some of the interactions between pairs of elements are independent of each other and can, therefore, be executed in parallel.

It is possible to specify an all-pairs computation as a *generic parallel algorithm* that implements process control and communication in a problem-independent manner. Such a generic algorithm can be glued together with domain-specific sequential code in order to derive particular all-pairs parallel computations. This methodology is facilitated by a concurrent message-passing language, *Paradigm/SP*, and by a compiler. *Paradigm/SP* [5, 6] is a high-level object-oriented language that allows the validation of parallel algorithms before they are converted into efficient cluster computing applications.

In Section 2 we propose a generic all-pairs pipeline algorithm for parallel computations on clusters of workstations. In Sections 3 we use this generic algorithm to derive specific parallel algorithms for three different problems: n-body simulation, bubble sort, and Gaussian elimination. In Section 4 we describe implementations of the algorithms on a homogeneous cluster of workstations using PVM, the parallel virtual machine software package. In the same section, we present performance measurements on an Intel Pentium II cluster of workstations. Concluding remarks are presented in Section 5.

2   A Generic All-Pairs Pipeline

We assume that an all-pairs computation in a system of *n elements* is defined by the type of the elements and by two sequential methods:

- a method *interact* to make two arbitrary elements exchange information and eventually update their states;
- a method to *integrate* the system of updated elements into a new system.

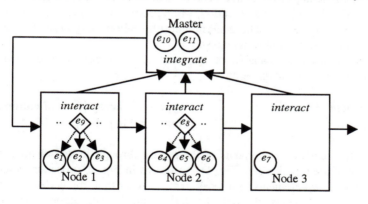

Figure 1. An all-pairs pipeline in progress.

An all-pairs computation on a system of n elements can be parallelized by means of a master and several pipelined nodes. The master sends all elements to travel left-to-right through the pipeline. Each node first retains its own subsystem of elements and makes them interact with each other, thus performing a sequential all-pairs computation on its retained elements. After that, the node continues to receive elements from its left neighbor, makes them interact with its own retained elements, and then sends them to its right neighbor. By traveling left-to-right through the pipeline, all elements finally become evenly distributed among the pipelined nodes. Then the master integrates the system of received elements by eventually performing additional problem-specific modifications on the elements. After that, the master may send the whole system through the pipeline again; the whole process is repeated a predefined number of steps. This type of computation can be efficient on a cluster of workstations provided the interaction between pairs of elements is computationally intensive and the individual elements are not very large.

We specify and test this generic all-pairs pipeline using the concurrent message-passing language Paradigm/SP [5, 6]. Procedures interact and integrate, and the element type are the principal parameters of the algorithm, together with the total number of elements n and the number of pipeline nodes p:

const n = ..; *{number of elements}* $\qquad$ p = ..; *{number of nodes}*
type *element* = ..; $\qquad$ *system* = *array[1..n] of element;*
procedure *interact(***var** *ei, ej: element);* **procedure** *integrate(***var** *s:system);*

Procedures *interact* and *integrate* are left unspecified in the generic algorithm because they vary significantly from one problem to another. The only assumption made in the generic algorithm is that procedure *interact* can operate and eventually update two individual elements, *ei* and *ej*, while procedure *integrate* can update the state of the whole system, *s*. The generic algorithm allows any desirable domain-specific *element* type without restrictions.

A net *c* of channels capable of transmitting messages of type *element* is declared and opened as shown below:

type *channel* = *(element);* $\qquad$ **type** *net* = **array** *[0..p]* **of channel**;
var *c: net*; $\qquad$ **for** $k := 0$ **to** p **do** *open(c[i]);*

The master sends all n elements of the system through its *left* channel to the leftmost node of the pipeline (see Fig. 1). As shown in Fig. 2, procedure *node* first retains a block of n/p elements in a local array, *e*. After that, the node continues to receive transient elements through its *left* channel. The node performs an application-dependent *interaction* between each transient element, *ej*, with every retained element, *e[j]*, eventually changing the states of the interacting elements. After the transient element interacts with all of the node's retained elements, the node sends it through its *right* channel and receives another transient element through its *left* channel. After handling all transient elements, the node sends, through its *top* channel, all retained elements to the master.

As shown in Fig. 3, procedure *master* repeatedly sends the whole system of elements to the pipeline through its *left* channel, so that each node can retain a block of elements and make these retained elements interact with transient elements. After these interactions, the master receives back all retained elements. Through a bottom net of channels that connect each pipeline node to the master. In order to make this communication more efficient, the master employs a whole net of bottom channels, one for each individual pipeline node. At the end of each cycle, the master performs an application-dependent *integration* of the whole system (see Fig. 3).

```
procedure node(                          for j := 0 to i-1 do
  steps, first, last: integer;               interact(e[i], e[j]);
  left, right, top: channel);            end;
const                                    for j := last+1 to n do
  max = n div p;                         begin
type                                       receive(left, ej);
  block = array                            for i := 0 to last-first do
    [0..max] of element;                     interact(ej, e[i]);
var                                        send(right, ej);
  e: block; ej: element;                  end;
  i, j: integer;                         for i := 0 to last-first do
begin                                      send(top, e[i]);
  repeat                                 steps := steps - 1;
    for i := 0 to last-first do          until steps = 0;
      begin                            end; {node}
        receive(left, e[i]);
```

Figure 2. **Pipeline node.**

```
procedure master(
  steps: integer;  var s: system;
  left: channel;  bottom: net);
begin
  repeat
    sendSystem(left, s);
    receiveSystem(bottom, s);
    integrate(s);
    steps := steps - 1;
  until steps = 0;
end; {master}
```

Figure 3. Master node.

```
procedure compute(
  steps: integer;  var s: system)
var
  c, b: net;
begin
  openChannels(c, b);
  parallel
    master(steps, s, c[0], b) |
    spawnNodes(steps, c, b);
  end;
end; {compute}
```

Figure 4. All-pairs pipeline.

Finally, the algorithm from Fig. 4 creates the pipeline displayed on Fig. 1 by first opening all channels and then running in parallel one master and p pipeline nodes.

Given this generic parallel algorithm, one can derive a parallel algorithm for a particular problem by specifying the particular type of its *elements* and the problem-specific, sequential procedures *interact* and *integrate*. Finally, procedure *compute* is invoked in the master to solve concrete problem instances.

A complete specification of the all-pairs pipeline algorithm in the form of a *Paradigm/SP* generic module can be found in [9].

3   Deriving Specific Cluster-Computing Algorithms

We use the generic all-pairs pipeline to derive specific cluster algorithms for three different all-pairs problems: n-body simulation, bubble sort, and Gaussian elimination. We achieve this by defining the type of the *elements* for each specific problem, and by defining concrete sequential versions of methods *interact* and *integrate*. The sequential versions of *interact* and *integrate* are linked together with the generic parallel algorithm in order to obtain a specific parallel algorithm. Complete specifications of all derived algorithms can be found in [9].

3.1   N-Body Simulation

We consider a discrete n-body simulation problem: compute the positions of n bodies in space at equal discrete time intervals, assuming that the bodies interact through gravitational forces only. From the generic all-pairs pipeline, we derive a *parallel n-body simulation* algorithm that is similar to the one presented in [4, Chapter 6]. The generic *element* from the all-pairs pipeline is specialized in the n-body simulation algorithm to represent a body with a particular mass m, relative distance r from the origin, velocity v, and cumulative force f acting upon the body:

element = **class** *m: real; r, v, f: vector;* **end;**

At each simulation step, procedure *interact* models force interaction between two particular bodies by (1) calculating the gravitational force between the two bodies at their current positions and (2), by correspondingly updating the cumulative forces acting upon each of the bodies:

procedure *interact(***var** *ei, ej: body);*
var *fij: vector;*
begin *fij := force(ei, ej); ei.f := sum(ei.f, fij); ej.f := difference(ej.f, fij);* **end;**

Procedure *integrate* simulates body moves as a result of body interactions by calculating the velocity and position increments at the end of each time interval.

3.2 Bubble Sort

We consider a standard internal sort problem: given an array of n elements, sort them in ascending or descending order. Starting again with the generic all-pairs pipeline, we derive a *parallel bubble sort algorithm*. For the derivation of bubble sort, we introduce a new generic parameter, a relation *less* that is capable of comparing any two generic elements. Then we define *interact* to swap elements ei and ej if *less(ei, ej)* is *true*:

```
procedure interact(var ei, ej: element);
begin if less(ei, ej) then swap(ei, ej); end;
```

This version of *interact* makes smaller elements move towards the end of the pipeline while large elements are kept closer to the beginning of the pipeline. As a result, the whole system becomes sorted in descending order.

The derived bubble sort algorithm is specialized yet generic version of the all-pairs pipeline because it can be used to sort any type of elements. As an example, we derive an integer bubble sort algorithm by defining an element to consist of a simple integer component:

```
element = class v: integer; end;
function less(ei, ej: element): boolean; begin less := ei.v < ej.v end;
```

3.3 Gaussian Elimination

Finally, we consider a standard numerical problem: find a solution for a system of n linear equations with n unknowns. Starting again with the generic all-pairs pipeline, we derive a *parallel Gaussian elimination* algorithm for solving such a system. We combine the system's n by n matrix and the right-hand side vector into a n by $n+1$ matrix. Then, the original all-pairs *elements* are specified to represent *rows* of the extended matrix:

Given two rows ei and ej, method *interact* eliminates xj from ei by multiplying and subtracting ej from ei. We have enhanced procedure interact with partial *pivoting* in order to reduce the numerical instability of Gaussian elimination:

```
row = array[1..n] of real;
element = class a: row; b: real;
    no: integer; {original row number} pos: integer; {current row position} end;
```

```
procedure interact(var ei, ej: element);
begin { pivot ei, and ej, then eliminate xj from equation i } end;
```

The LU factorization step of Gaussian elimination is done in parallel, and the final solution is obtained sequentially by back substitution, which is implemented in the method *integrate*. This sequential post-processing does not affect the parallel performance significantly. Like bubble sort, Gaussian elimination requires a single pipeline step.

4 Cluster Implementation and Performance Evaluation

We first derive and validate parallel algorithms in *Paradigm/SP*, then we convert them into efficient *C* code that runs in the PVM cluster computing environment [8]. We believe that this approach simplifies the development and debugging of cluster computing applications. Note that the cluster implementations of n-body simulation, Gaussian elimination, and bubble sort all use the same generic parallel implementation of the all-pairs pipeline. Each specific cluster algorithm defines its domain-specific sequential components: *element* type, functions *interact*, *integrate*, and functions to *initialize* and *finalize* the system of elements.

The number of operations per node is inversely proportional to its position in the pipeline, e.g., the first node performs the most work while the last performs the least. If nodes are mapped to processors in a one-to-one fashion, the parallel execution of the pipeline algorithm suffers from load imbalance. To remedy this problem, our cluster implementation of the generic pipeline algorithm maps nodes onto processors using reflected cyclic mapping, which corresponds to "folding" the pipeline. This ensures that work is divided more evenly among the processors throughout the computation.

We have obtained performance results on a dedicated 100Mbps Ethernet cluster of 400Mhz Intel Pentium II dual-processor workstations with 1GB RAM per workstation. Experiments were performed on $p = 1, 2, 4, 8, 16, 32$ processors with pipelines consisting of $(f + 1) *p$ folded nodes for different values of the folding factor f. Problems with larger number of elements can usually benefit from a larger folding factor. Table 1 shows the run time $T(p)$ and processor efficiency $E(p) = T(1)/(p*T(p))$ for the following randomly generated problems:

- n-body simulation of systems of size $n = 10,000$ with a fold factor $f = 7$;
- bubble sort of integer arrays of size $n = 30,000$ with a fold factor $f = 7$;
- Gaussian elimination of systems of $n = 6,000$ equations with a fold factor $f = 3$;

The speedup for the same experiments is illustrated in Fig. 5. Speedup is defined as $T(1)/T(p)$.

Table 1. Wall-clock time in seconds and processor efficiency.

p	N-Body Simulation		Bubble Sort		Gaussian Elimination	
	T(p)	E(p)	T(p)	E(p)	T(p)	E(p)
1	114	1.00	23	1.00	1525	1.00
2	42	1.36	7	1.64	815	0.94
4	22	1.30	4	1.44	486	0.78
8	12	1.19	2	1.44	295	0.65
16	7	1.29	2	0.72	199	0.48
32	4	0.89	1	0.72	186	0.26

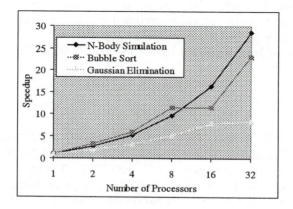

Figure 5. Speedup.

N-body simulation and bubble sort achieve super-linear efficiency because the total amount of available cache grows with the total number of processors. Gaussian elimination does not benefit much from a larger cache because its elements are considerably larger. Thus, only a small fraction of the node's retained elements can be retained in cache. The larger element size also leads to greater communication costs.

5 Conclusions

We believe that extending a *generic* parallel algorithm with *sequential* domain-specific code can result in good parallel performance in a cluster-computing environment. This parallel programming methodology leads to clean parallel solutions of a variety of problems that share the same parallel control structure. In ddition to providing good processor performance, genericity improves programming efficiency, allowing the application developer to focus on the

374

sequential implementation of domain-specific details, rather than on the more difficult parallel code development. These conclusions are founded on our experience with several generic parallel algorithms: the all-pairs generic algorithm (described in the present paper), a generic master-server probabilistic algorithm, a cellular automaton generic algorithm, and a generic branch and bound algorithm [9].

The work presented in this paper is similar but not identical to earlier results in parallel raster image processing[10]. The dependency graph of an all-pairs computation is analogous to a raster image processing dependency graph. The two kinds of algorithms are implemented by means of similar pipelines. Parallel raster image processing does not involve *interactions* as those found in an all-pairs computation. The all-pairs algorithm proposed in this paper is a rather generic solution that may be applied to a large variety of problems.

This work has been supported by NASA grant NAG3-2011 and NSF Grant CCR-9509223.

References

1. Amoura A., E. Bampis, J.-C. König. Scheduling Algorithms for Parallel Gaussian Elimination With Communication Costs, *IEEE Transactions on Parallel and Distributed Systems*, 9(7), July 1998, 679-686.
2. Arpaci-Dusseau A., R. Arpaci-Dusseau, D. Culler, J. Hellerstein, D. Patterson. High-Performance Sorting on Networks of Workstations, *Proc. 1997 ACM SIGMOD Conference*, ACM Press, 1997, 243—254.
3. Baiardi F., P. Becuzzi, P. Mori, M. Paoli. Load Balancing and Locality in Hierarchical *N*-Body Algorithms on Distributed Memory Architectures, *Lecture Notes in Computer Science*, 1401, Sringer, 1998, 284-294.
4. Hansen B. *Studies in Computational Science: Parallel Programming Paradigms*, Prentice Hall, Inc., Englewood Cliffs, NJ, 1995.
5. Radenski A. Module Embedding. Intl. Journal *Software - Concepts and Tools*, 19(3), 1998, 122-129.
6. Radenski A. Prototype Implementation of Paradigm/SP, www.rtpnet.org/~radenski/research/language.html, 1998.
7. Shih Z., G. Chen, R. Lee. Systolic Algorithms to Examine All Pairs of Elements, *Communications of the ACM*, 30, 1987, 161-167.
8. Sunderam V. PVM: A Framework for Parallel Distributed Computing, *Concurrency: Practice and Experience*, 2, No 4, 1990, 315-339.
9. Radenski A. Generic Parallel Message-Passing Algorithms and Their Applications, www.rtpnet.org/~radenski/research/algorithms.html, 1999.
10. Van Campenhout, J.M., Lasure, R., Kawahara, Y. PRIP - A Parallel Raster Image Processor, *Computer Graphics Forum*, 12, 1993, 95-104.

MANAGEMENT OF DISTRIBUTED DYNAMIC DATA WITH ALGORITHMIC SKELETONS

THOMAS RICHERT

rich@i2.informatik.rwth-aachen.de

Algorithmic skeletons are polymorphic higher-order functions that represent common parallelization patterns. In this paper, we consider the design and implementation of skeletons for the management of distributed dynamic data. Such skeletons are used by grid-managers of numerical solvers like multigrid algorithms with adaptive refinement techniques. We present three mechanisms to encapsulate the necessary communication in parallel implementations of those solvers. Further, we have integrated our skeletons in a single-grid example solver and have run it on a PC-Cluster against a pure C implementation. Run-time measurements show that the speedups and efficiency of the skeleton-based program are comparable to those obtained for the C implementation.

1 Introduction

Programming of parallel computers is still a difficult and erroneous task, because often developers of parallel applications have to rely on low-level message passing. However, those applications consist of complex computations, for instance consider simulations of aerodynamic behaviors of foils or weather forecasts. Those simulations require algorithms, which are difficult to implement. Thus, it would be a great simplification, if programming of parallel aspects were application-oriented instead of machine-oriented.

Our approach to facilitate parallel programming is based on *algorithmic skeletons* [5] as described in the next section. The main feature of a skeleton is to cover the low-level implementation of communication between processors by providing reusable functions that can be instantiated in different applications individually. In this paper, we present the advantages of skeletons by means of an implementation of a numerical solver of partial differential equations (pde's) for parallel machines with distributed memory.

With pde's we can describe simulations as those mentioned above. To compute these simulations with high precision we need fine-meshed grids and fast algorithms. It is well known that multigrid methods [4] with adaptive refinement techniques [7] are the fastest ones. Additionally, it is important for careful use of memory resources that the grid components like nodes or edges are *dynamic*, because to yield precise solutions the grids has to consist of some million nodes. If we want to run these algorithms on parallel computers with distributed memory, we have to solve the following problems:

1. To reduce the amount of communication during an iteration, parts of the grid are held by more than one processor. For keeping consistency, values have to be exchanged between copies of a distributed object after some iteration steps.

2. Adaptive refinement of a grid causes load imbalance on the processors. Because the grid consists of dynamic components we have to invoke a dynamic load-balancer that leads to a transfer of portions of the grid from one processor to another.

3. If we want to generate a grid in parallel, first we have to generate the parts of the grid locally and then connect it to a big global distributed grid. In order to do so we have to identify grid objects by a certain criterion, for instance the coordinates of grid nodes.

In Section 3 we work out the mechanisms needed to solve these problems and present suitable skeletons. After that we present a small example that demonstrates how to use these skeletons, compare it to an implementation based on DDD [1], and point out the differences between both approaches.

2 Algorithmic Skeletons with Skil

A *skeleton* is an algorithmic abstraction common to a series of applications, that can be implemented in parallel. Skeletons are embedded in a sequential host language, thus being the only source of parallelism in programs. The basic idea of algorithmic skeletons relies on the paradigm of functional languages: based on techniques like *higher order functions, type polymorphism,* and *partial application* we can write flexible and reusable skeletons that can be instantiated for each application individually.

Unfortunately, data-parallel functional languages like DPFL [6] are not fast enough [3] for computing expensive applications like adaptive multigrid solvers, for example. Hence, a better approach is to extend an imperative language by the above functional features. In this paper, we use Botorog's *Skil*[a] [3] to implement our skeletons. Skil is an extension of C, and the Skil compiler translates code from Skil into C by instantiating the skeletons with application-dependent types and functions. To use message passing in Skil we have to include a message passing library in the same way as in C. We prefer MPI [8] because it is available on many machines and architectures.

For example, consider the skeleton `fold` working on grids:

---

[a]**Skeleton Imperative Language**

```
$u fold(Grid <$t> g, $u conv_f($t), $u fold_f($u, $u)) ;
```

With that we can perform a *collect*-operation on all nodes of the `grid`. With `Grid <$t>` we declare a grid that contains polymorphic type `$t`. The skeleton performs a preliminary conversion of the data by calling the argument function `conv_f`. The data on all nodes are combined using the function `fold_f`, which must be associative and commutative, otherwise the result is unpredictable. For instance, after a few iterations the maximum of the residuals[b] on the nodes of a distributed grids is needed to check if the solution is precise enough or not. With `$t = $u = double`, the identy function `id` on `double` as `conv_f`, and the maximum function `max` on `double` as `fold_f`, we call in Skil

```
result = fold(grid, id, max) ;
```

Internally, if `fold` runs on more than one processor, two steps are performed. First, on all processors the values of the grid nodes which are stored on it are folded locally in one parallel step and then these results are folded together globally by communication.

Obviously, one advantage of using Skil instead of an imperative language is a reduction of the number of code lines because skeletons are reusable, abstract definitions of functions. Another benefit is the modularity. That means that someone who wants to write a multigrid solver doesn't have to think about low-level message passing implementation but about distribution of grids or about keeping computation data consistence.

3 Distributed Objects

In this section we present skeletons that encapsulate the communication mechanisms needed by parallel implementations for numerical solvers based on grids. First we give the meaning of *distributed objects*. We define an *object* as a piece of dynamic data that represents some entity, for instance a node, an edge, or a triangle of a grid. An object is called *distributed*, if more than one processor hold a copy of it. Regarding to the three kinds of communication needed in parallel numerical solvers mentioned above we specify three kinds of operations (see also [1]):

1. **Virtual Interface**
   During the computation the grid structure doesn't change. Thus, we can

---

[b]Numerically, the *residual* is defined as the difference between an approximate solution and the exact algebraic solution.

establish *virtual interfaces* between copies of distributed objects. The programmer of numerical software has the ability to define those interfaces and to use them to exchange some data.

2. **Object Migration**

   For dynamic load-balancing we need functions for sending an object from one processor to another, in fact the operations *copy*, *delete*, and *move*.

3. **Object Identification**

   If we want to generate a grid in parallel on all processors, it is necessary to identify objects like grid nodes with the same coordinates on different processors. Therefore, we need an *identifiy*-operation that finds out if two objects satisfy the same criterion or not.

Before we explain the design and implementation of these mechanisms we have to declare how we control the distribution of data. The simplest way is to assign an unique global identification number (gid) to each object. Each copy of a distributed object has the same gid. Additionally, each object has a table for saving the numbers of all processors, which hold a copy of it. We call this table *coupling table*. Note that both parameters are internal to the three mechanisms and thus hidden from the application programmer.

Virtual Interface

After an iteration has been performed we have to exchange the residual of the computation between the copies of the distributed nodes. Therefore we establish a virtual interface for nodes that indicate virtual connections between the copies of a distributed object. After these connections have been established the multiple copies of an object can send and receive data via the interface until the grid structure or it distribution changes. Hereby "establishing" means to pick up all distributed objects and insert references to them into a table, which drives the necessary communication. For working with virtual interfaces we need the following skeletons:

- `Interface define_interface(void);`
  defines an interface and allocates auxiliary memory.

- `void interface_data_exchange(Interface if,`
  `void pack_f(Buf*, $t2, int*),`
  `void unpack_f(Buf, $t2, int*));`

  establishes a virtual interface if if necessary and performs asynchronous communication. The message buffers are generated with `pack_f` and the data can be unpacked by `unpack_f`.

- `void disable_interface(Interface if);`
  destroys an interface `if` and frees auxiliary memory.

Object Migration

If we want to (re-)distribute a grid we have to transfer objects from some processors to some others. In the given example triangles are such objects. Note that dependent objects like corner nodes and side edges of a triangle have to be copied or moved additionally. The distribution algorithm can call the following operations:

- `void copy($t obj, int dest, void dep_f($t));`
  copies `obj` to processor `dest`. If further objects depend on `obj`, they possibly have to be copied or moved, too. That can be specified inside the function `dep_f`, which will be executed at last.

- `void delete($t obj);`
  deletes `obj`.

- `void move($t obj, int dest, void dep_f($t));`
  is a composition of `copy` and `delete`.

Clearly, if we execute copying or deleting immediately, we obtain communication overhead. A better approach is to collect all necessary data at first and then communicate in one step. Thus, we need the skeleton

`void execute_transfer(...)`

to send and receive all collected data, to delete objects, and to resolve dependencies. Further, the coupling tables have to be updated to keep consistency.

Object Identification

Turning back to our example, it is too expensive to generate the grid on one processor and then distribute parts of it to the others. To avoid this bottleneck we involve all processors in the generation process. After that we have to locate copies of the same object, for example nodes with the same coordinates, on different processors and have to assign them the same gid. Furthermore, the coupling table has to be updated. As for object migration we first collect all identification instructions and then evaluate them in one step:

- `void identify($t obj, int p, $t2 crit_f($t));`
  inserts necessary information in a table for the identification of `obj` with its copy on processor `p` with the criterion computed by `crit_f`.

- `void execute_identification(void);`
  sends and receives all identification information, adapts gid, and updates the coupling table, if both objects satisfy the given criterion.

4 Comparison of Implementations

We have implemented the skeletons and a small numeric application [c] on a PC-Cluster with 8 processor nodes using MPI [8]. We have compared our implementation with the one based on DDD [1]. In both programs the grid was generated on one processor and then divided into parts of equal size and mapped onto the others by object migration. Additionally, we have implemented a parallel grid generation on all processors, which is followed by an object identification phase. In all cases a virtual interface between distributed nodes was used during the iteration phase to add all residuals on the copies of the same node. The computation ends either after 2000 iteration steps or after the maximum of the residuals on all nodes is lower than 10^{-8}. In our implementations this maximum was computed after every 100 steps by calling the skeleton `fold` as mentioned above.

We have measured the run-times of the test programs for grid sizes between 50×50 and 360×360 on 1 to 8 processors. Additionally, we present the run-times of the object identification based program for a grid size of one million nodes on 4 and 8 processors. In the remaining cases the memory is too small to store the grid. The absolute run-times in seconds are given in Table 1, where bold entries stand for the times of the Skil program with object identification, roman font entries denote the times of the skeleton based implementation with object migration, and entries in italics represent the times of the DDD-based program using object migration.

First, it is easy to recognize that the Skil program based on object identification is much better than the other Skil program, if the programs run on more than one processor. We can even observe an acceleration of $30\% - 70\%$. Furthermore, the speedup rate of our implementations is rather good. If the grid is big enough, we can observe that the average factor of acceleration of the object identification based program is 1.85, if the number of processors grows with factor two. However, even if the DDD-based implementation has

---

[c]solution of the Laplace equation on a single uniform tringulated grid

#procs	50 × 50	100 × 100	264 × 217	360 × 360	1000 × 1000
1	**5.35**	**45.86**	**263.11**	**597.79**	—
	5.35	45.86	1263.11	597.79	—
	5.57	*46.30*	*276.34*	*615.81*	—
2	**3.19**	**22.31**	**156.99**	**307.02**	—
	5.09	31.58	201.51	400.11	—
	4.46	*26.06*	*162.13*	*353.85*	—
4	**2.73**	**12.99**	**78.73**	**184.68**	**1345.75**
	3.67	17.96	101.01	228.16	—
	5.28	*19.44*	*317.43*	*1416.48*	—
8	**3.30**	**7.77**	**38.32**	**96.81**	**639.20**
	3.99	11.70	65.78	148.71	—
	8.28	*16.16*	*113.56*	*433.27*	—

Table 1. Run-time results [**bold: distribution via identification**; roman: distribution with migration; *italic: DDD-based*]

a good speedup rate from one processor to two processors, it has a terrible slow-down from two to four processors. We suppose that this behavior results from an erroneous programming of the low-level communication mechanism. If we restrict our attention to the two processor case, we note that the Skil program based on object migration is somewhat slower than the DDD-based counterpart. With a reasonable grid size and enough processors this difference is smaller than 25%. This is caused by the declarative instead of the imperative paradigm, which leads in general to smaller and better readable programs. The price we have to pay are small losses in efficiency [3].

Although DDD uses the idea of encapsulating parallel aspects, the skeleton-based program has several advantages. First, the declarative program design given by the functional features of skeletons makes the code easier to understand and shorter. For instance, the skeletons can be called with any kind of object together with simple functions for accessing the object data as parameters. On the other hand, in DDD we must confirm types and sizes of object data manually. Additionally, in C we have to use "function handling" to simulate the higher-order feature in a very complicated manner. This disadvantages are caused by the imperative paradigm, that doesn't give any better possibility to manage these problems. Another advantage of our implementation is the reuse of code components, for example the generic list type that can be instantiated to any type of entry, or the skeleton `fold` that provides it functionality not only for the computation of maximal residual values, but also for any kind of data that have to be folded on a grid.

5 Conclusions and Future Work

We have presented algorithmic skeletons for coping with communication whenever distributed objects occur. The skeletons fit in three categories: communication via virtual interfaces, migration of (dynamic) data, and identification of distributed objects. Together with the existing skeleton fold we have used the skeletons in a numerical application. Furthermore, we have compared our implementation with another one written in the low-level imperative language C with respect to run-time and concepts. The results we have obtained support the idea that the use of skeletons leads to efficient programs, which are smaller and easier to understand than comparable low-level implementations.

The next step is to design and implement a multigrid solver with adaptive grid refinement for a "real word"-application using the presented skeletons. We want to investigate if such a project can be implemented in Skil with comparable efficiency but with less programming effort compared to a low-level implementation.

References

1. Birken, K. Rhle, R. (1995). *Dynamic Distributed Data: Efficient, Portable and Easy To Use*, In: Proceedings of the International Conference ParCo95, Gent, Belgium.
2. Botorog, G.H. Kuchen, H. (1998). *Efficient High-Level Parallel Programming*, Theoretical Computer Science, Vol 196, No. 1-2, pp. 71-107.
3. Briggs, W. L. (1987). *A Multigrid Tutorial*. Philadelphia: SIAM.
4. Cole, M.I. (1989). *Algorithmic Skeletons: Structured Management of Parallel Computation*. London: Pitman/MIT Press.
5. Kuchen, H., Plasmeijer, R., Stoltze, H. (1994). *Efficient Distributed Memory Implementation of a Data Parallel Functional Language*. In: Proceedings of PARLE '94, LCNS 817, pp 464-477. Springer, Berlin.
6. McCormick, S. (1989). *Multilevel Adaptive Methods for Partial Differential Equations*. Frontiers in Applied Mathematics, Vol 6. Philadelphia: SIAM.
7. Snir, M. Otto, S. Huss-Lederman, S. Walker, D. and Dongorra, J. (1998). *MPI: The Complete Reference, Vol. 1, The MPI Core, 2nd ed.* Cambridge MA: MIT Press.

EXPERIMENTS IN PARALLEL EVOLUTIONARY PARTITIONING

HENDRIK SCHULZE, REINER HAUPT, KLAUS HERING

Universität Leipzig, Institut für Informatik,
Augustusplatz 10-11, D-04109 Leipzig, Germany
email:{hendrik,haupt,hering} @informatik.uni-leipzig.de

Parallelization of logic simulation based on a replicated worker principle allows significant acceleration of functional verification in microprocessor design. Corresponding hardware model partitioning itself is an interesting subject for parallelization. In this paper we consider the application of Parallel Evolutionary Algorithms in the framework of a 2-level partitioning scheme. Applying a multiple subpopulation approach that permits various communication strategies we have reached promising experimental partitioning results for IBM S/390 processor models with more than 2 million elements at register-transfer and gate level.

1 Introduction

Due to challenging technological capabilities the complexity of VLSI designs is growing rapidly. Therefore, the use of verification tools in all design phases is unavoidable. Simulation is a very important but time-extensive verification method for the logic design of microprocessor structures. Based on the message-passing paradigm, we have developed a parallelization approach concerning particular logic simulation processes for functional verification[3]. Within a parallel simulation, several co-operating simulator instances run on a loosely-coupled system, each of them handling a part of a complex hardware model (replicated worker principle). The efficiency of the parallel simulation is essentially influenced by the corresponding model partitioning which is related to a NP-hard graph partitioning problem. Due to the complexity of processor models under consideration and a special cost function based on a formal model of parallel cycle simulation[4] we generally apply a 2-level partitioning strategy. Thereby, model partitioning appears as bottom-up clustering starting from possibly overlapping elementary model parts called cones. During a fast prepartitioning step cones are combined to super-cones. Prepartitioning represents a compromise between the advantage of reducing the problem complexity for the following partitioning step and a restriction of the solution space that lets one expect suboptimal partitioning results. Within our strategy prepartitioning establishes the precondition for the successful application of *Evolutionary Algorithms*[6] in final partitioning.

In Chapter 2 we describe the application of Evolutionary Algorithms in the field of model partitioning. A complex partitioning example is considered and a short retrospect of our previous work on Partitioning Algorithms is provided. The next chapter outlines advantages of the *multiple subpopulation approach* which naturally leads to *Parallel Evolutionary Partitioning Algorithms* (PEPAs). These algorithms are subject of Chapter 4. Selected experimental results concerning migration strategies and a special asynchronous communication mechanism called *lazy communication* are presented. Finally, in Chapter 5 conclusions are given.

2 Evolutionary Partitioning Algorithms

Using Evolutionary Algorithms we apply principles of the biological evolution theory to the field of computer science to tackle combinational optimization problems. Our *Evolutionary Partitioning Algorithms* (EPAs) work over a set (population) of individuals, which are represented by their genetic code describing a hardware model partition. Each evolution cycle starts with recombination (crossover) where pairs of individuals produce a set of offspring by reproducing and mixing their genetic code fragments[8]. Additionally, the genetic code is changed with a weak probability by a mutation operator. The new individuals are evaluated by a *fitness function*[1] which estimates the *parallel simulation time* per clock-cycle for the corresponding partitioned processor model. The best individuals, resulting from the offspring and a part of the parent generation, are selected to establish the following generation. During the evolution process the population improves its average fitness and converges towards the global optimum.

Due to the complexity of processor models under consideration the EPAs are embedded in a *2-level partitioning strategy*[3] in the context of our special partitioning problem. Combining cones as basic elements to super-cones at the first partitioning level (prepartitioning step) the problem complexity is drastically reduced but also the possibility to find acceptable solutions is restricted. At the first level, a fast and effective algorithm (STEP) is applied which makes use of special knowledge concerning the internal representation of the VLSI models. Based on this prepartitioning the number of elements to be partitioned is enormously reduced, from up to millions of cones at the first level to hundreds or thousands of super-cones at the second level.

At the second level super-cones are merged to a final partition, the set of blocks. Our partitioning aim (minimization of the partition-bound parallel simulation time) is related to a complicated cost function of a partitioning applied to a hypergraph representing a combination of an overlap and communication hypergraph the nodes of which are identified by the super-cones[1].

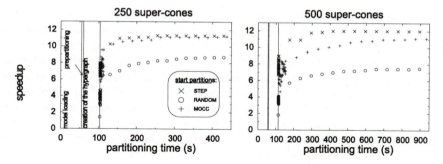

Figure 1. Complete partitioning procedure (model loading, prepartitioning, hypergraph creation, production of start population, EPAs) for 2 different numbers of super-cones and 3 different algorithms (STEP, RANDOM, MOCC) creating start partitions with 16 blocks at the second level. For all partitions of the initial population and the best individual per each 50th generation the speedup dependent on the partitioning time is shown.

Because of this complicated cost function, conventional partitioning tools as for instance METIS[5] are not applicable in our case. An intuitive way to get an acceptable partition at the second level is to produce a set of random partitions as initial population for the application of EPAs using the cost function as fitness function. But, the fitness landscape considered has many local minima and is rather jagged. Our intention was to include special model knowledge using several parameterized initial partitioning algorithms like MOCC, nBCC and STEP[3] to prepare an initial population with many rather good but concerning its genetic variety very different individuals. Hence, the partition quality at the beginning of the evolution is already a higher one than using random partitions. Simultaneously, we have an almost homogeneous distribution of individuals inside the search space which leads to a high improvement potential for evolution. In Fig. 1 examples for a full partitioning procedure[a] in dependence on the time consumption are shown including a constant phase comprising model loading, a short prepartitioning step and the creation of the hypergraph. The relative time slice for these phases is reduced with an increasing number of super-cones. For the two diagrams of Fig. 1 partition-bound speedup[b] values yielded by three different partitioning procedures are shown, each with 40 individuals using STEP, MOCC and RANDOM algorithms for

---

[a]concerning an IBM S/390 processor model with 2,7 million elements on gate level
[b]If not stated otherwise, throughout the paper *speedup* means the ratio between sequential simulation time (concerning the complete hardware model) and partition-bound parallel simulation time (to express the partition quality).

the initial population, respectively. In comparison to the evolution phase, which consumes the major part of overall partitioning time, the production of the initial population is very fast. For both diagrams, using knowledge-based algorithms (MOCC, STEP) the partitions of the initial populations are significantly better than those produced by RANDOM. Additionally, the partitions of initial populations based on MOCC and STEP provide an improvement potential by EPA application similar to that of randomly produced partitions. For all further experiments we use 250 super-cones, 16 blocks and the MOCC algorithms to generate the initial population. Furthermore, the processor model mentioned above is chosen in all cases.

Alternatively to EPAs as collective optimization methods, many single partitions can be produced and improved independently from another, followed by the choice of the best partition for a succeeding parallel simulation. For our purposes, we have developed iterative improvement algorithms such as TABU SEARCH and a FIDUCCIA-MATTHEYSES –like algorithm which handle single partitions. In contrast to EPAs, these algorithms strongly depend on the initial partition. Hence, if one performs a definite number of trials (containing an initial and improvement partitioning algorithm) no guaranty is given to get a final partition with acceptable quality. This main disadvantage is overcome using EPAs. Especially due to the effect of the recombination operator, EPAs almost always provide a sufficiently good final partition if the initial population is big and genetically diverse enough.

To achieve better partitioning results in shorter time using EPAs, we have integrated the concept of *superposition*[1] into the evolution strategy. Introducing a *local search operator*[2] based on an adaptation of an iterative partitioning algorithm of FIDUCCIA-MATTHEYSES we have enriched our EPAs to a hybrid technique. Both features work efficiently if the fitness function is very complex with many local minima as it is in our case. Using a *dynamic fitness function*[7] which includes an additional generation-dependent term favouring partitions with a higher potential of improvement especially at the beginning of the evolution, also better results are obtained.

In addition to that, a promising way to increase the probability to find a solution near the global optimum in a rich-structured fitness landscape is to broaden the population concerning the search space using a multiple subpopulation approach with an extended number of individuals.

3   Multiple Subpopulation Approach

The multiple subpopulation approach is based on the island model, a population genetic approach. Therein the individuals of one big population are distributed to n subpopulations. For each subpopulation a local evolution is computed. After a dedicated number of generations a few individuals can migrate to other subpopulations and translate their genetic code by proliferation. These migrating individuals are not integrated into the other subpopulation but can leave some genetic improvements by creating offspring with an individual from the target subpopulation. Applying this approach it is possible to get better optimization results than with one big population. This can be explained by the fact that, at early evolution time, a suboptimal individual can dominate the complete population and force the other individuals to remain in its surroundings. In our approach the isolation of the subpopulations and selective migration evade the mentioned disadvantage. Using the multiple subpopulation approach acceptable results can be found in shorter time, better results are found and the evolution converges with more reliability.

4   Parallel Evolutionary Partitioning Algorithms

Local evolution processes within a multiple subpopulation approach give a natural way to parallelize Evolutionary Partitioning Algorithms, using the same loosely-coupled system as target hardware where after partitioning the corresponding parallel logic simulation will be done. The subpopulations can be distributed to several nodes of the parallel hardware. Our implementation of the Parallel Evolutionary Partitioning Algorithms[8] (PEPAs) realizes migration by message passing, using a MPI library.

Several subpopulation approaches differ especially in their migration strategies. The PEPA implementation includes data structures which facilitate a dynamic and highly effective communication and allow to adjust all parameters relevant for migration, e.g. the number of migrating individuals, the communication structure between the single subpopulations and the period between migrations.

Based on our PEPA implementation we have examined a great variety of communication strategies. In the course of our experiments[c] the best partitioning results have been reached using a loosely connected communication structure and a static migration of 1%-30% of the individuals after every 1st up to 5th generation. Experimental results for examples with 8 subpopulations (each containing 40 individuals) are given in Table 1. Generally, if more individuals migrate they should do it in longer intervals. If communication is too strong, some suboptimal individuals can dominate all subpopulations and

---

[c] 8000 experiments have been done on an IBM SP2 using up to 112 nodes. Every experiment has been started 16 times with different initializations of the random number generator.

Table 1. Speedup related to special migration topologies (left). Speedup for selected migration strategies concerning migration frequency and number of migrating individuals (right).

Topology	Speedup after generation	
	250	500
Ring	11,36	11,39
Matrix	11,17	11,38
Torus	11,15	11,36
Star	11,88	11,29
AllToAll	10,86	11,17

Number of migrating individuals	Period between migrations (counted in generations)			
	1	5	10	25
	Speedup after 250 generations			
1	10,97	10,82	10,76	10,59
5	**11,03**	10,86	10,73	10,63
10	10,94	10,99	10,91	10,62
20	10,95	10,96	10,96	10,82

slow down the whole evolution. Compared to the huge expense for executing the fitness function (95% of the PEPA runtime) the communication overhead nearly disappears.

Our PEPAs include a special kind of asynchronous communication called *lazy communication*. Load influences and the heterogeneity of a workstation

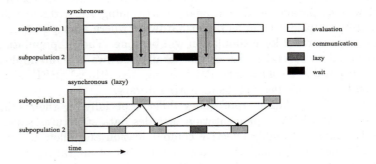

Figure 2. Synchronous vs. lazy communication.

cluster can cause PEPAs to wait at communication points. Lazy communication avoids such waiting periods by using nonblocking send and receive functions of the MPI-library. Before starting a new communication (sending individuals from one subpopulation to another) the success of the last communication to the same subpopulation is requested. If the last communication has not yet been successful, the new communication is rejected and evolution is going on without sending individuals (cf. Fig. 2).

Experiments show that evolution results don't get worse, if up to 35% of all communication actions fail (see Table 2). The lazy communication

Table 2. Dependence of the partition quality on communication loss.

communication loss	0%	5%	10%	20%	30%	40%	50%	60%
average speedup	12,26	12,3	12,28	12,32	12,38	11,56	11,35	11,12

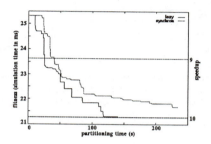

Figure 3. With 1 of 8 nodes slowed down by 50%, PEPAs on a ring topology using lazy communication reach the same fitness value as in the synchronous case in shorter time.

approach allows to use heterogeneous workstation clusters efficiently without implementing dynamic load balancing algorithms (see Fig. 3).

For the same IBM S/390 processor model as used in Fig. 1 PEPAs resulted in partitions about 10%-20% better (expressed in terms of the fitness function) than related EPA results. Compared to EPAs, generally it took PEPAs significantly less partitioning time to produce final partitions (cf. Fig. 4).

5 Conclusions

In the framework of a hierarchical strategy we have successfully applied Evolutionary Algorithms to the field of model partitioning for logic simulation in VLSI design. Based on a multiple subpopulation approach, in this paper we have presented Parallel Evolutionary Partitioning Algorithms taking advantage of dynamic communication structures and a special type of asynchronous (lazy) communication. Because of the small communication overhead and the potential of lazy communication these algorithms work very efficiently, even on a heterogeneous workstation cluster. By means of an IBM S/390 processor model we have exemplified that the parallel approach leads to better partitioning results in significantly shorter time.

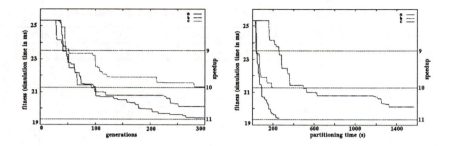

Figure 4. Partitioning results with a) PEPAs (8 subpopulations with 40 individuals and 100 children each) b) EPAs (320 individuals and 800 children) c) EPAs (40 individuals and 100 children) related to the number of generations and the partitioning time.

References

1. R. Haupt *et al*, Hierarchical Model Partitioning for Parallel VLSI-Simulation Using Evolutionary Algorithms Improved by Superpositions of Partitions, in *Proc. of EUFIT'97, Volume 1*, pages 804–808, (Verlag Mainz, 1997).
2. R. Haupt *et al*, Integration of a Local Search Operator into Evolutionary Algorithms for VLSI-Model Partitioning, in *Proc. of EUFIT'98, Volume 1*, pages 377–381, (Verlag Mainz, 1998).
3. K. Hering *et al*, Hierarchical Strategy of Model Partitioning for VLSI-Design Using an Improved Mixture of Experts Approach, in *Proc. of PADS'96*, pages 106–113, (IEEE Computer Society Press, Los Alamitos).
4. K. Hering, Parallel Cycle Simulation, *Tech. Report 13*, (Dept. of. Computer Science, Leipzig University, 1996).
5. G. Karypis and V. Kumar, MeTiS: Unstructured Graph Partitioning and Sparse Matrix Ordering System (1995).
6. I. Rechenberg, *Evolutionsstrategie - Optimierung technischer Systeme nach Prinzipien der biologischen Information*, (Fromman Verlag, Freiburg, 1973).
7. H. Schulze *et al*, Dynamic Fitness Function for Parallel Evolutionary Partitioning Algorithms in the Context of Parallel Logic Simulation, in *Proc. of EUFIT'99*, (1999).
8. H. Schulze, Entwicklung, Untersuchung und Implementierung von Algorithmen für die Modellpartitionierungskomponente parallelMAP, *Diplomarbeit*, (Leipzig University, Germany, 1998).

MG – A TOOLBOX FOR PARALLEL GRID ADAPTION AND IMPLEMENTING UNSTRUCTURED MULTIGRID SOLVERS

JÖRG STILLER AND WOLFGANG E. NAGEL

Center for High Performance Computing (ZHR)
Dresden University of Technology, D-01062 Dresden, Germany
E-mail: {stiller,nagel}@zhr.tu-dresden.de

We investigate parallel grid adaption and multigrid solvers based on the software system *MG*. Our results demonstrate the scalability of parallel grid adaption up to 512 processors and multigrids consisting of more than 10^8 tetrahedral elements. For the first time, we also present results obtained with a finite element multigrid solver based on *MG*. Though still under development, this solver proves to be an efficient tool for solving advection-diffusion problems.

1 Introduction

Adaptive multigrid methods comprise one of the most powerful approaches for solving partial differential equations. Their linear complexity makes them particularly well suited for "real world" problems. Unfortunately, the parallel implementation of these methods is a pretty complex task. Various projects have been devoted to aspects of unstructured grid solvers, grid adaption, parallelization techniques and multigrid methods [1–11]. However, only a few of these are concerned with parallel adaptive multigrid methods [2,9,11].

We have developed the software system *MG* (**MultiGrids**) which offers a lightweight interface for implementing parallel adaptive multigrid solvers [9]. *MG* provides methods for generating and adapting distributed multigrids as well as parallel intergrid transfer operators. The adaption algorithm includes a unique load balancing procedure which guarantees a uniformly balanced multigrid. Each load balancing step yields a set of independent multi-constraint graph partitioning problems which are solved in parallel. The current version of *MG* consists of less than 10000 lines of Fortran 90 code. All interprocessor communication is based on MPI.

In this paper, we focus on the following two topics: The adaption of distributed multigrids and parallel multigrid methods for advection-diffusion problems. For more details concerning the design principles and the implementation of *MG* we refer to [9].

2 Adaption of distributed multigrids

Efficient methods for adapting distributed multigrids are the basic foundation for the implementation of parallel adaptive multigrid solvers. *MG* supports multigrids consisting of tetrahedral cells. Curved boundaries are approximated by means of a quadratic rational interpolation method. In order to maintain optimal complexity in case of strongly local grid refinement, we have adopted the concept of *local grids* proposed by Bastian et al. [2].

2.1 Global grid refinement

First we consider the global refinement of a grid covering a cubic domain. The initial grid consisting of 27 nodes and 48 cells was refined using 5, 6, or 7 refinement cycles. Depending on the number of cycles, the resulting multigrid contained about 0.32/2.46/19.4 million nodes and 1.80/14.4/115 million cells, respectively. A simple, geometry based partitioner was used in this case. Figure 1a depicts the multigrid after two cycles. Figures 1b–c show the results of a test series performed on a Cray T3E-600 system. Using all 512 processors, it took about 12 seconds to create a multigrid of 115 million cells (Fig. 1b). As expected, the parallel efficiency degrades when the number of processors is increased in a fixed size problem (Fig. 1c). On the other hand, the same results clearly demonstrate the scalability of our approach.

2.2 Adaptive grid refinement

As a more realistic test case involving curved boundaries and local grid refinement, a rectangular domain with a cylindrical hole was considered. The initial grid consisting of 256 nodes and 766 cells was generated with *NETGEN* [12]. Using up to seven adaption cycles, the grid was locally refined in the vicinity of the cylinder. For dynamic load balancing we used a newly developed recursive procedure which has been shown to yield almost uniformly balanced multigrids [9]. For each grid level to be partitioned, this procedure leads to a set of independent multi-constraint graph partitioning problems which are solved in parallel using *Metis* [13]. Fig. 2a illustrates the multigrid after three adaption cycles. The final multigrids contained approx. 0.136/0.517/2.1 million nodes and 0.621/0.247/9.84 million cells after 5/6/7 cycles, respectively.

Fig. 2b shows the measured execution times. For example, on 256 processors, less than six seconds were needed for generating an adapted multigrid consisting of approx. 10 million cells (cycle 7). The obtained parallel efficiencies (Fig. 2c) are acceptable, but not as high as in the case of global grid refinement.

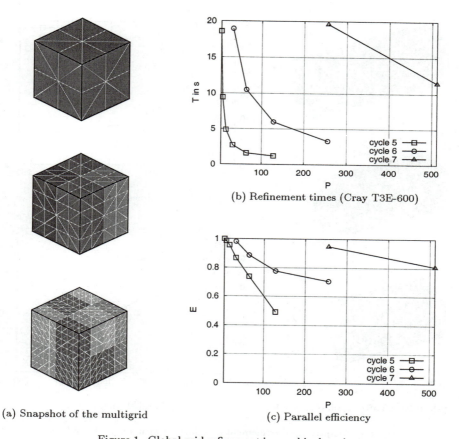

(b) Refinement times (Cray T3E-600)

(a) Snapshot of the multigrid

(c) Parallel efficiency

Figure 1. Global grid refinement in a cubic domain

3 Parallel multigrid solver

Moreover, we have implemented a multigrid solver for the scalar advection-diffusion equation,

$$\frac{\partial u}{\partial t} + \mathbf{a} \cdot \nabla u = \nu \nabla^2 u, \tag{1}$$

on top of *MG*. For discretization we used the Galerkin/least-squares method [14] with piece-wise linear elements in space, and a two-stage Runge-Kutta method for time integration. The discrete problem can be solved using either

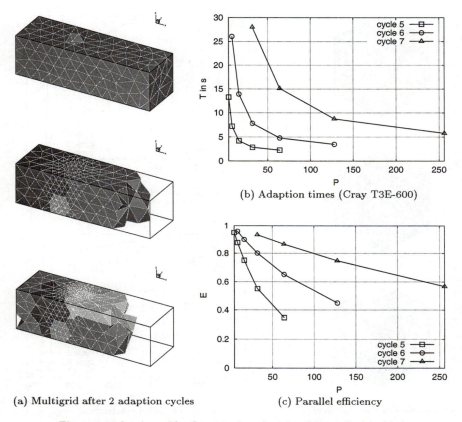

(a) Multigrid after 2 adaption cycles

(b) Adaption times (Cray T3E-600)

(c) Parallel efficiency

Figure 2. Adaptive grid refinement in a domain with a cylindrical hole

a Jacobi iteration or a full approximation storage multigrid method [15]. In the latter case, the Jacobi iteration serves as the smoother and as the coarse grid solver.

3.1 Diffusion problem

As the first test case for the multigrid solver we considered the following diffusion problem:

$$\frac{\partial u}{\partial t} = \nabla^2 u \qquad \text{in } \Omega = \{\mathbf{x} \in \mathbb{R}^3 : 1 < |\mathbf{x}| < 2\}, \qquad (2)$$

Level	Δx	cells	nodes	ε
1	1	689	255	1.4967E-01
2	1/2	5512	1448	4.4212E-02
3	1/4	44096	9410	1.1844E-02
4	1/8	352768	66930	3.0961E-03
5	1/16	2822144	510000	8.0983E-04

Table 1. Grid characteristics and spatial discretization error ε

with boundary conditions

$$u = 1 \quad \text{for} \quad |\boldsymbol{x}| = 1, \qquad \frac{\partial u}{\partial \boldsymbol{n}} = -\frac{1}{2} \quad \text{for} \quad |\boldsymbol{x}| = 2, \tag{3}$$

and initial condition

$$u(\boldsymbol{x}, 0) = 0 \quad \text{for} \quad 1 < |\boldsymbol{x}| \le 2. \tag{4}$$

The exact solution of (2–4) depends only on $r = |\boldsymbol{x}|$, and t. It can be explicitly stated for the limit case $t \to \infty$:

$$u_\infty(r) = 2/r - 1 \tag{5}$$

The problem was solved numerically using different solution techniques on multigrids composed of one to five grid levels (Tab. 1). The measured discretization errors confirm the second order convergence of the linear finite element method. Furthermore, the execution times clearly demonstrate the linear complexity of our multigrid solver (Fig. 3). For solving the steady state problem, it outperforms the best single grid solver (implicit Jacobi with cascadic grid refinement) by a factor of 33, and the standard explicit 2-stage Runge-Kutta method by a factor of more than 2000.

For parallel simulations, two different partitioning strategies were investigated:

1. $P_l = \min(4^{l-1}, P)$, i.e. a gradually increasing number of partitions

2. $P_l = P$, i.e. all grid levels are distributed over all available processors

The parallel efficiencies resulting from these strategies are shown in Fig. 4. Obviously, for this problem a significantly higher efficiency was achieved with the second strategy. However, this aspect should be investigated more detailed in future work.

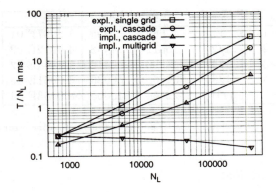

Figure 3. Computational complexity of different methods

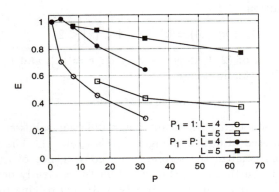

Figure 4. Parallel efficiencies for the diffusion problem

3.2 Advection-diffusion problem

In our second test problem, **a** represents the velocity of an incompressible potential flow around a spherical obstacle with radius R. The diffusion co-efficient is set to $\nu = a_\infty R/10$, where a_∞ is the velocity of the undisturbed flow. Further, we set $u = 1$ at the obstacle surface, and $u = 0$ at inflow boundaries. At outflow boundaries, homogeneous Neumann conditions are assumed. The computational domain is sketched in Fig. 5. The problem was solved using a globally refined multigrid consisting of 1.52 million cells and 264 thousand nodes on the finest level. This resolution was sufficient for cap-

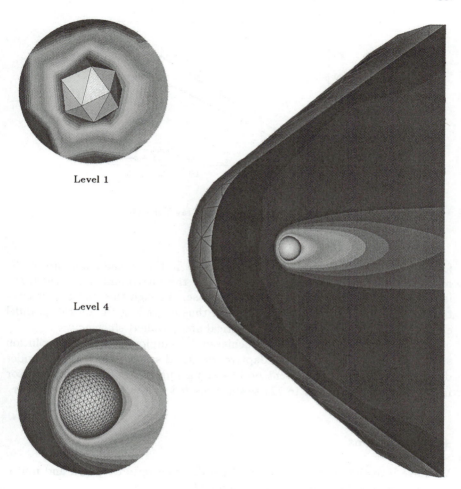

Level 1

Level 4

Figure 5. Computational domain and solution (flow from left to right)

turing the sharp boundary layer evolving at the surface of the obstacle. As in the previous example, the best performance was obtained by employing the multigrid solver with the second partitioning strategy $(P_l = P)$. The achieved parallel speedup is given in Fig. 6 for both, the overall solution procedure and a single time step. Despite of the excellent efficiency of a single step, the total parallel efficiency remains restricted to values between 0.7 and 0.8 (except

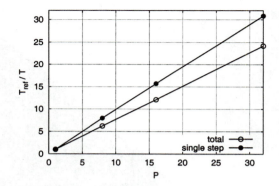

Figure 6. Parallel speedup (Cray T3E-900)

for $P = 1$). The reason for this behavior lies in the cascadic startup of the method: Starting with a single coarse grid, the final number of grid levels is reached only after the initial startup phase. Though this phase is characterized by a lower parallel efficiency, and thus degrading the overall parallel efficiency, it enhances the total (numerical and parallel) efficiency.

A further speedup could be achieved by employing adaptive solution strategies. In a first test, the adaptive multigrid solver, which is still under development, solved the present problem on a single Cray T3E-900 processor in 194 seconds, compared to 721 seconds needed by the non-adaptive solver.

4   Conclusions

We have investigated the efficiency of parallel multigrid adaption and multigrid solvers based on the software system *MG*.

The obtained results demonstrate the scalability of parallel grid adaption up to 512 processors and multigrids consisting of more than 100 million tetrahedral elements. In case of global grid refinement, parallel efficiencies of 90% could be achieved for any problem size investigated. Though with slightly reduced parallel efficiency, the scalability was confirmed also for the more complex case of local grid refinement.

For the first time we presented results obtained with a finite element multigrid solver based on *MG*. Though still under development, this solver proves to be an efficient tool for solving advection-diffusion problems.

Acknowledgments

We wish to thank F. Hoßfeld from ZAM (Forschungszentrum Jülich) for supporting the scalability tests on the large T3E systems.

References

1. R. Bank, *PLTMG Users Guide. Version 7.0.* (SIAM, 1994).
2. P. Bastian *et al*, Comput Visual Sci **1**, 1, 27–40 (1997).
3. J. Bey. Finite-Volumen- und Mehrgitter-Verfahren für elliptische Randwertprobleme. (Teubner, Stuttgart, 1998).
4. B. Erdmann *et al*, *KASKADE-Manual.* Konrad-Zuse-Zentrum für Informationstechnik Berlin (1993).
5. J.E. Flaherty *et al*, Appl Num Math **26**, 241–263 (1998).
6. J.Z. Lou *et al* in *Proc. NASA HPCCP Comput. Aerosciences Workshop*, pp 241–246. (NASA Ames Research Center, Moffet Field, CA, 1999).
7. D.J. Mavriplis and S. Pirzadeh, NASA CR-1999-208999 (1999).
8. L. Oliker and R. Biswas, NAS Report 97–020, NASA Ames Research Center (1997).
9. J. Stiller *et al*, in *Proc. 9th SIAM Conf. Parallel Processing*, ed. B. Hendrickson *et al* (SIAM, 1999).
10. A. Vidvans *et al*, AIAA J. **32**, 3, 497–505 (1994).
11. G.W. Zumbusch, in *Proc. 9th SIAM Conf. Parallel Processing*, ed. B. Hendrickson *et al* (SIAM, 1999).
12. J. Schöberl. NETGEN – An advancing front 2d/3d-mesh generator based on abstract rules. Comput Visual Sci **1**, 1, 41–52 (1997).
13. G. Karypis and V. Kumar. *Metis. A Software Package for Partitioning Unstructured Graphs, Partitioning Meshes, and Computing Fill-Reducing Orderings of Sparse Matrices. Version 4.0.* Univ. Minnesota, Dep. Comput. Sci. / Army Research Center, Minneapolis (1998).
14. T.J.R. Hughes *et al*, Comput. Meth. Appl. Mech. Engrg **73**, 173–189 (1989).
15. A. Brandt, *Multigrid techniques: 1984 guide with applications to fluid dynamics*, GMD, Bonn (1984).

STW: SWITCH TIME WARP. A MODEL FOR ROLLBACK REDUCTION IN OPTIMISTIC PDES

REMO SUPPI, FERNANDO CORES, MARIA SERRANO, EMILIO LUQUE

Computer Science Department - University Autonoma of Barcelona – Spain
Remo.Suppi@uab.es E.Luque@cc.uab.es {Maria,Fernando}@aows10.uab.es

STW (Switch Time Warp) is a mechanism to limit the optimism of the TW (Time Warp) method. The proposed method achieves significant time/performance improvements for rollback reduction in optimistic parallel discrete event simulation (PDES).

The STW uses a cost function to decide if a process is running in overoptimistic state. The STW mechanism will decide the LP's execution order within the processor and the amount of CPU time to assign to a logical process to reduce the number of rollbacks.

1   Introduction

Parallel Discrete Event Simulation (PDES) model we consider is a set of logical processes (LP) that manage a distributed event list, updating their logical virtual clock values (LVT: Local Virtual Time), and are interrelated by timestamped messages. As each logical process may advance its simulation time independently, LP event rates are different, so may generate causality errors: future could affect the past. It is the simulation mechanism's responsibility to ensure that the events for each LP are processed in nondecreasing timestamp order (local causality) on the parallel simulation.

Time Warp (TW) algorithm is an optimistic mechanism (events are processed at each LP when they become available) that employs a *rollback* (in time) mechanism to take care of proper synchronisation. If an external event arrives with timestamp in the local past (*straggler message*), the system *rolls back* to a previous "safe" state, undoing the effects of the straggler message (*annihilation*). The protocol generates cancellation messages (*antimessages*) for those output messages already sent during the wrong simulation interval (*cancellation*) [5,2].

The main performance pitfall of TW lays on overoptimistic event execution that may lead to a massive *rollback* production, a communication overhead (high number of antimessages) and so, to an inefficient simulation. The unbounded optimism of TW has to be restricted to an amount that improves overall execution performance, controlling the costs for potential future rollbacks. However, optimism control must not be too restrictive, since the potential gain of optimism progression over conservative blocking could be lost.

Several approaches have been developed to solve this problem: the Moving Time Window [10], the Breathing Time Window [11], the Adaptive Time Wrap

Concurrency Control Algorithm [1], the Probabilistic Cost Expectation Function Protocol [3], or the PADOC Simulation Engine [4].

Our idea is that if we can not predict the optimum event sequence for the global system, then we could obtain the better possible efficiency avoiding rollback (and its dangerous side effects). Because this prediction generates a high computation cost, our approach attempts to limit the overoptimistic event execution applying an algorithm with local information on each processor and to reduce the CPU time of those LPs that are involved in rollback [9].

Section 2 and 3 describes the model and implementation of the solution named Switch Time Warp (STW) mechanism. In section 4, we describe the experimental work developed and we show the most relevant obtained results. Finally, we will present the conclusions and the future work on the subject.

2   The model description

The only factor that prevents TW for achieving its performance limit is a scheduling policy that chooses wrong messages while correct computation is waiting to be handled [6].

If we previously knew the complete event sequence of a simulation application, from a static analysis of the system, we may be able to obtain the optimal event processing rate relation of each process and its causal predecessors. With this information, we can calculate the theoretical event simulation order that minimise the rollback probability. Moreover, we may calculate an optimal initial process assignment onto the available nodes that, theoretically, provides a balanced initial situation.

Consider a simulation S_i where there are **n** processes in the simulation distributed on **k** (n≥k) processors. At real time **t** we may create a list of processors as $p_1(t)$, $p_2(t)$,.....,$p_k(t)$ such that **TS(p1(t)) ≤ TS(p2(t)) ≤........≤ TS(pk(t))**.

Where **TS(p_i(t))** is the timestamp of the event executed by processor **p_i** at time **t**. Clearly, if **$t_1 \neq t_2$**, then TS($p_i(t_1)$) may be different of TS($p_i(t_2)$). That is, the place of a processor in ordered list {$p_1(t)$, $p_2(t)$,.....,$p_k(t)$} may change as time changes [6].

If we are able to execute the processes that maintain this order, we can obtain no rollbacks in this run. The main problem of this is to know all TS of each processor (global information) used in the simulation S_i. Moreover, this sequence is no static (the processor can change the order in the list for next time).

As we are not able to have this global information, we have developed an algorithm which, using LP local and temporary available information, tries to approximate to the optimal model (execution without rollbacks). It is a similar problem to the optimal algorithm in memory page replacement used in virtual memory systems and its real implementations, as the Last Recent Used (LRU).

The STW mechanism reduces the priority to access to CPU time for a process involved in rollback or that have received and/or processed antimessages. The process is penalised and therefore it will not increase your LVT. This situation can be exploited by the other processes (predecessors) to increase their LVT ratio and in a future do not generate rollbacks onto the penalised process.

3 Implementation issues

Our model is based on the general case, where the number of LPs required for a simulation (n) do not match the number of processors available to do simulation (p). In this case, the maximum simulation speed can be achieved by a full occupation of the available processors, performing correct simulation work.

We are going to consider an initial given mapping, so we shall try to achieve the best performance for such configuration. At least three solutions are possible to avoid wrong computation: *to block the faster process, to modify the CPU time assigned to the processes to maximise the CPU occupation or to change LP assignment (mapping) on the processors.*

We propose a solution based in the second option. Our proposal includes a manager process in each processor to locally monitor the dynamic behaviour of the LPs assigned to it. The main task of this manager is optimise the CPU-time occupation by balancing the relative execution time of those LPs involved in *rollbacks*. A local processing of the available information within each node, instead of the global data knowledge and processing (required for the optimal model) limits the global communication overhead.

Once a certain threshold value respect to the number of rollbacks and antimessages is detected in an LP, the manager process will try to adequate the relative speed of the implied processes. The manager will slowing down the fastest process (giving it less CPU time not to further advance its LVT), and so accelerating slower LPs. The threshold value is the point to decide when is necessary to limit the optimism of the TW.

Let's consider n LPs allocated on each processor. Each LP within a node locally provides a **cost function** value, Fc_{LPi}. Overstepping a certain threshold (mentioned previously) value means that such LP_i is running too fast. Then the manager will penalise it (and not the others) on its CPU-time assignment, so the rest of LPs mapped onto the processor will benefit from it. In other words, the relative LP's speed is modified "on-the-fly". Each logical process (LP_i) within a node locally calculates its Fc_{LPi} during each event processing, and writes the value on a specific shared memory. The scheduler manager will take this value to compose the scheduling decision. If the value of Fc_{LPi} is over a certain value, the LP will be penalised. In this situation, the TW optimism is not allowed to continue running free and CPU- time assigned to LPs is rebalanced.

The algorithm is performed dynamically (taking into account new arriving messages), and it introduces a fixed computation time to the local simulation time. Moreover, it also allows dynamic creation of LPs during simulation time.

This function Fc_{LPi} is described as following: $\mathbf{Fc_{LPi} = (rb + a\text{-})\, /\, PT_i}$

Where: **rb** is the *number of rollbacks* in the LP during the last period of the simulation (a period is from last time that the process was penalised up to the actual instant), **a-** is the *number of antimessages* sent by the LP in last period of the simulation and $\mathbf{PT_i}$ *period time* (period time = actual time - last time that the process was penalised).

Because the value of the Fc_{LPi} only represents the behaviour of this process, the threshold value will be calculated using the deviation (DFc_i):

$$\mathbf{DFci = FcLPi\, /\, FcLPT - 1}$$

The value of Fc_{LPT} is calculated for each processor as $\mathbf{Fc_{LPT} = \Sigma\, Fc_{LPk}\, /\, (N_{LP} - 1)\, \forall\, k \neq i.}$ (N_{LP} is the number of LPs in the current processor).

In conclusion, DFc_i shows behaviour of this process with respect to the rest of LPs in the current processor. This value will decide if the process will be penalised or not. When the DFc_i value of the processes mapped onto a processor are maintained under a certain value, the STW manager does nothing. The CPU time scheduling algorithm, assign CPU-time to each process without any restriction. The result is an unlimited optimistic Time Warp execution.

When the DFc_i value of a process exceeds the threshold value, the STW manager takes care of the number of quantum of CPU to be given to the process, by assigning it to a certain lower priority queue. The process will be penalised (decreasing their execution priority) and the STW mechanism will decide the relation of CPU quantum for a normal process and the penalised process.

In order to decide "how much" this process will be penalised the VLP_i (Velocity of LP) is calculated:

$$\mathbf{VLPi = (m1\ Im + m2\ Om + m3\ rb + m4\ a\text{-})\, *\, DFci\, *\, ET\, /\, PTi}$$

Where: **Im** is the *number of input messages* and **Om** is the *number of output messages* for the process, **rb** is the *number of rollbacks* in the LP during the last period of the simulation, **a-** is *the number of antimessages* sent by the LP in last period of the simulation, $\mathbf{m_1}$, $\mathbf{m_2}$, $\mathbf{m_3}$, $\mathbf{m_4}$ are *constant values* that respectively weight the variables, $\mathbf{DFc_i}$ is the *deviation* for the process, **ET** is the *event time* (average time to generate/process an event) and $\mathbf{PT_i}$ *period time* (period time = actual time - last time that the process was penalised).

The influence of $\mathbf{m_1}$, $\mathbf{m_2}$, $\mathbf{m_3}$ and $\mathbf{m_4}$ will be analysed on the experimental framework. Is the value of VLPi is high the process will be penalised because this process spent CPU-time in wrong work: this work will be made again. The VLP_i includes the DFc_i value because it indicates the excess speed for this process. The ET is include to weight "how much time" this process have spent in wrong events.

When a set of events is processed, the rest of processes placed in low priority queues must be aged to guarantee that a process will stay penalised when the rest of processes have balanced their LVT advancement. The penalised process will have the chance to re-evaluate its Fc_{LPi} and to enter again in the prior group for execution.

The algorithm for STW is similar to the TW mechanism. The difference is that two new function calls have been added in order to update FcLPi and VLPi each time the process is executed. These functions are locally executed on the node, which add a fixed compute to all the processes The overhead added by this process is very low for the effective utilisation rate improvement obtained.

The STW was implemented for Unix™ systems (SunOS 5.0™) using PVM libraries. PVM (Parallel Virtual Machine) permits to work with a heterogeneous network as a distributed machine. This virtual system is totally transparent for the programmer. Details of PVM operation and experiences in their use can be found in [8]. In our design of the STW mechanism, using PVM library, we associate a Unix process for each LP in our PDES scheme. This LP is a node in the distributed simulation application and communicates with others LP using the PVM library functions.

Another important part of the implementation of the SWT mechanism is the integration with the CPU scheduler of the operating system. The SWT oversees the behaviour of all LP processes and change, using the VLP_i value, the priority of the process that have a DFc_i greater that the threshold. This penalised process will receive CPU time in function of the priority level. When this process receives CPU time, will update your DFc_i and VLP_i and the SWT manager will change or not the priority level for it.

4 Case study and results

In order to test our STW mechanism with other algorithms in an exhaustive form we have used simulation techniques. The main problem to validate a PDES mechanism is the number of LP and the number of processor necessary to make some statistics analysis. The simulation approach can be suitable in order to make some proves with a higher number of LP and processors. For this task, we have use the Parallel & Distributed Algorithm-Architecture Simulator (PandDAAS) developed by the UAB [12]. The distributed simulation is specified by an application graph (logical processes). These processes are modelling the processes of the real system under simulation. The application will reach their objective once may have been arrived a given goblal virtual time (GVT).

The selected graph to analyse the TW & STW algorithms (simulation and real execution) has been a ring graph. This graph has a set of nodes that receives input messages, generates internal events (using an exponential probability function) and send output messages (using a normal probability function).

The first step to make the comparative study between the TW and STW is to analyse the influence of the constant values. However, these values depend on the application environment. In our case study, the better results are obtained for $m_1=1$, $m_2=1$, $m_3=5$, $m_4=5$. Using these values, the threshold value has been analysed. A study of the different threshold values reflects that a deviation of up to 10% with respect to the average of the others processes is adequate to fire the STW mechanism [9].

With these parameters, we can compare the results obtained from simulations of TW and STW mechanisms. In the figure 1 and 2 can see the evolution of the GVT (Global Virtual Time) and LVT (Local Virtual Time) for each process and with both methods. The TW is used in figure 1 and we can see that the processes runs fast but they are constantly making rollbacks. In the figure 2, we see the effect of including the STW mechanism. It can be verified as now the fastest processes are penalised, permitting that the slowest can advance their LVT. The occasional peaks that appear in the figure are generated by penalised process when it returns to normal state. Table 1 shows the results between both methods in function of the time used by distributed simulation. We can verify that in either case the method STW reduces notably the execution time of the simulation.

The analysis in real environment (SunOS & PVM) libraries, we have used graphs with 5, 10 and 20 nodes. The average improvement of STW is 25%. This speedup is obtained from small PDES graphs (5, 10 y 20 LPs) due to the limitations of PVM and the memory of the processor pool. The differences of this results with simulation results can be attributed initially to the communication model of PVM (all messages are centralised by the PVM daemon and this daemon is not present in simulation runs). In this sense, a change of the communication model is necessary to obtain better results. The possibilities are use of the direct communication method of PVM or use another communication library with a different communication model (i.e. MPI [7]).

5   Conclusions and Future Work

In this paper, we have shown that here is an optimal theoretical relation among the implied process speed in parallel and distributed discrete event simulation (PDES), which achieves best performance results, avoiding rollback chain production in optimistic simulation mechanisms.

To overcome rollback overhead, a solution based on the idea of "limiting the optimism" has been implemented. We have proposed an implementation of a dynamic synchronisation method, based on balancing the implied LP relative speed (STW mechanism). Our STW mechanism goes after the best CPU-time assignment

406

of the processes mapped on a certain processor that allows the maximum optimism besides the best simulation time. This CPU occupation time for each allocated process is decided from the evaluation of a local cost function in simulation run time that will penalise the process or will allow free optimistic execution.

The future work is divided in two lines:

- Improvement of the real simulation environment: we need to make some extensive proves to analyse the influence of the communication model.
- Mapping of the processes: The STW has a limit when all process in a processor must be penalised because the slowest processes are assigned to others processors. In this case, a load balancing technique is necessary.

This work has been supported by the CICYT under contract TIC-98-0433

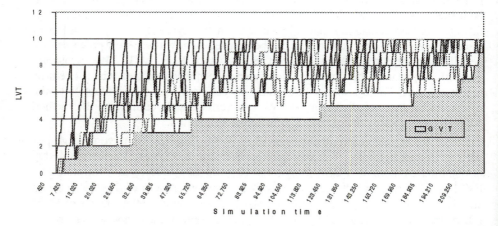

Figure 1. Lvt and Gvt evolution for Time Warp method (TW).

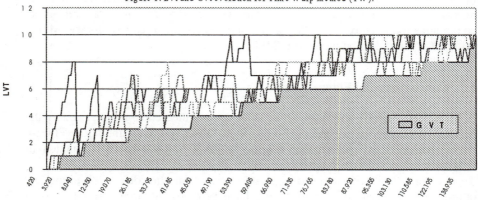

Figure 2. Lvt and Gvt evolution for Switch Time Warp method (STW).

Number of Processes	TW Simulation Time	STW Simulation Time	Improvement (%)
10	35368	14054	152
50	192907	126336	53
100	511615	349664	46

Table 1. STW & TW Simulation Time & STW improvement

6   References

1. Ball, D., and Hoyt, S., *The adaptive Time-Warp concurrency control algorithm.* Proc. SCS Multiconference on Distributed Simulation **22 1** (1990) pp. 174-177.
2. Ferscha A., *Parallel and Distributes Simulation of Discrete Event Systems.* Handbook of Parallel and Distributed Computing. McGraw-Hill (1995).
3. Ferscha A., Lüthi J., *Estimating Rollback Overhead for Optimism Control in Time Warp.* Proc. 28th Simulation Symposium, IEEE Press (1995) pp. 2-12.
4. Ferscha A., *Probabilistic Adaptive Direct Optimism Control in Time Warp.* Proc. 9th Workshop on Parallel and Distributed Simulation (1995) pp. 245-250.
5. Fujimoto. R.M., *Parallel Discrete Event Simulation.* Communications of the ACM **33 -10-** (October 1990) pp. 30-53.
6. Lin, Y-B., Lazowska, E., *Optimality considerations of "Time Warp" parallel simulation.* Proc. SCS Multiconference on Distributed Simulation **22, 1** (1990) pp. 29-34.
7. MPI: a message passing interface standard. MPI Forum. 94239, Computer Science Dept. University of Tennessee (April 1994).
8. PVM User's Guide. Oak Ridge Laboratory – University of Tennessee. ORNL/TM 1287 (September 1994).
9. Serrano M., Suppi R., Luque E., *Parallel Discrete Event Simulation: Rollback reduction in optimistic PDES.* Technical Report UAB (1999).
10. Sokol L.M., Briscoe D.P., and Wieland. A.P., *MTW: a strategy for scheduling discrete simulation events for concurrent execution.* Proc. SCS Multiconference on Distributed Simulation **19, 3** SCS International (July 1988) pp. 34-42.
11. Steinmann J.S., *Breathing Time Warp.* Proc. 7th Workshop on Parallel and Distributes Simulation, IEEE (1993) pp. 109-118.
12. PandDAAS - Parallel & Distributed Architecture-Algorithm Simulator - User's Guide, Caos, University Autonoma of Barcelona. www.caos.uab.es. (1999)

System Software and
Hardware Architecture

USING OPTIMAL PARTITION STRATEGIES FOR SKELETON ALLOCATION

S. ANTONELLI AND S. PELAGATTI

Dipartimento di Informatica, Corso Italia 40, I-56125 Pisa Italy
E-mail: antonell@di.unipi.it, susanna@di.unipi.it

In this paper, we formulate the allocation problem for skeleton programs, discuss its complexity and present a pseudo-polynomial strategy which solves the problem optimally. The complexity of the proposed strategy is $O(n^3 * S(P)^2)$ where n is the number of nodes in the task graph and $S(P)$ is a bound on the load on each processor. The strategy shows low execution time on typical skeleton programs.

1 Introduction

When executing a parallel program on a parallel architecture a critical problem to be solved is deciding the allocation of processes to processors. The goal is deciding such an assignment in order to optimize the response time of the system and/or the resource usage. In this paper, we focus on process allocation in parallel programs derived from skeleton-based parallel models. [6,8,12] In skeleton based models, a parallel computation is built by composing and nesting a small set of primitive structures, called *skeletons*. Typical skeletons are the *pipeline* skeleton, exploiting parallelism among different computation stages on a stream of tasks, or the *task farm* skeleton computing an independent pool of tasks on a set of identical worker processes. The implementation of a skeleton program is built by composing and expanding a set of parametric process networks (the *implementation templates*). Templates implement different skeletons on different target parallel architectures and are composed together to build the parallel implementation of the skeleton nesting defined by the user. The resulting parallel program (called the *skeleton program*) needs to be mapped efficiently on the target machine balancing the load of nodes and minimizing the communication delays.

The problem of mapping skeleton programs in an optimal way has not been addressed in the skeleton community yet. We propose a problem formalization in which the architecture is abstracted as a set of p identical processors with uniform communication costs among different processor pairs. This is sensible as technological factors are currently forcing a convergence of parallel architectures towards systems formed by a collection of essentially complete computers connected by a fast communication network. [7] Interaction between processors is done via explicit communication or through accesses to a shared address space. A skeleton program is modeled by a *task graph* with a node for each process and an edge for each pair of communicating processes. Weights are defined for nodes and edges of the task graph representing the amount of computation and communication required. In this setting, allocating a skeleton program on a given architecture means finding a partition of the corresponding task graph on the available processors in such a way that the overall completion time is minimized.

This allocation problem (or some close variants) has already been studied in the literature by different authors[4,10,13] even if usually for different architectural settings. The problem in its general formulation is NP-complete. [2] For the general model or its restrictions, different optimal algorithms and heuristics have been proposed in the literature. Bokhari[4] proposes two optimal polynomial algorithms which solve the problem for the case of a pipeline/chain of processes mapped on chains of processors and for trees of processes on host-satellite systems with the constraint that if a node is assigned to a satellite, all its children are assigned to the same satellite. Other authors[10,13] provide heuristics for arbitrary task graphs with slightly different assumptions and goals from the present work.

The paper is organized as follows. Sec. 2 introduces skeleton based parallel programming and the skeleton language p3l, formulates the skeleton allocation problem and discusses its complexity. Sec. 3 presents a pseudo-polynomial algorithm (UGA) which solves graph partitioning for *union graphs* (i.e., trees, cycles and constrained compositions of the two). Section 4 analyzes the structure of p3l skeleton programs and proposes an allocation strategy using UGA. Sec. 5 concludes the paper.

2 Allocating skeletal programs

In skeleton based languages, [6,8,12] a parallel computation is built by composing and nesting a small set of primitive structures, called *skeletons*. In this paper, we will focus on the skeleton language p3l. p3l[3,12] provides the following skeletons: the *pipeline* skeleton, exploiting parallelism among different computation stages on a stream of tasks; the *task farm* skeleton, computing an independent pool of tasks on a set of identical worker processes; the *loop* skeleton allowing the iteration of arbitrary skeleton nesting; and, a set of data-parallel skeletons (*map, reduce, scan, comp*) allowing data distribution/rearrangement and parallel computation on different parts of distributed data structures. A parallel application is defined by instantiating and nesting skeletons to build complex structures. We do not discuss the p3l programming model here, as it is not relevant for the skeleton allocation problem. The

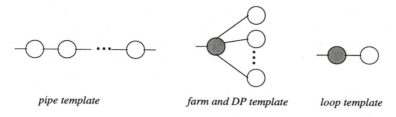

pipe template   *farm and DP template*   *loop template*

Figure 1. p3l templates: only white nodes can be further expanded with other templates.

interested reader may refer to[3,12] for details.

p3l skeleton programs are built from the templates shown in Fig. 1. In the picture, we see an abstract representation of the task graphs corresponding to the different templates. The node coloring shows the constraints on task graph composition due to template structure. All circles represent processes: gray circles are *control processes* and white circles are *user processes*. The dangling edges represent channels on which data are read and results are produced. In a pipeline, data are read from one end of the chain and results produced from the other end. In loops and farms, inputs and results are managed by a control process (the gray one) which takes care of load balancing between different executors and checks for the termination of the input task stream. Control processes are inherently sequential and cannot be further parallelized. User processes can be parallelized using any template. In this way, templates can be composed to build the implementation of any skeleton composition. We will discuss the rules governing template composition in detail in Sec. 4.

The p3l compiler[5] tunes the resource usage and performance of the different template instances to balance the load of each processor and minimize resource waste. This is accomplished using known properties of the skeletons and assuming an unbounded number of processors in the target machine. After the tuning phase, the resulting skeleton program needs to be mapped balancing the load of nodes and minimizing the communication delays.

The problem of allocating a skeleton program on a multiprocessor architecture can be formalized as follows. The program is modeled as a labeled *task graph* $G = (V, E)$ where $V = \{1, 2 \ldots n\}$ denotes the set of nodes and $E = \{a_1, a_2, \ldots, a_k\}$ the set of edges. Each node i represents a process and is labelled by an execution time $S(i)$. Each edge $a_k = [i, j]$ represents inter-processor communications and is labelled with a communication time $c(i, j)$. Direction of communications is not important so we define $c(i, j) = c(j, i)$ for each i and j. Skeleton processes are *all active during all the execution time,* thus the task graph G is undirected and communications can take place at any time during computation. The communication cost is zero if both nodes are allocated to the same processor. A parallel architecture is modeled as a set of p identical processors with uniform communication costs among different processor pairs. We suppose that the amount of computation that can be performed by a single processor is bounded by a value $S(P)$, such that $S(k) < S(P)$, for each k in V.

Def 1 *(skeleton allocation problem)* *The* skeleton allocation problem *consist in partitioning G in disjoint clusters and assign each cluster to a processor in such a way that: the computational cost on each processor do not exceed the threshold $S(P)$, the number of clusters do not exceed p and the sum of the edges among different clusters is minimized.*

More formally, we are looking for a partition Π of V in $V_1, \ldots, V_m$ disjoint subsets, such that the following three conditions hold: (1) $m \leq p$; (2) the sum of the computation costs in the same cluster V_i is less than $S(P)$ ($\sum_{k \in V_i} S(k) \leq S(P)$) and (3) the sum of inter processor communication costs, given by the sum of inter-cluster edges, is minimal (i.e. if $E' \subseteq E$ is the set of edges having their two endpoints in two different V_i, we minimize $\sum_{(i,j) \in E'} c(i,j)$). When $p \geq m$, the skeleton allocation problem becomes a *graph partitioning problem.* [9] The graph partitioning problem is NP-complete for $S(P) \geq 3$ and general graph structures, although for limited classes of graphs there exist algorithms of polynomial complexity. [4,9] However, for more complex graphs, we do not know any polynomial algorithm. An interesting algorithm solving the partitioning problem in pseudo-polynomial time for tree-structured graphs has been proposed by Lukes[11] (AT algorithm). Antonelli *et al*[1] generalize AT to partition a class of graphs built of trees and cycles (UGA algorithm). UGA operates on the graph structure to transform it into a sequence of trees which are partitioned using AT. Then, the results are combined to build the global result of the whole graph. In the next section, we formally define the class of graphs structures on which UGA works. Due to space limitation we cannot give an extensive description of the algorithm itself. The interested reader can refer to [1,11] for details.

3 Union Graphs and UGA

Consider n undirected connected graphs $G_i = (V_i, E_i)$, $i \in I = \{1, 2, \ldots n\}$. An undirected graph $G = (V, E)$ is called *union graph* of the n graphs G_i, if the G_i's are a partition of G, that is if G is connected, $V = \bigcup_i V_i$, $E = \bigcup_i E_i$ and $E_i \cap E_j = \emptyset$, $\forall i, j \in I$. We call *cut points* all the nodes in G connecting

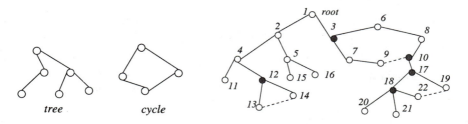

Figure 2. Base subgraph structures (tree and cycle) and a sample union graph (right).

two subgraphs.

The UGA[1] algorithm works on union graphs composed of only trees and cycles. A typical union graph of this class is shown in Fig. 2: dark nodes represent cut points. UGA works using a reference spanning tree of the graph (solid edges in Fig. 2) and a node numbering in which all children of a node in the reference spanning tree have label greater than the father. The root of the spanning tree is always considered a cut point. UGA inspects the cut points in decreasing order of labels. It uses AT to build a set of candidate partitions of each subtree rooted at a given cut point and a variant of AT working on cycles to build the same candidate set for the cycles a cut points belongs to. Then, all the candidate sets are combined to build the candidate set for the cut point. The process is repeated until the candidate solution for the root are computed, and the one with minimum communication cost is selected from this set. The complexity of UGA is $o(n^3 * S(P)^2)$ for a n node graph.

4   Allocating p3l skeleton programs

In this section, we show that all the task graphs coming from compilation of p3l programs are union graphs and thus they can be partitioned optimally using UGA when $p \geq m$. Then, we present a strategy to partition skeleton task graphs when $m > p$. Similar ideas can be used to find an optimal allocation of skeleton programs written in other languages, as different skeletal models use similar templates and UGA can be extended to other basic subgraphs.

Consider again the p3l templates shown in Fig. 1. For allocation purposes, a loop template can be seen as a farm with a single worker. Thus, in the following, we will discuss only pipes and farms. We first analyze the expansion process that builds p3l skeleton programs from templates and then characterize the corresponding task graphs. In Fig. 1, only nodes connected

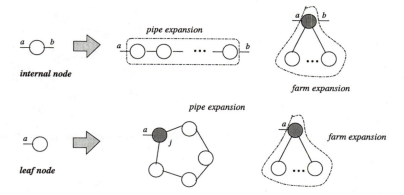

Figure 3. Node expansions in p3l template composition.

with one or two incident edges can be further expanded. We will call *internal nodes,* those with two incident edges and *leaf nodes,* those with a single incident edge. The expansion step substitutes an internal or leaf node using the rules in Fig. 3, which abstract the behaviour of a skeleton compiler. Notice that when a leaf is expanded using a pipeline template, we insert an extra *join* node (j in Fig. 3) to route in/out messages. In all the other cases, we simply substitute the selected node with an instance of the template. The following holds for all the p3l skeleton programs.

Theorem 1 *All the* p3l *skeleton programs are union graphs of cycle and tree structures in which only internal and leaf nodes can be further expanded and all the cut points are non-expandable nodes.*

Proof. By induction on the number of skeletons in the program P to be compiled. If P has only one skeleton, it is compiled in a graph G corresponding to one of the structures in Fig. 1, which obviously satisfies the thesis.

Suppose P has k skeletons. Choose a skeleton s in the innermost nesting level and delete it from P. The resulting program P' has $k - 1$ skeletons and by induction it is compiled in a task graph G' satisfying the thesis. Now, we build G by expanding a node x in G' with the template instance implementing s. Suppose G' is built by h subgraphs, and let G_i the subgraph of G' including x. If s is a *pipe*, we have two cases. If x is an internal node, expansion adds nodes to G_i without adding new subgraphs. Thus, the resulting graph G is still a union graph satisfying the thesis. If x is a leaf, then G_i is a tree and expansion inserts a join node as shown in Fig. 3. This means inserting a new subgraph G_{h+1} in G' and making x a cut point between G_i and G_{h+1}. x

has more than two incident edges and is now marked as non-expandable. x joins only two structures as required for union graphs, and in the future it will never be used to join more structures as it cannot be expanded further. Thus, G is again a union graph verifying the thesis.

If s is a *farm*, we again have two cases. If x is an internal node, expansion transforms it in a cut point and create a new tree G_{h+1} which is joined to the rest by a single node, making G again a union graph conform to the thesis. Finally, if x is a leaf, then G_i is a tree and expansion adds a new subtree to it. x becomes non-expandable and gets n new children (leaves). Also in this case, G is a union graph and verifies the thesis. ◇

From Theorem 1, it follows that UGA can be used to find the optimal partitioning when the number of partitions m is $\leq p$. Consider now the case $m > p$. In this case, the partitioning found by UGA is useless as some of the clusters cannot be allocated. This is due to the fact that the bound $S(P)$ to the computation that can be assigned to each processor is too small to accommodate all the processes in p clusters. Here we have two choices. If we do not accept a load greater than $S(P)$, G cannot be executed on p processors. However, usually the performance delivered by a node has a two phase behaviour. It first remain quite stable up to a threshold S_1, then decreases slowly up to a second threshold $S_2 > S_1$ and, finally, drops for loads exceeding S_2. Supposing to fix $S(P) = S_1$, if the number of partitions exceeds p we can increase $S(P)$ up to S_2 using UGA to find a new allocation. This can be done iterating the application of UGA using a binary search between S_1 and S_2 to find the allocation that fits in p processors and shows the minimum S (and thus the minimum degradation).

The complexity of the two strategies is pseudo-polynomial. However, in typical, skeleton program settings, the number of processors p involved is $\leq 10^3$, typical costs normalized with the minimum amount of computation required are $O(10^0)$ and $S_1, S_2 \leq 10^2$.

5   Conclusions

In this paper, we have formulated the problem of allocating skeletal programs, discussed its complexity and presented a solution strategy for the skeletons/template provided in p3l. We have proved that the UGA algorithm, [1,11] which partitions graphs constructed from combinations of trees and cycles in pseudo-polynomial time, can be used to find an optimal allocation of skeleton programs generated by a p3l compiler. The proposed strategy finds the optimal number of processors needed to execute the skeleton program in $O(n^3 * S(P)^2)$ where n is the number of nodes in the global task graph and S is the bound of processors load. When the number of available processors is bounded, the same UGA algorithm can be applied to find the allocation with the minimum performance degradation up to a given bound on processor load of $S_2 > S(P)$. Experimental results carried on a small sample of p3l programs show that the method works well in practical cases. Future work would be the extension of the method to other skeletal systems, the practical testing on a benchmark of real p3l applications and the analysis of the sensitivity of UGA to small perturbations of the estimated costs for communication and computation.

References

1. S. Antonelli *et al*, Un algoritmo per il partizionamento ottimo di una nuova classe di grafi. *Calcolo*, **20**, 85–100 (1983).
2. S. Antonelli and S. Pelagatti, On the complexity of the mapping problem for massively parallel architectures. *Int. J. Found. Comp. Sc.*, **3**, 379–387 (1992).
3. B. Bacci *et al*, P^{3}L: A structured high level programming language and its structured support. *Concurr. Pract. and Exp.* **7**, 225–255 (1995).
4. S. H. Bokhari, Partitioning problems in parallel, pipelined, and distributed computing. *IEEE Trans. on Comp.*, **37**, 48–57 (1988).
5. S. Ciarpaglini *et al*, ANACLETO: a template-based p3l compiler. In *Proc. of PCW'97*, Canberra (1997).
6. M. Cole, *Algorithmic Skeletons* (MIT Press, Cambridge MA, 1989)
7. D. Culler, *et al*, *Parallel Computer Architecture: a Hardware/Software approach.* (Morgan Kaufmann, San Mateo CA, 1999).
8. J. Darlington *et al*, Skeletons for structured parallel composition. In *Proc. of the 15th ACM PPoPP'95*, Santa Barbara CA (1995).
9. M. Garey and D. S. Johnson, *Computers and Intractability* (Freeman, S. Francisco CA, 1979).
10. V. M. Lo, Heuristic algorithms for task assignment in distributed systems. *IEEE Trans. on Comp.*, **37**, 1384–1397 (1988).
11. J. Lukes, Efficient algorithms for the partitioning of trees. *IBM J. of Res. and Dev.*, **18** (1974).
12. S. Pelagatti, *Structured development ,of parallel programs* (Taylor and Francis, London 1998).
13. C. M. Woodside and G. G. Monforton, Fast allocation of processes in distributed and parallel systems. *IEEE TPDS*, **4**, 164–174 (1993).

SWC: A SMALL FRAMEWORK FOR WEBCOMPUTING[1]

DAVID ARNOW, GERALD WEISS, KEVIN YING, DAYTON CLARK

Department of Computer and Information Science
Brooklyn College and CUNY Graduate Center
2900 Bedford Avenue
Brooklyn, NY 11210, USA

{kevin,arnow,weiss,dayton}@sci.brooklyn.cuny.edu

WebComputing is an approach to parallel computing that uses Java applets to automatically distribute a computation across the Internet. The promise of WebComputing is the potential for achieving an unprecedented degree of parallelism — in principle, a computation could harness every computer that is connected to the Internet. There have been a number of ambitious projects, including Charlotte, Javelin, and Bayanihan that have explored this platform.

SWC is a small, simple WebComputing framework that bears a number of distinct design approaches compared to the other WebComputing systems. The primary objective of the SWC system is to provide a layered system design that separates the programming interface from the underlying WebComputing architecture. This design approach shields application developers from the underlying dynamic and unreliable execution environment, makes the application programs portable, yet at the same time provides system developers freedom in architecture implementation.

The framework provided by the SWC system along with its simple programming interface allows WebComputing application developers to simply and conveniently implement and deploy a range of scientific programs and computationally demanding applications.

Keywords: WebComputing, distributed computing, Internet computing, Metacomputing, Parallel computing, Java applet, Java-enabled Web browser.

1   Introduction

The advent of the Java programming language, with its support for web-deliverable applets, has created a new, promising, though peculiar parallel-computing platform that some call *WebComputing*. The essential idea is that a master server, or collection thereof, in league with a collection of web servers coordinates the execution of tasks by applets running in parallel on an ever-changing set of unreliable, heterogeneous client machines (see Figure 1). The promise of WebComputing is the potential for achieving an unprecedented degree of parallelism — in principle, a computation could harness every computer that is connected to the Internet. There have been a number of ambitious projects,

---

[1] This research is supported by ONR grant N00014-96-1-1057 and National Science Foundation's CISE program #CDA-9522537.

420

including Charlotte [4], Javelin [5], and Bayanihan [8] that have explored this distributed computing platform.

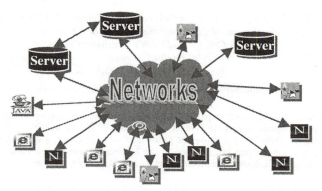

Figure 1. The Setting for WebComputing

SWC is a small, simple framework, originally developed as a tool for students, that simplifies developing and deploying WebComputing applications. The objective of the SWC system is to provide a layered WebComputing system design that separates the programming interface from the underlying WebComputing architecture. Figure 2 illustrates the SWC architecture. The large middle box represents the SWC system proper and contains two levels. The upper level, shown in the dashed box, provides the SWC programming API. The lower level provides the support for this API. This design approach shields application developers from the underlying dynamic and unreliable execution environment and makes the application programs portable, yet at the same time provides system developers freedom in architecture design.

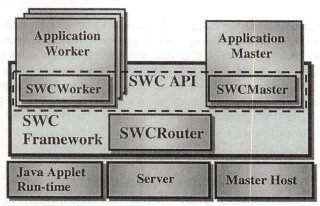

Figure 2. SWC Architecture

2 SWC System Design

The SWC framework provides a master-worker MIMD parallel programming model. At the programming interface level, the master process (SWCMaster) defines an initial set of tasks and integrates the results of those tasks, possibly defining new tasks along the way. The tasks comprising the computation are defined by lightweight data objects, received and carried out by workers (SWCWorker) that run as Java applets, and generated dynamically by both the master and the workers themselves. The master and any worker can also broadcast control information through the server (SWCRouter) to all workers. The workers do not communicate directly with each other — they simply return the results of the tasks and request new ones to carry out.

The master-worker programming model has a number of attributes that make it suitable for WebComputing:

1. It has been widely used and proven effective in many distributed computing systems.
2. It fits well with the Object-Oriented design methodology. Here in the SWC system, it is supported with the Java programming language.
3. It adapts well in an environment where communication is relatively expensive. Network latencies and bandwidth limitations on the Internet are extremely high.
4. It is a versatile and general parallel programming model and can be transformed to many other programming models, including Linda tuple space model [6].
5. A large set of problems can be parallelized using this model.

```
public interface SWCUnit extends Serializable {}
public interface SWCWorkUnit extends SWCUnit {}
public interface SWCResultUnit extends SWCUnit {}

abstract class SWCMaster {
  final void sendWork(SWCWorkUnit swu) {…}
  final SWCResultUnit receiveResult() {…}
  abstract void beTheBoss();
}

abstract class SWCWorker {
  final synchronized void send(SWCUnit su) {…}
  final synchronized SWCWorkUnit receiveWork() {…}
  abstract void doTheWork();
}
```

Figure 3. SWC Framework Programming API

To use the SWC framework, an application programmer must extend a set of framework-defined abstract classes (see Figure 3). The SWCMaster class defines the master's actions, while, the SWCWorker class defines the task computation. The SWCWorkUnit and the SWCResultUnit interface classes label the data needed to define a particular task or result, a mechanism for recognizing task equivalence, and a mechanism for recognizing task completion. Using these classes, the framework itself oversees the entire computation and handles all communications.

Because of its independent architecture design, SWC is able to provide three implementations of its architecture (see Figure 4). One is thread-based and runs on an SMP platform; it serves as development environment when a web-based one is not available or is inconvenient. Another implementation is based on independent Unix processes. The third implementation serves our main purpose — WebComputing. It consists of a multithreaded, servlet-enhanced HTTP server that provides an application control page, creates the master process, downloads the applets and handles all communication. It also provides the classes that define, for both the master process and the applets, their computational structure and their communication tools.

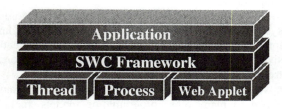

Figure 4. SWC Architecture Implementation

An SWC computation is initiated using a form in a web page provided by the server. A servlet responds by creating the necessary objects within the HTTP server along with an external master process. The master process and the server communicate using the connection-oriented TCP protocol and need not reside on the same machine. The master process, using programmer provided classes creates an initial set of task definitions, which are sent off to the server. The server maintains a collection of task definitions, and uses eager scheduling, as is commonly done in WebComputing [1,4,5], to assign them to applets that have been downloaded into volunteering web clients. Because of the unreliable nature of the applets themselves, the fact that the most obvious candidates for WebComputing will not require large quantities of data to define tasks, and the desire to eliminate system-imposed limits on the number of connections on the server as a potential bottleneck, plus the performance consideration [12], server-applet communication uses the connectionless UDP protocol. Because the server does not consider a task complete until the results are actually received, lost packets do not compromise the integrity of the application. To avoid failure to utilize an applet as a result of communication failure, applets use a timeout mechanism to repeatedly send the server their most recent response until the server provides additional work or instructs them to terminate.

As the server receives responses from applets, it determines whether these are additional task definitions, in which case they are added to its collection of task definitions, or results from completed tasks in which case they are passed to the master. The latter may, in response, generate new task definitions or control information for the server to distribute to the applets. Control information is immediately broadcast to applets and made available to all future ones. Figure 5 illustrates SWC communication between different modules.

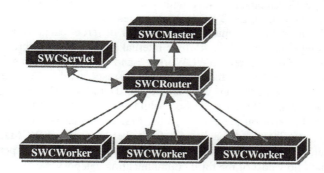

Figure 5. SWC Data Flow

3 Performance

The efficiency of a WebComputing application depends on many elements beyond the control of the implementer of a WebComputing system or framework. Among these are the appropriateness of the application to the platform because of the extreme network latency and bandwidth limitations of the Internet, the implementation of the Java Virtual Machines (JVM) that support the applets, and the network conditions that effect latency and bandwidth. To provide a sensible estimation of the system's performance, we need to quantify the communication overhead. Data transfers between different system modules constitute the dominant portion of the WebComputing system overhead. Data flow of the SWC system can be classified into three categories:

MW: The SWCMaster sends newly defined tasks to a SWCWorker.
WM: The SWCWorker sends SWCResultUnits to the SWCMaster.
WW: The SWCWorker sends SWCWorkUnits to the SWCRouter for rescheduling to another SWCWorker.

Evaluating the communication costs for these three categories can provide insight to the system's behavior. A WebComputing application developer may use this information and the communication pattern of the specific application to estimate its communication overhead.

To study these costs, performance measurements were carried out using JDK's Solaris Production Release version 1.1.7 and its default just-in-time (JIT) compiler, on two Sun Ultra-Sparc-10 workstations with 128 MB of RAM each, running Solaris 7 operating systems. One machine was employed as a server, the other as a client.

These machines were connected with 100Mbit Ethernet LAN. The network latency was below 1 millisecond (ms) (tested with UNIX ping facility). We also used Netscape Communicator 4.51 with a 1.1.5 Java run-time environment when applet implementation of the SWC system was tested.

Table 1 shows the communication costs for different categories of application data flow using an object with a 45-byte internal state. For both thread and process measurements, SWCMaster, SWCWorker, and SWCRouter ran on a single workstation as three threads and three processes respectively. For the Web Applet measurement, two workstations were employed. Both SWCMaster and SWCRouter ran on the server as different processes, while, a SWCWorker ran as a Java Applet in a Netscape browser on the client. In the first experiment (MW and WM), a 45-byte object was bounced back and forth between the SWCMaster and the SWCWorker. The cost of a round trip was recorded. The second experiment (WW) shows the data flow cost of the third communication category.

Table 1. Communication Costs of Different Application Data Flow Paths

45-byte state data object	Thread	Process	Web Applet
MW and WM	50 ms	50 ms	60 ms
WW	7 ms	8 ms	19 ms

4   Related Work

Since Java's inception, many distributed computing research projects have been designed to implement distributed systems using Java technologies. These research projects may be classified into two categories based on whether the system uses the World Wide Web as the distributed platform or not. Some projects from the first category like JavaPVM [10] and mpiJava [2] are direct extensions from traditional message passing distributed systems like PVM [7] and MPI [9]. While, some like ATLAS [3] extend the concept of thread, which is initially developed for SMP machines, to distributed computing by spawning "threads" onto remote hosts. These projects are developed solely based on Java applications running in a LAN environment. They can not be easily adopted for a large scale Internet Computing [11]. Projects from the second category use Java-enabled Web browsers as distributed platforms and deploy Java applets as primary computing units across networks. They are WebComputing systems.

The Charlotte project [4] pioneered the research on WebComputing in 1996. It uses the remote thread-programming model with distributed shared memory (DSM) that is implemented at the Java application programming level. The high price for migrating thread across JVM boundary renders the performance and scalability of Charlotte in question. On the other hand, Javelin [5] was developed from a system development point of view, using brokers to match computing resource donors with their consumers. It provides limited support for high level programming interfaces and expects WebComputing application developers to absorb most or all of the programming complexity imposed by the WebComputing programming environments. In addition, Javelin's ad hoc run-time library components use expensive Applet-to-Applet communication for load balancing between applet workers. This communication must be routed through the server because of the web-browser sandbox security restriction. The Bayanihan project [8] provides a highly object-oriented framework with replaceable components for its applications. Compared to Bayanihan, the programming interface of the SWC framework is less complex and more coherent, and the system itself is small and compact.

5 Usage

Although SWC applications must be written in Java and therefore can easily be developed in an object-oriented fashion, the framework is equally "friendly" to a procedural or imperative style. In particular, it is not terribly difficult to port C or even Fortran applications to run as SWC programs. Several projects (including Monte Carlo computations and classical Operational Research projects) are underway using SWC. Two CS courses in the spring of 1999 were taught using SWC and it is worth noting that students — graduate and undergraduate — took to it easily.

6 Conclusion

The SWC system provides a small framework for WebComputing. The system's source code is less than 80K and the total size of the compiled Java classes is less than 50K. Its layered design approach makes its application portable and provides freedom for robust underlying architecture development. At the upper layer, the SWC system provides a simple coherent programming interface. WebComputing application programmers simply extend four predefined classes of the framework using master-worker programming paradigm. Because of the robust lower layer implementation, the same application program can run as threads, processes, as well as applets for WebComputing. This provides a useful distributed program developing environment.

This paper also provides a communication performance measurement based on three categories of application data flows. Currently, we are extending the SWC framework and implementing more applications for this system. At the same time, we are extending current single SWCRouter architecture and adding multiple SWCRouter capability to the framework. This extension will greatly enhance the scalability of the system, and at the same time, be transparent to SWC WebComputing applications.

7 Reference

1. A. Alexandrov, M. Ibel, K. E. Schauser, and C. Scheiman. *SuperWeb: Research Issues in Java-Based Global Computing.* Concurrency: Practice and Experience, June 1997.
2. M. Baker, B. Carpenter, S. Ko, and X. Li. *mpiJava: A Java interface to MPI.* Presented at First UK workshop on Java for High Performance Network Computing, Europe 1998. `http://www.npac.syr.edu/projects/pcrc/mpiJava/mpiJava.html`
3. J. Baldeschweiler, R. Blumofe, and E. Brewer. *ATLAS: An Infrastructure for Global Computing.* Proceedings of the Seventh ACM SIGOPS European Workshop: Systems Support for Worldwide Applications, Connemara, Ireland, September 1996.
4. A. Baratloo, M. Karaul, Z. Kedem, and P. Wyckoff. *Charlotte: Metacomputing on the Web.* Proceeding Of the 9th International Conference on Parallel and Distributed Computing Systems, 1996.
5. P. Cappello, *et al. Javelin: Internet-based parallel computing using Java.* The 6th ACM SIGPLAN Symposium on Principles and Practice of Parallel Programming, 1997.
6. N. Carriero and D. Gelernter. *How to Write Parallel Programs: A First Course.* MIT Press, 1990.
7. A. Geist, *et al. PVM: Parallel Virtual Machine - A User's Guide and Tutorial for Network Parallel Computing,* MIT Press, 1994.
8. L. Sarmenta. *Bayanihan: Web-Based Volunteer Computing Using Java.* 2nd International Conference on World-Wide Computing and its Applications, Japan, March 1998.
9. M. Snir, *et al. MPI: The Complete Reference,* MIT Press, 1996.
10. D. Thurman. *JavaPMV: The Java to PVM Interface.* December 1996. JavaPVM was renamed to jPVM, `http://www.isye.gatech.edu/chmsr/jPVM/`
11. Kevin Ying and David Arnow. *A WebComputing Overview.* Brooklyn College Computer Science Department Technical Report #TR-3-99, March 1999.
12. Kevin Ying, David Arnow, and Dayton Clark. *Evaluating Communication Protocols for WebComputing.* Proceeding of 1999 International Conference on Parallel and Distributed Processing Techniques and Applications (PDPTA'99), CSREA Press, June 1999.

ON THE MEMORY PERFORMANCE OF PURE AND IMPURE, STRICT AND NON-STRICT FUNCTIONAL PROGRAMS

A. P. WILLEM BÖHM, JEFFREY P. HAMMES

Computer Science Department, Colorado State University

This paper reports on our experience with a Monte Carlo particle transport code, written in pure and impure, strict and non-strict styles in the functional programming languages Id, Haskell, and Sisal, and compares their performances to a multithreaded C version. We study a pure functional Id code, an impure Id code based on M-structures, a pure Haskell code, and three pure Sisal codes: a stream version, a loop version, and a stripmined loop version. The Id and Haskell codes are non-strict, whereas the Sisal codes are strict. We introduce the Monte Carlo particle transport problem and discuss the three implementations in functional language terms.

1 Introduction

There are at least three models for the evaluation order in functional programs. *Lazy evaluation* states that a value should be computed only if it is needed. This means that if a function specifies as its result an infinite list of values, any terminating execution of the program will use only a finite subset of these, and hence only a finite prefix of the list will be computed. Lazy evaluation is the default order of evaluation in Haskell [1]. In languages with lazy evaluation order it is hard to analyze whether two function calls can be evaluated in parallel. *Eager evaluation* states that a function can be evaluated as soon as its data are available. This is a "natural" model for parallel execution. There are two forms of eager evaluation. *Non-strict eager evaluation* performs the function call and the evaluation of the argument in parallel. This is the most aggressive parallel model of computation. The programming language Id [2] is based on it. A run-time penalty has to be paid, as a computation has to check the availability of its data, and has to suspend if the data are not available. A less aggressive parallel model is *strict eager evaluation*, where a function can start execution only if all its data are available. Sisal [3] was designed so that it can be implemented strictly. To accommodate non-strictness in principle, a stream data structure was provided in Sisal (*Streams* and Iteration in a Single Assignment Language).

Functional languages, especially eager ones, have the promise of efficient, machine independent parallelism, shielding the programmer from the bugs and booby traps of explicitly parallel, non-deterministic, machine dependent programming (for instance, in C with threads or C with message passing). Unfortunately, functional languages have not yet fulfilled this promise of efficient implicit parallelism. To study the expressiveness and efficiency of functional languages we have written a complex Monte Carlo photon transport code, MCP, in Id and Haskell [4], in Sisal and in multithreaded C. We discuss implementations in the functional languages, and study their performance compared to the multithreaded C version.

2   The Monte Carlo particle transport problem

The Monte Carlo radiation transport problem involves simulating the statistical behavior of certain particles while they travel through objects of user-specified shapes and materials. MCNP, the original Monte Carlo N-Particle code[5], was developed by physics researchers at Los Alamos over many years, and simulates the transport of photons, neutrons and electrons. It represents the *geometry* of the space in a recursive fashion, using planes, spheres, cylinders etc. MCNP is used to model problems in areas such as nuclear reactors, radiation shielding, and medical physics. MCP refers to *photon* transport codes, based on MCNP. Simulating the behavior of particles and their collisions with the nuclei of the material through which the particles travel is called *tracking*. Each collision has the potential for absorbing some of the photon's energy and changing the photon's direction of travel. It is also possible for a photon to *split* into multiple photons, each of which must be separately tracked, hence a source photon's track forms a dynamic, irregular tree. Track lengths and the degree of splitting are highly problem-dependent.

While tracking takes place, statistical information about certain events is accumulated in a process called *tallying*. The user of a Monte Carlo transport code describes a problem geometry, a radiation source, and the information that needs to be tallied. The program simulates individual source photons as they collide with the nuclei of the materials in the problem geometry, and each photon contributes information to the tallies being collected. A large number of particles, often in the millions, is needed to get statistically relevant results.

The user describes the *geometry* of a problem using *cells* with a specified shape and material composition. Each cell has a region, describing the space the cell occupies, its material composition and its material density. *Regions* are defined using *surfaces* such as planes, spheres and cylinders. A surface defines two primitive regions, one positive and one negative, such as the two half spaces defined by a plane or the inside and outside regions of a cylinder or sphere. More complex regions can be defined using *intersection, union*, and *complement* operators. To describe the material composition of the cells, a separate array of *materials* is defined and referenced by the cells, consisting of a list of *(nuclide, fraction)* pairs where the nuclide is in the range 1 (hydrogen) through 94 (plutonium). The *photon source* is described by its location, its direction (unidirectional or isotropic), and its energy distribution in the form of a cumulative histogram. An isotropic source emits photons evenly in all directions.

The user specifies a list of desired *tallies*, which describe the histograms to be gathered during simulation. Some tally types relate to surface crossings; others relate to collisions in the interior of cells. A tally can be partitioned by energy bands, or *bins*. Each tally has a *kind* (current, flux, collision count, etc.), a list of locations (surfaces or cells, depending on the kind of tally), and a list of energy bin partition values. When a photon passes through a tallied surface or cell, it contributes information to the appropriate tally. For example, a *current* tally simply counts the number of photons crossing a surface, in the appropriate energy bin. MCP reports the average source photon energy, the various kinds of photon *creates* and *losses*, and the values and error estimates for each of the user's tallies. The creates and losses give the user some insight into the kinds of tracks that are taking place, and demonstrate that all photons have been accounted for.

The most straightforward MCP code structure involves a direct encoding of the above description. Figure 1 shows a diagram of this pipelined, function-compositional approach, where each arrow can be implemented by either a stream or a list:

```
photons            =   photon_generator (n, init_seed);
event_lists        =   track (photons);
histogram_arrays   =   tally (event_lists);
result             =   reduce (n, histogram_arrays);
```

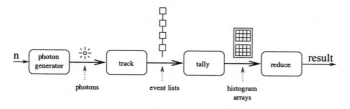

Figure 1. High level view of MCP

The evaluation order of a language has profound effects on the run-time behavior of this code structure. Strict evaluation forces each data structure (represented as an arrow in figure 1) to be built fully before the following stage can operate on it. Since an execution of the program easily may involve many millions of source photons, and each photon may produce thousands of events, the event lists in the center of the pipeline clearly grow to an infeasible size.

Non-strict eager evaluation allows consumers to work concurrently with producers, but the asynchronous, loose coupling of producers and consumers can allow a producer to run far ahead of its corresponding consumer, thereby using significant amounts of space. In fact, an unlikely but perfectly valid evaluation order could build each structure fully before it is used, resulting in the same space problems as in the strict version. In pure functional languages, there is no way to control the cooperation between the stages as they execute. This cooperation is usually implemented using buffers, and their size and use are not exposed at program level.

A non-strict eager evaluation of this code structure also causes problems if automatic garbage collection is not available. In the case where a user has specified multiple tally results, multiple concurrent traversals of the event lists will take place. Since these traversals are asynchronous, explicit deallocation is difficult and would seem to require either explicit reference counters (which takes the code outside of the pure functional realm), or a separate sweep to deallocate after all the traversals have completed. In the latter case, all event lists would live simultaneously in memory.

Non-strict lazy evaluation would appear to be ideal in its behavior. E-valuation would begin with a demand for the output, which would trigger a backflow of demands followed by a forward flow of evaluation. As evaluation takes place, the data structures that are created would seem to be short-lived and available almost immediately for deallocation. However, in the case where a user has specified multiple tally results, the demand for the first tally will cause the creation of all the event lists, and these lists cannot be deallocated immediately because computation of the second tally result must also traverse them. Thus the space requirements are at least as great as those of strict evaluation.

An alternative to the pipelined approach resembles a more imperative view of the problem. A top-level loop produces source photons, one per iteration. The photon is immediately tracked and its event list is then tallied into its histograms. Finally, these histograms are summed into the sum and sum-of-squares accumulator arrays. A strict language implementation of this code is forced to be largely sequential due to the loop-carried dependencies in the random seed and the accumulator arrays. A non-strict eager language may achieve useful parallelism because the loop iterations can be executed concurrently, though it is necessary to put a bound on the number of concur-

	Stream	Loop	Stripmined Loop
Haskell	pure		
Id	pure	impure	
Sisal	pure	pure	pure

Table 1. Implementations of the code versions in Haskell, Id and Sisal

rent iterations so as to prevent excessive space use. A non-strict lazy approach (done with a tail-recursive function if loops are not available in the language) will suffer from the same multiple-traversal problem as described above in the pipelined version, due to the multiple-consumer problem.

The loop-carried dependencies of the seed generation and the tally summing are easily overcome by a small amount of code restructuring. Since we use a random number sequence that allows easy *striding* [6], that is, an ability to efficiently jump ahead by a specified distance, the inherently sequential nature of the random number stream no longer holds. And since the tally array summing operations are associative, these operations also need not be sequential. This leads to a stripmined approach that breaks the problem into a number of chunks, where each chunk represents a subrange of iterations of the original loop. The number of chunks in our codes is specified as a run-time argument. The behavioral issues with regard to the language evaluation strategies are largely the same as for the straight loop version, since each chunk of work acts like a complete run of the straight loop.

Table 1 shows the various implementations of the above code versions in Haskell, Id and Sisal. Some comments are in order with respect to the impure Id loop version. Explicit deallocation was implemented using barriers and deallocate statements. The tally array accumulators were implemented using Id's M-structures (updatable memory cells [7]). Also, implementing a stripmined version in Id was unnecessary, because the eager non-strict execution model already provides ample parallelism, and Id's ability to k-bound loops allowed for control of that parallelism and hence of memory use.

3 Memory Performance

To acquire statistically relevant results, millions of particles need to be tracked, and the track of each particle can produce thousands of events. Hence, any execution model that forces the simultaneous existence of all event lists is useless for this application.

The stream version of the code has been implemented in all three languages. For each language, this version was rendered useless because of its excessive memory use, but each for a different reason. The Haskell version requires all event lists to exist simultaneously because of the multiple traversal problem mentioned earlier. The pure Id version dies for an obvious reason: this code does not deallocate memory. The Sisal stream version should perform well, were it not that Sisal streams have been given a strict implementation by the Sisal compiler. This renders streams completely useless in Sisal, because they actually are implemented as arrays. All three of these pure stream-based codes are able to run only a few thousand source photons before exhausting a reasonable amount of heap memory.

The impure Id version ran twenty million source photons on an eight processor Monsoon machine, staying within the machines memory resources. This was achieved by k-bounding the loop.

Both Sisal loop versions use in the order of 50K bytes memory for any number of particles when run sequentially. This use goes up to about 80K bytes for a four processor parallel execution.

4 Time Performance and Parallelism

The impure Id code ran 20 million photons in fifty hours on an eight processor Monsoon machine, which clocks at 10 MHz. In experiments with fewer photons, a seven fold speedup on eight processors was observed. We refrain from further timing analysis, as no comparison with multithreaded C on one common platform can be made.

As Sisal runs on many conventional, as well as experimental, parallel platforms including shared memory SUN/SPARC machines, its parallel timing performance can be compared to that of multithreaded C.

	50,000 photons					
	C parallel			Sisal parallel		
PEs	real	user	sys	real	user	sys
1	47.8	47.5	0.0	361.1	359.8	0.1
2	25.6	49.0	0.7	203.4	396.3	4.4
3	18.6	51.1	2.1	176.6	466.0	35.5
4	15.9	53.1	3.7	186.5	519.5	109.7

Table 2. Time performance, in seconds, of parallel codes

Table 2 shows time performance for a Sun SMP with four 50 MHz SuperSparc processors. In Sisal as well as in C, the time grows linearly with the problem size, both for sequential and parallel codes. The multithreaded Sisal uses the same threads package that was used for the explicit parallel C version of the code. In Sisal stripmining was necessary to get parallelism.

The C code speeds up as more processors are used, with a final speedup of three with four processors. However, the Sisal code slows down going from three to four processors. This is due largely to a strong increase in *sys* time, which is spent in suspending and wakening threads. A *mutex_lock* call suspends a thread if the lock is not acquired at the time of the call. We refer to this as a *failed* lock call. If the call does acquire the lock immediately, there is no *sys* time assessed, but there is still a *user* time cost. For the 5K problem, the Sisal program makes approximately 5.4 million lock calls. The number of lock calls is independent of the number of workers, whereas the number of *failing* lock calls is dependent on the number of workers. The vast majority of these are accesses to the reference count fields of the various data structures, with the intent of deallocating the structure when the count reaches zero. Many of the data structures, for example the photon cross sections and the geometry specifications, are created at the start of the run and persist throughout nearly the entire execution. Attempting to deallocate these structures is useless, but the compiler cannot determine that this is the case.

The reference count locks affect performance in a number of ways. First, since each lock access costs approximately 1.85 μsec of *user* time, approximately ten seconds of the 53.4 seconds of user time for the 4-processor 5K run of the stripmined code is due to lock calls. Second, since the cost of a failed lock call is approximately 45 μsec of *sys* time, the 9.7 seconds of *sys* time implies that approximately 216,000 lock calls failed to acquire the lock. Though the number of failing lock calls is only about 4% of the total number of lock calls, the performance cost is substantial. Third, the repeated accesses to the reference count fields undoubtedly contribute additional inefficiencies due to the cache effects of multiple processors writing to the same locations. Note that, aside from the reference count manipulations, the accesses to these Sisal read-only data structures should exhibit good cache behavior on an SMP since they should easily fit in a processor's L2 cache.

These problems do not occur, or are avoided, in the C version. The shared data structures are never deallocated, and hence do not need reference counts. Moreover, for some data structure types that are frequently allocated and deallocated, the C code avoids sharing (and thus the need for reference counts) by making copies. The tradeoffs between copying and sharing are not obvious. For large structures, sharing can have an obvious advantage. But sharing can incur two costs in an SMP: the reference count field requires mutex lock protection with its inherent costs, and the sharing of a memory location for writing by multiple processors can have bad cache effects.

434

5 Conclusions

We have studied the performance of a variety of functional implementations - pure and impure, strict and non-strict - of a complex Monte Carlo transport code, written in Haskell, Id and Sisal.

The pure functional Id and Haskell codes and the stream based Sisal code use an amount of space proportional to the number of particles simulated, whereas the non-strict impure Id code and the strict pure Sisal loop oriented codes run in a fixed amount of memory. On a four processor SMP the Sisal codes run about six times slower than multithreaded C.

It is interesting to note that the most straightforward and elegant approach to coding this problem, a compositional stream-based code, did not yield a satisfactory result in any of the languages. In the case of Id this could be avoided by providing automatic garbage collection, whereas in Sisal a non-strict implementation of streams would have alleviated the excessive space use.

References

1. Hudak, P., Peyton Jones, S., and Wadler, P. (editors). 1992. Report on the Programming Language Haskell, A Non-strict Purely Functional Language (Version 1.2). *ACM SIGPLAN Notices*, 27(5).
2. Nikhil, R. S. 1990. Id Version 90.0 Reference Manual. Computational Structures Group Memo 284-1, Massachusetts Institute of Technology.
3. J. McGraw et.al., SISAL: Streams and Iteration in a Single Assignment Language: Reference Manual Version 1.2, Lawrence Livermore National Laboratory, Memo M-146, Rev. 1, 1985.
4. Hammes, J., Lubeck, O., Böhm, W. 1995. Comparing Id and Haskell in a Monte Carlo photon transport code. *Journal of Functional Programming*, Vol. 5, Part 3, pp 283-316, July 1995.
5. Briesmeister, J. F. Editor. 1993. *MCNP–A General Monte Carlo N-Particle Transport Code, Version 4A*, Los Alamos National Laboratory Report LA-12625-M.
6. Hendricks, J. S. 1991. Effects of Changing the Random Number Stride in Monte Carlo Calculations. *Nuclear Science and Engineering*, 109(1), pp 86-91.
7. Barth, Paul S., R. S. Nikhil and Arvind, "M-structures: Extending a parallel, non-strict, functional language with state," *Proc. FPCA*, Cambridge, MA, Aug 1991.

ADVANCED VISUALIZATION AND DATA DISTRIBUTION STEERING IN AN HPF PARALLELIZATION ENVIRONMENT

P. BREZANY, P. CZERWIŃSKI AND K. SOWA

Institute for Software Technology and Parallel Systems, University of Vienna,
Liechtensteinstrasse 22, A-1090 Vienna, Austria
{brezany, przemek, sowa}@par.univie.ac.at

R. KOPPLER AND J. VOLKERT

GUP Linz, Johannes Kepler University Linz
Altenbergerstrasse 69, 4040 Linz, Austria
{koppler, volkert}@gup.uni-linz.ac.at

On distributed-memory systems, the quality of the data distribution has a crucial impact on the efficiency of the computation. Sophisticated visualization of large in-core and out-of-core data, and steering capabilities of the debugging system significantly reduce program development cycle, especially for *irregular applications*. In this paper we present an advanced system for visualization and steering of data distributions based on the Graphical Data Distribution Tool (GDDT) and the advanced HPF symbolic debugger DeHiFo. The development focused on efficient support for regular and irregular data distributions and brings several significant contributions: (1) on-line visualization of distributions and values of large in-core and out-of-core data structures, (2) quality control of data distributions using (re)distribution animation, and (3) dynamic data redistribution in parallel programs.

1 Introduction

Large-scale parallel applications, which typically use huge amounts of data, require special support for manipulation of global entities of the program. Since program performance on distributed-memory systems significantly depends on data distribution, the developer needs support for sophisticated visualization of large in-core and out-of-core data[a], and for steering data distributions. In particular, developers of *irregular applications* greatly benefit from on-line visualization and steering capabilities of the programming environment, since in such applications the distribution of major data arrays and their access patterns are known only at run time.

Despite of many activities in parallel software development – such as process mapping, performance analysis, debugging – data distribution has not been supported adequately. Most existing systems for visualization of data

---

[a]Out-of-Core data structures are too big to be kept in main memory, therefore they are stored on disks.

distribution (e.g., *HPF-Builder* [8]) are restricted to compile-time evaluation of data because of productivity reasons. Visualization and steering of dynamic data distributions still suffer from incomplete support. One of the most robust systems in this field is *DAQV* [6], which has been designed for HPF compilers. It provides a framework for accessing and modifying data at run time in order to simplify visualization and computational steering. The importance of distributed data visualization has been recognized in data-parallel debuggers. *Prism* [1] provides various displays based on histograms, multidimensional graphs, surfaces and vector representations of program's data including support for data-parallel programs written in CM-Fortran. Most existing HPF debuggers (e.g., *PDT* [5]), provide a global data visualization for viewing entire arrays and array segments allocated across processors.

So far, visualization has been concentrated more on a convenient, easily-interpreted representation of data. However, combining sophisticated facilities of the visualization tool with program execution control, data inspection, and distribution steering capabilities of the debugger gives the user a robust system for debugging and tuning programs. This paper presents an advanced system for visualization and steering of data distributions based on the Graphical Data Distribution Tool (GDDT) [7] and DeHiFo – an advanced HPF symbolic debugger [3]. The development focused on efficient support for regular and irregular data distributions and brings several significant contributions:

- on-line visualization of distributions and values of large in-core and out-of-core data structures by means of efficient parallel I/O software,

- quality control of data distributions at run time and program tuning using an animation facility, which replays the history of data distributions and redistributions with respect to data migration, and

- dynamic data redistribution in a program after stop at a breakpoint during a debugging session.

The rest of this paper is organized as follows. Section 2 outlines our approach and presents the software architecture and the capabilities of system. Support for debugging in the compiler and the run-time system, and the implementation of interfaces are discussed in Section 3. We conclude in Section 4.

2 System Design

2.1 Components and Interfaces

The overall system consists of the HPF debugger DeHiFo and the visualization tool GDDT. Both tools are loosely coupled. Up to now GDDT has offered communication with compilers and run-time systems via a socket-based data exchange protocol. In order to control GDDT from a debugger, the tool was extended by an additional text-based command interface. Whenever the programmer requests visualization of a distributed array, its distribution, or its values, the debugger sends a command to GDDT. The interprocess communication interface used allows remote steering, for example, opening and initialization of *Data Structure Editor* (DSE) windows using data gained from the interface, or opening of data array viewers. In order to let GDDT visualize a snapshot of the program, the debugger first converts the declarative part of the program into source form and issues an *open* command. This command causes GDDT to open a new DSE window. The program instrumented for debugging creates an additional file holding distribution histories of dynamically distributed arrays. On the user's request the debugger sends the name of this file to GDDT using the *add distributions* command. While the *open* command is issued once, the *add distributions* command is issued during each visualization request. Whenever the programmer requests visualization of the contents of an array, the debugger calls a run-time function that stores the array contents in a parallel file and passes the name of the array file on to GDDT using the *add values* command. GDDT accesses the file using parallel I/O and extracts arbitrary slices from it. This approach covers both in-core and out-of-core data.

2.2 Data Distribution Steering

In long-running applications the user should be able not only to inspect the program state at a given breakpoint but also to verify the data distribution quality and to change data distributions. Changing the distribution of an array during program execution may cause loss of the program consistency. As a result, the program may crash or produce wrong results. Loss of consistency may occur when the user redistributes an array that the compiler assumed to have an invariant distribution at this place, or somewhere later in the program the distribution specified in the source code is expected. The compiler can perform various optimizations based on the knowledge of distributions, producing code which is not transparent to an unexpected redistribution. In this section we specify conditions, under which an on-line redistribution is safe.

In HPF only arrays with the **DYNAMIC** attribute can be redistributed. The **DYNAMIC** attribute tells the compiler to generate code for this array that is distribution transparent, i.e., its behavior does not depend on the distribution of arrays and there are no distribution-driven optimizations. HPF also imposes that any array that is explicitly aligned to another array cannot be redistributed. On the other hand, the redistribution of an array triggers re-distribution of all arrays aligned to it.

Other limitations depend on the compilation strategy used in the given HPF compiler. An example of such a situation is a parallel DO loop (i.e., having the **INDEPENDENT** attribute) compiled using the inspector/executor strategy [2]. In the inspector phase communication schedules and iteration sets are com-puted according to the distribution of arrays used in the loop, and in the execution phase the schedules are used for data transfer among processors to enable fully parallel execution of the loop. Changing the distribution of arrays inside of the parallel loop makes all data precomputed in the inspec-tor phase useless and thus renders any further correct execution of the loop totally impossible.

All these conditions can be checked by the debugger using information obtained from static code analysis performed by the compiler. Unfortunately, compile-time code analysis is not sufficient when the programmer uses the **REUSE** clause or schedule variables. These tell the compiler that results of the computation of communication schedules can be preserved and reused in further executions of the loop to skip the time-consuming inspector phase. In this situation, changing the distribution of any array invalidates all schedules (both contained in schedule variables and implicitly used in **REUSE** clauses). Utilization of an invalid schedule leads to erroneous program behavior or a program crash. Decision about reusing given schedule variables can be made dynamically, so it is not possible, only through static analysis, to determine whether performing redistributions in the given program state is safe or not. So far, the problem remains unsolved and the current version of the system does not address it. A complete solution requires additional support in the run-time system and extension of the debugging system. We plan to address this problem in the future.

2.3 Data Visualization

GDDT provides facile navigation within distributed data arrays and logical processor arrays emphasizing mapping relationships between data and pro-cessors. GDDT displays arrays with arbitrary numbers of dimensions where up to three dimensions can be shown simultaneously. Data arrays and proces-sor arrays are shown in windows called *array viewers*. On the user's request separate viewers for each distribution of a data array can be opened, which allows the user to compare several distributions graphically. It is also possible to show a data array's distribution on another processor array shape than the one given in the distribution specification. The processor array viewer shows the shape of a particular logical processor array. The selection of a logical processor lets the data array viewer highlight all data blocks assigned to this processor. Besides exploratory displays, GDDT provides also displays for evaluation of data distributions, for example, a *data load diagram*.

Regarding visualization of post-mortem information GDDT concentrates on redistributions of data arrays. Visualization data cover redistributions and their locations in the source text. The HPF run-time system compiles all distribution changes and forwards them to GDDT. The user can see an animated replay of a redistribution sequence by opening a data array viewer and selecting the *animator tool*. The tool offers stepwise or continuous replay. The user can observe the migration of arbitrary array elements by selecting them in the data array viewer. At each redistribution the corresponding targets in the processor array viewer change their location, showing how array elements migrate from one set of processors to another.

While it is useful to inspect data distributions at run time, programmers usually use debuggers to inspect the contents of data arrays. Thus, GDDT provides an additional facility called *data array value viewer*. This viewer visualizes array values by mapping them to colors within a spectrum between blue and red. Low values are associated with "cool" colors such as blue, whereas high values are highlighted using "hot" colors such as red. Since small deviations between two snapshots can be hardly detected by looking at two similar pictures, GDDT also allows to visualize differences between snapshots. For this purpose, it provides a *contents file manager*, which holds up to seven snapshots and allows the user also to choose pairs of snapshots in order to show deviations between them. According to the above coloring scheme strong deviations are highlighted in red.

The data array value viewer does not restrict visualization to the array shape inherited from the data array viewer. Sometimes the user might want to clip pieces of a three-dimensional array in order to examine its interior. This can be achieved by specifying a sub-shape of the inherited shape. Whenever an appropriate slice has been found, it can be explored using scaling, translation, and rotation. Figure 1 shows an example debugging session where execution stopped at a breakpoint and the user requested visualization of the distribution and the values of the three-dimensional array a. The display shows a GEN_BLOCK/GEN_BLOCK/CYCLIC distribution.

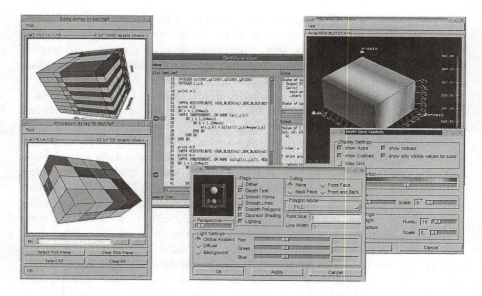

Figure 1. Example of a debugging session with DeHiFo.

3 Implementation

At the program level, the steering capability of the system requires an efficient implementation of a redistribution function in the run-time system. At the user level, we added a new debugger command which allows to change a distribution of the given array after stopping at a breakpoint. The debugger is responsible for checking the correctness of the redistribution at the given point in the program, using information generated by the compiler, stored in a symbol table file [4]. If the redistribution of the given array is safe, the debugger feeds the new data distribution specifications into the run-time system and executes the redistribution function. This function is defined in a module visible within a global scope of the program and linked with it.

A similar approach is used for data value visualization. On the user's request to display the contents of an array, the debugger calls a special subroutine in the program that stores the array contents or a section thereof in a parallel file, and passes the file name on to GDDT. The current implementation of parallel files is based on MPI-IO. Apart from the values of elements, the file contains metadata that are necessary for interpretation of its contents, i.e., the array rank, shape, size, and element type. The library executes I/O operations in two phases. First, a pair of complex MPI data types is prepared, one for the file layout and another for the memory layout. They describe a range of elements the operation affects and constitute the correspondence between elements in file and memory. Such a pair can describe the whole, even quite complex I/O operation that must be done on one I/O node. In the second phase, one collective call to MPI_File_Write or MPI_File_Read is made. This strategy reduces the number of I/O calls thus reduces overhead and gives the MPI-IO library a possibility for further optimization. On the other side, GDDT uses an I/O library for reading data from the parallel file. Here, the data type describes the linear multidimensional section that the application requests to read. The conversion from Fortran to C array layout is done on the fly. Data for post-mortem distribution visualization is collected by means of code instrumentation. During compilation the compiler inserts calls to an instrumentation library, and produces auxiliary files containing descriptions of data (re)distribution events[b]. Each event is described by its ID, type (array distribution or redistribution), and its position in the source code. The event ID is used to find the current location of the event in the source code and the name of the array. The instrumentation subroutine converts the information about an array (i.e., type of elements, rank, shape and type of distribution) taken from the run-time array descriptors, to a textual, HPF-like format and writes it to a trace file.

4 Conclusions

In this paper we presented the advanced debugging system DeHiFo integrated with the sophisticated visualization tool GDDT, which provides novel features for debugging and tuning large-scale, parallel applications: visualization of array distributions, array values, and parallel files, insight into redistributions performed during the program run by providing a replay of dynamic distributions, and advanced means for steering data distributions in a parallel program. Our work is presented in the context of HPF and the compilation environment VFC [2] (Vienna Fortran Compiler) developed at the University of Vienna, which supports HPF-2 along with a number of novel features for advanced irregular applications. However, the design concepts presented can be used in the development of programming environments for any high performance language based on the same programming model. In the next step we will develop an interface between the debugger, visualization tools and

---

[b]Here an event is understood as any change of data distribution.

the running program, built into the runtime system, that allows to extract information describing the conceptual state of the program. This will allow to fully address all issues related to safe data redistribution.

Acknowledgment

This research is being carried out as part of the research project "Visualization in Parallelization Environments" (grant P11157-TEC) and Special Research Program SFB F011 "AURORA" supported by the Austrian Science Foundation (FWF).

References

1. A Sun Microsystems, Inc. Business. *Prism 5.0 User's Guide*, July 1997.
2. S. Benkner, K. Sanjari, V. Sipkova, and Velkov B. Parallelizing Irregular Applications with the Vienna HPF+ Compiler VFC. In *Proc. Int. Conf. High Performance Computing and Networking*, volume 1401 of *Lecture Notes in Computer Science*, pages 816–827, Amsterdam, The Netherlands, April 1998. Springer.
3. P. Brezany, S. Grabner, K. Sowa, and R. Wismüller. DeHiFo - An Advanced HPF Debugging System. In *Proc. of the 7th Euromicro Workshop on Parallel and Distributed Processing*, pages 226–232, Madeira, Portugal, February 1999.
4. M. Bubak, W. Funika, G. Młynarczyk, K. Sowa, and R. Wismüller. Symbol Table Management in an HPF Debugger. In *Proc. of the 7th International Conference, HPCN Europe 1999*, pages 1278–1281, Amsterdam, The Netherlands, April 1999.
5. C. Clémençon, J. Fritscher, and R. Rühl. Visualization, Execution Control and Replay of Massively Parallel Programs within Annai's Debugging Tool. Technical Report TR-94-11, Swiss Center for Scientific Computing, 1994.
6. Steven T. Hackstadt and Allen D. Malony. DAQV: Distributed Array Query and Visualization Framework. *Special issue on Parallel Computing*, 196(1-2):289–317, 1998.
7. R. Koppler, S. Grabner, and J. Volkert. Visualization of Distributed Data Structures for HPF-like Languages. *Scientific Programming, spec. issue High Performance Fortran Comes of Age*, 6(1):115–126, 1997.
8. Christian Lefebvre and Jean-Luc Dekeyser. Visualisation of HPF data mappings and of their communication cost. In *Proc. VECPAR'98*, Porto, Portugal, June 1998.

ACTIVE I/O STREAMS FOR HETEROGENEOUS HIGH PERFORMANCE COMPUTING

FABIÁN E. BUSTAMANTE AND KARSTEN SCHWAN

College of Computing, Georgia Institute of Technology, Atlanta, GA 30332, USA
E-mail: {fabianb, schwan}@cc.gatech.edu

We are concerned with the attainment of high performance in I/O on distributed, heterogeneous hardware. Our approach is to combine a program's data retrieval and storage actions with operations executed on the resulting *active I/O streams*. Performance improvements are attained by exploitation of information about these operations and by runtime changes to their behavior and placement. In this fashion, active I/O can adjust to static system properties derived from the heterogeneous nature of resources and can respond to dynamic changes in system's conditions, while reducing the total bandwidth needs and/or the end-to-end latencies of I/O actions.

1 Introduction

The high performance computing community has identified I/O as a key limiting factor in the performance of future parallel and distributed systems. This *I/O bottleneck* arises from several trends in both technology and applications. For instance, there is an increasing speed mismatch between processing units and storage devices, which is only exacerbated by the use of multiple processors operating simultaneously in parallel machines. Furthermore, new classes of applications like multimedia, collaborative visualizations of large data sets, and computational solutions to Grand Challenge problems, are imposing steadily increasing demands on I/O. Finally, the attainment of high I/O performance is additionally complicated by the heterogeneous nature of many target platforms, the dynamically varying demands on resources, and the run-time variations in resource availability. The dynamically varying demands on resources are due to applications' data dependency and/or users' dynamic behaviors, while the run-time variations in resource availability are a consequence of failures, resource additions or removals, and most importantly, contention for shared resources.

The wide recognition of this problem can be seen in the growing number of large-scale research efforts addressing high performance I/O (see [1] for an extensive list). We contribute to such research with the introduction of adaptive *active I/O streams.* Applications I/O streams are made active through the association of application-specific or system-level operators to them. These operators are logically invoked by accessing the associated streams. The resulting *active I/O streams* permit us to exploit available computational resources and whenever possible and beneficial, to move computation toward the data sources and across the I/O Bottleneck. The ability to change, at runtime, these operations' behaviors and of their placement help us deal with dynamic variations in resource demands and availabilities.

This paper introduces active I/O streams and describes the design and implementation of *Adios*, a library for active I/O targeting parallel/distributed, heterogeneous computing platforms. Experimental evaluations of the active I/O concept and its realization are performed in the context of the Distributed Laboratories (DL) project[2] at the Georgia Institute of Technology.

2 Abstractions, System Architecture, and Implementation

This section briefly defines active I/O, presents some examples of its use, and describes the abstractions supported by the Adios I/O library, its architecture, and implementation. Performance results appear in Section 3.

Active I/O. By active I/O streams we refer to application-specific or system-level functionality associated with application I/O streams. This functionality is embodied in what we term *streamlets* and is implicitly invoked by accesses to the associated streams.

Examples of useful activities associated with streams include data-based filtering, conversion of data formats, adaptive prefetching, and adaptive declustering[3].

Many high-performance applications [4,5] work with large multi-dimensional datasets representing chemical concentration in the atmosphere or astronomical readings by different instruments. These applications rarely need the entire data set but perform data-dependent filtering to extract those items they are interested on. Although doing such application-specific filtering through active I/O streams does not reduce disk I/O, it may result in substantially less network traffic.

When data is exported into files or shared between cooperating programs, formats must be chosen for the data's representation. At the lowest level, this may involve choosing appropriate machine-specific or portable binary data formats. At the application level, this involves choosing record-based data representations most likely to be efficient for the programs that share data. In either case, active I/O can help by applying streamlets that implement data transformations 'in place'.

Weissman [6] proposes a scheme for application-specific remote file access. A Smart File Object (SFO) is user-level code intended to mitigate network performance problems through application-specific prefetching that can adapt based on application and network information. SFOs can be naturally implemented as streamlets in our active I/O streams.

As a final example of the use of activity, consider file declustering in a heterogeneous environment. The appropriate distribution of file data across storage nodes can be improved by considering the heterogeneity of such nodes and of network links connecting them, as well as the dynamic variation in resource availability across the data path. Activity could be used for declustering of data based on runtime-determined weights.

Abstractions. As depicted in Figure 1, Adios models an application's I/O as a directed network comprised of *high-level streams* originating at *sources*, arriving at *sinks*, and routed through a number of *intermediate* vertices. Each stream is a sequence of self-describing application-specific data units, such as complex data structures containing chemical concentration levels in an atmospheric model. Source and sink vertices may be application programs, or they may be devices such as disks, cameras, or satellites. Streamlets can be assigned for execution to sources, sinks, and/or intermediate vertices. By acting on the data units composing the stream, streamlets may modifying the stream's characteristics.

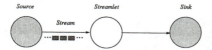

Figure 1. Streams and streamlets

Streamlets are registered with the I/O system at runtime and are subsequently attached to sets of one or more streams. The attachment of streamlets to I/O streams implicitly creates one or more additional streams (the streamlets' "output") which can then be accessed via read/write operations.

Adaptive I/O Streams. By managing I/O streams at runtime, it is also possible to cope with dynamic changes in resource availability and user needs[7]. The stream adaptations considered in our work exploit (1) the dynamic parameterization and/or specialization of streamlets that reduce/increase their execution times, while degrading/improving the fidelity or resolution of the results they produce, and (2) the migration of streamlets over the datapath in order to reduce a stream's composite bandwidth requirements or to adjust the computational/communication loads imposed by streams on the underlying

446

hardware to match the current resource availability.

The metrics used to evaluate and drive runtime stream adaptation in real-time or media applications typically concern total throughput or end-to-end latency[7]. Our work on I/O utilizes, among other metrics, a derived characteristic of a streamlet that we have found useful for both the initial allocation and the dynamic placement of streamlets. This metric, called *sprox*, *benefit from proximity to source*, indicates the potential benefit of having the streamlet placed closer to the source of data. Intuitively, there is a clear benefit in placing a streamlet that filters out the incoming messages as close to the source(s) as possible (and one that expands them as close to to the sink(s) as possible) in order to improve bandwidth utilization and/or end-to-end latency. Sprox tries to quantify this benefit as a weight function of the incoming and outgoing streams' data rates.

Adios Architecture and Implementation. Active I/O is realized in the Adios system. Adios high level design is depicted in Figure 2. Adios logically consists of a Directory Service, Client-Side Servers, Storage Servers, and Intermediate Servers.

The Directory Service acts as the contact point for all Adios components and the manager of files and stream metadata for the applications. Client-Side, Storage, and Intermediate Servers bind streamlets to their corresponding streams and perform resource monitoring and management functions.

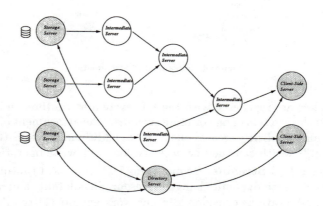

Figure 2. Adios architecture

Applications are linked with the Adios runtime libraries that translate their requests into lower level requests handled by Adios components.

Table 1. Response time to a client application's request

Streamlet location	Response time (sec.)
Part of application	62.8136
Streamlet at client	67.4798
Streamlet at server	49.4747

3 Experimental Results

The Importance of Activity in I/O. The following experiment validates the performance benefits derived from the association of activity with I/O streams and the potential advantages of adaptability. We measure the response time experienced by a visualization client requiring only a subset of the application's total data. An Adios operator performing the necessary data filtering is compared to a situation in which Adios and its filtering ability are not present.

In the experiment, a single server is connected to a single client via a 2-hop 10Mbps Ethernet link, and the client visualizes approximately 50% of the total (41.06 MB) data. The resulting performance differences are shown in Table 1.

Notice that, once the streamlet has been attached to the stream, the application can proceed as normal while the streamlet does the filtering on its behalf. This programmability improvement comes at a reduced cost, as can be seen by contrasting the first and second rows of Table 1.

Since activity is not associated with any particular device but with streams, we are able to dynamically change the placement of the filter streamlet. This application-specific filtering does not reduced disk I/O overhead but may result in substantially less network traffic. The resulting performance benefits are significant as can be seen by comparing the response times for both cases, when the streamlet is placed at the client or at server side (second and third row in Table 1). Since Adios currently uses runtime linking to migrate streamlets, however, adaptations will experience certain delays before they become effective. This delay was 20 milliseconds for the 10.7 KB streamlet used in this experiment.

Active I/O Streams for weight-based declustering. One way in which parallel I/O libraries address the I/O bottleneck is to aggregate multiple nodes with attached storage devices into one logical storage device. In our environment, the appropriate distribution of file data across such nodes must consider the heterogeneity of storage nodes and network links as well as the dynamic variation in resource availability for nodes and links. Consequently, the Adios library uses runtime-determined weights to decluster files across

Table 2. End-to-end bandwidths (in MBps) to I/O nodes

I/O Node	End-to-End		Disk		Network	
	Read	Write	Read	Write	Read	Write
lanai	0.155	0.156	1.65	3.85	0.164	0.164
micronesia	0.156	0.156	2.96	13.65	0.164	0.164
bimini	0.039	0.111	2.41	3.06	0.041	0.164
etna	0.156	0.156	1.43	2.93	0.164	0.164

Table 3. Effect of Weight-based declustering based on end-to-end bandwidths

Weight				Bandwidth (MBps)	
lanai	micronesia	bimini	etna	Read	Write
1	1	1	1	1.607	1.081
3	3	2	3	1.574	1.164
4	4	1	4	2.247	1.007

nodes; what we have termed *weight-based declustering*.

The effective bandwidths of heterogeneous storage nodes available in our lab are shown in Table 2. These bandwidths were determined by performing remote blocking reads and writes on a file in blocks of 8 KB.

From these measurements, it is clear that data must be declustered across storage engines based on the effective storage bandwidth. This is an example of useful parameterization of streamlets that route data. Comparisons of the base case of 'equal treatment' of storage engines to their unequal treatment with respect to bandwidth are depicted in Table 3.

From these experiments, it is clear that declustering files over a heterogeneous set of I/O nodes based on the nodes' performance characteristics can result in significant performance benefits. Several open issues remain concerning the appropriate assignment of weights to file components, including the fact that clients located on different nodes may experience different network connectivities to the same storage nodes. This implies that different clients sharing a single file may wish to use different weights for the file. However, the dynamic adaptability of other associated streamlets could cope with many of these situations.

4 Related Work

The potential performance benefits of moving computation across the I/O bottleneck and closer to the data has being recognized in a number of different areas including active disks, active networks, and file systems.

Active networks [8] provide a mechanism for running application code at the network routers and switches. Similarly, active disks [9,10,11] make possible to assign such functionality to empowered disk drives. In our work, activities are associated with applications' I/O data streams instead of a particular device. Once attached to their streams, the assignment of activities to specific "hosts" can be changed dynamically, adapting to the dynamic variation of resources demands and availabilities.

The Bridge file system [12] implements parallel interleaved files on the BBN Butterfly shared memory machine. One of the most innovative aspects of Bridge is its 'tool' interface, which allows application to create tool processes on the storage nodes on which the segments of a parallel file have been placed. Both Bridge and Adios allow the user to move functionality across the I/O bottleneck and towards the data. However, Adios provides an interface at a higher-level of abstraction than Bridge's tools, deals with heterogeneity, and makes use of dynamic adaptation to cope with the dynamically changing environments to which is targeted.

The dynamic placement and relocation of streamlets is a restricted type of code mobility. Code mobility raises a number of security issues and our work relies on solutions to some of those issues as proposed by projects like [13,14].

5 Conclusions and Future Work

In this paper we have introduced our ideas on *active I/O streams* and their runtime adaptation to deal with dynamically changing resource availability and with the distribution and heterogeneity of resources. Activity is supported through the association of application-specific/system-level operators with parallel/distributed I/O streams at runtime. Adaptation includes the dynamic variation of I/O streams' activities in terms of their assignments to execution sites and the precise actions performed by those computations.

We have presented our proposed programming model for active I/O streams, examples of useful activities associated with streams, and the results of our initial experimentations that validate the performance and programmability benefits of such ideas.

References

1. David Kotz. *Parallel I/O Archive.* Dartmouth College, ninth edition, February 1997. http://www.cs.dartmouth.edu/pario.
2. Beth Plale, Volker Elling, Greg Eisenhauer, Karsten Schwan, Davis King, and Vernard Martin. Realizing distributed computational laboratories.

to appear in The International Journal of Parallel and Distributed Systems and Networks.

3. Kenneth Salem and Hector Garcia-Molina. Disk striping. In *Proceedings of the IEEE 1986 Conference on Data Engineering*, pages 336–342, 1986.

4. John F. Karpovich, James C. French, and Andrew S. Grimshaw. High performance access to radion astronomy data; a case study. In *Proceedings of teh 7th International Working Conference on Scientific and Statistical Database Management*, September 1994.

5. Thomas P. Kindler, Karsten Schwan, Dilma Silva, Mary Trauner, and Fred Alyea. A parallel spectral model for atmospheric transport processes. *Concurrency: Practice and Experience*, 8(9):639–666, November 1996.

6. Jon B. Weissman. Smart file objects: A remote file access paradigm. In *IOPADS'99*, pages 89–97, Atlanta, GA, May 1999.

7. Daniela Rosu, Karsten Schwan, and Sudhakar Yalamanchili. Fara - a framework for adaptive resource allocation in complex real-time systems. In *Proceedings of the 4th IEEE Real-Time Technology and Applications Symposium (RTAS)*, Denver, CO, June 1998.

8. David L. Tennenhouse, Jonathan M. Smith, W. David Sincoskie, David J. Wetherall, and Gary J. Minden. A survey of active network research. *IEEE Communications Magazine*, 35(1):80–86, January 1997.

9. Anurag Acharya, Mustafa Uysal, and Joel Saltz. Active disks: Programming model, algorithms and evaluation. In *Eight International Conference on Architectural Support fo Programming Languages and Operating Systems*, pages 81–91, San Jose, CA, October 1998.

10. Erik Riedel, Garth Gibson, and Christos Faloutsos. Active storage for large-scale data mining and multimedia. In *Proceedings of the 24th VLDBL Conference*, August 1998.

11. Kimberly Keeton, David A. Patterson, and Joseph M. Hellerstein. A case for intelligent disk (IDISKs). 27(3), 1998.

12. Peter Dibble, Michael Scott, and Carla Ellis. Bridge: A high-performance file system for parallel processors. In *Proceedings of the Eighth International Conference on Distributed Computer Systems*, pages 154–161, June 1988.

13. George C. Necula and Peter Lee. Safe kernel extensions without run-time checking. In *Proceedings of the Second Symposium on Operating System Design and Implementation*, Seattle, WA, October 1996.

14. Rober Wahbe, Steven Lucco, and Thomas Anderson. Efficient software-based fault isolation. In *Proceedings of the 14th ACM Symposium on Operating Systems Principles*, pages 203–216, December 1993.

User Level Storage I/O :An experimental study of two storage protocols using the VI Architecture

Don Cameron, Ed Gronke, and Rob Knauerhase
{don.cameron,ed.gronke,rob.knauerhase}@intel.com

Server Architecture Lab, Intel Corporation Hillsboro, Oregon

Abstract

The emergence of low latency, low overhead, and high bandwidth interconnects based on the VI (Virtual Interface) architecture provides a new way for applications to interact with storage devices Techniques learned from supercomputing and parallel video servers recommend the placement of the computational part of the application on a separate node from that which performs the storage I/O. This separation allows for the specialization of these nodes to their intended purpose (computation or storage). As well, CPU speed increases are already causing difficulties in accessing locally attached storage and the industry is delivering technologies for commodity servers that encourage similar separation and specialization within the next 2 years.

We believe that the capabilities offered by such interconnects can provide significant benefits for applications that perform large numbers of storage I/O operations. This benefit derives from reducing the number of CPU instructions needed to initiate a storage operation, by avoiding context switches into and out of the kernel, and by minimizing the interference between the application requirements for storage I/O and the inclination of operating systems to use any opportunity to perform schedule recalculations at the end of all system transitions.

Introduction

The advent of high bandwidth, low latency and low overhead interconnects based on the VI architecture provide user applications direct access to interconnect hardware for speed-critical operations. This allows user-level applications to efficiently communicate with other user-level applications running on any other node on the same interconnect.

This paper examines two protocols implemented on a commodity operating system and compares their performance. The results demonstrate some of the difficulties of efficiently implementing storage protocols for VI-based interconnects and suggest ways to decrease the overhead, and maintain best performance for future implementations.

Section 1 will introduce the VI architecture and describe the storage problem. Section 2 will describe the two protocols. Sections 3 and 4 describe our experimental setup and results. Section 5 describes related work and the relevance of our results. Section 6 concludes the paper with some thoughts on the results as well as future work.

The VI Architecture

The Virtual Interface architecture sppecification (Version 1.0) was jointly defined by Compaq, Intel and Microsoft. Numerous hardware vendors (Fujitsu Systems, Giganet, NEC) have shipped products based on the architecture. As well, Fiber-Channel implementations based on the ANSI X3T11.4 subcommittee standard for VI over FiberChannel are shipping. As well, the Infiniband standard is expected to be VI compliant. A world record TPC-D 1000-scale result was published on 1/11/1999.

Vi requirements and guarantees

Applications establish connections between VIs. Data flows between two VIs once a connection is established. Normal messaging traffic as well as remote direct memory access (RDMA) are supported. There are various types of reliability supported. The protocols in this paper use Reliable Delivery, which requires that the interconnect deliver data at most once and in order. If the interconnect is unable to achieve this, the connection is broken, no more data is delivered and the application is notified.

An Experimental Study of two Storage Protocols using the VI Architecture

Work is enqueued via descriptors onto a VI send (send and RDMA requests) and a VI receive (receive requests) queues. Completion of work by the hardware marks a bit in the descriptor (for polling applications) or by an interrupt (for blocking applications). As well, there is a completion queue mechanism that allows for coalescing completion status from multiple VIs.

A more complete description of the architecture can be found in the VI Architecture Specification and the Intel VI Developer's Guide

Related Work

The VI Architecture is primarily based on lessons learned from the ASCI Red[18] work, as well as lessons learned by the SHRIMP [4] project. The VI focus on user level direct access is similar in approach to the U-net project[3].

The storage problem

As CPUs and memory buses get faster, scheduling storage requests and delivering status notification of those requests using locally attached storage devices is becoming problematic. The complexity and cost of attaching the number of disks to match the computational power of a commodity server is growing. (The CPU cycle cost of accessing the memory-mapped registers on these adapters is growing quite rapidly . As well, The sheer number of adapters required is a concern.) This growing concern forces one to examine message based I/O protocols on fabrics. These I/O protocols are most efficient if they utilize asynchronous request and status response notification to minimize the incurred message passing costs. Morever, the growing use of cluster services, each of which needs complete access to all available storage is another reason to move from direct attached storage to storage accessible over an interconnect.

The per operation cost of accessing the storage, given the large amount of storage requests generated by certain workloads (specifically database and web workloads) is also a growing concern. Recent studies have determined that a single storage request consumes approximately 4400 kernel processor instructions or about 8% of the number of processor instructions and 17% of the number of cycles (due to the higher measured kernel instruction CPI (cycles per instruction)). This leads one to examine user level (as opposed to kernel level) protocols for storage I/O.

Description of two storage protocols

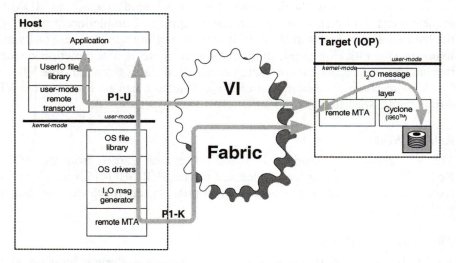

Figure 1 – Protocol 1 API and message flow (kernel and user-level)

Storage API Description

The implemented API calls are CreateFile, ReadFile, WriteFile, CreateIoCompletionPort, GetQueuedCompletionStatus and a few ioctls required in order to determine the size of the file or disk being opened. As well, additional API calls were created to initialize the library (create the VI and connect it to the target as well as register the communication memory) and to shutdown the library (disconnecting and closing the VI as well as deregistering the communication memory).

Protocol 1

The first protocol was designed to be used within a remote transport MTA (message transfer agent) for a host using an I_2O Block storage OSM (OS Service Module). As illustrated in Figure 1, this remote transport communicates across the interconnect to a target node that contains an I_2O IOP (I/O Processor) associated with locally attached storage adapters.

The MTA receives work requests from the OSM. A VI send operation transmits these requests to a remote MTA The MTA hands the request to a

An Experimental Study of two Storage Protocols using the VI Architecture

IO message layer on the IOP which hands the operation to a local adapter that performs the operation and then returns the status indication via the target messaging layer and MTA over the interconnect and through the host MTA to the OS messaging layer. The MTA and OS messaging layer then schedule a worker thread to perform an upcall to the OSM to indicate that the requested work is completed. (The upcall thread is required by OS driver model) The OSM notifies the user of the completion of the work via OS provided mechanisms.

For the user-level implementation of this protocol, the application issues the storage request to a user-level I/O library that then directly sends the message to the remote MTA. The behaviour on the IOP is exactly the same. When the response is received by the user-mode transport, a thread is scheduled to run an upcall which then notifies the application that the storage operation is completed.

In the case of a write operation initiated by the host, the IOP requests that the IOP fetch the data. The MTA performs an RDMA read to fetch the data and then schedules the actual storage operation. Upon completion, the status is returned to the host by a VI send operation from the MTA on the IOP to the MTA on the host. (For this prototype, the RDMA read is simulated by low-level software)

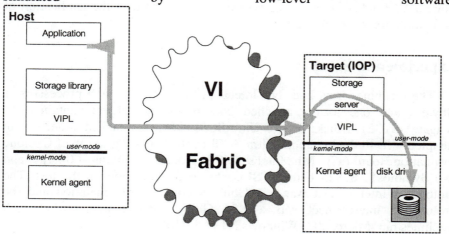

Figure 2 Protocol 2 API and Message Flow

Protocol 2

The second protocol is designed to provide the best possible performance with the storage API described above. This was achieved by minimizing the number of threads and thread context switches as well as minimizing the overhead needed to perform the storage operations.

The protocol is implemented as a user-level library on the host and an associated storage server on the target. After initialization, the client application on the host issue a read or write request to the library. Storage requests are sent to a user-level storage server running on the target. The storage request is translated into a local I/O operation and the response is generated upon completion of the I/O.

When an application requests a write operation, the host library allots a portion of a host-managed target buffer and the data are transferred using a RDMA write operation. The request to perform the disk write is then sent using a VI send operation. Upon completion of the actual write of the data on the target, a response is immediately sent to the host using a VI send operation. The host library frees the buffer allotment and notifies the application of write request's completion.

For a read operation, the request is sent to the target using a VI send operation. The target then performs a read operation and returns the data to the host using a RDMA write operation. The response is then sent to the host using a VI send operation. The host library then notifies the application of the completion of the request.

Experimental Setup

The machines used had four Intel® Pentium® II Xeon™ processors, 1 Gbyte , and one locally attached boot disk. The targets contained 12 Seagate* ST32171 disks on two Ultra SCSI channels attached either by an Adaptec* 3940 dual channel Ultra SCSI controller or by an Intel Cyclone Evaluation Board (a 33 Mhz Intel® i960™ processor running I_2O target and two Symbios* 87825 Ultra SCSI controllers) depending on the test. The protocol 1 interconnect was a 1 Gbit/s Myrinet* VI emulation and the protocol 2 interconnect was a 1.25 Gbit/s Giganet interconnect.. All machines ran Microsoft* Windows NT™ 4.0 SP3.

An Experimental Study of two Storage Protocols using the VI Architecture

All tests were performed with a target of 12 disks evenly distributed between two separate SCSI channels utilizing queue depths between 1 and 6 operations per disk. Workloads of 100% reads, 100% writes, and 50% reads/50% writes were performed using both protocols.

Test program

A single test program was used. This test program connected to the storage and registered the storage request buffers The measurement phase filled the queue using the modified ReadFile or WriteFile calls., then waited for operations to complete (using GetQueuedCompletionStatus) and immediately resubmitted the operation. Once the specified number of operations were submitted, the test waited for the outstanding operations to complete. Performance counters from Windows NT and cycle counters from the CPU were during the measurement phase. We ensured the validity of our test by comparing it to Iometer (a well utiliized Intel supplied I/O testing tool).

Experimental Results

The results shown in Figure 3 show the results of the two protocols for sequential and random reads of 2K. The results for P2 utilized the Cyclone board on the target to allow for valid comparison with P1 (which can only use the I₂0 board). The baseline local Adaptec and local Cyclone performance graphs are shown for comparison.

We expected P1 UL (user-level) to outperform P1 –K (kernel) because the P1-UL bypassed the entire host kernel storage stack. Secondly, we expected the P1-UL and P2 to have similar performance. Finally, we expected P1-UL and P2 not to achieve parity with local storage I/O because of the additional latency caused by the message passing between the host and the target.

Our first surprise was that P1-UL and P1-K performed similarly. This is due to the upcall requirement and matching this upcall to the NT completion port semantics. Secondly, P2 outperformed P1-UL and performed much closer to local I/O than expected (within 5% for a queue depth of 1, 2% for a queue depth of 2 and stastically insignificant for greater queue depths.

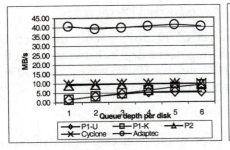 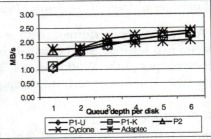

Figure 3: 2K Reads sequential (left) and random (right)

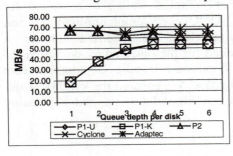 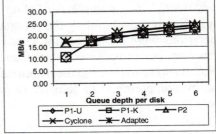

Figure 4 24K Reads sequential(left) and random (right)

Related Work

The work described here is applicable to MPP parallel file systems.because of its distributed nature. while the focus on user-level access for storage protocols is unexplored. The use of VI for IPC between nodes could speed synchronization of file pointers (as supported by MPI-IO, Intel's PFS, and others). This would lower the cost of storage operations for parallel applications even further.

Related work that distributes low level storage traffic across an interconnect include Frangipani and Petal. The idea of abstracting low level and using an RPC protocol is similar to our approach. NASD (Network Attached Secure Disks) is similar in approach with the additional separation of metadata management from data management.

Recent work has measured the performance improvements that can be achieved using VI to accelerate RPC. Specifically, RPC calls to remote nodes were found to be comparable to local RPC calls for packets of less than 8K.

Concluding Remarks

We have examined the performance characteristics of two user-level storage protocols and have found that careful attention must be paid to the implementation of these protocols, especially to the implementation of the status completion mechanism. We have seen that user-level protocols on a sufficiently capable interconnect can achieve similar performance to local disks even for low queue depths. Further work will examine how these protocols scale to larger number of target nodes as well as measure the average cost of each I/O when the system is under enough load to trigger significant scheduling contention between the storage threads and CPU-bound threads on the same systems

References

Intel Virtual Interface (VI) Architecture Developer's Guide. http://developer.intel.com/design/servers/vi/ index.html

Chandramohan A. Thjekkath, Timothy Mann and Edward K. Lee. Frangipani: A Scalable Distributed File System. In *Proc. 16th Symposium on Operating System Principles*. Pages 224-237, October 1997

Edward K. Lee and Chandramohan A. Thekkath. Petal: Distributed virtual disks. In *Proc. 7th Intl. Conf. on Architectural Support for Programming Languages and Operating Systems*, pages 84-92, October, 1996

Hemal V. Shah, Calton Pu, and Rajesh S. Madukkarumukumana, "High Performance Sockets and RPC over Virtual Interface Architecture", A. Sivasubramaniam, M. Lauria (Eds.): CANPC'99, LNCS 1602, pp. 91- 107, 1999.

Garth A. Gibson, David F. Nagle, William Courtright II, Nat Lanza, Paul Mazaitis, Marc Unangst, Jim Zelenka, NASD Scalable Storage Systems, USENIX99, Extreme Linux Workshop, Monterey, CA, June 1999. Available at http://www.pdl.cs.cmu.edu/Publications/publications.html#NASD

TPC 1000-scale results. http://www.tpc.org/new_result/d-result1.idc?id=99011101

The Shrimp Project, http://www.cs.princeton.edu/shrimp/

U-Net: project . http://www.cs.cornell.edu/Info/Projects/U-Net/

Infiniband Trade Association http://www.infinibandta.org/

DYNAMIC RUN TIME SUPPORT FOR SKELETONS

M. DANELUTTO

Department of Computer Science – University of Pisa
Corso Italia, 40 – I-56125 PISA – Italy
Email: marcod@di.unipi.it – Web: http://www.di.unipi.it/~marcod

We propose a new implementation model for skeleton based, structured parallel programming models based on macro data flow. The model overcomes some of the problems observed in traditional, template based implementations of skeleton languages, while preserving all the positive features of structured parallel programming models. We discuss some preliminary experimental results demonstrating the feasibility and effectiveness of our approach.

1 Introduction

Parallel, structured programming languages based on the skeleton concept [1] have been studied to provide the programmer with suitable tools to develop efficient and portable parallel applications in a reasonable time [2,3,4,5,6].

Basically, a skeleton is a known, reusable pattern of parallelism exploitation, and structured parallel programming languages based on the skeleton concept allow the programmer to code parallel applications by using proper compositions of skeletons. As the skeletons hide all the details involved in parallelism exploitation, such as process setup and scheduling, communication handling, load balancing, etc., the programmer can concentrate on the qualitative aspects of parallelism exploitation rather than on low-level, error-prone implementation details. Skeleton programs are usually compiled by generating a process network out of a known process network template for each of the skeletons appearing in the application code [7]. The process networks are then dimensioned (i.e. the parallelism degree of the network is computed) and mapped onto the processing elements (PEs) of the target architecture using heuristics derived from the information associated with the network templates. Once the mapping of processes to PEs has been devised, each PE in the target architecture becomes a specialized executor of some code belonging to the skeleton application.

However, this implementation strategy presents some problems. At compile time, the PEs of the parallel target architecture are dedicated to execute a particular part of the skeleton program and therefore they cannot be used for other purposes even when they stay idle (e.g. during pipeline startup, the

Work supported by the Italian MURST MOSAICO project and by the PQE2000 project

PEs dedicated to the execution of the final stages of the pipeline stay idle even if they could be used to perform the computations of the first pipeline stages). Furthermore, process networks are dimensioned statically. Any rearranging of the network at run time is impossible, even if the dimensioning turns out to be wrong, maybe due to the presence of irregular computations or in case the compiler performed an over and under-estimation of the parallelism degree of the skeleton. In this work, we discuss a new implementation technique for skeleton based parallel programming languages aimed at solving the problems arising from a number of choices performed at compile time, such as the ones stated above.

2 The skeleton framework

We assume to use the skeleton parallel language P3L [8]. This language provides both *stream* parallel skeletons (including pipe and farm skeletons) and *data* parallel skeletons[a] (including a map skeleton). The pipe and farm skeletons model usual pipeline and task farm parallelism exploitation patterns. The map skeleton models data parallel computations where a set of (possibly overlapping) data partitions are obtained from each input data item, then a set of results is obtained (by applying the inner skeleton on each data partition) and eventually a single result is computed combining the results in the set. P3L also includes a seq skeleton which is used to encapsulate sequential portions of code in such a way that they can be used as skeleton parameters (i.e. as a pipe stage). Other skeleton based programming languages/models include skeletons similar to those included in P3L [2,6,4]. P3L provides a template based set of compiling tools [8,9] that compile skeleton source code to a set of communicating processes. At compile time, the parallelism degree (i.e. the number of worker processes in the farms and the number of processes in the map) of all the skeletons is either computed or taken from user code. We can state that the computation of a skeleton program on a single input data item can be implemented as the coordinated execution of the sequential code appearing in the program in the order the seq skeletons appear in the normal visit of the application skeleton tree. Furthermore, the execution of sequential portions of code embedded in the seq skeletons is accomplished according to the plain data flow model: as soon as a new data set is ready, to be computed

---

[a]stream parallel skeletons exploit parallelism between computations performed on different data items appearing on some kind of input stream (ordered sequence of data items of the same type, possibly available at different times), while data parallel skeletons exploit parallelism between computations relative to (possibly overlapping) partitions of a single data item belonging to a given input data stream

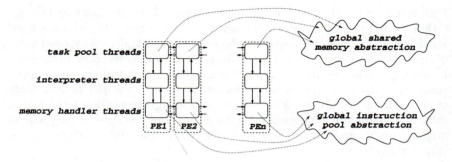

Figure 1. Target architecture abstraction

by using some `seq` code, a new process computing that code can be started.

3   A data flow implementation model for skeletons

The new model we propose to implement skeleton parallel programs is based on macro data flow, and can be summarized as follows: skeleton code is translated in macro data flow code, first. Then the macro data flow code is evaluated on a parallel architecture by a distributed interpreter of data flow code. The distributed interpreter is an enhanced version of a plain macro data flow interpreter. The enhancements basically consist in advanced memory management and macro data flow instruction pool management. They are possible just because of the exploitation of the knowledge deriving from the skeleton structure of the source code.

Skeleton programs are translated into data flow code by generating a macro data flow instruction from each `seq` skeleton appearing in the program. Such instructions wait for input data, compute the code embedded in the `seq` skeleton as soon as the input data are available and eventually deliver the output data to some other instruction. The input and output arcs to each instruction (i.e. the places where input data is taken from and output data is sent to) are determined by the skeleton structure of the program.

A collection of instances of an "interpreter" process is run on the target architecture, one process per PE. Each process has three distinct threads: a thread (the *task pool* thread) participates in managing a global macro data flow instruction pool, which is the union of all the instruction pools local to the different interpreter processes. A second thread (the *interpreter* thread) fetches fireable instructions (i.e. instructions with all the input data available) from the task pool thread, computes the instructions and deliver the results to the task pool thread. A third thread (the *memory handler*) manages a local data cache (Figure 1). In addition to the interpreter processes, two further processes are run on the target architecture: a first one delivering data items from the program input stream to the instructions that must eventually consume them, according to the skeleton structure of the program, and a second one, fetching results from the final instructions and delivering them onto the program output stream. The execution of a skeleton program compiled into macro data flow code proceeds with interpreter threads fetching fireable instructions from the task pool threads and delivering results to other instructions stored in the task pool.

We enhance this simple interpreter with some features exploiting the knowledge derived from skeleton structure of the program, in order to achieve better efficiency during skeleton program execution.

Data delivered as the result of the evaluation of an instruction, that may be reused in the evaluation of other instructions, is marked as `reusable`. Each interpreter stores received data marked reusable in a local cache handled by the memory manager thread. Further instructions referring to the cached data are scheduled with the name of the cached data in place of the input parameters. This mechanism requires some kind of centralized knowledge in the task pool managers to understand where pointers can be inserted in the instructions instead of real data. The mechanisms we want to exploit to this purpose, make use of "affinity scheduling" techniques, such as those used in SMP to enhance thread scheduling taking caches into account [10,11]. Furthermore, reusable data known to be used by a large number of data flow instructions, is broadcast to all the interpreters and stored in local caches before actually starting the scheduling of macro data flow instructions processing the data, in all those cases where broadcast communications are known to be more efficient than collections of point-to-point communications. Then, instructions using this data are scheduled to the interpreter processes with references in place of data.

The interpreter performance is also enhanced by a proper management of local task pools. Each local task pool has a low and a high water mark, representing the minimum and the maximum (suitable) number of data flow instructions that is to be stored in the local task pool. When the number of instructions falls below the low mark, new instructions are required to the other task pool threads. When the number of instructions exceeds the high mark, requests from other nodes are considered and consequently local instructions are delivered to other task pool threads. This mechanism allows dynamic load balancing to be achieved during program execution.

We organized things in such a way that instructions relative to the same input task are preferably kept local, even in case they become candidate for

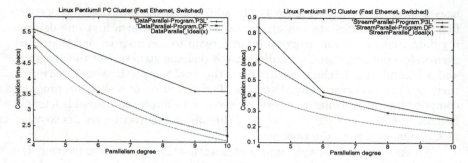

Figure 2. Performance results on a PC cluster

moving to other task pool threads. As a consequence, stream parallel computations relative to the single input data task happen to be performed onto the same PE. This allows communication overheads to be minimized.

Instructions deriving from data parallel `map` skeletons are scheduled to task pools by exploiting techniques derived from autoscheduling [12] in such a way that load balancing *and* communication optimization is achieved.

Last but not least, in our system we do not store in the task pools the complete data flow graph relative to the computation of any input data task. The first instruction only (the one fireable with the data coming from the input stream) is initially stored in the task pool. Then, interpreter threads know exactly the "continuation" of each data flow instruction[b] and each time they compute a data flow instruction they send to the task pool thread not only the result data but the result data embedded in the data flow instruction that will consume that data[c].

4 Experimental results

We evaluated our new implementation model for skeletons by "hand" compiling some sample programs and evaluating their performance. We considered simple "synthetic" programs instead of real applications, which are easy to be compiled according to our model, but having parameters that allowed us to measure different features of interest. We used P3L source code for the experiments, in such a way that the results achieved could be compared with

---

[b]such information can be easily derived (compiled) from the skeleton source code
[c]when evaluating instructions relative to a `map` skeleton, however, both the set of instructions computing the partial results and the instruction used to gather these partial results into the final `map` result are delivered to the task pool, in such a way that the partial results can be stored in the proper place.

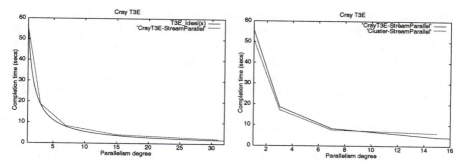

Figure 3. Performance results on a Cray T3E

the results achieved by using Anacleto [9], a prototype P3L compiler running on Linux PC clusters. Both the hand compiled code and the Anacleto object code were C programs with MPI calls [13]. We performed the tests on a cluster of Linux PCs (10 PentiumII PCs with a dedicated, switched Fast Ethernet interconnection network) and on a Cray T3E.

We discuss here the results of three different experiments. The first experiment was aimed at assessing the effectiveness of the reusable data caching mechanism. We wrote a program with a single data parallel skeleton inside. The map skeleton divided input data items into data sets in such a way that some of the input data were present only in a single data set (scattered data), some in more than one data set (multicast data) and some other data is simply included in all the data sets (broadcast data). The reusable data caching mechanism demonstrated its effectiveness on our PC cluster, showing good speedup values, and also showed better absolute performance than Anacleto in all those cases where the amount of reusable data is significant (Figure 2 left). The second experiment was aimed at evaluating the effectiveness of the low/high water marks in conjunction with the continuation based generation of data flow instructions. We run a plain stream parallel program (a pipeline with four stages: two sequential stages, the first and the fourth one, and two farm stages, the second and the third one). Again the performance measures turned out to be good and slightly better that the ones obtained by using Anacleto (Figure 2 right). The third experiment was aimed at assessing the scalability of our code on massively parallel architectures with a communication support much better than the support provided by the PC cluster. Therefore we run skeleton programs compiled according to our model on a Cray T3E. The typical results achieved are shown in Figure 3 (left): the performance achieved is very close to the ideal one. Although for small machine configurations the PC cluster demonstrated to be more efficient, as communication to computation ratio grows the Cray T3E performs better than the PC cluster, as expected (Figure 3 right). (Cluster sequential execution times are better than those of Cray T3E.) In Figure 3 right the parallelism degree of the cluster runs exceeds the number of machines in the cluster. Our code is designed to exploit a limited amount of node multiprogramming, by having a couple of interpreters competing for the usage of the same Linux machine.

5 Related work & conclusions

Recently, Serot et al. presented a coordination language based on skeletons for real-time image processing applications [6]. In their SKiPPER environment data flow graphs are generated that are subsequently submitted to a specialized tool scheduling fireable instructions for execution in such a way that real time constraints are satisfied. Although the approach is quite different, and despite the fact they claim that their environment is aimed at targeting special purpose applications, there are many contact points with our work. The work by Kasahara et al. [14] is also interesting, although it addressed compilation of FORTRAN code, because they also use a macro data flow execution model. Most of the works on skeleton systems describe very interesting and efficient optimization techniques for skeleton programs, that must be obviously taken into account in our work [2,15]. In this work we discussed a new implementation model for skeleton based parallel languages, based on the data flow execution model, extended to better exploit the locality proper of skeleton parallel computations. With this model, we achieved a better resource (PE) usage due to the reduced number of choices performed statically, better load balancing even in case of irregular computations, due to the dynamic run time support implemented, easier introduction of new skeletons in the language, as new skeletons should not require modifications to the macro data flow interpreter, and possibility of introducing shared memory features in the skeletons, exploiting the memory handler thread. Preliminary experimental results demonstrate that the approach is feasible and effective.

References

1. M. Cole. *Algorithmic Skeletons: Structured Management of Parallel Computations.* Research Monographs in Parallel and Distributed Computing. Pitman, 1989.
2. P. Au, J. Darlington, M. Ghanem, Y. Guo, H.W. To, and J. Yang. Coordinating heterogeneous parallel computation. In L. Bouge, P. Fraigniaud, A. Mignotte, and Y. Robert, editors, *Europar '96*, pages 601–614.

Springer-Verlag, 1996.

3. B. Bacci, M. Danelutto, S. Pelagatti, and M. Vanneschi. SkIE: a heterogeneous environment for HPC applications. *Parallel Computing*, to appear, 1999.

4. George Horatiu Botorog and Herbert Kuchen. Efficient high-level parallel programming. *Theoretical Computer Science*, 196(1–2):71–107, 1998.

5. M. Danelutto, R. Di Cosmo, X. Leroy, and S. Pelagatti. Parallel Functional Programming with Skeletons: the OCAMLP3L experiment. In *ACM Sigplan Workshop on ML*, pages 31–39, 1998.

6. J. Serot, D. Ginhac, and J.P. Derutin. SKiPPER: A Skeleton-Based Parallel Programming Environment for Real-Time Image Processing Applications. In *Proceedings of the 5th International Parallel Computing Technologies Conference (PaCT-99)*, September 1999. to appear.

7. S. Pelagatti. *Structured Development of Parallel Programs*. Taylor & Francis, 1998.

8. B. Bacci, M. Danelutto, S. Orlando, S. Pelagatti, and M. Vanneschi. P^3L: A Structured High level programming language and its structured support. *Concurrency Practice and Experience*, 7(3):225–255, May 1995.

9. S. Ciarpaglini, M. Danelutto, L. Folchi, C. Manconi, and S. Pelagatti. ANACLETO: a template-based P3L compiler. In *Proceedings of the PCW'97*, 1997. Camberra, Australia.

10. Srikant Subramaniam and Derek Eager. Affinity scheduling of unbalanced workloads. In *Supercomputing '94*. IEEE Computer Society, 1994.

11. K. M. Kavi, A. R. Hurson, P. Patadia, E. Abraham, and P. Shanmugam. Design of Cache Memories for Multi-Threaded Dataflow Architecture. In *Proceedings of the 22nd annual international symposium on Computer architecture*, pages 253–264, 1995.

12. D. S. Nikolopoulos, E. D. Polychronopoulos, and T. S. Papatheodorou. Enhancing the Performance of Autoscheduling in Distributed Shared Memory Multiprocessors. In D. Pritchard and J. Reeve, editors, *Proceedings of Europar '98*. Springer Verlag, 1998. LNCS No. 1470.

13. Argonne National Laboratory. MPICH home page. http://www-unix.mcs.anl.gov/mpi/mpich/index.html, 1999.

14. A. Yoshida, K. Koshizuka, and H. Kasahara. Data-Localization for FORTRAN Macro-Dataflow Computation Using Partial Static Task Assignment. In *Proc. of the 1996 Int. Conf. on Supercomputing*, pp. 61, 1996.

15. Mario Südholt, Christian Piepenbrock, Klaus Obermayer, and Peter Pepper. Solving large systems of differential equations using covers and skeletons. In *Proceedings of the 50th Working Conference on Algorithmic Languages and Calculi*. Chapman & Hall, February 1997.

ESTIMATING IPC OF A BLOCK STRUCTURED INSTRUCTION SET ARCHITECTURE IN AN EARLY DESIGN STAGE

LIEVEN EECKHOUT, HENK NEEFS AND KOEN DE BOSSCHERE

Department of Electronics and Information Systems (ELIS), University of Ghent
Sint-Pietersnieuwstraat 41, B-9000 Ghent, Belgium
E-mail: {leeckhou,neefs,kdb}@elis.rug.ac.be

Detailed performance analysis of an instruction set architecture (ISA) requires an optimizing compiler back-end as well as a cycle-by-cycle simulator. Unfortunately, developing a compiler/simulator environment is time-consuming. On the other hand, predicting the influence of the various architectural parameters on the attainable performance without a detailed performance model is a difficult task. Statistical modeling and simulation allow the investigation of the feasibility of a new ISA in limited time. In this paper, a statistical simulation model of a block structured architecture (BSA) is presented which allows us to explore various processor configurations in an early design stage. In this model, synthetic traces are generated based on real program characteristics, which are subsequently fed into a simple trace-driven simulator of a BSA. Performance is measured in the number of useful instructions retired per clock cycle (IPC).

1 Introduction

When designing a new microarchitecture, it is difficult to understand and predict the influence of the various architectural parameters on the attainable performance. Traditionally, this is done through cycle-by-cycle simulation which is accurate but time-consuming. Moreover, since microarchitectures are becoming more and more complex, the time to build a compiler/simulator environment is also increasing. Modeling in an early design stage is a possible solution to this problem, since only a few parameters have to be known to predict performance. Only recently, statistical modeling[1,2] was presented, which allows fast simulation and highly accurate IPC estimates. The basic principle of statistical modeling is to generate a synthetic benchmark trace based on a statistical profile, which is subsequently fed into a Markov chain based[1] or a trace-driven simulator[2]. The statistical profile consists of distributions which form a set of well chosen program characteristics. The simulator yields performance characteristics or IPC.

In this paper, we present a statistical model of a new microarchitecture, namely a block structured architecture (BSA), which allows us to explore the design space of BSAs in an early stage of investigation. The basic concepts of a BSA are explained in section 2; section 3 discusses some related archi-

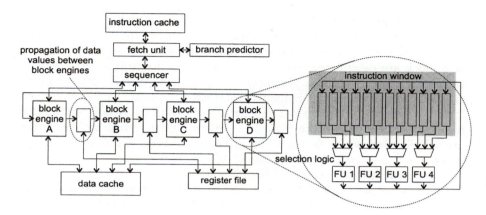

Figure 1. A possible microarchitecture of a multi-block BSA.

tectures. In section 4 the methodology of statistical simulation is elaborated. Section 5 presents the IPC estimates as a function of the various architectural parameters involved. Finally, we conclude in section 6.

2 Block Structured Architecture

A block structured architecture[3] (BSA) is a particular implementation of the control-driven decentralized paradigm[4], which means that several units of work of a single program are (speculatively) executed in parallel on separate processing elements. The units of work are assigned to the processing elements by a sequencer which uses a dynamic branch predictor to predict the follower units of work to be done. The unit of work in a BSA is called a BSA-*block*, and a processing element is called a *block engine*, see Figure 1. A BSA having multiple block engines, is called a *multi-block* BSA. In a multi-block BSA, a distinction is made between intra-block and inter-block communication. Intra-block communication is related to the communication flow within a single block engine; inter-block communication is concerned with the propagation of data values between different block engines and is slower than intra-block communication.

It is important to note that the length of a BSA-block is fixed (e.g. 16 instructions), that BSA-blocks are formed statically by the compiler, and that no control flow is allowed within a BSA-block. Moreover, the compiler is capable of grouping instructions from several control flow paths in a single block. And since no control flow is allowed within a single block, control dependencies have to be converted to data dependencies through predication, thereby eliminating unbiased branches. Once the instructions to be included in a block are determined, register renaming is performed by the compiler within the scope of a block. Register renaming removes false dependencies; only real data dependencies remain. This results in a static single assignment form allowing data-flow execution. Data-flow execution is however limited to a single block engine, see Figure 1. An instruction, which resides in the instruction window, is selected to be executed on a functional unit when all its operands are available (data-flow). After the execution, the results are sent to all the instructions in the instruction window.

Several properties of a BSA make it an interesting architectural paradigm. First, predication allows the elimination of unbiased branches[5]. Second, the architecture is partitioned reducing the complexity while preserving a high clock frequency[4]. Third, due to its hierarchical design, communication within a single block engine is hidden from the central register file reducing the number of register file ports required. The main disadvantage of block structured architectures is that higher memory bandwidths and bigger instruction caches will be needed since the inclusion of predicates and static register renaming requires more bits to encode an individual instruction. Applying compression techniques could possibly overcome these shortcomings, at the cost of (possibly) one additional pipeline stage.

3 Related Architectures

Data-flow execution has been proven to be an interesting paradigm in exploiting ILP, but a concrete hardware implementation of a pure data-flow computer seemed to be impractical[6]. Nevertheless, restricting data-flow execution to a subset of a program, which is called the instruction window, is feasible[7].

Notice that multi-block BSAs have some similarities with the multiscalar paradigm[8]. The compiler of a multiscalar architecture also partitions a program into *tasks* which comprises multiple basic blocks. The main difference between a BSA-block and a task however, is that a BSA-block has a fixed length—the number of instructions in a task is unbounded—and that no control flow is allowed within a BSA-block—control flow is converted statically into data flow through predication. Another important difference is that predicated execution is supported within a BSA-block, mitigating the consequences of mispredicting branches.

Note that multi-block BSAs also have some similarities with trace processors[9]. In both architectures, the unit of work—a BSA-block vs. a

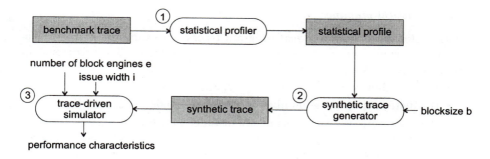

Figure 2. Statistical modeling and simulation. The parameters block size b, the number of block engines e, and the issue width i will be varied in the experiments of section 5.

trace—has a fixed length and can contain several basic blocks. But the main difference is that in a trace processor a trace is constructed at run-time and contains only one flow of control; BSA-blocks, on the other hand, are constructed statically and can contain multiple flows of control.

4 Statistical simulation

Statistical modeling and simulation is an interesting performance evaluation methodology due to its fast simulation property—IPC quickly converges to a steady state solution[2]—and its high accuracy—a relative error of only a few percents is reported by Noonburg and Shen[1] when compared to an accurate cycle-by-cycle simulator.

Statistical simulation consists of three phases, see Figure 2. First, programs are analyzed to extract a statistical profile. In a second phase, a synthetic instruction trace is produced à la Monte Carlo using that statistical profile. Subsequently, this instruction trace is fed into the trace-driven simulator modeling the architecture, which yields performance characteristics. These three phases are elaborated in the following sections.

It is also important to note that since we want to evaluate the BSA in an early design stage, we do not dispose of actual BSA-traces[a]. Consequently, the statistical profiles are taken from a traditional architecture, and the formation of BSA-blocks by the compiler will be emulated by the synthetic trace generator.

---

[a] An actual compiler/simulator-environment is still under development.

4.1 Statistical profiling

During statistical profiling, real program traces are examined and distributions concerning program characteristics are extracted. The distributions measured concerning individual instructions, are:

- the distribution of the instruction types,
- the distribution of the number of source operands per instruction,
- the distribution of the dependency distance between two instructions, or the distance (in the number of instructions in the dynamic trace) between a register instance use and its creation, and
- the probability that a memory operation is dependent on a preceding memory operation through a memory data value.

To be able to form synthetic BSA-blocks, we have incorporated two more distributions in our statistical profile, namely:

- the *basic-block-size* distribution, or the probability that a basic block contains x instructions; and
- the *biased-branch* distribution, or the probability that a conditional or indirect branch is biased to the same branch outcome.

4.2 Synthetic BSA-trace generation

As stated before, since we do not have actual BSA-traces to our disposal, the formation of BSA-blocks will have to be emulated by the synthetic trace generator. The first step of the synthetic BSA-trace generation process is adding basic blocks to a BSA-block until the maximum BSA-blocksize b is reached. Adding a basic block to a BSA-block is done in three phases. The first two phases emulate a BSA-compiler; the last phase creates a trace:

1. determine the size of the basic block to be included using the basic-block-size distribution,
2. determine the most likely path in the BSA-block using the biased-branch distribution, and add the basic block to that path, and
3. determine à la Monte Carlo if the basic block included, is part of the correct control flow path.

The process of adding basic blocks to the control flow graph of a BSA-block, is illustrated in Figure 3. First basic block **a** (path probability $p = 1.0$) is included, then **b** ($p = 0.65$), then **e** ($p = 0.40$), then **c** ($p = 0.35$), and finally **d** ($p = 0.25$). Notice that an actual compiler would add predicates to the instructions of the basic blocks to guarantee correct program semantics, e.g. p1 to b, ~p1 to c, p1&p2 to d, and p1&~p2 to e.

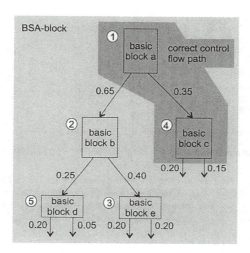

Figure 3. Building up a synthetic BSA-block as a collection of basic blocks. The probabilities determine the probability that the arrow is part of the actually executed path. The numbers in the circles show the order in which the corresponding basic blocks are included. The basic blocks shown in dark gray are marked to be part of the correct control flow path.

The second step of the synthetic BSA-trace generation process concerns the individual instructions. The instruction type, the number of operands and the dependency distance of each instruction are determined.

4.3 Trace-driven simulator

Once a synthetic BSA-trace is generated, this synthetic trace is fed into the trace-driven simulator which models a block structured architecture. The trace-driven simulator does not need to compute the actual values; only dependencies between instructions need to be taken into account. The architectural parameters of interest are the number of block engines e and the issue width i. The following instruction latencies were assumed: memory operations take 2 cycles, a multiply operation takes 3 cycles, a divide operation takes 20 cycles and all other integer operations take a single cycle to execute. All operations are fully pipelined, except for the divide operation. Further, the branch predictability was set to 90% in the experiments of section 5. The output of the simulator is the number of useful instructions retired per clock cycle (IPC).

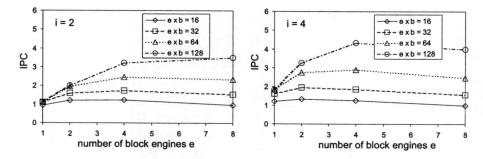

Figure 4. IPC (geometric average over the various benchmarks) as a function of issue width i per block engine, the number of block engines e, and the virtual window size $e \times b$. A point ($e = 4$ and $e \times b = 64$) on a graph denotes a 4-block BSA with a block size of 16 instructions.

5 Evaluation

5.1 Benchmarks

The traces used to collect statistical profiles were generated from the SPECint92 benchmarks on a DEC 5000/125 station with a MIPS R4600 processor. The SPECint92 benchmarks have been compiled with the DEC cc compiler with the optimization flag set to -O2. From all traces, 25 million instructions were used to generate statistical profiles. The biased-branch distribution showed that the fraction of conditional and indirect branches which are strongly biased, ranges from 50% to 80% over the various benchmarks.

5.2 Results

Experiments have been set up to estimate the attainable IPC as a function of three parameters: the issue width i per block engine, the number of block engines e and the virtual window size $e \times b$. The results are shown in Figure 4. From these results, we can conclude that as far as IPC is concerned:

- moving from an e-block BSA configuration with block size b to a $(2 \cdot e)$-block BSA with block size $\frac{b}{2}$, is only appropriate for large blocks ($b \geq 64$), since most register instances are read by nearby instructions[10];

- in general, a processor configuration with 8 block engines is not appropriate for virtual window sizes $e \times b \leq 128$, due to the inter-block communication overhead: small blocks ($b = 16$) result in much (slow) inter-block communication.

6 Conclusion

Statistical simulation allows the investigation of the feasibility of a new ISA in an early design stage with limited effort. In this paper, a statistical simulation model of a new microarchitecture, namely a block structured architecture, was presented which allows us to explore various processor configurations.

7 Acknowledgments

Lieven Eeckhout is supported by a grant from the Flemish Institute for the Promotion of the Scientific-Technological Research in the Industry (IWT).

References

1. D. B. Noonburg and J. P. Shen. A framework for statistical modeling of superscalar processor performance. In *Proceedings of the third International Symposium on High-Performance Computer Architecture (HPCA-3)*, pages 298–309, February 1997.
2. R. Carl and J. E. Smith. Modeling superscalar processors via statistical simulation. In *Workshop on Performance Analysis and its Impact on Design (PAID-98)*, June 1998.
3. H. Neefs. A preliminary study of a fixed length block structured instruction set architecture. Technical Report 96-07, Dept. of Electronics and Information Systems, University of Ghent, November 1996. Available through http://www.elis.rug.ac.be/~neefs.
4. N. Ranganathan and M. Franklin. An empirical study of decentralized ILP execution models. In *Proceedings of the 8th International Conference on Architectural Support for Programming Languages and Operating Systems (ASPLOS-VIII)*, pages 272–281, October 1998.
5. S. A. Mahlke, R. E. Hank, J. E. McCormick, D. I. August, and W. Hwu. A comparison of full and partial predicated execution support for ILP processors. In *Proceedings of the 22nd Annual International Symposium on Computer Architecture (ISCA-22)*, pages 138–149, May 1995.
6. Arvind, L. Bic, and T. Ungerer. *Evolution of Data-Flow Computers*, chapter 1. Advanced Topics in Data-Flow Computing. Prentice Hall, 1991.
7. W. Hwu and Y. Patt. HPSm, a high performance restricted data flow architecture having minimal functionality. In *Proceedings of the 13th Annual International Symposium on Computer Architecture (ISCA-13)*, pages 297–306, June 1986.
8. G. S. Sohi, S. E. Breach, and T. N. Vijaykumar. Multiscalar processors. In *Proceedings of the 22nd Annual International Symposium on Computer Architecture (ISCA-22)*, pages 414–425, June 1995.
9. E. Rotenberg, Q. Jacobson, Y. Sazeides, and J. Smith. Trace processors. In *Proceedings of the 30th Annual International Symposium on Microarchitecture (MICRO-30)*, pages 138–148, December 1997.
10. M. Franklin and G. S. Sohi. Register traffic analysis for streamlining inter-operation communication in fine-grain parallel processors. In *Proceedings of the 22nd Annual International Symposium on Microarchitecture (MICRO-22)*, pages 236–245, December 1992.

LINUX-CLUSTERS FOR LATTICE FIELD THEORY

N. EICKER AND TH. LIPPERT

Department of Physics, University of Wuppertal, D-42097 Wuppertal, Germany

C. BEST AND K. SCHILLING

John von Neumann-Institut für Computing, c/o Research Center Jülich,
D-52425 Jülich and DESY, D-22603 Hamburg, Germany

We benchmark two cluster systems both based on Alpha processors and operated under Linux as to their efficiency for simulations of lattice field theory. One systems consists of Alpha 21164 processors connected in a fast Ethernet mesh, the second system uses Alpha 21264 processors connected by Myrinet. Comparing price/performance ratios we arrive at the following estimates: an Alpha 21164 system, connected in a fast Ethernet mesh, would lead to a 4 Gflops (sustained) device for 128 processors with a price of about 80 k$ per Gflops. The 21264 Alpha-Linux-Cluster based on Myrinet, however, promises to reduce this cost to about 40 to 50 k$ per Gflops. As far as midrange systems are concerned we find that general purpose cluster solutions can come close to the performance of current dedicated QCD engines.

1 Introduction

In order to evaluate quantum chromodynamics (QCD), the component of the standard model of elementary particle physics that describes the strong interactions, non-perturbative techniques are indispensable. Solving QCD, the usual perturbative approach fails for situations where a momentum scale in the mass range of the nucleons is involved, because the strong coupling constant becomes large in that case.

Lattice gauge theory is a *non-perturbative* method invented to deal with QCD in an ab-initio manner. The quantum fields of the quarks and the gluons, the fundamental ingredients of QCD, are put on a space-time lattice and are simulated by Monte Carlo importance sampling techniques as known from statistical mechanics [1].

The costs of lattice QCD simulations are immense, in particular with the inclusion of dynamical fermions which necessitate frequent solution of a large sparse system of linear equations. Therefore, lattice QCD has become one of the largest application fields of practical parallel computing. State-of-the-art projects [2,4] require many Teraflops-weeks sustained floating point operations to generate samples of of $O(5000)$ field configurations on lattices of size up to $24^3 \times 48$ sites.

This urgent need for cheap sustained compute power provides a strong motivation to fathom the potential of PC or workstation clusters for QCD simulations. However, it is not a long time ago that PCs and workstations have become both speedy and cheap enough to render their clustering in commodity networks economical, in view of local performance, scalability and total system sizes. Moreover, to render clusters efficient one needs open source operating systems such as LINUX. The apparent success of Beowulf clusters and in particular the tremendous compute power of Alpha processors as realized in the Avalon cluster [9] immediately has called the attention of the lattice field theory community [7,8].

To give an example, if one could reach 10% efficiency on a 128 node Alpha 21164 system connected via fast Ethernet, one could build a 12 Gflops device that *today* would achieve a sustained price/performance ratio of $\approx$ 30 k\$ per Gflops for lattice QCD applications. Since this is the cost/performance ratio aimed at by the APEmille project (1998) [10], a dedicated QCD engine designed by INFN/Italy[a], prima vista, cluster solutions look very promising.

Unfortunately the estimation just given turns out to be by far over-optimistic as we are going to demonstrate for two different cluster approaches both based on Compaq Alpha processors for lattice QCD computations:

One system we have designed and benchmarked, using state-of-the-art lattice QCD codes, is a four-node cluster of 533 MHz 21164 EV56 Alpha processors, installed as a test-system at the *John von Neumann-Institut für Computing* in Jülich/Germany and operated under LINUX. Since QCD involves a nearest-neighbor interaction Lagrangian with fields living on a lattice with periodic boundary conditions, a mesh or a grid based connectivity appears to be the natural parallel architecture in order to handle the ensuing interprocessor communication between the nodes. While Avalon employs an all-to-all network using fast Ethernet switches connected by Gigabit Ethernet, the NIC-test-system (NICSE-TS) is built on a 2-D torus network. Thus, we have four Ethernet cards per node where Avalon uses only one. And, on the other hand, we do not require switches.

Our second test-cluster has been designed with respect to the experiences gained by NICSE-TS[b]. First of all, we shifted to 21264 EV6 Alpha processors, as provided in the Compaq DS10 workstations (and the UP2000 dual-processor boards offered by Alpha Processor Inc.). Furthermore, we are using Myrinet, a Gbit network to achieve an interprocessor connectivity which promised to be fast enough to compute lattice QCD on Alpha clusters. As

---

[a] assuming double precision arithmetics at 50% efficiency.

[b] The investigation of the Alpha 21264 systems has been carried out in the framework of the procurement and design for a follow up of the Connection Machine at Wuppertal University, Germany. This system is called ALiCE (Alpha-Linux-Cluster Engine)

Myrinet provides a multi-stage crossbar, we have given up the former mesh approach. Our test system (ALiCE-TS) consists of a cluster of four DS10 workstations.

We will show that ALiCE-TS is superior to the "cheap" NICSE-TS in terms of price/performance ratio by nearly a factor of two. This comes close to the price/performance ratio for APEmille, as mentioned above. Thus, we find that clusters today become competitive to specialized QCD engines for mid-range machines with a sustained power of up to 50 Gflops, however, they are limited by floorspace as well as by waste heat, and furthermore show advantages for coarse grained computations[c].

The paper is organized as follows: in Section 2 we give the specifications for the two variant clusters tested, Section 3 describes the computational problem as solved in our benchmark codes, in Section 4, we present the benchmark results and in Section 5, we give price/performance ratios and compare with special purpose QCD engines.

2 The Testbeds

The benchmark systems consist each of four single processor nodes but with two different generations of Alpha processors, the Alpha 21164 and Alpha 21264. The connectivity is fast Ethernet and Myrinet, respectively.

2.1 NICSE-TS

NICSE-TS is a four-node 21164 Alpha cluster with fast Ethernet connectivity in 2-dimensional mesh. The system is located at NIC, FZ-Jülich. The nodes are very similar to the Avalon-nodes, i.e. they contain:

- 533 MHz 21164A Alpha microprocessors on Samsung AlphaPC 164UX motherboards

- 2 Mbyte 3rd level cache per processor

- ECC SDRAM DIMMs (256 Mbytes total per node)

- 9.6 GB EIDE disk

- D-Link DFE 500 TX Ethernet cards with DEC Tulip 21140 chipset

- MPI based on MPIch

---

[c]The local QCD subsystems should be chosen not too small as the surface-to-volume ratio becomes disadvantageous for clustered RISC architectures.

The main difference to Avalon is the network-setup. Where Avalon has an all-to-all network using fast Ethernet switches connected by Gigabit Ethernet, the NICSE-TS uses a 2-D torus network. Thus we need four Ethernet cards per node where Avalon only employs one. Furthermore, we do not need any switch. We expect that the network performance scales to a large number of nodes for nearest neighbor communication. All-to-all communication can be achieved by using the routing capabilities of the Linux kernel.

2.2 ALiCE-TS

ALiCE-TS is a four-node 21264 Alpha-LINUX test-cluster with switched Myrinet connectivity. The system has been installed end of July 1999 at Wuppertal University. It includes

- 466 MHz 21264 Alpha microprocessors on Compaq DS10 motherboards

- 2 Mbyte 2nd level cache per processor

- ECC SDRAM DIMMs (128 Mbytes total per node)

- 10 GB EIDE disks

- 64-bit 33MHz Myrinet-SAN/PCI interface M2M-PCI64-2

- dual 8-port Myrinet-SAN switch M2M-DUAL-SW8

- MPI based on Myrinet GM library

ALiCE-TS has been purchased as prototype system for the design of the 128 node Wuppertal Alpha-Linux-Cluster Engine (ALiCE).

3 Computational Problem and QCD Benchmark

The computational key problem of lattice QCD is the—very often repeated—solution of a linear system of equations, leading to the so-called quark propagator [3]. The latter, on one hand, is used to construct the correlation functions of hadronic observables [1], on the other hand, its computation is needed in hybrid Monte Carlo simulation algorithms for the inclusion of dynamical quarks, i.e., the virtual quarks arising from quantum fluctuations.

The Wilson fermion linear system reads,

$$M X = \phi, \tag{1}$$

with

$$M_{nm} = \delta_{nm} - \kappa \sum_{\mu=1}^{4} (1 - \gamma_\mu) U_\mu(n) \, \delta_{n,m-e_\mu} + (1 + \gamma_\mu) U_\mu^\dagger(n - e_\mu) \delta_{n,m+e_\mu}. \quad (2)$$

The sparse matrix M is a tensor product of a combination of 4-dimensional 1st and 2st order derivative operators with *(i)* 3×3 matrices $U_\mu \in SU(3)$, the links, which vary from site to site and *(ii)* 4 variants of 4×4 Dirac matrices γ_μ [3].

With typical lattices sizes in the range of $16^3 \times 32$ to $24^3 \times 48$ sites of today's dynamical fermion simulations, the dimensions of the solution vectors X usually vary between $1.6 \cdot 10^6$ and $8 \cdot 10^6$ elements.

It has been shown, that such systems are most efficiently solved by Krylov subspace methods like BiCGStab [5]. State-of-the-art in this field is the application of parallel local lexicographic preconditioning within BiCGStab [6,4].

The results of this paper's benchmarks are based on two codes:

BiCGStab is a sparse matrix Krylov solver with regular memory access, where computation and communication proceed in an alternating fashion. In this case, DMA capabilities of the communication cards are not exploited.

SSOR is a sparse matrix Krylov solver with local-lexicographic SSOR preconditioning. The SSOR process leads to rather irregular memory access and extensive integer computations. The SSOR code is very sensitive to the memory-to-cache bandwidth, DMA can be exploited.

Both codes as written in C and compiled under the GNU egcs-1.1.2 C compiler, using those options that led to fastest code performance. They are executed in single and double precision arithmetics. We used MPI_Wtime for timing. Furthermore there are two versions for every code:

1. To test single node performance, the code runs without communication operations, otherwise carrying out exactly the same operations as the following parallel version. Only communication is omitted.

2. On the 4-node test machines, the physical system is laid out in a 2-dimensional fashion, consequently, communication is carried out along two dimensions, namely z and t directions. Assuming the processor grid is $N_{proc} = N_z \times N_t$, then the global lattice is divided in N_t slides in t direction and then every slide consists of N_z slides in z direction.

In the sequel, we are going to employ a local lattice of size $16^2 \times 4 \times 8$ on 2×2 processors such that we emulate a realistic $16^3 \times 32$ system on 4×4 processors.

4 Results

The results of our benchmarks are given for single nodes and for the four node system in order to determine the performance degradation by interprocessor communication for the two variant connectivities.

4.1 Comparison of single node performances

The basic operation in the iterative solution of Eq. 2 is the product of a 3×3 complex matrix $U \in SU(3)$ with two complex vectors of same dimension. The average number of FPOs per matrix vector operation $r_{1,2} = Uv_{1,2}$ is $N_{flops} = 171$. The number of complex words to transfer from memory to cache in order to carry out this process is $N_{cwords} = (9 + 2 \times 12)$ leading to $N_{bytes} = 528$ bytes for double precision arithmetics. Therefore we expect the maximal performance—that can be reached for a single node—to be limited by

$$P_{max} = \frac{B}{N_{bytes}} N_{flops} = \begin{cases} 97 & \text{Mflops for the UX 21164 board} \\ 420 & \text{Mflops for the DS10 21264 system} \end{cases} \tag{3}$$

in a steady state of computation and data flow, given a maximal memory-to-cache bandwidth of 300 and 1300 Mbyte/sec, respectively. Note that our problem size is chosen to be larger than the available caches. The real performances will be smaller due to BLAS-1 and BLAS-2 operations within BiCGStab.

Table 1 shows that, on the UX board, the performance of BiCGStab—with its regular memory access—comes close to the limiting value given, while the DS10 performance deviates by more than a factor of 2 from the limiting estimate. The local lattice size presumably is too small to lead to saturation of the bandwidth for the DS10. However, as a main result, we find that the improvement in performance going from the 533 MHz Alpha 21164 to the 466 MHz Alpha 21264 chip is around a factor of two, using identical codes. Furthermore, the SSOR preconditioner with irregular memory access is, as has been expected, less effective than the simple BiCGStab at the same absolute number of floating point operations.

	double precision		single precision	
Benchmark	UX 21164	DS10 21264	UX 21164	DS10 21264
BiCGStab	82	166	116	232
SSOR	57	115	90	182

Table 1. One processor benchmark.

4.2 Four-node results

The impact of interprocessor communication for both connectivities is determined on the four-node testbed systems. As shown in Table 2, the fast

Benchmark	double precision		single precision	
	UX 21164	DS10 21264	UX 21164	DS10 21264
BiCGStab	32	130	54	201
SSOR	30	100	53	164

Table 2. Four processor benchmark. UX results with fast-ethernet, DS10 with Myrinet.

Ethernet mesh performance is not sufficient for QCD. The performance of both codes, SSOR and BiCGStab, is reduced by more than a factor of two compared to the single node result. As global summation operations would lead to extensive communication on a large fast Ethernet mesh, we would expect a substantial decrease on a larger system. Varying the lattice extensions, we have verified that DMA is indeed working for SSOR. The main performance degradations are due to the massive protocol overhead stopping the processor doing other work while communicating.

User-level networking interfaces like U-Net [11] or VIA [12] promise to circumvent this problem in the near future, but are currently not available for our configuration. However, we ported a version of U-Net (without support for MPI) to Linux/Alpha and observed a sharp drop in system time (i.e. time spent in the kernel) as compared to full TCP/IP in a simple throughput measurement.

On the other hand, the Alpha 21264-Myrinet performance with Myrinet GM library only leads to decreases in the range of 10 to 20 % for the more powerful 21264 processor. We even expect a considerable improvement of these results by employing software with reduced protocol stack like SCore [13] or ParaStation [14] using Myrinet hardware.

5 Conclusion

Comparing price/performance ratios we arrive at the following estimates: An Alpha 21164 system, connected in a fast Ethernet mesh, would—as an optimistic estimate—lead to a 4 Gflops device (sustained) for 128 processors with a price of about 80 k$ per Gflops.

A 128 processor DS10 Alpha-Linux-Cluster connected by Myrinet, however, promises to reduce costs to 40 – 50 k$ per Gflops (estimated from list prices as of July 1999). These ratios are to be compared with that of APEmille, the European dedicated QCD engine built by INFN/Italy and DESY/Germany [10]. For APEmille one can expect a price/performance ratio of $\approx$ 30 k\$ per Gflops in double precision mode (offers from 1998). Thus, prima vista, general purpose cluster solutions can come close to the performance of dedicated QCD engines. Of course, the large scale generation of QCD field configurations by simulation is and will certainly remain the task of dedicated Teracomputers like APEmille, however, our results demonstrate that off-the-shelf PC clusters could represent cost efficient mid-range systems that might be an attractive substitute for the vector systems used so far to post-process QCD configurations for physics analysis.

References

1. I. Montvay and G. Münster: *Quantum Fields on a Lattice* (Cambridge Univ. Press, 1994. 491p.).
2. S. Güsken, Th. Lippert, and K. Schilling: 'Large Scale Simulations of Quantum Chromodynamics in a Europe Wide SIMD-MIMD Environment', *Seventh EUROMICRO Workshop on Parallel and Distributed Processing (EUROMICRO PDP'99), IEEE Computer Society Los Alamitos.*
3. Th. Lippert, K. Schilling, and N. Petkov: 'Quark Propagator on the Connection Machine', Parallel Computing **18** (1992) 1291.
4. N. Attig, S. Güsken, P. Lacock, Th. Lippert, K. Schilling, P. Ueberholz and J. Viehoff: 'Highly Optimized Code for Lattice Quantum Chromodynamics on Cray T3E', *Proceedings of Parallel Computing (ParCo) 97.*
5. A. Frommer, V. Hannemann, B. Nöckel, Th. Lippert, and K. Schilling: Int. J. of Mod. Phys. C Vol. 5 No. 6 (1994) 1073.
6. S. Fischer, A. Frommer, U. Glässner, Th. Lippert, G. Ritzenhöfer, and K. Schilling: Comp. Phys. Comm. 98 (1996) 20.
7. N. Eicker, C. Best, Th. Lippert, and K. Schilling: 'QCD on α-clusters', to appear in Nucl. Phys. B Proc. Suppl.
8. N. Christ: 'Machines', to appear in Nucl. Phys. B Proc. Suppl.
9. http://cnls.lanl.gov/avalon.
10. http://chimera.roma1.infn.it/apehdoc/apemille/APEmille.html.
11. T. v. Eicken, A. Basu, V. Buch, and W. Vogels, 'U-Net: A User-Level Network Interface for Parallel and Distributed Computing', 15th ACM Symposium on OS Principles, Copper Mountain, Colorado, 1995.
12. http://www.nersc.gov/research/FTG/via.
13. http://pdswww.rwcp.or.jp/dist/score.
14. http://ParaStation.ira.uka.de.

Novel Highly Parallel and Systolic Architectures using Quantum Dot-Based Hardware

Amir Fijany, Benny N. Toomarian, and Matthew Spotnitz

Jet Propulsion Laboratory, California Institute of Technology

4800 Oak Grove Drive

Pasadena, CA 91109, USA

Email: Amir.Fijany@jpl.nasa.gov and Nikzad.Toomarian@jpl.nasa.gov

In this paper, we present novel parallel architectures based on Quantum-dot Cellular Automata (QCA) hardware. We show that the QCA, by allowing co-planar line crossing, overcomes a major limitation of VLSI and, in this sense, it can potentially open a new direction in the design of parallel algorithms and architectures. In addition, the QCA is inherently suitable for pipeline and systolic computation. Exploiting these two unique features of QCA and as representative applications, we present systolic architectures for co-planar implementation of complex permutation matrices and computation of FFT by using QCA-based hardware.

1 Introduction

In VLSI design, memory and processing power are relatively cheap and the main emphasis of the design is on reducing the overall interconnection complexity since data routing costs dominate the power, time, and area required to implement a computation. Communication is costly because wires occupy the most space on a circuit and it can also degrade clock time [1]. In fact, much of the complexity (and hence the cost) of VLSI design results from minimization of data routing. Systolic arrays [1,2] are perhaps the best representative example of strengths and limitations of VLSI. Systolic arrays were originally devised as a novel paradigm for massively parallel computation to take advantage of and conform to the features of VLSI. Systolic arrays exploit massive parallelism in the computation by integrating a large number of simple processor elements interconnected with simple, recursive, and regular pattern. However, due to the inherent limitation of VLSI, many applications of interest are not amenable to systolic processing. There are two types of algorithms: the *local communication* type and the *global communication* type [1]. A large class of algorithms for signal/image processing, matrix operations, etc., belong to the class of local communication type. These algorithms can be classified based on their *planar graph*, that is, their graph can be mapped to another topologically equivalent graph with no *crossover* of wires. As a result, they require only local interconnection between the elements of the computing array. Such algorithms are highly suitable for systolic processing and consequently various systolic arrays have been proposed for their implementation [1,3]. However, a very important class of algorithms, the so called Fast Transforms including FFT, Hartley and Cosine Transforms, etc., are of global communication type, that is, they require global interconnection between the elements of the computing array and hence they cannot be mapped to another topologically equivalent graph with no crossover. Thus, this class of problem is considered as not suitable for systolic processing [1,3]. *It should be emphasized that the main obstacle in a systolic (and highly parallel) computation of this class of problems is the need for complex data permutations that arise in their implementation.* In fact, the so called Fast Transforms achieve their efficiency by exploiting the structure of their underlying operators through the use of permutation matrices.

There has been significant improvement in the performance of VLSI devices in recent years and this trend may also continue for some near future. However, it is a well known fact that there are major obstacles, i.e., physical limitation of feature size reduction and ever increasing cost of foundry, that would prevent the long term continuation of this trend. This has motivated the exploration of some fundamentally new technologies that are not dependent on the conventional feature size approach. Such technologies are expected to enable scaling to continue to the ultimate level, i.e., molecular and atomistic size. In particular, quantum dot-based computing by using Quantum-dot Cellular Automata (QCA) has recently been intensely investigated [8-13] as a promising new technology capable of offering significant improvement over conventional VLSI in terms of reduction of feature size and power consumption.

However, we strongly believe that the main advantage of QCA over VLSI is not in offering quantitative (and though significant) improvement in performance, i.e., feature size, integration, and power consumption. Rather, QCA offers a unique capability which overcomes the major limitation of VLSI, i.e., the data routing constraint. In fact, due to their cellular nature, it is possible to cross QCA wires in a plane (see §2). Such a capability then allows compact implementation of complex interconnection networks in a plane by using QCA wires, which has not been possible in VLSI. In this sense, QCA opens a new direction in designing novel and highly parallel algorithms and architectures. In this paper, in order to show the potential of QCA for designing novel parallel algorithms and architectures, we propose a hybrid VLSI/QCA architecture for systolic computation of FFT as a representative application. We first present QCA circuits for a *direct* hardware implementation of two fundamental permutation matrices: the *Perfect Shuffle* and the *Bit Reversal* permutation matrices which arise in FFT and many other signal and image processing applications [5]. We then consider a reformulation of FFT and a hybrid architecture for its systolic implementation. The hybrid architecture considered in this paper consists of a set of VLSI and QCA modules (chips).

2 A Brief Overview of Quantum-dot Cellular Automata

Here, we briefly review some pertinent features of basic functioning of and computation with QCA. More detailed descriptions can be found in [8-13]. The basic computational element in QCA is a quantum-dot cell (or molecule). A QCA cell consists of four quantum dots positioned at the corner of a square (Fig. 1). The cell contains two extra mobile electrons, which are allowed to tunnel between neighboring sites. Tunneling out of the cell is assumed to be completely suppressed by the potential barriers between cells. If the barriers between cells are sufficiently high, the electron will be well localized on individual dots. The Coulomb repulsion between the electrons will tend to make them occupy antipodal sites in the square. For an isolated cell, there are two energetically equivalent arrangements of the extra electrons which are denoted as cell state or polarization, P. The cell polarization is used to encode binary information (Fig. 1). The polarization of a non-isolated cell is determined based on interaction with neighboring cells. The interaction between cells is Coulombic and provides the basis for computing with QCA. No current flows between cells and no power or information is delivered to individual internal cells. Local interconnection between cells are provided by the physics of cell-cell interaction [9]. Previous results have shown the feasibility of fabricating quantum dots with single charges [6] and of making large arrays of dots and controlling their occupancy [7]. The design of universal logic gates and binary wire using QCA is presented in [8-10] (see Fig. 2). Experimental demonstartions of functioning QCA cell, QCA binary wire, and QCA majority gate are presented in [11,12,13]. More interestingly, however, QCA offers a unique capability which overcomes the major limitation of VLSI, i.e., the data routing constraint. In fact, due to their cellular nature and Coulombic interaction, it is possible to cross QCA wires in a plane (Fig. 3). We exploit such a capability of QCA for designing compact and complex interconnection networks in a plane.

In order to overcome some of the limitations of computing with QCA, an *adiabatic switching scheme* has been developed [9]. In this scheme, a QCA array is divided into subarrays and each subarray is controlled by a different clock. The proposed clock in QCA is *multi-phased*. This clocking scheme allows a given subarray to perform its computation, have its state frozen by raising of its interdot barriers, and then have its output as the input to the successor subarray. Such a clocking scheme implies a pipeline computation since different subarray can perform different parts of computation. In other words, QCA arrays are inherently suitable for pipeline and moreover systolic computations. The architectures presented in this paper exploit this feature of QCA to enable a systolic implementation of FFT.

3 QCA Circuits for Implementation of Perfect-Shuffle and Bit-Reversal Permutation Matrices

In this section, we present QCA circuits for implementation of the perfect shuffle and the Bit-Reversal permutation matrices which arise in Fourier transforms and other signal/image processing applications [5]. These circuits allow a co-planar (i.e., in a single layer), compact, and direct (i.e., hardwired) implementation of these permutation matrices. These circuits have been validated through extensive simulation by considering all possible combinations of the input vector. The simulations are performed by using AQUINAS (A QUantum Interconnected Network Array Simulator) which encapsulates the physics of Hartree-Fock model for simulation of QCA array [8].

3.1 Perfect Shuffle Permutation Matrix

A description of permutation matrix Π_{2^n} can be given by describing its effect on a given vector. If Z is an 2^n-dimensional vector, then the vector $Y = \Pi_{2^n} Z$ is obtained by splitting Z in half and then shuffling the top and bottom halves of the deck. Alternatively, a description of the matrix Π_{2^n}, in terms of its elements $\Pi_{2^n}(i, j)$, for i and $j = 0, 1, \cdots, 2^n - 1$, can be given as

$$\Pi_{2^n}(i, j) = \begin{cases} 1 & j = i/2 \text{ and } i \text{ even, or } j = (i-1)/2 + 2^{n-1} \text{ and } i \text{ odd} \\ 0 & \text{otherwise} \end{cases} \tag{1}$$

Figure 4 shows the schematic and the designed QCA circuit for implementation of Π_8. The circuit in Fig. 4.b has been validated through extensive simulation by considering all possible combinations of the input vector.

3.2 Bit-Reversal Permutation Matrix

The permutation matrix P_{2^n} can be described by its effect on a given vector. If Z is an n-dimensional vector and $Y = P_{2^n} Z$, then $Y_i = Z_j$, for $i = 0, 1, \cdots, 2^n - 1$, wherein j is obtained by reversing the bits in the binary representation of index i. Therefore, a description of the matrix P_n, in terms of its elements $P_{2^n}(ij)$, for i and $j = 0, 1, \cdots, 2^n - 1$, is given as

$$P_{2^n}(ij) = \begin{cases} 1 & \text{if } j \text{ is bit reversal of } i \\ 0 & \text{otherwise} \end{cases} \tag{2}$$

Figure 5 shows the schematic and the designed QCA circuit for implementation of P_8. Again, the circuit in Fig. 5.b has been validated through extensive simulation by considering all possible combinations of the input vector.

4 A Hybrid VLSI/QCA Systolic Array for FFT

The classical Cooley-Tukey Radix-2 FFT for a 2^n-dimensional vector is a sparse matrix factorization of DFT given by [5]

$$F_{2^n} = A_n A_{n-1} \cdots A_{i+1} A_i \cdots A_2 A_1 P_{2^n} = \underline{F}_{2^n} P_{2^n} \tag{3}$$

where

$$A_i = I_{2^{n-i}} \otimes B_{2^i} \tag{4}$$

$B_{2^i} = \frac{1}{\sqrt{2}} \begin{pmatrix} I_{2^{i-1}} & \Omega_{2^{i-1}} \\ I_{2^{i-1}} & -\Omega_{2^{i-1}} \end{pmatrix}$ and $\Omega_{2^{i-1}} = \mathrm{Diag}\{\omega_{2^i}^j\}$, for $j = 0, 1, \cdots 2^{i-1} - 1$, with $\omega_{2^i} = e^{\frac{-2\iota\pi}{2^i}}$ and $\iota = \sqrt{-1}$, and $\otimes$ indicates Kronecker Product. We have that $F_2 = W = \frac{1}{\sqrt{2}} \begin{pmatrix} 1 & 1 \\ 1 & -1 \end{pmatrix}$. The operator

$$\underline{F}_{2^n} = A_n A_{n-1} \cdots A_{i+1} A_i \cdots A_2 A_1 \tag{5}$$

represents the computational kernel of Cooley-Tukey FFT while P_{2^n} represents the bit-reversal permutation which needs to be performed on the elements of the input vector before feeding that vector into the computational kernel. The Cooley-Tukey FFT as given by (1), though optimal for a sequential computation, is not suitable for a systolic implementation. A suitable variant for systolic implementation is developed as follows. Using the permutation matrix Π_{2^i}, the matrices B_{2^i} can be reduced to a block diagonal form as

$$\Pi_{2^i} B_{2^i} \Pi_{2^i}^t = R_{2^i} \text{ or } B_{2^i} = \Pi_{2^i}^t R_{2^i} \Pi_{2^i} \tag{6}$$

where t indicates transpose and R_{2^i} is a block diagonal matrix given by $R_{2^i} = \mathrm{Diag}\{r(\omega_{2^i}^j)\}$, for $j = 0, 1, \cdots 2^{i-1} - 1$, with $r(\omega_{2^i}^j) = \frac{1}{\sqrt{2}} \begin{pmatrix} 1 & \omega_{2^i}^j \\ 1 & -\omega_{2^i}^j \end{pmatrix}$. Using (6), the matrices A_i given by (4) can be written as

$$A_i = I_{2^{n-i}} \otimes (\Pi_{2^i}^t R_{2^i} \Pi_{2^i}) \tag{7}$$

and using the identity

$$(A \otimes B)(C \otimes D) = (AC) \otimes (BD) \tag{8}$$

we then have

$$A_i = (I_{2^{n-i}} \otimes \Pi_{2^i}^t)(I_{2^{n-i}} \otimes R_{2^i})(I_{2^{n-i}} \otimes \Pi_{2^i}) \tag{9}$$

Let

$$S_i = (I_{2^{n-i}} \otimes \Pi_{2^i})(I_{2^{n-i+1}} \otimes \Pi_{2^{i-1}}^t) \text{ and } K_i = I_{2^{n-i}} \otimes R_{2^i}, \text{ for } i = n, n-1, \cdots i \tag{10}$$

Substituting (9) and (10) into (1), we then get

$$F_{2^n} = \Pi_{2^n} S_n K_n S_{n-1} K_{n-1} \cdots S_{i+1} K_{i+1} S_i K_i \cdots S_2 K_2 S_1 K_1 P_{2^n} \tag{11}$$

A hybrid VLSI/QCA architecture for a systolic implementation of (9) is shown in Fig. (6). The terms Π_{2^n}, S_i, and P_{2^n}, which represent data permutation operators, are implemented by using QCA modules. The terms K_i are implemented by using VLSI modules containing a set of simple bit-serial processing elements. Each processing element has two inputs and two ouputs. It reads data from its two inputs and produces two outputs by performing simple multiply and add operations. Aside being driven by the same clock, the processing elements are totally independent from each other. Due to this feature, the processing modules are highly suitable for a large-scale implementation with CMOS VLSI. In order to achieve the global synchronization, the VLSI and the QCA modules are driven by the same clock.

5   Conclusion

In this paper, we presented novel circuits for a compact, co-planar, and direct implementation of two fundamental permutation matrices by using QCA-based hardware. Using these circuits, we then presented a hybrid VLSI/QCA architecture for systolic computation of FFT. The architecture of this paper underlines the unique advantage of QCA. Although QCA offers significant quantitative advantages over CMOS VLSI, in terms of feature size and power consumption reduction, we strongly belive that one unique advantage of QCA is the capability of co-planar line crossing. This capability can potentially overcome a major limitation of VLSI, i.e., the data routing constraint. It can also opens a new direction in designing massively parallel algorithms and architectures. As it was shown for FFT, it can enable the design of novel systolic arrays for applications which have previously been considered not amenable to a systolic computation by VLSI. However, It should be emphasized that much more work remains to be done in developing a more systematic approach for the design of QCA-based circuits. Note that, in this paper and for the sake of proof of concept, we considered bit-serial circuits for computation and communication. However, many applications of interest might require a bit-parallel format resulting in more complex circuits which cannot be simulated and analyzed by the currently available simulators.

Acknowledgments

This research was performed at the Jet Propulsion Laboratory (JPL), California Institute of Technology, under contract with NASA. This work was supported by the Revolutionary Computing Technologies Program Element of the JPL Center for Integrated Space Microsystems (CISM). The authors greatfully acknowledge Professors C.S. Lent and P.M. Kogge from Notre Dame University for insightful discussions as well as for providing us with AQUINAS.

References

1. S.Y. Kung, *VLSI Array Processors*, Prentice Hall, 1988.
2. H.T. Kung,"Why systolic architectures?," *Computer*, vol. 15, p. 37, 1982.
3. D.I. Moldovan, *Parallel Processing: From Applications to Systems*. Morgan Kaufmann Publishers, 1993.
4. A.H. Karp,"Bit Reversal on Uniprocessor", *SIAM Review*, vol. 18(1), pp. 1-26, 1996.
5. C. Van Loan, *Computational Frameworks for the Fast Fourier Transform*. SIAM Publications, Philadelphia, 1992.
6. R.C. Ashoori *et al*,"N-electron ground state energies of a quantum dot in a magnetic field," *Phys. Rev. Lett.*, vol. 71, p. 613, 1993.
7. B. Meurer, D. Heitmann, and K. Ploog,"Single electron charging of quantum-dot atoms," *Phys. Rev. Lett.*, vol. 68, p. 1371, 199.
8. P.D. Tougaw and C.S. Lent,"Logical device implementation using quantum cellular automata", *J. Applied Physics*, 75, p. 1818, 1994.
9. C.S. Lent and P.D. Tougaw,"A device architecture for computing with quantum dots", *Proc. IEEE*, vol. 85(4), 1997.
10. C.S. Lent and P.D. Tougaw,"Line of interacting quantum-dot cells: a binary wire", *J. Applied Physics*, vol. 74, p. 6227, 1993.
11. I. Amlani *et al*, "Realization of a Functional Cell for Quantum-Dot Cellular Automata", *Science.*, vol. 277, p. 289, 1997.
12. A.O. Orlov *et al*, "Experimental demonstration of a binary wire for quantum-dot cellular automata", *Applied Physics Lett.*, vol. 74, p. 928, 1997.
13. I. Amlani *et al*,"Digital logic gate using quantum-dot cellular automata", *Applied Physics Lett.*, vol. 74, p. 2875, 1999.

a) Encoding Binary 1   b) Encoding Binary 0

Figure 1. Cell Polarization and Binary Information Encoding

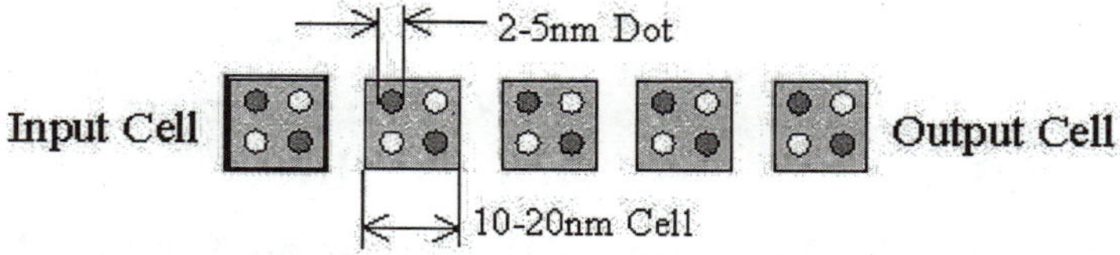

Figure 2. Binary Wire and Cell-Cell Interaction

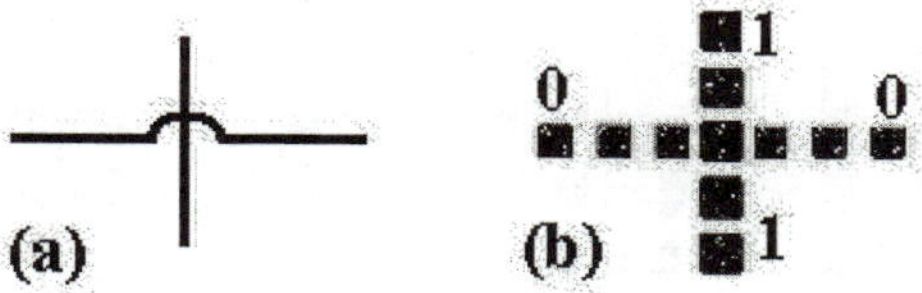

(a)   (b)

Figure 3. Co-planar Wire Crossing
a) Schematic   b) QCA Circuit

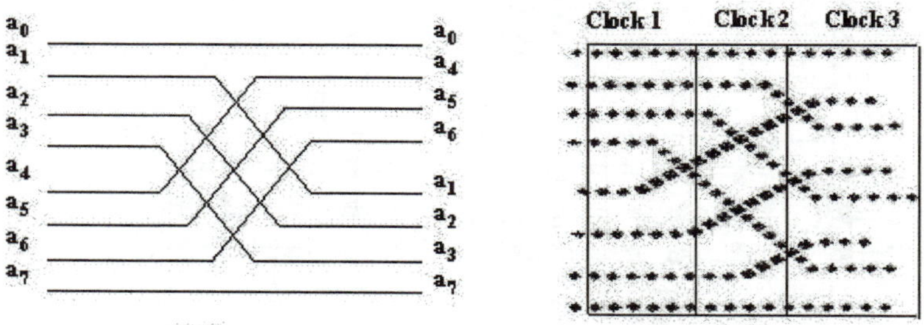

(a)   (b)

Figure 4. Implementation of Permutation Matrix Π_8
a) Schematic   b) QCA Circuit

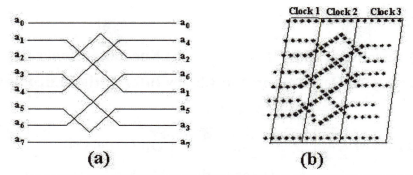

Figure 5. Implementation of Permutation Matrix P_8
a) Schematic   b) QCA Circuit

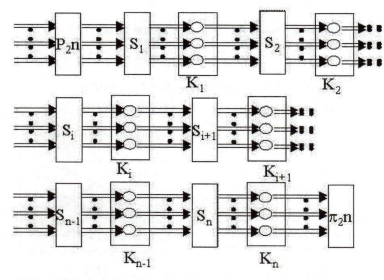

Figure 6. A Hybrid VLSI/QCA Architecture
for Systolic Computation of FFT

A CELLULAR ENVIRONMENT FOR STEERING HIGH PERFORMANCE SCIENTIFIC APPLICATIONS

G. FOLINO, G.SPEZZANO

ISI-CNR, c/o DEIS Università della Calabria, 87036 Rende(CS),Italy

This paper presents CARAVEL, a problem solving environment where simulation and steering are integrated to facilitate interactive exploration and modelling of complex applications on high performance computers. CARAVEL uses the cellular automata (CA) formalism both as a tool to model and simulate dynamic complex phenomena and as a computational model for parallel processing. It is an environment for CA programming and parallel execution. The system supports RUDDER, a purpose-built language for programming and steering cellular applications, and enables the parallel execution of the model.

1. Introduction

Many scientific areas, such as biology, physics, chemistry, geology, and engineering are using computational simulation as an essential tool in research and experimentation. Simulation consists of predicting the behavior of real physical systems in actual or hypothetical circumstances based on models of these systems. Moreover, simulations need to be accurate and often require massive amounts of computation. The integration of high performance computing systems with suitable modelling formalisms simplifies the development of new industrial or commercial applications and extends the scope of existing applications to more complex problems and to multidisciplinary simulation. However, the current methodologies for parallel computing are too complex and too specialised to be accessible for most engineers and scientists.

Problem solving environments (PSEs) provide a general, uniform framework allowing researchers to concentrate on their specific system of interest without to be involved in the lower level parallelization tasks (load balancing, distributed memory, message passing, parallelization of algorithms, etc.). A PSE provides a complete integrated computing environment for composing, compiling, running applications in a specific problem area [1]. Many PSEs are limited to post-processing of data sets and only some of them visualize the results as they are generated. However, without interaction with simulation during runtime she/he cannot modify input parameters to control and steer the computation to better match the experimental data or to perform a qualitative sensitivity analysis. A modern PSE must combine simulation, visualization, control and parallel processing into one tool that allows to interactively monitor and explore the program in execution, visualize the state of the computation as it progresses and allowing to change parameters, resolution or representation on the fly.

The CARAVEL system presented in this paper is a PSE where simulation and steering are integrated to facilitate modeling and interactive exploration of complex applications on high performance computers. CARAVEL is based on modeling formalism of cellular automata (CA) [2,3]. CA are very effective at solving scientific problems because they can capture the essential features of systems in which global behavior arises from the collective effect of numerous, simple, locally interacting components. They are discrete dynamic systems composed of cells in a regular spatial lattice, either one-dimensional or multidimensional. The cells are connected to their adjacent cells only. CA model a problem in a naturally parallel way as a collection of identical transition functions (set of rules) applied to all the cells of the automaton.

CARAVEL is an environment for CA programming and parallel execution. It is currently implemented on different distributed-memory parallel computers such as the MEIKO CS-2, CRAY T3E and LINUX cluster of workstations. The system supports RUDDER, a purpose-built language for programming and steering cellular applications, and enables the parallel execution of the model.

CARAVEL supports *exploratory*, *algorithmic* and *performance* steering [4] of cellular computations. Exploratory steering allows researchers to examine the state of a simulation as it proceeds through the interactive visualization of intermediate results and to guide the computation by the modification of model geometry, resolution, simulation parameters and boundary conditions. In this case, the decisional process is carried out by human users who interpret the data visualized and then issue, by a GUI, steering commands. The algorithmic steering approach automates the steering loop replacing the human with a decisional algorithm written in a steering language. Finally, performance steering allows to improve the performance of the application operating, for example, on the input parameters of the load balancing algorithm.

A number of computational steering environments such as VASE [5], SCIRun [6], Progress and Magellan [7,4], CUMULUS [8], CSE [9] have been developed. However, many of those support only exploratory steering. In Magellan the steering commands are specified in ACSL, an advanced computational steering language, and may also be bound to graphical user interfaces. Reference [10] surveys and compares those environments.

The main contribution of this paper is the development of a language-based approach to computational steering. Previous versions of CARAVEL support only exploratory steering. Here, we are interested to illustrate the steering constructs of the RUDDER language for algorithmic and performance steering of high performance cellular computations. Section 2 provides an overview of the CARAVEL system. Section 3 presents the RUDDER language for CA programming and the new constructs for computational steering. In Section 4 the numerical solution of Laplace's equation is presented in order to illustrate the language-based approach to steering. Section 5 concludes the paper.

2. Overview of CARAVEL

The CARAVEL prototype is derived from the CAMEL system [11], but offers additional functionality to perform program steering by a language based approach.

The CARAVEL environment consists of

1. a language, called RUDDER, which can be used to define cellular algorithms and to perform steering commands when complex space and time events are detected;
2. a graphical user interface (GUI) for editing, compiling, configuring, executing, visualising and steering the computation;
3. a load balancing algorithm to evenly distribute the computation among processors of the parallel machine.

To improve the performance of applications having a diffusive behaviour such as CFD, the CARAVEL run-time system implements a load balancing strategy similar to the scatter decomposition technique. The load balancing strategy is a trade-off between the static and dynamic approach. In fact, the cells partitioning is static, whereas the amount of cells mapped on each partition is dynamic. In CARAVEL, the grid of cells is first divided into n vertical folds; each fold is then partitioned into N strips, where N is the number of processors of the multicomputer. The i-th strip of each fold is assigned to the generic processor Pi. To avoid useless computation the user may change, at run time, the set of folds on which the state transition function must be applied. Each processor will compute only the strips of the specified folds. The set of active fold will be augmented or restricted just before some cells become active or passive. The choice of the active folds can be automatic including some tests.

3. RUDDER, a programming and steering language

CARAVEL supports the CA programming language RUDDER. RUDDER is an extension of the CARPET language [12], with new constructs to handle region-based programming and computational steering. It is a high-level language based on C with additional constructs to describe the rule of the state transition function of a single cell of a cellular automaton and steer the application. A RUDDER program is composed of a *declaration part* that appears only once in the program and must precede any statement, a *body program* that implements the transition function, and a *steering part* that contains a set of commands for extracting and analysing system information and performing steering.

The main features of RUDDER are the possibility to describe the state of a cell as a record of typed substates (*char, shorts, integers, floats, doubles* and mono-dimensional *arrays*), the simple definition of complex neighbourhoods (e.g., hexagonal, Margolus) and the specification of non-deterministic, time-dependent and non-uniform transition functions. In standard CA a cell can interact only with the cells defined within its neighbourhood. RUDDER extends the range of interaction among the cells introducing the concept of *region*. Regions are statically defined spatio-temporal objects which allow a cell to know, by aggregate functions, the behaviour of a substate within a set of cells put within a defined area.

The predefined variable *cell* refers to the current cell in the n-dimensional space under consideration. A substate can be referred appending the substate's name to the reserved word cell by the underscore symbol '_' (i.e, *cell_substate*). Cell substates are updated at each iteration only by the *update* function, in order to guarantee the semantics of cell updating in cellular automata. After an update statement, the value of the substate, in the current iteration, is unchanged. The new value takes effect at the beginning of the next iteration. The neighbourhood of a cell is defined as the maximum number of cells that a cell can access in reading. For example, in a 2-dimensional automaton defining the radius equal to 1 the number of the neighbours can be up to 8. To define time dependent transition functions or neighbourhood, the predefined variable *step* is used. Step is automatically updated by the system. Initially the value of step is 0 and it is incremented by 1 at each iteration. To allow a user to define spatially non-uniform CA, RUDDER defines the *GetX, GetY* and *GetZ* operations that return the value of X,Y and Z coordinates of a cell in the automaton. Parameter objects describe some global features of the system. The value of a global parameter is the same in each cell of the automaton.

In RUDDER, region objects are statically defined by the *region* declaration. A d-dimensional region is defined by a sequence of indices which represent the geometric coordinates, the time period (starting time and ending time) in which the region is defined, and the interval of monitoring. RUDDER implements also the aggregate functions *MaxRegion, MinRegion, SumRegion, AndRegion, OrRegion, AvgRegion,* which respectively allow to calculate the maximum, the minimum, the sum, the logical and, the logical or, and the average value of substates of the cells belonging to a region. Other functions can be added in the future. Furthermore, the *InRegion, InTempRegion* and *Distance* functions allow to know if a cell belongs to a spatial region, if the current iteration is within the temporal window and the monitoring step defined for the region, and calculate the distance between the cell and the region considered.

The steering commands are defined in the *steering* section that is performed by the runtime system at each iteration, after the transition functions of all cells have been evaluated. RUDDER allows to define significant events using the substates as variables as well as the parameters and the regions objects defined in the declaration part. Besides, it allows to take actions when an event is detected. The basic event-action control structure of RUDDER is **if** *<event_expr>* **then** *<steering_action>*. An *event_expr* is an expression that combines the aggregate functions defined on a region and the steering commands applied to the event variables by basic numerical expressions as well as relational and logical operators. An example is the following:

```
if MaxRegion(zone1_pressure,&suc1) == MinRegion(zone1_pressure,&suc2))
    steer_pause;
```

where the event expression checks if the maximum and the minimum values of the pressure substate in a region (*zone1*) are equal. If so, the computation is stopped.

Steering commands are of four types. Those for the control of the simulation are: *steer_pause* for stopping the computation, *steer_parameter* for changing the value of a parameter, *steer_view* and *steer_edit* to view and change the substate's value of a cell in a point of the automaton. Those for changing the visualization are: *steer_zoom* to set a region and zoom that region, *steer_changeplane* and *steer_changetype* to define the plane and the substate to visualize, *steer_colorange* to change the range of the colours associated with the values of a substate, *steer_openstate* and *steer_closestate* to open and close a window for the visualization of a substate. *Steer_load* and *steer_save* are used to load and save a configuration of an automaton from/in a file. For tuning the performance of the application the commands are: *steer_changefold* which sets the active folds, *steer_getstarfold* and *steer_getendfold* return the initial and final folds among those actives. The complete syntax of the steering commands is given in [13].

4. An example of program steering in RUDDER

In this section we describe a cellular automaton that solves Laplace's equation for equilibrium temperatures in a square area with fixed temperatures at the boundaries. Each cell represents the temperature at a single point in the region. In each time-step, the next temperature of every cell is defined by the average of its four neighbors (*Jacobi iteration method*). Figure 1 shows a RUDDER implementation. The *cadef* section defines a two-dimensional CA with two *float* type states (*A* and *Temp*), a von Neumann neighbourhood (*NEWS*) a global parameter (*epsilon*) and four regions (one (*err*) to delimit the area of computation and the other three (*edge[0]*, *edge[1]*, *edge[2]*) to automatically implement the activation of the folds of the load balancing strategy described in the section 2). When we define the size of the automaton we must allocate extra space to hold boundary elements. Therefore, if the size of *A* and *Temp* is N x N then the size of the CA will be $(N + 2)$ x $(N + 2)$. In our example the size of the CA is 600x600 and the size of A and Temp is 598 x 598. The program body begins by assigning 0.0 to *A* and *Temp* substates of all cells except for the boundary values at the west edge which values are 1.0. Then it calculates the next temperature for every cells in the *err* region. It also saves the difference between this value and the current in the *Temp* substate. *Temp* is used in the steering section to define the criterion for stopping the computation. In fact, the computation finishes when the maximum value of the *Temp* substate in the *err* region

```
cadef           /* definition part */
{
  dimension 2;
  radius 1;
  state (float A,Temp,P);
  neighbor NEWS[4] ([0,-1]North,[-1,0]West,[0,1]South, [1,0]East);
  parameter (epsilon 0.005);
  region (err(2,599,2,599,1,1,2,20000,1),
          edge[]{(149,150,2,599,1,1,1,20000,1),
                 (299,300,2,599,1,1,1,20000,1),
                 (499,450,2,599,1,1,1,20000,1)}});
}
int i; float tmp;  /* body program */
{
  if(step == 0)          /* CA initialisation  */
  {
    if (GetX == 1) {
        update(cell_A,1.0);
        update(cell_Temp,0.0);}
      else{
        update(cell_Temp,0.0);
        update(cell_A,0.0);}
  }
  else                          /* jacobi iteration */
      if(InRegion(err)){
        tmp = (North_A + South_A + West_A + East_A)/4.0;
        update(cell_A,tmp);
        update(cell_Temp, fabs(cell_A - tmp));}
}
steering                                /* steering part */
{
 int suc, foldin, foldfin; double par;

  if(InTempRegion(err))
   {
      par = MaxRegion(err_Temp,&succ);
      if( par < epsilon) {
          steer_openstate(Temp);
          steer_colrange(Temp,0.0,par);
          steer_pause;
        }
    }
 if (step==0){                  /* performance steering */
     steer_changefold(0,0);}
 else
   {
   foldin = steer_getstartfold();
   foldfin = steer_getendfold();
   if((foldfin < NumOfFolds -1)&&(MaxRegion(edge[foldfin]_A, &suc)>0))
    steer_changefold(foldin,foldfin +1);
       }
}
endsteering
```

Figure 1. The numerical solution of Laplace's equation in RUDDER.

is less than *epsilon*. When this event occurs, before stopping the computation, the steering system opens a window to visualise the *Temp* substate with the suitable range of colours. The steering part implements also the automatic activation of the folds through the defining of a region with size *N x 1* located at the end of each fold.

At the beginning, only the first fold is activated (*steer_changefold*(0,0)). Then when the max of the *edge[0]* region of first fold is greater than zero the second fold is activated. Afterwards, at the same way all the other folds will be activated.

We analyzed the performance of our RUDDER implementation of the Laplace's equation with the algorithm for performance steering and compared it to a version of the same application without the algorithm of steering. We executed each version on a partition of a MEIKO CS-2 parallel machine. Our partition was composed of five 200 MHz HyperSparc processors with 256MB of memory per processor. The algorithm is performed for different values of *epsilon* in order to obtain an increasing number of iterations and involve gradually all the folds of the automaton.

Table 1 shows the values of epsilon used, the number of iterations needed to reach the solution, the execution times (seconds) needed for computing the solution of the algorithm without and with the performance steering algorithm and the gain obtained using the performance steering algorithm.

Table 1. Execution times of the implementation of the Laplace's equation.

Epsilon	Iterations	Execution time without the performance steering algorithm	Execution time with the performance steering algorithm	Gain
0.005	51	25.11	15.83	36%
0.001	245	186.96	145.26	22%
0.0005	486	446.74	380.22	14%

5. Conclusions

We described the CARAVEL environment and we proposed a language-based approach to computational steering. This approach has been implemented extending the CA programming language RUDDER with new constructs that allow the definition of the steering commands. In the paper, we have shown how efficient steering algorithms for cellular computations can be designed by the definition of triggers that monitor the change of spatial data and the execution of actions when an event is detected. The performance gain obtained in the implementation of Laplace's equation demonstrates the advantage of this approach. Currently, this approach is used in the COLOMBO project within the ESPRIT framework. The main objective of this project is the application of parallel computing to the simulation of the bioremediation of contaminated soils using CA models.

500

References

1. Gallopoulos E., Houstis E.N., Rice J.R., "Computer as Thinker/Doer:Problem-Solving Environments for Computational Science", *IEEE Computational Science & Eng.*, vol. 1, n. 2, Summer 1994, pp. 11-23.
2. Hansen P. B., "Parallel Cellular Automata: a Model for Computational Science", *Concurrency: Practice and Experience*, vol. 5, 1993, pp.425-448.
3. Toffoli T., Margolus N., *Cellular Automata Machines A New Enviroment for Modeling*, The MIT Press, 1986.
4. Vetter J., Schwan K., "High Performance Computational Steering of Physical Simulations", *Proc. 11th International Parallel Processing Conference*, IEEE Computer Society Press, Los Alamitos, CA, 1997, pp.128-132.
5. Jablonowski D.J., Bruner D.J, Bliss B., Haber R.B., "VASE: The visualization and application steering environment", *Proc. of Supercomputing '93,* 1993, pp.560-569.
6. Parker S.G., Johnson C.R., "SCIRun: a scientific programming environment for computational steering", *Proc. of Supercomputing '95*, 1995.
7. Vetter J., Schwan K., "Progress: a toolkit for interactive program steering", *Proc. of the 1995 Int. Conf.* on *Parallel Processing,* 1995, pp. 139-142.
8. Geist G.A., Kohl J.A., Papadopoulos P.M.,"CUMULUS: Providing fault tolerance, visualizazion, and steering of parallel applications", *Int. J. Supercomput. Appl. High Performance Comput.,* vol. 11, n. 3, 1997, pp.224-235.
9. Van Liere R., Mulder J.D., van Wijk J.J., "Computational steering", *Future Generation Computer Systems,* vol.12, n.5, 1997, pp. 441-450.
10. Parker S.G., Johnson C.R., Beazley D., "Computational Steering Software Systems and Strategies", *IEEE Computational Science & Engineering*, vol.4 n.4 , 1997, pp.50-59.
11. Cannataro M., Di Gregorio S., Rongo R., Spataro W., Spezzano G., Talia D., A Parallel Cellular Automata Environment on Multicomputers for Computational Science, *Parallel Computing*, North Holland, vol. 21, n. 5, 1995, pp. 803-824.
12. Spezzano G., Talia D., "A High-level Cellular Programming Model for Massively Parallel Processing", *Proc. of the 2nd Int. Workshop on High-Level Programming Models and Supportive Environments HIPS'97,* IEEE Computer Society Press, pp. 55-63, April 1997.
13. Folino G., Spezzano G., "A Problem Solving Environment for Interactive Simulation and Steering of Parallel Cellular Computations", Technical report, CNR-ISI, n. 6, 1999.

Acknowledgements

This research has been partially funded by the CEC ESPRIT project n.24,907.

IMPLEMENTING A FUNCTIONAL APPROACH FOR PARALLEL RESOLUTION OF IRREGULAR PROBLEMS ON DISTRIBUTED MULTIPROCESSORS

LAURENT FOURNERIE   AND   BERNARD LECUSSAN

ONERA-CERT/DTIM
2 av. E. Belin, BP 4025 – 31055 Toulouse Cedex, France
e-mail: lecussan@cert.fr

A large class of complex simulations, those with irregular domains, cannot be efficiently implemented on parallel computers because their irregular and unpredictable runtime behaviour makes this type of computation difficult to distribute among each processor. This paper explores two issues: parallel lazy functional programming and multithreaded runtime as alternative complements to the efficient execution of irregular problems on (massively) distributed-memory multiprocessors. The single assignment feature and the absence of side effects allows one to overcome the difficulties of synchronised accesses to shared data and parallel computation distributions; it ensures that all processors get a consistent view of the memory hierarchy. Furthermore, this model of computation allows thread's execution without scheduling policy leading to efficient context thread switch, and consequently real overlapping of network latency by effective computations. We studied deeply a matrix multiplication program running in three alternative systems: a single processor using the function of BLAS library, a partition of an Intel/Paragon and an IBM/SP1.8.

1   Introduction

Functional approach achieves indeed high level of programming by abstracting over operational aspects and offers interesting features for parallel computing, such as the formal unicity of results whatever the number of concerned processors. In most parallel programming models based on imperative style, the algorithm is specified as a sequence of actions on a common store. In contrast, a declarative program does not specify such a sequence of operations, which allows the independent evaluation of function arguments (horizontal parallelism) as well as the simultaneous execution of a function with its argument (vertical parallelism). The compiler and the system are free to choose different evaluation order, provided the semantic is preserved. Furthermore, memory management is transparent to the programmer and high order functions provide an attractive way to specify parallel schemes. Moreover, lazy evaluation permits to execute not the entire calculus in place when defined in the code, but only the minimal part when necessary during the computation. Significant advantages can be taken with laziness to specify and run irregular applications. By example, domains can be specified in a recursive way without fixing area or required precision, although needed parts will be dynamically constructed until the necessary level for the desired quality of the final result [1] [2].

Generally, functional programs tend to run slowly because the language provides useful services to the programmer, in particular dynamic store allocation, lazy semantics or high order functions [3]. The goal of this paper is to give a technical overview to overcome those difficulties at the levels of language implementation and system design, underlining our main design choices and presenting first performance measurements on uniprocessor or multiprocessor computers running real cases. In the MaRS system, parallel tasks are explicitly specified using the only one annotation *process* but data management, thread distribution and dynamic multithreading are transparent to the programmer. Thus, the same program, once compiled for a platform, can be executed in various configurations with different number of processors. Yet available on several platforms, the system allowed the development of sizeable applications. It also proved its ability to efficiently link with pre-existing codes and to perform real speed-up.

Section 2 presents related works and the objectives of the approach. Section 3 offers a brief description of the language and the process of compilation. Section 4 discusses the multithreaded runtime and the link with graph reduction mechanism. Section 5 presents results obtained on Intel/Paragon and IBM/SP1.8 with different configurations of the parallel machine, using a matrix product program benchmark in order to evaluate the ability of the model to manage the computation distribution. This benchmark is not really representative of the applications aimed by the system (irregular computation, sparse system with lazy evaluation) but only enables one to study the efficiency of the multithreaded runtime. Then we have used the system to develop a Computational Fluid Dynamic application with dynamically auto-adaptive meshes which is not presented in this paper.

2   Related works and MaRS approach objectives

The execution model is a crucial point of the language definition and implementation; the computer's performance and the basic mechanisms depend on its features. Basically, program execution could be implemented using three models:
1. control flow model in which execution model is dependent upon the execution of the program instruction sequence;
2. data flow model in which computation is performed when data are ready to be computed [4][5]; where both models, instructions and data are explicitly split; the Threaded Abstract Machine (TAM) refines dataflow execution models to address the critical constraints that parallel architectures place on the compilation of general-purpose parallel programming language. TAM defines a self-scheduled machine language of parallel threads, providing a path from dataflow graph program representations to a conventional control flow;
3. reduction model which does not differentiate between data and instructions: everything is expression; program (data and code) and its result are the same

object in different representations; program computation consists of rewriting non-reduced expressions (*redex*) with their reduced form, under a set of rules control. Computation is done when no more rules can be. The reduction mechanism leads to graph reduction: a program is represented as a graph, each cell representing functional expression terms. The rewriting mechanism is carried out in a destructive way but in single assignment mode: the content of a cell is replaced by the computed value. In this way, shared subexpressions are reduced only once. Furthermore, this process could be done by lazy evaluation, i.e., only when the result is needed during the reduction of the graph [6].

The parallel reduction model combined with lazy evaluation of data structures and argument of functions could be efficient solutions for irregular computation applications in which data structures are not regular dense matrices and their data-access patterns are unknown until runtime. Furthermore, a pure functional language has no assignment operation: a memory cell cannot be explicitly modified by the programmer and responsibility for storage reallocation is completely left to the language implementation. This has the fundamental effect in parallel programming that, on one hand, the order of execution of the program is constrained only by data dependence between values and on the other, there are no need for mutual exclusion to support remote atomic updates and shared accesses.

3   MaRS-ML language and compiler overview

MaRS-ML is a lazy, pure, high order functional programming language but strict annotations can be used in order to obtain better time/space behavior: functions and data structure can be defined as lazy as well as (partially) strict in their arguments. Parallel tasks could be explicitly designed using the *process* annotation but parallelism management is transparent to the programmer. *Blocs* are provided to interface other language data implementations as arrays or records in order to delegate their management instead of performing costly data conversions; external functions written in C or Fortran languages for example, can be interfaced with MaRS-ML programs.

3.1   Stricticity

The compiler runs stricticity analysis and detects some arguments to be strict in order to optimize the target code. Stricticity annotations can appear:
- in function definition: a *n*-ary function is said to be strict in an argument x_i if and only if the value of the argument is essential to calculate the result.
- in type definition: a constructor with a strict component will compute its value before the data structure construction. Note that evaluating a value defined by a structure is not evaluating the whole structure, but only its first construction.

3.2 Process annotation

The *process* annotation provides the unique way to express parallelism but caution is required for a correct and efficient utilization. The rule below describes how an evaluation is performed. An expression is *hit* when the current evaluation process requires the value of this expression. When an expression $f\ e_1\ e_2\ ....\ e_n$ is hit for the first time the following operations append:

1. A new process is spawn for each e_i starting with *process*
2. Strict arguments still not evaluated or hit, are sequentially evaluated by the current thread,
3. The current thread applies the function f to its arguments. The arguments not yet evaluated will be reduced at the moment of being hit.

3.3 Compilation process

The compiler generate a Flat Intermediate Code (FIC) in C language which will be associated with the runtime in order to produce the parallel executable program. Let us now consider the following example that will be used to explain the main characteristics of the system.

> **fib n = if n < 2.0 then 0.0 else fib(n-1.0) + process fib (n-2.0) ;**
> **eval fib 34.0 ;**

The corresponding FIC code generated by the compiler is given in Table 1. The graph manipulation instructions (*MakeNode,Read*) are performed via pointer values that can be local or remote. The node is created with the tag *NRP* (*NonReducedReady*) that means the node has to be reduced by the first thread that need the value. In case of local pointers, the operation is immediately performed; otherwise, a message is sent to the node holding the cell. This is why the blocking operation (*Read*) is followed by the *STOP* instruction in order to allow a context thread switch instead of waiting the response in case of a distant pointer.

	Move (34.0) $\rightarrow$ R0		rtn1 :	DropP 1	
fib :	Prim lt_float R0 (2.0) $\rightarrow$ RegI0			Read P0 $\rightarrow$ RegR0	*get result of*
	Case RegI0 alt3 alt2			Stop	*fib(n-2)*
alt2 :	Move (1.0) $\rightarrow$ R0			Prim plus_float R0 RegR0 $\rightarrow$ R0	
	Jmp end		end :	Return	
alt3 :	MakeNode NRP (proc) R0 $\rightarrow$ P0		proc :		*Parallel thread entry*
	Stop	*thread creation*		Sget 0 $\rightarrow$ RegR0	*getting the*
	Prim minus_float R0 (1.0) $\rightarrow$ R0			Returning real	*argument n*
	RiseP 1			Prim minus_float RegR0 $\rightarrow$ R0	
	Mark rtn1	*function call to fib*		Jmp fib	*call fib (n-2)*
	Jmp fib	*with arg n-1*			

Table 1: FIC code generated from fib program.

4   MaRS multithreaded runtime

The runtime (RT) is divided into two main tasks: memory management (create, read and delete cells) and graph reduction processes management.

4.1   Memory management

Each distributed memory hierarchy contains part of the graph to be reduced and each cell of the distributed graph could be in one of the following states: *reduced, being reduced, non-reduced.* Data type used to represent the graph are the following: an entry table for cells, a heap for list of values, a cell descriptor table describing actions to perform (in light of cell's types and requests), a list of threads waiting for a cell being reduced and a buffer to manage partial applications. Thus, cell is made up of a fixed part (located in the entry table) and a variable part which is able to store a list of values or referenced data (situated in the heap). The entry table is visible to all processors so it is freed using the reference counter for distributed nodes, and the local heap is freed using an incremental generation-based garbage collector algorithm.

4.2   Graph reduction processes

The running parallel code is a collection of threads which represents the actions of graph reduction or the evaluations of function arguments in the high level language. Data structures contain a set of threads, each one comprising an identifier, four stacks (integer, real, pointer, addresses), a context (the four stack pointers) and an input buffer. They also contain a set of global registers for the intermediate code data, the running thread number with the associated context, and local variables.

All thread allocated with a same processor share a common address space containing an image of the intermediate code; so, the thread switch context consists only in the swap of the four stack pointers and the thread number. According to the model, the graph could be reduced out-of-order, without synchronisation latency and scheduling policy. For a full use of the processor resources, the network latency can be hidden by the activation of a ready thread in reading the input file message where messages are stored; a thread swap occurs each time a response is being await. An active thread cannot be interrupted until it reaches a message-sending instruction in order to limit the number of processor pipeline re-initialisations. Multithreading is used only when costly remote accesses are necessary, so as to minimize idle cycle time while maintaining long run-length threads.

4.3   Execution mechanism

The intermediate code does not contain any information about underlying computer architecture: only requests on graph management are formulated while the distribution and access management are runtime functions. Likewise, threads are not statically determined during compilation and the multithreading management is devoted to the runtime, but activated by reduction requests located in the intermediate code. Consequently, the object code can be portable on various multiprocessors, as there is no link to hardware resources of the parallel computer. The runtime will activate the intermediate code which call back to the runtime either for a memory operation, or for a thread operation. These solicitations can be either local or remote with message passing operations. The runtime so performs a main loop which processes memory messages (if any), reactivates an active thread (if any) and, if there is an inactive thread and a ready cell, allocates it for reduction.

The RT is thus activated by the intermediate code via the STOP instruction. Its role is to respond to the requests pertaining to its own graph management (cell reading, reference counter decrementation ...) but also to (re)activate threads. Further down, the mechanisms are illustrated through the previous example of the *fib* function shown on Table 1 computed with two nodes.

Thread allocation The *fib* program result is obtained by the evaluation of the cell starting at the label *begin*. During the reduction process, the tag's cell will obviously be *"being reduced"*.

Thread commutation The *mknode* instruction requests of another node, the creation of a *non-reduced-ready* cell in order to perform *fib(n-2)* computation in parallel. As the addressed node allocates the cell and sends back the pointer x, the thread is switched. When the thread is reactivated, the expected pointer is placed into P0 and calculus of *fib(n-1)* can begin.

Thread liberation The second node will allocate a thread to reduce the cell designed by x. After the reduction, the cell will become a reduced cell that will contain a real constant.

Cell creation The distribution of cell's creation must be as equitable as possible. There are two different allocators as the case may involve reduced or unreduced cells, so as to obtain a better layout of simple data on one hand and future works on the other hand.

Functions The instruction *read* is called following the computation of *fib(n-1)* to obtain the value of *fib(n-2)* which is computed in parallel, in order to produce the final sum. Thus, when the active thread requires the reduced value of x from node 2, three cases can appear:

- The reduced value is available and then the node 2 will transmit to the requesting thread, a message containing the expected value,
- the cell is being reduced, so the requesting thread will be added to the list of threads which must be responded to, after the cell has been updated,
- or, the cell has not changed since its creation (Unreduced tag). This means that the parallelization attempt failed and that the requesting thread will have to

reduce the cell itself. It will thus receive a CALL message in order to execute a remote procedure call for the computation of *fib(n-2)*, then updating the cell pointed by *x*, before resuming the *fib* computation. Note that this last case is a way to overcome the deadlock of all threads waiting for one-another because it guarantees that an active thread is always present.

5 Results

We sought to measure comparative performances of the system on an application as significant as possible. Nonetheless, we also wanted to demonstrate its ability to utilize pre-existing codes as well as its capability to process material examples. In light of this, we have chosen to write a MaRS-ML program of parallel multiplication of matrices in the C = A x B form. The algorithm we have used is hence, a decomposition of the initial matrix, into arborescent sub-matrices, the computations of the sub-matrices are made by addressing the *dgemm* primitive of the BLAS library. It would be interesting to examine the performances observed with this parallel multiplication on the full matrix regarding the peak performance reached by the *dgemm* on a single processor. The following results were obtained on an INTEL Paragon with 64 MO of memory per node and on IBM SP1.8 with also 64 MO per processor. Communication was implemented thanks the MPI package on both computers. Two matrix sizes of 1025*1025 and 2000*2000 are applied onto various configurations. The computation times are converted into MFLOPS per node, which allows us to assess the performance progress given a particular configuration.

Various attempts on the computation on a single node lead to a peak performance of 44 MFLOPS on Paragon and 94 MFOLPS on SP1.8. Table 2 reflects execution times of the matrix multiplication applied onto various configurations of the parallel computers.

n = 1025	4	8	12	16	20	24	28	32
Paragon	44.4	24.7	17.7	13.2	11.1	10.1	9.0	7.5
SP1.8	29.7	16.1	11.1	8.7	7.1	5.9	5.2	4.7

n = 2000	16	20	24	28	32	36	40	44
Paragon	45.8	37.1	31.8	24.7	24.7	23.6	22.5	20.0
SP1.8	35.2	28.3	23.8	20.5	18.7	-	-	-

Table 2: Execution times for C(n,n) = A(n,n) x B(n,n) (in seconds)

Efficiency defined by number of floating point operations/time/number of processors, is in the range of 20% to 25% for the first test, and 40% to 45% for the larger test, of the peak performance for each processor. With a benchmark program similar to both matrix configurations, the second test's granularity is greater, since only the size of the data differs. Those results show the significance of thread granularity on each processor throughput.

In order to study the behavior of the multithreaded system, we will focus on two specific measurements for 16 and 24 processors of the IBM SP1.8 with the larger test. The runtime's instrumentation for these two configurations produces the following results (Table 3): **Min** (resp. **Max**) corresponds to the processor offering the shortest (resp. the longest) execution time.

16 PE	T0	T1	T2	N0	N1	D0	Mem
Max	**33.6**	2.0	1.6	161	10,066	3,461	41,3
Min	**31.3**	4.3	1.7	180	10,790	3,300	42,5

24 PE	T0	T1	T2	N0	N1	D0	Mem
Max	**22.5**	1.3	0.8	139	6,644	3,588	27,7
Min	**20.9**	2.9	0.8	138	7,155	3,332	28,8

T0 = Effective execution time (s)   T1 = Overhead (idle time) (s)   T2 = Garbage collecting (s)
N0 = Total number of threads   N1 = Total number of thread interrupts
D0 = Thread mean duration (ms)   Mem = Memory size (Mbytes)

Table 3: Computation with 16 and 24 IBM/RS6000 processors.

The two values, Min and Max show that the execution time for each processor is always less than 7% of longest execution time. In addition the number of threads entailed onto each processor lies in the range [161-180] for a 16 PE configuration, and [138-139] for a 24 PE configuration. These results show a very good balance in threads, whether in the occupancy of processors or in memory allocation. The overhead denotes not enough parallel threads ready to execute and the thread context switch time; the garbage collecting of freed nodes seems not very costly.

Recall that each thread interrupt generates a context thread switch. We may deduce from both values T1 and N1 that the communication latency is really hidden by one another thread computation. Anyway the model generates an important effect in memory management, especially in cache memory: in fact, each thread context switch has a high probability to generate a miss on a line cache as many back and forth from the intermediate code and the runtime is made during thread executions. This may explain why each processor sustains only less than half of the peak performance of the best sequential execution. Trace cache presents in new modern processors could be a solution to this problem.

6   Conclusion

The programming and execution models presented in this paper offer a number of benefits in the programming of parallel computers, regardless of their architecture and type of memory (shared-address space or distributed). Functional programming and single assignment allow for a clear and high level of parallelism: the *strict* annotation, implies that the argument be assessed as early as possible since it is required for the computation. On the contrary, the absence of such a rule is an indication that the argument is lazy, and should be assessed as late as possible if, and only if, the result is required to carry on with the computation. Furthermore, lazy semantic allows manipulation of potentially infinite data structures or iterative processes.

The *process* annotation indicates that a task can be commenced, yet, competing with other tasks currently in process. In addition, there are no time-related dependencies between different tasks. This allows for an execution without having pre-established an order of execution, synchronised only according to the availability of graph nodes.

The implicit execution model of a graph's parallel reduction rests upon a shared-address space memory model; parallelism is generated by the reduction of unreduced cells. The mechanism implemented pertains to an adaptation of this model to a distributed memory model, the latency of the communication network being overlapped by effective thread computations within the processors.

However, the model generates important effects in memory management, from cache levels to main memory. On one side, given the fact that the contents of a shared-address memory cannot be rewritten, the data in the cache remain consistent without the need for a costly coherence protocol which cause excessive communication and overhead. On other side, frequent thread context switches cause an increase in the caches and TLB misses. It seems that the key point to improve parallel computation efficiency is to increase thread granularity without to sacrifice potential parallel tasks.

References

1. Jerzy Karczmarczuck, *Scientific Computation and Functional Programmin*, in IEEE Computing in Science & Engineering p. 64, May/June 1999
2. P.W. Trinder, K. Hammond, H.W. Loidl and S.L. Peyton Jones, *Algorithm + strategy = parallelism*, in Journal of Functional Programming, Volume 8(1) page 23, 1998
3. Paul Kelly, *Functional Programming for loosely-coupled Multiprocessors*, Research monographs in parallel and distributed computing, The MIT Press, Cambridge, Massachusetts ISSN 0953-7767, 1989
4. Arvind and R.A Ianucci, *Two fundamental issues in multiprocessing*, Memo 226-5, MIT Computation Structures Group July 1996
5. D. Culler, K. Schauser and T. von Eicken, *Two fundamental limits on dataflow multiprocessing*, in Proceeding of the IFIP Working Group 10.3 ; Conference on Architectures and Compilation Techniques for Fine and Medium Grain Parallelism. Elsevier Science, January 1993
6. S. Peyton Jones, *The implementation of Functional Programming Languages*, Series in Computer Science, Prentice-Hall International, 1987/1990.

DISTRIBUTED HIGH-SPEED COMPUTING OF MULTIMEDIA DATA

M. GAUS, G. R. JOUBERT, O. KAO, S. RIEDEL AND S. STAPEL

Technical University of Clausthal, Department of Computer Science
Julius-Albert-Str. 4, 38678 Clausthal-Zellerfeld, Germany

Distributed platforms are not necessarily well-suited for systems which handle large data sets, such as processed in multimedia applications. In this paper a specialised computation model, based on asynchronous transmission, is presented. As the necessary functions are encapsulated this system can be used without detailed knowledge of the system architecture. A dynamic strategy of task execution is utilised to adjust the number and size of the distributed data packages according to the computational load of the processing elements at transmission time. Thus more powerful PE's, or those whose resources are not fully utilised, will either receive packages more frequently or will be given larger packages. In large networks some nodes can be replaced by others or only a few data blocks may be sent to (a) particular node(s). The efficiency of the method is evaluated with a variety of practical run time measurements.

1 Introduction

Distributed systems consisting of a network of workstations are increasingly being used for solving compute intensive problems. Distributed platforms are, however, not always well-suited for systems which handle large data sets as can be found in, for example, multimedia applications. The limiting factor for processing of large data sets is usually network bandwidth. Thus, the distribution of huge amounts of data bounds the overall processing speed. This situation is made worse by the fact that data is transmitted only when requested or sent by the parallel processes. In order to reduce this effect, the transmission of data should be separated from the process synchronisation. Well-known software systems for parallel/distributed processing on existing computer networks are PVM, MPI, PVMPI, Condor, Mosix [1-5] and Treadmarks. An advantage of the PVM is its availability on nearly all important architectures and operating systems. On the other hand synchronous data transfers and type conversions are time consuming, making it unsuitable for the processing of large multimedia data sets.

1.1 Multimedia data

Multimedia data has become an important component of modern software systems. Static media (images, graphics, text) are combined with dynamic media (audio, video, animations) to obtain realistic representations of natural processes, for the visualisation of complex results or to depict dynamic processes.

In spite of the increases in memory sizes, processing and communication speeds, the processing and communication of multimedia data is still time and compute intensive. Some of the initial problems, essentially data compression, could be solved by the development of efficient compression algorithms, e.g. JPEG, MPEG, MP3. Many of these algorithms have been implemented in hardware, offering the possibility of real time encoding.

The next step resulted in parallelising numerous procedures for processing multimedia data. Static media, such as encountered in image processing applications, are usually subdivided into independent data fragments, which are then distributed among a number of processing elements. The results are gathered and combined to form the final result. In dynamic media, interdependencies between the different data blocks must be considered and resolved. An example for this is MPEG compression, which is based on finding and eliminating redundant information in consecutive frames.

Parallelisation by means of data segmentation is well-suited for parallel computers with shared memory, since little or no time is spent on communicating the data. Software for distributed computing in heterogeneous networks will have less of a performance gain, because of the slow synchronous transfers and greater variances in client resources. If the operations executed are simple these delay effects can be seen quite clearly. An example for this is the calculation of correlation coefficients for short term series [8]. Considering all combinations between 100 shares and a time difference of 5 days resulted in 681450 correlation terms and 27 megabytes of data. The performance gain by parallelising the algorithm with the PVM among 4 DEC Alphas was negated by the resulting administration overhead. This resulted in the run time on a single workstation being up to 6 times faster than the parallel PVM version.

These requirements (large data sets, simple operations) are also found in the management, retrieval and processing of multimedia data. Current approaches to multimedia databases are based on the extraction and management of specific characteristics. Queries compare the extracted characteristics with all images stored in the database, and return the most similar images. Each archival and retrieval process results in the computation of huge amounts of data. Performance gains through parallelisation are negated by transfer times and administration of the data, as described in the correlation example. This results in the necessity of a specialised model for parallel processing of huge amounts of data.

2 Processing model for static multimedia data

The proposed processing model aims to make development of parallel programs by non-experienced users easy, and minimise the communication and management effort, by using TCP/IP sockets directly. Similar to the work pile model [6], this model is based on the creation of pools of tasks, which are controlled by three special processes (*distribution* and *collection manager*, *computation client*). The information is divided into sections which are distributed to a number of processing elements (Figure 1).

512

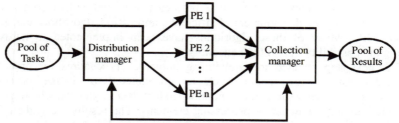

Figure 1: Schematic representation of the processing model

2.1 Distribution manager

The distribution manager is responsible for the division and management of the data packets to be processed. Push technology is used to minimise the transfer cost between server and clients. The responsibility of the distribution manager includes data packets definition, management of data packets in the local pool of tasks, processing of client requests and distribution of the data packets among the processing elements. The distribution strategy is set within this process. Essential requirements include the efficient use of available resources, as well as being failure tolerant. To circumvent problems related to processing element failures the data packets are subdivided into three groups: the first group consists of packages which were not yet distributed, the second group comprises transmitted, but unprocessed data, whereas the third group consists of processed data packets.

A simple distribution strategy of available data packets increases computing efficiency. If the first group is empty, but non-processed data blocks are still in the second group, then these are dispatched to idle clients, which have already completed their computation tasks. This can be achieved by generating a list of all available active nodes and of the status of their local pools of tasks. The number of distributed—but not yet processed—packets can be calculated from the number of packets sent, but not yet received by the collection task. This requires a direct connection between the distributor and the collector. The difference is analysed and compared to a given threshold values. If it is below the threshold the distribution manager sends new packets to the client. This strategy requires a time and/or workload oriented distribution of the data packets as well, since processing can only occur if the processing element has a low CPU load. A blocked client that does not satisfy this requirement is regarded as a node that has failed. The server will redistribute the data packets sent to this client.

2.2 Computation client

This component performs the computation on each processing element. A simple and compact structure reduces the management overhead and enables an important performance increase. The computation client consists of *a local pool of tasks, a processing object* and *a local pool of results.* In this pool the processed data packets are temporarily stored until a connection for the transfer to the collection manager becomes available.

2.3 Collection manager

This process accepts processed data packets from the computation clients and stores them until all data packets have been received in the pool of results. Once this occurs, it composes the processed original from the received data packets. A picture or a series of pictures would be composed at this point during e.g. JPEG-encoding. Furthermore, the collector sends a message giving the number of received data packets to the distributor. From this information the distribution manager determines the current workload of each client and redefines the distribution strategy. The distributor is also notified when all data packets have reached the collector and the processing is completed.

2.4 Arraying in multiple hierarchical levels

The described model consists of two hierarchical levels, containing the distribution and collection processes on one level, and computation clients on the other. This model will reach its capacities quickly with a large number of non-local processing elements. An alternative is to arrange servers hierarchically. The lower levels of this hierarchy contain not only clients, but subordinated servers as well, which distribute the data packets to lower level clients.

An example for the application of such a model are data distributions in corporate or university networks: *a super server* sends data packets to *subordinate servers* in each division. Each of these servers initiates the computation in its own domain. This significantly reduces the communication complexity, or at least binds it locally. The processed packets are still sent to a *central collector* making dynamic regrouping possible. The clients of a new group will then receive their packets from the server of the new group. Marking the processed data packets with the id of the *group* which processed them is mandatory. This allows the collector to find out which group processed each data packet so that this group is resupplied with data to process once it drops below a given threshold.

3 An adaptive distribution strategy

Heterogeneous networks consist of processing elements with different performance capabilities (CPU, memory etc). Information about the complexity of tasks being processed is usually not available. Furthermore, the number of users working on a particular workstation are continuously changing. Thus it is impossible to predict the performance of any particular workstation in a network at a given time. This makes it impossible to *a priori* schedule task processing. A *dynamic* distribution strategy of processing tasks is thus needed. The number and size of the distributed data packages must be adapted to the work load of the processing element at transmission time. Even this strategy may not be near optimal, as additional tasks can be started on the PE between the determination of the current load and the arrival of data packages. More powerful PE's or those with a small performance utilisation will receive packets more frequently or will be allocated larger packages. In large networks some low performance nodes can be skipped and the work distributed to more powerful PE's. If this is not possible the data blocks sent to the low performance nodes will automatically be adapted.

For the concrete realisation of this method *a performance ranking* must be generated. This can be done by calculating the difference between sent and processed packages as described above. In the first distribution run each processing element is supplied with n packages. After a certain time interval a performance rank list is created. The number of packets for the respective processing elements are then increased or decreased. This operation is repeated until the collector has received all data.

Alternatively the packet size can be adapted. Larger packets are sent to the PE's at the top of the performance list. This can minimise the communication and network traffic. However, this is not always possible. For example, an image is usually subdivided into n sections. If all sections are distributed during the first run a change of the package size is not possible without a loss of already processed data. This performance information can only be used if the image has large dimensions, or if a whole image sequence is to be processed. A disadvantage of this model is that additional logic for the management of dynamic block sizes is necessary in the clients. Furthermore the complexity of the model tasks and the requirements regarding the user knowledge are increased.

4   The usage of the system

The data flow of the proposed model for the parallel processing of multimedia data involves the following steps: The generated data packets are put into the pool of tasks when processing starts and the distribution manager is initialised. The data packets, received by the clients, are stored in the local pool of tasks, which is essentially a queue. Afterwards the computation starts. Processed data is stored in the local pool of results and sent to the collection manager. The collection manager informs the distribution manager of the receipt of the processed packets. When all data packets have been received, the so-called NULL-packet is distributed. Every processing element which receives a NULL-packet immediately terminates processing.

An object oriented system design will help making system components reusable and lessens the difficulty of using the distribution models. The most important class is the processing class. It does the actual processing and is the focal point of the model. All other classes support it by managing the administration, reception and distribution of data. The parameter of its run ( ) -method contains the data to be processed. The packet is processed in this method, stored in the local pool of results by means of a return call and is then sent back.

The usage of this system merely requires an overloading of the run ( ) -method of the processing class, adjusting the class for special problems. The distribution and collection manager have to be initialised at the beginning of a session. Furthermore, the required processes need to be launched in the processing nodes. These will then contact the distributor and collector on their own. At this stage the system will be idle. The pool of tasks is now filled with the required packets. Once this has been done, the distributor is activated and the data is processed. All processed packets are stored in the pool of results. Manipulating the packet size requires overloading of the methods that split and merge the packets.

5   Performance measurements

The measurements were performed on a cluster of Linux K6, 300 MHz PCs connected over a 10Mbit Ethernet. In a first attempt different block sizes and number of iterations as well as various configurations of the processing model were examined in order to obtain data about the efficiency and the run time behaviour of the proposed system.

Table 1: Measurement results (run times, speedup and efficiency) with the implemented prototype

Itera-tions	Time[s]: 1 PE	Time[s]/Sp/Ep : 2 PE			Time[s]/Sp/Ep : 3 PE			Time[s]/Sp/Ep : 4 PE		
10	35.693	25.373/	1.407/	0.703	22.100/	1.615/	0.538	22.455/	1.590/	0.397
30	43.153	27.213/	1.586/	0.793	24.640/	1.751/	0.584	22.252/	1.939/	0.485
50	51.373	31.373/	1.637/	0.819	27.739/	1.852/	0.617	24.050/	2.136/	0.534
70	61.534	34.993/	1.758/	0.879	30.220/	2.036/	0.679	25.540/	2.409/	0.602
90	69.813	39.493/	1.768/	0.884	31.519/	2.215/	0.738	27.919/	2.501/	0.625
110	76.353	42.301/	1.805/	0.902	34.430/	2.218/	0.739	30.370/	2.514/	0.629
130	85.553	46.779/	1.829/	0.914	35.820/	2.388/	0.796	30.591/	2.797/	0.699
150	93.713	50.519/	1.855/	0.928	39.039/	2.400/	0.800	32.081/	2.921/	0.730
170	102.233	55.369/	1.846/	0.923	42.080/	2.429/	0.810	34.179/	2.991/	0.748
190	110.733	60.659/	1.825/	0.913	44.100/	2.511/	0.837	35.100/	3.155/	0.789
200	115.953	59.819/	1.938/	0.969	45.849/	2.529/	0.843	35.130/	3.301/	0.825

Table 1 shows the run times needed for $10 - 200$ iterations of a simple inverting operation performed on a 10 Mbyte large block as well as the speedup factor S_P

and the efficiency E_p. The data is subdivided into 16384 byte large subsections and according to the strategy described distributed to the single PE clients.

Speedup values between 1.4 and 3.3 are reached in this simple application. At the beginning the network communication is the most influencing factor resulting in speedups between 1.407 (2 PE's) and 1.59 (4 PE's). With larger numbers of iterations a linear increase of the speedup values can be observed reaching top speedup values of 3.3 in case of 4 PE's and 200 iterations. The efficiency decreases only slightly, e.g. there is a difference of 0.24 between the mean values of the two and four PE systems. Thus the scalability of the system model appears to be good. A clearer description of the results is given in figure 2. The right hand diagram shows the run times of the different system configurations, the left hand diagram contains the mean speedup and efficiency values for the parallel configurations.

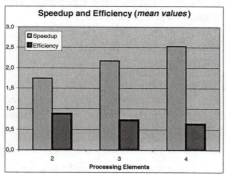
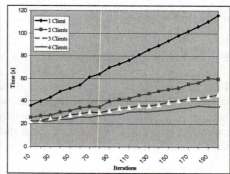

Figure 2: A diagram of the speedup and efficiency values achieved (left); run times for 1-4 PEs (right)

The achieved results are compared to the mean speedup and efficiency values of the PVM, which are shown in figure 3. The measurements are performed on the same configurations (K6 with Linux, distribution of 16384 byte large blocks) and type conversion disabled.

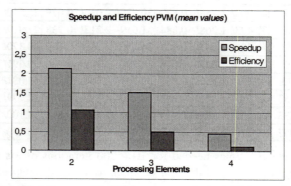

Figure 3: A diagram of the PVM average speedup and efficiency values

An analysis of the PVM results shows slightly better speedup and efficiency values in case of two processing elements. These decrease when larger numbers of PE's are used. The effort of management and transfer clearly reduces the performance. Thus the proposed system model reaches a five times better speedup and efficiency in case of configurations with four PEs.

6 Conclusions

In this paper a specialised computation model based on asynchronous transmission is presented, which automatically adapts to the workload of the elements in the parallel environment at transmission time, enables easy development of parallel programs and minimises the communication and management effort by direct use of TCP/IP sockets. It is based on the creation of pools of tasks, which are controlled by three special modules. A simple distribution strategy of the available packages increases the computing efficiency. More powerful processing elements or such with a small workload will more frequently receive packages. Additionally the package size can be adapted. The efficiency of the proposed method is evaluated through a variety of performance measurements. The results are compared with the results of the PVM.

Future work includes extensions, which primarily concern improving the system's performance. Storing the packets in the local file system, similar to a spool-directory, makes it possible to save all packets of the same type that are to be processed in a special directory. Furthermore, comparative benchmarks with other systems are to be performed.

References:

1. PVM Home page: Documentation, comparison between various packages, www.epm.ornl.gov/pvm
2. CONDOR Project description, documentation, www.cs.wisc.edu/condor/
3. MPI Project Home page: Documentation, tutorials, etc, www.mpi-forum.org
4. Mosix Home page: www.cs.huji.ac.il/mosix/
5. Information about PVMPI: www.cs.utk.edu/~fagg/PVMPI/
6. S. Keinman, D. Shah, Programming with Threads, Prentice Hall, 1995
7. B. Wilkinson, M. Allen: Parallel Programming: Techniques and Applications Using Networked Workstations and Parallel Computers, Prentice Hall, 1998
8. O. Sachs, Analyse von Aktienreihen mittels paralleler Korrelations-berechnungen, Master thesis, TU Clausthal, 1998

INCREASING THE EFFICIENCY OF VALUE PREDICTION IN FUTURE PROCESSORS BY PREDICTING LESS

BART GOEMAN, HENK NEEFS AND KOEN DE BOSSCHERE

Department of Electronics and Information Systems (ELIS)
University of Ghent
Sint-Pietersnieuwstraat 41, B-9000 Ghent, Belgium
E-mail:{bgoeman,neefs,kdb}@elis.rug.ac.be

Value prediction is a promising technique to increase the Instruction Level Parallelism (ILP) in future microprocessors. Most of the current work on value prediction is aimed at maximizing the prediction accuracy. However, in this paper, we show that a high prediction accuracy does not guarantee a high IPC (instructions executed per clock cycle), and that the relation between prediction accuracy and increase in IPC strongly depends on the benchmarks used, and on the underlying processor architecture. We show that values should only be predicted if their confidence is high, if the distance between the depending instructions is small, and if there are enough resources (execution units and prediction table entries) available to benefit from the increased ILP.

1 Introduction

Current microprocessor architectures use increasingly aggressive techniques to raise the average number of instructions executed per cycle (IPC). The upper bound on achievable IPC is generally imposed by true register dependencies: instructions that need input from other instructions have to wait until the latter are finished. Value prediction is a technique capable of pushing this upper limit by predicting the outcome of an instruction and executing the dependent instructions earlier using the predicted value. The producing instruction of the predicted value is only executed to verify the prediction. This is similar to branch prediction.

The concept of value prediction was introduced by Lipasti et al. [1,2] and by Gabbay et al. [3] They used respectively a last-value predictor and a stride predictor (excellent for counters, and pointers that scan an array).

2 Predicting less can increase efficiency

It is important not to predict every possible dependency because the value prediction requires quite some resources, and allocating resources to useless predictions creates competition with the useful instructions (comparable to cache pollution). This is especially important for value prediction because almost every instruction in a program is a candidate for value prediction (for branch prediction, this is approximately one out of five instructions), and because each entry in the value prediction table consumes considerable resources: a stride predictor needs a 32-bit last value, a 32-bit stride and a tag of some tens of bits to store extra information, and this is even worse for 64-bit CPU's. This is more than a magnitude bigger than a branch predictor that often requires little more than a two-bit counter for each entry.

Also, during the design process of a processor, the value predictor has to compete for silicon estate with other components, such as the branch predictor. In figure 1 the impact of a perfect value predictor is compared to the impact of replacing a good branch predictor (cf. section 3) with a perfect one. The latter change is obvious far more beneficial, so the hardware budget for a value predictor in a realistic processor can be expected to be rather small. Further on, sometimes the effect of the prediction on the execution speed is neutral, or even negative, because the instruction is not in the critical path. Predicting such a value will cause some instructions to become eligible for selection, and this might take away computing resources from the critical path.

Hence, in order to make value prediction feasible in real processors, it is mandatory to be able to distinguish between useful predictions, and useless predictions. We will investigate three heuristics that help to make this distinction: (i) prediction confidence, (ii) dependency distance, or the potential cycles that can be saved by predicting a value, and (iii) the amount of resources available to speed up the program.

3   Evaluation Methodology

An out-of-order simulator from the Simplescalar tool set [4] was modified for our purposes. This simulator models a general superscalar architecture, using an instruction set derived from the MIPS-IV ISA. The simulator is quite detailed, but is restricted to user-level code. We used the SPECint95 programs as benchmarks; each was run until 100M instructions had completed.

Target architecture

We model an aggressive architecture, capable of fetching, decoding and committing 8 instructions each cycle. Memory operations are put into a 64 entry reservation station, other instructions share a 128 entry reservation station. Up to 16 instructions can be issued to the functional units, i.e. 8 integer ALUs, 2 integer MULT/DIV, 4 FP ALUs, 2 FP MULT/DIV and 4

520

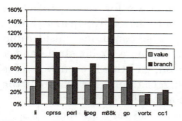

Figure 1. Perfect value prediction vs. perfect branch prediction.

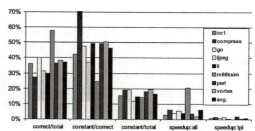

Figure 2. Totally predictable instructions (tpi's): results.

memory ports.

The memory subsystem has two levels of caches, a 1MB unified L2 cache and 64kB L1 cache, split into two equal parts for data and instructions. The latency of a load operation is 2 cycles for a L1 hit, 7 cycles for a L2 hit and 51 cycles for an access to the main memory.

The branch predictor is a hybrid one, using 1024 2-bit counters as a meta predictor to choose between a 2048 entry bimodal predictor and a 1024 entry gshare [5] predictor. The gshare predictor records 8 bits of global history.

Value predictor

The simulator models a last-value predictor using infinite tables, indexed by the program counter. The confidence mechanism is perfect; i.e. predictions are only used if they are right. Both 32 and 64 bit predictions are possible.

4 Heuristics that increase the efficiency

4.1 Confidence

All value predictors track the confidence of a prediction, using saturating or resetting counters, to avoid mispredictions. In this section, we show that even a confidence of 100% does not guarantee speedup. We illustrate this with a special class of instructions, the totally predictable instructions (tpi's).

Many instructions produce always the same value during the execution of a program. A prediction for the value produced by such an instruction has the highest confidence if we can statically prove that the instruction will always produce the same value. One could be tempted to predict these easy to predict values by means of compiler hints and a simple last value predictor which should guarantee us a 100% accuracy for these instructions. Because there is 100% confidence, there is no need for much extra hardware for a sophisticated prediction scheme, for a back-up of the non-speculative state, or for a recovery mechanism.

First, we have measured the accuracy of a last-value predictor. Measurements (Figure 3, first group of bars) show that 37% of all data dependencies can be removed using last-value prediction. Second, the share of those totally predictable instructions (tpi's) in the correct predictions done by a last-value prediction is shown (second group of bars). Almost half of those values (46%) are generated by tpi's.[a] Overall, one out of six data dependencies can be removed (figure 3, third group of bars) using this simple technique.[b]

The effect of predicting all dependencies on IPC is shown in figure 3, fourth group of bars, whereas the effect of predicting tpi's is presented in the last group of bars. It turns out that the speedup that can be attributed to the 100% confident predictions is less than 2%.

Why is the speedup so disappointing? The basic reason is that many of the totally predictable instructions have no input values, and hence, they do not belong to the critical path. For the MIPS R10000, the *lui* instruction (load upper immediate) is a major contributor: if one sorts the totally predictable instructions for *go* by their execution frequency, there are 17 *lui*'s in the top 20. This instruction sets the high-order bits of a registers and clears the others. Predicting it will almost never increase the IPC.

A similar observation was made by González: [6] the speedup using a stride predictor is far inferior to a hypothetical random predictor, both having the same average accuracy.[c] In both cases, there is a negative correlation between predictability and the impact on IPC of a correct prediction.

4.2 Dependency distance

The dependency distance is the distance (in the dynamic in-order instruction stream) between the producer and the consumer of a value. The prediction of a result (even if the confidence is 100%) only needed by an instruction that never belongs to the same instruction window is useless because the value will be produced before the consuming instruction can ever enter the instruction window. On the other hand, if an instruction needs the value of the preceding instruction, a correct prediction is likely to increase the IPC. The distribution

---

[a]This was investigated by profiling.

[b]This is however a maximum because results may be constant for one program input but not for a second. Also, the compiler has to be conservative in all cases and will not be able to identify all tpi's.

[c]If this random predictor has an accuracy of $p\%$, every instruction has a chance of $p\%$ of being correctly predicted.

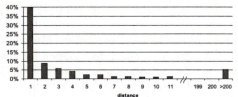

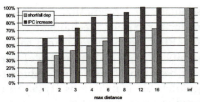

Figure 3. Dependency distribution for *go*.   Figure 4. Predicting short dependencies.

of the dependency distance (measured in instructions) is shown for the *go* (SPECint95 benchmark) in Figure 3.

Figure 4 shows the impact of restricting the predictor to short predictions. This is easy to implement in hardware, using the information available in the register renaming tables. The left bars show the number of dependencies examined by the predictor if only the short ones (*distance* ≤ *max distance*) are examined, relative to the total number of dependencies. The right bars show the speedup, relative to the achievable speedup by predicting all instructions. It is clear that restricting the number of predictions doesn't restrict the speedup in the same way.

If one chooses to predict only dependencies with *distance* <= 4, the speedup is 88% of the maximum achievable speedup, and one has only to predict 49% of the dependencies.[d]

4.3   Available ILP

A last heuristic is the available ILP. Predicting a value will hopefully enable a number of dependent instructions to become ready for execution, and hence increase the local ILP. If the local ILP is high, there is less need to predict a value because it is unclear whether the additional instruction will find the resources to execute. The predicted instruction can even block a non-speculative instruction. On the other hand, if the local ILP is low e.g., there is only one instruction executing, it might be worth trying to predict values in this area the next time this code is executed. A wrong prediction will also less likely cause resource pollution.

This idea can be put in practice by observing the functional units. If during a certain cycle only one instruction is executing, that instruction is marked as critical. Entries in the value predictor table are only allocated for such instructions.

---

[d]Arithmetic mean for the SPECint95 programs.

Figure 5 shows the effect on speedup from this technique, figure 6 shows the effect on the number of predictions. The first bar shows the reference case (all instructions are predicted), the second bar (labeled A) the proposed technique. On average (geometric mean), 40% of the predictions is eliminated, while still obtaining 81% of the available speedup.

A simple improvement is to check if the result of an instruction marked as critical is needed by another instruction currently in the reservation station,[e] before allocating an entry in the prediction table [7] (labeled B in both graphs). This affects the speedup somehow, the reduction in predictions is however far more distinct (38% predictions remain).

Observing the number of executing instructions is not efficient in all cases. This is because the processor selects instructions out of a finite instruction window, not out of the Data Dependency Graph (DDG). Most of the time, some instructions enter the reservation station. It's very likely that at least one of those has all its operands available and is immediately executable. Such a new instruction can hide the fact that the oldest instructions are critical and execute in a serial manner. A second problem is that if the oldest instructions are blocked by a cache miss, a non-critical instruction may be the only one executing and will thus be inserted in the table, while it is not critical at all.

A solution is to observe the age of instructions, compared to the oldest one still in the processor, and ignore the young ones. The new criterion can be formulated in two ways:

> *Bbf:* among the old instructions, is only one executing?
>
> *Baf:* is only one instruction executing, and if so, is it an *old* one?

Baf will handle the second problem and allow fewer instructions in the table, *Bbf* will also reject some instructions but allow others which are not the only ones executing to enter the table, handling the first problem.

For the results presented in figure 5 and 6, the 3 oldest instructions are considered *old*. The additional check is clearly an improvement as the average speedup raises again to 81% for *B3bf* while the number of predictions stays at 38%. *B3af* lowers the number of predictions (28%), but only 62% of the available speedup is left.

5   Related work

A plethora of work has been presented on prediction schemes besides the last value predictor used in this work. Gabbay et al. introduce a stride predictor and a register based predictor. [3] Other predictors have been proposed, many

---

[e]This information is available in the register renaming table.

524

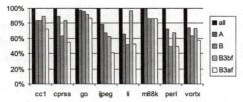 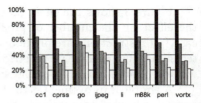

Figure 5. Speedups achieved over the baseline architecture, relative to *predicting all instructions.*

Figure 6. Available ILP heuristic:
number of predictions.

of them inspired by existing branch prediction techniques: (i) a finite context
method predictor (fcm) is based upon a (small) history sequence of preceding
values; the most likely next value in this sequence (from the recorded past) is
used as a prediction, [8] and (ii) hybrid predictors that combine two predictors
and select the more reliable prediction. [9]

Some authors study the impact of value prediction on the IPC [6,1,2,7,10] and
report speedups varying from 3% [2] to more than 2000.% [11] This enormous
gap can only be explained by the architectures: a real one (PowerPC 620)
vs. a hypothetical one that is only restricted by data dependencies. This
shows that the effect on IPC is strongly machine-dependent, and that raw
prediction accuracies as such (up to 91% has been reported [8]) are worthless
when investigating the beneficial effects of value prediction on IPC.

Some authors also try to use the prediction tables in a more efficient way,
by using simple predictors for easy to predict instructions. [12,13] In a study of
Gabbay, [13] prediction is not attempted for some instructions, but this decision
is based upon *confidence*, which is not such a good heuristic as we have seen.
Recently, Calder [14] has also attempted to reduce the number of predictions
by only predicting the ones in the critical path, but the classification method
is complex and hard to implement in hardware.

6 Conclusion

An accurate value predictor alone is not sufficient to speed up a program
execution. In order to save resources, one has to carefully candidates for predictions. This work tries to statically and dynamically identify the instructions that have the biggest impact on performance, when predicted. Three
heuristics are presented: confidence, dependency distance, and available ILP.
Confidence appears not to be an effective heuristic, the second and the third
are; both capable of doubling the efficiency of value prediction.

Acknowledgements

This work was supported by the Fund for Scientific Research – Flanders, project 3G003699.

References

1. M.H. Lipasti and J.P. Shen. Exceeding the dataflow limit via value prediction. In *Proceedings of the 29th Annual International Symposium on Microarchitecture*, December 1996.
2. M.H. Lipasti, C.B. Wilkerson, and J.P. Shen. Value locality and load value prediction. In *Proceedings of the 7th International Conference on Architectural Support for Programming Languages and Operating Systems*, October 1996.
3. F. Gabbay and A. Mendelson. Speculative execution based on value prediction. Technical Report 1080, Technion - Israel Institute of Technology, 1997.
4. Doug Burger, Todd M. Austin, and Steve Bennett. Evaluating future microprocessors: the simplescalar tool set. Technical Report TR-1342, University of Wisconsin-Madison, 1997.
5. Scott McFarling. Combining branch predictors. Technical Report TN-36, Digital Western Research Laboratory, 1993.
6. José González and Antonio González. The potential of data value speculation to boost ILP. In *Proceedings of the 12th ACM International Conference on Supercomputing (ICS)*, July 1998.
7. Bohuslav Rychlik, John Faistl, Bryon Krug, and John P. Shen. Efficacy and performance impact of value prediction. In *Parallel Architectures and Compilation Techniques(PACT)*, October 1998.
8. Yiannakis Sazeidis and James E. Smith. The predictability of data values. In *Proceedings of the 30th Annual International Symposium on Microarchitecture*, December 1997.
9. Kai Wang and Manoj Franklin. Highly accurate data value prediction using hybrid predictors. In *4th International Conference on High Performance Computing*, December 1997.
10. Yiannakis Sazeidis, Stamatis Vassiliadis, and James E. Smith. The performance potential of data dependence speculation and collapsing. In *Proceedings of the 29th Annual International Symposium on Microarchitecture*, December 1996.
11. Freddy Gabbay and Avi Mendelson. Using value prediction to increase the power of speculative execution hardware. *ACM Transactions on Computer Systems*, 16(3):234–270, August 1998.
12. Bohuslav Rychlik, John Faistl, Bryon Krug, Albert Y. Kurland, John J. Sung, Miroslav N. Velev, and John P. Shen. Efficient and accurate value prediction using dynamic classification. Technical report, Carnegie Mellon University, Microarchitecture Research Team, 1998.
13. Freddy Gabbay and Avi Mendelson. Improving achievable ILP through value prediction and program profiling. *Microprocessors and Microsystems*, 22:315–332, 1998.
14. Brad Calder, Glenn Reinman, and Dean M. Tullsen. Selective value prediction. In *Proceedings of the 26th Annual International Symposium on Computer Architecture*, pages 64–74, May 1999.

EXPRESSIVENESS VERSUS OPTIMIZABILITY IN COORDINATING PARALLELISM

A. GONZÁLEZ-ESCRIBANO, V. CARDEÑOSO-PAYO AND A. VACA-DÍEZ

Dept. de Informática, Universidad de Valladolid,
E.T.I.T. Campus Miguel Delibes, 47011 - Valladolid, Spain
E-mail: arturo@infor.uva.es

A.J.C. VAN GEMUND AND H-X. LIN

Dept. of Information Technology and Systems, Delft University of Technology,
P.O.Box 5031, NL-2600 GA Delft, The Netherlands
E-mail: a.vgemund@et.tudelft.nl

A number of interesting properties for scheduling and/or cost estimation arise when parallel programming models are used that restrict the topology of the task graph associated to a program to an SP (series-parallel) form. A critical question however, is to what extent the ability to express parallelism is sacrificed when using SP coordination structures only. This paper presents several basic task graph parameters that are the key factors to predict this loss of parallelism at the language modeling level. Our results indicate that a wide range of parallel computations can be expressed using a structured coordination model with a loss of parallelism that is small and predictable.

1 Introduction

It is well-known that the use of SP structured parallel programming models has a number of advantages with respect to cost estimation [1,2,3,4], scheduling [5,6], and last but not least, ease of programming. These attractive design properties, as outlined by Skillicorn and Talia [7], have led to a range of parallel programming models such as BSP [8], LogP [9], and SPC [2].

However, expressing a problem in a parallel language that imposes SP form may imply loss of parallelism since, compared to the original NSP version, additional synchronizations may have to be added. Although many algorithms already have SP structure (e.g., Divide & Conquer algorithms), still a considerable number of problems are typically solved using an NSP algorithm. For example, consider the NSP task graph associated with a Multilevel Paired Synchronization scheme as in Fig. 1(a). The SP graph, associated with the usual way this scheme is programmed in an SP language, is shown in Fig. 1(b). For many workload distributions of the tasks, the parallelism achieved in the SP structure is typically the same. However, in the often unpredictable event of a highly unbalanced workload (illustrated by black nodes having execu-

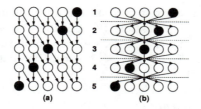

Figure 1. Multilevel Paired Synch. example (Bad workload distribution)

tion time τ, while the white ones have 0), the loss can be dramatic and only bounded on the same order as the problem size. (The critical path in *(a)* is τ, whereas in *(b)* it is 5τ). Although encountering this extremely unbalanced workloads in a real parallel computation is highly improbable, the critical question is to what extent one can expect high losses to appear and which parameters related to the graph topology and workload distribution are responsible for this loss.

For our study we use *AoN - DAGs* (*Activity on Nodes, Directed Acyclic Graphs*), denoted by $G = (V, E)$, to represent the set of tasks (V) and dependencies (E) associated with a program when run with specific input-data size. Each node represents a task and has an associated *load* or *delay* value representing its execution time. *SP* DAGs are a subset of task graphs which have only *series* and *parallel* structures, which are constructed by recursively applying Fork/Join and/or series compositions [10]. Let $W : V \rightarrow R$ denote the *workload distribution* of the tasks. For a given graph G and W, we define $C(G)$ (*Critical Path or Cost*) to be the maximum accumulated delay of any full path of the graph.

A technique to transform an NSP graph to SP structure without violating original precedence relations is called an *SP-ization* technique. It is a graph transformation $(T : G \rightarrow G')$ where G is an NSP graph and G' has SP form, and all dependencies expressed in G are directly or transitively expressed in G'. Due to the new dependencies an SP-ization introduces, the critical path may be increased. Let γ denote the relative increment in the critical path produced by a given T, and in general by the best possible T, according to

$$\gamma_T = \frac{C(G')}{C(G)} \quad , \quad \gamma = \min_T(\gamma_T)$$

For a given W, there exists a transformation T such that γ_T is minimal. However, in a usual programming situation the exact W is not known, and can therefore not be exploited in determining the optimal SP program. Thus, of more interest in our study into γ are the upper bound $\hat{\gamma}_T$ and the mean value $\bar{\gamma}_T = \mathrm{E}(\gamma_T)$ for *any* possible W. As there does not exist a generic optimal SP-ization for any G and W, we have conjectured in previous work that typically it holds $\forall G, \exists T : \gamma_T \leq 2$, except for pathological (extremely improbable) values of W [2].

In general, in absence of real W information, a fair assumption is to use *i.i.d.* (*independent identically distributed*) task loads. This model seems especially suitable for huge regular problems and topologies, and generally accurate enough for fine or medium grain parallelism. Previous empirical study [10] with random i.i.d. W identified certain structured topologies that present worse γ values than random unstructured topologies with the same number of nodes (where in some cases $\gamma \geq 2$). The exact topologies are those corresponding to the classical DAGs of *Macro-Pipeline* structure (MPipe), and *Neighbor Synchronization* structure from cellular automata (NSynch). The first lead us to the assumed worst problem topology called *Multilevel Paired Synchronization* (MPSynch), shown in Fig. 1(a), that yields, the worst loss of parallelism, according to our results, and has the inner features of the MPipe structure. Consequently, we chose these problems as starting point for our research on the topological factors that are responsible for the loss of parallelism as a result of SP-ization.

The rest of the paper is organized as follows. Section 2 concentrates on the effect of the problem size on γ. In Section 3 we discuss the high impact of a graph property called *synchronization density*. An analytical case study that supports the empirical results of the previous sections is presented in Section 4. The effect of the W parameter is then easily established. Section 5 presents our conclusions and future work.

2 The effect of problem size

As shown in Fig. 1 and discussed in Section 1, for certain topologies and W, $\hat{\gamma}$ increases with the problem size. In this section we concentrate on the influence on γ of the DAG depth D (DAG length or number of layers), DAG parallelism P (DAG width), and W variance.

The SP-ization technique (T) we use in all the experiments is, unless stated otherwise, a straightforward transformation (only suitable for regular structures) called *Wide Search Synchronization (WSSynch)* that typically adds barrier synchronizations between layers [10]. Task loads are modeled using Gaussian i.i.d. variables with relative variance Dev $= \sigma/\mu$ of 0.1, 0.2, 0.5, and 1.0. All results are based on averaging over 25 sample DAGs.

For fixed D, γ grows approximately logarithmically with P. Fig. 2(a)

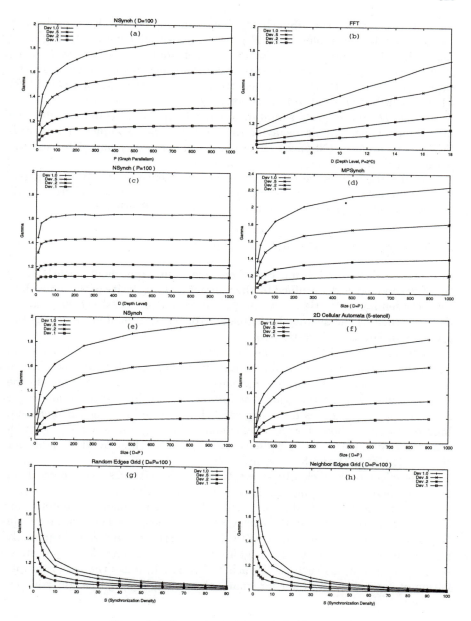

Figure 2. Effects of normal DAGs parameters on γ

shows this effect for the NSynch topology, and *(b)* for the FFT problem [a] (approximately linear plot since P grows exponentially with D). Fig. 2*(c)* shows that γ increases with D for the NSynch topology as long as $D < P$, after which γ levels off. This applies for all topologies tested except a special case discussed in Section 3. Consequently, we focus on the situation $D = O(P)$ where γ can be expected to have practically reached the worst case.

When D and P grow simultaneously, all topologies tested exhibit the same kind of logarithmic behavior as shown for the examples in Fig. 2*(d)* (MPSynch) and *(e)* (NSynch). The relative difference is caused by another parameter which is described in section 3.

At the same time we observe the large influence of the W parameter. As σ/μ increases, the curves go up, as the probability of an unfortunate W increases. This property will be further discussed in Section 4.

3   The effect of synchronization density

In a regular structured graph with fixed sizes, our experiments clearly show that the topology is determined by the number and regularity of the dependencies between layers [11]. Hence, we propose a parameter called *synchronization density*, which is the average in-degree and/or out-degree of all nodes, as key property of DAGs with respect to γ.

The parameter $S(G)$ indicates the propagation factor of dependencies and paths that arrive at a node. More edges, more dependencies between layers. More dependencies, less parallelism to lose when SP-ization is applied. In the extreme, when $S = P$, the graph has full barrier synchronizations, making it SP and $\gamma = 1$. Thus it is to be expected that γ decreases when S increases. Indeed, Fig. 2*(f)* shows how a *cellular automata* program in a 2D mesh with a 5-star-stencil ($S(G) = 5$) present lower γ values than previous plots for NSynch ($S(G) = 3$) and MPSynch ($S(G) = 2$).

The effect of S is clearly shown in Fig. 2*(g)*. It presents the result of an experiment with a synthetic grid of nodes with fixed size $P = D = 100$, changing the number of edges per node (S) up to 90, using a random uniform distribution to choose the target/source of the edges between layers. In Fig. 2*(h)*, the experiment is done with the same grid, but instead of randomly placed edges, they point to the neighboring nodes. The edge locality in most parallel computations such as NSynch or MPSynch, make the actual propagation of dependencies slower for small values of S, leading to slightly higher γ values.

---

[a] For FFT we use a specific SP-ization which slightly improves the results of WSSynch [11].

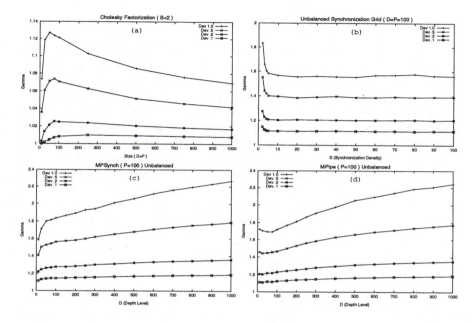

Figure 3. Special cases

The effect of S on γ is inversed when $S < 2$. In that case, there are series structures in the graph that can be exploited to minimize the increment of γ (using a more complex SP-ization than the simple WSSynch technique [10]). In Fig. 3(a) we show how γ is clearly affected by the small S parameter ($S \in [1.00, 1.17)$) in a Cholesky factorization where D and P are the dimensions of the input matrix. In the extreme case, where $S = 1$, only series structures are in the graph, which implies SP form and $\gamma = 1$.

Thus far we have considered edges that are unbiased in terms of their lateral preference. Topologies like the MPSynch (foundation of MPipe), have edges that *flow only in one direction* of the layers (see Fig. 1(a)). As dependencies do not propagate across the DAG in all directions, this has a large impact on the effect of S as shown in Fig. 3(b) (cf. Fig. 2(g)(h)). In fact, in this pathological case the impossibility to propagate dependencies to some nodes produces an unbounded effect when increasing D. Fig. 3(c)(d) show how in MPSynch and MPipe topologies γ keeps increasing whereas in Fig. 2(c) γ levels off. Again this illustrates our choice of topologies that show the worst characteristics.

4 Theoretical analysis

In order to support the empirical results previously presented, in this section we derive an analytic expression that approximates γ for NSynch and MPSynch topologies. A more detailed analysis is presented in [12].

Let $P = D$ and let W be modeled by an i.i.d. delay per node according to a Gaussian(μ, σ) distribution. The critical path (C) of SP graphs is derived using a well-known approximation of the cost of a P-node parallel section from order statistics [13] given by $C_P = \mu + \sigma\sqrt{2\log(0.4P)}$. Since the cost estimation of NSP stochastic DAGs is analytically untractable, we approximate the NSP DAGs by SP DAGs that capture the main inner features of the original. It turns out that the parallelism P' of the SP DAG approximation is directly related to S and P, according to $P' = S + \log(P/2)$ for NSynch and MPSynch topologies [b] (C_{NSP} is then approximated within 10% error [11]). Consequently

$$\bar{\gamma} = \frac{C_{SP}}{C_{NSP}} \approx \frac{D(\mu + \sigma\sqrt{2\log(0.4P)})}{D(\mu + \sigma\sqrt{2\log(0.4(S + \log(P/2)))})} \approx \frac{\mu + \sigma\sqrt{\log(P)}}{\mu + \sigma\sqrt{\log(S)}}$$

This formula agrees with our experiments within 25% [12]. The asympthotic influence of P is clearly logarithmic, while the effect of S is exactly inverse, which is in agreement with the results presented in Section 2. Also the effect of the workload distribution is in agreement with our measurements (considering the typical case where $P \gg S$).

5 Conclusion

In this paper we investigate the influence of several DAG parameters on the loss of parallelism (γ) as a result of SP-ization. Our experiments show that for a given task load distribution, the graph parameters P, D, and S predict the expected loss with a good degree of accuracy. Although γ is typically limited, there are situations in which $\gamma > 2$, corresponding to $S = 2$ and large values of $P,D,$ and σ. At the same time, one should note, that these circumstances only appear for DAGs with i.i.d. task loads that exhibit high variance. In particular, the assumption of statistical independence implies that our results are much too pessimistic. Future work includes a study into real codes and applications to determine the scope of this effect, as well as a study into irregular or dynamic codes.

---

[b]For NSynch $S = 3$, for MPSynch $S = 2$ [11].

References

1. R.A. Sahner and K.S. Trivedi. Performance and reliability analysis using directed acyclic graphs. *IEEE Transactions on Software Engineering*, 13(10):1105–1114, Oct 1987.
2. A.J.C. van Gemund. The importance of synchronization structure in parallel programs. In *Proc. 11th ACM ICS*, pages 164–171, Vienna, July 1997.
3. F. Hartleb and V. Mertsiotakis. Bounds for the mean runtime of parallel programs. In *Proc. 6th Int. Conf. Model. Techn. and Tools for Comp. Perf. Eval.*, pages 197–210, Edinburgh, Sept 1992.
4. Andras Salamon. Personal Communication, Jun 1999.
5. L. Finta and [et al.]. Scheduling UET–UCT series–parallel graphs on two processors. *DIMACS Series in DMTCS*, 162:323–340, Aug 1996.
6. R.D. Blumofe and C.E. Leiserson. Scheduling multithreaded computations by work stealing. In *Proc. Annual Symposium on FoCS*, pages 356–368, Nov 1994.
7. D.B. Skillicorn and D. Talia. Models and languages for parallel computation. *ACM Computing Surveys*, 30(2):123–169, June 1998.
8. L.G. Valiant. A bridging model for parallel computation. *C.ACM*, 33(8):103–111, Aug 1990.
9. D. Culler and [et al.]. LogP: towards a realistic model of parallel computation. In *Proc. 4th ACM SIGPLAN Symposium on PPoPP*, pages 1–12, San Diego, CA, USA, May 1993.
10. A. González-Escribano, V. Cardeñoso, and A.J.C. van Gemund. On the loss of parallelism by imposing synchronization structure. In *Proc. 1st Euro-PDS Int'l Conf. on Parallel and Distributed Systems*, pages 251–256, Barcelona, July 1997.
11. A. González-Escribano, V. Cardeñoso, and A.J.C. van Gemund. Loss of parallelism on highly regular DAG structures as a result of SP-ization. Tech. Rep. 1-60340-44(1999)-04, TU Delft, The Netherlands, July 1999.
12. A. Vaca-Díez. Tools and techniques to assess the loss of parallelism when imposing synchronization structure. Tech. Rep. 1-68340-28(1999)02, TU Delft, The Netherlands, Mar 1999.
13. E.J. Gumbel. *Statistical Theory of Extreme Values (Main Results)*, chapter 6, pages 56–93. Wiley Pub. in Statistics. John Wiley & Sons, 1962.

Dynamic Load Balancing with Self-Organizing Maps

ANDREAS HAIDT

Technische Universität Hamburg-Harburg, Technische Informatik 2
Harburger Schloßstraße 20, 21079 Hamburg, Germany
Haidt@tu-harburg.de

A modular environment was developed to support the dynamic load balancing of real parallel applications based on domain decomposition techniques. This environment was implemented on a Parsytec GC/PP-128 MIMD-multicomputer with distributed memory. For any parallel application to work within the environment an iterative structure of the application is precondition. This enables a migration to be delayed until the migrant reaches a consistent state, namely the end of an iteration. This contribution focuses on a new dynamic load balancing strategy based on Kohonen's self-organizing maps. For this Kohonen's sequential algorithm was parallelized and decentralized in a way that high scalability and low computational overhead were reached. This paper demonstrates that the self-organizing maps are an efficient method for generating solutions of the dynamic load balancing problem. The new strategy converges quickly even in the worst case, where the interacting execution entities of a parallel application are initially placed by random over the processing nodes. Some results from experiments are presented.

1. Introduction

The load balancing problem is a complex problem in parallel processing. The goal of dynamic load balancing is to dynamically assign workload of parallel applications to the processing network of the underlying parallel system. The load distribution decisions are made at runtime of the parallel application. Since a-priori information about runtime properties of the parallel application are not available, the dynamic load balancing procedure must run together with the parallel application. Thus, in order to provide scalability and high efficiency this dynamic procedure should be based on a decentralized parallel algorithm.

The intent of dynamic load balancing can be classified as system-oriented or application-oriented [1]. System-oriented load balancing is used to balance the workload of several applications in order to efficiently use the system's resources. Application-oriented load balancing deals with the distribution of parallel applications consisting of several interacting execution entities. It tries to reduce the execution time by exploiting the parallelism within the application.

The primary function of dynamic load balancing is assignment which can be classified as non-preemptive or preemptive [1]. In non-preemptive strategies new entities are placed once on any lightly loaded processor, whereas a preemptive strategy migrates entities at any time from a heavily loaded processor to a lightly loaded processor to reduce the load imbalance.

This contribution concentrates on the application-oriented preemptive load balancing in a massively parallel system with distributed memory. Such load balancing algorithms consider communication load so that the load balancing problem is usually modeled by two graphs: a processor graph representing a parallel architecture and a task graph representing the communication tasks of a parallel program [4].

Since the load balancing problem is known as NP-hard, heuristic methods are used to produce solutions that in general are suboptimal. As a heuristical approach this paper discusses the applicability of Kohonen's self-organizing maps to the dynamic load balancing problem. Self-organizing maps are a class of neural networks introduced by Kohonen in 1982 [2]. These maps were developed as an approximate model describing the self-organization of physiological neurons in the cerebral cortex, where neurons dynamically reorganize their spacial responsability according to sensory stimuli such that neighboring stimuli result in the excitation of neighboring neurons consequently leading to short signal paths [3].

In the past, self-organizing maps have already proven to be an efficient method for static mapping, where the load distribution of the parallel application is optimized before runtime of the application [4,5]. In an author's previous paper the applicability of self-organizing maps was extended to the dynamic load balancing problem and examined using a parallel simulator [6]. In the present paper an implemented parallel environment is described proving for the first time that dynamic load balancing with self-organizing maps is feasible with real parallel applications.

2. Applicability of Self-Organizing Maps to the Load Balancing Problem

The concept of self-organizing maps and the Kohonen learning rule based on these maps are introduced. Thereafter the necessary modifications of the Kohonen algorithm are described in order to be applied to the dynamic load balancing problem.

2.1. Self-Organizing Maps

Self-organizing maps are a well established class of neural networks in fields like robot control and speech recognition [7,3]. Besides the original publications [2,7]

Kohonen's learning rule was described several times. In the following the notation of Ritter et al. [8,9,3] is used. A self-organizing map defines a mapping $\Phi : V \rightarrow A$ of a metric input space V to a metric output space A. The self-organizing process being described by an iterative algorithm modifies a randomly chosen initial map such that the resulting map preserves two properties mentioned later.

While the input space V can be discreet or continuous, the output space A always is discreet. It consists of nodes r_j which are arranged in a topological order, e.g. as vertices of a lattice. For each node $r_j \in A$ there is a pointer $w_j \in V$. Now, each point $v \in V$ is mapped to that node $r_i = \Phi(v)$, whose pointer w_i lies closest to v, i.e.

$$\Phi(v) = \min_{r_j \in A} \left\{ d^V(w_j, v) \right\},$$ (1)

where $d^V(w_j, v)$ denotes the distance in the input space V between w_j and v. Hence, the map Φ is determined by the pointers w_j. During each iteration step these pointers are adjusted.

A single iteration step starts with the generation of a stimulus $v \in V$ according to a probability density function $p(v)$. In the next step the appropriate excitation center $r_e = \Phi(v)$ is calculated. It is that neuron r_j being most excited by the actual stimulus v. Under the condition that the stimulus v and all the pointers w_j are standardized, then r_e is that neuron r_j of which the pointer has the least distance to the stimulus v. Finally, all pointers w_j of nodes in the vicinity of r_e are adapted a small step toward v :

$$\Delta w_j = \varepsilon \, h(d^A(r_e, r_j)) \, (v - w_j) \qquad \text{for all } r_j \in A.$$ (2)

The extension of the vicinity of r_e is determined by the function $h(d)$ which depends on the distance $d^A(r_e, r_j)$ between r_e and r_j in the output space. A typical choice for $h(d)$ is

$$h(d) = e^{-d^2/(2\sigma^2)}.$$ (3)

The step-size ε with $0 < \varepsilon < 1$ and the vicinity radius σ are parameters influencing the convergence of the algorithm. They should decrease with an increasing number of iteration steps. Typically they decrease exponentially or hyperbolically.

The final map has two interesting properties: it tends to be neighborhood-preserving and distribution-preserving. During the iteration both preservation properties are gradually increased. A mapping preserves neighborhood, if neighboring pre-images are mapped to neighboring images. Because the condition is symmetric with respect to V and A, also the inverse map $\Phi^{-1} : A \rightarrow V$ of a neighborhood-preserving map Φ preserves neighborhood. The distribution preservation is a relation between the density $\lambda^V(\mathbf{v})$ of pointers $\mathbf{w}$ in the input space and the product of the density $\lambda^A(\mathbf{r})$ of neurons $\mathbf{r}$ in the output space and the probability density $p(\mathbf{v})$ of stimuli $\mathbf{v}$ in the input space.

Neighborhood preservation and distribution preservation can be contrary requirements. In that case the resulting map is a compromise minimizing the deviations from preservation of neighborhood and preservation of distribution.

2.2. Application to the Dynamic Load Balancing Problem

If used properly, the two introduced types of preservation provide solutions for the dynamic load balancing problem. The preservation of distribution can be used as load balancing mechanism. The neighborhood preservation reduces inter-processor communication significantly by assigning each pair of two directly communicating tasks to one processor or to a pair of directly connected processors.

The neurons are identified with the tasks of the parallel application. To embed the task graph into the output space an appropriate metric is used that distributes computation load and communication load homogeneously. The processor graph is embedded into a continuous input space which allows to map tasks to any virtual location on the processor network. This makes no sense in reality but improves the convergence of the load balancing algorithm. The desired map is the inverse of the self-organizing map $\Phi^{-1} : A \rightarrow V$.

2.3. Parallelization and Decentralization

In each iteration step Kohonen's learning rule requires the computation of a global minimum caused by the search of the closest task to a stimulus. In general this global search prevents an efficient parallelization for parallel systems with distributed memory [10]. Consequently, known approaches for parallelizing self-organizing maps are based on modifications of the original algorithm reducing or avoiding global instances. This leads to a higher scalability but also to a deterioration of neighborhood preservation and distribution preservation [11].

However, in the present case of assigning parallel tasks to processors the global search can be executed as a local search, because the structure of the input space and the structure of the parallel computer are identical. Thus, the Kohonen algorithm can be parallelized and decentralized efficiently.

Each processor asynchronously performs iteration steps consisting of the random generation of a stimulus, the search for the closest task to a stimulus, and the adaptation of pointers. The independent generation of stimuli on each processor implicates the simultaneous processing of several stimuli, so that each processor's search for an excitation center as well as each processor's adaptation of pointers can overlap. This contradicts to the requested processing of stimuli in the Kohonen algorithm. Next, for a stimulus to be processed quickly the number of communication messages caused by the search of the excitation center must be bounded. The search spreads out at most to the neighbored processors. This is a weightier contradiction to Kohonen's sequential algorithm than the one before. Finally, the parallelization of the pointers' adaptation showed to be the greatest challenge, because the evaluation of the shortest path between a task to be adapted and the excitation center can only be realized with considerable overhead. Thus, the basic idea is to adapt a task via all paths to the excitation center until the path length exceeds the vicinity radius. Physically this makes sense, since information are not only exchanged along the shortest path.

A dynamic load balancing algorithm based on the modifications described in the last paragraph results in another map than the original Kohonen algorithm would produce, at least at the beginning of the self-organizing process. But the difference over the time can only be minimal, since both algorithms behave similar with decreasing vicinity radius only making adaptations in the nearer surroundings of the stimulus.

2.4. Further Improvements

A self-organizing map assigns each task to a virtual task location. Virtual locations allow to migrate tasks gradually from one processor to another. If the closest processor to a task's virtual location changes, a migration to the new processor can be initiated. Since task migration produces additional computation load and communication load, a migration is delayed until the task's virtual location is closest to a new processor for a period of time. This period depends on the distance of the task's virtual location from the center of its executing processor. Therefore, this delay prevents the map from reacting too fast on load changes that last for a short time only. Such reactions would increase the execution time because the benefit of migration would be smaller than the cost. Furthermore, oscillations of the map are damped.

3. Environment for the Dynamic Load Balancing of a Parallel Application

An environment for dynamic load balancing of real parallel applications was implemented on the Parsytec GC/PP-128 MIMD-multicomputer with distributed memory. The application tasks are represented by light-weighted processes, so called threads. The environment combines three major modules which are executed on each processing node: 1. the *manager module* controls the progress of the load balancing and the parallel application, 2. the *load balancing module* decides whether a locally executed thread should migrate to another processing node, and 3. the *application module* executes the threads of the parallel application that are to be balanced. For any parallel application to work within the environment an iterative structure of the application is precondition. Because the state of a thread is easily catched at the end of an iteration, a migration will only be initiated at this point of time.

As the Parsytec-multicomputer does not support thread migration by itself, a novel migration mechanism was conceived [12]. The novelty of this mechanism is its ability to perform a migration, where instead of the whole parallel application only the migrant needs to reach a consistent state. Since the migration has minimal influence on the other execution entities, simultaneous migrations of unconnected and even directly neighbored entities are permitted. The migration time of an application thread averages 2.5 ms cpu-time.

4. Performance Results

An important result was to prove that self-organizing maps could be applied to the dynamic load balancing problem. The performance of the new algorithm is illustrated in Figure 1. The initial map (1) is generated randomly. In a series of pictures the effect of the dynamic load balancing algorithm is shown by (2)-(6), where (2)-(5) are intermediate states of the map and (6) is the equilibrium state which is optimal concerning the state of load.

Each picture shows the virtual position of tasks in the continuous input space containing the processor network. Thus, the processor graph always has an ordered look, while the task graph is reorganized in each step of the iteration. The tasks and their communication channels are represented by digitized circles and bold lines, respectively, where the circle area is proportional to the computation load of the corresponding task. The processors and their physical communication links are represented by squares and thin lines, respectively and are to be seen in the background.

540

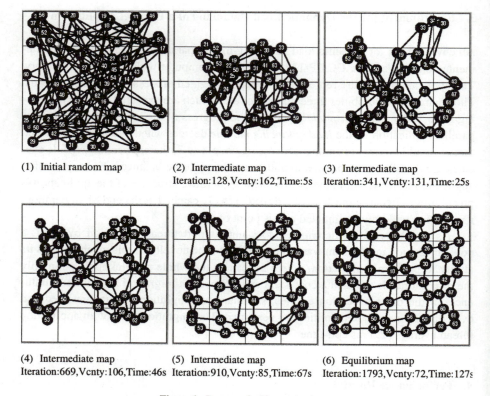

(1) Initial random map

(2) Intermediate map
Iteration:128,Vcnty:162,Time:5s

(3) Intermediate map
Iteration:341,Vcnty:131,Time:25s

(4) Intermediate map
Iteration:669,Vcnty:106,Time:46s

(5) Intermediate map
Iteration:910,Vcnty:85,Time:67s

(6) Equilibrium map
Iteration:1793,Vcnty:72,Time:127s

Figure 1. Process of self-organization.

Figure 1 shows a parallel application with a two-dimensional grid structure consisting of 8x8 tasks that are assigned to a 4x4 processor network. The time until an equilibrium state was reached could vary significantly, but always an equilibrium state was attained. The new load balancing algorithm demonstrates high convergence. It was even high for the worst case, where the communicating threads of the parallel application are initially distributed by random to the processor network.

5. Conclusion

An environment for dynamic load balancing of real parallel applications was implemented on a Parsytec GC/PP-128 MIMD-multicomputer with distributed memory. A new dynamic load balancing algorithm based on Kohonen's self-organizing maps was added to the environment as load balancing module. By an efficient parallelization Kohonen's sequential algorithm was adapted to the dynamic load balancing problem resulting in a local and decentralized algorithm offering high scalability and low computational overhead. Experimental studies demonstrated that self-organizing maps are an efficient method for generating solutions of the dynamic load balancing problem. The new strategy converges quickly even in the worst case, where the tasks of a parallel application are initially placed by random on the processing nodes.

References

1. Schnekenburger T., Stellner G., *Dynamic Load Distribution for Parallel Applications* (Teubner, 1997).
2. Kohonen T., *Self-Organized Formation of Topological Correct Feature Maps* in Biological Cybernetics 43 (1982), 59-69.
3. Ritter H., Martinez T., Schulten K., *Neuronal Computation and Self-Organizing Maps: An Introduction* (Addison-Wesley, 1992).
4. Quittek J.W., *Optimizing Parallel Program Execution by Self-Organizing Maps* in Journal of Artificial Neural Networks (1996).
5. Dormanns M., Heiss H.-U., *Topology Conserving Graph Mapping by Self-Organization* in Proceedings of the Conference on Artificial Neural Networks and Genetic Algorithms (Springer, 1993), 198-205.
6. Haidt A., Quittek J.W., *Dynamic Mapping with Self-Organizing Maps* in Proceedings of the International Conference on Parallel and Distributed Processing Techniques and Applications, ed. Arabnia H.R. (CSREA, 1996), 745-756.
7. Kohonen T., *Self-Organizing Maps* (Springer, 1995).
8. Ritter H., Schulten K., *On the Stationary State of Kohonen's Self-Organizing Sensory Mapping* in Biological Cybernetics 54 (1986), 99-106.
9. Ritter H., Schulten K., *Convergence Properties of Kohonen's Topology Conserving Maps: Fluctuations, Stability, and Dimension Selection* in Biological Cybernetics 60 (1989), 59-71.
10. Hodges R.E., Wu C.-H., Wang C.-J., *A Parallel Implementation of the Self-Organizing Feature Map Using Synchronous Communication* in IEEE International Symposium on Circuits and Systems (1990), 743-745.
11. Demian V., Mignot J.-C., *Optimization of the Self-Organizing Feature Map on Parallel Computers* in Proceedings of the International Joint Conference on Neural Networks (1993), 483-486.
12. Haidt A., Stellmann P., *Novel Migration Mechanism for Load Balancing of Parallel Applications* handed in at Mannheim SuParCup, (1999).

A FRAMEWORK FOR NESTING ALGORITHMIC SKELETONS

MOHAMMAD HAMDAN, GREG MICHAELSON AND PETER KING

Department of Computing and Electrical Engineering, Heriot-Watt University, Riccarton, Edinburgh EH14 4AS, UK

E-mail: {hamdan, greg, pjbk}@cee.hw.ac.uk

We propose a framework for compiling and executing arbitrary depth algorithmic skeleton nesting. It consists of schemes to be used at compile-time for the static-analysis of the source program and at run-time to execute nested skeletons in parallel. We report results for deeply nested programs for different platforms.

1 Introduction

It is well known that parallelism adds an additional level of difficulty to software development. Following Cole's characterisation [2] of algorithmic skeletons, there has been considerable interest in the association between skeletons and higher order functions (HOFs) as a basis for parallel functional programming. However, a major problem lies in the nesting of arbitrary skeletons to arbitrary depth, in particular in automatically generating nested skeleton instantiations from composed HOFs.

Many researchers have worked on skeletons. Pelagatti developed P3L [6] which is an explicit parallel programming language where the programmer has to craft skeletons together. The approach is static in nature as code generation depends on the abstract machine that has been fixed for the construct and on the target architecture at hand. In Rangaswami's HOPP (Higher Order Parallel Programming) model [7] for skeleton-oriented programming, nesting of skeletons was limited to three levels and code had to be generated manually. To [8] investigated optimising the combinations of algorithmic skeletons. A language for combining skeletons was proposed and a set of primitive skeletons was chosen. There have also been a number of approaches based on restrictions to the forms parallelism may take. In Blelloch's NESL [4], parallel operations may only be applied to sequences. In Jay's approach [5], all operations must be shapely, that is they must preserve the physical structure of their operands. Such limitations greatly ease both static analysis of programs and data communication between nested parallel control structures but necessarily constrain the language's parallel expressiveness.

The goal of this work is to allow **arbitrary depth** nesting of skeletons and automatically generate parallel code for the program prototype. Therefore, we propose a framework for compiling and executing arbitrary nested algorithmic skeletons. It consists of translation schemes used at compile-time for the static-analysis of the source program and schemes used at run-time to execute the nested skeletons in parallel.

2 The Programming Model

Our framework is demonstrated through **Ektran** (which means a function in Arabic), a simple functional programming language with polymorphic types which draws on Backus' FP [1]. Ektran provides a number of skeleton-HOFs (called operators) that perform general purpose operations on lists. These operators are inherently parallel and the programmer uses them to express programs as operator compositions along with user-defined functions. An Ektran program normally consists of constant bindings, function definitions and an expression to be evaluated. We define a subset of Ektran's grammar below:

<prog> ::= <constant_bindings>; <fun_definitions>; <exp>
<exp> ::= <value> | <operator> | (<exp> <exp>) |
      <unary_operation> | <binary_operation> |
      if <exp> then <exp> else <exp>
<operator> ::= map | fold | Fold | SFold | @

Expressions are the main part of the language and can be a value, an operator, a function application of two expressions enclosed by parentheses, a unary operation, a prefix binary operation or a conditional expression.

3 The Compile-time Framework

3.1 Engineering the Parallel Compiler

The Ektran compiler was engineered by plugging different components together and is organised in three stages. The purpose of the first stage (**Front End 1**) is to scan, parse, type-check, preprocess and transform an Ektran program into a CAML Light [3] source program with calls to the skeleton library using CAML Light's C interface. The next stage (**Front End 2**) generates a C program from the CAML Light source program using the Camlot (which is a high performance CAML Light to C) compiler. Finally, target code can be generated for different target architectures during the last stage (**Back End**) using an ANSI C compiler. The current compiler supports only the CRAY T3D, the Fujitsu AP1000 and a network of Linux workstations. The skeleton library is linked at compile-time to the generated code.

544

3.2 Preprocessing

To preprocess an Ektran program a number of schemes are applied to generate a nesting structure which can be used to combine the corresponding skeletons.

SymbolicBetaReduction, lifts all HOF combinations to the top level of the program. To do so, Ektran expressions are partially beta reduced by replacing all functions appearing in the main expression by their bodies. This greatly eases the **nesting deduction** stage. **PipelineNormalisation**, extracts pipeline parallelism which may arise from composed functions. This involves normalising the composed functions by generating a list of functions and flattening the generated list by deleting multiple occurrences of function compositions. **NestingDeduction**, annotates the skeleton-HOFs in the abstract syntax tree and generates a nesting structure which is used to combine the corresponding skeletons. For example, if HOF_1 has HOF_2 nested, then the scheme will simply annotate the first HOF in the following way HOF_1^N where N means that the function argument is a HOF. The annotations are used by the translator to set the proper flags for the skeleton's C interface. Figure 1 outlines the basic rules for this scheme in an ML-style notation. **FreeVariablesDetection**, annotates the outer skeleton-HOF in case free variables are found in the inner skeleton-HOF. The free variables will be transmitted at run-time to guarantee that closures being built are consistent across all processors.

4   The Run-time Framework

4.1   Supported Skeletons

The current supported parallel operators are the **map, fold, Fold, SFold** and **compose** HOFs with equivalent algorithmic skeletons realised as MPI process groups. Parallel communication between processes is effected through MPI and generic Camlot functions for flattening and unflattening data structures. **map**, which applies a function to each element of a list, is realised as a broadcast process-farm skeleton. The farmer process has access to a pool of worker processes, each of which runs the same function. The farmer distributes data to workers and collects results back. The effect is to apply the function on every data item. **fold**, which applies a function between each element of a list, is realised as a broadcast binary divide and conquer skeleton. The top level node (root) divides the original list into a fixed number of sub-lists and broadcasts the sub-lists to all nodes below it in the tree and keeps one sub-list for local processing. Next, the root will apply the function on its sub-list and receive the sub-results from its children. The leaf nodes in the tree will receive

NestingDeduction ⟦ constant_bindings | defs | exp ⟧ =
    ⟦ constant_bindings | defs | **Deduce** exp ⟧

Deduce ⟦ (exp1 exp2) ⟧ =
    if **LookFold** exp1
    then
        if (**IsHOF** exp2)
        then ⟦ ((**AnnotateHOF** exp1) (**Deduce** exp2)) ⟧
        else ⟦ ((**Deduce** exp1) (**Deduce** exp2)) ⟧
    else
        if (**IsHOF** exp1)
        then
            if (**IsHOF** exp2)
            then ⟦ ((**AnnotateHOF** exp1) (**Deduce** exp2)) ⟧
            else ⟦ ((**Deduce** exp1) (**Deduce** exp2)) ⟧
        else ⟦ ((**Deduce** exp1) (**Deduce** exp2)) ⟧
Deduce ⟦ (pipeline l) ⟧ = ⟦ **DeducePipeline** (pipeline l) ⟧

Figure 1. The nesting deduction scheme.

sub-lists from root, apply the function on the local sub-lists and then send sub-results to parents. The intermediate nodes will receive sub-lists from root, apply the function on their local sub-lists, receive sub-results from children then send the final result to parents. **Fold**, is a special case of **fold** where the function argument is of the form **fn** $h =>$ **fn** $t => f1\ (f2\ h)\ t$. **SFold** is a special case of **Fold**. In case the function argument for Fold is not associative it might be possible to replace it with two functions where one of them is associative. **compose**, where the result of one function is the argument for the next, is realised as a pipeline. It is usual to express an arbitrary depth composition as a folding binary compose over a list of functions, but this restricts the composed functions to having the same domain and range type. We have implemented an unrestricted compose, where the domain type of each function must be the same as the range type of its argument function. However, this will only work effectively when nested within another skeleton which generates a sequence of data values.

4.2 Skeleton Nesting

The run-time schemes for arbitrary depth nesting of algorithmic skeletons allocate processes to skeleton groups top-down through traversal of the HOF nesting structure. If a skeleton nests other skeletons then it reallocates processes in its group in order to support the nested skeletons. This involves dividing the group into sub-groups for each of its immediately nested skeletons, and creating a top group which connects all sub-groups. The process then continues recursively.

The **SplitGroup** divides or splits a given group (which is a set of processors) into a fixed number of sub-groups. It takes two parameters. The first is the original group and the second is the split value or key which determines how many sub-groups to be created out of the original group.

SplitGroup OriginalGroup Key =
let size = FindSize of OriginalGroup
Create key sub-groups
for i = 0 to (size - 1)
    add process i to the (i mod key)th Sub-Group
return Sub-Groups

The **CreateTopCommGroup** scheme creates a new group which consists of the first element in each sub-group that was created by the **SplitGroup** scheme. It takes two parameters. The first is the original group which was divided by the **SplitGroup** scheme, and the second is the same split value (key) used for the **SplitGroup** scheme.

CreateTopCommGroup OriginalGroup Key =
let size = FindSize of OriginalGroup
let CommGroup =
for i=0 to (size - 1) step Key
    add process i to CommGroup
return CommGroup

Figure 2 gives a simple visualisation of how a group can be divided into sub-groups and how a new group gets created from the existing sub-groups by applying the above schemes to a group.

5 Evaluation

5.1 Test Example I: Matrix Multiplication

Figure 3 shows the execution time and speedup results for an example of 3 levels of **map** nesting in solving matrix multiplication of 40-digit arbitrary length numbers for the Cray T3D, Fujitsu AP1000 and a network of Linux workstations. For this example we exploit parallelism for two cases: 1) running in parallel all nested HOFs (denoted by 3P on the graph) and 2) executing in parallel only the first two nested HOFs (2P). Note that running in parallel only the first two nested HOFs give better results compared to three HOFs.

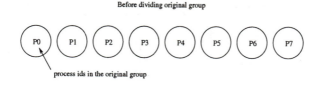

Before dividing original group

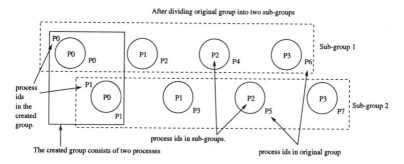

After dividing original group into two sub-groups

Figure 2. Dividing and creating groups from an existing group.

The reason is that the bottom HOF lacks useful parallelism. Also, note how speedup stays the same for a range of processors and then suddenly improves. This has to do with groups being balanced as more processors are added.

5.2 Test Example II: Merge Sort using a Pipeline

Figure 3 shows the execution time and speedup results for a merge sort of 50-digit arbitrary length numbers on a Fujitsu AP1000. In this example, we use a heterogeneous pipeline which consists of two stages: the first uses a **map** HOF and the second uses a **fold** HOF. The novelty here is in running the inner stages of the pipeline in parallel as well. However, the results are disappointing as the best speedup was 2.11 on 7 processors. Nonetheless, this speedup proves that running the inner stages in parallel improves the performance as speedup for 2 processors was 1.49. We think there are three reasons for the poor performance: 1) the parallelism exploited in the inner stages of the pipeline is poor 2) there are only two stages in the pipeline for this example and 3) it is possible that the pipeline is not load-balanced (i.e one stage needs more or less processors than other stages).

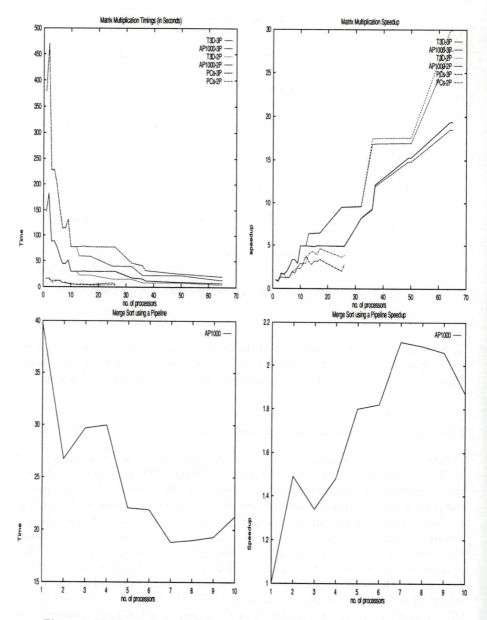

Figure 3. Matrix multiplication and merge sort execution times and speedups.

6 Conclusions and Future Work

We have outlined a framework for arbitrary depth skeleton nesting in which nesting is handled at run-time and the code generated does not depend on the target architecture. The results for the matrix multiplication suggest that good cross-platform portability and behavioural consistency can be achieved. However, the results for merge sort using a pipeline suggest that a better example is needed to study the behaviour of the heterogeneous pipeline. The current Ektran implementation is fully automatic. However, the run-time system uses a simple heuristic to divide the process groups. We are now developing a process allocation scheme, based on sequential Ektran program profiling, cost models for skeletons and performance characterisation of target architectures. The allocation scheme will decide how to divide the groups to achieve the best performance.

References

1. J. Backus. Can Programming Be Liberated from the von Neuman Style? A Functional Style and Its Algebra of Programs. *CACM*, 21(8):613–641, August 1978.
2. M. I. Cole. *Algorithmic Skeletons: Structured Management of Parallel Computation.* Pitman/MIT, London, 1989.
3. G. Cousineau and M. Mauny. *The Functional Approach to Programming.* Cambridge University Press, Cambridge, UK, 1998.
4. G. Blelloch et al. Implementation of Portable Nested Data-Parallel Language. In *Proceedings of the 4th ACM Conference (PPoPP)*, pages 102–111, San Deigo, CA, USA, 1993.
5. C. B. Jay. Shape Analysis for Parallel Computing. In *Parallel Computing Workshop: Imperial College*, September 1995.
6. S. Pelagatti. *Structured Development of Parallel Programs.* Taylor and Francis, London, 1998.
7. R. Rangaswami. *A Cost Analysis for a Higher-order Parallel Programming Model.* PhD thesis, University of Edinburgh, 1995.
8. H. W. To. *Optimising the Parallel Behaviour of Combinations of Program Components.* PhD thesis, Department of Computing, Imperial College of Science, Technology and Medicine, London, 1995.

REGISTER ALLOCATION IN HYPER-BLOCK FOR EPIC PROCESSORS

HANSOO KIM

New York University, 251 Mercer Street, New York NY 10003, USA

KANCHI GOPINATH

Indian Institute of Science, Bangalore 560012, India

VINOD KATHAIL

Hewlett-Packard Lab.,Palo Alto, CA 94304, USA

A hyper-block represents a linear sequence of predicated instructions with a single entry and multiple exit points. To exploit the high level of Instruction Level Parallelism(ILP) in EPIC architectures, hyper-blocks are often used as the unit of program presentation. In this paper, we study the impact of predication and the hyper-block representation in the register allocation phases. Our contributions can be summarized as we compare the effect of live range granularity in both hyper-block and conventional basic block. We show that predicate-aware liveness analysis can be used to obtain accurate interference graphs and to reduce false register pressure. Similarly, we demonstrate that a predicate-aware priority function can give a better register allocation performance over a predicate-insensitive one.

1 Introduction

Over the past decade, architectural innovations supporting *instruction-level parallel processing (ILP)* and compiler optimizations that work synergistically with them have become a technological reality[1]. Popularly referred to as *explicitly parallel instruction computing* or *EPIC*, key aspects of this technology have influenced the IA-64 architecture [2]. EPIC offers several advantages, notably performance that scales both in terms of architectural complexity, as well as the use of increasing levels of parallelism at the fine grained instruction level. However, compile-time analysis to enhance and detect the parallelism, as well as optimizations such as *instruction scheduling* and *register allocation* that exploit this parallelism play a central role in harnessing the performance opportunities offered by EPIC.

Since ILP within basic blocks is limited for control-intensive programs, techniques for exploiting ILP across basic block (BB) boundaries have been developed. Trace scheduling[3] or super-block (SB) scheduling[4] have been developed to achieve higher degree of instruction-level parallel processing by providing a wider scope for compile-time program analysis. Predication[5] has been included in EPIC-style architectures to enable modulo-scheduling[6] and hyper-block scheduling (HB)[7]. A hyper-block represents a linear sequence of predicated instruction with a single entry and multiple exit points. Hyper-block scheduling enables to handle branch intensive programs while trace scheduling or super-block scheduling cannot handle clusters of traces that should be considered together for interference optimizations. However, predicated instructions in hyper-block (HB)[7] pose new problems for register allocation(RA) and instruction scheduling(IS).

In this paper, we explore several aspects of register allocation such as liveness granularity, priority functions and different notions of live-range interference. The graph coloring approach is accepted as a good model for register allocation. In this, an *interference graph* is constructed from the program where each node represents a live range of a program variable. Two distinct nodes in the graph are connected if the two variables conflict with each other and they cannot be allocated to the same physical register.

A live range is a continuous group of nodes in the control flow graph where a variable is live. Liveness information can be presented at different granularities of a program, such as density of an operation or a basic block. The granularity of live range has a large effect on the number of edges (size) of interference graph and the execution performance. Our results show that this effect is larger for hyper-blocks and super-blocks. Predicated code used in "if-conversion" for hyper-block formation introduces another challenge to register allocation, since liveness analysis that is not predicate-aware may increase the size of graph also. In this paper, we explore the effect of predicate aware liveness analysis for hyper-blocks andthe predication on the *priority function* for hyper-blocks. By making Chow and Hennessy-style priority function predicate-aware, we obtain reduced spill code and improved execution performance.

2 Priority Function for Predicated Codes

Coloring assignment in register allocation assigns physical registers for live ranges by a certain order. Chaitin style register allocation assigns colors to the live ranges in the reverse order in which the live ranges are removed from interference graph during the *simplification* and *spill* [10]. In Chow and Hennessy style register allocation, which we have followed in our research, coloring assignment order is decided by a *priority function* [8].

The priority function models the savings in memory accesses when assigning a register to a live range as opposed to keeping the variable in memory. We use execution frequencies of instructions to guide register allocation (RA). In

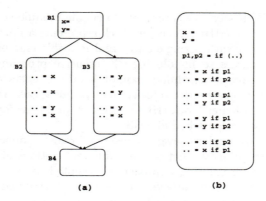

Figure 1. Change of priority with granularity

addition to the use of hyper-blocks to group together traces that are executed frequently (for more effective optimizations, including register allocation), we also use live range priorities based on the priority function due to Chow and Hennessy. For a given live range lr in blocks B_1 to B_i, the priority function can be defined as follows:

$$Priority(lr) = \sum_{lr \ \in B_1..B_m} \begin{array}{l} (D_i * ST\_COST \\ +U_i * LD\_COST) * w_i \end{array} \tag{1}$$

where D_i and U_i are the number of definitions, uses and function calls in block B_i respectively, and W_i is the weight of block B_i.

The above function captures the priority quite well in basic blocks (BBs) where all operations in a BB have the same weight. But in a hyper-block, where some operations can be nullified due to predication, these functions do not reflect predicated execution well. In Figure 1, the weights of B2 and B3 are 90 and 10 respectively. By using the above functions, $LiveRange(x)$ has a higher priority than $LiveRange(y)$ in B2. In the corresponding hyper-block, as in part (b) of figure, the priority of $LiveRange(x)$ and $LiveRange(y)$ is same, even if they are executed different number of times dynamically, if we use the traditional priority function using block weight. To correct this problem, we have modified the priority function as follows to reflect frequency information using the predicate expression:

Table 1. comparison between predicate-aware and predicate-unaware priority function (a) Dynamic spill code added (percentage) (b) Dynamic execution cycles

Benchmark	Predicate -Unaware	Predicate -Aware	Improvement
a5	59.97%	54.17%	5.80%
fir	25.00%	18.00%	7.00%
idct	27.82%	17.85%	9.97%
idea	38.58%	37.31%	1.27%
nbradar	141.57%	103.59%	37.98%
paraffins	103.15%	78.65%	24.50%
polyphase	205.85%	193.91%	11.94%
qsort	117.74%	101.10%	16.64%
wave	24.93%	23.96%	0.96%
SUM	435.45M	331.50M	31.36%

(a)

Benchmark	Predicate -Unaware	Predicate -Aware	Improvement
a5	195515	193519	1.03%
fir	188863	162823	15.99%
idct	12069	11388	5.98%
idea	8580	8199	4.65%
nbradar	462.56M	419.30M	10.32%
paraffins	155352	130073	19.43%
polyphase	1.08M	1.03M	4.89%
qsort	81.25M	69.10M	17.58%
wave	12996	11455	13.45%
SUM	545.47M	489.95M	11.33%

(b)

$$Priority(lr) = \sum_{lr \in HB_1..HB_n} \begin{aligned} &(D_i * ST\_COST * PR(D_i) \\ &+ U_i * LD\_COST * PR(U_i)) * w_i \end{aligned} \qquad (2)$$

where $PR(x)$ is the fraction of the time the variable access actually occurs due to predication.

Table 1 (a) shows dynamic number of instructions (spill code) added due to register allocation for predicate-aware priority function and predicate-unaware priority function. The two priority function for register allocation have been tested on a number of benchmarks. To quantify the spill code added, we measure the total amount of spill code (load, store and move instructions) added by a register allocation algorithm. The performance improvement of our algorithm is measured as the factor of reduction in spill

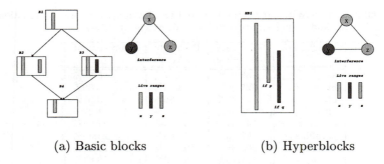

(a) Basic blocks   (b) Hyperblocks

Figure 2. Interference Graph

code achieved in comparison to past method.

Table 1 (b) shows total dynamic execution cycles (for the same set of benchmark) in a 9 way parallel machine with 4 integer units, 2 floating point units, 2 memory units and 1 branch unit. We obtained up to 20% performance improvement using our new priority function compared to using a predicate-unaware priority function.

3   Predicate Aware Liveness Analysis For Hyper-block

Predication has been included in EPIC-style architectures for supporting loops and for branch intensive programs. Hyper-block formation replaces a set of basic blocks containing conditional control flow between the blocks with a single block of predicated instructions [7].

One of the main issues with predicated code is computing accurate liveness information in order to build the sparsest possible interference graph. This is central for reducing compile time but more so for *performance*.

Consider the control flow graph and live ranges in Figure 2 (a) and the corresponding interference graph. In **B3** for example, **x** is live when **y** is defined. Therefore, there is an edge between vertices **x** and **y** in the interference graph. Notice that there is no edge between vertices **y** and **z** since the thread of execution moves exclusively to one of the two basic-blocks **B2** or **B3**. The accurate interference graph can be colored by no more than 2 colors.

Using if-conversion, the four basic-blocks of Figure 2 (a) are merged into the single predicated block of Figure 2 (b). The operations previously executed in **B2** and **B3** are guarded by the predicates **p** and **q** respectively.

An interference graph using traditional live ranges is also shown in Figure 2. This interference graph contains an edge between **y** and **z** because **y** and **z** are considered live simultaneously, as traditional analysis does not examine the predicate expressions. As a result, the register requirement of this predicated block increase from 2 to 3. This increase in register requirements is mainly due to two reasons. First, without knowledge about predicates, the data flow analysis must make conservative assumptions about the side effects of the predicated operations. Second, the solutions of the data flow analysis rely heavily on the connection topology among basic-blocks in the flow graph, which is altered by the If-conversion process used to construct hyper-blocks.

The problem of predicate aware liveness computation has been studied in the past [11] [12]. Eichenberger and Davidson[12] consider register allocation for predicated code assuming predicated registers. "P-facts" are defined to capture logically invariant expressions in straight line code (using both the predicated expressions in instructions and branch conditions) and analysis on these are used to define liveness. Our analysis differs in that we use a predicate query system rather than eagerly computing all the implications (the set of P-facts), which can be very expensive in larger regions. A more complex region like a loop is considered through "bundling" of virtual registers. A predicate insensitive RA is then used. Their framework does not consider spilling and emphasis is therefore placed on minimizing register requirements in the context of modulo-scheduled loops rather than on good register allocation with a fixed number of registers. Their data report show the reduction of registers needed for the Livermore kernel loops.

Gillies, Roy Ju, Johnson and Schlansker[11] also consider predicated register allocation but hyper-blocks are not used in their framework for region construction. Global analysis (on whole procedures) is performed on the standard control flow graph (CFG) with BB having (materialized) predicated code and control predicates representing the branch component from the CFG. The basis of a BB is the set of predicates used in the BB code stream. The basis of BB within a global scheduling region (GSR) are recursively merged to form a single common basis for data flow analysis (DFA). Interval analysis is used to guide this process. To avoid expensive global analysis, a limit (32) is imposed on the size of the basis during the recursive merging. Our approach uses a similar predicate analysis but HBs are constructed taking into account the frequency of execution. We perform local predicate analysis using a *Predicate Query System(PQS)* [13] in our region based register allocation. In both, due to the the artificial limit of the size of basis for each interval or the simplification used in PQS, the rest of the predicate expressions have to be approximated to what is in the basis or to TRUE.

Our study (see Table 2) shows that region based register allocation with

Benchmark	Function	predicate -Unaware	Predicate Aware	Improvement
a5	_clock_r1	70	62	12.90%
eqn	_fromto	5230	5206	0.46%
eqn	_eqn	4366	4350	0.37%
fir	_print	3042	3010	1.06%
huffman	_write_header	32300	27120	19.10%
huffman	_encode_codes_table	11404	10710	6.48%
tbl	_gettbl	14976	14966	0.07%
tbl	_runtabs	5372	5166	3.99%
yacc	_setup	11018	11006	0.11%
yacc	_defin	536	534	0.37%
yacc	_gettok	13166	12904	2.03%
yacc	_fdtype	74	56	32.14%
yacc	_cpyact	26132	26114	0.07%

Table 2. The number of edges in the interference graph for predicate-aware and predicate-unaware liveness analysis

local predicate-aware liveness analysis gives sometimes limited performance improvement. This can be explained in several reasons. First, hyper-block formation is not undertaken if there exists nested inner loops inside the selected block. Second, HB construction maximizes the potential of instruction scheduling and this disables many of the predicate-aware RA's careful interference calculations. For example, if a branch is weighted in one direction highly, the block on the opposite side may not be included in HB so as to maximize speculation. Third, if a block contains a function call with side effects, the block will not be included in a HB as it prevents code motion and instruction scheduling suffers. Last, many of predicate conditions are promoted to TRUE in our HB construction to get a good instruction schedule and this gives little chance to RA for accurate interference graph construction.

4   Conclusion

Our research has shown that fine grained live ranges reduce the number of interferences and hence allow both faster compilation and runtime execution. Similarly, a predicate-aware priority function gives a better register allocation. However, due to the heuristics used in hyper-block formation, predicate-aware liveness computations does not result in significant improvements. Hence, further study is indicated in developing hyper-block formation strategies that are both instruction scheduling and register allocation friendly.

Acknowledgments

This work is supported in part by awards for Hewlett Packard Corp, from Panasonic Corp. and by a NYU Research Challenge Grant

References

1. B. Rau and J. Fisher. Instruction level parallel processing: History, overview and perspective. *J. Supercomputing*, 7:9–50, 1993.
2. Intel Press Release. *Merced Processor and IA-64 Architecture*, 1998. http://developer.intel.com/design/processor/future/ia64.htm.
3. J. Fisher. Trace scheduling: A general technique for global microcode compaction. *IEEE Transactions on Computers*, C-30(7):478–490, 1981.
4. W.W. Hwu *et al*, The superblock: An effective technique for VLIW and superscalar compilation. *Journal of Supercomputing*, January 1993.
5. J.R.Allen *et al*, Conversion of control dependence to data dependence. In *Proceedings of the 10th ACM Symposium on Principles of Programming Languages*, pages 177–189, 1983.
6. B. Rau. Iterative modulo scheduling: An algorithm for software pipelining loops. *Proceedings of the 27th Annual Symposium on Microarchitecture*, December 1994.
7. S. A. Mahlke *et al*, Effective compiler support for predicated execution using the hyperblock. In *Micro-25*, pages 45–54, 1992.
8. Fred C. Chow and John L. Hennessy. The priority–based coloring approach to register allocation. *ACM Transactions on Programming Languages and Systems*, 12(4):501–536, 1990.
9. Trimaran Consortium. *Trimaran Web Site*, 1998. http://www.trimaran.org.
10. G. J. Chaitin. Register allocation and spilling via graph coloring In *Proceedings of the SIGPLAN '82 Symposium on Compiler Construction*, pages 98–105. ACM, ACM, 1982.
11. Johnson Gillies *et al*, *Global predicate analysis and its application to register allocation*, (MICRO-29, 1996)
12. Alexandre E. Eichenberger and Edward S. Davidson, *Register allocation for predicated code*, (MICRO-28, pages 180–191, 1995)
13. R. Johnson and M. Schlansker, *Analysis of predicated code* (Micro-29, 1996)

STUDY OF DATA LOCALITY FOR ITERATIVE METHODS

D.B. HERAS, V. BLANCO,
J.C. CABALEIRO AND F.F. RIVERA

Departamento de Electrónica y Computación
Univ. Santiago de Compostela, Campus Sur
15706 Santiago de Compostela, Spain
e–mail: dora,Vicente.Blanco,caba,fran@dec.usc.es

In this work we model the data locality in the execution of codes with irregular accesses. We focus on the product of a sparse matrix by a dense vector ($SpM \times V$) as this is the most relevant kernel in iterative methods for the solution of sparse linear systems. In this model, locality is initially established taking into account pairs of rows or columns of sparse matrices. In order to evaluate this locality three functions are introduced based on two parameters: number of *entry matches* and number of *line matches*. The model is generalized considering *windows* of locality (groups of consecutive rows/columns of the matrix). Although this model can be validated using any level of the memory hierarchy, the cache level was selected as a case of study.

1 Introduction

One factor that greatly influences the performance of a code, both in uniprocessor and in multiprocessor systems is the behavior of the particular memory hierarchy [4,6]. We are mainly interested on the behavior of codes with irregular accesses. The indirect addressing used in such codes, makes their efficiency difficult to predict and improve [1].

In this work we focus on the behavior of iterative methods for the solution of sparse linear systems. In particular, we concentrate the study on the product of a sparse matrix by a dense vector ($SpM \times V$) as this is the most relevant kernel in such codes. We develop a model of locality for this operation based on measures over consecutive groups of rows and columns of the sparse matrix. Although the model is general enough to be applied to any level of the memory hierarchy, the results are validated on the cache memory level. The model is analyzed through the variation of the relevant parameters and the results are validated on a particular cache configuration. They can be extrapolated to different cache organizations, to other levels of the memory hierarchy and to other memory organizations like multiprocessor systems.

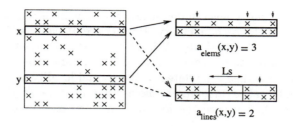

Figure 1. Measurement of locality parameters

2 Modeling the Locality Problem

Let N be the number of rows or columns of a sparse matrix and N_Z the number of non–zero entries. We work on a code for the sparse matrix–vector product when the matrix is stored in the *Compressed Row Storage* (CRS) format [2]. *DA*, *Index* and *PTR* are the three vectors (data, columns and row pointers) used by this storage format. The number of references to memory required by the different data structures in order to perform the product is $3 \times N_Z + 2 \times N$.

A detailed analysis of the locality of this algorithm shows that arrays Y, *PTR*, *DA* and *Index* present sequential accesses with a high spatial locality while array X exhibits a behavior that is difficult to predict and exploit as it is indirectly addressed by the *Index* array. Thus, the study of locality of the $SpM{\times}V$ must focus on analyzing the accesses to vector X.

2.1 Parameters to Model Locality: Distance Functions.

The locality of the $SpM{\times}V$ operation depends, among others, on features both of the memory level considered and of the sparse matrix. In order to model the locality, an approach in which the locality is defined over consecutive row or column pairs was used.

To reflect the locality induced in vector X when computing the product of X by any two rows of the sparse matrix, two parameters are introduced: the number of *entry matches* (a_{elems}) and the number of *line matches* (a_{lines}) (See Fig. 1).

The number of *entry matches* between two rows of a sparse matrix is defined as the number pairs of non–zero elements in the same column. The concept of *entry matches* can be extended to *line matches* replacing the term "elements" by "blocks (lines) with at least one entry". The size of these blocks depends on the memory level under study, and it will be the size of a cache line for the case of the cache memory. Both concepts can also be defined for columns in a straightforward way. When using these parameters in terms of rows, they are related to the temporal locality of X and, when they are used in terms of columns, they are related to the spatial locality of Y.

A magnitude called *distance between pairs of rows (x,y)*, denoted by $D(x,y)$ is defined to measure the locality. We propose three definitions of this distance.

$$D_1(x,y) = max(n_{elems}(x), n_{elems}(y)) - a_{elems}(x,y) \qquad (1)$$

$$D_2(x,y) = n_{elems}(x) + n_{elems}(y) - 2*a_{elems}(x,y) \qquad (2)$$

$$D_3(x,y) = n_{lines}(x) + n_{lines}(y) - 2*a_{lines}(x,y) \qquad (3)$$

Where $n_{elems}(x)$ is the number of elements of row x and $n_{lines}(x)$ is the number of groups of elements of row x.

These functions display some properties:

- If a relative order of the rows in terms of distance is established, the order in terms of locality for a fixed level of the memory hierarchy will be the inverse.

$$\forall \text{ rows } x, y, z \quad D(x,y) \leq D(x,z) \Leftrightarrow locality(x,y) \geq locality(x,z)$$

- The distance function is an injective application and defines a metric over the set $\mathcal{N}$ (the one made up of the N rows or columns of the matrix).

- They verify that the minimum possible value of the distance between two rows/columns will be zero and the maximum value will not exceed N.

For a given sparse matrix, the locality of the $SpM \times V$ can be modelled by summing the distances between consecutive rows/columns (D_{total}).

$$D_{total} = \sum_{i=0}^{N-2} D(i, i+1)$$

2.2 Results

The level of the memory hierarchy chosen for validating the results is the cache memory. Differences in locality among matrices may be established by the number of cache misses. So, we use cache misses as criterion to validate our model. Throughout this paper, the numbers of cache misses were measured using trace driven simulation considering a *2K* words cache, the line size was

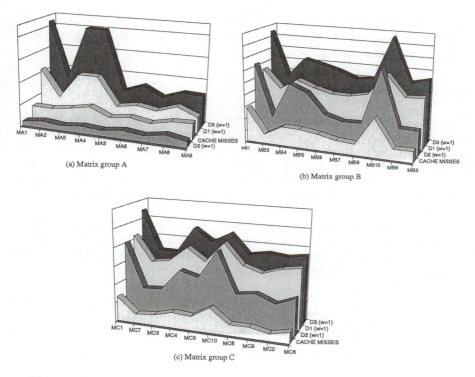

(a) Matrix group A

(b) Matrix group B

(c) Matrix group C

Figure 2. Cache misses and locality estimations for the different groups of matrices

8 words and the replacement algorithm LRU. The values of cache misses displayed do not include *compulsory misses* [5].

We made use of three groups of ten matrices. Matrices in each group present the same values of N and NZ but different patterns. One group (group A) includes matrices with nonzero elements confined to an almost band–like structure. In this case $N=4875$ and $NZ=105339$. Matrices in group B have their nonzero elements more uniformly distributed, $N=5300$ and $NZ=21842$. Finally, matrices in group C present elements very uniformly distributed, $N=4000$ and $NZ=13636$. All the matrices are symmetric, so the study is analogous for rows and columns.

In Fig. 2.2 the cache misses and the measures of locality D_{Total} using the distance functions D_1, D_2 and D_3 are shown. Note the similarity in the behavior between D_{Total} and the number of cache misses. The same general trend has been observed for other groups of matrices and other sizes and configurations of the cache memory. This observed behavior leads to the idea that a linear relationship between cache misses and D_{Total} exists.

3 Windows of locality

The model of locality introduced in the previous section provides results based only on the locality between pairs of consecutive rows/columns. However, at any level of the memory hierarchy, the reuse of elements of the vector X can be exploited by more than two columns/rows of the sparse matrix. In the case of the cache memory a cache line of vector X could probably be reused in the product of more than two rows of the sparse matrix before that line will be replaced.

For this reason we propose a generalization of the distance functions defining them over consecutive *windows of locality*, groups of w rows/columns of the matrix. Following this new approach we define the *distance between pairs of windows (g,v)*, denoted by $D(g,v)$, as:

$$Dw_1(g,v) = max(n(g), n(v)) - a_{elems}(g,v) \tag{4}$$

$$Dw_2(g,v) = n(g) + n(v) - 2*a_{elems}(g,v) \tag{5}$$

$$Dw_3(g,v) = nl(g) + nl(v) - 2*a_{lines}(g,v) \tag{6}$$

where:

$$n(g) = n_{elemsw}(g) - a_{elemsw}(g) \qquad nl(g) = n_{linesw}(g) - a_{linesw}(g)$$

In this case $n_{elemsw}(g)$ is the number of elements of window g. $a_{elemsw}(g)$ generalizes the concept of *entry matches* considering the matches that take place on two or more rows within window g. Introducing $n(g)$ the possible reuse of data inside g is considered. $a_{elems}(g,v)$ is a direct extension of the entry matches between groups g and v. For the particular case of $w = 1$ we have $D_1 = D_{w1}$, $D_2 = D_{w2}$ and $D_3 = D_{w3}$.

The selection of the best window size depends on the nonzero pattern of the matrix, the size of the particular level of the memory and the distance function used to model the locality and it is difficult to establish. We have sampled the space of possible values of w from $w = 1$, (the case of distance between pairs of consecutive rows), to $w = 2^6$. In Fig.3 we display the results obtained for the matrix group B and distance function Dw_2. We have arranged the matrices in the X-axis in increasing order of cache misses. Note that matrix *MB5* presents a behavior which is different from the general trend. It has a larger number of caches misses than *MB4* but lower measure of locality.

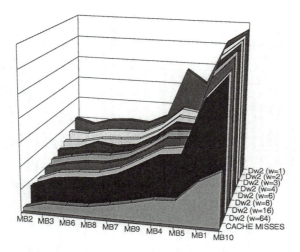

Figure 3. Results for the matrix group B and distance function Dw_2.

As the window size increases this effect decreases and the curves of locality are smoother. Similar results have been observed in the other groups of matrices.

4 Discussion and conclusions

Three distance functions (Dw_1, Dw_2 and Dw_3) with different window sizes were analyzed for the different groups of matrices. They are arranged in the X-axis of each graph in Fig. 4 in increasing order of adequateness. We have measured the adequateness of each prediction through a linear regression coefficient. This shows the linear relationship that exists between cache misses and D_{total}, as we have explained in Sect. 2.2.

Most of the predictions of locality present coefficients which are higher than 0.9 indicating very good predictions. For group A the better result obtained is only about 0.8. The reason is that this group of matrices presents closely banded nonzero patterns which lead to a more difficult modeling using our distance functions. Another reason is that these matrices present a greater percentage of nonzero elements than groups B and C and it will probably be necessary to consider a larger value of window size to achieve an adequate modelling.

Another interesting observation can be extracted from these graphs, the best value of window size and the best function to predict locality depend on

564

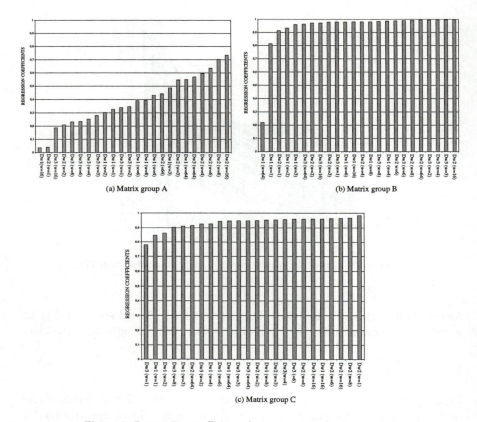

(a) Matrix group A

(b) Matrix group B

(c) Matrix group C

Figure 4. Regression coefficients for matrix groups A, B and C.

the nonzero structure of the matrices. In almost all cases the use of $w = 1$, leads to relatively bad results.

Our model can be employed to optimize the locality, and therefore, the number of cache misses, minimizing D_{total} by modifying the sparse matrix pattern. This modification could be performed by reordering rows and columns of the matrix [3].

Acknowledgements

The work described in this paper was supported by the Xunta de Galicia under project XUGA 20605B96 and by CESGA and FECIT under project

1998CP199.

References

1. R. Doallo B.B. Fraguela and E.L. Zapata. *Cache misses prediction for high performance sparse algorithms.* In *Proc. 4th Intl. Euro-Par Conference*, volume 1470, pages 224–233. LNCS, Sept 1998.
2. R. Barret, M. Berry, T. Chan, J. Demmel, J. Donato, J. Dongarra, V. Eijkhout, R. Pozo, C. Romine, and H. van der Vorst. *Templates for the Solution of Linear Systems: Building Blocks for Iterative Methods.* SIAM Press, 1994.
3. D.B. Heras, V. Blanco, J.C. Cabaleiro, and F.F. Rivera. Modeling and improving locality for irregular problems: sparse matrix–vector product on cache memories as a case study. HPCN99, 1998.
4. Mark D. Hill and James R. Larus. Cache considerations for multiprocessors programmers. In *Communications of the ACM*, volume 33, pages 97–102. 1990.
5. M.D. Hill. *Aspects of Cache Memory and Instruction Buffer Performance.* PhD thesis, University of California, Berkeley, 1987.
6. Evan Torrie, M. Martonosi, C. Tseng, and M.W. Hall. Characterizing the memory behavior of compiler–parallelized applications. *IEEE Transactions on Parallel and Distributed Systems*, 7(6), December 1996.

SUMA: A SCIENTIFIC METACOMPUTER

E. HERNÁNDEZ, Y. CARDINALE, C. FIGUEIRA AND A. TERUEL

Departamento de Computación y T. I., Universidad Simón Bolívar, Apdo. 89000, Caracas 1080-A, Venezuela.

E-mail: emilio@ldc.usb.ve

This article describes a metacomputing system for execution of Java bytecode, with additional support for scientific computing. The goal is to extend the Java Virtual Machine model, by providing both access to distributed high performance resources and execution of native scientific functions. SUMA currently executes three kinds of code: sequential Java bytecode, parallel Java bytecode (communicating with *mpiJava*) and SUMA native code, which includes standard mathematical libraries like Lapack and PLapack.

1 Introduction

There is increasing interest in using Java as a language for high performance computing [1]. Java provides a portable, secure, clean object oriented environment for application development. Recent results show that Java has the potential to attain the performance of traditional scientific languages [2,3,4]. In addition, the access to distributed high performance computing facilities through a metacomputing system has recently gained considerable acceptance [5]. A metacomputing system allows uniform access to heterogeneous resources, including high performance computers. This is achieved by presenting a collection of different computers as a single virtual machine.

We address the development of a metacomputing system for Java programs, called SUMA (Scientific Ubiquitous Metacomputing Architecture). The goal is thus to extend the Java Virtual Machine model to provide seamless access to distributed high performance resources. SUMA can be described as a "Datorr" project (Desktop Access to Remote Resources) [6]. SUMA middleware is object oriented and built on top of CORBA, a commodity communication platform. Other well-known metacomputing projects, like Globus [7] and Legion [8], provide their own communication platform. Using a standard communication platform allows us to benefit from a variety of implementations.

We focus on the development of the distributed services that comprise the middleware layer and on the design and development of easy-to-use clients. Apart from a modified *java* command, for remote execution, we developed commands for batch, off-line processing, and interactive clients like a scientific calculator with matrices as operands. SUMA executes three kinds of code: sequential Java bytecode, parallel Java bytecode (communicating with *mpiJava* [4]) and SUMA native code, which currently includes standard mathematical libraries like Lapack [9] and PLapack [10].

The rest of the document is organized as follows. Section 2 introduces the models underlying the execution of programs in SUMA. Section 3 shows different ways users can interact with SUMA. Section 4 describes some experiences with SUMA. Finally, in section 5 we present some conclusions and future work.

2 Execution of programs in SUMA

This section describes the execution model that any client of SUMA has to follow in order to execute Java programs and the environment on which these programs are executed.

2.1 ExecutionUnit

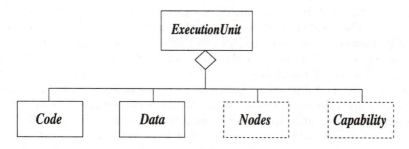

Figure 1. ExecutionUnit

A program in SUMA is represented by an object called an *ExecutionUnit*. An *ExecutionUnit* (figure 1) is an aggregate of the following components:

- *Code*: a collection of *SCode* objects that can be executed. An *SCode* (single code) object can be a sequential program (e.g., a Java class), a parallel program (a Java parallel application) or a native code (for instance, a Lapack routine).

- *Data*: a collection of data structures loaded by the user or generated by the programs.

- *Nodes*: a representation of the hardware on which the programs are executed, only visible to expert users and administrators. This object includes information on resource usage and performance.

- *Capability*: a capability list, which codes the permissions for using SUMA resources. This object is not visible to the users.

2.2 Execution Model

The basics of executing Java programs in SUMA are simple. The client machine executes *load* methods and *execution* methods. The class files are loaded in the *Code* component of the *ExecutionUnit*. It is possible to postpone loading a class to runtime[a]. Some of the data files may be loaded in the *Data* component of the *ExecutionUnit* as well. Any data structures different from files used by the class files (e.g. instances of SUMA native classes *SUMA_Vector* or *SUMA_Matrix*) must be loaded in *Data*.

After the execution of the static time actions, an execution method is invoked, initiating the execution of the *ExecutionUnit*. At run-time the class files that were not initially loaded, are loaded on demand from the client machine. The read and write operations on the data files that were not initially loaded in the *Data* object are routed to the client machine. This mechanism is useful if the data file is very big and the program needs only a few bytes from it. Output files can be created in the *Data* object in order to avoid excessive I/O operations between the server and the client machine.

Under the scheme described above we have two extreme cases. On the one hand the user only specifies the main class in the *ExecutionUnit*. The rest of the classes and data files are read from the client at run-time, on demand from the executing class. This scheme is communication intensive. On the other hand the user can load all of the class files and data files in the *ExecutionUnit* before invoking the execution method. The output files are stored in the *Data* object during the execution phase. After the execution has finished, the user can read the data structures (including files) contained in the *Data* object. Between these two extreme cases, the user can select the combination of pre-loading and run-time loading that (s)he prefers.

The *ExecutionUnit* exists until explicitly deleted. In this way, further class files loads, data file loads and execution actions can be performed.

A simplified scheme of the activities involved in executing a program is depicted on figure 2. A user invokes execution of a program through the modified

---

[a] In this case, at least a single reference to the main class must be passed, which will be loaded on starting the execution.

java command *SUMA_java*, which starts *Client*. This *Client* constructs an *ExecutionUnit* and passes it to the *SUMA_Engine*. Then, *SUMA_Engine* gets a server from the scheduler component (not shown on the figure) and contacts the *ApplicationServer* on this server, who will initiate the program execution. The *ApplicationServer* communicates with the *Client* to dynamically load classes and, depending on the execution mechanism used, to read/write files on the client. Note only some of the SUMA components are shown on the figure.

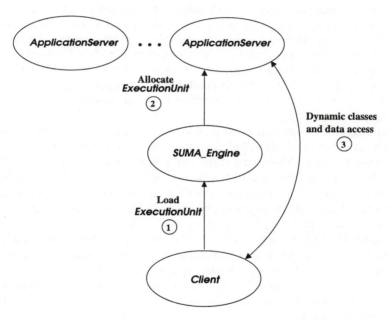

Figure 2. Basic activities involved in executing a program in SUMA

2.3 Execution Environment

Any Java class file that runs on a Java Virtual Machine also runs on SUMA. Additionally, a SUMA *ApplicationServer* always contains a number of classes that can be imported by any Java program executing in SUMA. Native classes contained in the *Data* objects must be explicitly declared and used.

Sequential *ApplicationServers* contain wrappers for BLAS and Lapack and will contain a larger set of native packages. Parallel *ApplicationServers* contain *mpiJava* and a wrapper for PLapack.

3 Interaction Models

The objects defined in SUMA are accessed through different interaction models, that we call *views*. These views are abstractions built on top of visible SUMA objects. The views are designed according to the user type or role. A non-expert user will see a single virtual machine, while the administrator view gives the necessary abstractions to configure SUMA, from user registration to installation of new services. Other views are also possible, for instance, a view that allows an expert user to do more specialized performance optimizations.

The views are supported by a single underlying object model. In this paper, we focus our attention on the non-expert user view. While SUMA will expose a greater number of details (mainly for tuning purposes) to an expert user, we are more interested in providing the right abstraction through the non-expert user view.

An authorized user can open a session in SUMA from a workstation, by creating an *ExecutionUnit*. The client machine becomes part of SUMA while the session is open. There are three main ways of interacting with SUMA. First, the user can open a SUMA session from a program executing on the local workstation. The program can then invoke any of the SUMA native services listed in the library catalog, which includes commodity scientific code. Second, the user can supply a Java bytecode for execution in SUMA. The component *SUMA_Scheduler* chooses the server on which the code is actually executed. The Java bytecode can include calls to the *mpiJava* package. The third option is actually a combination of the first two options. The user can supply a Java bytecode that invokes SUMA native services. The SUMA object model accommodates a number of basic mechanisms needed to support the aforementioned views.

4 Experiences with SUMA

We designed some experiments to evaluate the alternatives related to pre-loading and dynamic loading of data structures. We built a small scale testbed to simulate a SUMA environment. We used a prototype of SUMA built on top of JacORB[11], a freely available CORBA implementation. The hardware on which the experiments were conducted consists of several Sun Ultrasparcs 1 and a Sparc Classic connected with Ethernet. The Ultrasparcs played the role of high performance resources (servers) and the Sparc Classic simulated a low performance, desktop, client machine. *SUMA_Engine* runs in one of the Ultrasparcs, and one *ApplicationServer* on each of the other Ultrasparcs. The *SUMA_java* client runs on the Sparc Classic.

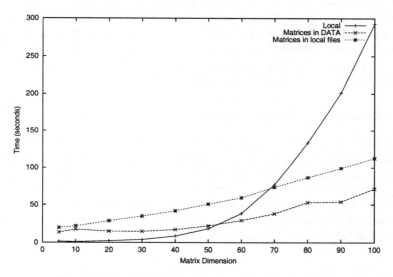

Figure 3. Matrix Multiplication execution time on SUMA

The experiment consists in running a matrix multiplication Java program on SUMA, varying the matrices size up to 100x100. We want to compare the following three cases:

Local: Running the program entirely locally (on the client). This situation stands for a machine out of SUMA.

Matrices in *Data*: The *ExecutionUnit* contains both input matrices (*Data*), and a reference to the main class (*Code*).

Matrices in local files: Same as before, but instead of passing along the matrices in the *ExecutionUnit*, only a reference to the files at the client machine are given.

The results are shown on figure 3. As expected, the SUMA versions on a more powerful machine soon outperform the local version of the matrix multiplication program. The version that loads the matrices in the *ExecutionUnit* is faster than the version which loads the matrices at run-time, on demand. The latter version implies a remote access for every matrix element access.

The communication overhead explains the large difference (a factor of about two) with respect to the "Matrices in *Data*" version, which loads both matrices on the remote node in a single communication operation. Even though the total number of transferred bytes is the same in both cases, pre-loading is much more efficient because it is done in a single communication operation. As the dynamic load version is necessary for cases in which a data structure is large and the program only needs a small portion of it, we plan to add caching in order to improve dynamic remote file accesses.

5 Conclusions and Future Work

In this work, we presented the development of a metacomputing system for execution of Java bytecode, through the definition of an object oriented interface and the efficient implementation of metacomputing services, for scientific and engineering application development. Tuning of clients and the middleware, as well as the design of other views of the metasystem, like the administrator view, are goals of future work in this project. More details on the SUMA project can be found at *http://suma.ldc.usb.ve*.

Acknowledgments

We thank Alana Aguirre, Luis Berbín, Roberto Bouza, Pedro García, Hector Rodríguez, and David Torres, who collaborated in the prototype implementation and the experiments.

References

1. Java Grande Forum Report: Making Java work for high-end computing. Technical Report JGF-TR-1, Java Grande Forum Panel, 1998.
2. José Moreira. Closing the performance gap between Java and Fortran in technical computing. In *Java for High Performance Computing Workshop, Europar 98*, 1998.
3. V. Getov, S. Flynn-Hummel, and S. Mintchev. High-performance parallel programming in Java: Exploiting native libraries. In *ACM 1998 Workshop on Java for High-Performance Network Computing*, 1998.
4. Mark Baker, Bryan Carpenter, Sung Hoon Ko, and Xinýing Li. mpiJava: A Java interface to MPI. In *First UK Workshop on Java for High Performance Network Computing, Europar 98*, 1998.
5. Mark Baker and Geoffrey Fox. Metacomputing: Harnessing informal supercomputers. In Rajkumar Buyya, editor, *High Performance Cluster*

Computing: Architectures and Systems, volume 1, pages 154–186. Prentice Hall PTR, 1999.

6. Gregor von Laszewski. Desktop Access to Remote Resources. http://www-fp.mcs.anl.gov/~gregor/datorr.

7. I. Foster and C. Kesselman. Globus: A metacomputing infrastructure toolkit. *The International Journal of Supercomputer Applications and High Performance Computing*, 11(2):115–128, Summer 1997.

8. A. S. Grimshaw, A. Nguyen-Tuong, M. J. Lewis, and M. Hyett. Campuswide computing: Early results using Legion at the University of Virginia. *The International Journal of Supercomputer Applications and High Performance Computing*, 11(2):129–143, Summer 1997.

9. http://www.netlib.org/lapack.

10. Philip Alpatov, Greg Baker, Carter Edwards, John Gunnels, Greg Morrow, James Overfelt, Robert van de Geijn, and Yuan-Jye J. Wu. PLAPACK: Parallel linear algebra package. In *Proceedings of the SIAM Parallel Processing Conference*, 1997.

11. Gerald Brose. JacORB: A Java Object Request Broker. Technical Report B 97-2, Institut für Informatik, Freie Universität Berlin, 1997.

COMET: A COMMUNICATION-EFFICIENT LOAD BALANCING STRATEGY FOR MULTI-AGENT CLUSTER COMPUTING

YU-KWONG KWOK[†], KA-PO CHOW[†], HAI JIN[†], AND KAI HWANG[†‡]

[†]*Department of Electrical and Electronic Engineering*
The University of Hong Kong, Pokfulam Road, Hong Kong

[‡]*Department of EE-Systems*
University of Southern California, Los Angeles, CA 90089-2562, USA

Email: {ykwok, kpchow, hjin, kaihwang}@eee.hku.hk

This paper proposes a new load balancing strategy, called *Comet*, for fast multi-agent cluster computing. We use a new load index that takes into account the cost of inter-agent communications. Agents with predictable workload are assigned statically to cluster nodes, whereas agents with unpredictable workload are allowed to migrate dynamically between cluster nodes using a credit-based load balancing algorithm based on the proposed load index. We have implemented and tested our load balancing strategy in a multi-agent cluster platform consisting of Linux PC machines. Experimental results indicate that the proposed Comet system outperforms traditional distributed load balancing strategies for applications with regular as well as irregular communication patterns.

1 Introduction

Balancing the computation and communication workload of a user application across the machines in a cluster is one of the most crucial resource management issue in realizing effective cluster computing[2,4,7]. Traditional "idle-cycle-stealing" approaches, which are based only on the computational workload, are not suitable for contemporary cluster applications. Indeed, it is widely envisioned that multi-agent systems will be a major paradigm in designing distributed software. In this paper, we propose a new load balancing strategy, called *Comet*, for balanced and communication efficient multi-agent cluster computing. In our Linux-based PC cluster platform (see Figure 1(a)), a user accesses the cluster with a Web browser. The agent name server (ANS) indicates the location of each agent in the system. An agent is essentially a light-weight software process running on a single machine. All drafted agents must interact with the database server, which updates the Oracle database of the addressed application. The final decision result is returned to the user by the ANS through the Internet.

Our multi-agent system has been designed to manage investors portfolio and provide customized alarming services. It monitors the risk level and expected return of the users portfolio continuously and gives advice to the investors on their portfolio selection. Alarming signals can be set according to the users criteria on the risk level of portfolio or other stock data. Different classes of agents are organized in the hierarchy. These agents are: portfolio management agents, economic performance agents, factor analysis agents, and indicator agents. At the lowest level of the hierarchy, the indicator agents acquire information from outside sources. There are now 33 indicator agents and ten factor analysis agents residing in our system.

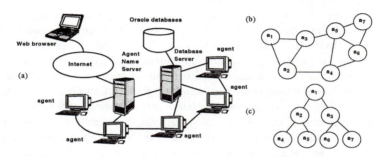

Figure 1. (a) A multi-agent cluster computing system; (b) a directed graph modeling the agent communication structure of the system; (c) an example tree-structured multi-agent system.

To efficiently response to user's queries, the agents are required to complete their designated tasks using the shortest amounts of time. However, if the mapping of agents to machines are not handled properly, it is likely that some machines will be overloaded with too many agents while some other machines may be idle. This results in unnecessarily long query response times. Thus, we need a judicious agents management scheme to monitor the execution of agents and properly balance the workload of machines.

In the proposed Comet load balancing algorithm detailed in the next section, we use a credit-based load index associated with each agent to keep track of the cost of inter-agent messages exchanged among the agents. We have implemented several multi-agent applications and the proposed Comet system using the Java programming language on a Linux PC cluster. Our extensive experimental results, as detailed in Section 3, indicate that the proposed credit-based approach outperforms a traditional distributed load balancing method in that the former always gives more balanced workload throughout the entire execution span of the applications. This in turn implies a much shorter response time can be obtained in servicing user's queries.

2 Communication Efficient Load Balancing

Unlike usual processes in a distributed system, an agent is a light-weight unit of execution capable of perpetually performing multiple functions in an autonomous manner. Agents are persistent software objects with long-lived missions[5,6]. Specifically, an agent consists of two parts. The first part is a set of data structures manipulated by the agent. For instance, in our financial database application, the set of data types might consist of a set of primitive attribute types (e.g., exchange rates) as well as some record types derived from those attribute types. The second part is a set of functions, may or may not be multithreaded, that manipulate the data types. These are typically function calls for gathering data and computing results. The distinctive feature of an agent is that the embedded computation in each agent is minimal compared with communication cost among agents. Although the agents are autonomous, they usually perpetually cooperate to collectively satisfy a user's query or command. Thus, the coordination among agents is represented by some structure (e.g., a tree or a mesh) rather than entirely disconnected. The difference between such a multi-agent software system from a message-passing parallel program is that agents are loosely coupled and there does not exist any strict precedence constraints as in among tasks of a parallel program.

In the multi-agent system considered in our study, we assume an application is composed of n agents executable on any of the p homogeneous machines of the cluster. The structure of the application is modeled by the interdependence relationships among the agents. More specifically, we use an undirected graph to model the application structure. For example, the undirected graph shown in Figure 1(b) can be used to model the structure of the multi-agent system depicted in Figure 1(a). Also, a binary tree structure, as shown in Figure 1(c), can be used to model most divide-and-conquer types of applications. An undirected graph is an appropriate generic model because a multi-agent application executes perpetually and produces results continuously in response to user queries (e.g., financial database queries). One particular feature in our multi-agent system is that the communication pattern among the agents is known. Even if it changes, all such changes will be registered on the Agent Name Server and JATLite Message Router. Using this feature, we can arrange the agents to minimize communication overhead through the inter-connection network. Notice that the computational load of an agent and the communication load between two agents may be different for processing different queries. Thus, the data or control dependencies among agents are not constant. Given these agent characteristics, we can also see that the application is inherently iterative in nature in that each iteration corresponds to the execution of the application for one particular query. Figure 2 illustrates the dynamics and structure of the multi-agent application.

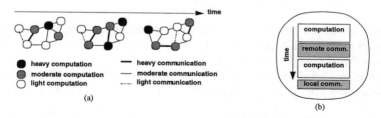

Figure 2. (a) Iterative and dynamic nature of a multi-agent application; (b) the structure of an agent.

Traditional load balancing strategies commonly use the computational load of a process as the load index based on the assumption that computation is the dominant activity in a process and communication can be fully overlapped with computation[8,9]. While this approximation might be valid for heavy weight processes in a distributed system, such a load index is clearly not appropriate for the multi-agent system considered in our study. Thus, we propose a composite attribute to indicate the load of an agent that takes into account the effect of remote and local communications among agents. Specifically, the load of an agent a_i executing on machine m_k is defined as the sum of its computational load w_i and the communication load u_i, where:

$$u_i = h_i + g_i = \sum_{M(a_i)=M(a_j)} c(a_i, a_j) + \frac{f}{2} \sum_{M(a_i)\neq M(a_j)} c(a_i, a_j) \qquad (1)$$

(note that a_j may be local or remote depending upon the value of $M(a_j)$). Here, h_i and g_i represent the intra-machine and inter-machine communication load, respectively. The factor 2 is included to avoid double counting the inter-machine communication. The value of w_i is computed statically by profiling the different execution instances of the agent and measuring the running times[3]. Note that the communication cost w_i can be computed by each agent using the message sizes. The scaling factor f (> 1) is system dependent and calculated based on the network bandwidth of the system (in our implementation, the point-to-point bandwidth of the ATM network is 155 Mbps so that inter-machine communication is approximately more than an order of magnitude slower than intra-machine communication). The load L_k of a machine m_k is defined as the sum of all its local agents' load. More specifically,

$$L_k = \sum_{M(a_i)=k} (w_i + u_i) \qquad (2)$$

The goal of a load balancing algorithm is to minimize the variance of load among all the machines in the cluster. This will in turn minimize the average response time of serving user's queries.

Given the definition of load index, we explicate below our proposed Comet load balancing algorithm by illustrating its important distinctive aspects.

- *Agents segregation*: During the start-up phase of an multi-agent application, the Comet system first segregates the agents with predictable workload from the others. Then, we map these agents to some dedicated machines statically in a balanced manner. The remaining agents are then assigned to the machines in a round-robin fashion and are subject to migration during the execution span of the application.

- *Information policy*: In the Comet system, we employ a distributed periodic information policy. Specifically, the machines in the system synchronize periodically and check their local aggregate load against the load thresholds, which are estimated high (T_H) and low (T_L) load levels computed during application start-up, where both T_H and T_L are computed based on the mean and standard deviation of load.

- *Transfer policy*: After the load information collection phase, the machines perform complete exchange to determine the machines with the highest load (and $L > T_H$). Agents then migrate from this sender machine to some receiver machines so as to reduce its load to a level below T_H.

- *Migration policy*: Each agent a_i is associated with a *credit* C_i which is defined as: $C_i = -x_1 w_i + x_2 h_i - x_3 g_i$, where x_1, x_2, x_3 are positive real value numbers and are application dependent coefficients. The rationale of this credit attribute is to capture the *affinity* of an agent to the machine in that the intra-machine communication component contributes positively to the credit whereas the reverse is true for the inter-machine communication. In the sender machine, the agent with the smallest credit is selected for migration because such an agent spends dominant amount of time communicating with a remote agent and hence, is a suitable candidate for migration in order to reduce the local load level.

- *Location policy*: After a migrating agent is selected, we need to determine the target machine. In the Comet system, each agent a_i keeps track of a

p-element vector V_i storing the value of remote communication (the local communication component is stored as the $M(a_i)$-th element) between the local machine and all other machines in the network. Specifically, each element v_s of the vector is simply $\sum_{M(a_i)=s} c(a_i, a_j)$. Suppose the y-th element ($y \neq M(a_i)$) is the largest element. Then, machine m_y will be chosen as the receiver of the agent.

Notice that the location policy of the proposed approach is novel in that we implicitly specify a receiver machine in the network for a migrating agent. By contrast, most existing load balancing schemes require the system to determine a receiver which is usually the one with the lowest load. It should be noted that for multi-agent systems in which communication is the dominant event, choosing the lowest load machine may not be a suitable strategy because such machine may not necessarily reduce the inter-machine communication overhead, which is a dominant part of the aggregate load.

3 Experimental Results and Interpretations

We have implemented the Comet system using Java for a Linux PC cluster. To evaluate the effectiveness of the system, several multi-agent financial-analysis benchmark applications have been developed in Linux cluster environment. We combine mirrored checkpointing[2] with the Comet strategy to balance benchmark workloads on two research clusters. We performed a number of experiments using a cluster with four Pentium Pro PC running Linux with 64 MB memory each. In all the experiments, we set the period of load monitoring and balancing to be ten seconds (i.e., $\tau = 10$). For comparison, we also implemented a classical sender-initiated computational workload based load balancing (abbreviated as WBLB) scheme[8]. In WBLB, the machines also synchronize periodically to identify sender (overloaded) cluster nodes and receiver (lightly loaded) cluster nodes. The sender node then transfers the agents with the greatest computational load to the receivers. Notice that in such a classical load balancing method, communication load is ignored.

We considered an irregularly structured financial application with 18 agents, which was executed under the control of the Comet system. We collected performance data for a time period of approximately 1400 seconds and the same process was repeated several times. To evaluate the performance of the proposed algorithm, we computed the standard deviation (SD) of the load over time normalized with respect to the mean load. The reason of normalization is that as the computation of the multi-agent application proceeds, the load level may fluctuate in that some extra workload may be generated or destroyed on-the-fly, depending upon the user queries. Thus, the normalized SD is a more accurate measure of the instantaneous degree of load balance.

Figure 3(a) shows the normalized SD of the two algorithms over time. As can be seen, the proposed Comet system almost always resulted in a lower normalized load SD. Indeed, a close scrutiny of the execution traces revealed that the WBLB scheme showed a moderate degree of thrashing—some agents were repeatedly being transferred among the machines without being actually executed until after the maximum number of transferrals was reached. Apart from instability and overhead, an adverse effect is that the resulting load was usually not balanced, as is illustrated by the wide range of load (normalized with respect to mean load) as shown in Figure 3(b).

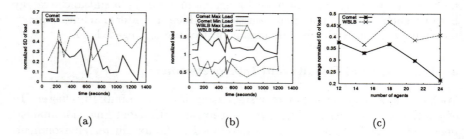

(a) (b) (c)

Figure 3. (a) Normalized standard deviation of load across all cluster nodes; (b) maximum and minimum load levels; (c) average normalized standard deviation of load across all machines over a time period of 1400 seconds with various number of agents.

Using the same four-node Linux cluster, we varied the number of agents in the application from 12 to 24. The results are shown in Figure 3(c). We can see that the Comet system outperformed the WBLB scheme in all cases. These results indicate that the proposed credit-based load index and balancing strategy are effective for efficiently executing applications composed of dynamic light- weight agents. Similar results were obtained for a tree structured application[1].

4   Conclusions

A novel load balancing strategy is presented for multi-agent cluster computing system. The proposed Comet system uses a load index that takes into account the effect of both intra-machine and inter-machine communication. This is important for agent-based systems because the embedded computation in each agent is minimal compared with communication cost among agents. The load balancing algorithm is credit-based and works by selecting the agent with the heaviest inter-machine communication for migration. We have also implemented the whole system using Java for a Linux PC cluster and tested it using several regular and irregular financial database applications. The experimental results indicate that the Comet system outperforms an existing distributed load balancing algorithm considerably.

Acknowledgments

This research was jointly supported by the Hong Kong Research Grants Council (under contract numbers HKU2/96C, HKU7022/97E, and HKU7124/99E), by the HKU Information Technology Development Fund, by a research initiation grant from the HKU CRCG, and by a special research grant from the Engineering School of the University of Southern California.

References

1. K.-P. Chow, *Load Balancing in Distributed Multi-Agent Computing*, M.Phil. Thesis, The University of Hong Kong, 1999.
2. K. Hwang, H. Jin, E. Chow, C.-L. Wang, and Z. Xu, "Designing SSI Clusters with Hierarchical Checkpointing and Single I/O Space," *IEEE Concurrency*, vol.7, no.1, pp.60–69, Jan./Mar. 1999.
3. K. Hwang, C. Wang, C.-L. Wang, and Z. Xu, "Resource Scaling Effects on MPP Performance: The STAP Benchmark Implications," *IEEE Trans. Parallel and Distributed Systems*, vol. 10, no. 5, pp. 509–527, May 1999.
4. K. Hwang and Z. Xu, *Scalable Parallel Computing: Technology, Architecture, Programming*, McGraw-Hill, 1998.
5. N.R. Jennings and M.J. Wooldridge, (eds.), *Agent Technology: Foundations, Applications, and Markets*, Springer-Verlag, Berlin, 1998.
6. A. Joshi, N. Ramakrishnan, and E.N. Houstis, "Multi-Agent System Support of Networked Scientific Computing," *IEEE Internet Computing*, vol. 2, no. 3, pp. 69–83, May/June 1998.
7. G.F. Pfister, *In Search of Clusters*, 2nd Ed., Prentice-Hall, 1998.
8. N.G. Shivaratri, P. Krueger, and M. Singhal, "Load Distributing for Locally Distributed Systems," *IEEE Computer*, vol. 25, no. 12, pp. 33–44, Dec. 1992.
9. P. Williams, *Dynamic Load Sharing within Workstation Clusters*, Honors Dissertation in Information technology, University of Western Australia, Oct. 1994.

PERFORMANCE COMPARISON OF FOUR SOFTWARE ARCHITECTURES FOR DISTRIBUTED COMPUTATIONS

JAN VAN KATWIJK

Delft University of Technology, 2600 AJ Delft, The Netherlands
E-mail: J.vanKatwijk@twi.tudelft.nl

YUN PENG AND JANUSZ ZALEWSKI

Dept. ECE, University of Central Florida, Orlando, FL 32816-2450, USA
E-mail: jza@ece.engr.ucf.edu

In the 1990s, several programming interfaces for distributed computing have been proposed, and various implementations have been realized and made public. In this paper, we concentrate on performance issues of packages for the support of distributed computations. The objective is to evaluate some of the current implementations of MPI, RMI, CORBA, and NetSolve in a client/server environment. Based on a set of measurements of communication time between hosts and computation time on a remote host, we address the question, what are the factors that determine performance of off-the-shelf distributed applications.

1 Introduction

Distributed computing requires that computations that run in different address spaces, on different hosts, are able to communicate with each other. Traditionally, sockets and *Remote Procedure Calls (RPC)* provided basic communication mechanisms, but the use sockets at the application level is cumbersome, while RPC does not translate well into distributed object systems.

MPI is a portable message-passing standard, based on the same principles, that facilitates the development of parallel applications and libraries [3]. MPI defines the syntax and semantics of library routines useful to a wide range of users writing portable message-passing programs in Fortran 77 or C.

RMI [2] is the protocol that goes beyond the RPC, taking it to object-oriented systems, specifically designed to operate in a Java environment. A remote method invocation is the action of invoking a method of a remote interface on a remote object. Most importantly, a method invocation on a remote object has the same syntax as a method invocation on a local object.

CORBA [2] is a standard for distributed object systems developed by the Object Management Group (OMG). It provides mechanisms by which objects transparently make requests and receive responses, as defined by OMG's Object Request Broker (ORB). The CORBA ORB is an application framework that provides interoperability between objects, built in different languages, running on different machines in heterogeneous distributed environments.

NetSolve is a new client-server application designed to solve computational science problems over a network [1]. It is still in an experimental stage of development. Interfaces have been developed to the NetSolve software so that users of C, Fortran, Java or MATLAB can easily use the NetSolve system.

The four systems mentioned above have different architectures and differ in performance. Due to space limitations, we refer the reader to the literature for more information on architectural details [1,2,3]. The objective of this study is to evaluate the performance of some of the current implementations of MPI, RMI, CORBA, and NetSolve in a client/server environment. In particular, we want to address the question, what are the factors that determine performance of off-the-shelf distributed applications, making them suitable for industrial use. The parameters selected in the comparison are as follows:

- The round trip time of data communication.
- The plain run time to perform local computations on a remote machine.

These two time intervals are collectively called execution time, in this paper. The same sample computational problem is used for each implementation: calculation of the average of a large number of integers. The experiments were performed on a cluster of Sun UltraSparc workstations running Sun Solaris 2.5.1, connected by 10 Mb/s Ethernet network.

2 The Experiments

The general setup of the experiments is that a server program, written individually for each of the packages, MPI, RMI, CORBA and NetSolve, calculates an average of input values. The calculations are called and parameters are sent from a remote client. After completing the computation, the server returns the result to the client.

This procedure is applied to the MPI parallel program, by sending an array of data of different lengths to the remote machines. RMI and CORBA client/server distributed programs, using a client with multiple threads connecting to different servers, are run for data arrays of different lengths. A NetSolve program is run with adding a new function to the system. Individual experiments are discussed in the following four sections.

2.1 The MPI Experiment

Results. The experiment was conducted using the MPICH 1.1.2 package. The results were obtained from execution on 1, 2, 4 and 8 machines. Results given in Table 1 show the data representing the execution time for sending arrays of different length as parameters to the remote machines. Execution time equals the communication time plus calculation time on the remote hosts. Results for communication time are only slightly smaller than execution time and are not shown here. The problem size corresponds to the amount of numbers in the parameter array. All results are averaged from 5 runs.

Table 1. MPI execution time (in seconds).

Size	10^1	10^2	10^3	10^4	10^5
1	.000345	.000374	.000579	.00289	.0262
2	.003	. 0048	0.02	.16	2.3
4	.005	.011	0.046	.53	8.4
8	.018	.023	0.12	1.2	14.6

To study problems that are computationally intensive, that is, where communication time does not have much impact·on the entire execution, we sent to the remote machines only the number indicating the array length, rather than the array itself. Tables 2 and 3 show the results (execution time and communication time) for such case.

Table 2. MPI execution time (in seconds).

Size	10^3	10^5	10^7	10^9
1	0.00073	0.0389	3.909	405.13
2 local	0.0023	0.0396	4.165	224.65
2 remote	0.0022	0.038	3.86	212.73
4	0.0033	0.023	1.9	192.0
8	0.0072	0.02	1.6	168.19

Table 3. MPI communication time (in seconds).

# of processors	1	2	4	8
time	0.00032	0.0018	0.0032	0.0069

Discussion. As might have been expected, the entire execution time for the problem with an array length from 1 to 10^5 is eaten by communication. Both execution time and communication time begin to increase linearly with the increase of array length for about 10^2 elements. For arrays with less than 10^2 elements, the length does not seem to have an impact on execution time. The increase of execution time with more processors added is easy to explain, because communication time is dominating, and almost all execution time is actually spent on communication.

For computationally intensive problems (Tables 2 and 3), when the problem size is less than a certain point in the range 10^4 to 10^5, the execution time increases with more processors. Execution time decreases with adding more processors for problem sizes bigger than 10^5, i.e., the processing power grows faster than the overhead. When the problem size is bigger than this cutoff point, the execution time increases linearly with the problem size.

2.2 The RMI Experiment

Results. The application using RMI was developed under JDK 1.1.7 and run on 1, 2, 4 and 8 machines. Table 4 presents the execution time with different numbers of processors for sending an array of parameters from a multithreaded client to the remote machines. All results are averaged from 5 runs.

Table 4. RMI execution time (in seconds).

Size	10^1	10^2	10^3	10^4	10^5
1	0.021	0.025	0.035	0.184	2.736
2	0.027	0.032	0.058	0.326	3.626
4	0.044	0.048	0.112	0.645	8.238
8	0.096	0.101	0.212	1.349	14.836

For studying computation intensive behaviour, we performed a second set of experiments sending a single number (problem size), rather than the whole array, as a parameter to the server. Results are given in Tables 5 and 6.

Table 5. RMI execution time (in seconds).

Size	10^3	10^4	10^6	10^8
1 local	0.021	0.031	2.896	290.12
1 remote	0.019	0.029	2.868	289.96
2	0.023	0.028	1.62	206.29
4	0.055	0.06	0.876	102.577
8	0.085	0.088	0.566	73.09

Discussion. Similar to what we have seen in the MPI experiments, the program communication time dominates the execution in case of multiple RMI servers receiving an array of input data. The execution time and communication time begin to increase linearly with the increase of array length from

Table 6. RMI communication time (in seconds).

# of processors	1	2	4	8
time	0.015	0.019	0.052	0.083

about 10^2 elements. Below that point, array length does not seem to have an impact on the execution time.

For computationally intensive problems (Tables 5 and 6), when problem size is less than a certain point below 10^5, the execution time with more processors is larger than the one with less. As in case of MPI, execution time begins to decrease with adding processors for problem sizes bigger than 10^5.

2.3 The CORBA Experiment

Results. The CORBA application was developed using the Visigenic Visibroker Developer for Java 3.1 (CORBA implementation). All programs were run under JDK1.1.7. The benchmark results are given in Table 7. The data represent the execution time for sending different-length arrays to the remote server machines (1, 2, 4 and 8 processors). Problem size corresponds to the amount of numbers in the parameter array.

Table 7. CORBA execution time (in seconds).

Size	10^1	10^2	10^3	10^4	10^5
1	0.018	0.021	0.057	0.482	6.53
2	0.021	0.026	0.085	0.846	9.65
4	0.039	0.045	0.135	1.32	14.94
8	0.086	0.091	0.261	2.81	30.02

As in case of MPI and RMI, a second set of experiments simulated computation intensive behavior of CORBA servers, by sending a single parameter (problem size) to the servers. Results are given in Tables 8 and 9.

Discussion. Results for CORBA are quite similar to those for RMI and we drop detailed considerations to save space.

2.4 The NetSolve Experiment

The experiments in this section were conducted using the NetSolve 1.2 development tool. In this implementation of NetSolve, we were able to run the remote part of the program only on a single server.

Table 8. CORBA execution time (in seconds).

Size	10^2	10^4	10^6	10^8
1 local	0.029	0.043	3.41	347.12
1 remote	0.024	0.03	3.35	346.3
2	0.023	0.033	1.71	172.9
4	0.043	0.047	1.31	138.1
8	0.096	0.1	0.52	69.42

Table 9. CORBA communication time (in seconds).

# of processors	1	2	4	8
time	0.016	0.021	0.037	0.091

Data in Table 10 show the execution time on a single server for various sizes of the parameter array. The execution time varies only slightly for significant changes in the array size. Since the communication time is a part of execution time, this means that in NetSolve most of the time is spent in an agent resolving access to a remote server.

Table 10. NetSolve execution time (in seconds).

Size	10^1	10^2	10^3	10^4	10^5
time	0.412	0.422	0.431	0.443	0.842

Table 11 gives results for a computationally intensive NetSolve program run on a remote machine with varying problem sizes. Communication time is of the order of that in Table 10, which confirms earlier observation that the time spent in an agent is significant and roughly independent of the problem size. Calculations for large problem sizes, however, are much faster than for other tools.

Table 11. NetSolve behavior for various problem sizes.

Time vs. size	10^3	10^5	10^6	10^8
Execution	0.3811	0.3911	2.367	42.372
Communication	0.3805	0.3805	0.3805	0.3805
Calculation	0.0006	0.0106	1.9865	41.992

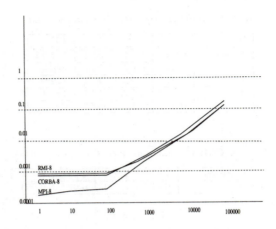

Figure 1. Execution time vs array size for 8 servers.

3 Conclusions and Future Work

In this study, we compared performance of four software tools for distributed computations: MPI, RMI, CORBA and NetSolve. Two principal parameters were used for comparisons: calculation time and communication time.

If large amounts of data, such as a long array, are sent to remote machines, the execution time is dominated by communication time that increases with the number of processors and higher array lengths. Thus, for communication intensive problems, we cannot reduce execution time by adding processors. This is shown in Figure 1, which compares the execution time versus the length of parameter array for 8 processors.

In all cases, when a long array is sent over the network to the servers, MPI demonstrates a slightly better performance than RMI, and significantly better than CORBA. This is shown collectively in Figure 2, for communication time versus the number of processors, with an array size of 10^5.

In cases where the calculation time dominates, it turns out that for bigger problem sizes the total execution time decreases with more processors and the minimum grain size of data to achieve this effect is around 10^5.

In general, MPI programs run faster than CORBA and RMI in both types of applications, mostly because RMI and CORBA in this study were interpretive Java programs. NetSolve programs execute much faster for large amounts of data, because uses an agent for server access resolution and this degrades the communication performance. However, for sufficiently large problems (10^6),

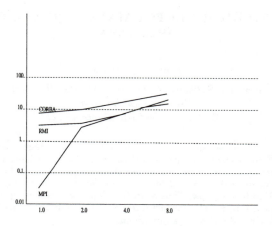

Figure 2. Communication time for array size 10^5.

calculation time begins to dominate and the execution time of NetSolve programs is smaller than that of RMI and CORBA programs.

In this paper, we report only a step to get a more clear picture of performance issues in distributed programs, built with standard packages. More research is required for an in-depth study and our current plans focus on:

- more complex problems to be used as benchmarks for the performance measurement of MPI, RMI and CORBA as support systems;
- the addition of multiprocessing capabilities to NetSolve to further improve its performance.

Acknowledgments

Thanks are due to H. Casanova, J. Dongarra, A. Karainov and J. Wasniewski for letting us use beta version of NetSolve and educating us on its use.

References

1. H. Casanova and J. Dongarra, International Journal **11**, 212-223 (1997).
2. R. Orfali and D. Harkey, *Client/Server Programming with Java and CORBA* (John Wiley and Sons, New York, 1998).
3. M. Snir *et al*, *MPI – The Complete Reference* (MIT Press, Cambridge, Mass., 1998).

DISTRIBUTED HIGH PERFORMANCE COMPUTING WITH OPUSJAVA

ERWIN LAURE

Institute for Software Technology and Parallel Systems
University of Vienna
E-Mail: erwin@par.univie.ac.at

The past few years have dramatically changed the view of high performance applications and computing. While traditionally applications have been targeted towards dedicated parallel machines, we see the emerging trend of building "meta-applications" composed of several modules that exploit heterogeneous platforms employing hybrid forms of parallelism. In this paper we present OpusJava, a Java based component framework that facilitates a seamless integration of high performance modules into distributed applications.

1 Introduction

Advanced scientific applications are often built by composing existing software components that exploit specialized computing and algorithmic resources[1,2]. In particular, high performance components are being employed and need to cooperate in distributed heterogeneous environments for generating a solution. We refer to such applications as *Distributed High Performance Computing (DHPC)* applications. Although several component frameworks are being developed that support DHPC applications (cf. Section 5), these systems are typically at a quite low level and do not provide a seamless and efficient integration of high performance modules (written e.g. in MPI or HPF).

In this paper we present the design of OpusJava, a Java interface to the coordination language Opus[3,4] that provides a high level, comprehensive model for DHPC. OpusJava combines the strengths of Opus (especially the integration of task- and data parallelism) with the strengths of Java (especially the dynamic networking features).

While Opus provides efficient support for coupling modules which exploit hybrid forms of parallelism on homogeneous systems, it lacks support for language interoperability and heterogeneous platforms[5]. OpusJava is designed to bridge the gap between efficient high performance computing and dynamic distributed computing by facilitating a seamless integration of high performance modules into larger distributed systems via a high level component model that hides low level details such as communication, data format conversion, or thread synchronization.

2 Overview of the Opus Language and Implementation Design

Opus[3,4] introduces a small set of extensions to HPF designed to coordinate an efficient parallel execution of multiple, independent program modules. At the heart of these extensions is an abstract data type called *ShareD Abstraction*, or *SDA*, whose purpose is to provide a means for encapsulation of data and methods (procedures) which act on this data. SDAs may exploit data parallelism in that the internal data of SDAs as well as the data of SDA methods may be distributed. By *creating* an instance of an SDA type an *SDA object* (or simply SDA) is generated. During its *lifetime* an SDA executes asynchronously in a separate address space and can be accessed through calls to its methods.

An SDA method can be invoked *synchronously*, where the caller is blocked until control returns, or *asynchronously*, where the caller does not have to wait for the completion of the method. Explicit synchronization is possible via *event* variables that can be bound to asynchronous method invocations. Arguments are passed with copy in/copy out semantics. In general, each method has *exclusive access* to the data of the SDA, much like in monitors. A method may have an associated *condition clause*, specifying a logical expression, which guards the method's activation.

At runtime, an SDA is conceptually represented by a (data parallel) thread of control[6]. This conceptual thread is realized by two independent threads that communicate via a shared memory area. In particular, the runtime components of an SDA are: (1) a shared memory area, which contains queues for temporarily storing Method Invocation requests (MIs). These queues, which are called *MI-queues*, are necessary because of the conditional method execution in Opus. (2) The *Server Thread* which receives MIs, unmarshals input arguments and places the request into the shared memory area (in the form of *execution records*, the runtime representation of MIs). (3) The *Execution Thread* which retrieves records from the shared memory area, evaluates the condition-clauses and executes the respective methods that are compiled to internal subroutines of the execution thread.

3 OpusJava

OpusJava is a Java framework that provides Opus functionalities. Thus, it can be seen as the Java binding of Opus. Similar to Opus, OpusJava provides a high level component model (SDAs) with plug compatibility among components, a hybrid parallelism model, and high level coordination means.

Moreover, OpusJava facilitates the integration of HPF modules in a distributed Java application by providing an interface to Opus. Language interoperability is furthermore ensured by the standardized Java Native Interface (JNI). OpusJava does not pose any restrictions to the Java programming style. In particular, Java's multithreading features may well be exploited within SDAs. The OpusJava API is modeled after the Opus syntax to provide a common look-and-feel.

By exploiting advanced Java features such as the reflection mechanism, we were able to avoid language extensions (that would have caused associated compiler development) and IDLs in our design of OpusJava. This fact favors a wide spread use of OpusJava by making the framework easily available on any platform providing a JVM. Moreover, the absence of compilation requirements allows the integration of dynamically loaded byte-code modules into OpusJava applications.

OpusJava introduces only two new objects visible to the user: the final class SDA, which defines a stub for remote SDA objects, and the final class Event, which is used to reference asynchronous method invocations.

A remote SDA is created by instantiating a new object of type SDA. After its creation, a remote SDA is accessible via the SDA stub. The SDA stub provides methods for calling remote methods in a synchronous (call) and asynchronous (spawn) way. The arguments of these methods are the remote method name and an array of input parameters for the remote method. A terminate method for gracefully destroying remote objects is provided as well. Although Java does not provide means for destroying objects, SDAs may be native (HPF) objects and thus support for explicit termination is desirable. The call method blocks the caller until the results are available, while the spawn method returns an Event object immediately and allows the caller to resume its execution. An Event is a pointer to a remote asynchronous method invocation and can be used for synchronization later on.

The remote counterpart of the SDA stub is the *SDA Implementation Skeleton* which is realized by the Java class SDAImpl. For every SDA object, an SDAImpl object is created automatically which handles all the interaction with the associated SDA. In particular, methods of the SDA are invoked via the SDAImpl counterpart rather than directly in the SDA. The skeleton is registered in the RMIRegistry, thus its methods can be invoked remotely. It exports a method for receiving and storing method invocation requests (insert).

SDAImpl skeletons are realized in a manner similar to Opus SDA objects (cf. Section 2; a detailed discussion can be found in[6]). In particular, a skeleton contains *MI queues* for managing *execution records* and operates an *execution thread* which is spawned upon creation. Method invocation requests are processed in a way similar to the Opus *Server Thread*: the `insert` method creates an *execution record* which contains references to the method to be executed, the input parameters, and some internal management data. This record is inserted into the *inqueue* of the skeleton. The *execution thread* retrieves the record from the inqueue and, after checking the associated *condition clause* (which is a logical function with the same name as the guarded method, postfixed with "_cond"), invokes the method in the SDA object exploiting Java's reflection mechanism. The skeleton also transfers results of a method execution back to the caller.

Finally, the OpusJava system requires an *SDA Server* which is a daemon that is installed on any system which may participate in an OpusJava program execution. This daemon is responsible for creating and terminating SDA objects for which two RMI methods (`create` and `terminate`) are exported.

In general, any Java object can be created as an SDA. The `create` method of the SDA Server, which is activated by the constructor of an `SDA` stub, has 3 arguments: the name of the SDA type, an array of input arguments for the SDA's constructor, and the number of processors to be used. Java's reflection mechanism is exploited to check whether appropriate classes are available. If not, dynamic class loading can be used to load the classes from user specified resources on demand. Subsequently, a new `SDAImpl` object is created, which in turn creates the new SDA object using the supplied arguments for the SDA's constructor. The `SDAImpl` object acts as a skeleton for the SDA and is registered in the RMIRegistry. The registered name is sent back to the caller, thus completing the `create` method.

In order to make Opus (i.e. F90 or HPF) SDAs accessible from OpusJava, the Opus compiler generates the necessary stubs and wrappers. More specifically, on the Java side additional *Java SDA classes* are generated that serve as wrappers to Opus objects. For every Opus SDA type, a Java counterpart is generated which is instantiated as an SDA (thus together with its associated SDAImpl object) for every Opus SDA object. Methods of these objects can be invoked just as of any other OpusJava SDA. However, instead of serving the request directly, it is forwarded to the wrapped Opus SDA. In doing so, the involved data is converted by means of *C wrappers*.

These C wrappers are generated by the Opus compiler and are based upon a generic JNI interface defined for OpusJava. Hence, all the required JNI compilation can be done when installing the framework rather than for every application. In particular, the wrappers marshal and unmarshal method arguments and construct the required Opus execution records.

On the Opus side, an *external SDA stub* is provided which is an Opus SDA through which external requests are routed. This stub acts as a multiplexer that transfers OpusJava requests obtained from the C wrappers directly to the respective Opus SDA and vice versa. For an Opus application, the stub appears as a normal SDA, thus any request admissible to SDAs can be posed to the stub, as well. But rather than serving the request directly, the stub routes it through the C wrappers to the associated OpusJava SDA for service.

4 Application Example and Experiments

We implemented a prototype of the OpusJava framework using the Java 2 platform and extended our Opus compiler[6] to provide the necessary interfaces. With this prototype environment we realized the coordination part of a simple online monitoring and steering application. Figure 1 to 3 illustrate the OpusJava/Opus skeletons: The main program (Figure 3), which is written in Java, instantiates a data parallel Opus simulation (Figure 1) with which it exchanges information via a buffer (Figure 2) that is used to temporarily store the actual status of the simulation as well as parameters that might be changed during a simulation run. Note, that the SDA constructors (line 4 and 6 of Figure 3) receive information about the machine to be used for object creation as well as the number of processors available to the HPF parts.

Based on these skeletons we measured the time needed for synchronous method invocation between (a) 2 OpusJava SDAs and (b) an OpusJava SDA and an Opus SDA, respectively, using two SUN Ultra 10 workstations connected by fast-Ethernet. The size of the input/output data set was in the range of 0 to 2000 floats. Figure 4 shows the mean time elapsed and, for comparison, the pure MPI based Opus results. Note, that these timings reflect the full OpusJava mechanisms as described above rather than pure communication times. Method invocation in pure OpusJava (a) is about a factor of 5 slower than in the Opus (MPI) version, however, using the full Opus interface (b) does not lead to a significant additional overhead; thus, the performance of OpusJava is almost exclusively bound to the performance of the underlying JVM. The overhead compared to MPI is on the one hand due to the unsatisfactory RMI performance for larger input data and on the other hand due to the less efficient thread implementation of Java. We expect the overhead to decrease when optimized Java thread implementations will be available and advanced RMI implementations[8] will be exploited.

5 Related Work

In this section we briefly review some systems, ranging from low level services and middle-ware to high level languages, that have been developed to support

```
SDA TYPE simulator(buffer)
  SDA (buffer_type) buffer
    ! simulation data
    ! HPF PROCESSOR directive
    ! HPF DISTRIBUTE directives
  CONTAINS
    SUBROUTINE simulate
      DO WHILE (.not. converged)
        params = buffer%get_parameters()
        ...
        buffer%dump_status(...)
      END DO
    END SUBROUTINE simulate
END SDA TYPE
```

Figure 1. The HPF Simulator

```
SDA TYPE buffer_type
  ! status data
  ! parameters
  CONTAINS
    FUNCTION get_parameters
    ...
    END FUNCTION
    SUBROUTINE set_parameters(...)
    ...
    END SUBROUTINE
    SUBROUTINE dump_status(...)
    ...
    END SUBROUTINE
    FUNCTION get_status
    ...
    END FUNCTION
END SDA TYPE
```

Figure 2. The Buffer

```
1:  public class Monitor {
2:    public static void main(String[] args) {
3:      // create SDAs
4:      SDA buffer = new SDA("buffer_type",machine, 1);
5:      Object[] args = new Object[] {buffer};
6:      SDA simulator = new SDA("simulator",
7:                        args, machine, nr_nodes);
8:      // initialize parameters
9:      buffer.call("set_parameters", params);
10:     // spawn the simulation
11:     Event ev = simulator.spawn("simulate");
12:     // monitor
13:     while (! ev.test()) {
14:       status = buffer.call("get_status");
15:       // visualize and analyze the status
16:       if (update_necessary)
17:         buffer.call("set_parameters",params);
    } } }
```

Figure 3. Main Program

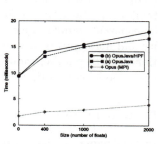

Figure 4. Elapsed Time for Method Invocation

distributed high performance computing.

Low level systems that support interoperation among heterogeneous components, such as *Globus*[9] and *Corba*[10], often lack efficient support for data parallel components and do not provide a high level hybrid programming model. In addition, interoperation with existing libraries is sometimes hampered. Nexus (the Globus communication module), for instance, prevents the exploitation of libraries (such as MPI) tuned to specific machine. Nevertheless, parts of these low level systems may well be exploited in higher level approaches like OpusJava in a selective way. The resource manager or the security module of Globus, for example, are valuable tools for OpusJava. Corba based communication could be exploited within OpusJava instead of Java's RMI, as well.

Higher level approaches such as *Legion*[11], which is based on a distributed object model, are more convenient to use than Globus or Corba. While Legion has similar aims as OpusJava, it lacks high level coordination of asynchronous remote procedure calls. In addition, Legion has problems with the integration of optimized data parallel code. In particular, Legion requires parallel libraries like MPI to be emulated using the underlying Legion runtime library. Moreover, parallel objects appear as simple sequential ones to other Legion objects which prevents e.g. optimized communication schedules between all components of such objects. Opus already supports data parallel objects and a port of this feature to OpusJava is planned in the near future.

The community has also seen the benefits of Java for coordinating distributed tasks resulting in a number of frameworks such as *WebFlow*[12] and *JavaParty*[13]. WebFlow is a high level graphical programming and program composition tool that exploits Java and builds upon Globus as back-end system, while JavaParty extends the Java programming language introducing transparent remote objects. Both approaches support language interoperability and high level composition techniques, however they lack efficient integration of data parallel modules and do not provide a comprehensive programming model supporting hybrid forms of parallelism.

6 Conclusions

In this paper we have presented OpusJava, a comprehensive programming model that supports hybrid parallelism (task and data parallelism) in the context of a multi-lingual framework for dynamic distributed high performance computing. In particular, OpusJava provides high level communication and coordination means and allows a seamless and efficient integration of high performance (Opus) components in larger, distributed environments. These high performance components need not be changed and can still exploit highly optimized communication mechanisms available on their target platforms. The user of OpusJava can focus on the algorithmic problem: all low level details like communication, RMI mechanisms, data format conversions, or JNI are completely transparent. Moreover, OpusJava employs Java's dynamic class loading features, which allow new modules to be plugged into a running application dynamically.

Future work will focus on the optimization of the currently RMI based OpusJava method invocation implementation by employing optimizations to enhance Java's object serialization and RMI mechanisms[8]. We will also investigate the use of Corba and JINI in this context. Moreover, we study the use of HPJava[7] for specifying data parallel Java SDAs.

Acknowledgments

The work described in this paper was partially supported by the Special Research Program SFB F011 "AURORA" of the Austrian Science Fund.
The author would like to thank Bernd Wender for many fruitful discussions on Java and the OpusJava design.

References

1. I. Foster and C. Kesselman, editors. *The Grid.* Morgan Kaufmann, 1999.
2. D. Gannon et al. Developing Component Architectures for Distributed Scientific Problem Solving. *IEEE Computational Science & Engineering,* 5(2), 1998.
3. B. Chapman, M. Haines, E. Laure, P. Mehrotra, J. Van Rosendale, and H. Zima. Opus 1.0 Reference Manual. TR 97-13, Institute for Software Technology and Parallel Systems, University of Vienna, October 1997.
4. B. Chapman, M. Haines, P. Mehrotra, J. Van Rosendale, and H. Zima. OPUS: A Coordination Language for Multidisciplinary Applications. *Scientific Programming,* 6/9:345–362, Winter 1997.
5. E. Laure, P. Mehrotra, and H. Zima. Opus: Heterogeneous Computing With Data Parallel Tasks. *Parallel Processing Letters,* in print 1999.
6. E. Laure, M. Haines, P. Mehrotra, and H. Zima. On the Implementation of the Opus Coordination Language. *Concurrency: Practice and Experience,* in print 1999.
7. B. Carpenter, G. Zhang, G. Fox, et al. Towards a Java Environment for SPMD Programming. In *EuroPar '98,* Southampton, 1998.
8. C. Nester, M. Philippsen, and B. Haumacher. A More Efficient RMI for Java. In *ACM 1999 Java Grande Conference,* San Francisco, June 1999.
9. I. Foster and C. Kesselman. The Globus Project: A Status Report. In *IPPS/SPDP '98 Heterogeneous Computing Workshop,* 1998.
10. OMG. *CORBA/IIOP 2.2 Specification,* June 1998.
11. A.S. Grimshaw, W.A. Wulf, et al. The Legion Vision of a Worldwide Virtual Computer. *Communications of the ACM,* 40(1), January 1997.
12. T. Haupt, E. Akarsu, and G. Fox. WebFlow: A Framework for Web Based Metacomputing. In *Proceedings HPCN Europe,* 1999.
13. M. Philippsen and M. Zenger. JavaParty - Transparent Remote Objects in Java. *Concurrency: Practice & Experience,* 9(11), November 1997.

MALLEABLE TASKS:
AN EFFICIENT MODEL FOR SOLVING ACTUAL PARALLEL
APPLICATIONS

RENAUD LEPERE, GREGORY MOUNIE, DENIS TRYSTRAM*

IMAG, Domaine Universitaire BP 53
38041 Grenoble Cedex 9, France

BORUT ROBIČ

Faculty of Computer and Information Science, University of Ljubljana
Tržaška 25, Ljubljana, Slovenia

The purpose of this paper is to promote the model of *Malleable Tasks* for efficiently solving actual parallel applications. Malleable Tasks are presented and discussed in regard to other classical models. We show how this approach has been applied to implement two actual applications, namely, the simulation of the circulations in the Atlantic ocean, and large sparse Cholesky factorization.

1 Introduction

Since the eighties, many works have been developed for parallelizing actual large scale applications. All parallel implementations are based on algorithmic studies where scheduling and load-balancing issues have to be considered. The resolution to this problem is crucial to the design of a high-performance parallelization, since it deals with deciding where (i.e., on which set of processors) and when the tasks will be executed. Many works have been developed, ranging from theoretical studies on abstract and idealized models to practical tools consisting of actual implementations on most parallel and distributed platforms. Among the various possible approaches, the most commonly used is to consider the tasks of the program at the finest level of granularity and apply some adequate clustering heuristics for reducing the relative communication overhead. The main drawback is that communications are explicitly taken into account (they are expressed assuming a model of the underlying architecture of the system which is very difficult to establish and often far from the actual asynchronous and non-deterministic behaviour). It is well-known that the introduction of explicit communications leads to harder problems [1].

Recently, a new computational model has been proposed [2]. It is based on *Malleable Tasks* (denoted MT in short). Informally, MT are computational

*THIS RESEARCH WAS SUPPORTED BY THE FRENCH-SLOVENE PROTEUS PROGRAM UNDER GRANT NO. 98019.

units which may be themselves executed in parallel. MT are closely related to two other models, namely multiprocessor tasks and divisible tasks. The difference is the freedom to choose the number of processors to execute each task. Each multiprocessor task [3] requires to be executed by a fixed integer number of processors, while the divisible tasks share the processors as a continuously divisible resource [4,5].

2 Motivation

A parallel application is traditionally modeled by a weighted *precedence task graph* where the nodes represent computations and arcs represent precedence constraints between tasks with communication costs (determined by a dataflow analysis). In practice, however, it is hard to generate these graphs because they are usually too large, in spite of the fact that some approaches for reducing their size do exist (e.g., parameterized representation [6]).

The execution of an application requires to decide where and when tasks will be executed. This decision usually involves hard optimization problems because opposite objectives must be met, such as load balancing and minimization of communications. On one side, the minimization of communication and synchronization overheads is important for the efficiency: if the application involves only small amount of communication and synchronization, more time can be spent on computation. However, to keep all the processors busy all the time, load balancing generally requires distribution of data over the network. Since the parallel data management requires communications, an increase of data distribution also increases the number of communications. As a result, due to the intractability of the problem, the impact of the parallelization overhead is usually partially ignored.

There are several reasons for introducing Malleable Tasks (MT) as a way to design efficient parallel applications:

- malleable tasks reflect the structure of some actual parallel applications such as domain decomposition and all hierarchical methods. The MT model unifies the usual single-processor tasks and tasks that may require more than one processor for their execution. The hierarchy is naturally contained in the MT model and the user does not need to specify when to use one or the other. This is, malleable tasks automatically adapt to the right *granularity* of the tasks.

- the MT model simplifies the expression of problems in the sense that the user does not have to explicitly express the communications. In addition, the same formalism can be used at different levels of granularity.

- the MT model can be easily augmented to take into account additional assumptions about the architecture and capabilities of the target parallel system (e.g., heterogeneity, clusters of SMPs).

- the MT model allows to hide the complex behaviour of the execution of a subset of tasks by using a parameter to abstract the overhead incurred by the management of the parallelism (e.g., communication, synchronization, idle times due to internal precedence constraints, etc.).

3   The Malleable Tasks (MT) model

Let $G(V, E)$ be a directed graph where V represents the set of tasks of an application and E represents the set of precedence constraints among the tasks. Let m denote the number of processors of the target machine. A *schedule* of $G(V, E)$ on a m-processor machine is a pair $(date, proc)$ of functions $date : V \rightarrow R^+$ and $proc : V \rightarrow \{1, 2, \ldots, m\}$ which assign, to each task, its *starting time* of execution and the *number of processors* that will execute the task. The time required to execute a task T on p processors is denoted by $t(T, p)$, Given a schedule, the *completion time* of a task T is $comp(T) = date(T) + t(T, proc(T))$. A schedule $(date, proc)$ is *valid* if, at each moment, at most m processors are engaged in the computation, and all precedence constraints are respected.

The *makespan* C is defined to be $C = \max_{T \in V} comp(T)$. Given $G(V, E)$, m, and t, the objective of the scheduling problem is to find a valid schedule that minimizes C.

3.1   Inefficiency function

The efficiency of the execution of a parallel application depends on many factors such as the structure of the algorithm, the data size, the data partitioning between available processing units, communication volume, network latency, topology, and throughput. Ideally, a parallel system with m processors would complete the execution of an application m times faster than a single-processor system. In reality, however, such a speedup is not achieved due to the overhead introduced by the inter-processor communications.

The idea behind MT model is to introduce a parameter that will implicitly describe the communication overhead and, consequently, the average behavior of the parallel execution of a task. The parameter is called *inefficiency function* (denoted by μ) and is defined to be the ratio between the actually achieved parallel execution time $t(T, p)$ and the theoretically achievable parallel execution time $t(T, 1)/p$, where $p = proc(T)$. Since the inefficiency function depends on the number p of processors as well as on the size N of the task, it will also be denoted by $\mu(p, N)$ (cf fig. 1). Generally, the inefficiency function increases with the number of processors (at least up to a certain threshold) and decreases with the size of the parallel task.

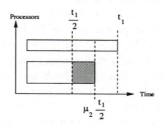

Figure 1. Inefficiency factor interpretation

3.2 Geometrical interpretation

A natural way to represent a malleable task T in simple cases is to use rectangle, with alloted processors $proc(T)$ in one dimension and achieved execution time $t(T, proc(T))$ in the other dimension (see Figure 1). This geometrical interpretation is also a nice way to consider scheduling and load-balancing problems. For example, task scheduling corresponds to the problem of setting (packing) rectangles into a box.

This kind of representation requires the *continuity* assumption. However, the assumption may be relaxed without penalty if the parallel machine may be viewed as a complete graph, such as most workstation networks and parallel machines. For most real applications, the way of object clustering (data and control) is the important factor, much more than the location of each cluster on homogeneous environment.

When the number of processors varies, the general shape of the μ function can be divided into three regions of consecutive intervals: the start-up overhead region, the region where adding extra processors costs almost nothing (here, speedups are generally linear), and the region of rapid degradation due to the lack of parallelism (e.g., for too small malleable tasks).

In order to simplify the scheduling problem, several assumptions can be made about the inefficiency function. A practical assumption is the *monotony*: *If the number of alloted processors increases, the parallel execution time of a task decreases and the work increases.* The *Convexity* of the μ function permits to obtain some general graph results.

3.3   Related work and some theoretical results

As said, MT is related to multiprocessor tasks and divisible tasks problems. Thus, some results may be transposed from these problems to MT.

The multi-processor problem is a hard problem: some results exist [7], but none of them is general. In MT problem, however, the allotment is chosen by the scheduling. Thus, the problem is to find any allotment close to the optimal for the task graph to be able to schedule it with some guarantee. This may be possible for some specially structured task graphs, such as chains and trees, or for specially shaped μ functions, such as convex ones. The monotony assumption may even be sufficient for some simple cases.

The divisible tasks model allows each task to use a fraction of the number of processors. Some general-graph results do exist, but they assume a special shape of μ function, namely p^{α} [4]. This model is unrealistic in the $[0, 1]$ interval because such a function induces a super-linear speedup. On the other hand, there are results that hold for any convex function, but can be applied to some special classes of graphs, such as graphs of independent tasks [5]. Although any continuously divisible solution can be transformed into an integer solution by simply rounding the number of processors, this does not guarantee to produce a better solution than any other discrete algorithm presented below.

The MT problem is fully approximable for any set of independent MT assuming fixed number of processors [8], but with quite a high factor in front of the polynomial complexity. In practice, independent MT may be scheduled using two techniques: simple allotment and 2-dimensional bin-packing, or complex allotment but a simple packing.

Turek et al. [2] sought an allotment close to the optimal allotment and applied a 2-dimensional bin-packing heuristic. The allotment is a trade-off between the length of tasks and the sum of task works divided by the number of processors. Using this allotment, any 2-dimensional bin-packing algorithm schedules the tasks. The problem is that 2-dimensional bin-packing is an NP-complete problem in the strong sense and, to our knowledge, the best 2-dimensional bin-packing algorithm [9] has a performance bound of 2

Another method to choose the allotment is to use a pseudo-polynomial algorithm [10], such as the algorithm for the knapsack problem. With n tasks and m processors the complexity is $O(nm)$, and is therefore easily tractable for reasonable numbers of tasks and processors: the packing is just a list algorithm. With the monotony variation of the μ function schedules are achievable that are guaranteed to be at most $\sqrt{3}$-times the optimal ones, as well as to be good approximations on average [10] The general problem of finding a good heuristic for arbitrary task graphs and arbitrary μ functions is still open.

4   Using MT in some applications

In the following we briefly present two actual applications for which we currently develop parallel program code based on the MT model. For both applications, preliminary experiments show some direct gains in computation using MT model. First, malleable tasks with or without inefficiency factor allow to easily handle efficient scheduling of the application. Second, MT-oriented implementation allows to easily change the scheduling strategy used by the MT model. Third, the case of small-sized malleable tasks is handled gracefully without penalty.

4.1   Simulation of Ocean circulation

This work deals with the parallel implementation of a code for large scale simulations of ocean circulation. It started two years ago by a cooperation with E. Blayo and L. Debreu within a team of numericians of our Institute. The principle is a discretization of finite difference equations with adaptive meshing. Today, adaptive meshing is one of the most challenging problems in parallel and distributed processing. It is of real interest for ocean modelers because it could reduce the computational cost of models by taking advantage of the spatial heterogeneity of oceanic flows and thus using a fine mesh only where and when necessary. Moreover, this would allow local zooms on some limited areas of particular interest. Like in all major ocean general circulation models, we used a finite difference method on structured grids. The objective is to develop a fortran 90 package, which will provide to any finite difference ocean model the capability of adaptive meshing and local zooming. The method is based on the adaptive mesh refinement (AMR) algorithm [11] [12], which features a hierarchy of grids at different resolutions, with dynamic interactions. Since the mesh refinement is adaptive over the time step, the number of grids as well as their sizes and resolutions vary during the simulation. Thus, the computational load is also varying in time, and a dynamic load balancing is necessary to implement efficiently this AMR method on a parallel computer.

Here, a malleable task corresponds to the resolution of one step of a sub-grid. Thus, scheduling the application is scheduling a serial-parallel graph (fork-join trees) of malleable tasks. The knowledge of task size helps to schedule without using costly strategies such as gang scheduling (all malleable tasks are executed by all processors). The knowledge of the μ function allows to limit MT's processor usage to the degree that is really needed.

4.2 Sparse Cholesky factorization

The second target application is the parallel implementation of the well-known large sparse Cholesly factorization. This work was initiated with B. Dumitrescu, M. Doreille and JL. Roch [13]. Recall that a sparse Cholesky factorization is usually performed in three successive stages. First, the matrix is permuted in order to reduce the fill-in. Second, the symbolic factorization is computed. Finally, the numerical factorization is performed. The third stage is the most time consuming and is therefore the first to be parallelized. In order to get efficient computations using BLAS of level 3 columns with the same structure are grouped into supernodes. The elimination tree represents the task graph execution of the Cholesky factorization. Each node represents a column; the father of a node j is node i where L_{ij} is the first subdiagonal nonzero element on column j of the Cholesky factor L. It illustrates the intrinsic parallelism of the sparse Cholesky factorization.

On one hand, 2-dimensional block partitioning allows to distribute the same block column to several processors. Here, MT are computations of block columns. On the other hand, a block panel on more than one processor induces some additional communications. Thus, the distribution of a node is used in general only on the top (big) nodes. Local subtrees improve efficiency but may also unbalance the load. Most existing algorithms have to separate the subtree distribution and the top tree node distribution. Our idea was to use malleable tasks to efficiently manage the two different levels of hierarchy: the trade-off is a result of the load-balancing MT function.

5   Concluding remarks

Both of the applications we briefly presented, simulation of circulations in the Atlantic Ocean and Sparse Cholesky factorization, have been implemented on large parallel systems with the help of MT model. For both applications it was difficult to get a good estimation of the inefficiency function. For the first application we used an empirical function based on a large number of systematic experiments. For the second application an analytical expression based on the complexity analysis of the parallelization of the Cholesky factorization is used. Initial experiments validate this approach using a simple adaptation of (well-known) load-balancing policies, namely level by level mapping and proportional mapping. Our short term perspective is to develop other heuristics and integrate them into the actual program code to improve the performance. Another important issue is to study the behavior of scheduling policies in regard to perturbation of the data, since μ functions are not precisely known.

References

1. J. Hoogeveen, J.-K. Lenstra, and B. Veltman. Three, four, five, six, or the complexity of scheduling with communication delays. *Operations Research Letters*, 16:129–137, 1994.
2. J. Turek, J. Wolf, and P. Yu. Approximate algorithms for scheduling parallelizable tasks. In *4th Annual ACM Symposium on Parallel Algorithms and Architectures*, pages 323–332, 1992.
3. M.R. Garey, R.L. Graham, and D.S. Johnson. Performance guarantees for scheduling algorithms. *Ope. Research*, 26(1):3–21, January 1978.
4. G. N. Srinivasa Prasanna and Bruce R. Musicus. Generalised multiprocessor scheduling using optimal control. In *3rd Annual ACM Symposium on Parallel Algorithms and Architectures*, pages 216–228. ACM, 1991.
5. J. Blazewicz, K. Ecker, G. Schmidt, and J. Weglarz. *Scheduling in Computer and Manufacturing System*. Springer-Verlag, 1985.
6. M. Cosnard and E. Jeannot. Automatic coarse-grained parallelization techniques. In Kowalik Grandinetti, editor, *NATO workshop: Advances in High Performance Computing*. Kluwer academic, 1997.
7. M. Drozdowski. Scheduling multiprocessor tasks - an overview. *European Journal of Operational Research*, 94:215–230, 1996.
8. K. Jansen and L. Porkolab. Linear time approximation schemes for scheduling problems. *SODA 99*, 1998.
9. A. Steinberg. A strip-packing algorithm with absolute performance bound 2. *SIAM Journal of computing*, 26(2):401–409, 1997.
10. G Mounie, C Rapine, and D Trystram. Efficient approximation algorithms for scheduling malleable tasks. In *Eleventh ACM Symposium on Parallel Algorithms and Architectures*, pages 23–32. ACM Press, 1999.
11. M. Berger and J. Oliger. Adaptive mesh refinement for hyperbolic partial differential equations. *J. Comput. Physics*, 53:484–512, March 1984.
12. E. Blayo and L. Debreu. Adaptive mesh refinement for finite difference ocean models: first experiments. *J. Phys. Oceanogr.*, 1998. to appear.
13. B. Dumitrescu, M. Doreille, J.-L. Roch, and D. Trystram. Two-dimensional block partitionings for the parallel sparse Cholesky factorization. *Numerical Algorithms*, 16(1):17–38, 1997. Sparse matrices in industry (Lille, 1997).

FILE MAPPING IN SHARED VIRTUAL MEMORY USING A PARALLEL FILE SYSTEM

RENAUD LOTTIAUX, CHRISTINE MORIN, THIERRY PRIOL

IRISA, Campus de Beaulieu, 35042 Rennes Cedex (France)
e-mail: {$rlottiau, cmorin, priol$}*@irisa.fr*

In this paper, we propose a one level storage parallel file system (PFS) using mapping as a new PFS interface for a Shared Virtual Memory system. Such an interface offers many advantages which are described in this paper. To evaluate the feasibility of such a system, we have developed a prototype which is described in this paper. Preliminary results are presented.

1 Introduction

The growing performance gap between processors and disks has led to the design of Parallel File Systems (PFS) [1] [2]. Their goal is to increase bandwidth by using parallel accesses to several disks, located on different nodes of a parallel architecture.

Existing PFS offer a traditional interface for accessing files: *open, read, write, close* and are designed for distributed memory architectures using the message passing paradigm. At the same time, there is a renewed interest for Shared Virtual Memory (SVM) [3] [4]. The SVM paradigm provides a global address space on top of physically distributed memories. Data sharing between processes located on different nodes is transparent as data is automatically migrated or replicated in the node memory of the processor using them.

Typical PFS interfaces are in contradiction with the principle of transparency and simplicity of the SVM programming model. The programmer must indeed explicitly manage data transfers between memories and disks.

In this paper, we propose file mapping as a new PFS interface for SVM based clusters. In Section 2, we explain the advantages of file mapping in an SVM using a PFS. In section 3 we present the architecture of the proposed system. Section 4 gives an overview of the prototype that we have implemented and describes the preliminary performance evaluation. Section 5 presents related works and section 6 concludes.

2 A New Interface for PFS : File Mapping

Single level storage operating systems [5] provide *file mapping* to offer a uniform access to memory and disk using *virtual memory* mechanism. The mapping operation consists of creating a link between a file and a memory region. Once a file is mapped, accesses to this memory region behave as if they were accesses to the corresponding file region.

The shared memory paradigm offers a common address space to several nodes. This vision of a single shared memory can be brought closer to the vision offered by parallel file systems of a single very large disk with high bandwidth. Memories and disks unification mechanisms existing, it seems natural to integrate them to offer an interface for accessing disks via file mapping into SVM. Such an interface offers many advantages, discussed in the remainder of this section.

Simple access : File access is simply done by memory access. No parallel file pointer is managed.

Concurrence : The coherence of concurrent accesses to the same file is automatically managed by the SVM.

Distribution : Data being loaded automatically in the memory of the processor accessing it, the programmer does not have to explicitly manage initial data distribution.

Overlap : With the traditional file system interface, during a file access a process is blocked until the last byte of data is transferred. With file mapping, the process is blocked only during the time needed to load a single page corresponding to the data accessed by the processor. By using page prefetching, the process will not be blocked when accessing next pages. This automatic overlap of computing and loading from disks increases the performance.

Out-of-core : Programming an algorithm which deals with an amount of data larger than the physical memory is a difficult problem. In order to avoid page swapping (which leads to a performance collapse), the programmer explicitly manages data transfers between memories and disks to ensure that data needed for the computation is in memory. When memories and disks are distributed in the nodes of a cluster, out-of-core management is complex. Using mapped files in an SVM system eases the programmer task, since data accessed by a processor is automatically loaded in memory or write back to disk.

Checkpointing : Many scientific applications require a large processing time: from several hours to several weeks. For these applications, programmers usually manage *checkpoints* manually, i.e. save the computation state periodically to tolerate the failure of a node component. In the event of a breakdown, computation is restarted from the last checkpoint. However, establishing checkpoints is expensive as many disks accesses are required to save data. When using an SVM, establishing a checkpoint is all the more complex that the programmer does not have any information on the physical data location in memories. When a file mapping mechanism is implemented, data location in memories is known by the system, as well as its location on disks. Thus, high level, efficient and easy to use checkpointing primitives can be offered by the system to the programmer.

3   System Architecture

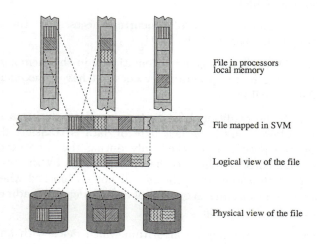

Figure 1. *Mapping of a parallel file in SVM*

The aim of the proposed system is to allow the mapping of parallel files in an SVM. Thanks to this mapping, a parallel application running on different nodes of a cluster can access a file simply with memory accesses (fig 1). In the remainder of this section, we describe the architecture of this system.

3.1   Architecture

The system consists of two logical components: the SVM which manages shared memory mechanisms and the PFS which ensures parallel access to storage units.

The SVM is composed of a *fault handler*, a *page manager* and a *page server* (see fig 2). The fault handler is activated when a processor accesses a page which is not in the local memory. If the page is present in the memory of a remote node, the SVM mechanism is used to resolve the page fault, else a load request is sent to the PFS. The page copies localization in the cluster is handled by page managers which deal with a statically distributed directory. This directory contains the page owner location and the set of existing copies. Lastly, a page server is present on each node to answer to page request from remote nodes.

On each node, the PFS is composed of a *PFS manager* and a *PFS server*. The PFS manager deals with a list of open files and their corresponding mapping address. It makes the correspondence between a page number in the SVM and its location on disks. It may also decide to prefetch pages to improve performance. The PFS server accesses data of the local disk. It is used as an interface between storage units and PFS managers.

3.2 Interface

Three high level functions are offered to the programmer to manage mapping mechanisms :

- *file_map (file name)* : create a mapping and return the corresponding mapping address.

- *file_unmap (mapping address)* : delete a mapping.

- *check_point (mapping address)* : make a checkpoint.

The *file_map* and *file_unmap* functions allow to create and remove a mapping. The mapping function allocates a memory area in SVM and adds an entry in the mapped files list. This entry contains the mapping address of the file, its size and a file descriptor. Initially, no data is loaded in memory, all pages are invalid and the copy set of each page is empty.

The *check_point* primitive allows the checkpointing of data associated to a file mapping. Only modified data is written back to disks.

3.3 Data access

When a page fault occurs, the fault handler is activated. It sends a request to the page manager, which checks if there exist a copy of the page in the memory of a remote node. If a copy exists, the standard SVM protocol is used. If not, the page manager sends a page loading request to the local

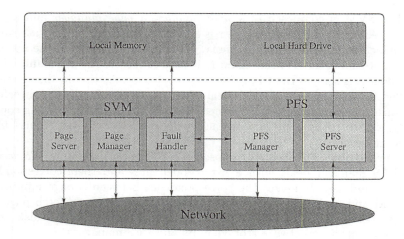

Figure 2. *Software architecture of the prototype*

PFS manager. This one searches in the list of mapped files, the one which is associated with the requested page. It determines on which disk the page is stored and sends a read request to the corresponding PFS server. Then, the page is read from disk and sent back to the fault handler of the faulting machine. Lastly, the page copy is placed in a free page frame and the faulting process is restarted.

Writes are carried out in two cases. The first one is the closing of a mapping. In this case, the PFS writes on disks all pages which have been modified and close the file. Page writes can also occur in the event of a page replacement, i.e. when there is no more available page frames to store a new page copy. Thus, the SVM must remove a page copy from the local memory. If the page selected to be removed has not been modified, it is simply evicted. If this page has been modified but there exists another up-to-date copy, it is also evicted. Lastly, if this page has been modified and is the only up-to-date copy, it must be written back to disk before being evicted. In order to limit the number of disks accesses, the system checks if it is possible to place the page in the memory of a remote node, before writing this page on disk. If this is not possible, the page is written to disk.

3.4 Performance Optimizations

To optimize the performance of a file system, several techniques exist like caching and prefetching [6]. In caching mechanisms the cache size being limited, only the most recently used data is kept in the cache. Replacement algorithms are used to remove from cache the least often used data. An SVM uses exactly the same mechanisms. When space is needed in memory, the least often used pages are written back to disk. Thus, the SVM acts as a high capacity disk cache. So, it is no more necessary to implement a page cache for the PFS. The file system cache is integrated in the SVM.

4 Performance Evaluation

In order to check the feasibility of the proposed system, we have developed a simple prototype. In this section, we describe this prototype and results obtained from preliminary performance evaluations.

4.1 Prototype Description

A first prototype of the proposed system has been developed on the PACHA cluster, which is composed of PCs interconnected by a high bandwidth (200 MB/s) SCI [7] network and running Linux SMP. Each node is composed of two PENTIUM II 266 MHz processors, a 128 MB memory and a 2 GB hard drive. The hard drive bandwidth is 5 MB/s.

This prototype consists of a strict consistency SVM and a basic PFS implemented at user level. The PFS striping unit size is equal to the size of a memory page (4 KB). A *one block lookahead* prefetching mechanism is implemented : when a page is loaded, the next n pages are prefetched ($n = $ *number of disks used to store the file - 1*).

A write-invalidate coherence protocol similar to [8] is implemented. A *right access* is associated to each page. There are three possible right accesses : *invalid*, the page is not accessible by the processor; *read*, the page can be read and multiple copies may exist; *read/write*, the page can be read and written and only one copy of the page exists. When a processor tries to write a page which is not in *read/write* mode, all the page copies are invalidated and the right access changes to *read/write*.

4.2 Experiments

Our experiments consist of n nodes reading a file stored on d nodes (i.e. disks). Three types of experiments have been carried out. In the first one, one node

($n=1$) reads a file stored on several disks ($d=2,3,4$) in a sequential way. In the second one, several nodes ($n=d=2,3,4$) read a file in a sequential way. In the last experiment, several nodes ($n=d=2,3,4$) read a file in a random way. In the case of a sequential read performed by several nodes, each node accesses an independent and sequential part of the file.

To read the file, each process accesses the memory area where the file is mapped. For each experiment the file size varies from 10 MB to 200 MB, and the disk cache is flushed before each run thus, data is really loaded from disks.

4.3 Results

Results obtained from a sequential read performed by one node are presented in Figure 3.a. The best bandwidth obtained is 14 MB/s when the file is stored on 4 disks. This bandwidth is close to 3 times the bandwidth of one disk, which is a good result for such a simple prototype but higher performance could be obtained, using a more aggressive prefetching mechanism. A prefetching mechanism allowing to prefetch more than one page per disk should offer higher performance, by increasing the size of disk accesses.

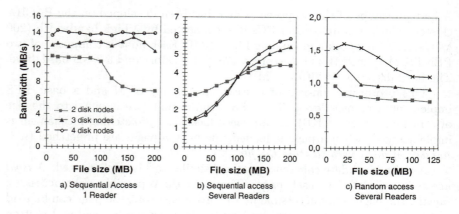

a) Sequential Access
1 Reader

b) Sequential access
Several Readers

c) Random access
Several Readers

Figure 3. *Experimental results*

Results obtained from a sequential read performed by several nodes are presented in Figure 3.b. In this case, performance collapses: the best bandwidth obtained is 6 MB/s when a 200 MB file is stored on 4 disks. This bandwidth is close to the bandwidth of a single disk, so the system does not take benefit from the use of a PFS. This poor bandwidth is a result of the concurrent accesses made by the different processes. When a process accesses a page in the mapping area, the process is blocked until corresponding data is loaded. Thus, disk requests cannot be buffered and must be performed without delay. If several processes access simultaneously different parts of a file, the PFS must access successively different disks cylinders, leading to many disk seeks and then to poor performance.

Results obtained from a random read are presented in Figure 3.c. The best bandwidth obtained (1.6 MB/s) is low, which is typical for a random access. Higher performance could further be obtained with an adaptive mechanism which disable prefetching when a random access is detected.

4.4 Design of a New Architecture

Preliminary results obtained by performance measurements on our prototype have highlighted two specific problems of the file mapping interface in a parallel architecture. The first one is the small size of disk accesses induced by the mapping interface. The second one is the high number of disk seeks caused by simultaneous access to a file by several processes.

To solve these problems, implementation of efficient prefetching and disk scheduling strategies is required. But these mechanisms need high level information on the application data access pattern. With a mapping interface, this information is not explicitly given by the application programmer. So, we are currently working on a mechanism to automatically find a close approximation of a parallel application logical data access pattern at execution time. To achieve this automatic pattern detection, we investigate different approaches, in particular artificial neural networks and Markov chains [9].

5 Related Works

Very few other works on file mapping in SVM systems with a PFS are described in the literature [10,11]. In [10], mapped files are proposed as the basis of a PFS but the standard file system interface (*read/write*) is kept. Moreover, there is no integration with a SVM as a hardware-implemented shared memory is assumed. In [11], the design of BFXM, a PFS relying on a SVM mechanism, is roughly presented. To the best of our knowledge, BFXM has not been implemented.

6 Conclusion

In this paper, we have presented file mapping as a new interface for parallel file systems and explained advantages of this method. The prototype we have implemented has been detailed and preliminary results have been discussed. These results show the necessity to get high level information on application data access pattern to achieve high performance.

Our future research directions include the design of an adaptive prefetching mechanism and the implementation of the proposed system inside Linux kernel to improve performance. Moreover, fault tolerance mechanisms will be integrated.

References

1. N. Nieuwejaar and D. Kotz. The Galley parallel file system. In *Proceedings of the 10th ACM International Conference on Supercomputing*, pages 374–381, August 1996.
2. P. F. Corbett and D. G. Feitelson. Design and implementation of the Vesta parallel file system. In *Proceedings of the Scalable High-Performance Computing Conference*, pages 63–70, 1994.
3. C. Amza, A. L. Cox, S. Dwarkadas, P. Keleher, H. Lu, R. Rajamony, W. Yu, and W. Zwaenepoel. TreadMarks: Shared Memory Computing on Networks of Workstations. *Computer*, pages 18–28, February 1996.
4. R. Stets, S. Dwarkadas, N. Hardavellas, G. Hunt, L. Kontothanassis and S. Parthasarathy. Cashmere-2L: Software Coherent Shared Memory on a Clustered Remote-Write Network. In *Proceedings of the 16th Symposium on Operating Systems Principles*, pages 170–183, December 1997.
5. P. J. Leach, P. H. Levine, B. P. Douros, J. Hamilton, D. L. Nelson, and B. L. Stumpf. The architecture of an integrated local network. *IEEE Journal on Selected Areas in Communications*, 842–856, November 1983.
6. David Kotz. *Prefetching and Caching Techniques in File Systems for MIMD Multiprocessors*. PhD thesis, Duke University, April 1991.
7. D. B. Gustavson. The Scalable Coherent Interface and Related Standards Projects. *IEEE Micro*, pages 10–21, February 1992.
8. K. Li and P. Hudak. Memory coherence in shared virtual memory systems. *IEEE Transactions on Computers*, 7(4):321–359, November 1989.
9. T. M. Madhyastha and D. A. Reed. Exploiting global input/output access pattern classification. In *Proceedings of High Performance Networking and Computing*, 1997.
10. O. Krieger, K. Reid, and M. Stumm. Exploiting mapped files for parallel i/o. In *Workshop on Modeling and Specification of I/O*, October 1995.
11. Q. Li, J. Jing, and L. Xie. BFXM: A parallel file system model based on the mechanism of distributed shared memory. *ACM Operating Systems Review*, 31(4):30–40, 1997.

SCALABLE SIMULTANEOUS MULTITHREADING (SCSMT)

J.C.MOURE, D.I.REXACHS, E.LUQUE

Computer Architecture and Operating Systems Group,
University Autónoma of Barcelona. Barcelona, 08193. SPAIN
E-mail: (iarqp, d.rexachs, e.luque)@cc.uab.es

R.B.GARCÍA

Departamento de Ciencias de la Computación, Universidad Nacional del Sur
Avenida Alem 1253, Bahia Blanca, 8000. ARGENTINA
E-mail: rbg@cs.uns.edu.ar

This paper explores the design space of high-performance multithreaded processors. Two microarchitectural proposals are subject of intense research: chip multiprocessing, and simultaneous multithreading. We propose a scalable multithreaded design approaching the high instruction rate of a simultaneous multithreading processor and the low cycle time of a chip-multiprocessor, integrating mechanisms from both proposals in a balanced design. Quantitative results obtained from simulation are presented and discussed.

1 Introduction

IC processing technology advances increase the integration density of chips, and allow including more computation logic on a microprocessor. To effectively use this logic, current processors add control hardware to dynamically find independent instructions on sequential portions of a single thread. This superscalar execution model, though, does not scale well with issue width. First, dependencies among adjacent instructions and long-latency memory accesses limit the amount of instruction-level parallelism (ILP) exhibited at runtime by most of the applications [4]. Second, since technological trends indicate that wire delays will soon dominate gate delays, [5], the complexity of the centralized control logic will ultimately affect cycle time, [6]. Very fast clock frequencies will only be achieved on distributed microarchitectures composed of high-speed execution clusters working more or less asynchronously and connected by slower, infrequently-used wires, [3].

Multithreaded (MT) architectures represent a high-performance alternative that runs multiple control flows sharing the on-chip resources. They widen the window of independent instructions that can be found for parallel execution, and bypass the local dependencies among instructions in a single thread, providing TLP when a single thread does not expose enough ILP. In addition, long-latency operations, like cache misses, are overlapped by executing instructions from other threads, allowing to sustain large instruction per cycle (IPC) rates. Finally, their inherent distributed organization makes them suitable for low cycle-time implementations.

Apart from improving a chip's performance, multithreading provides hardware support for general-purpose parallel programming, building a parallel execution model where several virtual processors share the resources of a host chip, and facilitating asynchronous programming. Emerging automatic parallelization technology and more widespread use of inherently parallel applications (like multimedia) and multitasking operating systems should make feasible the provision of threads to MT architectures. MT processors will further fuel the development of better parallelizing compilers and parallel languages.

We address the design of a scalable, complexity-effective, [6], MT processor whose microarchitecture must provide flexibility to exploit both ILP and TLP. Achieving these two goals suppose complex tradeoffs among different design issues: (1) control logic to feed the execution hardware with independent instructions, (2) number of supported thread contexts, and (3) how to share processor resources.

The hardware expended by MT processors either to exploit ILP, TLP, or both, must be balanced in order to maximize overall performance. Superscalar processors are biased to only exploit ILP. Chip-multiprocessors, CMPs, [3], represent the other extreme of the design space. They integrate multiple, relatively simple, single-thread processor cores into a single chip. Each core exploits the ILP of a single thread, while the execution of several threads on different processor cores at the same time exploits TLP. Simultaneous multithreading (SMT), [7], combines the two previous approaches, augmenting wide-issue superscalar processors to allow multiple threads sharing almost all the processor resources every cycle. An SMT processor behaves like a superscalar processor when only one thread is available, and behaves like a CMP when many threads are ready. In a CMP, if a thread lacks ILP to fill its processing core, then some or all of its resources will be wasted. Conversely, in a SMT, the lack of per-thread ILP can be compensated with excess of ILP from other threads. The SMT capability of exploiting ILP and TLP interchangeably maximizes resource utilization and execution throughput.

Sharing all the resources, though, require centralized scheduling logic and long interconnection paths, complicating processor design and increasing cycle time. Conversely, CMPs have a more distributed organization (not all the resources are connected), allowing higher clock frequencies. SMT gains in cycle count are at the expense of increasing cycle time and design complexity, while CMPs sacrifice cycle count to reduce cycle time.

This paper addresses the design of a Scalable Simultaneous MultiThreaded (ScSMT) processor that achieves the high IPC rate of a SMT processor with the low cycle time of CMPs. The basic idea guiding the design is assigning each thread the same execution resources as in a CMP, but allowing any thread to access some of its neighbor's resources when the owner thread does not need them, maybe with a penalization cycle. The overall goal is not to sacrifice fast intra-cluster execution, which is expected to be very frequent, by infrequent, slow inter-cluster execution.

2 Specification of the CMP and SMT Microarchitectures

The number of hardware threads is fixed to 4, a compromise between 8 threads, which demands too much TLP on the workload, and 2 threads, which might not highlight all the advantages of MT processors versus single-threaded processors. As a result, the CMP will consists of four 2-issue cores, and the SMT processor will share a full, 8-issue core among 4 hardware threads (figure 1).

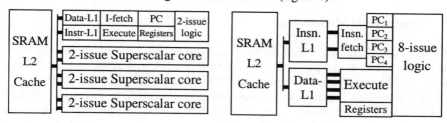

Figure 1. CMP and SMT microarchitectures

We use a real processor, the alpha 21264, [2], to fix many of the design parameters for our MT processors. Since we are designing for a next generation of processors, we assume two times the transistor budget and the peak IPC rate of the alpha 21264. Table 1 shows the parameters of the 8-issue and 2-issue cores that form the basis of the CMP and SMT processors. Branch prediction uses a combined predictor with size and organization scaled with respect to the alpha 21264.

Table 1. Latencies, Issue rates and Bandwidths of an 8(2)-issue processor, and Memory System

	BW-8 (2)	Size-8 (2)
Fetch queue	8 (4)	8 (4)
Decode	8 (2)	-
Retire (active list)	12 (3)	160 (40)
Memory ROB	-	64 (16)
Branch queue	-	24 (6)
Integer queue	8 (2)	40 (10)
Float queue	4 (1)	30 (8)
Integer Reg. File	16 (4)	31+82(21)
Float Reg. File	8 (2)	31+82(21)
Branch misprediction penalty	7(6) cycles	

Operation Types	Lat	issue rate	BW-8 (2)	
simple integer	1	1	8 (2)	8(2)
address compute	1	1	4 (1)	
shift	1	1	4 (1)	4(1)
branches	1	1	4 (1)	
integer multiply	7	1	1 (1)	
float addition	4	1	2 (1)	2(1)
float move/branch	2	1	2 (1)	
float divide	12/15	12/15	1 (1)	
float multiply	4	1	2 (1)	2(1)

	# ports	size	lat.	line size	assoc.	bus width	bus lat.	TLBs	MHT
Instr. Cache	2 (1) ports	128 Kb	2	64 bytes	2-way	8 bytes	1 cycle	256	16
Data Cache	2x2 banks	128 Kb	2	64 bytes	2-way	8 bytes	1 cycle	256	
L2 Cache	1 port	4 Mb	10	64 bytes	direct	16 bytes	3/2 cycles	256	fully-assoc.
Memory	unlimited	unlimited	60	-	-	8 bytes	3/2 cycles	-	

The CMP design is very simple, with four 2-issue cores coupled with a shared L2 cache. Preliminary simulation results have demonstrated that using a direct-mapped, shared, L2 cache generates too many conflicts among those threads using the L2 cache significantly. Therefore a 4-way associative L2 cache has been used.

On the SMT design, the associativity of the shared L1 caches has also been increased (8-way) to mitigate the interference among threads. The shared register file has been enlarged to accommodate at the same time the state of 4 threads (maintaining the total number of renaming registers). As a consequence, the branch misprediction penalty is increased to 8. The total size of the queues, some of them partitioned among the threads, is maintained with respect to the CMP design.

3 Experimental Methodology

We have developed *MTScalar*, an execution-driven simulator of alpha code based on release 3.0 of the *SimpleScalar* simulation tools, [1], with added support for non-blocking caches, MT execution, and the mechanisms presented in this paper.

Multithreaded benchmarks are built using single SPEC benchmarks. We have first simulated the execution of each single benchmark on superscalar processors with different issue width. Only fifty million instructions are simulated to reduce simulation time, and some instructions are skipped to avoid unrepresentative startup behavior, (table 2). The execution rate for the 2-, 4-, and 8-issue processors (IPC_2, IPC_4 and IPC_8, respectively) provide significant data that will be used later to model performance on the CMP, SMT and ScSMT designs.

Table 2. SPEC benchmarks: IPC, branch prediction rate, L1 hit rates, L2 and memory bus occupancy (subindexes refer to the processor's issue width)

	IPC_2	IPC_4	IPC_8	Prd_8	$iL1_8$	$dL1_8$	$L2bus_2$	$Mbus_2$	skipped insns	Input data
compress	1.30	1.62	1.93	0.94	1.00	0.87	30.21	0.74	2000M	reference
gcc	0.96	1.38	1.72	0.87	1.00	0.99	12.15	0.90	10M	expr.i
go	1.16	1.52	1.82	0.82	1.00	1.00	4.48	0.82	1M	reference
ijpeg	1.45	2.12	2.85	0.89	1.00	1.00	0.67	0.36	100M	penguin.ppm
li	1.28	1.99	2.65	0.93	1.00	1.00	3.25	0.06	1M	deriv.lsp
m88ksim	1.50	2.37	3.19	0.96	1.00	1.00	0.15	0.09	4M	dhrystone
perl	1.32	1.99	2.50	0.94	1.00	1.00	2.29	0.13	1M	primes.pl
vortex	1.21	2.29	3.60	0.97	1.00	0.99	13.67	1.36	500M	reference
applu	1.13	1.68	2.37	0.86	1.00	0.93	5.65	10.42	100M	reference
apsi	1.33	1.87	2.56	0.98	1.00	0.89	12.15	1.06	20M	reference
fpppp	1.49	2.31	3.22	0.96	1.00	1.00	3.25	0.10	1M	reference
hydro2d	0.96	1.48	2.45	0.99	1.00	0.77	10.81	6.68	200M	reference
mgrid	1.50	2.21	2.78	0.97	1.00	0.96	7.62	5.51	5M	reference
su2cor	1.12	1.45	1.88	0.90	1.00	0.92	9.02	5.82	2100M	reference
swim	1.18	1.94	2.74	1.00	1.00	0.94	5.21	8.90	50M	reference
tomcatv	0.88	1.38	2.07	0.99	1.00	0.86	11.35	11.00	2100M	reference
turb3d	1.15	1.93	2.79	0.97	1.00	0.80	31.43	10.49	1M	reference
wave	1.29	1.54	1.75	0.95	1.00	0.99	1.48	0.04	20M	reference

A multithreaded benchmark is built with four SPEC applications (table 3 lists). There are ten heterogeneous MT benchmarks, combining 4 different threads to stress particular characteristics of the workload (low IPC_2 or IPC_8, high memory bus utilization, etc.). There are also 8 homogeneous benchmarks consisting of 4 copies of the same application, trying to maximize conflicts among threads.

Table 3. Heterogeneous and Homogeneous Multi-tasking Workloads

A	B	C	D	E	F	G	H	I	J	Homogeneous MT	
comp	comp	ljpeg	gcc	ijpeg	applu	li	comp	perl	Apsi	go	fpppp
gcc	go	m88k	go	m88k	swim	perl	perl	go	Hydro	li	tomc
ijpeg	su2cor	Fpppp	su2cor	fpppp	tomc	swim	mgrid	li	mgrid	m88k	turb3d
vortex	wave	Vortex	wave	apsi	turb3d	applu	applu	m88k	swim	vortex	wave

4 IPC Comparison of CMP and SMT

The IPC rate on a CMP processor is bounded by the sum of the IPC of each single thread running alone in a 2-issue processor (IPC_2 in table 2). Figure 2 shows the percentage of this reduction. For the heterogeneous benchmarks the IPC reduction is always less than 12% and, for 80% of the benchmarks, it is less than 5%. IPC reduction is due to conflicts on the access to the shared L2 cache and busses. The bus occupancy, shown in figure 2, indicate that performance is more related to high memory bus utilization (benchmarks F and J) than high L2 bus utilization (A, B and H). L2 cache accesses due to L1 misses are better tolerated using the available ILP and TLP than memory accesses due to L2 misses. For the homogeneous benchmarks, as expected, the IPC reduction is greater due to more conflicts on the L2 and memory busses (30% and 45% for *turb3d* and *tomcatv*).

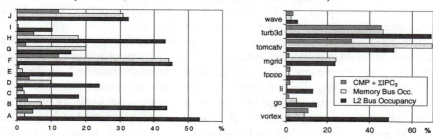

Figure 2. IPC reduction (%) on a CMP versus ΣIPC_2, and L2 and memory bus occupancies (%)

The ability of SMT processors to share resources should increase the effective execution bandwidth per thread, allowing it to surpass the IPC_2 bound. However, reduction in the lookahead capability of each thread and competition for shared resources will limit the IPC increase per thread.

Figure 3 compares the CMP and SMT designs. The IPC increase of SMT with respect to CMP on the heterogeneous benchmarks ranges from 10 to 25%. The increase on the homogeneous benchmarks, except for *vortex*, is less than 5% or negative (*turb3d* and *tomcatv*). Some threads benefit from sharing resources more than other threads in the same MT benchmark, while some of then reduce their IPC bellow the IPC_2 threshold. Greater benefits correspond to threads with higher IPC_8/IPC_2 ratios. Additionally, we have quantified the utilization of the (expensive) mechanisms allowing threads to share the pipeline and have found that <u>a single</u>

620

thread decodes or issues more than four instructions less than 10% of the execution cycles. These results prove that most of the SMT hardware is wasted, a hardware that, as the next section will illustrate, may affect cycle time.

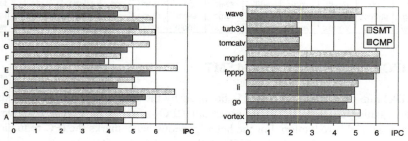

Figure 3. IPC rates on the CMP and SMT processors

5   Complexity Comparison

To get the ultimate measure of a processor's performance it is necessary to model the effects of microarchitectural decisions on both the IPC and the cycle time, T_c. Modeling T_c accurately requires a full implementation using a specific technology. Relative measures, though, can be obtained by quantifying the delays and analyzing the pipelineability of critical portions of a microarchitecture, [6].

The most critical elements in a microarchitecture are instruction wakeup, instruction selection and operand bypass, whose delay grows quadraticaly with issue width, [6]. Register renaming and register access latencies may be tolerated with pipelining, with the only effect of increasing the branch misprediction penalty.

CMPs limit the issue width of each thread to a small value, avoiding the critical hardware bottlenecks exposed previously. Using 8-issue logic instead of 2-issue, like in a SMT processor, multiplies by 16 the delays of bypassing, wakeup and select. Wakeup and bypassing, whose main delay is only a function of the wire length, will be a harder bottleneck on advanced technology.

6   ScSMT Proposal

In this section, we present an scalable SMT design, ScSMT, which limits support for sharing resources among threads to make its complexity realizable (figure 4). The fetch stage is separate, like in a CMP, with a peak bandwidth of 4 insns/cycle per thread. The decode and rename stages are shared, like in a SMT, but providing each single thread a peak decode rate of 4 insns/cycle of the total decode bandwidth (8). Instructions are dispatched to separate instruction queues and read their operands from separate register files, like in a CMP. The ScSMT allows each thread issuing up to 4 insns/cycle of the total issue bandwidth (8) to a subset of shared functional units. This doubles the available execution bandwidth per thread of the CMP with the same total number of functional units.

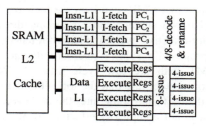

Figure 4. ScSMT processor

The complexity added to the CMP design includes doubling the number of ports of register files, renaming tables, and instruction queues, and also doubling the number of connections among queues, register files, and functional units. The SMT design, however, requires 4 times the number of ports and connections.

7   Results

Figure 5 compares the IPC increase (%) of SMT versus CMP, with the increase of ScSMT versus CMP. The ScSMT reduces the IPC increase of the SMT between 10% and 35% on the heterogeneous benchmarks (except for benchmark I, where the ScSMT increase is higher). The homogeneous benchmarks *go* and *li* executed on a ScSMT double and treble, respectively, the increase of SMT, and *turb3d* achieves an 8% speedup on a ScSMT versus a negative 9% speedup on a SMT.

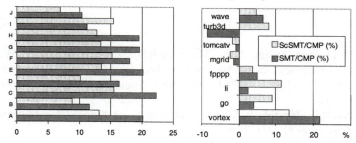

Figure 5. IPC increase relative to the IPC of a CMP for the SMT and ScSMT designs

We have traced the waiting time of instructions in their queues, and have found an average 15-20% reduction on the ScSMT with respect to the SMT. This result demonstrates that the ScSMT organization inherently exhibits a better instruction scheduling policy than SMT. While a SMT processor permits a thread to saturate the pipeline, the ScSMT processor assures a minimum amount of resources to each thread, providing a fair utilization of the processor resources.

622

8 Conclusions

Results in this paper show that CMPs can increase their performance up to 20-30% by integrating mechanisms to share resources among threads. The SMT design, though, is not complexity-effective due to the hard bottleneck that supposes its wide-issue logic. We have proposed a ScSMT microarchitecture that combines the IPC rate advantages of SMT with the low cycle time of CMP. Experimental data obtained from simulation corroborate that the total IPC reduction over a pure SMT design is typically less than 6%, and sometimes the IPC even increases.

As a conclusion, it is not complexity-effective to provide full issue capability for every single thread, like a SMT processor does, and threads must share the processor resources with care. It is necessary to investigate on selection policies that maximize the use of the processor resources. In some situations, the processor should inhibit the sharing of resources and work as a pure CMP to avoid the negative interference of threads, which may be greater than the benefits obtained by sharing resources. Also, it could be worth to stall the decode stage of a given thread when it is probable that new instructions will degrade the processor utilization and waste resources that could be put in better use for other threads.

9 Acknowledgements

This work has been supported by the CICYT under contract number TIC 98-0433 and partially supported by the "Comisionat per a Universitats i Recerca" (Grups de Recerca Consolidats SGR 1997)

References

1. Burger, D., and Austin, T.M., The SimpleScalar Tool Set, Univ. Wisconsin-Madison Computer Science Department, Technical Report #1342, (1997).
2. Gwennap, L., Digital 21264 Sets New Standard, *Microprocessor Report* (1996), 1-6.
3. Hammond, L., Nayfeh, B.A., and Olukotun, K., A Single-Chip Multiprocessor, IEEE *Computer* (1997), 79-85.
4. Lam, M.D., and Wilson, R.P., Limits of Control Flow on Parallelism, Proc. of the *Int. Symp. on Computer Architecture* (1992), 46-57.
5. Matzke, D., Will Physical Scalability Sabotage Performance Gains?, IEEE *Computer* (1997), 37-39.
6. Palacharla, S., Jouppi, N.P., and Smith, J.E., Complexity-Effective Superscalar Processors, Proc. of the *Int. Symp. on Computer Architecture* (1997), 206-218.
7. Tullsen, D.M. *et al.*, Simultaneous multithreading: Maximizing on-chip parallelism, Proc. of the *Int. Symp. on Computer Architecture* (1995), 392-403.

Achieving Multiprogramming Scalability of Parallel Programs on Intel SMP Platforms: Nanothreading in the Linux Kernel

Dimitrios S. Nikolopoulos, Christos D. Antonopoulos,
Ioannis E. Venetis, Panagiotis E. Hadjidoukas,
Eleftherios D. Polychronopoulos, Theodore S. Papatheodorou
High Performance Information Systems Laboratory
Department of Computer Engineering and Informatics
University of Patras, Rion 26500, Greece
http://www.hpclab.ceid.upatras.gr

This paper presents the design and implementation of a *nanothreading* interface in the kernel of the Linux operating system for Intel Architecture-based symmetric multiprocessors. The objective of the nanothreading interface is to achieve robust performance of multithreaded programs and increased throughput in multiprogrammed shared memory multiprocessors, where multiple parallel and sequential programs with diverge characteristics and resource requirements execute simultaneously. The interface lets a multithreading runtime system and the kernel exchange critical scheduling information through loads and stores in shared memory, in order to enable parallel programs to adapt to dynamically changing resources and minimize their idle time. The same interface enhances the capability of the kernel scheduler to allocate resources evenly between competing programs. We discuss the main design and implementation issues concerning the nanothreading interface and provide experimental evidence which substantiates the efficiency of our implementation.

1 Introduction

Small-scale symmetric multiprocessors (SMPs) based on commodity Intel microprocessors are widely adopted as high performance and cost-effective compute servers. Proprietary and freeware operating systems for IA-based servers are SMP-compliant and provide operating system support for multithreading, typically implemented on top of kernel-level execution vehicles (EVs)[a] that share the same address space. At the same time, SMP-compliant operating systems support transparent multiprogramming, through time and space sharing of the system processors and memory.

The integration of multithreading with multiprogramming has been a hot spot in high performance computing research during the last decade[6]. Since modern SMPs are heavily multiprogrammed, the need for achieving scalability of parallel programs under multiprogramming is intensified[b]. The burden of

---

[a] We use the more general term *execution vehicle* instead of the term *kernel thread*, to cope with the inconsistencies in threads terminology between different operating systems.
[b] In this paper the term *scalability* is used in a broad sense, to characterize the ability of a

effectively integrating multithreaded programs in multiprogrammed environments is shared between the operating system and the runtime system layers. Unfortunately, most multithreading runtime systems are oblivious of multiprogramming and most SMP-compliant operating systems are oblivious of the fine-grain interactions between threads in multithreaded programs. This lack of coordination between runtime systems and operating systems has proven to be severely harmful for the performance of both individual applications and systems as a whole.

This work addresses the problem of integrating parallel programs in multiprogrammed environments, via the use of a lightweight shared memory interface, called the *nanothreading interface*[7], which lies between a multithreading runtime system and the operating system kernel. The nanothreading interface implements a communication infrastructure that enables a multithreaded program to automatically and transparently adapt to changes of the system resources allocated to it from the operating system at runtime. Adaptability is attained by matching the granularity of user-level threads to the number of processors available to the program at runtime and resuming maliciously preempted threads that execute on the critical path of the parallel computation. The same interface, used in the opposite direction, assists the kernel scheduler to apply sophisticated resource distribution strategies, by taking into account the actual resource requirements and the exploitable parallelism of each parallel program. The kernel gracefully grants parallel programs the authorization to use their EVs in the most effective way, while it maintains the responsibility of distributing system resources evenly. Put simply, the kernel acts like an advisory rather than as an explicit coordinator of the concurrency of parallel programs. The nanothreading interface architecture is adaptable and extensible, as it is not based on operating system or architecture-specific mechanisms. It thus promises to be a viable alternative for the effective integration of multiprocessing and multiprogramming in contemporary operating systems.

We present the main design and practical issues regarding the implementation of the nanothreading interface in the Linux operating system. These include the shared memory interface, mechanisms for processor allocation and affinity scheduling of nanothreaded jobs, mechanisms for fast resuming of maliciously preempted threads and the integration of the nanothreading jobs scheduler with the native time-sharing kernel scheduler. Our working prototype runs in Linux version 2.0.36 and is integrated with a user-level threads library that uses compiler knowledge to match the number of running user-level threads to the number of EVs granted to the program by the kernel [3]. We provide

---

parallel program to sustain robust and predictable performance when the load of the system due to multiprogramming is increased.

results from experiments with multiprogrammed workloads consisting of parallel jobs. The results show that the nanothreading Linux kernel achieves solid throughput improvements of up to 41% compared to the native Linux kernel.

The rest of this paper is organized as follows: Section 2 overviews the design and implementation of the nanothreading kernel interface. Section 3 provides experimental results and Section 4 discusses related and ongoing work.

2 Nanothreading Kernel Interface Design and Implementation

Three design principles guide the implementation of the nanothreading kernel interface. The first principle is that parallel programs should communicate with the kernel through loads and stores in shared memory in an asynchronous manner, since shared memory is the most efficient communication medium on a SMP. The second principle is that each parallel program should be armed with mechanisms that assist the program to effectively utilize the available processors and execute through the critical path, in the presence of preemptions of EVs from the operating system and blocking system calls. The third design principle is that the scheduler of the adaptive nanothreading programs should be seamlessly integrated with the native time-sharing scheduler of the operating system.

The nanothreading shared memory interface is organized around a *shared arena* [2,7]. Each multithreaded program reserves a portion of memory in its address space, which is shared between the program and the kernel. Care is taken so that the shared arena is situated in a single memory page. The pages containing shared arenas are pinned to physical memory in order to avoid paging out critical scheduling information at runtime. The shared arena is logically divided into a read-only and a read-write region. In the read-write region, each multithreaded program stores requests for processors, which are guided from the degree of parallelism that the program can effectively exploit and may vary during execution. In the same region, the program designates its EVs as *workers*, or *idlers*, depending on whether the EVs have user-level threads to execute in their run queues or not.

The processor requirements of a parallel program can be different from the number of processors allocated from the operating system to the program at runtime. The instantaneous number of physical processors allocated to each program is kept up-to-date from the kernel, which stores the associated information in the read-only region of the shared arena. A nanothreading program retrieves snapshots of this field by polling the shared arena whenever it initiates a parallel execution phase. In this way, the program is able to arrange its parallelism by creating as many user-level threads as the actual instantaneous number of physical processors allocated to it from the operating system. The read-only region is also used by the kernel in order to communicate the number of undesirably preempted EVs to the program.

A virtual memory page in the Intel x86 architecture can be either read-only or read-write. In order to achieve both goals of using one memory page per application for the shared arena and protecting read-only information from accidental overwriting, the kernel keeps a private copy of the shared arena page and trusts only the data residing on it. The read-write region of the kernel copy is updated each time the application loses control of a processor. The read-only region of the application copy is updated when the operating system scheduler selects an EV belonging to that application to be given a processor for the next time quantum. The application copy is updated with a copy-on-write strategy to avoid some expensive TLB flushes.

The disposition of the shared arena page in the application's virtual address space is communicated to the kernel via a system call. This system call informs the kernel that the application uses the nanothreading interface and serves as a request to the kernel to create as many EVs as the application expects to use during its execution lifetime. All EVs needed are created at once, using a modified version of the native kernel code for cloning. This reduces the overhead of multiple system calls and results to significantly faster EV creation. The return address in the kernel stack of each created EV is set to point to the function the EV must upcall to when running for the first time i.e. the threads runtime library scheduler loop. The newly created EVs are not unblocked until the kernel decides to grant some processors to the application.

The assignment of runnable EVs to applications is a duty of the nanothreads kernel-level scheduler, which is invoked in four cases: when a nanothreading application leaves or enters the system, when an application changes its processor requirements and upon expiration of the nanothreads scheduler time quantum. The scheduling takes place in three phases. During the first phase, the scheduler decides how many runnable EVs will be assigned to each nanothreading application. A dynamic space sharing policy is used for this purpose [8]. Each program is granted processors according to the number of processors it requests and the overall system load. The second phase results to an indirect assignment of physical processors to the nanothreading applications selected in the first phase. More specifically, the nanothreading applications are granted the right to compete with other, non-nanothreading applications, for some specific processors. This strategy is used to integrate the nanothreading jobs scheduler with the native time-sharing scheduler of the operating system. In other words, the nanothreading jobs scheduler is solely responsible for deciding how many and which specific processors should be allocated to each parallel program. Granting actual CPU time to the programs and managing priorities is a responsibility of the native time-sharing scheduler of the operating system. The major objective of the nanothreading scheduler in the second phase is to preserve the spatial and temporal locality of the processor sets in which each parallel program executes, via a strong affinity link maintained for each EV of a nanothreading program. In the final phase, a specific EV of an application chosen in the first phase is selected to serve as an EV during the next time quantum. A priority scheme is applied between the threads of each nanothreading application. Given a physical processor, if an EV was during the last time quantum executing on that physical processor, it is automatically selected. Otherwise the EVs that have previously been preempted while they were executing useful work, have the highest priority. The EVs that were previously preempted while idling constitute the next priority class. The two types of preempted EVs are distinguished with the worker/idler field in the shared arena. The EVs with the lowest priority are the ones that were previously voluntarily suspended at an idling point.

The nanothreading interface provides mechanisms to ensure that worker EVs which were undesirably preempted by the operating system scheduler are quickly resumed with application intervention. Each EV reaching an idling point of execution checks the shared arena for preempted worker EVs of the same application. If such EVs are found, the currently executing EV handoffs its processor in favor of a preempted worker, via a system call. EVs that find themselves idling for long also yield their processor in favor of an EV belonging to another nanothreading application, with the prospect that this EV will utilize the processor better. With this technique, nanothreading programs cooperate with the kernel to increase system throughput.

A common problem of user-level thread libraries is that when a user-level thread blocks in the kernel, e.g. while waiting for I/O, the corresponding EV also blocks. However, the user-level library has no means to be informed and activate another EV in order to keep using the processor efficiently. This can result to low processor utilization. In our implementation, when the kernel detects that an active EV of a nanothreading application is blocked, local scheduling, i.e. a scheduling having effect only on the processor assigned to the blocked EV, takes place. This leads to the selection and resumption of another EV. When the blocked EV is unblocked, it is either immediately resumed, or marked as a high priority preempted EV in the shared arena.

Several kernel services were added in the Linux kernel to support an efficient implementation of the nanothreading interface, including binding and unbinding of EVs to or from physical processors and an implementation of share groups for handling prematurely terminated EVs. The user-level side of the nanothreading interface, was implemented in a research prototype of the Nanothreads runtime library [3], customized for Linux. Details on the implementation can be found in an extended version of this paper [5].

3 Performance Evaluation

We used a Quad Pentium Pro for the evaluation of the nanothreading Linux kernel. Each processor was clocked at 200 MHz and equipped with 512 Kbytes of L2 cache, while the total physical memory of the system was 512 Mbytes. We used the Pentium Pro hardware counter to measure time in our experiments.

The overhead for cloning EVs in the nanothreading kernel is 26 μs, which is about 4 times faster than the native Linux cloning overhead. Blocking and unblocking EVs from physical processors cost from 1.4 to 8 μs, depending on the previous state of the EVs. A full handoff from an idler EV to a worker EV costs 54 μs. In general, the nanothreading kernel services pose minimal system overhead, which is comparable to the overhead of well tuned user-level lightweight thread libraries.

We evaluated the overall performance of the nanothreading kernel in terms of the throughput achieved by the kernel scheduler for multiprogrammed workloads consisting of several multithreaded programs. We selected four applications from the SPLASH-2 suite [9], LU, FFT, Raytrace and Volrend as benchmarks. These applications either follow a task queue execution paradigm, or constitute of parallel regions separated from each other with global barriers. The changes needed in these applications in order to use the nanothreading interface were minor. The workloads used consisted of 1, 2, 4 and 8 identical copies of each application. All copies requested all processors of the system to execute, therefore the degree of multiprogramming was always equal to the number of copies of the program used in the workload. For each workload, we measured the throughput in terms of average turnaround time for our nanothreading kernel and the native Linux kernel (version 2.0.36) with the LinuxThreads POSIX 1003.1c-compliant threads package.

The results are depicted in Figure 1. Two observations are worth commenting in the charts. First, we witness that the nanothreading kernel demonstrates a solid improvement of throughput compared to the native Linux kernel. The increase of system throughput ranges from 9% to 41% with an average of 18% over all the experiments. Second, the throughput improvement achieved by the nanothreading kernel tends to magnify as the degree of multiprogramming and the load of the system increase. The improvements are mainly attributed to the effectiveness of the handoff strategy and the strong affinity scheduling mechanism which is employed in our nanothreading interface.

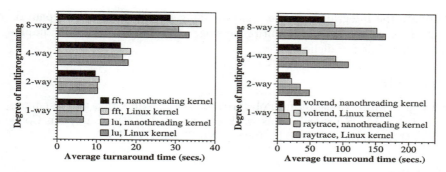

Figure 1: Results from executions of multiprogrammed workloads of SPLASH-2 benchmarks with the native and the nanothreading Linux SMP kernel.

4 Related and Ongoing Work

The idea of interfacing the user-level and kernel-level schedulers in order to provide adaptability of parallel programs in multiprogrammed environments is not new and has been used in the context of dynamic space-sharing processor scheduling strategies [1,4,10]. Our approach differentiates from these works in three critical aspects. Unlike previous implementations that relied on coarse-grain mechanisms like signals and upcalls, we implement the communication path between the runtime system and the kernel using just loads and stores in shared memory. We rely on a completely asynchronous mechanism based on polling to realize user-kernel communication. This mechanism minimizes the communication overhead and provides adequate means to parallel programs in order to readapt in the presence of frequent changes of system load and fine-grain interactions between threads. Second, the nanothreading interface is oriented towards providing efficient mechanisms to speedup the execution of parallel programs in the presence of undesirable preemptions from the operating system. The nanothreading interface as such is not coupled with a specific kernel scheduling policy. It rather enhances any scheduling policy with mechanisms for efficient multiprogrammed execution of parallel programs. Third, the nanothreading interface is seamlessly integrated with a UNIX time-sharing scheduler and enables efficient simultaneous execution of both nanothreading and non-nanothreading jobs. Integration of sophisticated parallel job scheduling strategies with time-sharing has not attracted considerable attention in previous research works on multiprocessor scheduling.

Our current efforts focus on integrating the nanothreading interface with the POSIX threads standard in order to extend its applicability to out-of-core multithreaded programs, including networking applications and Java. We also

630

investigate the integration of the nanothreading interface with the OpenMP standard for shared memory multiprocessing, as an infrastructure for implementing dynamic parallelism.

Acknowledgments

We are grateful to Constantine Polychronopoulos, David Craig and our partners in the NANOS project. This work is supported by the European Commission, through the ESPRIT IV Project No. 21907 (NANOS).

References

1. T. Anderson et.al. *Scheduler Activations: Effective Kernel Support for the User-Level Management of Parallelism.* ACM Trans. on Computer Systems, 10(1), pp. 53–79, 1992.
2. D. Craig. *An Integrated Kernel-Level and User-Level Paradigm for Efficient Multiprogramming.* Master's Thesis, CSRD Technical Report 1533, University of Illinois at Urbana-Champaign, 1999.
3. X. Martorell et.al. *A Library Implementation of the Nanothreads Programming Model.* Proc. of Euro-Par'96, pp. 644–649, 1996.
4. C. McCann, R. Vaswani and J. Zahorjan. *A Dynamic Processor Allocation Policy for Multiprogrammed Shared-Memory Multiprocessors.* ACM Trans. on Computer Systems, 11(2), pp. 146–178, 1993.
5. D. Nikolopoulos et.al. *Achieving Multiprogramming Scalability of Parallel Programs on Intel SMP Platforms. Nanothreading in the Linux Kernel.* Technical Report HPCLAB-021298, Available at http://www.hpclab.ceid.upatras.gr, 1998.
6. C. Polychronopoulos. *Multiprocessing vs. Multiprogramming.* Proc. of the 1989 Int. Conf. on Parallel Processing, pp. II-223–II-230, 1989.
7. C. Polychronopoulos, N. Bitar and S. Kleiman. *Nanothreads: A User-Level Threads Architecture.* CSRD Technical Report 1297, University of Illinois at Urbana-Champaign, 1993.
8. E. Polychronopoulos et.al. *An Efficient Kernel-Level Scheduling Methodology for Multiprogrammed Shared Memory Multiprocessors.* Proc. of the 12th ISCA Int. Conf. on Parallel and Distr. Computing Systems, 1999.
9. S. Woo et.al. *The SPLASH-2 Programs: Characterization and Methodological Considerations.* Proc. of the 22nd Annual Int. Symposium on Computer Architecture, pp. 24–36, 1995.
10. K. Yue and D. Lilja. *An Effective Processor Allocation Strategy for Multiprogrammed Shared Memory Multiprocessors.* IEEE Trans. on Parallel and Distributed Systems, 8(12), pp. 1246–1258, 1997.

PERFORMANCES OF HOLE BASED, CHAOTIC AND MINIMAL FULLY-ADAPTIVE ROUTING ALGORITHMS UNDER CONSTANT RESOURCE CONSTRAINT

P. PALAZZARI

ENEA - HPCN project, Via Anguillarese, 301, 00060 S. Maria di Galeria (Rome)

M. COLI, F. MARRA

Electronic Engineering Department – University "La Sapienza" – Rome

Simulation under significant traffic loads is often used to estimate performances achievable by a routing algorithm: the same traffic loads are offered to different routing algorithms which are compared through (average) message latency and throughput. Usually simulations neglect the actual HW cost of a routing algorithm: in this work we consider three routing algorithms based on the virtual cut-through flow control technique (Hole Based (HB), Chaos and the Minimal Fully-Adaptive (MFA)) and we show that HW cost must be taken into account in order to make reasonable comparisons among different routing algorithms.

1   Introduction

In parallel systems processors share data through a high bandwidth communication network. A typical computational node is configured with a high-performance CPU and some amount of local memory. The interconnection network consists of channels and routers, which move messages from sources to destinations.

Store-and-forward flow-control mechanism was used in first generation multicomputers. Each time a message reaches a node, it is buffered into a local memory. Second generation multicomputers use wormhole routing [6]: each message is divided into flow control units (flits). The flit at the head of a message determines the route and, as the header is routed, the remaining flits follow in a pipelined mode. When the header is blocked, all the flits of the same message stop advancing and, consequently, block the progress of any other message requiring the channels they are occupying. Virtual Cut-Through (VCT) ([9],[8]) is similar to wormhole routing but, when the header is blocked, the message is completely stored in the buffer containing the header flit. Thus each buffer must be large enough to store the whole message.

Interconnection networks may vary significantly in size and topology, but most of them belong to the class of k-ary d-cubes (radix k, dimension d networks). This class of networks contains $N=k^d$ nodes. In general, a k-ary d-cube with open edges is known as d-dimensional Mesh, and as d-dimensional Torus if the edges are wrapped around. The case $k=2$ produces a d-dimensional Binary Hypercube.

The bisection of a network is defined as the minimum number of channels that must be cut to separate the network into two symmetric equal halves. The Bisection

Bandwidth (BB) is the amount of data crossing a bisection of the network in the time unit. The probability of a message to cross the bisection border is equal to one-half in the case of uniform random traffic. To avoid overloading bisection channels, nodes cannot inject more data than the bisection channels can handle. Thus, the total amount of data injected into the network per time unit can not be greater than 2BB (Max Load).

The routing of a message is specified as an ordered list of nodes, $(n_{source}, n_2, n_3, \ldots, n_{dest})$, which describe a path starting at the source node and ending at the destination node. This path may be selected "off-line" by a mechanism which has information on the network, or "on-line" by a distributed mechanism within the network nodes. Deterministic path routing algorithm is completely determined by the source and destination node addresses. However, realizing the need for adaptability in routing around congested or faulty nodes and links, several researches have proposed adaptive algorithms, in which a packet is permitted to change its routing path if a blocked channel is encountered. Adaptive algorithms can be classified into minimal and not-minimal algorithms. Minimal algorithms always use the shortest-length paths to reach destination: they are called fully-adaptive if they use all the possible minimal paths, partially-adaptive otherwise. Not-minimal algorithms are also allowed to use non-minimal paths.

Deadlock and livelock are the most common problems which can arise in such routing schemes. A deadlock occurs when there is a cyclic dependence in the network and no packet can progress toward its destination because it is blocked by some other packet in the cycle. Livelock can happen only in not-minimal algorithms and arises when a message is transmitted an arbitrarily high number of times without ever reaching its destination. Usually, in minimal routing schemes (adaptive [7], [10], [11] or deterministic [6]), deadlock is avoided by using virtual channels and forcing the communication graph to be acyclic. In not-minimal routing schemes (like Chaos routing [1] and Hole-Based (HB) routing [4], [5]) deadlock freedom is achieved by allowing misrouting of blocked packets. In this paper we compare the routing algorithm we developed (HB) with the Chaos and the Minimal Fully-Adaptive (MFA) algorithms, because they are among the most representative in the class of not-minimal (Chaos) and minimal adaptive (MFA) routing policies.

2 Definitions

A parallel machine (PM) is described through the graph PM=$\{$P,Ls$\}$, being P=$\{P_1, P_2, \ldots, P_N\}$ the processor set and Ls$\subseteq$P$\times$P the interprocessor communication set. Given the ordered couple $(P_i, P_j) \in$ Ls, we denote with c_{ij} the channel connecting P_i to P_j. Each processor P_i has the set of input and output channels $C_{in}(P_i) \cup C_{out}(P_i)$,. HB routing assumes Ls to be connected; Chaos assumes Ls to be a connected graph with bidirectional channels; MFA considers only the Mesh, Hypercube and Shuffle-Exchange topologies.

Each processor has a set of buffers $B_{in}(P_i) \cup B_{out}(P_i) \cup B_{alg}(P_i)$, being $B_{in}(P_i)$ and $B_{out}(P_i)$ the set of input and output buffers, with $|B_{in}(P_i)| \neq |B_{out}(P_i)|$ (possibly) in HB routing, and $B_{alg}(P_i)$ a set of auxiliary buffers depending on the algorithm ($B_{HB}(P_i)=\{\}$).

We denote with L the maximum length of a message (expressed in flits) and with $0<=Free(B,P_k)<=L$ the number of free positions in buffer B of processor P_k; a buffer cannot receive the header flit of a new message if it contains the tailing flits of another message, i.e. a buffer can receive a new message only if it is empty.

We say that B is in a deadlock state if it never succeeds in transmitting the message to the following buffer.

Furthermore, we indicate with Dest(B) the processor to which the message in B is directed, $B_{in}(P_i,P_j)$ the input buffer for P_j connected to channel (P_i,P_j), $B_{out}(P_i,P_j)$ the output buffer for P_i connected to channel (P_i,P_j), Neigh(P_k) the set of processors adjacent to P_k, Dist(P_i,P_j) the minimum distance between the node P_i and P_j, Cap(B_i,P_j) the capacity (in flits) of the buffer B_i in the node P_j, R(P_i,P_j) the routing function which returns the set of processors to which a message, stored in P_i and directed toward P_j, can be transmitted and $S(B)=\{E,H,NH\}$ the state of buffer B ($S(B)=E$ if $Free(B)=L$, $S(B)=H$ if B contains the header of a message and $S(B)=NH$ if $Free(B)<L$ but the header flit of the message is not more contained in B).

3 Hole Based routing

HB is a deadlock and livelock free, fully adaptive, not minimal routing algorithm [4], using the VCT flow control technique [5]. It has a buffer associated to each input or output channel, one injection and one delivery buffer; input and injection buffers are connected through a crossbar switch to output and delivery buffers. HB derives its name from the 'hole' concept: a hole is a free buffer (the equivalent of the hole concept in silicon devices). A time-out T_0 is connected to the output of each input buffer and a misrouting is performed whenever a message cannot succeed in moving one step toward its destination within T_0 (there is the suspicion of a deadlock occurrence). In [5] it is demonstrated that, once ensured that an hole is always present in the network and is subjected to random movement, the hole is able to reach each buffer and remove the deadlocks within a finite time. A hole is subjected to random motion if, being $Free(B_{out})=L$, the B_{in} which transmits a message to B_{out}, in the same processor, is chosen in a random and equiprobable way. Furthermore, livelock freedom is demonstrated in a probabilistic way.

HB routing algorithm has fault tolerance capabilities (connection is the only hypothesis on the network), it does not need virtual channels, it presents low HW requirements (extra queues of buffers are not necessary) and supports any topology. Outline of the HB-VCT algorithm:

1. In the presence of one message to inject, insert it into an output buffer on a direction bringing it closer to the destination. Routing function is

$R(P_i,Dest(B_{in}))=\{P_j\in Neigh(P_i)|Dist(P_j,Dest(B_{in}))=Dist(P_i,Dest(B_{in}))-1\}$.
Injection can be performed only if at least two holes are present in the node (i.e. two buffers must be in the E or NH state);

2. As soon as the header flit of a message is received in an input buffer, retransmit it (or deliver it if it is arrived) to one of the output buffers with $S(B)=E$ and bringing the message closer to the destination processor; if it is not possible to find such an output buffer, after a time T_0 being elapsed try to transmit the message to the first empty output buffer;

3. As soon as a header flit enters in an output buffer, it must be retransmitted to the next empty input buffer; all the other flits will follow the header flit in a pipelined way.

4 Chaotic routing

Chaotic routing is a deadlock and livelock free, fully adaptive non-minimal routing algorithm using the VCT flow control technique [2], [3].

Chaos router has three main components: input/output buffers, a crossbar, and a multiqueue. Each buffer and multiqueue slot holds one fixed-size packet. The basic operation of the Chaos router is similar to a typical oblivious cut-through router: packets entering a router input buffer, are connected through the crossbar to an output buffer and have their header updated, to reflect their progress, as they exit. Virtual cut-through allows packets to proceed through the router as soon as their header is received and decoded; it is not necessary for the entire packet to be buffered before moving to the next router. In a Chaos router packets may be routed to any output channel that brings them closer to their destination. Thus, in this mode of operation, the Chaos router acts as a minimal adaptive router, and the routing function can be written as:

$R(P_i,Dest(B_{in}))=\{P_j\in Neigh(P_i) \mid Dist(P_j,Dest(B_{in}))=Dist(P_i,Dest(B_{in}))-1\}$.

The central buffer of the Chaos router, the multiqueue, stores packets waiting for profitable channels to become free. Immunity from deadlock and livelock is demonstrated in [2]. Packets in the multiqueue have priority over packets in input frames when competing for a free channel. Moreover, whenever the multiqueue becomes full, a packet in the multiqueue is randomly selected to be sent to the next free output channel, regardless of the packet destination. Misrouting is accomplished through this mechanism and randomization is used to prevent livelock.

5 Minimal Fully Adaptive routing

MFA is a deadlock free, fully adaptive, minimal routing algorithm, using the VCT flow control technique [10], [11]. A routing algorithm is fully-adaptive and minimal if all possible minimal paths between source and destination nodes can be used. Minimal paths followed by messages depend on the local congestion encountered in each node of the network. It is shown in [11] that MFA routing algorithm can be implemented in Mesh and Hypercube topologies using with two central queues per routing node (q_A, associated with the fully-adaptive phase, and q_B, associated with the partially-adaptive (i.e. acyclic) phase, see below).

The algorithm for the Hypercube is the following.

1. Each injected message starts moving through the q_A queues of the nodes it is visiting, correcting any 0 (1) of his binary source address into 1 (0) to match the destination address (fully-adaptive phase); in such a phase the following routing function is used:
   $R(P_i,Dest(B_{in})) = R_1(P_i,Dest(B_{in})) \cup R_2(P_i,Dest(B_{in}))$ with
   $R_1(P_i,Dest(B_{in}))=\{P_j \in Neigh(P_i)|Dist(P_j,Dest(B_{in}))=Dist(P_i,Dest(B_{in}))-1,P_j>P_i\}$ (0-to-1);
   $R_2(P_i,Dest(B_{in}))=\{P_j \in Neigh(P_i)|Dist(P_j,Dest(B_{in}))=Dist(P_i,Dest(B_{in}))-1, P_j<P_i\}$ (1-to-0).
2. When the message is not more able to find a place in the q_A queues, it is switched into the partially-adaptive phase (q_B queues) and the routing function is
   $R(P_i,Dest(B_{in}))=R_1(P_i,Dest(B_{in})) \rightarrow R(P_i,Dest(B_{in}))=R_2(P_i,Dest(B_{in}))$,
   i.e. all the 0-to-1 changing are done before ($\rightarrow$) the 1-to-0 changing.

The number of hops is exactly the Hamming distance between the source and the destination nodes, so the algorithm is minimal. The algorithm for the two-dimensional Mesh is similar.

In our simulation we adopt the MFA implementation given in [10]. Each input and output buffer is divided into three different buffers: the A (ascending phase), B (descending phase), and C (adaptive phase) buffers.

6   Simulation Methodology

Simulations for the three algorithms were performed using a flit-based simulator written in C. Each node of the network consists of a processor, its local memory, a router and several channels. Simulations are synchronized by the cycle time unit. One cycle is the time necessary to transmit a single flit across a channel. We assume that a routing decision must be taken within a single cycle so, if a message header enters a router at cycle t, it may enter the next router at cycle $t+1$. In each router a crossbar connects each of the input buffers to all the output buffers. At each cycle, all the routing decisions are taken simultaneously. A packet which has a profitable output buffer may be immediately sent to that output buffer, i.e. all possible new paths through the router can be established at a time.

We assume that the channels are implemented as bidirectional busses of W wires, and one flit of data contains W bits (W=32).

Being interested to network bandwidth and not to local node memory management, we do not consider contention in the delivery buffer. When a message arrives to its delivery buffer B_{del}, it is immediately removed from the network (i.e. we suppose $Cap(B_{del},P_i) \rightarrow \infty$ or $Free(B_{del},P_i) \rightarrow \infty \ \forall \ P_i \in P$).

Each node of the network can inject a finite length packet (with L flits), according to the simulated traffic pattern. The flow-control mechanism adopted is VCT routing, so $Cap(B_i, P_j) = L$.

Times are reported as an integer multiple of the cycle time unit (which is the external clock period; a reasonable value for today's technology is $T_{ck} = 10ns$).

In our simulations we used two synthetic workloads. The first is uniform random traffic which is often used to compare routing performances. The second workload is the transpose traffic, occurring in many numerical computations. The node with address $a_{n-1}a_{n-2}...a_0$ transmits to node $a_{(n/2)-1}a_{(n/2)-2}...a_0a_{n-1}a_{n-2}...a_{n/2}$.

The simulator returns average latency and average throughput. The average latency is the mean value of the time elapsed between the generation of each packet and the delivery of its header flit, including (if present) the stalling time in the injection buffer. Throughput is the sustained data delivery rate (flits /second) for a given applied load.

Simulations, with L=20 flits, gave the same results reported in the literature [2] for the case of Chaos router and showed that Chaos routing performs better than HB and MFA algorithms.

7   HW cost of routing algorithms: the constant cost constraint

Previous simulations do not make any assumption on actual HW implementation cost of the routing algorithms. In order to have more meaningful comparisons, we introduce a rough estimation of the HW costs of HB, Chaos and MFA routing algorithms.

We express the HW cost in terms of flip flops (FF) needed to implement buffers, being the most of the HW in a router chip devoted to buffers. W is the width (in bit) and L the length of each buffer; by counting the number of needed buffers it is easy to obtain the number of FF needed in each node of HB, Chaos and MFA routing circuits: in the case of 2D-Torus $(k=4)$, we have $N_{FF}(HB)=10WL$, $N_{FF}(Chaos)=15WL$, $N_{FF}(MFA)=30WL$. Similarly, for a Binary Hypercube $(d=6)$, we obtain $N_{FF}(HB)=14WL$, $N_{FF}(Chaos)=19WL$, $N_{FF}(MFA)=42WL$.

We assume W=32 (dimension compatible with the pin-out of a state-of-the-art FPGA) and the maximum number of available flip-flops is denoted as $Nmax_{FF}$; the length of the buffers is given by

$$L = \left\lfloor \frac{Nmax_{FF}}{32N_B} \right\rfloor \qquad (1)$$

N_B being the number of buffers required (10, 15 and 30, respectively, for the 2D-Torus and 14, 19, 42 for the 6D-Hypercube). In the case of $Nmax_{FF} = 10000$ (reasonable number for the current technology), expression (1) yields L=31 (HB), L=20 (Chaos), L=10 (MFA) flits in the case of 2D toroidal topology $(k=4)$ and L=22 (HB), L=16 (Chaos), L=7 (MFA) flits in the case of Binary Hypercube $(d=6)$.

8   Realistic Simulation Results

In order to show the impact of the constant HW constraint on performance comparison, we simulated the behavior of HB, Chaos and MFA algorithms in the cases of toroidal and hypercubic topologies with either 16 or 64 nodes using the buffer lengths obtained from expression (1).

We simulated the simultaneous transmission of messages with constant length (typical communication operation in MPI programs, where, after a possible synchronization, processes within a communicator exchange messages).

We considered the all to all transpose and complement traffics and the one to many scatter and many to one gather traffics. We chose the length of messages to be 64 KB (trade-off between the necessity to manage large messages, reducing start-up communication overhead, and necessity to exchange frequently small messages).

Figures for algorithm performances are the Excess Completion Time T_C (i.e. the difference between the actual completion time AT_C, when the last flit is delivered to destination, and the minimal theoretical completion time TT_C) and the average Excess Latency T_L (i.e. the difference between the mean value of the actual mean latency AT_L and its minimal theoretical value TT_L). In the case of a message of m flits it is easy to verify that

$$TT_C \approx m \quad \text{and} \quad TT_L = \frac{1}{m}\sum_{i=1}^{m}(n_i + i) \approx \frac{1}{m}\sum_{i=1}^{m} i = \frac{m+1}{2} \approx \frac{m}{2}$$

(for m>>network diameter; n_i<<m gives a negligible contribution to the summation, being the path length of the ith message).

Summarizing, for messages of m flits, we have

$$T_c = AT_C - TT_C \approx AT_C - m \quad \text{and} \quad T_L = AT_L - TT_L \approx AT_L - \frac{m}{2}$$

Messages of 64×10^3 bytes and W=4 bytes are split in $m = 16 \times 10^3$ flits, so $TT_C \approx 16 \times 10^3$ cycles and $TT_L \approx 8 \times 10^3$ cycles.

As we see in table 1, HB routing gives (nearly) always better performances than Chaos and MFA algorithms (the best values are bolded). This fact is due to the minor buffer requirements of HB, allowing the implementation of larger buffers (with the same HW resources): as a consequence, the same traffic pattern applied to HB, Chaos and MFA routers generates, in the HB case, less messages which are delivered in a shorter time.

9   Conclusions

This work concerns with the use of simulation to compare routing algorithms. The main idea introduced, after a brief review of three routing algorithms, is that actual HW costs, connected to the implementation of a given algorithm, must be taken into account whenever simulating and comparing different routing algorithms. In this

638

paper we show how simulated routing performances change when HW constraints are taken into account; for example we discovered that HB is better than Chaos when the two algorithms are compared on a basis of a fixed amount of silicon area.

Table 1: Excess Completion Time (T_C) and Excess Latency (T_L) for different topologies and traffic loads

Routing	2D-Torus $k=8$			Binary Hypercube $d=6$		
	HB	CHAOS	MINIMAL	HB	CHAOS	MINIMAL
T_C Gather	**711**	1198	2057	**707**	1200	2291
T_L Gather	**267**	520	926	**228**	531	940
T_C Scatter	**845**	1305	2822	**823**	1301	2740
T_L Scatter	**443**	704	1574	**399**	651	1451
T_C Complement	**27283**	31857	41561	5885	**2379**	Not Done
T_L Complement	**9871**	11620	14659	1985	**1129**	Not Done
T_C Transpose	**16477**	20192	31666	1953	**1707**	4659
T_L Transpose	**2833**	4804	1287	**570**	649	1498

References

[1] K.Bolding, L. Snyder: *Mesh and Torus Chaotic Routing*. Advanced Research in VLSI and Parallel Systems: Proc. Of the 1992 Brown/MIT Conference, March 1992.
[2] K.Bolding: *Chaotic Routing: Design and Implementation of an Adaptive Multicomputer Network Router*. PhD thesis, University of Washington, Seattle, WA, 1993.
[3] K.Bolding, W.Yost: *Design of a Router for Fault-Tolerant Networks*. Proceedings of the 1994 Parallel Computer Routing and Communication Workshop - May 1994.
[4] M. Coli, P. Palazzari: *An Adaptive Deadlock and Livelock Free Routing Alghoritm* Proceedings of the 4th Euromicro Workshop on Parallel and Distributed Processing. January 1995, Sanremo (Italy). IEEE CS ed.
[5] M. Coli , P. Palazzari: *Virtual Cut-Through Implementation of the HB Packet Switching Routing Algorithm*. Proceedings of the 6th Euromicro Workshop on Parallel and Distributed Processing. January 1997, Madrid (Spain). IEEE CS ed.
[6] W.J. Dally, C.L. Seitz: *Deadlock Free Message Routing in Multiprocessor Interconnection Networks*. IEEE Trans. On Computers, vol C 36, May 1987.
[7] J.Duato: *A Necessary and sufficient Condition for Deadlock-Free Adaptive Routing in Wormhole Networks*. IEEE Trans. Parallel and Distributed Systems, vol 6, 10, Oct, 1995.
[8] J.Duato: *A Necessary and sufficient Condition for Deadlock-Free Routing in Cut-Through and Store-and-Forward Networks*. IEEE Trans Parallel and Distributed Systems, 6, 1996.
[9] P.Kermani, L. Kleinrock: *Virtual cut-through: a new computer communication switching technique*. Computer Networks, vol. 3, 1979.
[10] T.D. Nguyen, L.Snyder: *Performance Analysis af a Minimal Adaptive Router*. Proc. Of he 1994 Parallel Computer Routing and Communication Workshop – May 1994
[11] G.D. Pifarré, et al: *Fully Adaptive Minimal Deadlock-Free Packet Routing in Hypercubes, Meshes and other Networks: Algorithms and Simulations*. IEEE Trans. Parallel and Distributed Systems - March 1994.

A TOOL FOR SPMD APPLICATION DEVELOPMENT
WITH SUPPORT FOR LOAD BALANCING

A. PLASTINO

Department of Computer Science - Universidade Federal Fluminense
R. Passo da Pátria 156, Niterói 24210-240, RJ, Brazil
E-mail: plastino@dcc.ic.uff.br

C. C. RIBEIRO, N. RODRIGUEZ

Department of Computer Science - Catholic University of Rio de Janeiro
R. Marquês de São Vicente 225, Rio de Janeiro 22453-900, RJ, Brazil
E-mail: {celso,noemi}@inf.puc-rio.br

This paper describes SAMBA, a tool for supporting the development of SPMD applications. A predefined SPMD skeleton invokes application-dependent routines, which must be coded by the programmer, allowing him to concentrate on the specific problem at hand. The tool includes a library of load balancing strategies, all of which can be automatically incorporated to any SPMD application written with SAMBA. In this paper, SAMBA is used to compare several load balancing strategies for two specific applications.

1 Introduction

The SPMD (Single Program, Multiple Data) model has been widely deployed in parallel programming, due to the ease of developing and controlling a single code running on several processors (over different data sets). Moreover, data decomposition is a natural approach for the design of parallel algorithms for many problems [1]. Different SPMD applications typically present a common structure. However, parallel programmers usually write the entire application from scratch, replicating the associated development and debugging work.

The central contribution of this work is SAMBA (Single Application, Multiple Load Balancing), a tool for supporting the development of SPMD applications. The first goal of SAMBA is to allow the reuse of common code in SPMD applications. In SAMBA, a predefined SPMD skeleton invokes application-dependent routines, which must be coded by the programmer, allowing him to concentrate on the specific problem at hand.

Different applications and architectures give rise to specific unbalancing factors which must be taken care of by a *load balancing strategy*. A difficulty in the design of a new SPMD application is to find, among the variety of available strategies [2,3,4,5], the one that best fits the characteristics of the application.

Another important purpose of SAMBA is to help the programmer in identifying an appropriate load balancing algorithm for the application under development. With this purpose, the tool offers a library which contains several load balancing strategies, all of which can be automatically incorporated to any SPMD application written with SAMBA.

Other tools for supporting development of parallel applications have been proposed [6,7]. SAMBA focuses on SPMD applications and on facilitating the experimental evaluation of different load balancing strategies.

2 SAMBA

The code of an SPMD application can typically be structured in three major components: the code which is replicated for the execution of a task (In this work, we use the term *task* to identify a subset of data which corresponds to a unit of work in an SPMD application.); the load balancing strategy; and a skeleton (which initializes and terminates the application, and controls the execution of the other parts). The first of these components is specific to each application, but the other two are usually not.

We designed SAMBA (figure 1) bearing this commonality in mind. Once the programmer has written a specified set of routines – the *user module* –, SAMBA can generate different versions of the associated SPMD application for each load balancing algorithm in its library. In the user module, the programmer must define routines for generating the tasks, executing a single task, and dealing with the results.

The tool uses a predefined *control module* and offers a library of different load balancing strategies. Any one of them may be chosen to define the *load balancing module*. The control module is responsible for initializing and terminating the application, as well as for activating the other modules.

The tasks which compose the application are stored in task pools at each processor. The control module also manages these pools (currently implemented as lists) and transfers tasks between processors as required by the load balancing algorithm. The procedures which manipulate these pools have been isolated in a submodule. This allows the user to easily substitute them, if the application requires a specific data structure.

3 Programming Model

A SAMBA-generated SPMD application executes a control code which contains calls to functions defined by the user. In this section we discuss the routines which must be coded by the user. The central routine is the one for processing a single task (the kernel of the "single" program). Besides this function, the user must necessarily code the generation of tasks. Other routines,

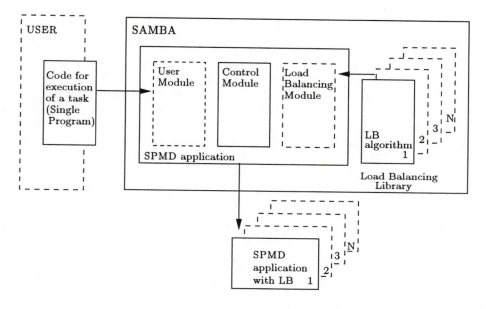

Figure 1: Architecture of SAMBA.

which may be optionally defined with empty bodies, have been specified in an effort to capture the full generality of the SPMD model.

A set of routines is reserved for initialization chores. One of these must take care of task creation. Each new task must be registered by calling a routine in the control module. Before calling this routine, the task description must be packed into a contiguous block of data (The control module knows nothing about the semantics of such description.). Besides the creation of tasks, other common initialization chores include initialization of global variables, parameter verification, and data input and argument checking.

The task execution routine will be continuously invoked at each processor during the application execution. When invoked, it receives the task to be executed as a block of bytes. It unpacks this block to obtain a task description, executes the task, and finally stores results in global variables or sends them to other processors. In some cases, such as in search tree or recursive applications, this function may also register new tasks generated by the current one.

Last, there are routines reserved for finalization procedures, which are invoked after all tasks have been executed. Such procedures may include sending results to a central processor or storing them in files.

4 Load Balancing in SAMBA

One of the assumptions behind the development of SAMBA was that it is possible to use the architecture and programming model described in sections 2 and 3 independently of the chosen load balancing strategy. To validate the hypothesis, we implemented load balancing algorithms with a wide variety of characteristics. The development of SAMBA's load balancing library was guided by a taxonomy of load balancing algorithms for SPMD applications which we had previously proposed[8]. This section describes seven implemented algorithms. SAMBA also allows new algorithms to be included in its library.

1 STATIC: The central processor distributes the initial set of tasks in equal parts among all processors, including itself. Each processor simply executes the tasks it has received, without any dynamic load balancing.

2 DEMAND-DRIVEN: A central processor first allocates a block of tasks to each other processor. Each time a processor finishes executing a block of tasks, it requests and receives a new one.

3 DISTRIBUTED, GLOBAL: A central processor distributes the complete set of initial tasks in equal parts among all processors, including itself. Whenever any processor consumes its tasks, it sends a message to all others, asking them to execute a load balancing step. At this point, each processor sends to all others its internal load index, i.e., the remaining number of tasks to be executed. Load balancing takes place only if the load index of at least one processor exceeds a certain threshold, which is given as an argument in the activation of the application. In this case, each processor computes the necessary task exchanges and performs the exchanges in which it is involved.

4 CENTRALIZED, GLOBAL: This algorithm is similar to the previous one, except that all decisions are taken by a central processor. Whenever any processor consumes all its tasks, it sends a message to all other processors asking them to send their internal load index (number of remaining tasks) to a central processor. After receiving this information from all processors, this central processor checks the need for load balancing, in the same way as before. If load is to be balanced, the central processor defines the necessary exchanges, and informs each processor of the task transfers in which it is involved.

5 DISTRIBUTED, GLOBAL, INDIVIDUAL: Once again, load balancing is triggered by the end of tasks at a processor. However, instead of aiming at balancing the load of all processors, here the goal is to correct the load problem at this single underloaded processor. Whenever a processor consumes all its tasks, it sends a message to all others and they send back their internal load indexes. Based on the received information, the underloaded processor will choose one

from which it will request new tasks. After receiving load information from all processors, the underloaded processor checks whether load balancing is to take place or not, in the same way as in algorithm 3. If load balancing is necessary, a request for load transfer is sent to the most loaded processor.

6 DISTRIBUTED, LOCAL, PARTITION-BASED: This algorithm is basically the same as algorithm 3, except that processors are partitioned in disjoint groups. Load balancing takes place inside groups defined by the user.

7 DISTRIBUTED, LOCAL, NEIGHBORHOOD-BASED, INDIVIDUAL: This strategy is similar to algorithm 5, except that load information and load exchanges occur only between processors in the same group. Groups are defined by a logical neighborhood (which could reflect physical connections) and processors may belong to more than one group. This strategy requires the use of a termination detection algorithm, since there may still be global load to execute even when neighboring processors have no remaining load. Dijkstra's termination detection algorithm[9] was used in our implementation.

5   Experimental Results

The current version of SAMBA was written using C and MPI[10]. It has been executed on an IBM SP2, on a network of Sun workstations, and on a cluster of IBM PCs. As an initial evaluation of the tool, we have used it to develop and analyse load balancing strategies for well known and understood SPMD applications. In this section we report the results obtained with two applications: computation of $\int_0^{15} e^x dx$ by the adaptive quadrature method with a tolerance of 10^{-16} (application #1) and computation of the product of two integer valued square matrices of dimension 2000 (application #2).

The choice of these two applications was due to their simplicity, which allowed us to focus on load balancing issues, and to their different task creation characteristics. While in application #1 tasks are generated dynamically (and their total number is previously unknown) by the execution of other tasks, in application #2 the number of tasks is fixed from the beginning.

The seven strategies described in the previous section have been tested and compared. For the last strategy, two logical topologies have been evaluated: ring (R) and hypercube (H). Each group of the local partition-besed strategy is formed by exactly four processors. The computational experiments we present have been carried out on a cluster of 32 Pentium II-400 running Linux.

Application #1 computes $\int_0^{15} e^x dx$ using the adaptive quadrature method. Numeric quadrature computes the definite integral of a function over an interval by dividing it into subintervals and approximating the area of each subinterval using a method like the trapezoidal rule. The creation of subintervals is dynamically determined. The approximation of the area in an interval is compared to the sum of the two areas corresponding to the two subintervals obtained by dividing this interval at the middle. If the difference is small enough (below the tolerance limit), the approximation is returned. Otherwise, recursive (and parallel) computations proceed over the two subintervals.

In our experiment, the original interval was initially divided into 64 subintervals, generating 64 tasks. The computational effort of these 64 tasks is not the same, since there are different levels of recursion for each subinterval. In the static run with four processors, each processor received 16 tasks. The total number of executed tasks was 110 933 464. However, the number of tasks executed by each of them was quite different, giving rise to the need for dynamic load balancing: 1 793 764, 6 281 112, 22 816 968, and 80 041 620 tasks. Table 1 shows elapsed times in seconds for different load balancing strategies, using 4, 8, 16, and 32 processors. The experiment was performed in exclusive mode (i.e., with no other applications sharing the cluster) - the only unbalancing factor was the dynamic generation of tasks. The demand-driven strategy (lb2) led to the best results, independently of the number of processors. The poor behavior of strategies based on task migration (lb3 to 7) seems to be natural for small granularity applications with a large number of dynamically generated tasks. To illustrate this point, we notice that the load balancing was activated 548 times along the distributed strategy (lb3) using four processors. Also, the very bad behavior of the partition-based strategy (lb6) is due to the fact that different processor groups receive initial subsets of tasks with different computational demands, but are not able to redistribute them to other groups.

Table 1: Application #1 using 4, 8, 16, and 32 processors.

Proc.	lb1	lb2	lb3	lb4	lb5	lb6	lb7R	lb7H
4	248	114	126	132	115	126	117	117
8	162	49	82	82	74	122	91	81
16	103	23	49	51	56	88	68	58
32	52	13	32	32	39	53	49	36

Application #2 computes the product of two integer valued square matrices of dimension 2000. The basic parallel multiplication algorithm is used. The second matrix is replicated on all processors. Each task is defined by a row in the first matrix and corresponds to computing one of the 2000 rows of the resulting matrix. In this case, all tasks present roughly the same computational demand, and the only unbalancing factor is the external load.

Table 2 presents execution times for application #2 with different load balancing strategies, using 4, 8, 16, and 32 processors. External load was simulated by load processes which continuously computed arithmetic expressions. In each group of four processors, a first processor executed no load process, the second executed one process, the third executed two processes, and the fourth, three processes. The static case (lb1) reflects the external load - with four processors, each of them executing 500 tasks, execution times at each processor were 170, 412, 618, and 762 seconds.

Table 2: Application #2 using 4, 8, 16, and 32 processors with external load.

Proc.	lb1	lb2	lb3	lb4	lb5	lb6	lb7R	lb7H	lb8	lb9
4	762	496	391	383	379	391	386	386	374	374
8	410	261	247	252	244	252	245	260	241	248
16	265	168	189	190	196	177	191	195	187	171
32	182	128	171	163	175	145	153	166	166	140

With four and eight processors, the algorithms based on task migration (lb3 to 7) presented comparable results, and were more appropriate than the demand-driven algorithm (lb2). This possibly occurs due to the fact that, with few processors, the communication overhead imposed by the exchange of load indexes is low. On the other hand, in the demand-driven strategy, one processor is dedicated to task distribution and does not contribute to the computation itself. With few processors, this represents a heavy loss in computing power.

As the number of processors grows, the demand-driven strategy again achieves the best results. However, it is interesting to note the relatively good performance of the partition-based strategy (lb6). In this experiment, the same load unbalance was generated inside each group. In this setting, a group strategy can attain the same balancing results as a global one and implies less communication overhead. The comparison of strategies 3 and 6 thus reflects the communication overhead due to a totally distributed computation.

We modified algorithms 3 and 6 to take the external load into account, originating strategies 8 and 9, respectively. The external load index used is the number of tasks executed per unit of time, which reflects the computational capacity of each processor. The gain in performance obtained with the new algorithms is still very small. However, we believe this gain can be higher if we eliminate the observed "ping–pong" effect. When a processor is handling little external load, there is a tendency for too many processors to send it their load, causing the previously underloaded processor to become a bottleneck in the system, and eventually to have to send back part of the load it received.

6 Final Remarks

We presented a tool for supporting the development of SPMD applications and the evaluation of different load balancing estrategies. SAMBA's implementation has shown that it is possible to integrate different load balancing strategies to the single code of an SPMD application. Once the user has written the set of routines described in section 3, several different versions of his SPMD application can be generated with no further programming effort.

The analyses reported in section 5 show how the tool can help in identifying the appropriate strategies for specific applications and environments. The computational results also show significant reduction in elapsed times due to the use of appropriate load balancing algorithms.

References

1. T. G. Mattson, "Scientific computation", *Parallel and Distributed Computing Handbook* (A. Y. Zomaya, editor), 981–1002, McGraw-Hill, 1996.
2. M. A. Franklin and V. Govindan, "A general matrix iterative model for dynamic load balancing", *Parallel Computing* 22 (1996), 969–989.
3. S. Lifschitz, A. Plastino, and C. C. Ribeiro, "Exploring load balancing in parallel processing of recursive queries", *Proceedings of the III EUROPAR*, LNCS 1300, 1997, 1125–1129.
4. M. A. Willebeek-LeMair and A. P. Reeves, "Strategies for dynamic load balancing on highly parallel computers", *IEEE Trans. on Parallel and Dist. Systems* 4 (1993), 979–993.
5. M. J. Zaki, W. Li, and S. Parthasarathy, "Customized dynamic load balancing for a network of workstations", *Journal of Parallel and Distributed Computing* 43 (1997), 156–162.
6. T. Decker, "Virtual Data Space – a universal load balancing scheme", *Proceedings of the IRREGULAR IV*, LNCS 1253, 1997, 159–166.
7. C. Fonlupt , P. Marquet, and J. Dekeyser, "Data-parallel load balancing strategies", *Parallel Computing* 24 (1998), 1665–1684.
8. A. Plastino, C.C. Ribeiro, and N. Rodriguez "Uma taxonomia de algoritmos de balanceamento de carga para aplicações SPMD", Technical Report PUC-RioInf.MCC49/98, Department of Computer Science, Catholic University of Rio de Janeiro, Brazil, 1998.
9. E. Dijkstra, W. Seijen, and A. Gasteren, "Derivation of a termination detection algorithm for a distributed computation", *Information Processing Letters* 16 (1983), 217–219.
10. Message Passing Interface Forum, "MPI: A message passing interface", *Proc. Supercomputing'93*, 878–883, IEEE Computer Society, 1993.

EFFECTIVE PERFORMANCE PROBLEM DETECTION OF MPI PROGRAMS ON MPP SYSTEMS: FROM THE GLOBAL VIEW TO THE DETAILS

ROLF RABENSEIFNER

High-Performance Computing-Center Stuttgart (HLRS),[*]
University of Stuttgart, D-10550 Stuttgart, Germany
www.hlrs.de/people/rabenseifner, rabenseifner@hlrs.de

PETER GOTTSCHLING, WOLFGANG E. NAGEL AND STEPHAN SEIDL

Center for High Performance Computing (ZHR),
Dresden University of Technology, D-01062 Dresden, Germany
www.tu-dresden.de/zhr, [gottschling\nagel\seidl]@zhr.tu-dresden.de

This paper presents an automatic counter instrumentation and profiling module added to the MPI library on Cray T3E systems. A detailed summary of the hardware performance counters and the MPI calls of any MPI production program is gathered during execution and written on a special **syslog** file. The user can get the same information on a different file. Statistical summaries are computed weekly and monthly. The paper describes experiences with this library on the Cray T3E systems at HLRS Stuttgart and TU Dresden. It focuses on the scalability aspects of the new interface: How to obtain the right amount of performance data to the right person in time, and how to draw conclusions for the further optimization process, e.g. with the trace-based profiling tool Vampir.

1   Counter-Based Profiling

Today, job accounting on MPP hardware platforms does not provide enough information about the computational efficiency nor about the efficiency of message passing (MPI) usage for both, users and computing centers. There is no information available on bandwidth and latency or integer and floating point operation rates obtained in real application runs. Therefore, users and hotline centers have no reliable information base for technical and political decisions with respect to programming and optimization investment. For a first glance at an application, the existing trace-based profiling tools are too complicated. They can be used in small test jobs only, but not in long-running production jobs.

To solve this problem, the High-Performance Computing-Center (HLRS) at the University of Stuttgart has combined the method of counter-based pro-

---

[*]Part of the work was done while the author was a visiting research associate at ZHR, Jan.-Apr. 1999.

filing with the techniques of writing system log-files. For each MPI routine, the number of calls, the time spent in the routine and the number of transferred bytes are written at the end of each parallel job to a syslog file at the computing center and, optionally, to a user file. The integration of the PCL library[1] allows the automatic instrumentation with the microprocessor's hardware performance counters (e.g. floating point instructions) to receive information about the computational efficiency of each program.[10]

An analysis tool reads the syslog file and, on a weekly basis, sends a summary to each user about his jobs and writes a web-based summary for the computing center. The results of the first half-year have shown the MPI usage on the CRAY T3E 900-512 at the HLRS.[9]

The profiling was implemented, tested and installed as default library on the T3E systems at HLRS Stuttgart and TU Dresden, and it is now ported to the Origin2000 at TU Dresden. The counter-based profiling only has a minimal overhead. The memory requirements on a T3E-900 are 200 kBytes. The counting requires $0.3 - 0.5\,\mu$sec per MPI call and writing the syslog file requires about 0.1 sec for each job. The overhead was 0.03 % of the application CPU time in the first half-year average in Stuttgart. Including the hardware counters, the overhead is about 300 kBytes memory, $2\,\mu$sec per call and about 0.1 - 0.2 % (expected) in all.

2 Scalable User-Interface

The user interface is designed so that the cost-benefit ratio is scalable for the user. This means that one is able to receive the most important information about an MPI application with an effort that is nearly zero, and if more information is wanted, there are several levels of support:

Level 1: Reading the first lines of an e-mail yields the MPI percentage, the instruction rate of all completed hardware instructions, the floating point instruction rate, and the level 2 cache miss rate of the jobs in the last week, if they have used the MPI default library.

Level 2: Reading the details of the e-mail yields for each MPI routine a summary of the calling count, execution time, and transferred bytes. Additionally, an estimate of the transfer and synchronization parts of the execution time is given. For each hardware performance counter, the total number of events and the rates are printed for the application part and for all MPI routines together.

Levels 1 and 2 could be implemented because the instrumentation is added to the default MPI library and writes the counters via the syslogd daemon to a syslog file.

Level 3: The user has to set a special environment variable in the MPI job before calling mpirun. As a consequence, the user gets all the information mentioned above (except the synchronization part estimate) for each parallel application run that uses the environment variable. For the future it is planned to implement a Web interface for the database created upon the syslog information. Then the user can view each job without setting the environment variable, and for levels 1-3 the user does not need to modify anything in the programs or job commands.

Level 4: The application can call MPI_Pcontrol to print out the state of the counters at any location inside the application. This gives all the information not only at the end of the application run, but also at any time and on each individual process (and not only the average of all processes).

Level 5: Setting one more environment variable, the user can choose other hardware performance counters, e.g. the integer instruction rate, level 1 data cache hits, and misses.

The levels 1 to 5 provide the information base to decide whether other tools should be used. Therefore, the next level is not part of the automatic MPI profiling, but part of the scalability strategy:

Level 6: Using trace based tools, e.g. Vampir, the user gets detailed insight into the computation and communication structure of the application. Using the PCL library directly or using other performance visualization tools can give a detailed insight into the computation efficiency and any problems of the application. PAT and Apprentice can also be used to locate and analyze the computational kernel of the application.

One of the key issues for this design is that on average the instrumentation overhead is in the range of a thousandth of the CPU time consumed by the applications. The automatic MPI profiling is a method to get enough information to decide whether the application is running as expected, one more chance to detect major bottlenecks and a basis to decide whether trace based tools or direct hardware counter instrumentation should be applied.

3 Comparing Counter-Based and Trace-Based Methods

The major differences between the counter and trace-based profiling can be seen by comparing the following characteristics: *Automatic counter-based MPI profiling* analyzes the whole MPI application. The analysis of long-running production jobs is not a problem. The extent of instrumentation must be restricted in time and memory to about a thousandth of the application because the tool is used for all MPI application runs. Only a small amount of data is written for each application run on the system's disk. The computing center and the users can get an overview about all jobs parallelized with MPI.

Trace-based profiling can normally be used to analyze short test jobs only. The instrumentation overhead can vary within the range of 5 to 10 percent because the user decides whether or not the tool is applied. Each trace can produce a large amount of data, written on the user's disk. The computing center does not get any information and long running parallel jobs can not be viewed, although these jobs are more important because they consume most of the computing resources.

4 Optimizing User Applications

In the case that the reported application performance does not correspond to the user's expectation, the per-job counter-based profiling output should also be examined. From the user's point of view, typical results of counter-based profiling are: 1) The application does or does not spend a lot of time in MPI routines. 2) The application might not seem to be load-balanced since a lot of time is spent inside of MPI receives, barriers or collective operations. 3) The overall and the user part MFLOP rates are or are not as expected.

To localize such effects of MPI routines, or to figure out other critical parts, the application can be instrumented to be analyzed by means of Vampir, for example. For instrumenting codes, there are different options, depending on the particular platform. On Fujitsu, Hitachi, and NEC systems, it is sufficient to switch on an appropriate compiler flag. On Cray T3E, the software tool PAT can do this job. In general, the Vampir visualization and trace system from Pallas GmbH will help or, in order to solve special tracing problems, one could contact the TU Dresden for an alternative binary trace library.

An example: At our center, the relatively low floating-point rate associated with a user who is investigating linear solvers based on a new algebraic cascadic conjugate gradient method (ACCG) has induced more detailed studies. Besides the floating-point rate, the level-1-analysis showed that the ratio of the total weekly MPI-time to the corresponding application time was 0.328. With respect to a multigrid-like application where a significant part of the computing time is spent on small linear equations, this result seems to be acceptable.

The examination on level 2 displayed that most of the 9640 MPI-seconds were consumed by three routines: MPI_Bcast with 5120 s, MPI_Alltoallv with 1410 s and MPI_Allreduce with 1270 s. For all three functions, the number of calls and transferred bytes did not explain this time consumption. Instead, it

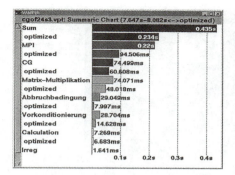 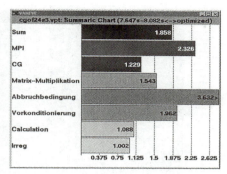

(a) Comparison of the two versions of the solver (without initialization)

(b) Quotient: Original/optimized time

Figure 1. Parts of the ACCG solver

might be an indicator for a load-imbalance.

On level 3, we considered the per-job statistic of a test case which solves a linear equation with 253,000 unknowns on 24 processors. The test case computes the stationary solution of a ground-water flow simulation instead of the in-stationary solution. In the investigated job, the same three MPI-functions took a significant part of the computing time: MPI_Bcast 6.323 s, MPI_Allreduce 163 ms and MPI_Alltoallv 142 ms. The trace-based analysis showed that the time spent on MPI_Bcast originates in reading the input files on one processor. In this phase of the program, all other processors are waiting at MPI_Bcast. This fact explains the large idle times of this function in the weekly statistic.

Since the discretization of the differential equations and therefore, the construction of linear equations is not part of our research area, we are solely interested in the run-time behavior of the linear solver (i.e. the ACCG solver). With MPI_Pcontrol (level 4), we got the same counters as in the per-job statistic, but now at the beginning and the end of the linear solver. The differences of the corresponding counters in the two snapshots indicated that only 0.435 s of the 8 seconds are spent in the solver. Moreover, we saw that MPI_Bcast only took 0.2 ms during the computation of the solver. Unfortunately, most of the time of MPI_Allreduce (159 ms) falls in this phase. Since MPI_Alltoallv required only 60 ms in the solver it seemed most promising to optimize the allreduce computation.

Replacing the call of MPI_Allreduce with a function using a similar shmem-routine, the allreduce computing time could be reduced from 159 ms to 36 ms. For a better comparison, we grouped the new function to MPI in

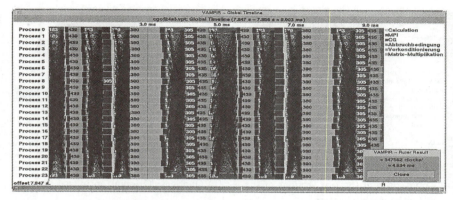

Figure 2. Two iterations of the conjugate-gradient solver (original implementation)

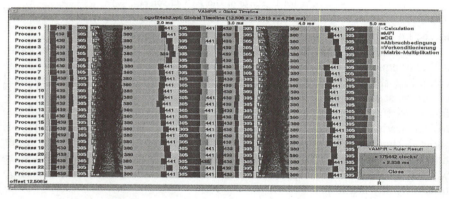

Figure 3. Two equivalent iterations in the optimized implementation

Figure 1. Together with several numerical optimizations – like storing the inverse of the diagonal of the matrix to replace divide operations by multiplications – the computing time of the linear solver could be reduced from 0.435 s to 0.234 s. Figure 2 and 3 display the timeline diagrams of two iterations on the second finest grid of the cascadic solver. On the fine grid, mainly the numerical part of the iteration is significant whereas the communication plays the most important roll on the coarser grids of the cascadic algorithm. On all grids, the average of the communication part was 40 % of the computing time in the optimized implementation.

The optimization of the communication was mainly based on the counter profiling. Additional tools – here trace-based profiling with Vampir – helped to optimize the numerical part.

5 User Feedback

The first feedback we received from our users by calling our MPI hotline to get help in optimizing their MPI programs after they noticed in the profiling e-mail that their MPI percentage was worse than expected. For a detailed feedback from our users we made a survey with 20 questions; finally, we received results from 28 of our users.[11] Major results of the survey are:

- The automatic profiling was regarded as *useful* in most answers.
- In the past, automatic profiling was only occasionally used for optimization because it came too late for most users, i.e. the application development was already completed and the programs are used in production.
- 75 % of those interviewed believe that the counter profiling can help to improve their applications in the future.
- Our weekly mail should be improved, too.
- We should provide the users with reference values. This would simplify the decision as to whether one should focus on further optimization.
- The analysis of the instruction rates of the applications' numerics and the MPI timings of the applications' communication are similarly important for the users.

For this survey, we have chosen customers who had computed at least four parallel jobs between February and April '99 and who already had received weekly mails from the automatic counter profiling system. The survey was taken by phone. Out of the 28 customers, 26 users are familiar with the automatic profiling. Out of these 26 users, 9 users always read the weekly mail, 9 users only sometimes, and 7 users rarely. Additional answers have shown that this depends on whether the users are testing their applications or, whether they have production jobs. This means that the level 1 and 2 of the profiling system is well accepted, which is also expressed by the average rank of 1.9 chosen by the 26 customers in the range of 1=*very useful* to 6=*not useful*. The third level was used by 8 users. The fourth level was used by one person. The fifth level never was used (perhaps because of the default that shows the total instruction rate and the floating point instruction rate). But the answers to the question whether instruction rates or MPI timings are more important were: *MPI timings are more important* (37 %), *both equal important* (53 %) and *instruction rates are more important* (10 %). The counter profiling is used to get information about the behavior of the users' programs (18 answers) and for optimizing the programs (11 answers). 4 users said that the profiling had really helped to improve their programs, 2 persons indicated that the MPI profiling was available too late, i.e. after they had finished the development. For the future, 21 users believe that the profiling will or may help to improve their programs. Additional optimization and analyses tools were used by

11 customers, i.e. only about 42 % have stepped to level 6. But only one user said that the MPI profiling had helped for the decision to use additional tools and 4 users told us that the profiling was available too late so that it could not help make this decision. On our system, mainly Vampir and Apprentice are used as additional optimization tools.

The last questions examined aspects of the interaction of the computing center with its customers. We also asked whether our customers – they all have publicly funded computing time on our systems – feel disturbed because the computing center also might look at the profiling information. Nobody was upset about this. Should the computing center use the overview and select optimal applications to learn about the optimization strategies used by the developers? 19 users would appreciate this, 5 don't care and 2 would be bothered. Should the computing center use the profiling information to contact the user with applications that could be inefficient? To our surprise, 22 users would like this, 2 don't care and 2 would be bothered.

Major wishes mentioned by the users are: To obtain reference values for the instruction rates, e.g. the minimum, maximum and average achieved by the other users; the layout of the weekly mail should be improved and should support html-based and ASCII-based mail readers; and it would be nice if the per-job information could be acquired from a database with a web interface.

6 Related and Future Work

Riek et al.[12] give a comprehensive overview about monitoring and profiling systems. The hardware counters are accessed by using the PCL library.[1] Trace-based systems are described in the references[2,3,7,8]. HP[4] has developed a local, user callable MPI counter profiling. Li and Zhang[5] combine counter profiling and a virtual clock approach to minimize the intrusiveness of the instrumentation. Further papers about the counter-based MPI profiling focus on the technical principles and statistical results of half a year of profiling nearly all MPI applications running on a CRAY T3E 900-512 (instrumented without the hardware counters)[9] and on the integration of the hardware counters and the implementation on different MPI library interfaces.[10] The scalability of the user interface has an analogy in the level-structured approach to learning, described in Shneiderman's[13] Principle 1.

In the future we plan to generate global half-year statistics that include hardware counters. Also, it is planned to implement a user interface, which allows to read the data on the syslog file directly via a web interface. This reduces costs in level 3 to few clicks in the web browser. Based on the technology of TOPAS[6], the hardware counter profiling can be extended from the MPI applications to *all* applications.

Acknowledgments

We gratefully acknowledge the support of the PCL library from R. Berrendorf
and H. Ziegler which we have integrated into the new profiling interface. The
authors especially would like to thank Roland Rühle from HLRS for placing
major resources at the project's disposal.

References

1. R. Berrendorf and H. Ziegler, *PCL – The Performance Counter Library: A Common Interface to Access Hardware Performance Counters on Microprocessors*, internal report FZJ-ZAM-IB-9816, Forschungszentrum Jülich, Oct. 1998.
   www.fz-juelich.de/zam/docs/autoren98/berrendorf3.html
2. M. T. Heath, *Recent Developments and Case Studies in Performance Visualization using ParaGraph*, Proceedings of the Workshop Performance Measurement and Visualization of Parallel Systems, G. Haring and G. Kotsis (ed.), Moravany, Czechoslovakia, Oct. 1992, pp 175–200.
3. V. Herrarte and E. Lusk, *Studying Parallel Program Behavior with Upshot*, Argonne National Laboratory, technical report ANL-91/15, Aug. 1991
4. *HP MPI User's Guide*, 4.1 Using counter instrumentation, HP, B6011-90001, Third Ed., June 1998.
5. K-C. Li and K. Zhang, *Supporting Scalable Performance Monitoring and Analysis of Parallel Programs*, The Journal of Supercomputing, 13, pp 5–31, 1999.
6. B. Mohr, *TOPAS – Automatic Performance Statistics Collection on the CRAY T3E*, Proceedings of the 5th European SGI/Cray MPP Workshop, Sept. 9–10, 1999. www.cineca.it/mpp-workshop/abstract/bmohr.htm and
   www.fz-juelich.de/zam/docs/autoren99/mohr.html
7. W.E. Nagel et al., *VAMPIR: Visualization and Analysis of MPI Resources*, Supercomputer 63, Volume XII, Number 1, Jan. 1996, pp 69–80, and technical report KFA-ZAM-IB-9528, www.fz-juelich.de/zam/docs/printable/ib/ib-95/ib-9528.ps
8. W.E. Nagel and A. Arnold, *Performance Visualization of Parallel Programs: The PARvis Environment*, technical report, Forschungszentrum Jülich, 1995.
   www.fz-juelich.de/zam/PT/ReDec/SoftTools/PARtools/PARvis.html
9. R. Rabenseifner, *Automatic MPI Counter Profiling of All Users: First Results on a CRAY T3E 900-512*, Proceedings of the Message Passing Interface Developer's and User's Conference 1999 (MPIDC'99), Atlanta, USA, March 1999, pp 77–85.
   www.hlrs.de/people/rabenseifner/publ/publications.html#MPIDC99
10. R. Rabenseifner, *Automatic Profiling of MPI Applications with Hardware Performance Counters*, in J. Dongarra et al. (eds.), Recent Advances in Parallel Virtual Machine and Message Passing Interface, Proceedings of the 6th PVM/MPI European Users' Group Meeting, EuroPVM/MPI'99, Barcelona, Spain, Sept. 26–29, 1999, LNCS 1697, pp 35–42. www.hlrs.de/people/rabenseifner/publ/publications.html
11. R. Rabenseifner, *Umfrage zum automatischen MPI Counter Profiling auf der T3E*, only online: www.hlrs.de/mpi/umfrage_results.html
12. M. van Riek, B. Tourancheau and X.-F. Vigouroux, *Monitoring of Distributed Memory Multicomputer Programs*, University of Tennessee, technical report CS-93-204, and Center for Research on Parallel Computation, Rice University, Houston Texas, technical report CRPC-TR93441, 1993. http://www.netlib.org/tennessee/ut-cs-93-204.ps and ftp://softlib.rice.edu/pub/CRPC-TRs/reports/CRPC-TR93441.ps.gz
13. B. Shneiderman, *Designing the User Interface: Strategies for Effective Human-Computer-Interaction*, 3rd ed., Addison-Wesley, March 1998.

EXECUTION REPLAY FOR AN MPI-BASED MULTI-THREADED RUNTIME SYSTEM

M. RONSSE AND K. DE BOSSCHERE

RUG-ELIS, St.-Pietersnieuwstraat 41, B9000 Gent, Belgium

J. CHASSIN DE KERGOMMEAUX

LMC-IMAG, B.P 53, F38041 Grenoble Cedex 9, France

In this paper we present an execution replay system for Athapascan, an MPI-based multi-threaded runtime system. The main challenge of this work was to deal with nondeterministic features of MPI - promiscuous communications and varying number of test functions - without compromising the efficiency of an existing solution for execution replay of shared memory thread based programs. Novel solutions were designed and implemented in an efficient execution replay system for Athapascan programs.

1 Introduction

This paper describes an execution replay system for Athapascan [1], a runtime system for parallel systems composed of shared memory multiprocessor nodes connected by a network. Athapascan exploits both inter node and inner node parallelism. The nodes communicate using a communication library such as MPI and each node consists of different POSIX threads communicating through shared memory.

Athapascan is built on top of a POSIX thread library and an MPI communication library (Figure 1). The thread library offers mutexes and condition variables for synchronization purposes, while the communication library takes care of message passing. The Athapascan kernel extends the POSIX & MPI layer in two ways: (i) semaphore functions are added and (ii) mutually exclusive versions of the MPI functions are provided. The latter is necessary as most MPI implementations are not thread-safe (the functions are non-reentrant) and most thread-safe MPI implementations are not thread-aware: each time a thread calls a blocking communication primitive, it also blocks the other threads of the same node (Unix process). Therefore Athapascan uses a daemon thread that transforms all communications into non blocking communications and that regularly checks for incoming messages.

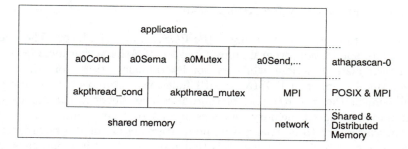

Figure 1. Athapascan is built using a layered approach, extending the functionality offered by POSIX threads and MPI messages.

2 Cyclic Debugging

Developing applications for such a complex system is difficult and error prone but it is possible to alleviate the debugging task by providing adequate debugging support. The basic support that comes to mind is cyclic debugging (watchpoints, breakpoints, stepping through the application, ...). Unfortunately, cyclic debugging assumes that a program execution can be faithfully re-executed any number of times, which is not the case for the class of non-deterministic parallel and distributed programs we envision. Even if two executions produce the same output, they are not guaranteed to have the same internal program flow which is essential if one wants to debug the application.

Known sources of nondeterminism are: certain system calls (such as random() and date(), ...), signals, unsynchronized accesses to shared memory (for parallel programs) and message exchanges (for distributed programs). There exists effective and fairly efficient ways to remove the sources of nondeterminism that are not caused by the parallel nature of the program (e.g., nondeterministic input can easily be recorded). This paper will only address nondeterminism caused by the parallel and distributed execution, i.e., race conditions between threads and processes. The standard technique to guarantee reproducibility of an execution is to implement an execution replay system [2]. Such a system makes a program execution reproducible by tracing a first execution (*record phase*) and by using the traced information to enforce equivalent re-executions (*replay phase*). The main challenge is to maximally limit the overhead during the record phase to limit as much as possible the probe effect.

3 Execution Replay for Athapascan

The abstraction level of recording is the POSIX and MPI layer. The reason is that the application programming interface of Athapascan includes many nondeterministic functions while its nondeterminism arises from the use of a very small number of POSIX or MPI functions. Moreover, this allows us to implement the record/replay method as a layer between the Athapascan layer and the shared memory and message passing layer and it allows the Athapascan layer[a] to be changed without worrying about the record/replay layer. The drawback of this choice is that more low-level function calls have to be considered than if recording were performed at the Athapascan level of abstraction. However, the amount of tracing could remain very low by combining the most efficient recording techniques for shared memory with novel solutions designed for the combination of nonblocking communication and test functions.

3.1 Shared memory

Replaying shared memory programs is possible by logging the order of the memory operations, and by imposing the same ordering during replay. It is obvious that this is very intrusive. Therefore, we only log the ordering of a subset of all memory operations: the synchronization operations. Forcing the same order during replay will guarantee a correct re-execution, provided the program contains no data races. The latter requirement can be tested using data race detection tools. These tools are very intrusive, but they can be used during replay as replay guarantees a correct execution up to the first data race [3].

The replay system used for Athapascan is based on ROLT (Reconstruction of Lamport Timestamps) [4] an execution replay system that only traces the partial order of synchronization operations by attaching a scalar logical timestamp to these operations. To get a faithful replay, it is sufficient to stall each synchronization operation until all synchronization operations with a smaller timestamp have been executed.

3.2 Message passing

As Athapascan uses LAM[5], an MPI implementation that is not thread-safe, for sending and receiving messages, Athapascan grabs a mutex while executing an MPI function. This causes these functions to be executed in a serialized

---

[a]Still in development.

way. Since the order of the mutex operations is traced during the record phase, the same serial ordering will be imposed during the replay phase. However, this is not sufficient for a deterministic replay: promiscuous receive operations –operations that do not specify the sender– and nonblocking communication operations require special attention.

Sending Messages MPI uses FIFO channels for its communication. This means that if a single thread sends two messages to a node, the messages will always be received in the same order. Even if the two messages are sent by two different threads on the same node, they will still arrive in the same order during replay because the MPI send operations are serialized per node by the Athapascan kernel. Hence, since messages are assumed to be produced deterministically, receive operations in a private point-to-point communication that specify the sender are also deterministic.

There is however a problem with messages sent by different nodes to a single node. In that case, the events are not serialized by the MPI library, and hence the order of events is not recorded, and might be replayed incorrectly. Fortunately, this problem can be solved at the receiver side.

Receiving Messages On the receiving side, events are also serialized. This time however, they are not serialized by the mutex guarding the MPI functions, but by the mutex of the Athapascan kernel daemon thread. As such, the order of the receive operations is automatically recorded and can be replayed. However, problems arise if the receive operation is promiscuous. A receive operation is promiscuous if a message can be received from any possible source (e.g. `MPI_Recv(...,MPI_ANY_SOURCE,...)`). These operations are nondeterministic which means that the order in which communication events are taking place can differ between two executions, leading to different execution paths (see Figure 2). In a sense, they play the role of 'racing' memory operations in nondeterministic programs on multiprocessors.

These messages should be received by replayed executions in the same order as during the recorded ones. We solved this problem by additionally recording the sender of a message for a promiscuous receive and by replacing a promiscuous receive by a regular receive operation (from the sending node) during replay.

Nonblocking operations A last source of nondeterminism is introduced by the nonblocking receive and send functions. This class of functions has been overlooked in previous papers on record/replay for message passing libraries [6]. Nonblocking test operations are however intensively used

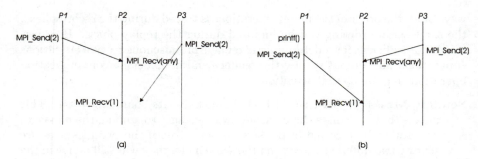

Figure 2. The result of a promiscuous receive operation can depend on small timing variations, e.g. caused by adding a `printf()` statement

in message passing programs, e.g., to maximally overlap communication
with computation: a nonblocking receive operation returns a request object as soon as the communication is initiated, without waiting for its
completion. The request objects can be used to check the completion
of the nonblocking operations by means of test operations, which can in
turn be blocking (*Wait*), or nonblocking (*Test*).

By the very fact that the test operations are nonblocking, they can be
used in polling loops. The actual number of calls will depend on timing
variations of parallel program, and is thus nondeterministic. Although
many programs will not base their operations on the number of failed
tests, some could do so (e.g., to implement some kind of time-out), and
hence cannot be correctly replayed when not recorded (see Figure 3).

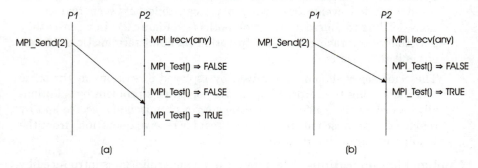

Figure 3. The number of nonblocking test operations can depend on small timing variations.

For the nonblocking test operations, ordering driven replay implies that the setting of the condition that is tested for (e.g., the arrival of a message), must be postponed until the required number of test operations is carried out. Only then, the operation that sets the condition can be allowed to resume. Replaying these test functions is no problem for a pure ordering driven replay system, where the order of *all* message operations is logged.

This approach has however a serious drawback. Nonblocking test operations are typically used in polling loops where they can in theory run for a very long time. Every iteration of the polling loop will add a bit of information to the trace file, although the polling loop is actually used to wait on a particular event. The fact that the trace file grows while the process is just waiting is not acceptable. It turns out that contents driven replay is actually more efficient for test functions than ordering driven replay. This is because a test function normally reports a series of failures, followed by a success unless the program finished before the test succeeds, when the request is cancelled (MPI_Cancel) or when the application stops polling and uses an MPI_Wait to wait for the completion of the request. Since all test functions (for one request) are identical we can count them and log this single number (n). This greatly reduces the amount of information that has to be stored in the log files. It also has a positive effect on the replay speed: since all these test operations are now collapsed into one single execution of the operations, their replay can be many times faster than in the original execution. During this phase, the first $n - 1$ tests simply return FALSE and the last test returns TRUE and forces an MPI_Wait. For an unsuccessful series of test functions, we log a number that is bigger than the number of executed test functions. This will force all test functions to fail during the replay phase. A similar solution was adopted to record the number of unsuccessful calls to MPI_IProbe. Note that this approach is possible because the test functions have no side-effects: replaying less test functions than during the original execution introduces no problems.

Special care needs to be taken so that the number of unsuccessful tests is read from the traces as soon as the first MPI_Test of a series is performed. Similarly, in case of a nonblocking promiscuous receive operation MPI_IRecv, followed by a series of tests, the identification of the sender node needs to be read from the traces at the time the receive operation is called. These two problems were addressed by assigning request numbers to the first MPI_Test of a series as well as to each promiscuous MPI_IRecv call. These request numbers are stored in the trace files with the number of unsuccessful tests (resp. sender node identification) and the trace files are sorted before the first replayed execution. This approach dramatically reduces the trace size of test operations, especially in applications that use the nonblocking operations intensively.

4 Evaluation

An execution system has now completely been implemented in Athapascan and has already proven helpful in locating bugs in Athapascan itself. The execution replay system was tested on several Athapascan-0 programs featuring all possible cases of nondeterminism of the programming model. It was also tested on the available programming examples of the Athapascan-0 distribution, and it was used to debug the Athapascan system itself.

Preliminary test results show that the time overhead during both the record and replay executions remain acceptable while the sizes of the trace files are fairly small. The table below shows execution times (wall time in seconds) for three test programs, measured with a confidence range of 95 %. Mandelbrot computes a Mandelbrot set in parallel; queens(12) computes all solutions to a size 12 queens problem while scalprod computes the scalar product of two vectors of 100,000 floating point numbers each. The experiments were performed on two PCs running the Linux operating system and connected by a 100 Mbps Ethernet connection.

| program | execution time (s) | | | trace |
name	normal	record	replay	size (b)
mandelbrot	1.858±0.003	1.914±0.037	1.864±0.002	3912
queens(12)	6.70 ±0.15	6.58 ±0.05	6.86 ±0.17	1710
scalprod	4.38 ±0.04	4.44 ±0.07	4.66 ±0.03	874

5 Related work

One of the first implementations of a replay mechanism for MPI was proposed in [7]. The tool uses a technique that is comparable to ours in order to deal with nonblocking operations, and uses the technique of Netzer and Miller to detect racing messages [8]. As such, a vector clock is attached to each message. The authors don't discuss the implications of this approach: what if messages become too big? The techniques used in [6] is also comparable to ours, but test functions are not dealt with. As such the number of test operations can vary between different replayed executions.

6 Conclusion

We have implemented execution replay for Athapascan, a runtime system using messages and shared memory for communication. We solved the problem of reconstructing the order of messages received from different (unsynchronized) nodes, and of efficiently recording and replaying nonblocking operations. We solved the first problem by not only recording the order of receive operations, but also the identification of the sending node per successful receive. We solved the latter problem by not recording individual nonblocking operations, but by counting the number of failed tests.

References

1. J. Briat, I. Ginzburg, M. Pasin, and B. Plateau. Athapascan runtime: Efficiency for irregular problems. In *Proceedings of the EuroPar'97 Conference*, pages 590–599, Passau, Germany, August 1997. Springer Verlag.
2. Thomas J. LeBlanc and John M. Mellor-Crummey. Debugging parallel programs with Instant Replay. *IEEE Transactions on Computers*, C-36(4):471–482, April 1987.
3. Michiel Ronsse and Koen De Bosschere. Recplay: A fully integrated practical record/replay system. *ACM Transactions on Computer Systems*, 17(2):133–152, May 1999.
4. Luk J. Levrouw and Koenraad M. Audenaert. An efficient record-replay mechanism for shared memory programs. In *Proceedings of the Euromicro Workshop on Parallel and Distributed Processing*, pages 169–176. IEEE Computer Society Press, January 1993.
5. Gregory D. Burns, Raja B. Daoud, and James R. Vaigl. LAM: An Open Cluster Environment for MPI. In *Supercomputing Symposium '94*. Toronto, Canada, June 1994.
6. Dieter Kranzlmueller and Jens Volkert. Debugging Point-To-Point Communication in MPI and PVM. In *Proceedings of EuroPVM/MPI 98*, volume 1497 of *LNCS*, pages 265–272, September 1998.
7. Christian Clemencon, Josef Fritscher, Michael Meehan, and Roland Ruhl. An Implementation of Race Detection and Deterministic Replay with MPI. Technical Report CSCS TR-94-01, Swiss Scientific Computing Center, January 1995.
8. R.H.B. Netzer and B.P.Miller. Optimal tracing and replay for debugging message-passing parallel programs. In *Supercomputing '92*, pages 502–511, November 1992.

A PRACTICAL METHODOLOGY
FOR DEFINING HISTOGRAMS
FOR PREDICTIONS AND SCHEDULING

Jennifer M. Schopf

Computer Science Department
Northwestern University
Email: jms@cs.nwu.edu

Current distributed parallel platforms can provide the resources required to execute a scientific application efficiently. However, when these platforms are shared by multiple users, the performance of the applications using the system may be impacted in dynamic and often unpredictable ways. Performance prediction becomes increasingly difficult due to this dynamic behavior. Even performance modeling techniques that are built specifically for distributed parallel systems often require parameterization by single (point) values. In shared environments, point values may provide an inaccurate representation of application behavior due to variations in resource performance.

This paper address the use of **practical histogram stochastic values** to parameterize performance models. Whereas a point value provides a single value representation of a quantity, a stochastic value provides a set of possible values to represent a range of likely behavior. In previous work we investigated using either normal distributions or an upper and lower bound to represent stochastic data. In this work we examine using a combination of those methods, namely histograms, to represent this data. We define a practical approach to using histograms in a production setting, and then give experimental results for a set of applications under different load conditions.

1 Motivation

Current distributed parallel platforms can provide the resources required to execute a scientific application efficiently. However, when these platforms are shared by multiple users, the performance of the applications using the system may be impacted in dynamic and often unpredictable ways. In order to obtain good performance, accurate performance prediction models for distributed parallel systems are needed. Most performance prediction models use parameters to describe system and application characteristics such as bandwidth, available CPU, message size, operation counts, etc. Model parameters are generally represented as a single likely value, which we refer to as a **point value**. For example, a point value for bandwidth might be 7 Mbits/second.

In some situations it may be more accurate to represent system and application characteristics as a *range* of possible values which we refer to such values as **stochastic values**. Whereas a point value gives a single value for a quantity, a stochastic value gives a set of values, possibly weighted by probabilities, to represent a range of likely behavior [1].

One way to represent stochastic values is by using **histograms**, which consist of a set of intervals with associated probabilities. In this paper we present a practical definition for histograms and demonstrate their use when predicting the performance of parallel distributed applications. This paper is organized as follows: Section 2 gives a brief overview of a modeling technique called structural modeling that can be parameterized by stochastic information. Section 3 details a practical definition for histograms. We describe the arithmetic needed to combine histograms in Section 4. Section 5 presents experimental results, and conclude in Section 6.

2   Overview of Structural Modeling

In order to predict an application's behavior on shared resources, we need both good models of the implementation and accurate information about the application and system with which to parameterize the models. In previous work [4] we developed a technique called **structural modeling** that uses the functional structure of the application to define a set of equations that reflect the time-dependent, dynamic mix of application tasks occurring during execution in a distributed parallel environment. A structural model consists of a top-level model, component models, and input parameters. A top-level model is a **performance equation** consisting of component models and composition operators. This allows us to abstract away details into the top level models and the parameters, but still accurately model the performance by showing the inter-relation of application and system factors through the component models and their parameterizations. We parameterize these models with stochastic values represented as histograms, which requires not only compute-efficient definitions of histograms but the needed arithmetic as well.

3   Defining Histograms

A stochastic value X may be specified using a one-dimensional histogram $H(X)$ as follows:

$$
\begin{aligned}
&H(X) = X_1, X_2, ... X_m; \quad with \\
&X_1 = [\underline{x_1}, \overline{x_1}] : p_1; \quad X_2 = [\underline{x_2}, \overline{x_2}] : p_2; \quad ...; \quad X_m = [\underline{x_m}, \overline{x_m}] : p_m \\
&where \sum_{i=1}^{m} p_i = 1
\end{aligned}
\tag{1}
$$

Each X_i entry in the definition of $H(X)$ is a pair consisting of an interval $[\underline{x_i}, \overline{x_i}]$, and an associated probability, p_i. One of the primary difficulties in defining histograms for dynamic system values is the determination of the appropriate intervals and probabilities for each histogram. A tradeoff exists between adding detail to the histogram description, which may be more accurate, but increases the computational complexity.

3.1 Previous Histogram Definitions and Related Work

There are a number of guidelines for defining histograms in the literature[5,3,6,7]. These "rules of thumb" concentrate on ways to *display* the information, as opposed to *using* the information as a summary technique in a practical setting, and do not provide a rigorous approach to choosing the number of intervals in a histogram. The collective experience of these researchers indicates that the "best" number of intervals to select is data-dependent, application-dependent and system-dependent, as well as dependent on how the histogram will be used and the granularity of measurement [8].

In the most closely related work to our research[9], histograms are defined initially based on the number of intervals provided by the user. The intervals are then split, using interval splitting [10,11] and a user supplied procedure to produce more sub-intervals for intervals with high probabilities and fewer for intervals of the same width but lower probability. This procedure is iterated for each defined histogram until splitting the interval further does not change the resulting predicted value. For their purposes, "Computational complexity is reasonable given that the number of parameters specified as histograms is not too high" [8]. However, this is not practical for our setting as we do not have a good splitting routine or the compute time to spend on an iterative method.

3.2 Practical Histograms

When defining histograms for use in making predictions to determine schedules at run-time, we need an approach that uses few, if any, user supplied parameters, is computationally efficient, and yet can adequately capture the behavior of the system being described. Furthermore, since the number of partial results for arithmetic functions over histograms can be quite large (as described in the next section) we need to limit this factor as well.

In our approach we used a two-pass method and limited the number of intervals in the histogram as well as the partial results. The first pass over the data was used to evaluate an upper bound and a lower bound, and to determine the size of the individual interval bins. The second pass was used to sort the data into the interval bins, and define the histogram for the stochastic data.

To select the number of intervals, we experimentally evaluated a range of intervals on a preliminary set of data. The primary source of varying behavior for this data was the available CPU values for the contended system. This data was supplied by the Network Weather Service (NWS) [12], an online tool that provides a time series of data for CPU availability, bandwidth and latency. We experimentally examined the accuracy of the histogram for a range of interval sizes and measured both the time to compute the prediction, which included the time to determine the histograms for the input parameters, and the accuracy of the prediction. For load characteristics commonly seen on networks of workstations [4], we determined that the predictive accuracy of more than five intervals did not increase significantly, although the computational expense grew quite large at that point. Therefore, in the following, we used five intervals divided evenly over the range unless stated otherwise.

3.3 Arithmetic over Histograms

Arithmetic over extended histograms involves combining all possible sets of probabilistic choices, which given the set D of stochastic values represented as histograms, each with k_D intervals, this results in $\Pi k_i * k_j$ for all $i, j \in D$. This value can be quite large, depending on how we define the number of intervals the histogram for a given stochastic value should have.

Given a set of k stochastic valued parameters, $D_1 \ldots D_k$, represented by histograms, assume that parameter D_i has m_i intervals $\{D_{i,1}, \ldots, D_{i,m_i}\}$ with $D_{i,j} = [\underline{d}_{i,j}, \overline{d}_{i,j}] : p_{i,j}$, i.e.:

$$D_i = \{D_{i,1}, D_{i,2}, \ldots, D_{i,m_i}\} with \ D_{i,j} = [\underline{d}_{i,j}, \overline{d}_{i,j}] : p_{i,j} \atop for \ i = 1 \ \ldots \ k \ and \ j = 1 \ \ldots \ m_i \qquad (2)$$

Since histograms are just sets of intervals, the interval arithmetic rules [13] can be used to combine them arithmetically. However, every interval has an associated probability. Hence, when calculating $F = D \odot E$ for some arithmetic function $\odot$ and histogram values D and E, it is necessary to calculate intermediate results for all possible combinations of intervals for each histogram.

4   Predictions Using Histograms

Given a structural model for an implementation parameterized by point value and stochastic value system and application characteristics, we can calculate a prediction for applications running in contentious environments. This section details our experimental results, and compares using a histogram to represent stochastic values to other methods.

We examined three applications on a distributed network of Sparc workstations located in the UCSD Parallel Computation Lab. The machines are connected with a mix of 10 Mbit (slow) and 100 Mbit (fast) ethernet. Both the CPU and the network were shared with other users. For each application we ran a series of experiments under different load conditions. To show the execution time trends, we show the results of the actual execution times with the upper bound and lower bound of the histogram predictions, and in Table 1 give the percentage of values which fell into each probability interval of the histogram predictions for that graph. In categorizing the multiple background workloads seen for each experiment set, we define a machine with a **low** variation in CPU availability as having a variation of 0.25 or less, on a scale from 0 to 1, a **medium** variation when the CPU availability varied more than 0.25, but less than 0.5, and a **high** variation when the CPU values varied over half the range.

Figure	Highest	2nd	3rd	4th	Lowest	Outside
SOR1 Figure 2	32	20	25	3	12	4
SOR2 Figure 3	18	23	21	13	14	11
GA 1 Figure 4	21	28	10	15	0	25
GA2 Figure 5	33	21	20	12	0	14
LU 1 Figure 6	55	26	8	7	4	0
LU2 Figure 7	42	38	0	12	8	0

Figure 1: Percentage of actual values falling in each probability interval for histogram predictions.

The three applications we used were an Successive Over-Relaxation (SOR), A genetic algorithm (GA), and an LU solver. The SOR code is a Regular SPMD code that solves Laplace's equation. Our implementation uses a red-black stencil approach where the calculation of each point in a grid at time t is dependent on the values in a stencil around it at time $t - 1$. The GA solved the Traveling Salesman Problem [14] using a global population and synchronizion between generations [15]. All of the Slaves operate on a global population (each member of the population is a solution to the TSP for a given set of cities) that is broadcast to them. Each Slave works in isolation to create a specified number of children, and to evaluate them. Once all the sets of children are received by the Master, some percentage are chosen to be the next generation, and the cycle repeats. The LU benchmark is a simulated CFD application that solves a block-lower-triangular/block-upper-triangular system of equations, and is one of the NAS Parallel Benchmarks [16]. This system of of equations is the result of an unfactored implicit finite-difference discretization of the Navier-Stokes equations in three dimensions. It has the feature that it tests the communication aspects of the system well by sending a relatively large number of 5 word messages.

Figures 2 and 3 stochastic value predictions and the actual time of the SOR application. These experiments show the benefits of stochastic predictions when the execution times exhibit an extreme variance, in this case variance production over 300%. Figures 4 and 5 show the stochastic value predictions and the actual time for the GA experiments. These experiments show how well

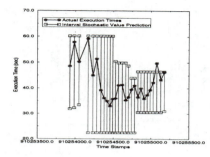

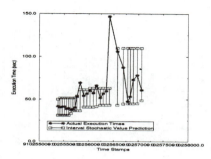

Figure 2: SOR1- stochastic value prediction for the SOR with 2 high, 1 medium and 1 low variability machines.

Figure 3: SOR2- stochastic value prediction for the SOR with 1 high, 2 medium and 1 low variability machines.

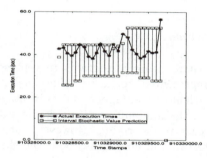

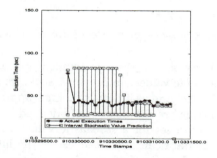

Figure 4: GA1- stochastic value prediction for the GA code with 3 high and 1 low variability machines.

Figure 5: GA2- stochastic value prediction for the GA code with 1 high and 3 low variability machines.

our methodology deals with non-deterministic applications. Figures 6 and 7 stochastic value predictions and the actual time for the LU experiments, and show that our approach can take into account communication time variability as well as CPU variability.

4.1 Summary of Experiments

In summary, for the majority of the experiments, we achieved predictions that captured the execution behaviors using histogram representations for the stochastic information. In addition, the shape and percentages of the histogram intervals were close to the actual execution values, and seemed to add valuable information to the prediction. Future work involves examining how these values affect scheduling decisions as well as adaptive methods for defining histograms.

670

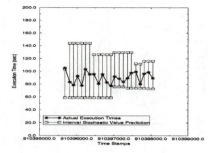
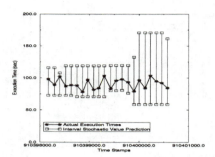

Figure 6: LU1- stochastic value prediction for LU with 2 high and 2 low variability machines.

Figure 7: LU2- stochastic value prediction for LU with 1 high, 1 medium and 2 low variability machines.

4.2 Comparison of Stochastic Representations

This work has given a detailed approach to using histograms to represent stochastic values. In previous work, we represented stochastic values as distributions[17] and as intervals[18]. Each approach has advantages and disadvantages. Intervals are the most easily defined since the minimum and maximum value in a data set for a stochastic value are easy to determine. However, outliers in the data can affect the size of the interval, and no details about the shape of the data are included in a simple range. Histograms allow the shape of a stochastic value to be elucidated, and lend themselves to the grouping of values, but even with out approach, can be difficult to accurately define in a practical setting. Distributions can be defined using well understood metrics for the data, but in order to be tractable arithmetically, we must assume that the associated data fits a well-defined and computationally efficient family of distributions, such as the family of normal distributions, which is not always a valid assumption.

5 Conclusions

This work has presented a practical way to represent stochastic data in a way that gives more information than using a standard interval, but is computationally simpler than using a full distribution. The results from three distributed applications show that this technique has a high accuracy, and can be of use in scheduling.

References

1. Howard M. Taylor and Samuel Karlin. *An Introduction to Stochastic Modeling.* Academic Press, 1993.
2. J. Luethi. Histogram-based characterization of workload parameters and its consequences on model analysis. In *Proceedings of the Workshop on Workload Characterization in High-Performance Computing Environments, jointly with MASCOTS'98*, 1998.
3. Leland Blank. *Statistical Procedures for engineering, management, and science.* McGraw-Hill Book Company, 1980.
4. Jennifer M. Schopf. *Performance Prediction and Scheduling for Parallel Applications on Multi-User Clusters.* PhD thesis, University of California, San Diego, 1998.
5. William Mendenhall, Richard L. Scheaffer, and Dennis D. Wackerly. *Mathematical Statistics with Applications*, pages 4–6. Duxbury Press, 1981.
6. H. A. Sturges. *Journal of American Statistical Ass.*, 21, 1926.
7. D.W. Scott. On optimal and data-based histograms. *Biometrika*, 66, 1979.
8. J. Lüthi, S. Majumdar, and G. Haring. Mean value analysis for computer systems with variabilities in workload. In *Proceedings of the IEEE International Computer Performance and Dependability Symposium, IPDS '96*, 1996.
9. J. Lüthi and G. Haring. Mean value analysis for queuing network models with intervals as input parameters. Technical Report TR-950101, Institute of applied science and information systems, university of Vienna, July 1995.
10. S. Majumdar and R. Ramadoss. Interval-based performance analysis of computing systems. In *Proceedings of the Third International Workshop on Model Analysis and Simulation of Computer and Telecommunication Systems*, 1995.
11. Stig Skelboe. Computation of rational integer functions. *BIT*, 14, 1974.
12. R. Wolski. Dynamically forecasting network performance to support dynamic scheduling using the network weather service. In *Proc. 6th IEEE Symp. on High Performance Distributed Computing*, August 1997.
13. Arnold Neumaier. *Interval methods for systems of equations*, chapter Basic Properties of Interval Arithmetic. Cambridge University Press, 1990.
14. Lawler, Lenstra, Kan, and Shmoys. *The Traveling Salesman Problem.* John Wiley & Sons, 1985.
15. Karan Bhatia. Personal communication, 1996.
16. David Bailey, Tim Harris, William Saphir, Rob van der Wijngaart, Alex Woo, and Maurice Yarrow. The nas parallel benchmarks 2.0. Technical Report Report NAS-95-020, Numerical Aerospace Simulation Facility at NASA Ames Research Center, December 1995.
17. J. M. Schopf and F. Berman. Performance prediction in production environments. In *Proceedings of IPPS/SPDP '98*, 1997.
18. J. M. Schopf and F. Berman. Using stochastic intervals to predict application behavior on contended resources. In *Proceedings of the Workshop on Advances in Parallel Computing Models, ISPAN 99*, 1999.

WORKLOAD CHARACTERISTICS AND EFFECTIVE SCHEDULING IN LARGE PARALLEL COMPUTER SYSTEMS

JOHN S. SOBOLEWSKI

University of New Mexico, Albuquerque, NM 87131 USA

SANTOSH MAMIDI

Cisco Systems, Inc., San Jose, CA 95132 USA

WILLIAM SMITH

Maui High Perf. Computer Center, Kihei, HI 96753 USA

This paper describes the collection and analysis of usage data for a large (hundreds of nodes) distributed memory machine over a period of 31 months during which 178,000 batch jobs were submitted. A number of data items were collected for each job, including the queue wait times, elapsed (wall clock) execution times, the number of nodes used, as well as the actual job CPU, system and wait times in node hours. This data set represents perhaps the most comprehensive such information on the use of a 100 Gflop parallel machine by a large (over 1,200 users in any given month) and diverse set of users. The results of this analysis provide some insights on how such machines are used and on workload profiles in terms of the number of nodes used, average queue wait times, elapsed and CPU times, as well as their distributions. A longitudinal analysis shows how these have changed over time and how scheduling policies affect user behavior. Some of these results confirm earlier studies, while others reveal new information. That knowledge has been used to develop a new scheduler for the system which has increased system node utilization from the 60% to the 90-95% range if there are sufficient jobs waiting in the queue.

1 Introduction

Implementation of effective batch scheduling policies for large distributed memory (shared nothing) parallel systems is a difficult problem. The main objective is to schedule jobs both for efficient system performance and fairness to users. In an N node system, a long sequence of large jobs each requiring $(\lceil N/2 \rceil + 1)$ nodes can reduce the node utilization to about 50% since under such circumstances the system can run no more than one job at a time, leaving the remaining $(N - \lceil N/2 \rceil - 1)$ nodes idle. On the other hand, scheduling small (in terms of nodes) but long running jobs on idle nodes as soon as they become available may forever block large jobs from running, creating unfairness to the class of users requiring many nodes.

Although various solutions have been proposed to solve these problems, they are far from perfect [1-3]. Difficulties arise when user profiles and job mixes are heterogeneous and when certain classes of users need priority processing. Heterogeneity of nodes (e.g. systems with different types of nodes, memory, and local desk configurations) introduces additional complexity to the scheduling problem since certain jobs may not be able to run on any node but may require specific nodes with specific configurations. The development and validation of effective scheduling algorithms for such systems requires an understanding of how they are used and the characteristic of the workload.

2   System Description

The job data were collected at the Maui High Performance Computing Center (MHPCC) which consisted of five interconnected IBM SP systems totaling 480 nodes. The main production system consisted of 368 nodes, of which 30 were dedicated to NFS and HIPPI connected I/O services, 28 formed an interactive pool for development and testing of new codes, leaving 310 nodes for batch processing of parallel jobs. The results presented here are confined to jobs submitted to this 310 node batch pool.

Submission of jobs was controlled by IBM's LoadLeveler [4] which is a modified version of the CONDOR scheduling system [5], originally developed to run a large number of single node jobs on clusters of workstations. It has been modified by IBM specifically for SP machines, which essentially consist of a collection of N workstations ($N \leq 32,768$) connected by means of a high performance switch. LoadLeveler allows the system to be divided into interactive and batch partitions, and can schedule serial and parallel jobs on the batch partitions. It requires the user to specify the type and number of nodes needed for a job, the expected elapsed run time, and the batch queue to which the job should be submitted.

Table 1 shows the six batch queues that were implemented and which were used by LoadLeveler to run the vast majority of batch jobs submitted between June 1995 and June 1997. It shows the minimum and maximum number of nodes jobs can use, the range of elapsed run times allowed, as well as the available memory per node. These queues were set up based upon an initial estimate of the workload characteristics. After June 1997, the so called "Maui Scheduler" was implemented and installed. It has a single queue for the entire system, supports improved backfill algorithms, a range of scheduling policies and communicates with LoadLeveler via the EASY-LoadLeveler Application Programming Interface [3]. It should be noted that jobs with characteristics different from those given in Table 1 could be run, but only by special arrangement.

Table 1. MHPCC Queue Configuration

Queue Name or Job Class	Number of Nodes	Memory per Node	Job Characteristics		
			Min Nodes/Job	Max Nodes/Job	Max Elapsed Time
Large	129	128 MB	64	128	8 Hrs
Medium	80	64-256 MB	8	64	4 Hrs
Long	47	64-256 MB	1	32	24 Hrs
Small Long	16	128 MB	1	8	8 Hrs
Small Short	30	64-256 MB	1	8	2 Hrs
Large Memory	8	1,024 MB	1	8	8 Hrs
Batch (after June 1997)	310	64-1,024 MB	1	256	36 Hrs

3 Data Collection

In any given month, there were 1,000-1,200 users of the system, mostly from government agencies, national laboratories and academic institutions, with some representation from the commercial sector. The range of applications was very broad, ranging from all branches of computational science and engineering to datamining and image rendering for the entertainment industry. The statistics collected used LoadLeveler's historical data, which included the time at which, and the queue to which, a job was submitted; the time spent in the; the number of nodes used (n_j); the elapsed run time; the total application (user) and system CPU times used on all nodes assigned to the job measured in user and system CPU node seconds; and the completion status.

An ORACLE database was created using the LoadLeveler data and SQL (Standard Query Language) was used to extract appropriate data subsets for further analysis. From this data, a variety of information may be derived, including job profiles, system utilization, elapsed and CPU times in node hours, the efficiency of the various queues, as well as the efficiency of the overall system.

4 Job Characteristics

Between June of 1995 and December of 1997, a total of 178,062 jobs were submitted for execution. Of these, 160,831, or 90.32%, started execution and it is these jobs that are included in the subsequent analysis since they contributed to resource utilization. The 9.68% of jobs that did not start were removed either by the user or by the system because they requested resources that were not available (e.g. more than eight "Large Memory" nodes). Of the 160,831 jobs that started execution, 131,966, or 74.70%, were completed successfully. The remaining jobs were terminated because they exceeded the maximum elapsed run time limits for the queue to which they were submitted, or because they encountered some fatal error condition during execution.

Figure 1 shows the distribution of the 160,831 jobs that started execution as a function of the nodes used. Although jobs could use any number of nodes up to 128, and any number up to 310 by special arrangement, 82% of all jobs used a number of nodes that was some power of 2. Eight node jobs were by far most numerous, representing 38.8% of the sample, followed by one node jobs which represented a surprising 15.5% of all jobs. The great majority of jobs (77%) used eight nodes or less and only 5.3% used more than 32 nodes.

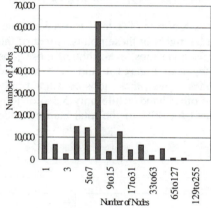

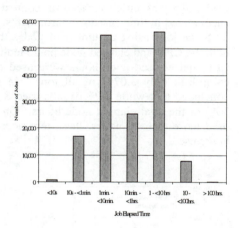

Figure 1. Distribution of jobs as a function the number of nodes used.

Figure 2. Distribution of jobs as a function of elapsed time.

The distribution of jobs as a function of their elapsed (wall clock) run times is shown in Figure 2. The distribution is bimodal with the large majority of jobs running between 1 and 10 minutes (32.9%) or 1 and 10 hours (33.5%). However, 42.8% of all jobs consumed less than 10 minutes of elapsed time each, while only 5% consumed more than 10 hours.

Figure 3 shows the distribution of the elapsed and CPU node hours accumulated by jobs of different sizes in terms of nodes used. Here, the elapsed time in node hours is obtained from $t_{ej} \cdot n_j$ where t_{ej} is the elapsed wall clock time and n_j is the number of nodes used by some job j. The CPU node hours for job j, on the other hand, are obtained by summing the actual user CPU times across all n_j nodes used by job j. The ratio of (Σ CPU node hours for jobs using n_j nodes/Σ Elapsed node hours for jobs using n_j nodes) therefore gives a measure of the average efficiency of jobs using n_j nodes and, in the ideal case, should be close to 1.

Comparing the CPU and elapsed node hours, Figure 3 clearly shows that the smaller the job size in terms of nodes used, the more efficient the jobs tend to be.

676

Not surprisingly, one node jobs tend to be most efficient, averaging 91.5% efficiency. Power of 2 node jobs (8,16,32) tend to be quite efficient (67% or better) but the average efficiency tends to fall rapidly beyond 32 nodes to a low of 35.8% at 128 nodes. Not much can be concluded for jobs larger than 129 nodes since they were relatively few in number, consumed a small fraction of the resources, and represented benchmark runs that tended to be highly optimized and therefore not indicative of user applications. The average efficiency for all jobs was 70%. While not shown, the CPU overhead (system time) was almost constant at 2% for all jobs, irrespective of the number of nodes or elapsed node hours used. The small system overhead should not be surprising since the nodes are not running in time sharing mode, implying little overhead for context switching, swapping or paging normally encountered in time sharing environments.

Since jobs using a number of nodes that is a power of 2 tend to predominate, both the CPU and elapsed node hours tend to be higher at these points. Most of the CPU and elapsed node hours were used by 64 node jobs, even though those jobs comprised only 3.07% of all jobs. In comparing Figures 1 and 3, it may be concluded that while 77% of jobs used 8 nodes or less, these jobs consumed only 30% of the total elapsed node hours. On the other hand, while only 5.3% of jobs used more than 32 nodes, these jobs accounted for 40% of the total elapsed node hours used.

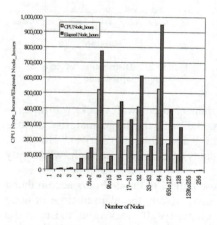

Figure 3. Distribution of CPU and elapsed node hours accumulated as a function of the number of nodes.

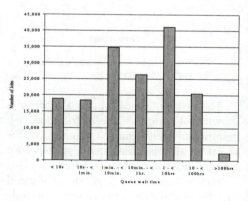

Figure 4. Distribution of jobs as a function of queue wait time.

The distribution of jobs as a function of queue wait time is also bimodal, with most jobs waiting either 1-10 minutes (21.1%) or 1-10 hours (24.8%), as shown in Figure 4. While 59% of jobs had queue wait times of less than 1 hour, the *average* queue wait times were relatively long, ranging from 2 hours for 2 node jobs to 60 hours for 128 node jobs. The reason is that users can submit a job to a queue but defer its execution for some reason, then "undefer" it much later so it can be executed. This deferring of jobs has the effect of artificially increasing average queue wait times. The implication is that average queue wait times are not a good measure of either scheduling effectiveness or quality of service provided in systems where users can defer jobs at will. In such cases, the percentage of jobs that wait for less than a certain time provides a much better measure of the quality of service.

Summary statistics for the various classes of jobs or queues defined in Table 1 are shown in Table 2. "Small Short" jobs predominated, but they made up only a small portion of total elapsed node hours. "Large" jobs used most of the elapsed mode hours and had the longest average queue wait times. In all cases, the average queue wait time was greater than the average elapsed (wall clock) time but, as mentioned in the previous section, this is artificially inflated by users who submit but defer execution of their jobs. In this table, the average job efficiency for a given queue is the ratio (Average CPU Node Hours/Average Elapsed Node Hours).

Table 2: Statistics By Job Class

Queue or Job Class	No of Nodes	Max El. Time Hrs	Max Nodes	Total # Jobs	Ave # Nodes per Job	Ave El. Time Hrs	Ave Q. Time Hrs	Ave CPU Node Hrs	Ave El. Node Hrs	Ave Job Efficiency
Large	129	8	128	5,007	76.25	3.78	41.03	130.48	274.78	47.48%
Medium	80	4	64	30,189	19.06	2.22	9.11	20.04	33.05	60.64
Long	47	24	32	11,454	7.33	9.00	26.12	33.63	53.89	62.40%
Sm Long	16	8	8	10,947	5.07	3.10	7.96	10.11	15.55	66.91%
Sm Short	30	2	8	74,860	6.02	0.65	1.12	2.90	3.96	73.23%
Lrg Mem	8	8	8	3,609	2.80	3.47	8.31	5.41	8.21	65.90%
Batch (after 6/97)	310	36	256	24,765	11.19	3.56	13.20	25.16	35.97	69.95%

5   Longitudinal Analysis

A longitudinal analysis of the data to determine changes over time showed the following trends over the 31 months during which data were collected:

- There was virtually no change in the average number of nodes used per job.
- The average elapsed time per job showed an increase of 69% from 2.09 to 3.54 hours.
- The average job efficiency showed an increase of 61% from 42.4% to 68.4%.
- With the single "Batch" queue implemented after June, 1997, the scheduling efficiency (see next section) improved from the 60% to the 90-95% range if there are sufficient number of jobs waiting in the queue.

The above trends suggest that, over time, users increased the size of their jobs by increasing their elapsed run times rather than the number of nodes used, and tuned their jobs over time to achieve greater job efficiencies as measured by the ratio of CPU to elapsed node hours.

6 Scheduling Efficiency

Given a diverse job mix and many jobs waiting in job queues at all times, a measure of scheduling efficiency over some sufficiently long period of time T can be defined as (100 * Total elapsed node hours provided during period T/ Total elapsed node hours available during period T). Performing this calculation with the original 6 queues, resulted in scheduling efficiencies of about 60% over one month periods, implying that at all times there was an average of 124 nodes idle, even though the queues were full.

The reason for this low scheduling efficiency is that LoadLeveler supports a strict first in, first out queuing system which means that a sequence of long running jobs could block other jobs for long periods of time. Partitioning the system into six separate queues, as shown in Table 1, guarantees that at least six batch jobs can concurrently run on the system assuming all queues have jobs to run. While this helps ensure some degree of fairness to all classes of jobs, it also has the effect of reducing the scheduling efficiency. For example, a single 66 node job running in the "Large" queue will prevent another "Large" job from running, leaving 63 nodes idle (too few nodes to meet the 64 mode minimum for a LARGE job) and resulting in a scheduling efficiency for this particular queue of 66/129 or 51.1% for the elapsed duration of the 66 node job.

The fact that a large portion of jobs use a small number of nodes and run for relatively short times, suggests that such jobs could be scheduled preferentially without significantly affecting other jobs. In such environments, the scheduling efficiency should approach 100% given a sufficiently large number of computational nodes and a sufficiently large number of jobs in the queue. To accomplish this, a preprocessor was written to interface with LoadLeveler using the available programming interface (API) [3]. This preprocessor, also known as the "Maui Scheduler" [6], uses a number of configurable parameters, including job and user limits, node configurations, identities of high priority users, as well as a number of algorithms to determine the priority of job execution based upon a combination of authorized user priority, the type and number of requested nodes, the elapsed run time limit as defined by the user, and the number of times the job has been by passed by other jobs to ensure jobs are not forever blocked. Once a job starts to execute, the elapsed run time limit provided by the user allows the preprocessor to calculate the time at which the nodes used by that job will once again become available. The preprocessor uses the API to get information on node and job status from LoadLeveler, as well as to command it to start a job on a (reserved) set of nodes, to cancel a job, or to collect job statistics.

All jobs are submitted to a single queue which is examined by the preprocessor every few seconds to:

1. Attempt to run high priority jobs that have previously reserved nodes.
2. Create a new prioritized list of jobs in the queue to include any new jobs submitted since the last time priorities were calculated.
3. Run the highest priority jobs if the required nodes are available.
4. Reserve the set of nodes for the highest priority job remaining, based upon the earliest projected availability of appropriate nodes.
5. Determine the earliest possible start time for that highest priority job.
6. Run smaller and shorter jobs on any available reserved nodes without moving back the earliest possible start time (calculated in step 5) for the highest priority job (back fill) using scheduling priority (step 2) to influence the back fill order.

The preprocessor performs the above actions after it has first obtained all necessary node and job status through the API and collected all statistical data for completed jobs.

In effect, the combination of the preprocessor and LoadLeveler creates a single queue scheduling system that is deterministic, supports priority processing, is completely parameter driven, and makes effective use of job backfill to schedule jobs for both efficient performance and fairness. Additional features include the ability to schedule jobs on multiple machines from a single queue, and a simulation capability that allows management to determine the effects of changes in scheduling policies or system configuration.

The new scheduler has been in operation since June 1997, and has increased the scheduling efficiency from about 60% to the 90-95% range if there are a sufficiently large number of jobs in the queue. In addition, it has allowed users to run jobs as large as 256 nodes and 36 elapsed hours without having to make special arrangements. The increase in scheduling efficiency is very significant in that it has allowed the center to provide an additional 40,000-50,000 elapsed node hours each month without any additional investment for hardware or measurable performance degradation to the users.

7 Conclusions

An understanding of the workload characteristics for large parallel systems can result in more effective capacity planning, help establish design parameters for future generations of parallel machines, and help implement more effective job schedulers. The fact that, in a diverse user environment, a large percentage of jobs use 8 nodes or less and run for relatively short times can be used to help off load large machines by using small clusters of workstations or Symmetric Multi Processors with 8 CPU's or less. This information can also be used to develop more effective schedulers that allocate resources more efficiently without blocking large jobs, and are deterministic in that users can obtain a worst case estimate when their jobs will start executing. Such a scheduler has been implemented, and described, and has greatly enhanced the throughput of the MHPCC system without a large capital expense for new equipment.

References

1. J. Subhlock, T. Gross, T. Suzuoka, "Impact of Job Mix on Optimizations for Space Sharing Schedulers," Proceedings of the Supercomputing '96 Conference, November 1996.
2. D. Feitelson, "A Survey of Scheduling in Multiprogrammed Parallel Systems," Technical Research Report RC 19790, IBM T.J. Watson Research Center, 1994.
3. J. Skovira, W. Chan, H. Zhou, D. Lifka, "The EASY-LoadLevler API Project," IPPS '96 Workshop on Job Scheduling Strategies for Parallel Processing, April 1996.
4. "LoadLevler Users' Guide," IBM publication number SH26-7226-02.
5. M. Livny, M. Litzkow, "Making workstations a Friendly Environment for Batch Jobs", Third IEEE Workshop on Workstation Operating Systems, April 1992, Key Biscayne, Florida.
6. For more detailed information on the Maui Scheduler see:
   http://www.mhpcc.edu/maui

A MESSAGE ORIENTED RELIABLE MULTICAST PROTOCOL FOR J.I.V.E.

GUNTHER STUER, FRANS ARICKX, JAN BROECKHOVE

University of Antwerp, Groenenborgerlaan 171, 2020 Antwerp, Belgium

In this paper, a message oriented reliable multicast protocol to support a distributed virtual reality project in Java (JIVE) is presented. Performance studies show that it fulfills the requirements for the virtual reality goals set forward.

1   Introduction

In this paper, we report on work that is part of the JIVE project (Java Implementation of Virtual Environments). The key features of this VR system are that (1) it supports desktop VR on a generic PC platform in a local area network, (2) it enables multiple participants to join a shared world and (3) it is dynamical i.e. it allows the construction of the virtual world, including participants leaving and entering, at run-time. Processes that are distributed over a network of computers represent the constituent entities of the virtual environment. Human participants (or "viewer") are also regarded as entities, leading to a homogeneous structure and design.

From the implementation point of view a secondary, but equally essential, goal is to base the project on an object oriented design, with implementation in Java to achieve platform-independence. Java also provides the support of a very large set of class libraries. We are convinced that, with the recent speed boosts and the expected increase in performance of Java, desktop VR in Java will eventually rival implementations that are more traditional. Java features such as multithreading, late binding of classes, class-loading over the network and remote execution provide additional advantages for a sound development. The current implementation relies heavily on separate threads for all naturally parallel objects.

The overall system can be divided in three main areas of development: (1) rendering i.e. visualization of the current state of the virtual world based on the Java 3D API, (2) information management i.e. taking care of the status information of the world constituents (objects) and (3) communication i.e. delivery of messages between the constituents. The communication component is split up in two layers. The message transfer layer deals with the delivery of messages between groups of interacting objects in the VR world. The reliable multicast transmission protocol deals with packing and unpacking of messages into packets and with the reliable transmission of individual packets with IP multicast. In the remainder we will focus on the communication scheme.

To support the type of virtual environment outlined above, we have implemented a reliable message oriented multicast protocol [1]. The protocol presented here will be tuned to virtual reality applications. The average message size expected is small since most of the information concerns changes in position and orientation. Undelivered messages within a preset time interval are dropped, simply because totally out of date information is as bad as no information. Objects send messages at an expected maximum of 30 per second because when visualizing the world frame rates need be no higher anyway[2].

In the classification of reliable multicast protocols [3,5] the proposed type is most closely related to the Transport Protocol for Reliable Multicast. When we classify on data buffering mechanism [4], it is known as a receiver-initiated approach. This means that no ACKs are used. The receivers transmit NACKs if retransmission is needed, detected by an error, a skip in sequence numbers, or a timeout. Two problems can arise: (1) a NACK implosion due to the detection of a missing packet by many receivers, and (2) too limited buffersize at the sender side: as one never knows that messages are received by all receivers, buffers should in theory be infinite. Waiting a random wait interval before transmitting the NACK can solve the first problem; the second one is solved heuristically by assuming messages to be of no further interest after a configurable timeout interval.

2   Multicast Protocol Details

Usually new applications are tailored to fit the properties of the existing communication (class) libraries provided. In the context of multicast protocols this could be in the way groups are assigned, the allowed number of groups, limitations on message content. The current protocol is tailored to fit seamlessly in the JIVE application. In this way one is assured that communication-oriented limitations on the VR application are kept to a minimum.

The communications layer has been designed for ease of use. The number of user-callable methods has been kept to a strict minimum. They include joining and leaving a multicast group, creating a new message, sending and receiving messages in a blocking or non-blocking mode.

The VR constituents or VR-objects, determine the communication "channels". Each VR-object is assigned a unique socket number (SN) on its host, and exclusively sends messages over this socket; as such an (IP, SN) pair, forming the object identifier OI, identifies a VR-object.

As messages are independent and will occur in parallel, a separate thread is used for each message. Due to this design decision one will be faced with a heavily threaded multicast system. Each message is uniquely characterized by the originating OI and a message identifier (MI). A message is split in a number of data packets of specified maximum byte-size, which are then characterized by the OI, MI, a packet identifier (PI), and the message size. The combination of (OI, MI, PI) is always unique. Both MI and PI are implemented as sequence numbers.

The JIVE implementation of a message concerns three distinct elements: the unique message-id as described above, the message buffer and the message timer. The behavior of buffer and timer

depends on the send or receiver mode. Figure 1 summarizes the internals of the multicast protocol.

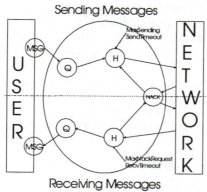

Figure 1. The internals of the multicast protocol

2.1 Part 1: Sending Messages

A new message leads to the creation of a new message object. Initially the object has a passive behavior, corresponding to an as yet inactive timer. One of the parameters at creation time is the multicast group for which the message is aimed at. An outputstream then becomes available in which the message content can be put; when filled, the **Send** command is executed, which closes the message buffer, and transfers it to the **SendQueue**. The latter contains complete messages waiting to be transmitted, when the necessary resources to do so are available.

The next component in the sending process is a hashtable in whose slots all messages under transmission are kept. The message-id is used as the hash-key. The extent of the hashtable is determined by the **maxsending** parameter, and its value will be chosen so as to keep the system busy, but not overloaded. Whenever a slot becomes available, it is filled with a new message from the **SendQueue**, and the message changes its state from passive to active.

When a message is transferred from the SendQueue to the hashtable, the message timer is starter, with a time-out limit given by the parameter **sendtimeout**. The value of the latter will be chosen large enough to handle possible NACKs, but small enough so as not to keep the hashtable slots unnecessarily occupied.

The transmission of a message amounts to breaking up the message content in packets of equal length, adding a unique packet header to each of them and transmitting the packets sequentially.

Incoming NACKS, containing the corresponding message-id and missing packet-ids, are readily traced in the hashtable, so that the list of missing packets can be resent; the message timer is reset.

As NACKs are sent on the same multicast address the original message was sent, all senders should listen to all groups on which active messages are being transmitted. This is implemented by a list of multicast groups each carrying a counter containing the number of currently active messages for that group. The list is updated each time a message becomes active by incrementing the corresponding multicast group counter or adding a new multicast group to the list with its counter set to 1.

If during the **sendtimeout** interval no packets are (re)sent, the active message is considered to be properly transmitted and removed from the hashtable. The corresponding counter in the list of multicast groups is decremented, and if the counter becomes zero, the multicast group removed from the list.

2.2   Part 2: Receiving Messages

Incoming packets are transferred immediately to a receive queue to account for possible (hardware) buffer limits on the network interface card.

Packets are retrieved from the receive queue and passed to a hashtable of incoming messages. Again the message-id is used as a key. If a corresponding message already occurs in the hashtable, the packet is appended to the message content in its proper position. If it concerns a new message, a new slot is added to the hashtable. The system checks for possibly missing messages from the same sender, which can easily be done as message-ids are sequentially ordered. For each missing message-id a new slot is added.

When adding a new slot to the hashtable, the message timer is started with a time-out limit given by the **recvtimeout** parameter. This value will be chosen in such a way that NACKs for missing packets are transmitted soon enough, but not before they can be received if still underway. After the time-out interval a check for possibly missing packets in the message is initiated. If so, and if currently less than **maxnackrequest** resend requests have been transmitted to the message originator, a NACK is transmitted containing all missing packet-ids and the timer is reset. If more than **maxnackrequest** attempts are necessary, the message is considered to be lost, and removed from the hashtable.

When a message has been received completely, its content is transferred to a queue of received messages, from which it can be retrieved by the "user".

3   A First Performance Study

An initial implementation of the communication layer was tested to investigate whether the performance goals to support the JIVE platform could be met. In the context of low-level communications in VEs, the amount of messages that objects can send to each other (the throughput) is the most important performance measurement. In order to make everything work smoothly we need a throughput of 30 messages a second. With our communication protocol this proved to be no problem at all. Although a throughput of 30 is sufficient in a VE, which we can easily achieve, throughput is used in this performance study to scan the outer limits of the protocol. Further optimization to improve efficiency and communication throughput will be considered later. All performance measures are made in terms of throughput[6], defined as the number of bytes per time unit transferred for complete messages. Resent packages are not accounted for and neither are incomplete messages at the end of the test.

The protocol results depend on a number of implementation parameters discussed previously, on message size and on the characteristics of the underlying physical communication system. To obtain comprehensible results, variation on two parameters only is considered for each test situation. All tests were performed on a 100Mbps Ethernet LAN with error rates simulated from the sender side.

3.1   Throughput vs. Maxsending And Sendtimeout

This accounts for a performance study depending on the protocol characteristics on the sending side. The results are shown in figure 2.

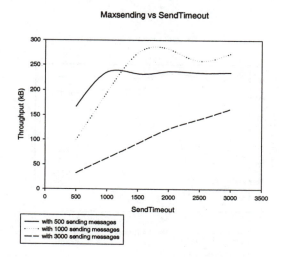

Figure 2: The effect of maxsending and sendtimeout on the throughput

Both parameters considered here are clearly correlated. For large **sendtimeout** values messages remain in the buffer for a relatively long time interval in a passive state waiting for possible potential NACKs. To keep the system busy **maxsending** should consequentially be sufficiently large. Remember however that large values for both parameters require important buffer resources.

The observed effect by variation of **sendtimeout** is twofold. A too small value leads to throughput loss as active messages are removed too soon: NACK requests arrive too late and are left unhandled. Increasing **sendtimeout** beyond some limit shows a slow degradation of throughput because of the many messages waiting passively.

For now **sendtimeout** has been determined statically and thus has a constant value throughout the lifetime of the Virtual Environment. Future improvements will include an algorithm to determine the optimal value dynamically through statistics.

Variation on **maxsending** shows an initial steep increase of throughput evolving to a constant value. This is easily understood as it represents the filling up of idle processing time up to full system load; increasing the number of active message slots beyond this point has no additional effect due to the limitations on processing power.

3.2   Throughput vs. Receivetimeout And Errorrate

These results describe the effect on the main parameter on the receiving side, and on physical communication hiccups. They are shown in figure 3.

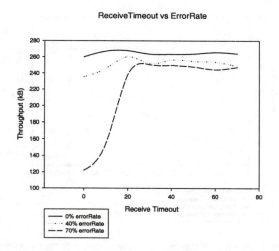

Figure 3. The effect of receivetimeout and the errorrate on the throughput.

The influence of both parameters is seen to be limited. As long as one of both parameters is kept small the influence of the other is restricted. Only when the error rate is unrealistically high and **receivetimeout** is small one obeserves a dramatic decrease in throughput. This is as expected because **receivetimeout** is only of importance when transmission errors occur and NACK requests have to be sent. Too small a value for this parameter at high error rates leads to premature NACK requests leading to unnecessary duplicate packets and possible instability of the system if all **maxnackrequest** NACKS are emitted before full reassembly of messages. One observes large standard deviations on the gathered data in these cases confirming the increasing instability.

3.3 Throughput vs. Message Size And Error Rate

One important parameter that was left undiscussed up to now is the message size, as it determines the number of constituent packages to be sent for a message. Its correlation to the error rate is again clear, as chances for a successful transmission are lowering for an increasing number of packets and for non-zero error rates.

A closer look at the figure indicates throughput to be larger for larger message sizes. This is probably an indication that message thread creation carries an important overhead, and should be considered for future optimization. Results are shown in figure 4.

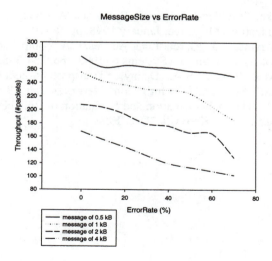

Figure 4. The effect of the messagesize and the errorrate on the throughput.

688

4 Conclusions

This paper outlines a Java implementation for a reliable multicast protocol aimed at supporting a distributed virtual reality platform. The requirements of this kind of application are quite different from more traditional parallel system applications in that messages have "relevance" only for some limited time period. This has interesting consequences for the design of the multicast protocol.

Some initial experiments have been performed which look promising. The performance analyses clearly shows that parameter values for the protocol can be chosen in sufficiently large intervals, even in extreme situations. It also indicates that the performance goals for supporting JIVE are already met.

Future work on the communication system will be mainly focused to optimization.

5 References

1. Donald P. Brutzman, Michael R. Macedonia, Michael J. Zyda, "Internetwork Infrastructure Requirements for Virtual Environments", http://www.stl.nps.navy.mil/~brutzman/vrml/ vrml_95.html
2. Kris Demuynck, Jan Broeckhove, Frans Arickx, "The VEplatform system: a system for distributed virtual reality", Future Generation Computer Systems 14 (1998), pp. 193-198.
3. Katia Obraczka, "Multicast Transport Protocols: A survey and taxonomy", IEEE Communications Magazine, January 1998, pp. 94-102.
4. Brian Neil Levine, J.J. Garcia-Luna-Aceves, "A comparison of reliable multicast protocols", Multimedia Systems 6 (1998), pp. 334-348.
5. B. Sabata, M.J. Brown, B.A. Denny, "Transport Protocol for Reliable Multicast: TRM", Proc. IASTED Int'l. Conf. Networks, Jan. 1996, pp.143-145.
6. Kara Ann Hall, "The implementation and Evaluation of Reliable IP Multicast", University of Tennessee, Knoxville, Dec. 1994.

Evaluation of File Access Patterns using Realistic I/O Workloads for a Cluster Environment

R. Todi[†], G. Prabhu[‡], Y. Alexeev[†], and J. Gustafson[†]

†Ames Laboratory, ISU, Ames, IA 50011, USA.

‡Department of Computer Science, ISU, Ames, IA, USA

With the rapid development of microcomputers and fast networking with high-speed switches, parallel processing on distributed clusters of workstations has e-merged as a cost-effective method of high performance computing. The lower price-performance ratio of clusters makes them a viable and affordable alternative for a variety of scientific, engineering, and commercial applications. In this paper realistic Input/Output (I/O) workloads from quantum chemistry code, General Atomic and Molecular Electronic Structure System (GAMESS) is used, to study the effect of a network file system on the ALICE cluster at the U.S. Department of Energy sponsored Ames Laboratory facility. The primary goal of the research is to identify I/O patterns of the application and to use these patterns in selecting the appropriate parallel file systems. The other goal is to tune the selected parallel file system for the ALICE cluster that is being used to implement these applications. The study finds that ratio of I/O over computation increases rapidly with the size of basis function of the molecules. There are I/O intensive phases that tend to be a bottleneck. We are able to effectively relate the different patterns captured the corresponding code.

1 Introduction

Rapid advances have been made in the hardware and software aspects of cluster computers. On the hardware side, most of the research on clusters has been based on building an efficient cluster configuration, selecting the right computing node, and the network hardware. On the software side, there has been work on writing device drivers for various operating systems, porting parallel libraries, compilers, and performance tools. Unfortunately, many scientific applications that run on these clusters do not benefit in terms of overall speedup because of their I/O requirements. To take care of such I/O requirements better parallel file systems should be developed.

The workloads we plan to trace are some scientific problems

in chemistry, physics and related fields. Many of these workloads are I/O intensive which limits the scalability and overall speedup of these applications. To the best of our knowledge, very few such realistic workload studies have been carried out on cluster environments. The workload we present here is from the quantum chemistry program GAMESS (which forms the basis of the SPEC high performance group benchmark SPECchem'96). We have obtained the file access patterns or characteristics for this application by trapping file access operations on all nodes of the cluster. We use the Pablo [10] Instrumentation tool to characterize the I/O performance of the input-output of GAMESS.

2 Cluster as a High Performance Contender

In order to understand better why I/O is a bottleneck we take a case study of a cluster such as ALICE [1] to illustrate the problem.

1. *Large File Size support*: Since the Pentium-Pro is a 32-bit processor, the largest file size supported by the operating system is 2^{31}, that is equivalent to 2 gigabytes. Parallel file systems such as IBM PIOFS overcome this problem by supporting file sizes up to 128 terabytes.

2. *Limited Memory Bandwidth*: The most commonly used protocol TCP, adapted from distributed computing has a number of limitations for the cluster environment. On a Pentium-Pro with fast ethernet the maximum achievable performance is 150 megabits/sec [4]. This is mainly due to protocol stack overhead and memory bandwidth as TCP tends to do data copy during transmission and reception.

3. *Limited Bus Bandwidth*: Since PCI bus (with limited bandwidth) is the gateway for the I/O, it can easily become a bottleneck for the increased requirement.

4. *Lack of scalable file system support*: An NFS file server is designed to provide a low-latency service to a large number of

nodes. It can tend to become a bottleneck if the number of nodes is increased due to limited transfer bandwidth or in the case of parallel applications where concurrent access to a single file is made by a large number of compute nodes.

5. *Lack of parallel file system:* Lack of global and concurrent file access, high speed access to a large amount of data, file stripping over multiple nodes, efficient data caching and prefetching techniques, and ease of administrative workload of maintaining multiple data are some of the problems of using the UNIX file system. A file system like GFS[13] can provide scalability but has special hardware requirements such as fiber channel supported network interface and disks. A distributed file system like Coda[9] improves availability but may not deliver high performance for cluster computing.

3 GAMESS

3.1 Introduction to GAMESS

GAMESS[12] is a program for performing ab initio quantum chemistry calculations. The starting point for the majority of quantum chemistry methodologies is RHF (Restricted Hartree Fock) wavefunction. So an understanding of RHF I/O obstacles can give useful information for choosing an appropriate parallel file system. Hartree Fock calculates non-relativistic interactions in Born-Oppenheimer approximation. There are three types of interactions: nuclei-nuclei, nuclei-electrons, and electron-electron. In the first step a molecule is specified as a set of nuclear coordinates, atomic numbers, number of electrons and a basis set. The second step is calculations of one-electron and two-electron integrals and electron density. In the third step the Fock matrix is constructed from one-electron (core) integrals, two-electron integrals and electron density. The diagonalization of Fock matrix to obtain electron density and energy of the molecule is the fourth step. The above steps are iterated until electron density or energy converges to an acceptable threshold. This procedure is known as SCF (Self Consistent Field) method.

3.2 I/O Requirements

The I/O and computational bottlenecks come from the calculation and storing of one electron integrals and two electron integrals.

There are simple formulas to estimate the disk storage requirements:

$$No.\ of\ Integrals = 1/Sigma * 1/8 * N^4 \qquad (1)$$

$$Disk\ Storage\ (in\ megabytes) = No.\ of\ Integrals * 12/2^{20}\ (2)$$

Here N is the total number of basis functions. $Sigma$ accounts for the point group symmetry (sigma=1 for C1 symmetry). The number of integrals grows as $O(N^4)$. and that symmetry significantly affects on the number of integrals to calculate. We choose three different computational time molecules to run: CH2, luciferin and HEDM (High Energy Density Material) molecule (Table 1).

Table 1. Number of basis function versus % I/O

	Basis function	% I/O
CH2	7	4.53
Luciferin	294	6.03
HEDM	630	50.23

Table 2. Number of nodes versus % I/O for Luciferin

No. of nodes	% I/O
16	43
32	9
64	6

It is shown in Table 1 that I/O grows rapidly with an increase in number of basis functions. Table 2 shows that I/O contribution decreases as number of nodes increases. So the more nodes you have the better I/O distribution you achieve that leads to decreasing percentage of I/O.

The HEDM molecule is choosen for analysis. By equation 1 the total number of integrals is $1.96 * e^{10}$. Thus by equation 2 total disk storage required for this molecule is 225347 megabytes. This estimate is an upper bound for I/O for HEDM molecule. The real disk storage requirement is hard to predict. It is far less for chosen molecule (1087 megabytes) because integrals close to zero are not stored. In case of large molecule the number of integrals grow as $O(N^2)$ and not $O(N^4)$. The requirements for disk storage grow fast with increasing size of problems up to 23 terabytes for 2000 basis functions. The only alternative for such molecules is recomputing of two electron integrals on each iteration due to limited storage capacity and I/O limitations. This is a relatively large molecule to run nowdays, but for real biological molecules like proteins, DNA will need petabytes storage. The development of a parallel file system for a cluster can play a crucial role in solving this problem.

4   Experimental Data and Discussion

GAMESS accesses information from files both directly and sequentially. Every GAMESS run opens a sequential access input file that is reset often, two output files and a direct-access master dictionary file that stores information including: atomic coordinates, gradient vectors, electron integrals and so on.

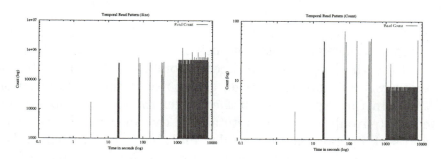

Figure 1. Temporal Read (Size)   Figure 2. Temporal Read (Count)

The HEDM molecule is representative of all the molecules in GAMESS with respect to their access patterns. Thus only the results of HEDM are presented. The electron integrals can be

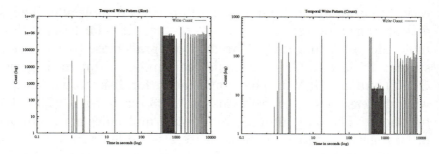

Figure 3. Temporal Write (Size)   Figure 4. Temporal Write (Count)

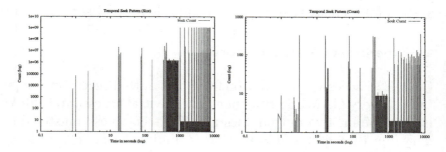

Figure 5. Temporal Seek (Size)   Figure 6. Temporal Seek (Count)

computed once and stored on disk or recomputed each time. Historically the integrals have been recomputed each time because there was not enough storage, giving rise to more computational time. In the experiment on the cluster the electron integrals are computed only once. The details of the amount of read, write, and seek operations are provided in Table 3, 4. As seen in Table 4, I/O operations are divided into two categories: for request sizes smaller than 4K and request sizes between 64K and 256K, they are significantly larger in number than for request sizes outside these ranges.

For the rest of article the discussion will be based on Figures 1, 2, 3, 4, 5, and 6. They show the temporal read, write and

Table 3. Basic I/O Instrumentation Summary on 64 nodes

Oper	Count	IO time	MBytes
Read	18205606	221247.61	10921477
Seek	5427569	917.49	-
Write	1519620	4973.86	68399
All I/O	25153131	227139.32	11605466

Table 4. Distribution of Read and Write Requests by Size on 64 nodes

Oper	Sz < 4K	4K <= Sz < 64K	64K <= Sz < 256K	256K <= Sz
Read	9100187	5242	9099904	273
Write	934500	16334	568744	42

seek patterns of node 0 with respect to the size (time window of 0.1 second) and the respective counts for HEDM molecule. Node 0 has an additional overhead as it handles output of the results. Other nodes have uniform file access. From these access patterns one can see that at the beginning GAMESS writes a huge chunk of data that corresponds to calculation and writing of two-electron integrals on the local hard disk. After initializing the integrals the Fock matrix is constructed and SCF procedure begins. As clear from the figures, massive reading, writing, and seeking take place during each SCF iteration. At the end of SCF procedure GAMESS calculates molecular properties and writes output to files as can be seen from writing pattern. The overall read, write and seek access patterns are superposition of sequential access of two electron integral file and direct-access master dictionary file.

We summarize the requirements for parallel file systems for GAMESS in the following statements.

- There are a large number of read, write, and seek intensive phases.

- Request sizes vary from extremely small to extremely large.

- Size of local disk on cluster is not sufficient for molecules with large basis functions.

- Presence of global file access can significantly reduce the total requirement for disk space and also reduce message-passing traffic.

5 Acknowledgment

This work was made possible in part by the Scalable Computing Laboratory which is funded by Iowa State University and the Ames Laboratory - USDOE under Contract W-7405-Eng-82. The authors acknowledge Professor Mark Gordon, Dr. Michael W. Schmidt, and Dr. David Halstead for their guidance on GAMESS.

References

1. D. Halstead et. al., "*ALICE Cluster*", http://www.scl.ameslab.gov/Projects/ALICE/
2. M. Baker, R. Buyya, and D. Hyde, "*Cluster Computing: A High-Performance Contender*", IEEE Computer, July 1999.
3. P. M. Chen, D. A. Patterson, "*Storage Performance–Metrics and Benchmarks*", Proceedings of the IEEE, vol. 81, no. 8, August 1993.
4. G. Helmer et. al. , "*SCL Cluster Cookbook* ", http://www.scl.ameslab.gov/Projects/ClusterCookbook/
5. P. Crandall, R. Aydt, A. Chien, and D. Reed, "*Input/Output Characteristics of Scalable Parallel Applications*", Proceedings of SC'95, December 1995.
6. G. Pfister, "*In Search of Cluster*", Prentice-Hall, Upper Saddle River, NJ, 1995.
7. Raj Jain, "*The Art of Computer Systems Performance Analysis: techniques for experimental design, measurement, simulation, and modeling*", John Wiley & Sons, INC, 1991.
8. N. Nieuwejaar, D. Kotz, A. Purakayastha, C. S. Ellis, and M. Best, "*File-access characteristics of parallel scientific workloads*", IEEE Transactions on Parallel and Distributed Systems, 7(10):1075-1089, October 1996.
9. M. Satyanarayanan, "*Coda: A Highly Available File System for a Distributed Workstation Environment*", Proceedings of the Second IEEE Workshop on Workstation Operating Systems Sep. 1989, Pacific Grove, CA.
10. D. A. Reed, R. A. Aydt, et. al., ""*Scalable Performance Analysis: The Pablo Performance Analysis Environment*", Anthony Skjellum(ed), Proceedings of the Scalable Parallel Libraries Conference, IEEE Computer Society, pp. 104-113, October 1993.
11. "*Scalable I/O Initiative* ", http://www.ccsf.caltech.edu/SIO/index.html
12. M. Schmidt, K. Baldridge, J. Boatz, S. Elbert, M. Gordon, et. al. "*General Atomic and Molecular Electronic Structure System*", J. Comput. Chem., 14, 1347-63, 1993.
13. S. Soltis, T. Ruwart, M. O'Keefe, "*The Global File System*", Proceedings of the Fifth NASA Goddard Space Flight Center Conference on Mass Storage Systems and Technologies, September 17-19, 1996, College Park, MD.

PARALLEL PROGRAM MODEL AND ENVIRONMENT

V. D. TRAN, L. HLUCHY, G. T. NGUYEN

Institute of Informatics, Slovak Academy of Sciences
Dubravska cesta 9, 84237
Bratislava, Slovakia
E-mail: upsyviet@savba.sk

In this paper, we present a new powerful method for parallel program representation called Data Driven Graph (DDG). DDG takes all advantages of classical Directed Acyclic Graph (DAG) and adds much more: simple definition, flexibility and ability to represent loops and dynamically created tasks. With DDG, scheduling becomes an efficient tool for increasing performance of parallel systems. DDG is not only a parallel program model, it also initiates a new parallel programming style, allows programmer to write a parallel program with minimal difficulty. We also present our parallel program development tool with support for DDG and scheduling.

1 Introduction

Advances in hardware and software technologies have led to increased interest in the use of large-scale parallel and distributed systems for database, real-time, and other large applications. One of the biggest issues in such systems is the development of effective techniques for the distribution of tasks of a parallel program on multiple processors. The efficiency of execution of the parallel program critically depends on the strategies used to schedule and distribute the tasks among processing elements.

Task allocation can be performed either dynamically during the execution of the program or statically at compile time. Static task allocation and scheduling attempt to predict the program execution behavior at compilation time and to distribute program tasks among the processors accordingly. This approach can eliminate the additional overheads of the redistribution process during the execution. With the support of program models such as Directed Acyclic Graph (DAG), Iterative Task Graph (ITG), static scheduling can produce optimal or nearly optimal task schedule [1, 2, 5] because the scheduling process has enough time and information to consider. Unfortunately, static scheduling algorithms require exact data about execution times and communication delays of each task. In most cases, the data cannot be predicted because it depends on the actual loads of processors and interconnection networks. Furthermore, the behavior of many programs depends on their input data and cannot be determined at compile time.

On the other hand, dynamic task scheduling is based on the distribution of tasks among the processors during the execution, with the aim of minimizing communication overheads and balancing the load among processors. The approach is especially beneficial if the program behavior cannot be determined before the execution. However, the lack of program model for dynamic scheduling forces dynamic scheduler to make a "blind" decision, i. e. to assign tasks to processors only on the basis of load of processors, regardless of program structure [8]. That can lead to increasing communication, especially when tasks are fine-grained. Some dynamic scheduling algorithms are based on DAG, so they have the same restriction as DAG [9]. In the addition, the scheduling process also uses processor time and that increases the total execution time of the parallel program. The crisis of program models can threaten the existence of the dynamic scheduler: some approaches remove the separate scheduler and leave the task allocation for the program itself [6,7]. Finding a dynamic program model is the vital problem for scheduling and parallel programming in general.

2   Parallel program models

Most of static scheduling algorithms use a directed acyclic graph (DAG) to represent the precedence relationships and the data dependencies of tasks of a parallel program [1, 5]. Each node of the graph represents a task and each edge represents the precedence relationship and communication between the tasks. DAG model is simple but it can represent only programs with static behavior and without loops. It cannot represent programs with loops or dynamically created tasks.

2.1   Data Driven Graph model

For a flexible model, which contains all advantages of the existing models and can represent also loops and dynamical behavior, we propose new approach to representation of parallel program called Data Driven Graph (DDG). The main ideas of DDG are following:

- Each task is defined by its input and output data. The set of input and output data creates a task interface, which hides all implementation details of the task. No relationship among tasks is explicitly defined.
- A scheduler manages all tasks and data of the parallel program. It determines the relationship among tasks according to their interfaces, i.e. their input and output data. The behavior of the parallel program is defined by its data. A data on a processor is ready when it is produced by a task and is sent to the processor. When all input data of a task are ready, the scheduler will execute the task.

The relationship between task interface and task implementation is like the relationship between function calling and function implementation in HLL (High Level Language). The task interface of task A says "Task A reads data X and produces data Y" without information how it is done, when the task implementation says "Tasks A reads a floating number and produces its square root" without information what real data it manipulates. That allows tasks to share their implementation, if they have the same functionality but manipulate with different data. The separation of task interface from task implementation is especially beneficial for tasks in loops and for dynamically created tasks, when tasks do the same work with different data and we do not know in advance, what real data they manipulate.

2.2 DDG versus DAG

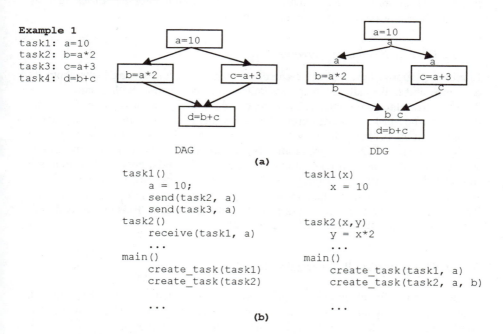

Example 1
```
task1: a=10
task2: b=a*2
task3: c=a+3
task4: d=b+c
```

DAG   DDG

(a)

```
task1()                          task1(x)
    a = 10;                          x = 10
    send(task2, a)
    send(task3, a)
task2()                          task2(x,y)
    receive(task1, a)                y = x*2
    ...                              ...
main()                           main()
    create_task(task1)               create_task(task1, a)
    create_task(task2)               create_task(task2, a, b)

    ...                              ...
```

(b)

Fig. 1 Similarities and differences between DAG and DDG

Fig. 1 shows the similarities and differences between DAG and DDG. For the simplicity, each task is represented by one command line. At the first sight of the graphs (Fig. 1a), there is no difference except that DDG gives more information about communication. Because most of existing scheduling algorithms is based on DAG, the compatibility with DAG is very important for DDG. Despite that DDG uses a different method from DAG for definition, existing scheduling algorithms can be applied for DDG as for DAG.

The largest advantage of DDG is the style of source codes (Fig. 1b). The source code of DDG is very similar to the source code of a normal sequential program. The task implementation does not contain any communication routines, which are typical of parallel programs. If the task creation create_task(task1, a) is replaced by function calling task1(a), the source code of DDG is actually the source code of a sequential program. It means that transforming a sequential program to a parallel program in DDG is done with minimal difficulty. Programmers can write a parallel program in the style of the sequential program, which they are used to, then replace function calling by task creation. For DAG, the situation is different. Each task contains communication routines and has to know which tasks it communicates with and where the tasks are. That requires major modification in the source code when transforming a sequential to a parallel program. Programmers have to learn to use new communication libraries such as PVM, MPI or new parallel programming languages.

2.3 DDG and dynamic task creation

In classical approaches, a newly created task has to inform existing tasks about its existence and makes all necessary communication connection with existing tasks. That increases the communication overhead and requires a lot of work in the source code of the task. Furthermore, the scheduler has no information about communication between the new task and existing tasks, so it cannot produce a good schedule. In DDG, programming with dynamically created tasks is as easy as with static tasks. Tasks in DDG do not have an explicit relationship, thus adding a new task does not affect existing tasks. The new task can be created anywhere in the parallel program by adding the command like that `create_task(task2, a, b)`. The scheduler will add the new task to DDG, and schedule it. Existing tasks do not have to be notified about the newly created task.

3 DDG Application Programming Interface

To demonstrate the advantages of DDG, we have implemented a set of routines in programming language C/C++ for programming in DDG. The aim of our implementation is to make a simple, robust and effective interface for DDG. All frequent errors, such as incompatibilities between task interfaces and implementations or attempts to modify input or to read output variables, have to be detected in compilation time. An example of programs in DDG API is as follows:

```
void ddg_config(void)
{   a = ddg_create_varriable(float);
    b = ddg_create_varriable(int);
    ...
    ddg_create_task("task 1", task1, input(a), output(b));
    ...
}
void task1(import(float) x, export(int) y)
{   y = x*10;
}
```

Each task is implemented as a function in C. As the program starts, it will call the ddg_config() routine, which contains definitions of variables and tasks. The ddg_create_varriable(int) creates an integer variable. The ddg_create_task("task 1", task1, input(a), output(b)) creates a task with name "task 1", implementation in function tasks1, floating-point input variable a and integer output variable b. The task name is useful for task identification in trace files, visualization graphs and resource files. The task implementation task1(import(float) x, export(int) y) shows that task1 has a floating-point input variable and an integer output variable. Macros input, output, import, export do not have only implementation functionality but also make the parallel program easier to read.

The classical main() function in C/C++ is as follows:

```
void main()
{
    ddg_config();
    scheduler();
}
```

Note that the only work the user has do is to write ddg_config() and tasks functions and to link them with DDG API. Other functions, including main() and scheduler() are the part of DDG API. When parallel programs run, the scheduler will spawn on other processor, schedule and execute tasks in parallel. The presence of the scheduler in parallel programs also makes them more effective and easy to adapt to new hardware configurations. An optional trace file can be generated, which is used for visualization and further optimization.

4 Scheduling

In Section 2, we assume that the scheduler will manage all communication. In this section, we will describe how the scheduler does it.

Scheduler in DDG consists of two parts: task management modules, which synchronize data, control communication among processors, supply proper data for tasks and execute tasks; and scheduling algorithms, which assign tasks to processors and determine priorities of tasks.

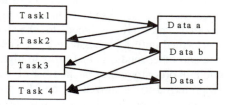

Fig. 3 Data structure in scheduler of Example 1

Scheduler has one task management module on each individual processor. The task management module maintains a structure of tasks and data on the processor such as in Fig. 3. When a task is created, the task management connects it with its input and output data. When a task finishes, its output data is ready. The task management will check all consumers of the data. If a consumer is already assigned to another processor and the processor does not contain the data, the task management module will send a copy the data to the module on the processor. Each task management module has also a queue of task waiting for execution. If a consumer has all its input data ready, it will be assigned to the waiting queue. When a processor is idle, the task management module will choose the task with the highest priority from the waiting queue and execute it. The task management is a part of DDG API.

The program runs in one of the following scheduling modes:

- External scheduling mode: The processor assignments and execution orders of all tasks are defined in the configuration file. That is the case the schedule is generated by an external scheduler, or is extracted from the trace file of the previous execution. No scheduling is performed during the program execution

- DAG-based static scheduling mode: This is the default mode, when the program runs for the first time or the hardware environment is changed. The configuration file contains the execution times of the tasks, but no schedule is defined. In this case, a DAG is generated after executing the ddg_config() function and a DAG-based scheduling algorithm is performed on the DAG. Users can choose one of the built-in scheduling algorithms, or write their own one. After executing scheduling algorithm, the program runs as in external scheduling mode.

- DAG-based dynamic scheduling mode: The program runs in this mode if it has dynamic tasks or the estimated execution times of tasks are not accurate. The task management modules periodically call the scheduling algorithm (default 10s) and change schedule dynamically. If a new task is created, it is assigned to the local processor where it is created. No notification is sent to other processors until the next scheduling step. If too many tasks are created or the tasks are created recursively, the program switches to lazy scheduling mode.

- Lazy scheduling mode: When too many tasks are created, especially when the tasks are created recursively, the program enters to lazy scheduling mode. In this mode, processors are supposed to have enough work to do, so all dynamically created tasks are assigned to the local processors and no scheduling is performed until a processor is idle. The main difference of lazy scheduling mode and other modes is that tasks in higher level will be executed as soon as possible in order to reduce the number of waiting tasks while tasks in lower level are preferred to be moved to the idle processor because tasks in lower level are potential to produce larger number of new dynamic tasks (tasks created by a task in level n will have level n+1, tasks created in ddg_config() have level 0).

5 Comparison with existing projects

There are some projects which have similar goal like DDG. The nano-threads project [10] uses Hierarchical Task Graph (HTG) [12] to express multi-level parallelism. HTG is composed of simple and compound nodes. Simple nodes contain sets of operation, which need to be executed sequentially. Compound nodes contain more complex operation and can be further decomposed into simple and compound nodes. During the execution, each node is instantiated through a nano-thread. However, a nano-thread can execute several nodes one after another at a specific level of hierarchy, if the application lacks processors to execute them in parallel.

The main difference between DDG and nano-thread project is that nano-thread project is oriented to shared-memory systems. In distributed systems, e.g. clusters of workstations, it is impossible to move a thread from a processor to another one. Another difference is that threads have to be scheduled at operating system kernel level, so the scheduling is limited and depends on the operating system. DDG offers more flexible scheduling with several modes and is independent from operating systems.

Other project is CODE [11], which has visual parallel programming language and development environment. The dependence among tasks is expressed by communication ports and firing rules. DDG uses variables to expresses the dependency among tasks, so it is simpler and closer to the classical sequential program and allows to reuse existing code of the sequential program. Another advantage of DDG is that DDG API is implemented directly in C language, so it is easier to integrate to a parallel compiler in future.

6 Conclusion

This paper has presented the new program model DDG, which has many advantages over classical DAG, ITG models. The definition of DDG is simple, flexible, tasks in DDG are independent, easy to write, and parallel programs in DDG are clear, easy to modify, maintain and upgrade. DDG model is also compatible with classical DAG model, so existing scheduling algorithms can be applied for DDG. DDG API initiates a new parallel programming style, allows programmers to write flexible, effective parallel program with minimal difficulty. DDG is not only a parallel program model, it also opens a new space for research and development in parallel programming, for example automatic parallelization a sequential program by a parallel compiler based on DDG.

Acknowledgements

We thank the Slovak Scientific Grant Agency which supported our work under Research Project No.2/4102/99.

References

1. S. Darbha, D. P. Agrawal: Optimal Scheduling Algorithm for Distributed-Memory Machines, IEEE Trans. Parallel and Distributed Systems, vol. 9, no. 1, pp. 87-95, 1998.
2. T. Yang, C. Fu: Heuristic Algorithms for Scheduling Iterative Task Computations on Distributed Memory Machines, IEEE Trans. Parallel and Distributed Systems, vol. 8, no. 6, pp. 608-622, 1997.
3. G.M. Megson, X. Chen: Automatic Parallelization for a Class of Regular Computations, World Scientific 1997.
4. S. Ha, E. A. Lee: Compile-Time Scheduling of Dynamic Constructs in Dataflow Program Graph, IEEE Trans. Parallel and Distributed Systems, vol. 46, no. 7, pp. 768-778, 1997.
5. Y. Kwok, I. Ahmad: Dynamic Critical-Path Scheduling: An Effective Technique for Allocating Task Graphs to Multiprocessors, IEEE Trans. Parallel and Distributed Systems, vol. 7, no. 5, pp. 506-521, 1996.
6. C. D. Polychronopoulos, D. J. Kuck: Guided Self-Scheduling: A Practical Scheduling Scheme for Parallel Supercomputers, IEEE Trans. Computer, vol. C-36, no. 12, pp. 1425-1439, 1987.
7. B. Hamidzadeh, D. J. Lilja: Self-Adjusting Scheduling: An On-Line Optimization Technique for Locality Management and Load Balancing, Proc. International Conference on Parallel Processing, Volume II: Software, pp. 39-46, 1994.
8. M. Wu: On Runtime Parallel Scheduling for Processor Load Balancing, IEEE Trans. Parallel and Distributed Systems, vol. 8, no. 2, pp. 173-185, 1997.
9. E. Maehle, F. Markus: Fault-Tolerant Dynamic Task Scheduling Based on Dataflow Graphs, Proc. IPPS'97, Workshop on Fault-Tolerant and Distributed Systems, Switzerland 1997.
10. X. Martorell, J. Labarta, N. Navarro, E. Ayguade: A Library Implementation of the Nano-Threads Programming Model, Proc. of the Second International Euro-Par Conference, vol. 2, pp.644-649, France 1996.
11. P. Newton, J.C. Browne: The CODE 2.0 Graphical Parallel Programming Language, Proc. ACM Int. Conf. on Supercomputing, 1992.
12. M. Furnari, C. Polychronopoulos: Run Time Management of Lisp Parallelism and the Hierarchical Task Graph Program Representation, CSRD Report 1133, 1991.

THE ASYNCHRONOUS OBJECT-ORIENTED PROGRAMMING MODEL FOR PARALLEL SYSTEMS

BRUNO WÉRY, FERNAND QUARTIER

Spacebel Informatique S.A., Parc Scientifique du Sart-Tilman, B4031 Angleur, Belgium
E-mail: Fernand.Quartier@spacebel.be, Web: http://www.spacebel.be/products

1   Introduction

While the distributed programming techniques are evolving, hiding the client-server aspect behind object-oriented concepts, intensive parallel computing is still significantly governed by old operating concepts. When a cluster of processors is considered, message-passing techniques are often the only solution. Of course, message-passing middleware evolves. Smart interfaces have been introduced. But the user has still to manage explicitly synchronisation and communication between processes.

This makes the application programmer community spending a lot of resources on something that is not clearly a part of its applications. Often, debugging a parallel application is more debugging the structure of the software than considering the computing algorithms themselves.

When Digital Signal Processors are involved, the situation is getting even more complicated. Hardware that supports these processors falls usually into the category of embedded systems. The software environment for these systems, if satisfactory for hardware and system engineers, provides very limited facilities if compared with those available on general-purpose systems.

This paper presents a programming model that simplifies parallel programming by introducing both an object-oriented concept and an asynchronous mode of operation. In our model, we transpose the concepts of event driven programming towards intensive computing.

This system is not the single approach for a smart parallel-programming environment. Moreover, our approach is not new by itself. Our main contribution is the fact that our model allows very efficient implementations.

SPACEBEL has used the AOO model to build a middleware called ARBEOS. This middleware implements a very light weight object request broker concept. This middleware has a very small footprint and reduced overhead. Consequently, it is adapted for medium to fine grain parallelism (20µs). Moreover it is portable towards various platforms, including Digital Signal Processors, and system topologies.

706

2   The Model

The basic idea behind the Asynchronous Object Model is the fact that event-driven programming can be applied to parallel programming. Event driven programming has been demonstrated to be a very efficient way to organise and synchronise large set of concurrent processes. This is particularly demonstrated in the area of user interface programming.

When using the Asynchronous Object-Oriented (AOO) programming model, the application software must be split into *objects*. The AOO objects are autonomous programming units, which are known by other units only through an interface and which can be duplicated. Note that this object definition is very general, and does not relate to the concepts used in object-oriented languages.

An object is composed of a set of *activable functions*. An activable function is a function that is triggered by a message, sent by another object. When the function is triggered, it performs an action. The function triggering through the transmission of a message is called the *activation*. A function may trigger more than one function. Through group broadcast mechanisms, a function may trigger functions of multiple objects at the same time.

Figure 1 represents the way the objects are communicating together.

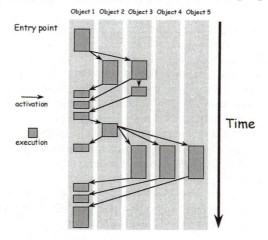

Figure 1: Object Communication in the AOO Model

An object that activates another never waits for returned data. It continues its execution until it has nothing more to do. If the activated object must return data to the object that has activated it, it must reactivate a function of this object.

Between two activations, no code execution is associated with an object.

Note that the programming model does not include any assumption about the way object execution is performed. The functions belonging to different objects may be executed within a single process or within multiple ones, on a single machine or on multiple ones, sequentially or in parallel.

3   The AOO Model versus Message Passing and Shared Memory Models

In parallel and concurrent programming, synchronisation is probably a major source of trouble in development. Developers spend a lot of time in order to verify that their system cannot enter a deadlock state. Often, debugging a parallel application is debugging synchronisation.

The AOO model makes a break-through because the programmer has to manage only a single kind of relations in the system: the causality. Efficiency of this approach can be understood when comparing the proposed model with message-passing and shared memory models. Such a comparison is presented on the Figure 2. This figure represents the operations to be performed when a software component (object 1 or process 1) requests a service to another component (object 2 or process 2).

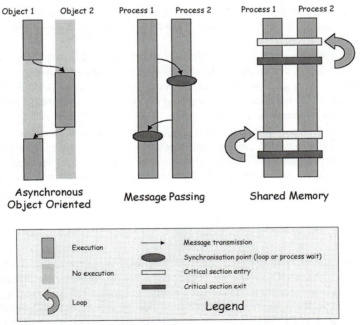

Figure 2: The AOO Model versus the Message Passing Model and the Shared Memory Model

When using the AOO model, the requesting object generates a message towards the second one. The second one executes the service following the activation and sends back a message towards the requester. Note that there is no explicit synchronisation code and that the underlying process execution is managed automatically.

When using the message-passing model, a synchronisation point must be implemented in each process for the reception of the messages. On these synchronisation points, the processes must wait for the required message to be present. Moreover, the fact that a message of a given kind is to be received must be known "a priori" by the process. If not known "a priori", the application programmer must implement himself a mechanism to determine the nature of the received data and the appropriate processing.

When using the shared memory model, things are even more complex. Request and results must be transmitted through a shared memory. Access to this shared memory must be protected by insertion in a critical section. Moreover it is not always possible to stop execution of processes while waiting data through memory arrays. It is of course possible to create more efficient schemes, but this implies often an increase of the complexity of the application code.

Managing synchronisation points or critical sections becomes very difficult when the size of the system grows. Then a significant amount of effort must be spent to ensure that deadlock is not possible at the system level. Therefore, the significance of the benefit of the AOO model increases with the system size and complexity.

Another significant benefit is that the programmer does not longer manage synchronisation and communication objects like semaphores, queues, signals, etc. The communication and synchronisation paradigms are unified into a single one, simple to master. Consequently, the learning curve for a programming environment based on the AOO model is short.

Note that it was required to solve the problem of object re-entrance: if more than one activable function can be simultaneously executed, the programmer would have again the problem of managing shared variables and critical sections. This may be solved through a rule that forbids the simultaneous execution of two functions within a given object.

4   Creating a Scalable System using the AOO based Programming

Having the capability to create scalable application is essential for a large set of applications. The AOO model is appropriate for a natural implementation of scalable applications, using a "serve-when-ready" programming scheme (Figure 3).

To allow it, the system must implement the "group of objects" concept. This means that the user can design an object and duplicate it at configuration time. The duplicates are then incorporated into a group.

On the figure, the Object 1 (the requester) activates the initialisation function of all processing objects belonging to a target group (here Objects 2 to 5). When initialised, these objects activate a function of the requester to indicate they are ready to proceed.

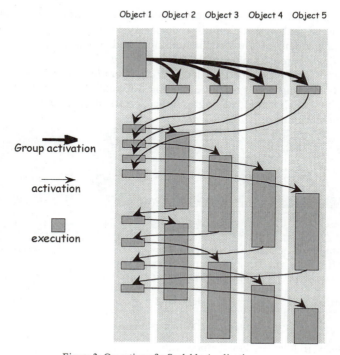

Object 1   Object 2   Object 3   Object 4   Object 5

Group activation

activation

execution

Figure 3: Operation of a Scalable Application

Every time the requester is activated by a ready processing object, it activates it back to request it the execution of a part of the job.

5   The ARBEOS Middleware

SPACEBEL has developed prototypes of minimal systems based on the core of the object request broker concept. In these experiences, we have implemented the AOO model and we have reduced the system functionality to the essential. From these experiments, we came to the conclusion that it is possible to design a kind of object request broker that could be

_ efficient enough for use in parallelisation of computing algorithms,

_ compact enough to be implemented on embedded platforms,

_ simple enough to be implemented without an underlying operating system.

Of course such a system is a lot simpler than a conventional ORB, even when characterised as "minimal". There are of course no compatibility nor interoperability issues between such a system and an ORB.

This led us to the development of a commercial middleware, called ARBEOS.

ARBEOS is a software environment oriented towards the writing of highly computational software for multi-processor systems. It provides an environment that is independent of the system topology, and is based on the Asynchronous Object-Oriented programming model.

ARBEOS is a layer to be installed over an Operating System. ARBEOS integrates multiple computing nodes (may be running different Operating Systems and using different style of CPUs) into a single application frame (Figure 4), to create a virtual distributed machine.

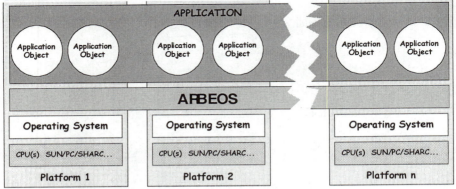

Figure 4: The ARBEOS Virtual Machine

The ARBEOS middleware key features are:

Object location independence, topology independence and heterogeneous clustering support: Except for optimisation purposes, no information about which machine executes the code, about the communication media available in the system or about the architecture of the participating machines is included into the application code. The same application code runs on a Symmetric Multi-Processor (SMP) Workstation or a cluster of single-processor personal computers. System related information is introduced during a configuration procedure that takes place before compilation.

API simplicity: Thanks to the AOO model, we were able to define a very simple API for ARBEOS. It includes 24 general calls (plus 6 for "control-oriented" extensions and 6 for the "distributed I/O service). With this call set, it provides a distributed operating system functionality.

Small footprint: ARBEOS code is small. Its size makes it suitable for most embedded systems. Particularly, it is compatible with recent Digital Signal Processing hardware (~25 Kwords on SHARC processor and 100 Kbytes on an Intel x86 processor, including code and data structures).

Small overhead: ARBEOS has been designed for efficiency. The ARBEOS overhead is so small that ARBEOS can be used to split the heart of the algorithms. (On a dual Pentium-III machine (500 MHz), we have observed that the ARBEOS latency (half the round trip delay) is around 12 µS, while the computing overhead is below 5 µS[1]).

Note that all these nice features have a price: ARBEOS is a static system. This means that the system configuration is established during the configuration phase and cannot change during execution: a new object cannot be declared at run-time and the communication paths cannot be modified. Note that this limitation has very little impact on most intensive computing applications.

ARBEOS already supports a range of systems and topologies: Single processors workstations, SMP multi-processor workstations and cluster of such workstations connected over a TCP/IP network. Today, ARBEOS has been implemented on the following environments: SOLARIS (x86 and SPARC – supports SMP), LINUX (x86), Windows NT (x86 – supports SMP), ADSP21060 (DSP - running without OS), ERC32 (specific processor for space applications - running without OS).

ARBEOS appears as a library. This library includes the ARBEOS run-time core. The application objects must be written in C^2. ARBEOS includes a distributed I/O system, interactive configuration tools and a code pre-processor, which creates a few extensions to the C language in order to ease ARBEOS based programming.

6   The AOO Model for Real-time Control Software ?

We have developed initially the AOO model in order to solve problems related to parallel intensive computing. The initial development of ARBEOS was oriented towards operation in a batch-oriented environment.

As we have already pointed out, AOO programming is a form of event driven programming. Most applications in real-time control relate mainly to event-processing. From these considerations, we imagined that the AOO model would provide a natural framework for the design of such applications.

Therefore, we have created extensions to ARBEOS, in order to transform it into a valuable tool for building multiprocessor control systems. These extensions relate mainly to the control of the system behaviour in time (activation priorities), the catching of external events and the communication with other software components that are not built using the ARBEOS concept.

Introduction of these extensions is only a first step. We need now to develop tools to determine and control precisely the behaviour in time of the systems. Particularly, simulation tools will be required. Nevertheless, the simplicity of the ARBEOS core makes us confident of the potential of ARBEOS in this application range.

---

[1] When using a cluster of workstations, the latency and overhead are mainly constrained by the interconnection system. Using TCP/IP on fast Ethernet, we have observed latencies that may grow up to a few hundreds of µs. We believe that these latencies are not linked mainly to the specific processing introduced by ARBEOS. There is a major dependency from the communication protocol stack, and from the way events and scheduling are managed by the Operating System.

[2] Or C++, but ARBEOS do not take advantage of the object-oriented features of the language.

7 Program Example

In order to improve the reader perception of ARBEOS programming, we present an small example in this section. The following example is the code of a simple objects implementing a scalable processor, using the principle presented in the previous sections. Because of limitations of the length of this paper, the documentation is reduced to a strict minimum. Nevertheless, it is hoped that it provides a feeling about the simplicity of ARBEOS.

Two objects are presented here:

  _ The "processing object", which can be duplicated (objects 2..4 on Figure 3)

  _ The "supervisor object", which controls the execution (object 1 on Figure 3)

This very simple piece of code executes the processing of a matrix that can be parallelised on a line-by-line basis. We do not consider the processing code itself.

The presented code uses the C extensions introduced by the ARBEOS pre-processor. These extensions use keywords beginning by the character '@'. In this example, we find the following keywords

  _ @init and @!init: surround an initialisation sequence executed at system start-up. It includes the first activations to initiate the execution event chain.

  _ @object_function: indicates that the following routine is not a standard C routine but an object activable function

  _ @create_message: build an activation message using an activable function prototype.

  _ @body: indicates where the pre-processor may insert active code (between variable declarations and actual code)

Arbeos defined symbols, types and library functions are presented using a *bold-italic* font. C standard symbols are presented using a bold font.

Processing Object Code

```
static float32 working_buffer[LINE_LENGTH];
static ARBEOS_address working_buffer_address;
static ARBEOS_activation_message message;
@object_function processor_init()
{
@body
working_buffer_address = ARBEOS_pointer_to_address(working_buffer);
@create_message[message] distribute_work(working_buffer_address, 0);
ARBEOS_activate(&message);
}
@object_function processor_execute(ARBEOS_address result_destination)
{
  @body
    ...
  @create_message[message] distribute_work(working_buffer_address, 1);
ARBEOS_data_transfer(ARBEOS_FLOAT32, LINE_LENGTH, 1,
                        Local_object_id,
                        Received_message.source_id,
                        working_buffer_address,
                        result_destination, 0, 0, &message);
```

```
}
```

Supervisor Object Code
```
static ARBEOS_activation_message message;
static ARBEOS_group_identifier group_id;
static float32 data_matrix[NUMBER_OF_LINES * LINE_LENGTH];
static float32 result_matrix[NUMBER_OF_LINES * LINE_LENGTH];
static ARBEOS_address data_matrix_address, result_matrix_address;
@init
ARBEOS_group_get_identifier("PROCESSORS", &group_id);
@create_message[message] processor_init();
ARBEOS_group_activate(group_id, init_message);
@!init
@object_function distribute_work(ARBEOS_address buffer_address,
                                 int32 line_processed)
{
  @body
  static int32 distributed_lines = 0;
  static int32 processed_lines = 0;
  ARBEOS_address origin_address, destination_address;

  processed_lines += line_processed;

  if (distributed_lines < NUMBER_OF_LINES)
  {
    origin_address = ARBEOS_address_offset(data_matrix_address,
                ARBEOS_FLOAT32, (LINE_LENGTH * distributed_lines));
    destination_address = ARBEOS_address_offset(result_matrix_address,
                ARBEOS_FLOAT32, (LINE_LENGTH * distributed_lines));

    distributed_lines++;
    @create_message[message] processor_execute(destination_address);

    ARBEOS_data_transfer(ARBEOS_FLOAT32, LINE_LENGTH, 1,
                         Local_object_iD, Received_messagE.source_id,
                         origin_address, buffer_address, 0, 0,
                         &message);
  }
  if (processed_lines == NUMBER_OF_LINES)
      ....
}
```

8   Conclusions

In this paper, we have presented an efficient programming model for parallel processing. Using this model, we have developed a "brooking middleware", called ARBEOS, oriented towards portability, compactness and efficiency. We believe that using such a middleware, it is possible to shorten significantly the development cycle of parallel applications.

The initial development of ARBEOS has been funded by ESA / ESTEC through the "Scalable SAR Processor for the Ground Segment (SCASAP)" project under contract n°11370-95-NL-FM

COMPILING FOR FAST STATE CAPTURE OF MOBILE AGENTS

Christian Wicke, Lubomir F. Bic, Michael B. Dillencourt

Information and Computer Science, University of California,
Irvine, CA 92697-3425 USA
E-mail: {cwicke,bic,dillenco}@ics.uci.edu

Saving, transporting, and restoring the state of a mobile agent is one of the main problems in implementing a mobile agents system. We present an approach, implemented as part of our MESSENGERS system, that represents a trade-off between the unrestricted use of pointers and the ability to perform fully transparent state capture. When writing the code for an agent, the programmer has a choice between two types of functions. C functions are fully general and may use unrestricted pointers, but they are not allowed to invoke any migration commands. Messengers functions may cause migration but their use of pointers is restricted to only a special type of a dynamic array structure. Under these restrictions, the local variables, the program counter, and the calling stack of an agent can all be made machine-independent and can be captured/restored transparently during migration.

1 Introduction

Saving, transporting, and restoring the state of a mobile agent is one of the main problem in implementing a mobile agents system[1]. While it is quite easy to capture and transport the state of all agent variables, transporting the program counter and the stack is difficult. The reason is that returning addresses and pointers stored on the stack are machine dependent and must be translated to appropriate memory addresses on the destination machine. Hence many systems leave it up to the programmer to capture, transport, and restore the agent state.

In this paper we propose a novel approach to state capture in mobile agents. The main idea is to differentiate between two types of functions, *C functions* and *Messengers functions*. C functions are fully general: they may be arbitrarily nested, they may involve recursion, and they may use unrestricted pointers. However, they are not allowed to invoke any migration commands. Any C function invoked from the Messenger's main function (the script level) is treated as a block box—it must return to the script level before any migration can take place. In contrast, Messengers functions may include any number of migration statements. They may also be nested and may even invoke regular C functions. But they are not allowed to use free pointers. To permit dynamic memory management inside of Messengers functions, a special type of a dynamic array structure is provided. Under these restrictions, the compiler is able to represent the local variables, the program counter, and the calling stack of an agent in a machine-independent form, which may be captured and restored transparently during migration.

2 Overview of MESSENGERS

MESSENGERS [2,3] is a system that supports the development and use of distributed applications structured as collections of autonomous objects, called Messengers[a]. Each Messenger is a self-contained thread of execution, represented by its own Messengers control block, and capable of moving among different nodes of the underlying network by issuing migration commands.

Each Messenger consists of a program called a script. This corresponds to the *main()* function of conventional C programs and consists of three types of statements: computational statements, function calls, and migration statements. Computational statements include all standard C assignment and control statements involving arbitrary variables and constants except pointers. Function calls permit the dynamic loading and invocation of arbitrary precompiled functions written in unrestricted C. They also permit the invocation of Messengers functions. Finally, migration statements endow the Messenger with mobility, permitting it to move within the network. The most important migration statement is the *hop* statement, which transparently captures the state of the Messengers on the current machine and restores it at the destination machine. The main contribution of this paper is a mechanism that permits migration statements to be invoked not only at the script level but from within Messengers functions, which may be arbitrarily nested.

The MESSENGERS system distinguishes two kinds of variables: *Messenger variables* are local to each Messenger and are automatically carried with the Messenger as it travels through the network. *Node variables* are local to each node and are shared among all Messengers residing on that node. These two basic kinds of variables clearly separate the state of a Messenger from the state of a node.

As already stated above, Messengers are not allowed to use pointers at the script level or inside of Messengers functions. To compensate for the lack of free pointers, the MESSENGERS system supports a special variable type, called a *dynamic array*. This behaves like a regular array in C, except that the array size can arbitrarily be changed at runtime using the *setSize* command. Dynamic arrays enable Messengers to allocate and use dynamic memory at the

---

[a]individual autonomous objects are denoted by mixed case (Messengers), while the system as a whole is denoted by small capitals (MESSENGERS).

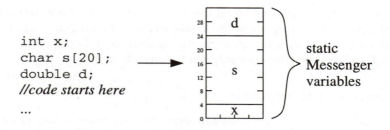

Figure 1: Generation of memory structure from variable declaration

script level and withing Messengers functions. This similar to using malloc() in C functions. However, unlike memory acquired using malloc(), memory managed using dynamic arrays cannot be transferred to other Messengers.

3   Saving the State

The current version of MESSENGERS is fully compiled. All MESSENGERS-code is compiled first to C code and then to machine code using gcc. With the aim of achieving a high migration speed a special compiling technique has been developed, based on keeping the full state of the Messenger in one memory block, called *Messenger Control Block* (MCB). This block does not contain any machine-dependent information such as pointers, so that it can be transported easily to a new machine.

The state of a mobile agent consists of three parts: (1) The values of its local Messenger variables, (2) the program counter, and (3) the function calling stack (file handles are only allowed as node variables). The MESSENGERS compiler transforms these three parts to satisfy the above requirements as explained in the remainder of this section.

3.1   Transformation of the Messenger Variables

The state capture and restoration of the variables is the easiest of the three tasks. The MESSENGERS compiler puts scalars and arrays of fixed size into one memory block by generating a C-struct and declaring all Messenger variables as members of that struct. Figure 1 displays the transformation of a simple example code.

More difficult is the implementation of dynamic arrays. To put them into the struct of the Messenger control block, the space must be able to grow and shrink at one end so that the array sizes can change. The MESSENGERS

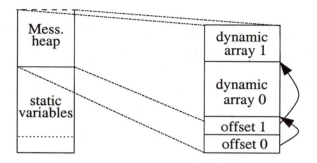

Figure 2: Adding dynamic variables to MCB

compiler achieves this by adding an empty character array at the end of the struct. This character array becomes the Messenger's *private heap*. Whenever an MCB is needed for a Messenger with at least one dynamic array the compiler allocates extra memory to accommodate the arrays. The total size of the MCB is the normal size plus the size of all dynamic arrays stored in the Messenger heap. The bottom portion of the heap contains an integer variable for each dynamic array to store the offset of that array.

Figure 2 illustrates the structure of the MCB with a Messenger heap containing two arrays and their corresponding offset values. Using these offsets, the compiler transforms references to dynamic arrays. With these transformations we achieve our goal of storing all Messengers variables in one block.

3.2   Transformation of the Program Counter

The program counter must be stored inside the Messenger control block during migration. It cannot be stored as a pointer, since pointers are machine dependent. The MESSENGERS compiler solves this problem by breaking the code into smaller *function blocks* such that state saving will only occur at the end of a function block. Execution can easily be continued if it is known which block has to be executed next. These blocks are implemented as an array of C functions. A Messenger is then executed by invoking the function blocks in the appropriate order. Because of branches, the execution order can only be determined at runtime. For that reason, each function block returns the index of the function block to be executed next. This index, called *nextFB*, is stored inside the Messenger control block. Unlike a regular program counter, this index is not machine dependent and thus a Messenger is capable of resuming its execution correctly even after a hop to another machine.

718

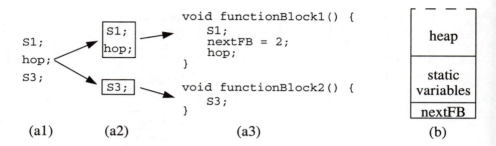

(a1)　　　(a2)　　　　　　(a3)　　　　　　　(b)

Figure 3: Dividing code on function blocks

Figure 3 illustrates this principle for a sequence of three instructions. The sequence (a1) shows a fragment of MESSENGERS source code that containing a migration command (**hop** statement). The compiler separates the code at this hop statement, resulting in two function blocks as seen in figure 3 (a2). Figure 3 (a3) displays the C-Code of the two resulting function blocks. Before performing the hop, the function block 1 stores the index of the next function block (*nextFB = 2;*) in the MCB, which is shown in 3 (b).

The general rules followed by the MESSENGERS compiler when transforming the Messengers code into C code are the following:

- The first function block starts at the beginning of the Messenger code.
- A new function block starts following every migration statement.
- Each function block continues from its starting point along all conditional branches. Each branch terminates when a migration statement is encountered.

Enforcing these rules requires special care when compiling loops and conditional statements. The techniques required to ensure correct behavior in the presence of arbitrarily nested loops and conditional statements have been discussed elsewhere [4,5].

3.3 Transformation of the Stack

The previous section showed how the program counter can be made machine independent by transforming code between any two migration statements into separate function blocks. If migration statement are restricted to only the script level of any Messenger, as was the case with earlier implementations, then state capture does not need to include the calling stack, because the stack is always empty at the top level. However, this kind of restriction can be cumbersome to the programmer: for example, it means that a program to traverse a spanning tree in a network must be written as an iterative loop rather than as a recursive function. To eliminate this restriction, we have introduced Messengers functions, as described in the introduction, that may contain migration statements and may be arbitrarily nested. Supporting these functions requires additional transformations as explained in this section.

The introduction of the dynamic arrays into MESSENGERS opened the opportunity of capturing and restoring the calling stack during migrations. The basic idea is to store all the information normally kept on the system stack in a special dynamic array called the *Messenger Stack*. This way the system stack remains empty, while the relevant information about the calling sequence of a given Messenger is maintained in the Messenger Stack.

Storing the information on the Messenger Stack requires that calls and returns have to be transformed to jumps. Since simple jumps would be machine dependent, function blocks are used again. Function calls and returns are treated as special state-capture statements. For a function call, the nextFB variable is set to the first function block of the called function. The index of the function block that follows the call statement is stored as a return index on the Messenger Stack. Any parameters for the called function are also stored there. The called function accesses the parameters through the Messenger Stack and also keeps its local variables there. A return statement causes the Messenger to pop the top element from the Messenger Stack and to set the nextFB variable to this value. This causes the execution to return to the next higher calling function, and continue executing the function block that follows the earlier function call.

Figure 4 shows an example with two functions. The main function calls the function myFunc, in which a migration statement occurs. Figure 5 displays the states of the Messenger control block during execution. The main function starts with function block 1. The call to myFunc terminates this function block. At the end the return index is stored on the Messenger Stack (Figure 5(a)). The Messenger continues with function block 3. Since the function myFunc contains a migration statement (hop), it is separated into two function blocks (3 and 4). Figure 5(b) shows the state of the MCB when the hop is executed. The nextFB variable is set to 4 and the return index remains on the Messenger Stack. The execution then continues with function block 4. At the end of function block 4, the nextFB variable is loaded with the value popped from the Messenger Stack. This ensures that execution continues with function block 2, which performs the computation S2.

Using the above transformation assures that the system stack is always empty at the point of migration. In other words, all function blocks are ex-

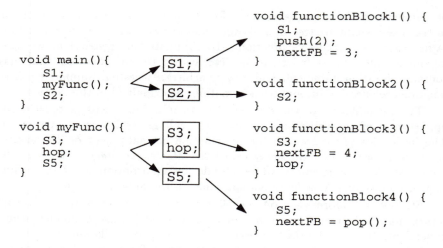

```
                                    void functionBlock1() {
                                        S1;
                                        push(2);
void main(){           S1;            nextFB = 3;
    S1;                              }
    myFunc();
    S2;                S2;          void functionBlock2() {
}                                       S2;
                                    }
void myFunc(){
    S3;                S3;          void functionBlock3() {
    hop;               hop;             S3;
    S5;                                 nextFB = 4;
}                      S5;             hop;
                                    }

                                    void functionBlock4() {
                                        S5;
                                        nextFB = pop();
                                    }
```

Figure 4: Handling code with functions

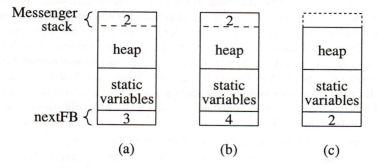

(a)   (b)   (c)

Figure 5: The state of the MCB before the function call (a), during the hop statement (b) and at the end of the function (c)

ecuted as a linear sequence of function blocks by being called from a loop in the MESSENGERS daemon. No function block ever calls another function block directly. For example, in the above program, the daemon would call the four blocks in the following order: 1,3,4,2. This transformation is similar to compiling code for a basic RISC processor, which doesn't know anything about calls or a stack.

4 Conclusion

We have presented a compilation-based approach to capturing the state of a Messenger automatically and transparently each time the Messenger wishes to migrate between machines. This flexibility comes at a price: we need to restrict the use of pointers, so at the script level and within Messengers functions the programmer is allowed to use only a special dynamic array for space management. This causes memory management to become slower, because changing the size of dynamic arrays is expensive.

We are presently experimenting with various approaches to reducing this memory management overhead. We can avoid frequent changes of the array size by extending the Messenger Stack and dynamic arrays generously when more space is needed. Shrinking of the stack and dynamic arrays is generally not necessary while the Messenger remains on one machine. When a Messenger moves to another machine, only the part of the Messenger Control Block that actually contains data (dynamic array entries or Messenger Stack entries) must be moved through the net. By maintaining a profile of changes in the sizes of the various dynamic arrays and the stack, it may be possible to proactively guess an appropriate size when the Messenger hops to a new machine (and the MCB must be allocated anyway), thus reducing (or even eliminating) subsequent reallocations of space on the new machine. Such optimizations will be the subject of our future research.

References

1. K. Rothermel, editor. *MA '98: Second International Conference on Mobile Agents*, Springer-Verlag, Lecture Notes in Computer Science, Stuttgart, Germany, Sept 1998.
2. L.F. Bic, M. Fukuda, and M. Dillencourt. Distributed computing using autonomous objects. *IEEE Computer*, 29(8), Aug. 1996.
3. M. Fukuda, L.F. Bic, M. Dillencourt, and F. Merchant. Distributed coordination with messengers. *Science of Computer Programming*, 31(2), 1998. Special Issue on Coordination Models, Languages, Applications.
4. C. Wicke, L. F. Bic, M. B. Dillencourt, and M. Fukuda. Automatic state capture of self-migrating computations in messengers. In *MA '98: Second International Conference on Mobile Agents*, Springer-Verlag, Lecture Notes in Computer Science, Stuttgart, Germany, Sept 1998.
5. C. Wicke. Implementation of an autonomous agents system. Master's thesis, Dept. of Information and Computer Science, University of California, Irvine, Irvine, CA, 1998.

A SCALABLE MULTITHREADED COMPILER FRONT-END

A. WINDISCH

Technical University of Chemnitz, Department of Computer Science, 09107 Chemnitz, Germany

T. SCHNEIDER, K. YANG

Darmstadt University of Technology, Institute of Microelectronic Systems, 64289 Darmstadt, Germany

J. MADES, W. ECKER

Infineon Technologies, Otto-Hahn-Ring 6, 81739 Munich, Germany

In this paper we present a parallel scalable compiler front-end the implementation of which was based on an existing sequential compiler front-end. Our objective was to reduce compilation time by using a multithreaded compilation approach on shared memory multiprocessor computers. In the presented approach, multithreaded analysis of syntactic and static semantic information is based upon a newly developed weighted dependency graph allowing load balancing to be applied to the threads during the analysis process by using different thread priorities. The parallel compiler front-end was implemented for VHDL which is an ADA-like hardware description language. Our approach, however, can also be applied to other modular languages such as ADA, MODULA or JAVA.

The presented compiler front-end was implemented in JAVA. Due to its excellent support for threading, the multithreaded version of the presented compiler front-end required only 11 additional JAVA classes, containing approximately 2.500 lines of code, to be implemented. Consequently, the implementation of the multithreaded compiler front-end was completed within one man month. In comparison to the sequential compiler front-end, the multithreaded counterpart achieves an overall mean speed up of factor 1.8 using a 4 processor SMP machine. However, performance improvements vary between factor 1.4 for memory allocation dominated parsing, factor 1.9 for computation intensive tasks such as symbol generation and type checking, and factor 2.0 for IO-dominated data storage.

1 Introduction

The increasing complexity and size of today's hardware and software systems is reflected by the large quantities of the source code required to implement them. The modification of a widely used or referenced piece of code can cause several hours of compilation time that is unacceptable especially in the debug phase. Therefore, new approaches to the syntactic and static semantic analysis of implementation languages must be applied in order to reduce compilation time. Parallelisation of compilation is one solution to reduce today's high computation times. Applicable solutions in the field of parallel parsing already exist [1], [2], [3]. However, our effort is extended to the parallel analysis of static semantic information such as symbol generation and type checking. The development of such new parallel applications is more feasible today than it was a decade ago due to the decreasing price and increasing availability of shared memory multiprocessor computers running UNIX or Windows-NT.

We present in this paper our effort in implementing a multithreaded VHDL compiler. Section 2 explains the overall architecture of our compiler front-end and our intermediate data structure. In section 3 we focus on the presentation of the different multithreaded front-end components and section 4 gives test results for the multithreaded front-end version.

2 Compiler Aspects

2.1 Front-end Architecture and Intermediate Data Structure

The compiler architecture is based on the front-end / backend structure [4]. The front-end consists, in maximum, of five components. Through these compiler phases the intermediate data structure, subsequently called database, is build up. Our database is organized as a concrete syntax tree according to the grammar described in [5], [6], [7].

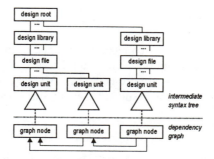

Figure 1. The compiler intermediate data structure.

The root of the syntax tree is a list containing all design libraries. A design library is a collection of design unit nodes ordered by design file nodes. The concrete syntax tree of a VHDL design unit is positioned below the corresponding design unit node as shown in Fig. 1. The database is annotated with a dependency graph. Exactly one dependency graph node is attached to every design unit node and each dependency graph node is linked to the dependency graph nodes upon which it is dependent from.

2.2 Weighted Dependencies

For reasons of performance optimizations, described in detail in Sec. 3, the nodes of the dependency graph are annotated with weights. The weight w_k of a single node is calculated according to the equation

$$w_k = s_k + \sum_{i=0}^{n} w_i \tag{1}$$

where

n ... is the number of dependent nodes

s_k ... represents the size of the attached design unit in bytes and

w_i ... denotes the weight of the ith dependent node of node k.

The semantics of a dependent node are such that its attached design unit depends on all the design units attached to its dependency nodes in the dependency graph. The calculated weight of a particular design unit is used as a heuristics for determining the amount of analysis required for that design unit. Thus, the critical path in terms of the amount of analysis required in a design is represented within the dependency graph by the path ending at the design unit with the biggest weight.

3 Multithreading the Frontend Components

Based on the compiler front-end architecture explained in the previous section, we now focus on a detailed description of the multithreaded algorithm of each front-end component. The algorithms are presented by UML sequence diagrams because this notation is, in our opinion, well suited for expressing concurrency.

3.1 Parser

Parsing does not rely upon any dependencies since, for the construction of the syntax trees, no static semantic information such as symbolic or type information is needed. Thus, analysis of the VHDL design files by the parser can be done concurrently.

The multithreaded parsing algorithm is shown in Fig. 2. The main application process creates and starts n parse threads (a). After start-up each parse thread requests a design file from the main process (b). The main process synchronizes access to the database and returns a new design file on each request (c) by calling method `getDesignFile` of the database instance. After receiving a design file the parse thread parses the design file (d) and inserts the generated syntax tree into the database (e). Access to the database is synchronized by the implementation of method addDesignFile. Steps (a) to (e) are repeated by each parse thread as long as there are design files left to be processed. In case all design files are processed already, the parse thread notifies the main process about termination (f) and terminates.

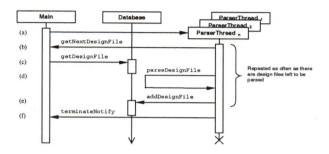

Figure 2. The multithreaded parsing algorithm.

3.2 Dependency Generator

After parsing, the database contains not only the syntax trees of all parsed design units but also the names of all design libraries and all design units. Based on the partial symbolic information, the dependency generator performs a worst case dependency analysis for each design unit as described in [8]. Multithreaded dependency generation is equivalent to multithreaded parsing except that the main application initially adds a dependency node to each design unit which are then concurrently inter-linked by the dependency threads.

3.3 Symbol Generator, Type Checker, and Expression Evaluator

For symbol generation and all subsequent front-end analysis steps the order of processing of design units is significant. Since the algorithms for symbol generation, type checking, and expression evaluation are equivalent in regard to thread control only the multithreaded algorithm for symbol generation will be explained.

As shown in Fig. 3 the main process retrieves an initial set of dependency graph nodes from the database (a). These nodes represent design units that do not depend on any other design units in the design. All nodes in the set are added to a node queue (b) that is used as a temporary store for design units ready to be processed. Subsequently, the symbol threads are created and started (c). After start-up each thread tries to retrieve a dependency graph node from the node queue (d).

In case a symbol thread does not succeed in getting a graph node it is suspended until new graph nodes are added to the node queue. Otherwise the symbol thread requests a new priority calculation from the main process (e) that results in new priorities to be set for all running threads (f). With its new priority set, the symbol thread starts generation of symbolic information that is added to the database (h). Since every symbol thread processes a different design unit, no write conflicts can occur in the database and therefore no extra synchronization mechanism is required. Once processing of the design unit is finished by a symbol thread, nodes dependent upon the currently processed dependency graph node are added to the node queue (i). Finally, the symbol thread notifies the main process that a unit was processed (k) by calling method `decUnitCount` and tries to acquire a new dependency graph node from the node queue. After the processing of the last dependency graph node by one of the symbol threads, the main thread resumes all suspended symbol threads and signals that all design units in the design were processed. This leads each symbol thread to send a termination notification to the main process (l) and to terminate thereafter.

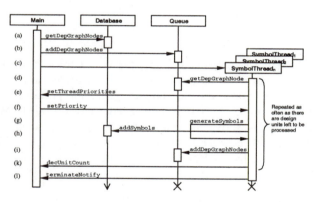

Figure 3. The algorithm for dependency sensitive symbol generation.

The above outlined algorithm uses thread priority setting to achieve load balancing of the symbol threads based on the weights of the dependency graph nodes. The priority p_i of a single analysis thread i is calculated as

$$p_i = p_{MIN} + \frac{w_i \times r}{w_{MAX}} \qquad (2)$$

where

p_{MIN}	... denotes the minimum possible thread priority
w_{MAX}	... denotes the maximum weight currently processed
w_i	... denotes the weight to be processed by thread i and
r	... denotes the resolution factor used for thread priority scaling

4 Selected Test Results

We subsequently present test results taken from the multithreaded analysis of the DLX microprocessor design which consists of approximately 6000 LoC distributed over 38 design units. Several tests with a different number of threads were performed on a 4 processor SPARCserver 1000 (60MHz version) containing 512 MB system memory. The resulting speedup of the multithreaded front-end version in comparison to its sequential counterpart are shown in Fig. 4.

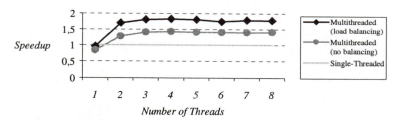

Figure 4. Speedup test results for DLX microprocessor design

The test results clearly illustrate that load balancing based upon thread priority control gains an additional speedup of approximately 20 percent in comparison to the unbalanced approach. Equivalent test results were achieved on different VHDL designs. Furthermore, the presented test results show that in this particular example the highest speedup is reached with a 4 thread configuration. However, different examples delivered different test results for speedup in relation to the number of threads used. This can be explained by considering the overall execution time of a front-end component T_{EXEC} that is determined by the execution time of its slowest thread

$$T_{EXEC} = \overset{t}{\underset{i=1}{MAX}} \ T_{EXEC,i} \tag{3}$$

where

t ... denotes the number of threads

Given that the execution time of a single thread $T_{EXEC,i}$ is given by

$$T_{EXEC,i} = T_{INIT} + T_{RUN,i} + T_{BLOCK,i} \tag{4}$$

where

$$T_{INIT} = \sum_{i=0}^{t} T_{INIT,i} \tag{5}$$

and

$T_{INIT,i}$ ... represents the initialization time of thread i and
$T_{RUN,i}$ ... represents the running time of thread i and
$T_{BLOCK,i}$ ... represents the blocking time of thread i

728

it follows that the optimal execution time does not merely depend on the degree of parallelism exploited but on the relation between the overall initialization time T_{INIT} and the overall running time T_{RUN} and the relation between overall blocking time T_{BLOCK} and T_{RUN}. The overall blocking time T_{BLOCK} is in turn determined by the number of threads used for processing and the average branch factor F_{BRANCH} and average join factor F_{JOIN} in the dependency graph. A heuristic found regarding the selection of the optimal number of threads needed for the analysis of a particular design is

$$t = \left| \frac{F_{BRANCH} + F_{JOIN}}{2} + 0.5 \right| \tag{6}$$

Selected test results showing the relations between T_{INIT}, T_{RUN}, and T_{BLOCK} and measured queue depths for multithreaded symbol generation are given in Table 1.

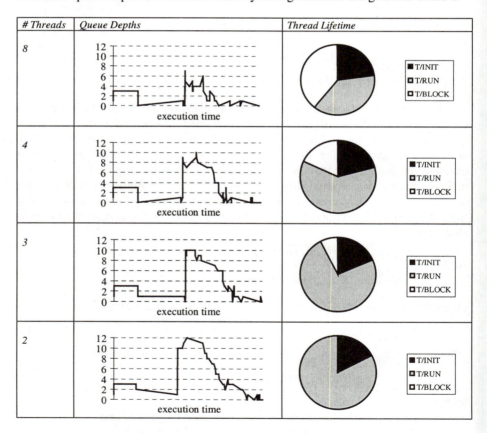

Table 1. Queue depths and thread lifetime analysis for multithreaded symbol generation.

5 Summary and Outline

We presented a multithreaded compiler front-end for the hardware description language VHDL that was developed out of an already existing sequential implementation. It was shown that based upon dependency information, analysis of static semantic information can be performed in parallel. In the presented approach, dependency information is stored in a newly developed weighted dependency graph that is also used for the implementation of a load balancing algorithm based on thread priority calculation. Tests performed on several hardware designs showed that the multithreaded front-end reached an overall mean speedup of factor 1.8 in comparison to its sequential counterpart. However, the tests also revealed that speedup reached on a particular VHDL design depends on the number of threads used for analysis. Therefore, a heuristic for the selection of an appropriate number of analysis threads based on dependency information was presented.

Future work will focus on the refinement of the heuristic and its implementation in our multithreaded compiler front-end. Furthermore, a new distributed compiler front-end implementation based on multiple processes will be investigated.

References

1. Dowsing R. D. and Anderson M. T., *Writing concurrent assemblers – A case study in Path Pascal*, Software Practice and Experience Vol. 16(12), pp. 1117-1135.
2. Fischer C. N., *On parsing context free languages in parallel environments*, TR 75-237, Cornell University, Department of Computer Science, 1975.
3. Sarkar D. and Deo N., *An optimal parallel parsing algorithm for a class of block-structured languages*, ConPar 87, pp. 585-588.
4. Aho A. V. *et al*, *Compilers, principles, techniques, and tools*, Addison-Wesley, ISBN 0-201-10088-6, 1986.
5. The Institute of Electrical and Electronics Engineers Inc., *IEEE Standard 1076-1993. VHDL Language Reference Manual*, 1987.
6. The Institute of Electrical and Electronics Engineers Inc., *IEEE Standard 1076-1993. VHDL Language Reference Manual*, 1993.
7. The Institute of Electrical and Electronics Engineers Inc., *Definition of Analog and Mixed Signal Extensions to IEEE Standard VHDL (Draft Version)*, 1998.
8. Ecker W. *et al*, *A Dependency Graph for VHDL Design Files and Design Units and its Application in a VHDL Design Environment*, HDLCON, 1999.
9. Oaks S. and Wong H., *JAVA Threads*, O'Reilly, 1997.

A 3D-JAVA TOOL TO VISUALIZE LOOP-CARRIED DEPENDENCES

YIJUN YU

Parallel Information Systems, University of Ghent,
St-Pietersnieuwstraat 41, 9000 Ghent, Belgium
E-mail: Yijun.Yu@elis.rug.ac.be

The interactive tool presented allows programmers to visualize and manipulate the three-dimensional iteration space dependence graph (ISDG). Constructed from the runtime analysis, it reveals the potential parallelism and permits the programmer to find suitable loop transformations which maximize the speedup.

The tool manipulates it with a number of graphical operations such as rotations, zooms, cutting planes and projections. Once the runtime trace of the program is generated, the new iteration space of a unimodular or non-singular transformation can be constructed without having to rewrite and execute the transformed program. In addition the temporal behavior of the program is revealed by a step-by-step traversal animating the iterations presently executed as well as the past and the future iterations in either data-flow, loop-wise or plane-wise order. From the ISDG, a dependence distance matrix is derived for both uniform dependence and non-uniform dependence problems.

It has been used to speedup a real-life computational fluid dynamics(CFD) program which is hard to parallelize with traditional compiler.

Keywords iteration space, program visualizing, loop transformation

1   Introduction

In the last decade, many loop transformation techniques have been developed, such as the unimodular [1] and non-unimodular transformations [2] for perfectly nested loops; and transformations for non-perfectly nested loops [3]. These techniques are based on the data dependence analysis to find the parallel loops and optimize their execution. However, the array subscript expressions, the loop bounds, and the conditional branches are often too complicated for a compiler to detect precisely all the loop dependences [4]. Therefore the runtime dependence analysis technique has emerged [5]. Unlike the compile-time dependence analysis, the runtime dependence analysis gathers more accurate information. Although the run-time analysis has to sacrifice the independence from the program input, the accurate runtime information aid to study the difficult loops which are hard for the compiler.

In this paper an interactive tool is presented for three-dimensional(3-D) iteration space dependence graph(ISDG). Presently, the tool has the following functions to construct, visualize and manipulate the ISDG: constructing an

ISDG from run-time analysis of the program; visualizing the dependences of a multi-level nested loop; manipulating the ISDG by a number of graphical operations; detecting parallelism or loop transformation by data-flow, loop-wise or plane-wise traversal of the graph; extracting distance matrix from the loop dependences; constructing a new iteration space without rewriting and execution of the transformed program; testifying and evaluating the loop transformations for maximum speedup.

Section 2 discusses the basics of iteration space and iteration space dependence graph. Section 3 discusses the technique to derive an ISDG from the run-time analysis of the program. Section 4 explores the visualizing and manipulating functions; As a result, section 5 shows the application to the most time-consuming loop nest of a computational fluid dynamics (CFD) program which is hard to parallelize by a traditional compiler.

2 The iteration space dependence graph

The *iteration space dependence graph* is a directed acyclic graph $< \mathcal{N}, \mathcal{E} >$ with nodes $\mathcal{N}$ representing iterations and edges $\mathcal{E}$ representing the dependences among them.

For a m-level normalized nested loop with i_j as index variable, L_j, U_j as lower and upper bounds of loop j and all loop steps are 1, the node set is:

$$\mathcal{N} = \{\mathbf{i} = (i_1, \ldots, i_m) | \forall 1 \leq j \leq m : L_j \leq i_j \leq U_j\} \tag{1}$$

In sequential loops, the iteration $\mathbf{i}$ executes before $\mathbf{j}$ if $\mathbf{i}$ is *lexicographically less than* $\mathbf{j}$, denoted as $\mathbf{i} \prec \mathbf{j}$, i.e., $i_1 < j_1 \vee \exists k \geq 1 : i_k < j_k \wedge i_t = j_t \ for \ 1 \leq t < k$. The lexicographical order of two dependent iterations $\mathbf{i} \prec \mathbf{j}$ also defines a lexicographically positive *distance vector* $\mathbf{d} = \mathbf{j} - \mathbf{i}$.

If both iterations $\mathbf{i_1} \prec \mathbf{i_2}$ read or write to the same array element $A(f(\mathbf{i_1})) = A(g(\mathbf{i_2}))$ and at least one of the iteration write, no intermediate iteration $\mathbf{j} \mid \mathbf{i_1} \prec \mathbf{j} \prec \mathbf{i_2}$ overwrite the same array element by any reference $A(h(\mathbf{j}))$, there is a direct *loop carried dependence* between the iterations $\mathbf{i_1}$ and $\mathbf{i_2}$, denoted as $\mathbf{i_1} \ \delta \ \mathbf{i_2}$. Therefore, the edge set of is defined as:

$$\mathcal{E} = \{(\mathbf{i_1}, \mathbf{i_2}) | \mathbf{i_1}, \mathbf{i_2} \in \mathcal{N} \wedge \mathbf{i_1} \ \delta \ \mathbf{i_2}\} \tag{2}$$

3 Constructing an ISDG from run-time analysis

To construct an ISDG from the program, the tool extends the run-time method described in [5] with treatment of non-perfectly nested loops.

First, a statement is inserted for each array reference $A(f(\mathbf{i}))$ in the loop to output in the execution order the sequential counter for iteration $\mathbf{i}$, the array name A, the subscript expression $f(\mathbf{i})$ and the type of reference (Read/Write).

Then, for all references outside the innermost loop body of an m-level non-perfectly nested loop: $A(f(i_1, \ldots, i_k))$ where $k < m$, it records the next iteration count so that these references are treated in the same manner with the references within the innermost loop body. The converted perfectly nested loop, whose ISDG is constructed in this way, subjects to the unimodular transformation and code generation as described in [3]. For example, the ISDG of the non-perfectly nested loop in Figure 1(a) has nodes $(i_1, i_2, i_1 + 1)$ which summarize all the references in both instances of the statements $S_1(i_1, i_2)$ and $S_2(i_1, i_2, i_1 + 1)$.

The graph is constructed from the records: (1) the tool keeps a record in a stack, for each array element, the last iteration that writes the element; (2) it marks the loop-carried dependence edges from the records to construct the graph: (2.1) Before pushing each new write reference in an iteration $\mathbf{j}$ to the stack, it pops up each the references to the same array element in iteration $\mathbf{i}$ and marking an output- or an anti- dependences edge $\mathbf{i}\ \delta\ \mathbf{j}$ if the reference in iteration $\mathbf{i}$ is a write or read reference. Then the iteration $\mathbf{j}$ is remembered as the new last write iteration; (2.2) Before pushing each new read reference in an iteration $\mathbf{j}$ to the stack, if iteration $\mathbf{i}$ is the last iteration that writes to the same array element, it marks a flow-dependence edge from $\mathbf{i}$ to $\mathbf{j}$.

For the programmer, the pragma *C\$doisv* before the innermost loop of the selected iteration space is the only required modification to the program.

4 Exploring the ISDG

There are two ways to expose loop parallelism. One way is looking into the graph to see if there are any parallel partitions of the iteration set $\mathcal{N}$. Rotating the graph to a certain angle may expose the partitions of independent iterations to eyes for simple programs like matrix multiplication.

Another way to detect loop parallelism is traversing the iteration space in the *data-flow, loop-wise* or *plane-wise* order. The execution of the loop is animated through step-by-step highlighting the traversal iterations presently executed as well as the past and the future iterations.

4.1 Traversing ISDG in data-flow order.

The data-flow orders of iterations are calculated as the following. Since the ISDG is a directed acyclic graph, that is, each iteration $\mathbf{i}$ can not start execu-

```
        do i1=1,n
          do i2=1,n
            if(i1.ne.i2) then
S₁          f=a(i2,i1)/a(i1,i1)
C$doisv
              do i3=i1+1,n+1
S₂            a(i2,i3)=a(i2,i3)-f*a(i1,i3)
              enddo
            endif
          enddo
        enddo
```

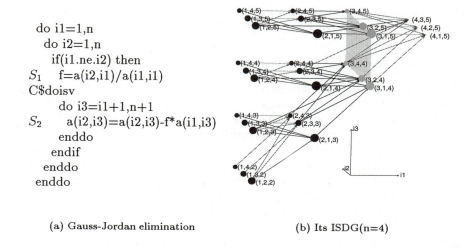

(a) Gauss-Jordan elimination   (b) Its ISDG(n=4)

Figure 1. (a) the loop to be visualized; (b) The graph showing all types of dependence, the data-flow execution at the third sequential step highlights a plane $i_1 = 3$.

tion until all its precedent iterations $prec(\mathbf{i}) = \{\mathbf{j} \mid (\mathbf{j}, \mathbf{i}) \in \mathcal{E}\}$ in the dependence edges $\mathcal{E}$ have been executed. Therefore, the optimal schedule time $T(\mathbf{i})$ for each iteration $\mathbf{i}$ is recursively defined as the topology order of the graph:

$$T(\mathbf{i}) = \begin{cases} 1 + max\{T(\mathbf{j}) \mid \mathbf{j} \in prec(\mathbf{i})\}, for \quad prec(\mathbf{i}) \neq \{\} \\ 1, \qquad\qquad\qquad\qquad\quad for \quad prec(\mathbf{i}) = \{\} \end{cases} \quad (3)$$

In principle, if the loop is executed by a data-flow machine, the data-flow parallelism is defined as the total number of iterations divided by the number of data-flow steps. Therefore, the number of data-flow steps tells the programmer how much potential parallelism lies in the loop.

For example, the Gauss-Jordan elimination has a 3-level loop as shown in Figure 1(a). There is a conditional statement in the non-perfectly nested loop. A non-perfect-to-perfect conversion is automatically applied to visualize an equivalent perfectly nested loop, as shown in Figure 1(b).

After detecting the data-flow parallelism, the tool will find a proper parallel execution by traversing the parallel loop iterations or traversing the parallel planes. The traversal of parallel iterations detects if there are any dependences carried by a certain loop; the traversal of parallel planes finds a unimodular transformation which makes the loop parallel while keeping the lexicographical ordering of dependent iterations.

4.2 Traversing parallel loop iterations

If all the dependences are not carried by a loop as testified, the loop can run in parallel, otherwise the iterations of the loop must traverse sequentially.

The tool not only testifies the loop parallelization specified by the programmer, but also judges the parallelizability of each loop automatically. Each loop can be run as a parallel DOALL loop or a sequential DO loop. Therefore for the 3-level nested loops, there are 8 possible DOALL/DO combinations. It testifies all the combinations in the outer-first parallelizing order to detect as much coarse grain parallelism as possible.

The amount of loop parallelism revealed by the loop parallelization is reported once it's testified. If it is equal to the data-flow parallelism of the data-flow execution, the detected loop parallelization has realized the data-flow parallelism under given loop boundaries.

For example, the ISDG of Gauss-Jordan elimination loop in Figure 1(b) shows that the two innermost loops can be parallelized, which has also revealed as much parallelism as the data-flow execution.

4.3 Defining and traversing planes

A *plane* in a 3D iteration space is defined by the equation:

$$ai_1 + bi_2 + ci_3 = d \qquad (4)$$

where a, b, c, d are any integers. The iteration space is divided into three subspaces by the plane: $\{(i_1, i_2, i_3) \mid ai_1 + bi_2 + ci_3 < d\}$, $\{(i_1, i_2, i_3) \mid ai_1 + bi_2 + ci_3 = d\}$ and $\{(i_1, i_2, i_3) \mid ai_1 + bi_2 + ci_3 > d\}$.

Given a, b, c, there are a number of parallel planes with d ranging from $min(ai_1 + bi_2 + ci_3)$ to $max(ai_1 + bi_2 + ci_3)$. Traversing these planes, one may find parallel *partitions* without inter-plane dependences or sequential *wavefronts* without intra-plane dependences. In other words, the partitions corresponds to the parallel outermost loop, the wavefronts corresponds to the sequential outermost loop with the two inner loops parallel. If neither partitions nor wavefronts exist, the loop can not parallelize without an index reordering transformation.

The tool distinguishes the three cases by filtering dependence according to the specified plane: hiding dependence edges between different planes may reveal partitions if the edge set of the graph becomes empty; hiding dependence edges within all the parallel planes may reveal wavefronts if the edges set of the graph becomes empty.

Traversing the planes gives one more insights into inter-partition or intra-wavefront parallelism. For Gauss-Jordan elimination in Figure 1(a), the planes $1 \leq i_1 \leq 4$ are wavefronts, meaning that the outermost loop is sequential, the two inner loops are parallel.

4.4 Extracting distance matrix and evaluating loop transformations

The tool is able to extract a distance matrix from the smallest basis cone of all the distance vectors in the iteration space. It is not only useful for judging the parallelizability of the outermost or the innermost loops, but also for finding a proper unimodular transformation.

A unimodular or non-singular loop transformations correspond to coordinate transformations of the iteration space. As long as the transforming matrix T is specified from either the plane-wise traversal or the distance matrix, the new iteration coordinates are recalculated as $\mathcal{N}' = \{\mathbf{j} | \mathbf{j} = \mathbf{i}T\}$.

However the edges set $\mathcal{E}'$ of the transformed iteration space is not easy to obtain without executing the transformed program. This difficulty is solved by reusing the trace records generated from the program and construct the graph according to the new coordinate system. If the new dependence graph is inconsistent to the dependence constraints, the illegal transformation is rejected and the dependence graph is restored. Rapid prototyping of the loop transformation is useful to testify and evaluate the parallelism in the transformed program without rewriting and execution of the transformed program.

5 Application

The tool has been used to detect parallelism in a CFD program that is hard to parallelize by a traditional compiler. This program has a 3-level loop nest whose computation consumes most execution time. The loop body contains 176.5 array references in average for each iteration that has to be analyzed at run-time. To avoid the graph being over-crowded, the run-time generated ISDG was zoomed to show the first $N = 4$ part of the whole iteration space so that there are $N^3 = 64$ visible iterations, see Figure 2(a).

To detect the parallelism, the iteration space was traversed in data-flow order and there are 19 sequential steps for the 64 iterations. Testing the data-flow execution for dimensions $N = 5, 6, \ldots$, the sequential steps were found to be $25, 31, \ldots$, as shown in Figure 2(c), or $6N - 5$ in general. Therefore, there is $N^3/(6N - 5) \approx N^2/6$ data-flow parallelism, as shown in Figure 2(d).

Looking for intra-plane wavefront parallelism, it found that the iterations in planes $6 \leq 3i_1 + 2i_2 + i_3 \leq 6N$ are parallel intra-plane, since there is no more dependence edge after hiding inter-plane dependence edges. According to these planes, and the extracted distance matrix whose rows are the bases of all the distance vectors of the dependences: $\begin{pmatrix} 1 & -1 & 0 \\ 0 & 1 & -1 \\ 0 & 0 & 1 \end{pmatrix}$, it found a unimodular transformation $\begin{pmatrix} 3 & 0 & 1 \\ 2 & 1 & 0 \\ 1 & 0 & 0 \end{pmatrix}$.

Finally, it constructed the ISDG after such a unimodular transformation without rewriting and execution of the transformed program. The reshaped iteration space after this unimodular transformation is shown in Figure 2(b). The figure shows that the reordered iterations are parallelizable for the inner two transformed loops because no intra-plane dependence exists for each plane i_1'. There are also $6N - 5$ planes as testified by the tool, thus all the data-flow parallelism has been revealed by this transformation.

6 Conclusion

An interactive tool for exploring 3-D iteration space dependence graph of nested loops is presented. Using runtime analysis method, it helps programmers to accurately study the loop dependence and to detect parallelism of the loop. It has been applied to the difficult but significant loop nest of a CFD program, as result, a unimodular transformation is found to generate the parallelism that the compiler could not find. This web accessible tool [6] has been added into the parallel programming environment of FPT [7].

References

1. Utpal Banerjee. *Loop Parallelization*. Kluwer Academic Publishers, 1994.
2. J. Ramanujam. Non-unimodular transformations of nested loops. In *Proceedings, Supercomputing '92*, pages 214–223, Nov 1992.
3. Jingling Xue. Unimodular transformations of non-perfectly nested loops. *Parallel Computing*, 22(12):1621–1645, February 1997.
4. William Pugh and David Wonnacott. Constraint-based array dependence analysis. *ACM Trans. on Prog. Lang. and Sys.*, 20(3):635–678, May 1998.
5. L. Rauchwerger and D. A. Padua. The LRPD test: Speculative run-time parallelization of loops with privatization and reduction parallelization. *IEEE Trans. on Parallel and Distributed Systems*, 10(2):160–180, February 1999.
6. Yijun Yu. The iteration space visualizer. Technical report, ELIS, University of Ghent, Belgium, http://sunmp.elis.rug.ac.be/ppt/isv/, 1999.
7. E. D'Hollander, F. Zhang, and Q. Wang. The Fortran Parallel Transformer and its programming environment. *J. Information Sciences*, 106:293–317, 1998.

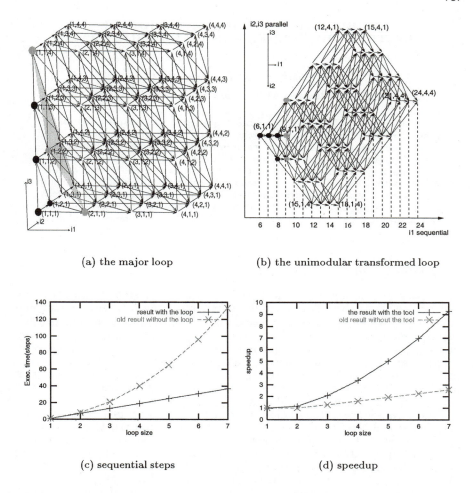

(a) the major loop

(b) the unimodular transformed loop

(c) sequential steps

(d) speedup

Figure 2. The CFD application:ISDG (a) shows the iteration space of CFD major loop with dimension $N = 4$, the current wavefront plane is $3i_1 + 2i_2 + i_3 = 9$, (b) shows the iteration space of the transformed loop, where the iterations in 19 planes form parallel loops in the new iteration space. The new plane $i'_1 = 9$ is highlighted with 3 parallel iteration nodes. Comparison between 2-D and 3-D transformation (c) The number of sequential steps is the minimum execution time of the parallel program. (d) The speedups are the sequential execution time divided by the minimum parallel execution time.

BUBBLE-DRIVEN OPTIMIZATION OF
INSTRUCTION LEVEL PARALLEL PROGRAMS

N.ZINGIRIAN AND M.MARESCA

Dipartimento di Elettronica ed Informatica – University of Padua, Italy

This paper proposes an instruction reordering scheme, called *Bubble-Driven Optimization* (BDO), suitable for programs targeted to superscalar and pipelined microprocessors that issue instructions in order. This scheme represents a novel instance of profile-driven optimizations because it optimizes the code taking advantage of a specific execution profile extracted through a novel technique, called *Bubble Detection* (BD), able to determine the occurrence of execution stalls, also called *bubbles*, at a single instruction level. This paper first presents the BD technique, and finally shows the speedup delivered by the reordering scheme proposed to a number of Livermore Kernels running on HP PA-7100 microprocessor adopting BDO.

1 Introduction

Instruction reordering is a crucial code optimization step if programs are targeted to instruction Level Parallel microprocessors (i.e. superscalar and pipelined)[1]. Instruction reordering takes advantage of an instruction *scheduling algorithm*, typically the "list scheduling", which determines the instruction schedule that minimizes some *cost functions*, e.g. latencies, critical path length, etc. Cost functions need to receive in input a set of cost parameters extracted by a *Functional Model*, that quantitatively describes the target processor, e.g. in terms of number of functional units, instruction type and throughput, maximum issue value (see e.g. [2]), etc.

As a consequence the choices of scheduling algorithms, cost functions and Functional Models determine the effectiveness of instruction reordering. The point is that even though algorithms are efficient and cost functions are appropriate, unfortunately, inaccurate Functional Models may introduce heavy inefficiencies in the code generated. This is the case for many compilers, especially the retargetable ones that adopt Functional Models general enough to describe a wide spectrum of architectures but not suitable for capturing the peculiarities of specific machines[3]. We propose an approach to instruction reordering that does not need any Functional Model and consists of

- a first step, called the *Bubble Detection* (BD), which automatically identifies all the execution inefficiencies, also called *bubbles*, and in particular those that the compiler ignores due to the limited accuracy of its CPU *Functional Model*, through a set of preliminary runs and

- a second step, called the *Bubble-Driven Optimization* (BDO), that adopts a simple algorithm that exploits the exact knowledge of the processor behaviour estimated during the previous step for that specific program.

This technique is an original instance of a class of optimizations, called profile-driven (see e.g., [45]), that take place after compilation and take advantage of execution profiles extracted at run time. BDO allows *i)* equipping compilers with more generic, portable and retargetable Functional Models, relying on the fact that Bubble Detection compensates the limited accuracy of Functional Models, and *ii)* allows testing the compiler Functional Model accuracy during compiler development. This technique is excellent for optimizing basic blocks which belong to critical paths of computing intensive programs.

The paper is organized as follows. First it introduces the basic concepts and the terminology adopted in the paper (Sect. 2). Then it describes the technique devised to detect the bubbles occurring during program execution (Sect. 3) and the optimization technique based on the bubble detection (Sect. 4). Finally it presents a set of experimental results to validate the techniques proposed and reports some concluding remarks (Sect. 5).

2   Concepts and Terminology

The technique proposed in this paper applies to superscalar and pipelined processors. Such processors can issue up to M instructions at each clock cycle, where M corresponds to the *maximum instruction issuing degree*. Equivalently, we can think that these processors issue always M instructions per clock cycle, some of which represent the actual program instructions while the others represent *bubbles*. Coherently to this point of view we adopt the following definition of instruction schedule.

Definition 1 *An instruction schedule of a program lasting T cycles and targeted to a specific processor able to issue M instructions per clock cycle is a table of T rows by M columns. Each table entry, called issuing slot, can contain either exactly one actual program instruction or exactly one bubble. In particular, if n instructions are scheduled to be issued at cycle t , then issuing slots $(t, 1), \ldots, (t, n)$ contain the n instructions (in any order), while the issuing slots $(t, n + 1), \ldots, (t, M)$ contain bubbles.*

The scheduler of an optimizing compiler aims at minimizing the number of bubbles present in the instruction schedule. It uses a set of parameters and rules describing the target CPU, called the *Functional Model*, to fill out the schedule of the program it is arranging. We call the schedule filled out using the Functional Model *Expected Instruction Schedule* (EIS).

When the program is executed, the target CPU issues the instructions according to one specific instruction schedule. We call this schedule *Actual Instruction Schedule* (AIS), because it describes the actual issuing time of each program instruction executed by the target CPU.

If the Functional Model does not perfectly describe the target CPU, then the EIS evaluated by a retargetable compiler is not equal to the corresponding AIS. In this case the optimization can be less effective because of the inaccuracy of the model.

The technique proposed directly extracts the AIS of a sequence of instructions (a basic block) by detecting the bubbles present in the AIS and

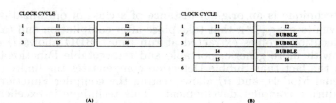

Figure 1. The Actual Instruction Schedule : a) bubble-free , b) in presence of bubbles

optimizes the code using no Functional Models. The technique works only for processors which do not reorder the instructions dynamically.

3 Bubble Detection

In this section we present our technique to extract the Actual Instruction Schedule (AIS) of a specific program running on a specific processor. This technique is called *Bubble Detection* (BD) because it detects the occurrence of the execution stalls (bubbles) during program execution. In this section first we describe the principle of the BD technique (Sect. 3.1), then we present an algorithm for BD (Sect. 3.2).

3.1 Bubble Detection Principle

Ideally, if programs were bubble-free, the AIS of any program would easily be determined. In particular, the i-th instruction of the program would be issued at the $\lceil i/M \rceil$-th clock cycle, where M is the maximum number of CPU instructions issuable at the same clock cycle. In other words, all the M *issuing slots* available at each clock cycle would be actually used to issue program instructions, as in the instruction schedule depicted in Figure 1(a) .

Unfortunately, during real program execution, the instruction interlock or the lack of available functional units leave some execution slots unused (bubbles) as depicted in Figure 1(b) and make the extraction of the AIS not immediate. In fact the AIS can be determined only if the issuing slot occupied by each bubble is exactly known.

The crucial point is that the bubbles cannot be detected directly measuring the time interval elapsing between two consecutive instructions by means of a real-time system clock. This is due to the difference of time granularity between the CPU clock and the system clock, and due to the interferences between the execution of the measured instructions and the instructions inserted to measure the latencies[a] These two limitations make it possible only to measure the execution time of code segments consisting of a large number

---

[a] The second shortcoming makes it impossible even to use hardware performance counters.

```
for each instruction I_n of Code from I_N to I_1 do
    for each type T of padding instructions do
        for each instr J ∈{ I_n }∪{padding instrs between I_{n-1} and I_n } do
            repeat
                insert padding instr of type T before J into Code;
            until (execution time of Code > initial execution time ) ;
            remove last padding instr inserted from Code;
        endfor
    endfor
endfor
```

Figure 2. The algorithm of bubble detection

of instructions repeated a large number of times, as a whole. Unfortunately such measurements allow evaluating the total latencies due to the overall bubbles present in the measured code but they are not sufficient to determine the exact location (at the instruction level) of such bubbles and, eventually, to extract the AIS.

The technique proposed detects the bubbles occurring during the program execution by inserting some specific *padding instructions* in the program and measuring the execution time of the resulting code. The principle behind this technique is the following. If a *padding instruction* is inserted at a particular position of the code and does not cause any execution slow down in the overall program, then it is necessarily filling a bubble present in the original program and thus it reveals the presence of a bubble.

In the rest of this section we present an algorithm based on the principle above.

3.2 Bubble Detection Algorithm

The Bubble Detection (BD) Algorithm is depicted in Figure 2. The algorithm scans the instructions of the inspected code from the end to the beginning backwards and inserts the padding instructions of different types between any pair of instructions until the program execution time[b] overrides the original program execution time.

The input of the algorithm is a basic block of assembly instructions $(I_1, \ldots, I_N)$, denoted also as *Code* in Figure 2. The output of the algorithm is a new assembly code which contains the instructions of the input code augmented with a number of padding instructions. The execution time of the output code is equal to the execution time of the input code. This output code is such that no instruction of somewhat type can be added without increasing the execution time of the code.

---

[b]In this paper we assume that no cache miss occurs during the code execution. The occurrence of cache misses could be detected by bubble detection as well, but it is beyond the scope of this paper.

In this section we describe the algorithm in depth. In particular we characterize the *padding instructions* with their types and discuss the insertion order of the padding instructions.

Padding instructions are machine instructions selected within the instruction set of the CPU. An instruction can be selected as a padding instruction if it satisfies all the following conditions:

1. it does not modify the semantics of the program in which it is inserted;

2. its latency is one cycle;

3. it does not cause data interlock either with other program instructions or with other padding instructions.

In addition, the padding instructions must be differently typed, as will be discussed in the next section, because superscalar architectures execute instructions of different types (ALU, Floating Point, Load/Store) by means of different functional units. In particular for each functional unit we select one representative padding instruction such that *i)* it satisfies the above three conditions and *ii)* it is issued if and only if at least one functional unit of its same type is available.

A few measurements of the execution time of programs containing only padding instructions are enough to determine if an instruction works correctly as a padding instruction. For example in many architectures, the *nop* instruction works correctly as a padding instruction for the ALU; similarly floating point conversion instructions operating on special registers have been tested to work correctly as padding instruction for the FPU.

To describe the insertion of padding instructions we suppose first that the target processor features only one functional unit type, then we consider the case of multiple functional unit types. Given a pair of consecutive program instructions (say I_n and I_{n+1}) a new padding instruction, (e.g. a *nop*) is added between I_n and I_{n+1} until its insertion does not increase the total program execution time. In this way we are sure that each padding instruction inserted is executed in the place of a bubble present in the original code.

However, to make bubble detection effective, a stricter requirement must be observed. In fact the padding instructions must be inserted in the program in such a way that the number of padding instructions inserted between I_n and I_{n+1} is equal to the number of the issuing slots wasted after or during the execution of I_n instruction and before the execution of I_{n+1} in the original program. Figure 3 shows that this result can be obtained only inserting the padding instructions from the last instruction to the first backward.

The BD algorithm takes into account also the different functional units present in superscalar processors. In fact the padding instructions of one type may keep busy all the functional units of that type before filling all the issuing slots available. In order to avoid this shortcoming, given a pair of program instructions, say I_n and I_{n+1}, the BD algorithm adds a padding instructions of the same type (say t) between I_n and I_{n+1} until the execution time increases (i.e., it *pads the pair* (I_n, I_{n+1}) *with type* t). The resulting sequence is $(I_n, P_1^t, \ldots, P_m^t, I_{n+1})$, where P_i^t is the i-th

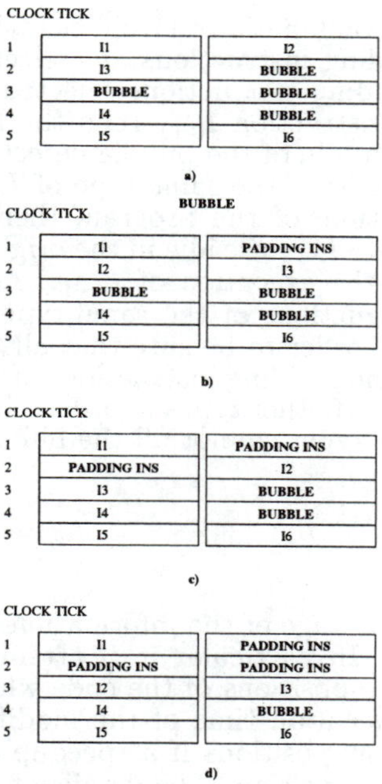

CLOCK TICK

1	I1		I2
2	I3		BUBBLE
3	BUBBLE		BUBBLE
4	I4		BUBBLE
5	I5		I6

a)

CLOCK TICK BUBBLE

1	I1		PADDING INS
2	I2		I3
3	BUBBLE		BUBBLE
4	I4		BUBBLE
5	I5		I6

b)

CLOCK TICK

1	I1		PADDING INS
2	PADDING INS		I2
3	I3		BUBBLE
4	I4		BUBBLE
5	I5		I6

c)

CLOCK TICK

1	I1		PADDING INS
2	PADDING INS		PADDING INS
3	I2		I3
4	I4		BUBBLE
5	I5		I6

d)

In AIS (a) the first three bubbles are caused by a data hazard between instruction I_1 and instruction I_4. When BD algortihm inserts a padding instruction between instruction I_1 and instruction I_2, it produces the schedule (b). Since the schedule length does not increase, the BD algorithm inserts another padding instruction between I_1 and I_2 obtaining the AIS (c) and then, after inserting another padding instruction, the AIS (d). Then no more padding instructions can be inserted without increasing the schedule length. The location of the padding instructions of (d) does not correspond to the position of the bubbles present in the original AIS (a). This is due to the fact that the padding instructions inserted can make the successive instructions shift through the issuing slots and fill some bubbles located in the rest of the program. BD algorithm avoids this shortcoming by inserting the padding instructions starting from the last basic block instruction backward.

Figure 3. Why BD inserts padding instructions backward

padding instruction of type t inserted. Then BD algorithm pads each pair $(I_n, P_1^t), \ldots (P_i^t, P_{i+1}^t), \ldots (P_m^t, I_{n+1})$ with a new type, different from t. In general for each type x of padding not yet inserted, the BD separately pads each pair of padding instructions previously inserted between I_n and I_{n+1} with type x. The algorithm in Figure 2 implements this technique. The instructions are inserted in this way because between any pair of padding instructions of types different from t there can be one ore more bubbles which can be filled by padding instructions of type t.

It is worth noticing that the number of bubbles occurring between the execution of I_n and the execution of I_{n+1} in general is not equal to the sum of the maximum number of operations that each functional unit could perform after or during the execution of I_n and the execution of I_{n+1}. This is due to the fact that generally the architectures are equipped with a number of functional units larger than the number of instructions issuable at each clock cycle. As a consequence there can be several combinations of padding instructions of different types that can pad a pair of program instructions. In any case, the total number of padding instructions is constant and corresponds to the number of instructions that could have been issued and were not issued due to data and structural hazards regardless their combination. This fact makes the order according to which the types of padding instructions are selected not relevant. However, if the first type of padding instructions selected to pad pair (I_n, I_{n+1}) is the same as the type of instruction I_{n+1} then the BD algorithm extracts more information about the origin of the bubble detected. In fact, if BD can insert some padding instructions of the same type of I_{n+1} before I_{n+1} without increasing the execution time of the program then it means that the functional units that could execute I_{n+1} are idle in the original program because the issuing logic is deferring the execution of I_{n+1}. As a consequence the bubbles filled by padding instructions of the same type as I_{n+1} are necessarily caused by data hazards. In order to be sure that all the data hazards are filled, it is necessary to insert the padding instructions of the same type of I_{n+1} before the padding instruction of other types in order. This choice ensures that padding instruction of other types cannot fill the bubbles due to data hazards.

4 Bubble-Driven Optimization

The Bubble Driven Optimizer (BDO) takes advantage of the information extracted by BD to improve the code efficiency. In particular it *i)* attempts to move appropriate program instructions to the positions of the code where the bubbles were detected, *ii)* measures the execution time of the modified code and *iii)* leaves the instructions at their new positions if a speedup occurred, otherwise it restores them at the original position. The details of the algorithm, although presented at the conference, are omitted due to space limitations in the proceedings.

5 Experimental Results and Concluding Remarks

In order to evaluate the speedup delivered by bubble driven optimization, we applied the BD and BDO algorithms described in previous sections to the first seven Livermore Kernels[6]. We selected Hewlett-Packard PA-RISC 7100 as target processor, because it is a superscalar processor equipped with hazard detection logic and performs in order instruction execution, thus satisfying the BD/BDO's operating conditions. The processor features, i.e. double instruction issue, double ALU, single FPU, etc., can be found in [7]. First, we compiled the Livermore Kernel, written in C language, using the HP native optimizing compiler of HP-UX 9.05 operating system, activating the most aggressive optimizations (i.e. +O4 flag). Then we compiled the same source programs using the GNU C Compiler, version 2.7.2, activating the most aggressive optimizations (i.e. -O3 flag). Surprisingly, we noticed that all the programs compiled by native compiler ran slower than the ones compiled by GNU C compiler, with 13% average slowdown. Then we manually unrolled the kernels (with degree 4) and repeated the experiment. The average slowdown of native compiler versus GNU C was 18%. This motivated us to discard the native compiler and compare the performance of GNU C before and after Bubble

Livermore	Plain Code			Unrolled Code (degree 4)		
	gcc -O3	+BDO	SpUp (%)	gcc -O3	+BDO	SpUp (%)
Kernel 1	22.1	20.1	9.0	13.4	12.2	9.2
Kernel 2	21.8	20.5	6.0	17.0	16.3	3.5
Kernel 3	10.3	9.0	12.9	8.7	8.1	7.1
Kernel 4	36.8	30.5	17.0	27.2	24.5	9.8
Kernel 5	18.0	18.0	0.0	9.1	8.8	3.4
Kernel 6	21.2	19.5	8.1	*Unrolling not applicable*		
Kernel 7	52.8	51.5	2.4	43.2	38.1	11.7

Table 1. Results of the Experiments on Livermore Kernels: execution times and Speedups delivered by BDO

Driven Optimization. Table 1 reports the execution times of the first seven Livermore Kernel, in the cases of both plain and unrolled source programs. The table shows that 17% is the peak speedup delivered by BDO, while 7.9 % and 7.4% are the average speedups for the plain and unrolled codes of the Livermore Kernels, respectively. These results show that, in both cases of small and large basic blocks, the exact knowledge of bubble position drives a simple instruction reordering algorithm to highly efficient schedules.

As a conclusion we propose BDO as a final optimization phase which takes place after regular model-driven optimizations. Such a phase allows optimizing the code taking account of the the target architecture peculiarities without requiring to encapsulate the details in the functional model, that can be too expensive to be included in retargetable compilers.

References

1. J.L. Hennessy and D.A. Patterson. *"Computer Architecture:A Quantitative Approach"*.MorganKaufmann Publishers, Inc., San Mateo, Ca 94403, 1996.
2. R.M Stallman. *"Using and porting GNU CC"*.GNUFree Software Foundation, 1997.
3. John C. Gyllenhaal, Wen mei W. Hwu, and B. Ramakrishna Rau. Optimizationof machine descriptions for efficient use. *International Journal of Parallel Programming*,26(4):417–430, 1998.
4. William Y. Chen, Scott A. Mahlke, Nancy J. Warter, Sadun Anik, and Wen-Mei W. Hwu. Profile-assistedinstruction scheduling. *International Journal of Parallel Programming*,22(2):151–181, April 1994.
5. J. A. Fisher. Tracescheduling : A technique for global microcode compaction. *IEEE Trans. Comput.*,C-30(7):478–490, 1981.
6. Joanne L. Martin. *Performance evaluation of supercomputers*,volume 4 of *Special topics in supercomputing*. ElsevierScience Publishers, Amsterdam, The Netherlands, 1988.
7. T. Aprey, G.S. Averill, E. DeLano, Mason R., B. Weiner, and J. Yetter. " Performance Features of the PA7100 Microprocessor". *"IEEE Micro "*,pages 22–35, June 1993.

Industrial Perspective

COMPAQ AND QSW SCALABLE SCIENTIFIC COMPUTING

PARETI J, *IT CONSULTANT, HIGH PERFORMANCE TECHNICAL COMPUTING, COMPAQ COMPUTER CORPORATION*
FERSTL F, *DIRECTOR, RESOURCE MANAGEMENT, GENIAS SOFTWARE GMBH.*
DR TAYLOR J, *PH D, TECHNICAL MARKETING, QSW LTD.*

This paper describes the scalable computing environment provided for by combining Compaq Alpha microprocessor technology within SMP systems and the amalgamation of these through the highly scalable systems using QSW System Area Networks (SAN). It starts at the microprocessor and describes the architecture and development environment within SMP systems. The SAN is then described along with the integration of Resource Management software and Genias Global Resource Director to support production level computing.

1   The Alpha processor (21264)

The 21264 Alpha processor [1,2] is at the time of writing in production in its 0.35 u process implementation while samples 0.25 u are being tested. This is the basic building block of high performance SMP systems which are in turn connected together in low latency System Area Networks (SAN). In addition to a clock rate of 500-730 MHz [1] the 21264 uses advanced micro-architectural techniques, including out-of-order and speculative execution with many in-flight instructions. It also includes a high-bandwidth memory system to quickly deliver data values to the execution core, providing robust performance to many applications, including those without cache locality.

The 21264 is the last high-end CPU optimized for a 0.35-micron process. The current wave of high-performance CPU designs consume a large 0.25-micron die with a bigger transistor budget than the 21264's. Meanwhile Intel is advancing to 0.18 u technology(Pentium III "Coppermine"). To take full advantage of a new process technology, a microprocessor vendor must redesign its core to consume the maximum available transistor budget. Simply shrinking a previous-generation processor provides a performance gain due to higher clock speeds, but the per-cycle throughput is not increased. Within Alpha, the full capability of the 0.18 u technology will only be realized with the 21364 „ev7" chip. Nonetheless two shrink-down implementations of ev6 are planned, i.e. the ev6/7 and ev6/8 (0.25 and 0.18 u technologies). The current transistor count is 15.2 million; although most are

---

[1] 730 MHz is the expected clock rate for the 0.25 u part

in the large caches and branch predictor, the CPU core contains about 6 million transistors. Compared to EV5 (9.5 M transistors) EV6 performs a larger amount of work per cycle and can sustain a larger percentage of peak performance. A key to achieving this is that ev6 can execute in an order different than that specified by the program. The decode unit arbitrates among several instructions in-flight, giving priority to those which have operands and overlaps load/store instructions with arithmetic instructions, thereby masking the latency associated with memory operations. A 64K, dual set-associative D-cache delivers data at a rate of 8GB/s and is backed up by an L2-cache that can be configured for different speeds and sizes (commonly 4MB). The latter has a dedicated 128-bit bus that when operated at 2/3 of clock provides a bandwidth of 5 GB/sec. The enhanced logic, including a ground-breaking branch-prediction unit [3] allows more parallelism among instructions to be realized. The improved interface to main memory[2] allows programs using data structures in excess of L2-cache sizes to achieve a larger percentage of peak performance when compared with 21164 performance. This translates in advantage McCalpin „Stream" benchmarks [4]. Another key performance parameter is the load-use latency that appears e.g. in „reduction-intensive" applications. An EV6 based system performs similar tasks up to 3x more efficiently.

The following example illustrates some functional differences between the 21164 (ev5) and 21264 (ev6) Alpha processors :

assume a program computing the following in a loop :

a(i)=b(i) + c(i)

This will get unrolled by the compiler to amortize the overhead. Where is the ev6 performance advantage ? *In a nutshell, EV6 is better at memory references.*
Each iteration requires two loads, a store, and an add, as well as some loop-overhead instructions such as pointer increments, conditional branches, etc. Unrolling reduces the number of overhead instructions per iteration. In every iteration, EV5 can issue a floating add, a floating multiply, and two integer operations. The two integer operations can include a store (integer or floating), or one or two loads (integer or floating), along with other non-floating instructions.
For the loop a(i)=b(i)+c(i), each iteration needs two loads, one store, one floating add, and some loop overhead. If we unroll enough so that one overhead instruction per cycle is enough, EV5 can complete one iteration every 2 cycles:

EV5
add b3+c3, store a1, overhead
load b5, load c5

---

[2] The Tsunami chipset that provides the data switch in midrange systems is connected to ev6 on a point to point link that operates as a 64-bit bus at 2/3 of clock

add b4+c4, store a2, overhead
load b6, load c6
add b5+c5, store a3, overhead
load b7, load c7
add b6+c6, store a4, overhead
load b8, load c8
add b7+c7, store a5, overhead

Getting this level of performance also requires that the memory system cooperate. The data must all be in an on-chip cache (the on-chip caches can deliver 128 bytes every cycle; off-chip caches can deliver 128 bytes about every 5-7 cycles). The schedule above works if the data is in the 8KB primary cache, but if it's in the 96KB level-2 cache you would need to move each load about 8 cycles earlier, which uses up a lot more registers.

EV6 can complete two iterations in 3 cycles:
load,load
load,load
store,store
There are plenty of slots for the floating add and overhead instructions.

Going from 2 cycles on EV5 to 1.5 cycles on EV6 isn't much of an improvement. The real difference is that EV5 achieves this level of performance only if everything works out exactly right. EV6's out-of-order execution absorbs cache misses much better. Rather than making everything wait if the $b(i)$ fetch misses, EV6 will run on ahead, perhaps starting a memory fetch for $c(i+3)$ before the $b(i)$ fetch has completed. This ability to keep multiple memory operations in flight at once helps performance on a lot of real programs.

2 Midrange systems.

Here's an architectural view of the ES40 system. The CPU's connect to the Tsunami cross-bar switch via independent 64-bit 333 MHz point-to-point channels - providing up to 2.6 GB/sec per channel. An implementation of the 21264's 4MB L2 cache uses 200-MHz late-write Static RAM (SRAM) chips, providing 3.2 GBps of peak bus bandwidth. When the CPU does miss the on-chip caches, it accesses the L2 cache over the 128-bit backside bus. A higher performance implementation of the L2-cache interface calls for Dual Data Rate SRAM (DDR-SRAM) chips. This runs at 166 MHz, but transfers data on both edges of a clock signal to achieve an effective data rate of 333 MHz, for 5.3 GB/sec of peak bandwidth. The chip set also connects to 4 banks of main memory over a pair of 256-bit buses, operating initially at 83MHz, providing a peak memory bus bandwidth of 2.6 GB/S per memory bus and a total available memory bus bandwidth of 5.2GB/S. The chip set also operates two 64-bit busses at 33MHz. The system supports up to 10 PCI slots.

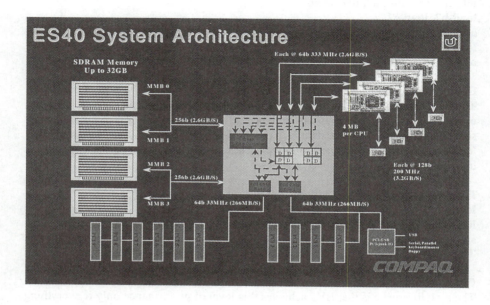

3   GEM and related compiler technology

A key element in the software strategy is the GEM compiler [5] that on 21264 takes advantage of cache prefetching instructions and improved scheduling features. GEM is the common base of languages such as Fortran, C and C++. A single optimizer, independent of the language and the target platform, transforms the intermediate language generated by the front end into a semantically equivalent form that executes faster on the target machine.The GEM system supports a range of languages and has been retargeted and rehosted for the Alpha and MIPS architectures and for several operating environments. To efficiently handle C and C++ GEM uses *alias analysis* [6]: through the use of type information, the compilers can assume that a pointer assignment can modify only those objects whose type matches that referenced by the pointer. To exploit the parallelism in the Alpha processor GEM employs a *dominator-path scheduling* [7] which does not require copying of operations to preserve program semantics. Compiler parallelization uses *SUIF's analysis* and memory optimization techniques [8], exploiting coarse-grain parallelism. Further, SUIF uses a technique called *compiler-directed page coloring* to get the OS to make each processor's data contiguous in its address space. Tools for SMP parallelization include (i) a debugger to detect incorrect variables declarations in parallel regions, e.g. thread-private vs. global, and (ii) a profiler to detect load-umbalances and threads synchronization effects. These tools known as KPTS are available at Kuck and Associates, Inc.

4   Basis for data lay-out in a NUMA architecture: The High Performance Fortran view.

Here we describe some optimization techniques in future SMP's roll-out. NUMA is an acronym for Non-Uniform Memory Access. In NUMA machines, the time to access a memory location may vary with the memory address being accessed. Usually, there is some memory that is considered "local", and some memory that is "non-local", or "remote", for which the access time is longer. There is generally a difference in both latency and bandwidth for remote memory accesses; both factors contribute to the longer access time. This is quite different from the UMA model, in which the time to access any memory location is the same regardless of which memory location is being accessed. In both the NUMA and UMA cases, the actual time to access a memory location may vary from access to access with system load, but in the NUMA case it also varies by memory address.

For a stencil code as shown below, Harris [9] demonstrates the effect of data-layout on performance in a NUMA architecture with a performance factor of 2.5 between ‚good' and ‚bad' layout.

```
C  simplified Jacobi method – only first j-loop shown below – the
C  example is mathematically incomplete and
C  is meant to illustrate the data access effect only - declare double
C  precision arrays x,y 1002x1002
      C Initialize arrays:
        read *, ((X(i,j), i=1,n), j=1,n)
      C Main loop:
        do iter=1,20000
        do j=2,n-1
        do i=2,n-1
          Y(i,j) = (X(i-1,j) + X(i+1,j) + X(i,j-1) + X(i,j+1) + 1.0) * 0.25

        end do
        end do
```

For this loop it is reasonable to assume that the operate time is effectively zero, since the operates can overlap in pipelined fashion with the reads and writes. The total time for the loop nest is dominated by the time for the remote read of X. Assuming X is laid out in the local memory of 1 quad , the 4 processors in the other quad will have to share the single bandwidth connection to the second quad in order to read their columns of X. If however X had been laid out half locally to each quad, the time to read X would have been ¼ and the total time for the "DO J..." loop would have been 2.5 x shorter.[3]

The above analysis omits many real-life details, such as the increased latency for remote accesses, most of which will only make the effect of poor data layout even more visible.

5   Atom

Tru64 UNIX provides a basic profiling tool *uprofile* that uses on-chip performance counters. However in order to learn about program-specific behaviors (e.g. data-access patterns, memory leaks, number of floating point divisions, etc.) it is necessary to instrument the application binary so that specific instructions can be monitored. This capability is provided for by the Atom tools [10]. Atom tools allow the programmer to build custom tools that instrument programs in specific ways. Some of these tools come off-the-shelf with the OS, such as *pixie* and *hiprof*, for basic-blocks counting and hierarchical profiling respectively. Further information can be obtained in the atom manpages, as well as in the manpages for atom_application_instrumentation,   atom_instrumentation_routines, atom_application_navigation, etc.

In order to build an Atom tool the programmer has to supply:

- An instrumentation file. This is used to modify the program by inserting calls to procedures that are found in the analysis file.
- An analysis file. This defines procedures and data structures used in the instrumentation file.

The application program and the analysis routines run in the same address space. Atom is independent of any compiler and language system because it operates on object-modules. It is based on extending the intermediate representation of OM, a link –time code modification system. The AddCall primitives annotate the intermediate representation. Next the procedure calls are inserted. To deal with programs that contain inlined procedures, Atom provides a wrapper routine for each analysis procedure to save and restores the necessary registers. This is the default mechanism that works with dbx too. For highly-optimized programs no wrapper routines are created and the saves and restores of caller-save registers are added in the analysis routines. One major goal of Atom is to avoid perturbing the addresses in the application program. Therefore the analysis routines are put in the space between the application's text and data segments. The data sections of the

---

[3] Assuming that the cost of stores is identical in both cases

application are not moved, so that the data addresses are not changed. Moreover all stack and heap addresses are unchanged.

6 Continuous Profiling Infrastructure (inlcuding a sample problem)

This is a low overhead profiling tool [11] designed to collect performance data on production systems.Time intervals or epochs are defined for data gathering upon images or shared libraries. It uses periodic sampling method via the alpha performance counters to gather data on cycles, cache misses, branch mispredicts, etc. DCPI analyzes CPU use down to the instruction level including stall analysis information. The following features are provided:

DCPI data collection and control tools: *dcpid, dcpictl, dcpiscan*
DCPI data analysis tools: *dcpiprof, dcpistats, dcpilist, dcpicalc, dcpitopstalls, dcpidiff*
DCPI data analysis support tools: *dcpisource, dcpi2ps, dcpicc, dcpi2pix, dcpisumxct*

DCPI allows to profile at different levels, i.e (i) Coarse details: system by image, image by procedure, and (ii) Fine details: image by instruction, procedure by basic block/instruction.

The following stencil is the critical part of a bit-manipulation program. DCPI identifies the high load latencies at a given assignment in the source code:

```
do s = 0, max_adrs
    ...
    do k = 0, min0 (max_lgls, i-1)
    x=ieor(ishft( a(k),2*max_bits-64),ts(s))
    y=iand(x,max_adrs)
    y1 = ieor (ieor (al(k), tl(s)), tl(y))
```

DCPI reports 55 cycles in the following assignements.

  207:   y1 = ieor (ieor (al(k), tl(s)), tl(y) 1118485 55.0cy

so the problem load is one of al(k), tl(s), or tl(y) .

- tl(s) - s only changes in the OUTER loop, so for every iteration of the inner do k loop, tl(s) is the same location. Therefore, tl(s) has been loaded on the previous iteration, and will be in the cache. No problem.

- al(k) - this is the first reference to al(k) in the do k loop. However, since k is increasing regularly by 1 on each iteration, the CACHE LINE containing al(k) has most likely already been read from memory (32 bytes/cache line, al(k) is 4 bytes, there are 8 elements of al(.) in each cache line, so 7/8 of the time there is a cache hit. No problem.

- tl(y) - y gets some totally different value on every iteration, so we probably haven't loaded tl(y) before. Furthermore, since tl is significantly larger than 4 mbytes, the whole array is NOT contained in the cache. This is the problem load.

Another way to interpret DCPI data is to look at the assembler listing and relate it back to the high-level language source line.

7   The SIERRA programme.

When the US Department of Energy set up the Accelerated Strategic Computing Initiative, DoE scientists analyzed their applications to determine what latency, bandwidth, and size would be needed to sustain high computational rates at each level of the computer system memory hierarchy. The results are expressed in terms of CPU cycles or seconds(for latency), and bytes per cycle or bytes per operation (for bandwidth and size).The DoE then did a survey of US computer manufacturers to find out whether computer builders planned to meet the required memory hierarchy performance in their future products. In the areas of **latency** (30-80 cycles to access *local main memory*, 300-500 cycles to access *nearby nodes*, and 1000 cycles to access *far away nodes*) and of **bandwidth** (2-8 bytes/flop peak) industry did not meet the required performance. The Sierra programme addresses those issues, as well as the related software components to operate the clustered compute resource as one system. The SAN components and software tools are explained below.

8   DEC and QSW MPI and other libraries

For cluster-wide parallel applications using domain decomposition and message passing, specific implementations of MPI [12] and other libraries on UNIX clusters have been undertaken to minimize the message transfer latency and optimize the bandwidth. COMPAQ-QSW MPI implementation has been demonstrated on a cluster of 64 twin-processors systems (DS20) to provide latencies between 5-6 microseconds on a ping-pong program. The QSW link with the current PCI implementation achieves a bandwidth of 200 MB/sec.

9   Features of the Quadrics System Area Network

Such large SuperCluster systems like Sierra are provided by the integration of commodity SMP technologies with the QSW System Area Network environment. In essence the QSW SAN provides two distinct elements, a High Performance communication sub-system and a Resource Management System. Effective co-operation between processing nodes is the most important factor influencing the overall sustained performance of a parallel system. Specifically, this requires both **high bandwidth** and **low latency** from the communications network. The QSW network provides this capability in a highly scalable and flexible configuration. This is constructed using two components:

A **Network Communications Processor or Adapter** that allows each node in the system to transfer data over the network. The basic primitives of the adapter are supported by:

- *Remote read and remote write*: **the direct transfer of data from a user virtual address space on one processor to user virtual address space on another processor. This does not cause or require synchronization between the processes.**
- *Protocol handler*: **A user programmable "thread" processor which can directly generate network operations, and execute small pieces of code to perform protocol handling without interrupting the main processor.**
- *Synchronization operations*: **These can be set or tested locally or remotely, and can cause scheduling of processes on the thread processor, or interrupts to the main processor.**

The adapter handles all the network traffic, freeing the main processor from communications processing. It also has sufficient local processing power to implement the high-level message passing protocols required in parallel processing.

The Network switch: is an arity-4 cross-bar switch used to construct a multi-stage network of links connecting all nodes. The switch configuration allows simultaneous connectivity between all nodes.

Each adapter provides access for nodes to connect to a logarithmic network constructed from 8-way crosspoint switches with each switch chip rolling up the functionality of eight of the unidirectional two way switches with provision for two virtual channels to minimize contention. Bandwidth is constant at each stage of the network, and there are as many links out (for expansion) as there are processors. Larger networks are constructed by taking four (sub-) networks and connecting them with a higher stage of switches. A 64-node network is illustrated. 64 systems are connected to stage 1, 64 links connect stage 1 to stage 2, and similarly stage 2 to stage 3, 64 links are available at the *top* for expansion. The bi-directional nature of the links localizes traffic to a sub-tree large enough to span both nodes. The uplinks in the top stage of a switch network can either be used for expansion or they can be used as additional downlinks doubling the number of nodes that can be connected without reducing the bi-sectional bandwidth. The data network can be replicated to increase bi-sectional bandwidth (using the nodes multiple independent PCI buses) and in the tolerance of failures. Each node can have 2 or more network adapters connecting them to separate layers (sometimes called rails).

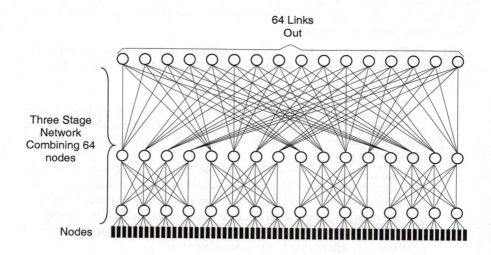

64 Node QSW SuperCluster *Data Network: Each node has dedicated communications processor(s) that links to other communications processors via an independent QNS network. One such network is shown in this diagram.*

Processor (nodes)	Elements	Switching Layers (l)	Network Switches(n/4*l)	Latency Factor
4	1	1		1
16	2	8		3
64	3	48		5
256	4	256		7

9.1 The role of the Resource Management System (RMS)

The RMS provides a single point interface to the system for resource management. This interface enables a system administrator to manage the system resources (CPUs, memory, disks, and so on) effectively and easily. The RMS is implemented as a set of Unix clients and daemons, programmed in C and C++, using sockets for communications. All the details of the system (its configuration, its current state, usage statistics) are maintained in an SQL database as discussed below.

System View of the RMS

Machine management	controlling and monitoring the nodes in the network (known collectively as the *machine*) to ensure the correct operation of the hardware
Fault diagnosis	automatically diagnosing faults and isolating errors; instigating fault recovery and escalation procedures
Monitoring	recording statistics on system performance and maintaining an audit trail
Resource allocation	determining the role of each node to optimize the use of system resources
Access control and accounting	controlling user access to resources and recording usage details for accounting purposes
Scheduling	providing the software support required to load and run parallel programs and resolve their conflicting requests for resources

Users Viev of the RMS

Resource information	querying the resources of the system
Resource access	gaining access to system resources
Running programs	Loading and running parallel programs on a given set of resources

Program monitoring	monitoring the execution of parallel programs

10 Global Resource Director of Genias Software, GmbH.

The Global Resource Director (GRD) is an unique resource management product designed to support the Enterprise mission with two ground-breaking features:

- fine-grained policy management - whereby Enterprise goals such as on-time completion of critical work or fair resource sharing are expressed as policies that determine how computing resources are used and shared.
- dynamic scheduling - where GRD allocates resources among jobs when a job is dispatched and throughout its lifetime. This insures that the most important work at any instant receives its deserved system share by allowing newly-arrived, more important work to take resources away from less important executing jobs.

Thus, an organization can arrange its computing tasks based on their importance to its mission, while efficiently utilizing the available computing resources. This, coupled with the reduced administrative cost that results from automating policies, provides a quick return on investment.

GRD policy statements allow data centers to equitably regulate routine resource usage while promptly handling high priority work through these resource-sharing paradigms:

- Relative priority of departments, projects, job classes, and users
- Relative resource entitlement based upon budgeted share over time and usage to date (expressed through a hierarchical share tree)
- Relative urgency based on job deadlines.

GRD benefits:

- Centralized workload and policy management to promote organization goals
- Global workload management strategies including share-based, priority and deadline scheduling
- Advanced job-queuing and load-balancing
- Automated policy enforcement
- Global resource management
- Immediate response to priority work
- Maximum utilization of all computing resources.

10.1   GRD Integration with RMS

To leverage the high level resource management facilities of GRD for QSW - Compaq clusters, an implementation of GRD on top of RMS is planned, delivering full hardware resource control through RMS while providing leadership resource management interface through GRD. The integration will be supported by a close cooperation between Compaq, QSW Ltd. And Genias, to provide an optimal solution. It will include:

- Full awareness of RMS-managed resources in GRD.
- Automatic and transparent forwarding of GRD jobs to RMS (the user and administrator only needs to see GRD).
- High level GRD policy and job management while RMS allocates resources and executes and controls jobs.
- Support for concurrent interactive usage of RMS.
- Transparent integration of other computational resources available at a site into a single system image.
- Specialized GRD submission support encompassing a representation of all RMS job start options.
- Full GRD resource limit control and accounting via RMS.
- Dynamic resource utilization data collection and on-line reflection in the share management database.
- Turn-key installation, administration and trouble shooting procedures as well as specific documentation.

11   References

1. Kessler et al. " The Alpha 21264 Microprocessor Architecture"
2. Gwennap,L "21264 sets new standard" Microprocessor Report, October 1996
3.McFarling, http://www.research.digital.com/wrl/techreports/abstracts/TN-36.html "Combining Branch Predictors"
4. STREAM: Sustainable Memory Bandwidth in High Performance Computers http://www.cs.virginia.edu/stream/
5. Noyce W. et al. " The GEM Optimizing Compiler System" Digital Technical Journal, vol. 4, 1992
6. Reinig A. „Alias Analysis in the DEC C and DIGITAL C++ Compilers" Digital Technical Journal, Vol 10, No 1 1998
7 Sweany P." Compiler Optimization for Superscalar Systems: Global Instruction Scheduling without Copies" Digital Technical Journal, Vol 10, No 1 1998

8. Hall M. et al. „Maximizing Multiprocessor Performance with the SUIF Compiler" Digital Technical Journal vol 10, 1998

9 Harris J. „Why Data Layout is Important in NUMA Machines" Internal memo of Digital Equipment Corporation, 1996

10 Srivastava, A "ATOM: A system for building cusomized program analysys tools" Proceedings of the ACM SIGPLAN 1994

11 Anderson et al." Continuous Profiling: where have all the cycles gone ?" Proceedings of the 16th ACM Symposium on Operating Systems Principles- 1997

12 J. Lawton et al. "Building a High-Performance Message Passing System for MEMORY CHANNEL Clusters" Digital Technical Journal vol. 8 no 2. 1996

Extended Abstracts

PARALLEL INEXACT NEWTON AND INTERIOR POINT METHODS

LUCA BERGAMASCHI AND GIOVANNI ZILLI

Dipartimento di Metodi e Modelli Matematici per le Scienze Applicate,
Università di Padova, via Belzoni 7, Padova, Italy
E-mail: berga@dmsa.unipd.it, zilli@dmsa.unipd.it

Given a non-linear system of equation in the form $F(x) = 0$ where $F : R^n \to R^n$ is a non-linear function, the Newton method linearizes the problem yielding a number of linear systems to be solved at each non-linear iteration. The coefficient matrix is represented by the Jacobian matrix $J(x)$. The inexact Newton method relies on the iterative (and hence 'inexact') solution of such linear systems, and proves to maintain, under suitable hypotheses, the quadratic, or at least superlinear, convergence of the Newton method. In this paper we present the results obtained in the solution of sparse and large systems of non-linear equations by inexact Newton methods, combined with a p-block row-projection linear solver of Cimmino type [2]. Let us consider the linearized system $Ax = b$. the row projection algorithm can be written as a Conjugate Gradient iteration applied to the preconditioned system $HAx = Hb$, or,

$$\sum_{i=1}^{n} A_i^+ A_i x = \sum_{i=1}^{n} A_i^+ b \tag{1}$$

where $A_i^+ = A_i^T (A_i A_i^T)^{-1}$ is the Moore-Penrose pseudo inverse of A_i and the blocks A_i are such that $A^T = \left[A_1^T, A_2^T, \ldots, A_p^T \right], 1 \leq p \leq n$. We also propose a suitable partitioning of the Jacobian matrices. In view of the sparsity, we obtain a mutually orthogonal row-partition of A in such a way that $A_i A_i^T = I, i = 1, \ldots, p$, and consequently, $A_i^+ = A_i^T$. We provide numerical evidence of the good conditioning of such a preconditioned matrix and present numerical results obtained on a CRAY-T3E when this method is used to solve both non linear problems and a non-linear complementary problem (the obstacle Bratu problem)[1]. It is indeed well known that the solution of the primal-dual interior point method for mixed complementary problems cam be viewed as a variant of Newton's method applied to a particular system of non-linear equations. Due to the presence of a logarithmic penalty, this problem can be written in the framework of the inexact Newton methods.

References

1. Dirske S. P., and M. C. Ferris Tech. Rep., CS Depth., University of Winsconsin, Madison, WS, 1994.
2. Zilli, G. and Bergamaschi, L., in: *M. Bubak, J. Dongarra, J. Wasniewski (Eds.), Recent advances in PVM and MPI, Lectures Notes in Computer Sciences,* 1332, Springer, 390-397, 1997.

PARALLEL SAR PROCESSING ON LINUX PCS ENABLES OPERATIONAL RADAR REMOTE SENSING

J.P. GESCHIERE, M. BAGNI

Program Operations - Remote Sensing, Fokker Space B.V., P.O. Box 32070, 23030 DB Leiden, The Netherlands

R.A. VAN MAARSEVEEN, M.P.G. OTTEN

TNO Physics and Electronics Laboratory, P.O. Box 96864, 2509 JG , The Hague, The Netherlands

Abstract

Current tools for processing Synthetic Aperture Radar (SAR) data are both computation- and memory intensive. Taking radar remote-sensing into operational use requires processing of a relatively large number of large images within a limited time frame. Moreover, operational remote-sensing applications are not always fully automatic, but may require frequent interactions with the user, which requires a fast delivery of intermediate remote-sensing results. Commercial radar image processing systems need to cover these operational needs: increased performance in combination with low operational costs are a competitive asset. When trying to implement this challenge, an infrastructure of Linux PCs appeared to be a very promising possibility to fulfil the system level needs in a cost-effective way. Also, since this solution is based on industry standard hardware and software, future upgrades and maintenance do not depend on the developments and prices of one or a limited number of specific vendors.

This paper examines specific technology and operationalization aspects of parallel processing to be applied to a future radar remote sensing system. First, we describe the main elements of a typical end-to-end radar remote sensing system. Next, an overview is given of the radar image processing software in this end-to-end chain: the Core Generic SAR Processor (CGSP). Subsequently, the parallelization of the CGSP targeting a cluster of Linux PCs is detailed, together with its actual implementation in a separate software system: the CGSP Controller. The sequential CGSP software was originally targeted towards SUN Sparc systems. We present the cost benefit results obtained using the Linux cluster compared to price/performance results on SUN systems. Next, we look again at the general radar remote sensing system and focus on the operationalization aspects when using the parallel CGSP as part of its end-to-end chain. Finally, follow-up activities are described.

Author Index